ROYAL COMMISSION ON HISTORICAL MANUSCRIPTS

JP19

THE LEDGER OF

JOHN SMYTHE

1538–1550

FROM THE TRANSCRIPT MADE BY

JOHN ANGUS, BA

EDITED BY

JEAN VANES, BA

LONDON

HER MAJESTY'S STATIONERY OFFICE

1974

© *Crown copyright 1974*
ISBN 0 11 440014 8*

This volume, which has been prepared for Joint Publication by the Bristol Record Society, forms No. XXVIII in the series of that Society and No. 19 in the Joint Publications series of the Historical Manuscripts Commission.

Acknowledgments

The Society is indebted to the Bristol Archives Office and in particular to Miss Elizabeth Ralph, the City Archivist, for permission to edit the manuscript.

Acknowledgments are also due to Mr and Mrs John Farrell for compiling the index.

Contents

Acknowledgments   iii

Abbreviations used in the notes   vi

Notes on transcription   vii

Introduction   1

Text   30

Appendix I   The Family of Smythe of Long Ashton, Somerset   319

Appendix II   Bristol Occupations as shown in the Ledger   321

Appendix III   A Comparison between the Customs Accounts and the Ledger   322

Appendix IV   A Table of Prices to show the Effects of Inflation   324

Glossary   326

Saints' Days and Festivals used in dating   333

Weights and Measures   334

Currency   336

Index of Persons, Places and Ships   339

Abbreviations used in the notes

AC.	Ashton Court Manuscripts.
Add. MSS.	Additional Manuscripts, British Museum.
B.A.O.	Bristol Archives Office.
B. & G.A.S.	*Transactions of the Bristol and Gloucestershire Archaeological Society.*
B.M.	British Museum.
B.R.S.	Bristol Record Society Publications.
C.P.R.	*Calendar of Patent Rolls.*
Ct. of Aug.	Court of Augmentations Records, Public Record Office.
D.N.B.	*Dictionary of National Biography.*
E.H.R.	*English Historical Review.*
Ec.H.R.	*Economic History Review.*
Inq. P.M.	Inquisitions Post Mortem, Public Record Office.
K.R. Customs	King's Remembrancer, Customs Accounts, Public Record Office.
L. & P. H. VIII	*Letters and Papers, Foreign and Domestic of the Reign of Henry VIII.*
N.E.D.	*New English Dictionary.*
P.C.C.	Prerogative Court of Canterbury.
P.R.O.	Public Record Office.
S.P.	State Papers.
T.R. Misc. Bks.	Lord Treasurer's Remembrancer, Miscellaneous Books, Public Record Office.

Notes on transcription

1 The rules followed are those set out in the *Bulletin of the Institute of Historical Research*, Vols. 1 and 3.

2 Each folio is clearly numbered by Smythe. The letters 'L' and 'R' have been supplied to distinguish left- and right-hand pages, and right-hand pages are indented. Pages out of order have been rearranged so that debit and credit entries correspond. Papers found inside the ledger have been given the page number of the folio next to which they were found together with a letter, 'A', 'B' or 'C'. Smythe has numbered two consecutive folios '9' and the second of these has been called '9A'.

3 Most abbreviations have been extended in the form usual in the manuscript and all letters supplied have been printed in italics. Where Smythe uses a standard form of abbreviation throughout the ledger these have been retained to give more of the flavour of the original. r. is always used for 'received' where Smythe uses r., rec., or recd. Itm. is always used where Smythe uses it. d'd is used for 'delivered'; pd. for 'paid'; fo. for 'folio'; S. for 'Summa'; h'd for 'hogshead' and S.S. for 'San Sebastian'. w°, wᵗ and c° are spelt-out as 'which', 'with' and 'credito'.

4 Capitals have been modernised, as have v and u, i and j which are used indiscriminately. Punctuation has been modernised where Smythe uses a great many oblique strokes. ⟨ appears frequently but has been extended as '*th*'. Smythe uses two signs for 'and', ⁄~ and ⁄. These have both been shown as '&'.

5 Smythe uses a mixture of Roman and Arabic numerals but these have been printed in Arabic for reasons of economy and for clarity of presentation. Errors of arithmetic have not been footnoted.

6 Dates have not been modernised but left as Old Style throughout.

7 To avoid overloading the text with footnotes, single sums of money and short passages crossed out have been crossed through in the printed text, but where a whole item has been crossed through with a diagonal line this is indicated with a footnote.

8 Where there is a column of figures in the left-hand margin relating directly to items in the text this has been left to show the importance of this development in accounting technique. Marginal dates and such words as 'Memorandum' have been inset at the appropriate point in the text. Other marginalia are footnoted.

9 Notes on the terms and abbreviations used for money, weights and measures will be found at the end of the Glossary.

Introduction

1 The Ledger

The John Smythe ledger which is now in the keeping of the Bristol Archives Office[1] is one of the treasures found among the family archives in the muniment room at Ashton Court, the house near Bristol which Smythe bought. It is a large, leather-bound volume originally fastened with a strong buckle and strap. The leather has an all-over pattern of tooled rectangles and diamonds, the pattern larger on the front than on the back. The ledger is in excellent condition, though some of the pages (folios 173–177 and folios 183–187) are out of order. It has three hundred folios of $13 \times 8\frac{1}{2}$ inches with the water mark 'J. Nivelle' which shows that the paper was manufactured at Troyes in north-eastern France,[2] where the ledger may have been made and then exported to England. It covers the years 1538 to 1550 and is apparently one of a series, though it seems to bear no distinguishing letter A, B or C, as one might expect.[3] Most of the earlier accounts were brought forward from an 'old boke which began in a*nno* 1533' and many accounts end with 'This cownt is passed into my newe booke fo . . . the ijde day of July a*nno* 1550'.

The first folio records only that 'This boke of accowmpt*es* ap*er*teynith to Jo*h*n Smythe, m*ar*chant of Bristowe' and carries a mark which seems to be a monogram of Smythe's initials with a cross superimposed.[4] Each folio is headed with a cross and, occasionally, having despatched a particularly valuable consignment, Smythe adds, 'God send hit saff.'[5] The typical medieval ledger contained frequent invocations to the deity, such as the long prayer in the Borromeo ledger of 1436, 'to the salvation of our souls and with honour and profit to our bodies',[6] and Ympyn adds when he notes his profits, 'Praise and honour to Almighty God who granted me this. Amen'.[7] By the sixteenth century, however, 'God and Profit', the twin deities of the fourteenth century Florentine merchant, Datini,[8] were already beginning to part company, as modern business ethics and the sole pursuit of profit drove out medieval practice.

2 Family and early life

The family of John Smythe of Bristol came during the fifteenth century from Aylburton near Lydney in the Forest of Dean. Family tradition, based on records which have now

---

[1] B.A.O. AC/B63.
[2] C. M. BRIQUET, *Les Filigranes*, Vol. III, 12·058 (Geneva 1907).
[3] A distinguishing letter on each volume was usual.
YMPYN, Ch. IV, quoted by B. S. YAMEY, H. C. EDEY and H. W. THOMSON, *Accounting in England and Scotland 1543–1800* (London 1963), p. 23. WEDDINGTON quoted Yamey and others, pp. 27–28. J. PEELE, *The maner and fourme . . .* (R. Grafton, London 1553), Ch. III.
J. MELLIS, *A Briefe Instruction . . .* (J. Windet, London 1588), Ch. IX.
There is on the inside of the front cover a symbol which may represent an 'A'.
[4] Such marks were often used as merchant marks. Smythe seems to have used this mark for leather and cloth but other marks on lead and on one occasion yet another mark on wine. Ledger, fos. 126, 222, 290.
F. A. GIRLING, *English Merchant Marks* (London 1964), p. 11.
A. E. HUDD, 'Bristol Merchant Marks', *Proceedings of the Clifton Antiquarian Club*, Vol. VII, pt. 2, pp. 101, 159, 161, 183 (Exeter 1912).
[5] For example, Ledger fo. 290.
[6] P. KATS, 'Double entry Book-keeping in England before Hugh Oldcastle', *The Accountant*, LXXIV (1926), p. 92.
[7] P. KATS, 'The "Nouvelle Instruction" of Jehan Ympyn Christophle', *The Accountant*, LXXVII (1927), pp. 267 and 269.
[8] I. ORIGO, *The Merchant of Prato* (London 1957), p. 114.

disappeared, reports that a John Smythe was living at Aylburton in 1422 and that in 1440 he gave all his lands there to his son Robert, whose son John was the father of Matthew. Matthew Smythe moved to Bristol where he became a merchant.[1] The family retained lands in the Forest of Dean which Matthew Smythe left to his son, John, in September 1526.[2] These lands do not appear in John's will in 1556[3] nor are they referred to in the ledger so it is possible that John sold them soon after his father's death.

Matthew Smythe married Alice, the daughter and heir of Lewis John, a Bristol merchant of the late fifteenth century. They lived in a house on the south side of Corn Street in St. Leonard's parish, which Alice inherited in 1520 under the terms of the will of Lewis Mors.[4] Matthew and his brother, Thomas, were hoopers, though they also engaged in trade, occasionally exporting wine and cloth to Ireland and importing small quantities of fish.[5] In the subsidy rolls of 1524 and 1526 Matthew figures among the lesser merchants and tradesmen, assessed at £16 and in 1526, after his death, his widow was assessed at only £3.[6] Alice seems all her life to have done some weaving, however, and to have invested her profits in the occasional trading venture.[7] Items in the ledger sometimes mention cloth of her making and oil and wine imported by her, as well as 'money which my mother Alice Smythe ... lent'.[8] In later subsidy rolls she was assessed at £8 and £10 and gave 13s 4d to the Benevolence of 1545.[9] When the Corn Street house was sold to John Cutt in 1549, three years after her death on 9th April, 1546, 'toto le draperye wurke cum omnibus aliis implementis et necessariis' were mentioned in the deed[10] and John included cloth, wool and yarn in her inventory on fo. 246 of the ledger.

The only surviving children of Matthew and Alice, as far as is known, were John and a daughter, Elizabeth, who married Thomas Phelips,[11] son of Richard Phelips, M.P. for Melcombe Regis in Dorset.[12] The youngest son of Elizabeth and Thomas was Sir Edward Phelips, Speaker of the House of Commons in 1604, Master of the Rolls in 1611, Chancellor to Prince Henry and the builder of Montacute House.[13]

Even in the sixteenth century each community seems to have included at least one 'John Smith' and it has not been possible to discover much about John's early life. He must have been apprenticed to a merchant in the Spanish trade, possibly in Bristol, as a 'Johannes Smyth' de Bristoll' marchaunt' was admitted to the Bristol Staple Court at Michaelmas 1513.[14] It was, however, quite usual for a boy to be sent to another town to be apprenticed and he does not appear in the Bristol customs accounts until the arrival of a cargo of 4 tons of wine on 7th December, 1525.[15] The ledger shows that the Bristol man had some ties with Bridgwater. In 1538 he paid £2 6s 8d to Sir Thomas Crane, priest, for 'kepyng of an obbyt this 7 yeres' for Thomas Hoper, merchant of Bridgwater,[16] who seems to have gone there

---

[1] See genealogical table p. 319. L. U. WAY, 'The Smythes of Ashton Court', in *B. & G.A.S.*, Vol. XXXI (1908), p. 244. The documents of 1422 and 1440 seem to have disappeared from the family papers though there is a deed of 1436, B.A.O. AC/D2.
J. COLLINSON, *The History and Antiquities of the County of Somerset* (Bath 1791), Vol. II, p. 292.
[2] Will of Matthew Smythe, B.A.O. AC/F7/1.
[3] Will of John Smythe, B.A.O. AC/F7/3 and P.C.C. 14 Ketchyn.
[4] B.A.O. Bundle of Corn Street Deeds. AC/Box 8, XII. B.A.O. 04421(1), Great Orphan Book, Vol. I, pp. 182–183, the will of Lewis Mors.
[5] P.R.O. K.R. Customs, Bristol, E122/199/1, E122/21/1, E122/21/4.
B.A.O. 04026(1), Mayor's Audits, Vol. I, fo. 46. Two former apprentices of Matthew Smythe granted freedom.
[6] P.R.O. Lay Subsidy, Bristol, E179/113/192, E179/113/205.
[7] P.R.O. K.R. Customs, Bristol, E122/21/5, E122/21/7, E122/199/3, E122/21/15.
[8] Ledger fos. 162, 183, 254, 262.
[9] P.R.O. Lay Subsidy, Bristol, E179/114/256, E179/114/269, E179/114/274.
[10] B.A.O. 00566(12).
[11] Ledger fo. 9A.
[12] *Return of Members of Parliament* (London 1878), Parliament of 1529.
[13] *D.N.B.*, Vol. XV, p. 1029. This gives Elizabeth as the daughter instead of sister of John Smythe.
[14] E. E. RICH (ed.), *The Staple Court Books of Bristol*, B.R.S., Vol. V (Bristol 1934), p. 172.
[15] P.R.O. K.R. Customs, Bristol, E122/21/5.
[16] Ledger fo. 9A.

from Bristol some years earlier.[1] In the Bridgwater customs accounts a John Smythe appears, sometimes in partnership with John Dowding[2] whose name occurs on fo. 43 of the ledger among the 'Dessperid dettes'. At about the same date a petition in the Chancery Court records that 'John Smyth, late of Bridgwater, merchant' had been unable to collect a debt from John Dowding,[3] while a petition from John Dowding accused 'John Smyth and Johan his wife, late the wife and executrix of Simon White' of the detention of the deeds of a house and garden in Bridgwater.[4] Simon White's wife, Joan, was the daughter of Thomas Hoper. Dowding, who had married her sister, Elizabeth,[5] was a witness of Simon White's will when White, one of the wealthiest men in the town, died in 1529.[6] It may be that John Smythe was apprenticed in Bridgwater either to Thomas Hoper or to Simon White and on Simon's death married his widow and brought her to the house in Corn Street where his first son Hugh was born in 1530.[7] The property Joan inherited would have given him an excellent start in the Spanish trade and would have enabled him to undertake the expensive office of Sheriff in 1532.[8]

3 Trade

The John Smythe ledger presents a remarkable picture of the nature of Bristol's trade and industry in the decade 1540–1550. Overseas trade was divided clearly into two parts; the trade to Ireland, for which Bristol was the great entrepôt, and the long-distance trade to Biscay, Lisbon and Andalusia. The Irish trade seems mainly to have been carried on in Irish ships[9] while the greater Bristol merchants traded to Gascony and Spain. These men of the mid-sixteenth century were obviously less wealthy than such merchants as William Canynges in the fifteenth century[10] or Robert Thorne in the early sixteenth.[11] Each man seems to have owned one ship of about 100–150 tons and the Bristol fleet of 1545 was considerably smaller than those of earlier times.[12] The merchants formed a close-knit group and it was unusual for one merchant's goods to be the whole freight of a ship. They wisely shared the cargo space, spreading their goods in several ships to avoid the risk of crippling losses.[13] The decline in Bristol's wealth was partly the result of the concentration of English trade through London to Antwerp in these years and partly the result of the increasing difficulties and dangers of the trade to Bordeaux and to Spain during a period of war with France and growing religious and nationalist rivalry with Spain.[14]

Another reason for a considerable change in the prosperity of the town is illustrated in the ledger. There are some references to Bristol cloth workers and to cloth made in Bristol but it is clear that Bristol merchants bought most of their cloth in the Somerset or Wiltshire

---

[1]P.R.O. Early Chancery Proceedings, C1/810/52.
[2]P.R.O. K.R. Customs, Bridgwater, E122/27/10.
[3]P.R.O. Early Chancery Proceedings, C1/673/15.
[4]P.R.O. Early Chancery Proceedings, C1/627/37.
 A Tristram Hoper also accused a John Smythe of the detention of the deeds of a house—C1/818/12.
[5]P.R.O. Early Chancery Proceedings, C1/589/15.
[6]Will of Simon White, P.C.C. 10 Jankyn.
[7]Family album made by Lewis, J. U. Way 1904, B.A.O. AC/F1/4. This gives the wife of John Smythe as Joan, daughter of John Parr, Esq. but I have been unable to trace Joan or John Parr.
[8]See below p. 22.
[9]P.R.O. K.R. Customs, Bristol, E122/21/10, E122/199/4.
 A. K. LONGFIELD, *Anglo-Irish Trade in the Sixteenth Century* (London 1929), pp. 38–57.
[10]E. M. CARUS WILSON, 'The Overseas Trade of Bristol', in E. POWER and M. M. POSTAN (eds.), *Studies in Fifteenth Century Trade* (London 1933), pp. 183–246.
[11]G. CONNELL-SMITH, *Forerunners of Drake* (London 1954), pp. 67–76.
[12]P.R.O. S.P.1, Vol. 205, fo. 47.
[13]P.R.O. K.R. Customs, Bristol, E122/199/3, E122/21/10, E122/199/4. For example, Ledger fos. 108, 114, 144, 145.
[14]G. D. RAMSAY, *English Overseas Trade during the Centuries of Emergence* (London 1957), pp. 9, 135–137.

villages and that, in general, only the finishing processes were carried out in Bristol.[1] Many other trades are mentioned in the town, such as soap-making, beer-brewing, tanning and point-making; there are smiths and rope-makers, carvers, bakers and shoemakers,[2] but the loss of much of the cloth manufacture must have been a considerable blow. Though it is hardly necessary to take at face value the statement of the Mayor in 1530, when he was suing for special fiscal concessions, that the town was 'yerely fallyng more and more into Ruyn and decaye',[3] yet the decline must have been noticeable and, for the merchants, the risks of the mid-sixteenth century unusually severe.

This may be why the Bristol Merchant Venturers made in 1552 such a 'lamentable representation' to the King and secured a Charter giving them a monopoly of the overseas trade.[4] With Edward Pryn as Master and Thomas Hicks and Robert Butler as Wardens, there can be little doubt that Smyth was included in the Company and the lists of names of Bristol merchants at the end of the ledger[5] may well have been compiled in about 1550 when discussion must have been taking place to determine who was eligible for membership.

It seems to have been the general opinion in the first half of the sixteenth century that Spain had an adverse balance of trade with England,[6] that 'all the gold went from Castille to England, and nothing came in return but English cloth'.[7] During the 1540s this can hardly have been true. Smythe regularly seems to have sent gold in quite large sums to complete his purchases in Northern Spain and in Gascony,[8] though this was forbidden by English law, and he sometimes lost money on consignments of cloth for which there was no ready sale.[9] Export of gold from Spain was forbidden but merchants frequently carried gold earned by sales in Seville to the north to complete their purchases there.[10]

Cloth was, nevertheless, Smythe's most important export. Much of it was obtained from the villages on the borders of Somerset and Wiltshire which experienced a 'boom' in the manufacture of cloth during these years.[11] As early as the end of the fourteenth century such villages as Bath, Wells, Pensford and Frome were producing 1,000–2,000 cloths a year and Taunton, Bruton, Bridgwater, Beckington, Shepton, Mells and Rode produced 200–800.[12] The Mayor of Bristol blamed the rural industry for the merchants' losses, 'the marchaunt men daylly have and have had so great losses in the sale of their clothes beyond the see which is onely by reason of the untrue and faltie making therof'.[13]

---

[1] G. D. RAMSAY, *The Wiltshire Woollen Industry in the Sixteenth and Seventeenth Centuries* (Oxford 1943), p. 23, suggests that by the sixteenth century few Wiltshire cloths were sold in Bristol.
E. M. CARUS WILSON, 'The Woollen Industry before 1550', in *The Victoria County History of Wiltshire*, Vol. IV (London 1959), pp. 115–147.
R. PERRY, 'The Gloucestershire Woollen Industry 1100–1690', in *B. & G.A.S.*, Vol. 66 (1945), pp. 73–76.
E. LIPSON, *The History of the English Woollen and Worsted Industries* (London 1921), pp. 138–142, cloth making processes; pp. 233–235, the W. of England industry.
[2] See below, App. II, p. 321.
[3] P.R.O. S.P.1, Vol. 236, fo. 262. Petition of the Town of Bristol.
[4] P. McGRATH (ed.), *Records relating to the Society of Merchant Venturers of the City of Bristol in the Seventeenth Century*, *B.R.S.*, Vol. XVII (Bristol 1952), pp. xii–xiii. C.P.R. 6 Edw. VI, Vol. IV, p. 258.
[5] Ledger fos. 300A, 300B.
[6] J. LYNCH, *Spain under the Habsburgs*, Vol. I (Oxford 1965), p. 122.
[7] L. & P. H. VIII, I, pt. i, 6, p. 5.
[8] For example Ledger fo. 55 and see below pp. 13, 20.
[9] Ledger fo. 92 L.
[10] Ledger fos. 261, 271. A Bill of Exchange from Cadiz to Bilbao. See also Ledger fo. 127—money transferred to another Bristol merchant to be repaid in Bristol.
[11] G. D. RAMSAY, *The Wiltshire Woollen Industry in the Sixteenth and Seventeenth Centuries* (Oxford 1943), pp. 1–3.
E. M. CARUS WILSON, 'The Woollen Industry before 1550', *The Victoria County History of Wiltshire*, Vol. IV (London 1959), pp. 115–147.
[12] K. G. PONTING, *A History of the West of England Cloth Industry* (London 1957), pp. 22–26.
H. L. GRAY, 'The Production and Exportation of English Woollens in the XIVth Century', *E.H.R.*, Vol. XXXIX (1924), pp. 30–31.
[13] P.R.O. S.P.1, Vol. 236, fo. 262. Petition of the Town of Bristol.

Much of the cloth which was sent to London for export to the Netherlands was exported unfinished, but the cloth sent from Bristol to Spain and Gascony was already dyed and dressed, either in the villages or in Bristol.[1] Smythe supplied the country clothiers not only with the wool oil used to dress the raw wool before carding[2] but also with alum, woad, madder and other dyestuffs. In Bristol he seems to have owned a 'setting' or dyeing vat, at the dye house of John Lawrence, where his cloths were dyed with woad and where he charged William Shipman 2d a lb for dyeing cloths of 88 lb weight.[3] He also employed dyers for 'grazing' or 'grassing' green cloth, for 'wodyng of a clothe & for the hand of the same to be a vyolet', also for 'reffreshyng of the collowrs of ij old gownes'. Richard Tipper, tucker, was employed for 'rowyng' the truckers Smythe bought from Yerbery and Hasche and for 'bryngyng up of . . . northens' and then Davy Hart might have the task of 'barbyng and sheryng'[4] these cloths.[5] The Redcliffe and Temple suburbs to the south of the River Avon seem to have been the main cloth-working district and many houses there had the 'racks' or tenters used when drying the cloth to bring it to the correct size.[6]

During the years 1540 to 1545 Smythe's main supplier of cloth was John Yerbery of Bruton in Somerset,[7] from whom he bought an average of about seventy cloths a year. In 1545 Yerbery supplied only about forty cloths, in 1546 twenty-five and in later years very few, though there is no indication in the ledger of any reason for the decrease. These were mainly cloths which Smythe called 'penny hewes' and 'truckers'. For 'penny hewes' he paid £3 11s 8d a cloth in 1540–1541, £3 13s 4d a cloth during 1542 and 1543 and £3 11s 8d in 1544 to 1545.[8] In 1542 he paid £2 for 'truckers' but in later years they were exchanged for certain quantities of woad and the exact price is difficult to determine. It is not possible to show from the ledger a series of variations in the price of cloth according to the fluctuations in wool prices. Accounts for William Buchar of Cowley in Somerset, which cover the period 1538 to 1550 show that cloths which seem normally to have cost £3 6s 8d in the years 1538 to 1545 were £3 10s 0d for one consignment in 1541.[9] This, and Yerbery's 1542–1543 price could be the result of a rise in wool prices in 1540.[10] By 1549 Smythe was paying Buchar £5 6s 8d and in 1550 £5 8s 4d[11] which certainly does reflect the later rise in wool prices due to the inflation. The total cost of a cloth 'clere abord' ship in Bristol rose from £4 in 1540 to £6 in 1549.[12]

Other occasional suppliers of cloth were Thomas Hasche of Batcom, James Bysse of Stokelane and William Brydges of Weston.[13] For Brydges the ledger records sales only from

---

[1] E. M. CARUS WILSON and O. COLEMAN, *England's Export Trade 1275–1547* (Oxford 1963), p. 15, 'panni sine grano' does not necessarily mean undyed cloth but it could be in various colours, grain not being used. This is clear also from a comparison of the ledger and the customs accounts.
G. D. RAMSAY, *The Wiltshire Woollen Industry in the Sixteenth and Seventeenth Centuries* (Oxford 1943), pp. 23–24.
[2] K. G. PONTING, *A History of the West of England Cloth Industry* (London 1957), pp. 38, 94.
[3] For the use of the word 'setting' see T. P. WADLEY (ed.), *Notes or abstracts of the Wills . . . in . . . the Great Orphan Book* (Bristol 1886), p. 140, 'unu' settyng woode', see glossary p. 331, Ledger fo. 7.
[4] See glossary, pp 326, 331 for barbing and rowing.
[5] Ledger fos. 18, 57, 160.
[6] B.A.O. AC/M21/7. Rent rolls of Lord Lisle and Temple Fee.
[7] For the later importance of the Yerbery family in the cloth industry see K. G. PONTING, *A History of the West of England Cloth Industry* (London 1957), pp. 78–86.
G. D. RAMSAY, *The Wiltshire Woollen Industry in the Sixteenth and Seventeenth Centuries* (Oxford 1943), pp. 40–42.
P.R.O. Court of Requests CXV 51. P.R.O. Early Chancery Proceedings, C1/1171/1517, C1/1430/28.
G. D. RAMSAY, 'The Distribution of the Cloth Industry in 1561–2', *E.H.R.*, Vol. 57 (1942), p. 368.
[8] Ledger fos. 48, 125, 163, 201, 233.
[9] Ledger fos. 4, 187.
[10] P. J. BOWDEN, *The Wool Trade in Tudor and Stuart England* (London 1962), p. 219.
[11] Ledger fo. 187.
[12] Ledger fos. 56, 290.
[13] Ledger fos. 38, 115, 169, 286, 293.

August 1549 to June 1550 during which time the price of 'penny hewes' rose from £5 6s 8d to £6 the cloth.[1] There is no indication that Smythe supplied any of the wool for cloth making or that he had any agreement with the clothiers for the exclusive purchase of cloth, though similar agreements were not unknown in the local wool trade.[2]

Smythe also purchased Manchester 'cottons' for export from Thoman Abeck of Bolton and others.[3] These are unlikely to have contained any true cotton, but were coarse, light-weight woollens, cheap and brightly-coloured, manufactured mainly around Bolton.[4] 'Kendallmen' and 'Northernmen' brought in Kendall cloths and Northern dozens[5] and Welsh and Bristol friezes were also exported, sometimes as linings or wrappers for the more valuable cloth.[6] The bundles or 'fardells' of cloth were marked with one of Smythe's merchant marks[7] and loaded ready for the voyage to Biscay. It is clear from the ledger that the cloth did not always command a ready sale. The losses recorded on fo. 92 L are mainly on cloth, while an analysis of profitable voyages during the period 1539 to 1546 on fos. 92 and 200 shows that a loss or a small profit on cloth exported was often far outweighed by a considerable gain on wheat or leather exported at the same time. Sometimes when a voyage account was closed Smythe noted that cloth remained unsold in the hands of an apprentice or factor in Spain.[8]

Leather was obtained for Smythe from the Forest of Dean and the Welsh borders by John Spark of Newnham and from Gloucestershire by William Bullock of Elmore and Thomas Machin of Berkeley, who seem to have acted as his agents. Calf skins cost less in the Forest of Dean than on the Bristol side of the Severn; in 1547 Smythe paid 6s 8d a dozen to Spark for skins worth 10s in England.[9] Hides were also frequently exported and on occasion hides 'of my owne slawghter'[10] were tanned for export. Conditions for the export of leather were laid down by a statute of 1535–1536.[11] Few licences were granted direct to merchants but were given to Royal officials and favourites who then sold them to the merchant at a high price.[12] Smythe bought a licence for the export of leather in 1539 from Antonio de Manuela, a Spaniard. Shares of the licence were sold to other merchants and Smythe made a profit of 24s 8d on the whole transaction.[13]

A licence was also needed for the export of wheat,[14] and in 1540 he paid £25 to Alvaro de Astodillo, another Spaniard, for a licence to export 100 quarters.[15] In 1541 Thomas Shipman travelled to London to obtain for Smythe another licence to export wheat for which £50 was paid to Mr. Secretary Paget. This licence was shared with Robert Pole and Thomas Webb.[16] Spark, Bullock and Pole obtained wheat and beans for Smythe and sometimes contracted to be ready to deliver consignments straight on board ship at Hungroad or

---

[1] Ledger fo. 293.
[2] P.R.O. Early Chancery Proceedings, C1/386/43, C1/396/40, C1/1117/33, C1/1186/2.
[3] Ledger fos. 168, 274.
[4] A. P. WADSWORTH and J. de LACY MANN, *The Cotton Trade and Industrial Lancashire* (Manchester 1931), pp. 4–5, 16–17.
G. W. DANIELS, *The Early English Cotton Industry* (Manchester 1920), pp. 2–7.
[5] J. THIRSK, 'The Farming Regions of England', in J. THIRSK (ed.), *The Agrarian History of England and Wales*, Vol. IV, 1500–1640 (Cambridge 1967), p. 21.
[6] Ledger fos. 174, 196, 290.
T. C. MENDENHALL, *The Shrewsbury Drapers and the Welsh Wool Trade in the XVI and XVII Centuries* (London 1953), pp. 2, 26, 27.
[7] See above p. 1, note 4.
[8] For example Ledger fos. 56 and 91 when cloth was left with William Ostriche in Seville.
[9] Ledger fo. 264.
[10] Ledger fos. 67, 196.
[11] Statute 27 H. VIII, c.14.
[12] A. EVERITT, 'The Marketing of Agricultural Produce', in J. THIRSK (ed.), *The Agrarian History of England and Wales*, Vol. IV, 1500–1640 (Cambridge 1967), p. 530.
[13] Ledger fo. 71.
[14] Statutes 25 H. VIII, c.2 (1533), 34–35 H. VIII, c.9 (1542).
[15] Ledger fo. 71.
[16] Ledger fo. 133.

Kingroad whenever it was needed.[1] Food seems frequently to have been scarce in Spain during these years, especially on the northern coast where most of Smythe's trade lay. There, successive poor harvests in 1539 and the following years made the export of grain even more profitable than usual.[2] Smuggling of grain from the West coast ports seems to have been endemic in spite of a series of Acts forbidding export without a licence and decreeing that none should be loaded from the Severn creeks but only from the Quay at Bristol.[3] It may be that the wheat loaded into the ships down river was uncustomed and not covered by a licence. The shipping of wheat down the Severn to Bristol in time of scarcity was a frequent cause of complaint in Gloucester, where it was said that cockets were on sale in the market for 7d or 8d and 'they repayre unto Kyngrode which is a port of Bristoll' and there 'delyver the said greyne into some shippe there redy'.[4] Certainly the export of wheat even with a licence seems to have needed the distribution of a number of gifts to the customs men at Gloucester and Bristol.[5]

The ledger shows that lead was another important export which increased in volume considerably in the years 1543–1550. Smythe had three sources of lead. It seems from a letter in the Ashton Court archives that he sold the lead from the Long Ashton Chantry Roof.[6] Then, in 1546, he received 100 fothers of lead in payment for the sale to the King of the ship *Trinity*. This lead came from John Scudamore who was in charge of the store of lead kept at Bristol for the Court of Augmentations.[7] His other source of supply was the lead mines of Mendip, which, though reported in 1539 to be dead, began to resume working in the 1540's, perhaps to supply gun shot for which the Mendip metal was particularly suited.[8] The suppliers were usually small men, yeomen or farmers, such as John Lane of Priddy in the parish of West Harptree, a husbandman, for whom mining was a secondary occupation.[9] The lead was delivered by the supplier at Redcliffe where the sows were marked and 'powncyd' with Smythe's marks before export.[10] The markets of Antwerp and the north may by this time have been saturated with monastic lead and Henry VIII's agents able to obtain only £4 or £4 10s 0d a fother,[11] but the Bristol merchants seem to have found a steady market in Biscay and the lead 'made in smawle sowyes'[12] rose slowly in price, though not by any means in proportion to the inflation of the later years.[13]

One of Smythe's most important imports was Gascon wine. The Bristol customs accounts show that in September each year a small fleet of ten or a dozen ships set out from Bristol for the vintage at Bordeaux. They were usually loaded with cloth and leather, sometimes also

---

[1] For example Ledger fo. 87. Hungroad is an anchorage in the R. Avon about three miles below Bristol Bridge and Kingroad an anchorage at the mouth of the river about seven miles from Bristol Bridge.
[2] B.M. Vesp., C. VII, 87.
J. LYNCH, *Spain under the Hapsburgs* (Oxford 1964), Vol. I, pp. 113–114.
A. EVERITT, 'The Marketing of Agricultural Produce', in J. THIRSK (ed.), *The Agrarian History of England and Wales*, Vol. IV, 1500–1640 (Cambridge 1967), pp. 526–527.
[3] Statutes 25 H. VIII, c.2, 34–35 H. VIII, c.9.
N. S. B. GRAS, *The Evolution of the English Corn Market from the Twelfth to the Eighteenth Century* (Cambridge, Mass. 1915), pp. 138–139.
[4] P.R.O. Star Chamber, H. VIII, XXXII 96. P.R.O. Early Chancery Proceedings, C1/993/16.
[5] Ledger fo. 71 L.
[6] B.A.O. AC/C2/1–6.
[7] See below p. 16 for the sale of Smythe's ship *Trinity* to the King.
W. C. RICHARDSON, *The History of the Court of Augmentations, 1536–1554* (Baton Rouge 1961), p. 239, n.8.
[8] J. W. GOUGH, *The Mines of Mendip* (Oxford 1930), pp. 64–65, 83, 89, 134, 178.
[9] Ledger fos. 210, 216, 266, 283, 284, 297.
J. THIRSK, 'Industries in the Countryside', in F. J. FISHER (ed.), *Essays in the Economic and Social History of Tudor and Stuart England* (Cambridge 1961), p. 73.
[10] Ledger fos. 222, 290.
[11] W. C. RICHARDSON, 'Some Financial Expedients of Henry VIII', *Ec.H.R.* new series VII, pp. 33–48.
[12] Ledger fo. 273.
[13] See App. IV, pp. 324–325; A. C. FEAVERYEAR, *The Pound Sterling* (London 1931), pp. 48–70.

with lead or wheat. On two occasions Smythe also sent a horse for sale in Bordeaux.[1] Sometimes, especially in time of war, the Mayor was ordered by the Privy Council to ensure that the ships sailed in convoy.[2] They also faced attack by pirates and possible confiscation by the authorities in foreign ports[3] as well as the natural hazards of the Biscay voyage during the Autumn gales.[4] In January 1543, for example, after sixteen English ships had been taken by the Scots, the others were ordered to remain at Bordeaux for some time.[5]

In normal times, the English merchants seem to have been welcome at Bordeaux and were given many privileges, including a lower rate of customs duty than that paid by other aliens.[6] It was said in 1495 that when all the English merchants and sailors went ashore at the time of the October fair there were 7–8,000 Englishmen in the city.[7] About twenty years later an observer put the figure at 6–7,000.[8] They lodged mostly in the suburb of the Chartrons which, according to the French historian, Jullian, 'en temps de foire . . . devait ressembler à une ville anglo-saxonne, avec ses auberges, ses brasseries, le parler étrange de ses habitants et de ses hôtes'.[9] Smythe, like the other English merchants, must have searched the surrounding countryside for its best wines. The ledger shows that he dealt in white, red and claret wine from Bordeaux.[10] The Englishmen also loaded the woad of Toulouse which was needed for dyeing their cloth. Bordeaux notaries' records quoted by Michel show Bristol merchants of the period 1538–1550 dealing, as Smythe did, in cloth and lead, woad and wine.[11]

After a stay in Bordeaux of about two months, the Englishmen left, to return to their home ports towards Christmas time.[12] Some returned to Bordeaux for the rack vintage of January or February and the March fair.[13] At this time and throughout the summer months the ships also visited La Rochelle for wine and salt[14] and the northern ports of Spain for iron. Some also went on to Lisbon, San Lucar and Seville for wine, oil, soap, fruit, dyestuffs and spices. The ledger shows that Smythe imported sherry[15] from Seville and from San Lucar de Barrameda, where the English merchants had for many years carried on their trade under the protection of a charter from the Duke of Medina Sidonia.[16] While prices of Gascon wine seem to have been affected as much by war and uncertainty as by inflation, the price of sherry shows a fairly steady rise from 1539 to 1546, followed by a steeper jump

---

[1] Ledger fo. 104.
[2] J. R. DASENT, *Acts of the Privy Council of England* (London 1890), new series IV, p. 138, VI, p. 145.
[3] L & P. H. VIII, XX, pt. i, 459, 494, 981, 1003, pt. ii, 874, L. & P. H. VIII, XXI, pt. ii, 371, 509.
F. MICHEL, *Histoire du Commerce et de la Navigation à Bordeaux* (Bordeaux 1867), Vol. I, pp. 406–407.
[4] Statute 23 H. VIII, c.7, stated that no wine was to be imported between Michaelmas and Candlemas because of the dangers of the voyage.
[5] L. & P. H. VIII, XVIII, pt. i, 19, 28, 33, 57, 71, 113.
B.A.O. 13748(4) Adams's Chronicle of Bristol, 'The Bourdeaux fleet was arrested in Gascoyne and likewise the Frenchmen here'.
[6] T. MALVÉZIN, *Histoire du commerce de Bordeaux* (Bordeaux 1892), Vol. II, pp. 185–190.
F. MICHEL, *Histoire du Commerce et de la Navigation à Bordeaux* (Bordeaux 1867), Vol. I, pp. 389–390.
[7] P. BOISSONADE, 'Le mouvement commercial entre la France et les Iles Brittaniques aux seizième siècle', *Revue Historique*, Vol. 134 (1920), pt. 2, p. 215.
[8] B.M. Add. MSS. 11716, 11717 printed in G. SCHANZ, *Englische Handelspolitik gegen Ende des Mittelalters . . .* (Leipzig 1881), Vol. II, pp. 526–528.
[9] C. JULLIAN, *Histoire de Bordeaux* (Bordeaux 1895), pp. 440–442.
[10] For example fo. 211 L.
[11] F. MICHEL, *Histoire du Commerce de la Navigation à Bordeaux* (Bordeaux 1867), Vol. I, pp. 256–257, 290.
[12] P.R.O. K.R. Customs, Bristol, E122/21/10, E122/199/4.
[13] T. MALVÉZIN, *Histoire du commerce de Bordeaux* (Bordeaux 1892), Vol. II, pp. 53, 79–80.
M. K. JAMES, 'The fluctuations of the Anglo-Gascon wine trade during the fourteenth century'. *Ec.H.R.* 2nd series IV (1951).
[14] For an account of 'Salt of Rochell' see Ledger fo. 54. This may be salt from the Bay of Bourgneuf.
[15] Smythe usually calls it 'seck', but also 'Seckes of Sherys' as on fo. 114.
[16] G. CONNELL SMITH, *Forerunners of Drake* (London 1954), pp. 81–82.

in 1548–1550.¹ Some other wines are mentioned, mainly 'osseys' and bastards, both probably wines of Portugal, and taynt from Alicante,² but quantities of these were generally small.

The main import from San Sebastian and Renteria in northern Spain was iron. Early in the sixteenth century the use of water power caused a minor industrial revolution in the area, producing far more iron than the native industry could absorb.³

The quantities brought to England were large and profits were high. During the years 1539 to 1543 covered by the profit and loss account on fo. 92 the total profit on iron was almost £500 compared with just under £300 on all kinds of wine. The layout of the iron accounts in the Ledger makes the determination of precise costs and average selling prices difficult. In addition, price depended on quality, iron of San Sebastian always selling for slightly more than iron of Renteria. In general, selling prices remained fairly steady around £6–£6 13s 4d a ton throughout the period 1539 to 1544. The rise after this date is best shown from one account in the ledger, that of Edward Rowley of Kingsnorton, since comparison of the figures is then less likely to be falsified by expenses of carriage and other costs. In 1542 Rowley paid £5 13s 4d a ton for Renteria iron and £6 6s 8d for San Sebastian iron; by 1550 he was paying 'won with Another' £12.⁴

The iron was distributed throughout the whole area around Bristol, from Bridgwater to Birmingham and from South Wales to the villages of Wiltshire and Somerset. Much went northwards in Severn trows to the Forest of Dean and the Midlands. Historians of the Midlands iron industry make little mention of this source of supply, following Leland's account that smiths of Birmingham 'have yren out of Staffordshire and Warwickshire'.⁵ The evidence of this ledger suggests that the amount of Spanish iron used in the Midlands may not have been altogether negligible.

Three types of woad are mentioned in Smythe's ledger, according to their places of origin: Toulouse or 'Tullus' woad imported from Bordeaux; woad from 'the Yles of Surrys'—the Azores, and, once, 'Jeaner' woad, presumably from Genoa.⁶ Woad was imported into Bristol in large quantities and town regulations governed its storage and processing. It was sold to dyers and to cloth makers like John Yerbery often in part payment for cloth supplied. To obtain regular supplies at a reasonable price, a company was formed in 1540 to import woad from the Azores. The company was set up for six years, each share costing 650 ducats (£162 10s 0d). Nicholas Thorne, William Sprat, Smythe, Francis Blanckeley and Pedro Gonçalez each held one share, while Edward Pryn, Robert Butler, Francis Codrington, William Car, William Ballard and Francis Fowler each took half shares. Francis Blanckeley and Pedro Gonçalez were to represent the company overseas and Edward Pryn in England. It is an interesting early example of Bristol merchants in a company for overseas trade.⁷ There are few later mentions of the company, only a reference to 'the Portingall's freight which browght *owr* wood' and the payment of £25 to Smythe by Edward Pryn in 1547 'for my cowmpt of the Yland wood'.⁸ The later customs accounts

---

¹See tables, App. IV, p. 324.
²See glossary for types of wine, p. 332. P.R.O. Early Chancery Proceedings, C1/872/13–14.
³J. LYNCH, *Spain under the Hapsburgs*, Vol. I (Oxford 1964), p. 117.
⁴Ledger fos. 167, 248, App. IV, p. 324.
⁵W. H. B. COURT, *The Rise of the Midland Industries 1600–1838* (Oxford 1938), pp. 33–50.
H. R. SCHUBERT, *The History of the British Iron and Steel Industry* (London 1957), p. 313 mentions Spanish iron for making anchors.
R. A. PELHAM, 'The Migration of the Iron Industry towards Birmingham during the Sixteenth Century', *Birmingham Archaeological Society Transactions*, Vol. LXVI (1945–1946), pp. 142–149.
⁶Ledger fos. 48, 52, 101. 'grenewood' is also sometimes mentioned as on fo. 48.
⁷Ledger fo. 149.
C. A. COOKE, *Corporation, Trust and Company* (Manchester 1950), pp. 45–50.
W. R. SCOTT, *English, Irish and Scottish Joint Stock Companies* (Cambridge 1910–1912), Vol. I, pp. 12–13.
⁸Ledger fos. 89, 271.

show some very large shipments of woad to various Bristol merchants which may have resulted from the formation of the company.[1] Other dyestuffs and mordants, such as alum, madder and orchil, appear in small quantities in the ledger.[2]

Oil was another important commodity in Smythe's import trade. Some of it went to the clothiers for use in working the raw wool and some went to Bristol soap-makers, such as William Beryn, Thomas Thurston and Nicholas Shee.[3] The selling price of oil varied from £12 to £15 a ton during the years 1539 to 1547. In 1548 to 1549 it was £18 to £22 and in 1550 it rose to £28 and £29.[4] Occasionally, soap was imported and was usually sold either to another merchant or to a Bristol apothecary.[5]

Smythe dealt occasionally in fish but the quantities were small and it may have been mostly for his own use in the household or for his ship.[6] Salt seems not to have been particularly profitable. There is a short account for Rochelle salt on fo. 54 but it ends with a loss and it seems possible that Bristol imported less salt than had been found profitable in the Middle Ages.[7] Miscellaneous 'luxuries', such as sugar, marmalade, raisins, figs and almonds—even once 'a jar of oyle berys'—appear occasionally in the ledger and were often distributed as gifts to friends.[8]

Costs were high. The detail of freight charges, customs duties, the 'averia' in Spain,[9] costs of loading and stowing cargo, the expenses of apprentices, agents or factors abroad and the occasional loss on the exchange of gold are all shown in the voyage and imported commodity accounts and make up a considerable proportion of the total purchase price. Smythe's ledger shows payments for the insurance of cargo and, when shown, insurance is normally 6%,[10] though an earlier London merchant's account from Bordeaux and the later 'Marchants Avizo' both take 7% as the usual rate.[11] Smythe gives no indication of who his insurers were, whether they were English or foreigners or of how the rate was fixed.

The ledger shows in a remarkable way the importance of Bristol as a centre of distribution and that this was firmly based upon a good system of coastal and river transport. Much of Bristol's local trade was by water which was considerably cheaper than land transport. By 1635 the Severn was said to be navigable as far as Shrewsbury and the Wye as far as Hereford.[12] It was the only great English river whose navigation was not impeded by weirs, floodgates, locks or sluices.[13] In the early sixteenth century a series of Acts forbade tolls on the river and on the towing paths on its banks and protected mariners from the dangers of the dumping of ballast in its main waterways and anchorages.[14] The most usual boat on the

---

[1] For example P.R.O. K.R. Customs, Bristol, E122/21/10, consignment to Pryn, Gonsalves and partners, 14 June, 1542 in the *Harry* of Bristol—114 tons of 'woad of the islands' value £760. See App. III, p. 323.
[2] Ledger fos. 18, 27, 30, 31, 173.
[3] Ledger fos. 85, 185, 294, 129, 164, 165.
[4] Ledger fos. 84, 97, 156, 164, 179, 183. In 1550 oil cost £21 16s 6d a ton to import. Profit on 18 tons was £101 13s 0d and the average selling price £28 6s 0d. Smythe's valuation of stock to close the account was £22 a ton. Ledger fo. 185.
[5] Ledger fos. 9, 97, 146.
[6] H. A. INNIS, *The Cod Fisheries: the history of an international economy* (Yale 1940), p. 12 implies that Bristol ships were still sailing regularly to Iceland in the sixteenth century. There is no trace of this in the ledger. All fish mentioned seems to have been caught around the coats of England, Wales and Ireland, except for occasional 'Newland' fish.
[7] A. R. BRIDBURY, *England and the Salt Trade in the later Middle Ages* (Oxford 1955), pp. 110–115, 117, 121–122.
[8] Ledger fos. 17, 24, 27, 109, 146, 195, 197, 259, 271, 273.
[9] For 'averia' see glossary.
[10] Ledger fos. 222, 232, 234, but Ledger fo. 52 'for shewrance of 500 ducats £3.15.0'—only 3%.
C. F. TRENERRY, *The Origin and Early History of Insurance* (London 1926), p. 264.
[11] P.R.O. S.P.1, Fol. J(2).
P. McGRATH (ed.), *The Marchants Avizo* (Cambridge, Mass. 1957), p. 53.
[12] T. S. WILLAN, *River Navigation in England 1600–1750* (London 1964), pp. 99, 119, 147.
[13] T. S. WILLAN, 'River Navigation and Trade of the Severn Valley 1600–1750', *Ec.H.R.*, Vol. VIII (1937), pp. 68–79.
[14] Statutes 19 H. VII, c.18, 23 H. VIII, c.12, 35 H. VIII, c.9.

Severn was the trow, a large, often unwieldy sailing barge with a square sail and a square top sail on its main mast.[1] About thirty 'trowemen' and owners of boats are mentioned in the ledger, not usually Bristol men but from riverside towns and villages like Tewkesbury, Bewdley and Bridgwater. Some carried heavy cargoes of iron, woad and wine to the river ports of Worcestershire for transport overland to the Midlands. They sailed to the Forest of Dean and South Wales bringing their leather and cloth, wheat and timber in to the Welsh Back on their return. Yet others went south to Bridgwater and Minehead with many of the commodities imported by the Bristol merchants. Those Bristol certificate books which are still extant also show this flourishing coastal and river traffic. Smythe, in partnership with his former apprentice Giles White, sent northern dozens and other cloth to Bridgwater and another apprentice, Hugh Hamond, also appears several times, sending cargoes to Bridgwater, his home town.[2]

A number of carriers plied regular journeys from Bristol, for example Sheward of Bedminster travelled to Wells and the Somerset villages, Byrcom of Doddington went as far as Cirencester, while others travelled further afield, to Oxford, Reading and London.[3] Trowmen and carriers sometimes seem to carry on business on their own account, act as Smythe's agents in the supply of leather and buy small quantities of iron, woad or wool–oil as though for re-sale.[4] There is no indication in the ledger as to who usually paid the costs of carriage, though Smythe sometimes paid Spark the costs of shipping leather or timber from Newnham. On one occasion he notes 'bote hier from the Forrest at 12d per ton', on another a payment of 3s 10d a butt on wine shipped to Tewkesbury.[5]

A study of the ledger reveals some interesting effects of the debasement of coinage and the price rise of 1542 to 1550. Perhaps more questions are raised than answered. Why the difference, for example, between the rate of price rise of oil, which more than doubled in price in a couple of years, and that of woad which remained relatively stable?[6] Freight rates, though fixed by law in 1540, vary from ship to ship but do not rise very much by 1550.[7] The changing value of English currency in these years is frequently shown in comparison with the ducat which in 1540 was worth 5s then in 1548 6s and finally in 1550 6s 8d.[8]

To compare the record of Smythe's trade in the ledger with that in the Bristol customs accounts is not easy, although some accounts remain for these years. The dates given for the various consignments are usually near enough to identify them but the amounts given are rarely the same. The valuations are, as one would expect, rather out of date.[9] Many ships were freighted by several merchants in partnership and sometimes the whole cargo is assigned in the customs accounts merely to 'John Smythe and his partners'. These difficulties

---

[1] H. MORTON NANCE, 'Trows past and present', *Mariners' Mirror*, Vol. II (1912), pp. 201–205.
G. FARR, 'Severn Navigation and the Trow', *Mariners' Mirror*, Vol. XXXII, No. 2 (1946), pp. 66–95.
H. D. BURWASH, *English Merchant Shipping 1460–1540* (Toronto 1947), p. 140.
T. S. WILLAN, *River Navigation in England 1600–1750* (London 1964), p. 98.
[2] P.R.O. K.R. Customs, Bristol, E122/22/7, E122/23/3, E122/22/19.
For Giles White and Hugh Hamond see below p.12.
[3] Ledger fos. 3, 10, 68, 112, 225, 267.
[4] Similarly some of the craftsmen mentioned seem to have two trades. They 'tended to diversify' rather than put more capital into their existing businesses.
F. J. FISHER, 'Tawney's Century', in F. J. FISHER (ed.), *Essays in the Economic and Social History of Tudor and Stuart England* (Cambridge 1961), p. 7.
[5] Ledger fos. 6, 20, 34, 70, 128, 152, 264.
[6] Ledger fos. 147, 169, 185.
For price changes, E. H. PHELPS BROWN and S. V. HOPKINS; 'Seven Centuries of the Prices of Consumables . . .', *Economica* 1956, reprinted in E. M. CARUS WILSON (ed.), *Essays in Economic History*, Vol. II (London 1962), pp. 179–196 especially tables p. 194. Presumably, prices of sherry, oil and iron reflect changing conditions in Spain.
[7] The Statute, 32, H. VIII, c.14, however, fixed rates only to and from London and stated that rates might be increased by agreement in time of war. Spanish and Portuguese freight rates were lower than English, Ledger fos. 180, 185, 202, 255.
[8] Ledger fos. 56, 88, 91, 103, 126, 183, 185, 287.
A. E. FEAVERYEAR, *The Pound Sterling* (London 1931), pp. 47–70.
[9] T. S. WILLAN (ed.), *A Tudor Book of Rates* (Manchester 1962).

are clearly shown in the comparison of imports and exports in 1541 to 1542 as shown in the accounts of the Royal customs collected at Bristol[1] and the same consignments as shown in the ledger. It has been argued that in spite of smuggling and corruption it is possible from the customs accounts 'to measure precisely at certain times and places imports of . . . an infinite variety of . . . commodities'.[2] It seems from the evidence of Smythe's ledger that Bristol in the 1540's was not such a place and time.

4 The Apprentices

Several of John Smythe's apprentices are mentioned in the ledger and some interesting details of their work can be found there. The earliest surviving Bristol apprentice book begins in 1532[3] and therefore does not mention Thomas Shipman or Giles White who were apprenticed to Smythe before that date. Thomas, who was the son of William Shipman, Smythe's friend and neighbour in Corn Street,[4] received the freedom of Bristol in July 1540.[5] Giles was the cousin of John White, a wealthy Bristol merchant[6] and may also have been the nephew of Simon White of Bridgwater.[7] The later apprentices of whom the apprentice book gives details were none of them from Bristol. Robert Tyndall, apprenticed in 1535 for nine years, was the son of a husbandman of Belton in Lincolnshire.[8] Hugh Hamond, apprenticed in July 1537 for eight years, was the son of John Hamond, a merchant of Bridgwater, friend of Thomas Hoper and Simon White.[9] Robert Leight, apprenticed in January 1540 for ten years, was the son of a tailor from Kingsnorton[10] and Henry Setterford, apprenticed in July 1540 for ten years, came from Wolverhampton and was the son of a weaver.[11]

During the 1540's Smythe seems not to have taken any more apprentices but to have waited until these young men were trained. Then in 1550 he accepted John, son of John Blande, a London merchant tailor,[12] and in 1551 Thomas, son of John Horner of Stokelane in Somerset.[13] There is no record of what happened to Blande and Horner when Smythe died, though Horner received his freedom in the usual way in April 1558 'because he was the apprentice of John Smythe alderman and late burgess'.[14] It is interesting to see that three of these young men came to Bristol from the Midland counties and that only four of the eight came from merchant families. They were apprenticed for seven to ten years; the indenture was supposed to be enrolled at the Guildhall within a year of the young man's arrival in Bristol. He lived in his master's house, receiving bed and board valued at 13s 4d and at the end of his term was to receive the freedom of the city on payment of 4s 6d.[15] The apprentices might be quite comfortably lodged. In Smythe's house, even the chambers

---

[1] P.R.O. K.R. Customs, Bristol, E122/21/10, App. III, pp. 322–323.
[2] E. M. CARUS WILSON and O. COLEMAN, *England's Export Trade 1275–1547* (Oxford 1963).
[3] B.A.O. Apprentice Book, 04352(1).
  D. HOLLIS (ed.), *Calendar of the Bristol Apprentice Book (1532–1565), Pt. I. 1532–1542*, B.R.S., Vol. XIV (Bristol 1949).
[4] William Shipman witnessed Matthew Smythe's will, B.A.O., AC/F7/1.
[5] B.A.O. 04026(2), Mayor's audits, fo. 192.
[6] Will of John White, P.C.C. Welles 12. His inventory is printed in *B. & G.A.S.*, XLIII (1921), pp. 267–278.
[7] See above p.3
[8] B.A.O. 04352(1), Apprentice Book, fo. 51.
[9] B.A.O. 04352(1), Apprentice Book, fo. 99, and see above p. 3.
[10] B.A.O. 04352(1), Apprentice Book, fo. 166.
[11] B.A.O. 04352(1), Apprentice Book, fo. 178.
[12] B.A.O. 04352(1), Apprentice Book, fo. 458.
[13] B.A.O. 04352(1), Apprentice Book, fo. 481. Ledger fo. 297 mentions 'my sarvant Thomas Horner' on 1st March, 1550, although he was not formally apprenticed until 25th May, 1551.
[14] B.A.O. 04026(5), Mayor's Audits, fo. 178. 04359(1), Burgess Book, fo. 4. The ledger also mentions William Clerk and Humfrey Swift but they cannot be traced in the apprentice book and were probably household servants.
[15] HOLLIS, *Calendar*, pp. 13–14.

'for servants' had beds with flock and feather mattresses, blankets, bolsters and coverlets,[1] and when Thomas Horner was apprenticed a coffer was made for him.[2]

In the shop the apprentices sold goods and made payments, entering each transaction in date order in the shop book from which Smythe copied the details into the ledger. Sometimes they descended into the cellar to record and value the stock.[3] They learned to use the 'beme of yron', the scales and weights, they learned the varied and often complicated measures, 'cahisses' of salt, 'fodders' of lead, 'serons' of soap and 'ballettes' of woad.[4] Many of the notes in *The Marchants Avizo*, a handbook for apprentices abroad written by a Bristol merchant, John Browne,[5] must have been only a reminder of lessons already well learned at home.

Most merchant apprentices in Bristol seem to have spent some-time overseas. Shipman was already at Bordeaux in 1535.[6] Tyndall was there in 1537, only two years after his apprenticeship, acting as purser of the *Trinity*, Smythe's ship.[7] By 1539 he was 'Robert Tyndall, my prentis resydent at S.S. in Spayne'.[8] That October Hugh Hamond sailed in the *Trinity* with leather and a horse for Tyndall to sell and over £70 for him to use in buying wine at Bordeaux. A further £25 in gold was sent by land.[9] In all, Tyndall accounted for £600 of his master's money that autumn. Sales overseas were by no means always for cash and apprentices sometimes took a list of debts to collect.[10] *The Marchants Avizo* makes it clear that an apprentice acting as a factor in this way might expect a 2½% commission.[11] There is no trace of this in the ledger, though there is one reference to Giles White's 'wayges'[12] and provision was made for expenses. In 1539 Thomas Shipman was also in Spain and his account shows 'for his owne exspences untill the last day of Awgost 1539, 11250 *maravedis* and for Tyndalls tables 1975 *maravedis*'.[13]

It seems probable that Smythe's apprentices were allowed to do some trading on their own account and to act as factors for other merchants.[14] Thomas Shipman, in 1535, sent wine from Bordeaux not only to 'Jehan Semyth, son maître', but also to Guilham Schipman, son parent' and to 'Francisco Codryngthon' and 'Eddoouard Knotsford',[15] Some accounts compiled by William Tyndall in 1544 and 1545 show that he and his brother were already in partnership[16] although Robert's apprenticeship did not end until 1544. He received his freedom on 9th August that year[17] but in the ledger Smythe was still calling him 'my *sarvant*[18] and Robert continued to act as Smythe's factor in Spain.

For such young men the responsibility was very great and John Browne's advice to 'Be curteous and lowly to all men' and to forswear 'Wine, Wealth and Women'[19] was probably not always easy to follow. Smythe makes no complaints of his apprentices, though other masters were less fortunate. When a factor was led astray with 'riotous meanes and

---

[1] B.A.O. AC/F1/8. Inventory of John Smythe.
[2] Ledger fo. 280.
[3] Ledger fos. 265A, 289A.
[4] For these weights and measures see glossary.
[5] P. McGRATH (ed.), *The Marchants Avizo* (Cambridge, Mass. 1957).
[6] Archives départementales de la Gironde—3E 9826, fo. CCXLIX^vo, notaire—Nicolas Poyrou, 6 Nov. 1535.
[7] Ledger fo. 8 L.
[8] Ledger fo. 55 L. 'S.S.' is San Sebastian.
[9] Ledger fo. 55.
[10] Ledger fo. 221.
[11] P. McGRATH (ed.), *The Marchants Avizo* (Cambridge, Mass. 1957), pp. xvii–xviii and the account on p. 28.
[12] Ledger fo. 42.
[13] Ledger fo. 50.
[14] Ledger fos. 70, 229.
[15] Archives départementales de la Gironde 3E 9826, fo. CCXLIX^vo (see n. 6 above).
[16] B.A.O. St. John's Misc. Papers 187, 188, 189.
[17] B.A.O. 04026(3), Mayor's Audits, fo. 161.
[18] For example Ledger fo. 221.
[19] P. McGRATH (ed.), *The Marchants Avizo* (Cambridge, Mass. 1957), pp. 11, 56.

mysguydyng of hymselfe' losses might be considerable.[1] By the mid-sixteenth century, religious differences added to the young man's problems. In 1537 Hugh Tipton wrote to his master, William Sprat, that he and Thomas Shipman, Smythe's apprentice, had been sentenced by the Inquisition to go to the Church at San Sebastian and 'duringe the tyme of the masse and sermon stonde at the highe altar with tapers in their handes with owte cappes and capes, girdles and shoes' and to pay a fine of 600 ducats within three days and 120 ducats costs. They were forbidden to leave San Sebastian for two years or they would face a fine of 10,000 ducats. Tipton reported that their offence was that six years beforehand they had denied the authority of the Pope and had declared that King Henry's laws were in accordance with the laws of God.[2] In Tyndall's account for 1542–1543 an item notes his costs and 'his truble at Bilbo', but there is no indication as to what kind of trouble he had met with at Bilbao.[3]

Experiences of this kind do not seem to have made these young men wish to settle down quietly at home when their years of apprenticeship were ended. Among Smythe's former apprentices, Giles White was ordered by the Privy Council on 22nd September, 1556, not to undertake the forbidden Guinea voyage.[4] The final codicil to White's will was written on 1st May, 1564 'at my last Departing to Sea'.[5] Robert Tyndall seems to have spent many years at San Sebastian in the Biscay trade and in a Spanish notarial document of 1558 was described as 'vezino'—resident—of that town.[6] In 1589 a 'Henry Sekeford', who may have been Smythe's former apprentice, Henry Setterford, complained of his losses in Spain and Portugal during Elizabeth's reign.[7]

5 John Smythe's ship, the *Trinity*

There is in the ledger an inventory of the ship *Trinity* which Smythe compiled in 1539.[8] The total cost of the ship 'her hull, mastes, takle, sayles, iiij ankers, iiij cables' and all the monycions and abyllymentes' was reckoned at £250 but there is no indication of when or from whom Smythe purchased her[9] and the 1539 inventory may indicate only that she was temporarily in the King's service that year. She was certainly well prepared for war with a formidable equipment of 'gret gouns' as well as 'bowes, arrowes, bills, morys pikes & dartes'. She may also have had at her stern a 'scuchyn of the Kynges armes in tymber gilltyd' such as Smythe sold to William Sprat for the *Nicholas*[10] before this ship was purchased by the King[11] and she probably had flags and a 'streamer' like the *Nicholas*.[12]

Normally, the *Trinity* was regularly engaged in the Spanish trade and many references appear in the ledger to freight charges when she brought cargoes for other Bristol merchants. Timber for use in shipbuilding was sent to Bristol from the Forest of Dean by John Spark of Newnham.[13] In 1543 Smythe bought a load which included 'a kelle & stem and stern

---

[1] P.R.O. Early Chancery Proceedings, C1/66/98, C1/66/230.
G. CONNELL SMITH, *Forerunners of Drake* (London 1954), pp. 12–14.
[2] P.R.O. S.P.1/124, fo. 252.
[3] Ledger fo. 174 L.
[4] J. R. DASENT, *Acts of the Privy Council* (New Series), Vol. V, pp. 357, 358, 385.
[5] Will of Giles White, P.C.C. 18 Crymes.
[6] B.A.O. St. John's Deeds, 659, a notarial act from Bordeaux 1569.
B.A.O. St. John's Misc. Papers, 178—a notarial act of San Sebastian 1558.
J. ALBAN FRASER, *Spain and the West Country* (London 1935), pp. 92–94.
[7] B. M. Lansdowne II, CXLIV, fos. 386, 387.
[8] Ledger fo. 61.
[9] There are records of an earlier *Trinity* of about the same size in Bristol.
L. & P. H. VIII, I, Vol. I, 1577(1)(2), 1728, L. & P. H. VIII, I, Vol. 2, 1982(4), 2304.
[10] Ledger fo. 30.
[11] B. M. Arundel 97, fo. 100v.
P.R.O. Exch. T.R. Misc. Books, E 36, Vol. 143, fo. 124.
[12] P.R.O. S.P.1/150, fo. 113, S.P.1/153, fos. 94–95.
[13] For example, Ledger fos. 186, 230.

post for my bote' and seven 'knees' the shaped timbers so important in shipbuilding.[1] At other times he bought oars, cordage, canvas 'owllrons' for sails, anchors, gunpowder, a 'botehook', a 'gra*per*' and other iron work, and tallow and the special 'betakyl' candles for the lantern which hung by the compass.[2] Victuals for the ship are frequently mentioned; biscuit and wheat and beans; beer and cider; beef and fish.[3] Ships in distress were ready to help each other then as now, for in 1537 Robert Tyndall, acting as purser of the *Trinity*, gave John Enyon, purser of the *Mary Grace*, two butts of beer, a quarter of 'Newland' fish and a 'great seame of wood' at Bordeaux 'in theyr greate nede'. There is no record that her owner ever paid Smythe for this help.[4] Crew members are sometimes mentioned; the purser. the 'boteswain' and a succession of masters. In 1539 the master was a Scot, William Logan, whose receipt for victuals was left by Smythe inside the relevant pages of the ledger.[5] There is no indication of how the crew was paid, except that the master sometimes seems to have laden cargo on his own account[6] and on occasion Smythe bought goods from mariners which may have been their 'portage', the part of the cargo space they were allowed as a proportion of their wages.[7]

In 1539 the *Trinity* was probably among the Bristol ships employed as hired merchantmen in the King's service. The Truce of Nice between France and the Empire in 1538 left England exposed to the danger of a Roman Catholic Crusade. The Exeter conspiracy that Autumn, the despatch of Cardinal Pole to urge Francis I and Charles V to action and the gathering of a hostile fleet in the Netherlands all led to a serious invasion scare in England. Henry VIII and Cromwell took strong defensive measures and in the Spring of 1539 Henry had almost 150 ships in his service.[8] By the beginning of April 1539 the little fleet from Bristol, organised and fitted out by John Winter,[9] was ready to set out for Portsmouth.[10] At the end of the month, four were already there, waiting for the *Saviour*, the *Nicholas* and two others to come in, 'which ships be very well trymmyd as may be in good order to *serve* the kyn*ges* grac*e* & spesyally the ships of Brystowe & Wallis gret Joy to see them', Richard Abbis wrote from Portsmouth.[11] By 10th June they had all arrived and some are mentioned in a list of that date, though the *Trinity Smythe* is not included there.[12] War did not break out in 1539, however, and the Bristol ships returned to their usual trading voyages. In the following years unsettled political conditions brought several interruptions of normal trade by the impressment of shipping for the King's service, for example on 23rd February, 1541 and again in January 1543, John Winter received instructions to fit out ships for the King[13] and, after war had been declared against France in July 1543, ten ships went out from Bristol in November of that year to intercept a French fleet[14] but it is not certain that the *Trinity* was among them.

---

[1] Ledger fo. 186.
[2] Ledger fos. 11, 30, 50, 65, 82, 97, 99, 106, 129. See glossary for canvas Olerons and bittacle candles, pp. 330, 326.
[3] Ledger fos. 11, 13, 50, 78.
[4] Ledger fo. 8.
[5] Ledger fos. 11 R, 11 A. A foreign master was unusual.
 H. D. BURWASH, *English Merchant Shipping 1460–1540* (Toronto 1947), p. 21.
 Logan later distinguished himself in a fight against the French when he was captain of the *Murderer*. P.R.O. S.P., Ireland, H. VIII, Vol. 12, fos. 15 and 151.
[6] Ledger fos. 62, 65, 146.
[7] Ledger fo. 146.
 H. D. BURWASH, *English Merchant Shipping 1460–1540* (Toronto 1947), pp. 43–50.
[8] R. B. WERNHAM, *Before the Armada; The Growth of English Foreign Policy 1485–1588* (London 1966), pp. 141–144.
[9] Ledger fos. 11 L, 11 R, 11 A.
[10] P.R.O. S.P.1, Vol. 150, fo. 113.
[11] P.R.O. S.P.1, Vol. 151, fo. 141.
[12] B.M. Royal MSS. 14 B, XXVIII.
[13] P.R.O. Augmentations Office Payments, E 323/2B, pt. I, fo. 92 v.
 J. R. DASENT, *Acts of the Privy Council* (New Series), Vol. I, p. 76.
[14] B.M. Add. MSS., 32, 653, fo. 50.

In 1545 the *Trinity* was again prepared for action against the French.[1] Lists, dated 3rd and 10th August, of the ships gathered at Portsmouth both include the *Trinitie Smith* of 150 tons with a complement of 100 men, her captain James Parker.[2] In the original fighting instructions she was placed among the ships of the third rank, bearing, with the others there, the 'flag of Saint Georg*es* Crosse in his mesyn topp mast'.[3] She was later placed among 'the vauwarde'. The watchword for the battle was to be 'God save King Harry' and the answer 'And long to reign over us'.[4] In the event the French did not stay for a battle.[5] On 9th November, 1545, the Privy Council granted Smythe and Anthony Payne a licence for each to import and sell 200 tons of Gascon wine through any port in the Kingdom, 'which licence the Kinges Highnes grawnted them in consideration of theyre dommages by serving his Majeste this sommer upon the see', though this may be only a means of paying for the hire of the ship. It required further instructions from the Council before the customers of Bridgwater would permit the entry of the wine.[6]

In 1546 Smythe sold the *Trinity* to the King, then purchasing several vessels for the replacement of royal ships which during the war with France had been found unreliable or too old for further service in the royal fleet. On 20th March, 1546, a royal warrant ordered Edward North at the Court of Augmentations to deliver to John Smythe a hundred fothers of lead in payment for 'his ship called *Trinitie Smithe* with all her ordonaunce, takell and apparell received all readie by our Officers for us and to our use. And also for two hundreth poundes of Sterlinge money alreadie paid unto us by the said John Smithe'.[7] At this date Smythe was paying about £5–£6 a fother for lead,[8] so possibly the ship was valued at about £350. Already in March 1546 the *Trinitie Smith* was listed among the 'Ships for the North Seas'[9] and Lord Lisle reported that on the 11th or 12th March, 'being a parfect good sailer and well appoynted for the warres', she was sent out of the Thames to the coasts of Norfolk and Suffolk 'to be a continuall wafter of the king*es* m*ajestys* victuallers to be conductid to Calleise, Boulloign or Dov*er*. The capitaign of the same his name is Gilbert Grice a gentleman born in those p*ar*ties and hath good skyll of the Sees'.[10]

Finally, in the reign of Mary, the *Trynytie Smythe* of Bristol appears in a list of royal ships 'decayed' between the 36th year of Henry VIII and the end of Edward's reign.[11]

6 Accountancy as shown in the Ledger

Sixteenth century text books of accountancy suggest that a ledger should begin with an inventory. Smythe has no inventory, and he transfers personal accounts direct from his old book with no attempt at a balance. A later page of the ledger is given up to the enumeration of his plate in 1539, 1542 and that which was in his 'powar' in May 1549,[12] some of it possibly as pledges for debts. When his mother died in 1546 he made a list of her possessions and a note of the legacies he must pay according to her will,[13] but there is no attempt to estimate

---

[1] Ledger fo. 11. J. R. DASENT, *Acts of the Privy Council* (New Series), Vol. I, p. 192.
[2] P.R.O. S.P.1, Vol. 205, fos. 47 and 160.
[3] Historical Manuscripts Commission, *Salisbury (Cecil) MSS.*, Vol. I, No. 56. The Calendar dates this document 1539 but it seems to refer to the 1545 fleet.
[4] P.R.O. S.P.1, Vol. 205, fo. 160.
[5] Calendar of State Papers Spanish, Vol. VIII, No. 101, pp. 190–191.
[6] J. R. DASENT, *Acts of the Privy Council* (New Series), Vol. I, pp. 267–296. Ledger fo. 240.
[7] P.R.O. Augmentations Office Books, E315/472, fos. 13 and 14.
[8] Ledger fos. 254, 261. A fother was $19\frac{1}{2}$ cwt.
[9] P.R.O. S.P.1, Vol. 216, fo. 45.
[10] P.R.O. S.P.1, Vol. 216, fo. 114.
[11] P.R.O. S.P.11, Vol. I, fos. 59–60.
[12] Ledger fo. 63.
[13] Ledger fo. 246.

the value of all his possessions, such as Mellis suggests there should be in a 'solempne Inventorie'.[1] It is possible that such an inventory would be in a 'Secreat greate Boke'. Similarly, the 'Kalendar', 'Abecedario' or index was often a separate sheet or separately bound pages in the front of a Ledger[2] and, if Smythe kept one, it has been lost. The entries are not in alphabetical or date order and when a page was full the balance of the account was simply transferred to the next empty page. It is not unusual to find, as on fo. 245, an account of 1549 or 1550 pushed in between two earlier accounts.

Smythe sets out his accounts clearly in the correct bilateral form; the folios numbered across the double page from 1 to 300, the left-hand side for Debit, the right-hand side for Credit. Although his accounts are set out 'alla veneziana'[3] and in many ways they resemble the fifteenth century venture accounting of Venetian merchants like Andrea Barbarigo, accountancy was for Smythe almost certainly the 'Reconynges of Spayne'.[4] He may well have spent several years of his apprenticeship abroad, as John Browne described in *The Marchants Avizo*[5] and as his own apprentices did. Many Bristol merchants, such as Robert and Nicholas Thorne, Thomas Howell, Roger Barlow, Thomas Batcock and Hugh Tipton, lived for a time in Spain and Smythe had dealings with most of them as well as with William Ostriche, the London merchant who was the Governor of the English merchants at San Lucar near Seville.[6] Edward Pryn, with whom Smythe and some other English and Portuguese merchants formed a company in 1540, spent many years in Portugal and must have had a good knowledge of accounts to be 'admyttyd for mynes*ter*' of the company 'here in Ynglande'.[7] Early manuals of accountancy are lacking in Spain as in England[8] but it is the presence of an important colony of Genoese at Seville from the thirteenth century[9] which may provide the link through which Bristol merchants learned Italian techniques. That these methods were well understood in Spain by the mid-sixteenth century is shown by the ledgers of Simon Ruiz, which begin in 1551.[10]

Many such ledgers probably already existed in England. That of Thomas Howell, the Bristol merchant who became a member of the London Drapers' Company, covers the years 1517 to 1529.[11] Account books are mentioned in the will of Robert Thorne who was a partner with a Genoese in a soap-making company in Seville.[12] In the John Smythe ledger, references are made to the account books of such humble people as Robert Jackson, haulier, and Moris Appowell, smith, no doubt very crudely kept, in which Smythe signed, agreeing their accounts and admitting his own liabilities.[13] Among the miscellaneous

---

[1] J. MELLIS, *A Briefe Instruction* . . . , Ch. II and III.
[2] YMPYN, Ch. III quoted P. Kats, *The Accountant*, Vol. LXXVII (1927), p. 266. In 1522 Thomas Howell, the London Draper, paid 3s 4d for his ledger and 8d for the kalendar. I owe this reference to the kindness of Mr. J. Brierley, who is editing Howell's ledger.
[3] R. de ROOVER, 'The Development of Accounting Prior to Luca Pacioli', in A. C. LITTLETON and B. S. YAMEY (eds.), *Studies in the History of Accounting* (London 1956), p. 139.
[4] Will of J. Kydermyster, P.C.C. 37 Pynnyng, quoted by P. Ramsey in Littleton and Yamey, p. 185, n.2.
[5] P. McGRATH (ed.), *The Marchants Avizo* (Cambridge, Mass. 1957), pp. xvi–xxiii.
[6] G. CONNELL SMITH, *Forerunners of Drake* (London 1954), pp. 68, 95–99.
[7] Ledger fo. 149. Pryn's nephew married a Portuguese lady and became aide to Don Antonio, the Portuguese pretender.
F. W. WEAVER, *Visitations of the County of Somerset 1531 and 1573* (Exeter 1885), pp. 125–126.
B. M. Lansdowne MSS. LIII 24, LIV 74.
[8] H. LAPEYRE, *Une famille marchande; Les Ruiz* (Paris 1955), p. 342.
[9] R. PIKE, 'The Genoese in Seville and the opening of the New World', *Journal of Economic History*, Vol. XXII (1962), pp. 348–378.
A. GIRARD, 'Les étrangers dans la vie économique de l'Espagne au XVIe et XVIIe siècles', *Annales d'histoire économique et sociale*, Vol. V (1933), pp. 567–578.
[10] H. LAPEYRE, *Une famille marchande; Les Ruiz* (Paris 1955), pp. 342–346.
[11] A. H. JOHNSON, *The History of the Worshipful Company of the Drapers of London* (Oxford 1915), Vol. II, pp. 44–45, App. II, p. 251.
The Will of Robert Thorne, P.C.C. 18 Thower, also P.R.O. Early Chancery Proceedings, C1/798/8.
[12] G. CONNELL SMITH, *Forerunners of Drake*, p. 67.
[13] Ledger fos. 45, 65.

papers inside the ledger are accounts in bilateral form from John Wylly, Chamberlain of Bristol, and another, probably from Thomas Hickes. These seem to have been copied from personal accounts in ledgers similar to that of Smythe.[1]

Smythe's daily purchases and sales were recorded in a 'shop-boke', though, unfortunately, none of the shop books has survived. The sixteenth century manuals recommend that three books should normally be kept; the shop book or Memorial, the Journal and the 'Leager' or 'Quaterne'—the 'great boke of accompts'.[2] However, they admit that 'howe be it, some marchauntes there be, that use but small feate of marchandise, which do occupie but onely the Journall and Leager'.[3] A 'jornal' is mentioned once[4] by Smythe but, as there are no other references to it, this may be an error for the shop book. In the shop book, only once called 'my memoryall',[5] every transaction was noted in detail by himself or by his family, apprentices or servants and this daily information was later transferred to the ledger. This was often done much later and not within the prescribed five or six days and this may account for some of the errors in the ledger.[6] Although Smythe does not strictly follow the instruction that 'in the Journall or Leiger book there may not be any alteration of Cyphers, blotting (nor places left blanke in the Journal) . . . otherwise the books are of no credit in Law',[7] his corrections are usually carefully made. The wrong figure is erased and the correct one inserted and at the end of the entry it is often repeated, 'I sey £6'.[8] Sometimes he was in a hurry and merely crossed out and there are many blank spaces, but the constant naming of witnesses and sureties suggests that, unlike the Chancery Court,[9] the Bristol Courts of Staple and Tolzey did not accept the unsupported evidence of a merchant's book.

From a study of the John Smythe ledger it seems clear that Smythe was using a system of venture accounting similar to that described by Professor Lane from the account books of Andrea Barbarigo of Venice.[10] This system, which was the 'most practical form for merchants much of whose wealth was coming and going on the seas',[11] enabled Smythe to keep account of his obligations and claims through the various personal accounts which include also a few family and household expenses. In addition, by means of the 'Voyage' accounts, he could compare, year by year, the relative profitability of the various overseas markets to which he sent his goods. Accounts for apprentices and factors overseas would enable him to correlate his accounts with theirs, while commodity import accounts showed clearly the profit received on iron, the various kinds of wine, fruit, woad and oil. Whenever he wished to do so, Smythe could calculate his total profit over any given period in a Profit and Loss Account to which he closed the voyage and imported commodity accounts.[12]

---

[1] Ledger fos. 222 B, C, D, E.
[2] J. PEELE, *The manner and fourme* . . . , Ch. V.
[3] J. MELLIS, *A Briefe Instruction* . . . , Ch. V.
   B. S. YAMEY, 'John Weddington's "A Breffe Instruction . . . 1567"', *Accounting Research*, Vol. IX (1958), pp. 124–133.
[4] Ledger fo. 30.
[5] Ledger fo. 293.
[6] For example, see note on Ledger fo. 198.
[7] MALYNES, *Lex Mercatorial* (1656), quoted in Yamey and others, p. 49.
[8] For the correction of a credit entry wrongly placed to debit see Ledger fo. 168.
[9] P.R.O. Early Chancery Proceedings, C1/598/43, 'theire bookes of theire owne wrytyng to be of lyke forsse as is a specialtie'.
[10] F. C. LANE, *Andrea Barbarigo, Merchant of Venice 1418–1449*, Johns Hopkins University Studies in Historical and Political Science, Series LXII, no. 1 (Baltimore 1944).
   See my article 'Sixteenth Century Accounting', *The Accountant*, Vol. CLV (1967), pp. 357–361 for a more detailed account of the system used.
[11] F. C. LANE, 'Venture Accounting in Medieval Business Management', *Bulletin of the Business Historical Society*, XIX (1945), pp. 168, 173.
   A. H. WOOLF, *A Short History of Accountants and Accountancy* (London 1912), pp. 117–118, comments on the convenience of venture accounting when the merchant did not specialise, trade was uncertain and insurance rates high.
   B. S. YAMEY, 'Scientific Book-keeping and the Rise of Capitalism', *Ec.H.R.*, 2nd series, I (1949), pp. 111–112.
[12] Profit and loss accounts are Ledger fos. 92 and 200.

This double entry system is not complete in the ledger because there is no cash account and no account for his ship.¹ There are no accounts for expenses nor for the profits of money lending and sometimes he failed to copy in full in the ledger the factors' accounts and the commodity accounts. Thus there are a great many entries in the ledger for which it is impossible to trace a corresponding debit or credit, though it is possible that separate books were kept for cash and for the ship.²

There are necessarily a large number of personal accounts in the ledger. These are clearly set out and in the accepted form, though the pages are not ruled into columns. Most items are dated and the exact amount and type of commodity is specified. The cost and total value of each purchase is stated, often in Arabic numerals, sometimes in a mixture of Arabic and Roman, and then set out, usually in Roman numerals in the final column.³ Generally, all foreign currency is changed into sterling in the totals column, though on one occasion the whole of Thomas Shipman's account from Biscay was copied into the ledger in maravedis.⁴

Some personal accounts include freight charges, house rents, purchases of victuals and stores for his ship, expenses connected with his civic duties and accounts of money lending. Although valuables, such as 'a flat cup & a smawle standyng cup of sylver'⁵ were often taken as pledges for loans, no profit is shown from these transactions, since to take interest on a loan was for most of this time illegal. Only once does he write,

'Itm. for M*aster* Bowen 5 nobles *the* pr*i*nsypall & the cost*es* 3s 7d'⁶

as though interest of approximately 10% was being taken. It seems probable that the money lender found some way to take a concealed profit when interest was forbidden. Professor de Roover has suggested that in Italy the borrower actually received something less than the sum recorded in the ledger.⁷

Very rarely was anything paid for in ready money. Apart from 'barter' agreements, '3 monthes and 3 monthes' was usual or 'half in hand and half at O*wr* Lady Day' or at one of the local fairs.⁸ The amount owing was recorded on a bill or obligation stating the agreed days of payment. As payments were made—very rarely on time—they were recorded on the back of the bill and, when all was paid, the bill was returned.⁹ Smythe recorded the details of his own obligations in the ledger and often crossed off the amounts owing as he paid

---

¹Smythe began an account for the ship on Ledger fo. 61 but crossed it through.
²It was usual in Florence to have a separate book, used both as cash book and as cash account, called the 'libro dell' entrata e dell' uscita', R. de ROOVER, 'Development of Accounting Prior to Luca Pacioli', in Littleton and Yamey, p. 119.
See also R. de ROOVER, 'New Perspectives in the History of Accounting', *Accounting Review*, Vol. XXX (1955), p. 413.
I. ORIGO, *The Merchant of Prato* (London 1957), p. 114. Datini had 'libri d'entrata e d'uscita della cassa grande'.
Weddington and Peele both recommend a separate cash book.
³Roman numerals were felt to be less liable to error or falsification.
R. de ROOVER, 'Aux origines d'une technique intellectuelle; la formation et l'expansion de la comptabilité à partie double', *Annales d'histoire économique et sociale*, IX (1937), p. 191.
⁴Ledger fo. 50. The maravedi was a coin of Moorish origin and it is noticeable that Smythe always uses arabic numerals when dealing with maravedis.
A. P. USHER, *The Early History of Deposit Banking in Mediterranean Europe* (Cambridge, Mass. 1943), pp. 212–217.
⁵Ledger fo. 11.
⁶Ledger fo. 278. This entry is dated 1548. During the years 1546–1553 interest of 10% was legal in England, Statutes 37, H. VIII, c.9 and 5 and 6 Edw. VI, c.20.
⁷R. de ROOVER, 'Accounting Prior to Luca Pacioli', in Littleton and Yamey, pp. 120–121.
⁸For an example of methods of payment and the use of bills obligatory, see fo. 201—the account of John Yerbery.
⁹M. M. POSTAN, 'Private Financial Instruments in Medieval England', in *Vierteljahrschrift für Sozial und Wirtschaftsgeschichte*, Band XII, pp. 26–75 (Stuttgart 1930) and 'Credit in Medieval Trade', in *Ec.H.R.*, Vol. I (1928), pp. 234–261.
H. VAN DER WEE, *The Growth of the Antwerp Market and the European Economy* (Louvain 1963), Vol. II, pp. 334–350.
J. M. HOLDEN, *The History of Negotiable Instruments in English Law* (London 1955), pp. 4–29.

them, a practice which drew the censure of a seventeenth century writer who complained that thereby 'the Beauty of their Books is turned to Deformity'.[1]

Prices vary a great deal but one can only suppose that the price was lowered on the unusual occasion when someone paid cash. There are times when so much is 'discowntid' or 'rebatid' in the price but whether this is the result of prompt payment or poor quality is difficult to discover. Payment was sometimes by a 'circular' or 'giro' method, well established among Italian merchants in the fifteenth century.[2] Thus it was quite usual for Smythe to supply wine to William Northe or Stevyn Chick who then paid John Yerbery for the cloth he had sent to Smythe. With some of his customers Smythe waited years for payment and there is a formidable list of debts in the inventory taken at his death.[3]

Some of the more interesting accounts in the ledger are the Voyage accounts. Each time he sent a large consignment, usually in a particular ship or fleet of ships, he opened a new account.[4] This contained on the debit side full details of all the goods sent; their cost and quality; how they were packed and sometimes their merchant marks,[5] and the names of the ships and their masters. All the costs and expenses were added here, including the carriage to Bristol, the dyeing and finishing of cloth, and licences and insurance. The credit side was completed when the whole consignment was sold or when accounts were received from the factor. If the account was closed before all the goods were sold those remaining were debited to the following year's account at their cost price. The debit side or sometimes both sides of an account had left-hand columns in which the goods were briefly listed so that none was forgotten when the account was closed. Any profit or loss was then posted to the profit and loss account.

An account was opened for the apprentice or factor who was then debited with the value of the goods sold and any money sent to him and credited with the purchases he made on his master's behalf. It usually seems to have been necessary to export gold in order to complete the purchases for the year. In 1539 Francis Codryngton carried 110 crowns of the sun by land to Smythe's apprentice, Robert Tyndall, at Bordeaux, while 196 ducats and 97 crowns were sent by sea.[6] In 1546 Edward Pryn as 'taker' made Smythe as 'remitter' a Bill of Exchange which the purser of the *Trinity* of Wales carried to Hugh Hamond in Andalusia so that Hamond as 'payee' was able to obtain £25 from Pryn's agent, Hugh Tipton.[7] This was money Pryn owed Smythe from the profits of the company importing woad. In 1547 when Hugh Hamond sent money from Andalusia to Bilbao, he sent 600 ducats in cash carried by Tyndall and 200 ducats in a bill made by John Swetynge of Cadiz to be paid to Henry Setterford at Bilbao by Robert Jeffarson, merchant of London.[8] These are the only occasions when bills of exchange are mentioned, though Smythe sometimes notes a loss on the exchange of gold.[9] Smythe obviously followed Weddington's advice when he received his factors' accounts, first to 'peruse diligentlie and se yf in all thingis they be just'[10] because he sometimes notes an error,

Itm. more 1 d*ucat* which he r. of the purs*er* of the P*ri*mros & gave me no cowmpt of hit 5s.[11]

---

[1] MONTEAGE, 'Debtor and Creditor' 1675 preface, quoted in Yamey and others, p. 12.

[2] P. KATS, 'Double entry book-keeping in England before Hugh Oldcastle', *The Accountant*, Vol. LXXIV (1926), p. 95.
M. M. POSTAN, 'Private Financial Instruments . . .' especially p. 49 describing debts 'set over'.

[3] B.A.O. AC/F8/1.

[4] F. C. LANE, *Andrea Barbarigo* gives an example p. 166, 'Shipments to Constantinople entrusted to Carlo Capello'.
J. MELLIS, *Briefe Instruction* . . . , Ch. V, 'Viages', 'Per viage, commyted to such a man, by name, holding accompt as author and factor of all such marchandise, goods and money to him sent . . .'.

[5] As on Ledger fo. 290.

[6] Ledger fo. 55.

[7] Ledger fos. 254, 271.
R. de ROOVER, *Gresham on Foreign Exchange* (Cambridge, Mass. 1949), pp. 99–102.

[8] Ledger fos. 261, 271.

[9] For example, fos. 104, 195.

[10] Weddington, 'Breffe Instruction . . .', quoted by Yamey and others, p. 97.

[11] Ledger fo. 174.

Professor Lane found in studying the Venetian merchants' records that factors were very slow to send in their accounts, possibly from negligence but possibly also because of delays in settling local expenses, taxes and freight charges.[1] This may be one of the reasons why so many of the voyage accounts in the second part of the Smythe ledger have no credit entries and the second profit and loss account on fo. 200 is incomplete. On the other hand, the war with France may have caused losses at this time and Smythe was granted a licence to import Bordeaux wine in 1545 because of the great losses he had sustained, 'by serving his majeste this sommer upon the see'.[2] It may be that some of these consignments were lost but he makes no note of it. Only one brief account for salmon from Ireland carries the note, 'my foreseid cabow being employed was taken with Scot*tes*'.[3]

Occasionally accounts were opened for the main exports, cloth, wheat, leather and lead, as these commodities were purchased and recorded in various personal accounts. However, this was by no means general and where no such commodity account exists it is very difficult to trace an individual purchase of cloth, for example, from the supplier's account straight to the debit side of a particular voyage account. In the second part of the ledger, even where they exist, these export commodity accounts are often not complete.

Commodity accounts for imports are usually very detailed. Separate accounts were opened for the various types of wine; Gascon, sack, bastards, taynts and osseys. There are many accounts for iron and for wool oil[4] as well as those for woad, soap, raisins and figs and salt. The debit side of such an account gives the price of the goods 'clere aborde' the ship, then all the expenses of freight, taxes, insurance, hauling and stowing. The credit side usually gives a detailed list of purchasers, with dates of purchase, amount and total cost and the folio reference of the customer's account. Both sides of the account have left-hand columns in which the quantity is recorded so that Smythe could be sure that the total amount on each page coincided.[5] The credit sides of the iron accounts were often summarised, unlike the others.[6] When these commodity accounts were closed it was often necessary to value the remaining stock to carry forward to a new account. The basis for this valuation was usually the cost price but seems sometimes to have been a possible selling price. Finally, any profit or loss on the imported commodity account was carried to the profit and loss account.

Lines drawn under three of the totals on the profit and loss account[7] show that Smythe could at any time roughly calculate his profit or loss over a given period without actually closing the account in the ledger. The account on fo. 92 was closed when he reached the bottom of the page in January 1544[8] to show a profit of £1,427 16s 0½d. No account is taken here of profits on the ship, from the company importing woad or from money lending, since none of these accounts appears in the ledger. Smythe was, in fact, including as 'profits' a lot of money which he had not yet received. Folio 43 gives a list of 'dessperid dett*es*' from his old book which totals over £76 and a study of the ledger shows that a very large number of his customers paid very slowly.[9] However, only a token amount of £60

---

[1] F. C. LANE, *Andrea Barbarigo . . .* , p. 167.
[2] J. R. DASENT, *Acts of the Privy Council* (New Series), Vol. I, pp. 267, 296. Above p. 16.
[3] Ledger fo. 281. For 'cabow' see glossary, p. 326.
[4] 'Wool oil' was the olive oil used in preparing the raw wool for carding and spinning.
[5] Weddington was the first English writer to recommend a left-hand column—B. S. YAMEY, 'John Weddington's "Breffe Instruction" 1567', *Accounting Research*, Vol. IX (1958), pp. 124–133.
[6] For example, fo. 176 R. This is an additional proof that Smythe was concerned to determine profitability and not merely to record transactions.
[7] Ledger fo. 92 R. The lines are drawn after entries dated 14 January, 1541, mid-December, 1541, and 3 January, 1543, and the account is closed on 30 January, 1544, almost as though Smythe were totalling his profits for each year.
[8] Ledger fo. 92 gives January 1543 because in the old calendar the year began in March.
[9] For example, John Wells, fo. 29.

'lost by dett*ers* and o*ther*wise' is included here[1] and no provision is made for the other sums not paid.

There is no evidence that the ledger was checked and balanced. It seems as though Smythe sat down quietly in his 'cownter' on the first few days of July 1550 and transferred each account separately into his new book, noting at the end of each account in the old book the new folio number. Very few fifteenth or sixteenth century merchants balanced their books each year as the manuals advised.[2] For such men, who well knew the whole state of their trade, the ledger was still used mainly to record transactions. It was not yet 'the glasse of a mannes state wherein all men maie se clerely in what case thei stande'.[3]

7 Civic Duties

It has not been possible to trace when John Smythe obtained the freedom of the town of Bristol or when he became one of the forty members of Common Council. At Michaelmas 1532 he became one of the two Sheriffs for the year during which Clement Base was Mayor.[4] The office of Sheriff seems to have been both arduous and expensive and Latham suggests that it was 'in practice reserved for recently elected councillors'. In 1519 the complaint of William Dale at the great expense in 'his youthe and yong begynnyng' came before the Star Chamber and a compromise was reached but no doubt the expense remained considerable.[5]

Smythe must have found it an eventful year. On the second Sunday in Lent, Latimer preached at St. Nicholas' in the morning, at the Black Friars in the afternoon and on the following Monday at St. Thomas' 'dyv*er*s sysmatyke & yronyous opinions'. At Easter Hubbardine arrived to preach in St. Thomas' and St. Nicholas' against Latimer, 'And where as yt was very yll from the seyd seco*n*de sonday yn lente tyll Est*er* . . . yt hathe ben wors sens Est*er*'.[6] The townsfolk were divided into two factions and there were threats and even blows,[7] so that many people were imprisoned for 'sedycyous and skla*n*derus wordd*es*'.[8] Eventually in July Cromwell appointed a group of the leading men of the town to enq Iire into the trouble and statements were taken. Only John Smythe seems to have been prepa ed to testify against Latimer; 'Master Lattymer p*r*echyd that Sowlies in purgatery may meryt to pray for us as we may for them.

p*er* me John Smythe'.

The whole bundle of manuscripts is endorsed, 'The bokes & byll*es* Agaynste Huberdyn Only with owte Any matt*er* Agaynste Latymer save on J*o*hn Smyth Sheryff of Bristow'.[9] If this incident means that at this date Smythe was against any change in religion, then his

---

[1]Ledger fo. 92.

[2]B. S. YAMEY, 'Scientific Book-keeping and the Rise of Capitalism' (*cf.* p. 18 note 11 *supra*), p. 106 states that many books were not balanced regularly even in the seventeenth century.

H. LAPEYRE, *Les Ruiz*, p. 354.

F. C. LANE, *Andrea Barbarigo*, p. 180.

[3]YMPYN, *A Notable . . . Woorke . . .* , Ch. 29 quoted by Yamey and others, p. 7.

A. C. LITTLETON, 'Social Origins of Modern Accountancy', *Journal of Accountancy*, Vol. LVI (1933), p. 267.

B. S. YAMEY, 'Scientific Book-keeping and the Rise of Capitalism', p. 110, n.6, suggests that a too exact poring over ledgers could be the antithesis of enterprise.

[4]B.A.O. Mayor's Audits, 04026(1).

B.A.O. Copy of Adams' Bristol Chronicle, 13748(4).

[5]R. C. LATHAM (ed.), *Bristol Charters 1509–1899*, *B.R.S.* Vol. XII (1947), pp. 14–16.

H. BUSH, *Bristol Town Duties* (Bristol 1828), pp. 43–47.

I. S. LEADAM (ed.), *Select Cases before . . . the Court of Star Chamber*, Vol. II (Selden Society, London 1911), pp. 142–165.

[6]B. M. Cotton MS. Cleop, E IV, fo. 56.

[7]P.R.O. Early Chancery Proceedings, C1/872/51.

[8]P.R.O. S.P.1, vol. 119, fos. 184–197.

[9]P.R.O. S.P.2/0/11.

views were probably modified very soon, as he was later concerned with the surrender of monastic lands.

The Mayor's Audits for the year show the even tenour of life continuing[1] but Smythe, as Sheriff, must have been concerned in the discussions when, in August 1533, perhaps to show their loyalty after the troubles, the Mayor and Aldermen thought it wise to invite Thomas Cromwell to be their new Recorder. The fee was to be £19 6s 8d and 'hitt shal be butt to yow litill labors', William Appowell assured him.[2]

John Smythe's interest in town affairs is shown by his signature and his seal with the griffin's head on a variety of documents, such as the petition in 1543 of the merchants and tradesmen of Bristol against the Candlemas fair.[3] The ledger records two occasions on which he gave or lent money to the town. In 1542 he made a contribution to the repair of the Quay and in 1544 he lent £20 towards the purchase of the Lord Lisle's lands.[4] The presence among the Ashton Court manuscripts of a copy of the Lisle rent rolls and a draft of the petition of the City to the King for the grant of these lands shows the extent of his interest.[5] In addition, the lands of the Friars, of Temple Fee and various monastic properties were secured for the city, partly by the influence of his friend Dr. Owen, and Smythe was one of the Commissioners appointed to receive the surrender of the Hospital of St. John in March 1544 which Dr. Owen later leased to the city.[6] In 1546 Smythe was a member of the Committee of Aldermen set up to organise the purchase of land with money partly borrowed and partly received from sales of church plate. From the resulting income in rent the city was able to abolish the tolls, a long-standing grievance and a serious bar to trade.[7] After Smythe's death, ten years later, the Chamberlain, John Sebright, repaid to his widow two more sums, one of £20 and one of £23, which had been lent to the Chamber.[8]

In 1549, a year of risings in many parts of the country against enclosures and against the religious changes, 'there was a great Insurrection' in Bristol '. . . and many Young men pluck'd up Hedges and thrust down Ditches which enclosed Grounds near the City, & afterwards Rebell'd against the Mayor, so that he and all his Brethren with him were forced to go into the Marsh with weapons, and there the matter was closed up'. The rebels were imprisoned but none was executed, though the walls and gates of the city and the castle were strengthened and armed 'with great ordnance' and a watch kept night and day.[9] It must have been then that Smythe recorded in the ledger that 'at the tyme of the uprore' he had lent the Chamber £13 6s 8d and sent a hogshead of wine to Mr. Kingston's, presumably for the refreshment of the Mayor and Councillors after the fight.[10]

In 1547 Smythe became Mayor for the first time, an office he was to hold again in 1554 to 1555. The position of Mayor of the Staple seems to have been held concurrently and, since the Staple Court met three times a week, this with his other duties as Mayor and as Vice-Admiral must have been a considerable responsibility.[11] One of Smythe's first acts as Mayor

---

[1] B.A.O. Mayor's Audits, 04026(1), fos. 129–236.
[2] P.R.O. S.P.1/78, fo. 110.
[3] P.R.O. Exchequer Misc., E163/12/2.
[4] Ledger fo. 73.
[5] B.A.O. AC/M21/7.
[6] L. & P. H. VIII, XIX, pt. i, p. 157.
[7] H. BUSH, *Bristol Town Duties* (Bristol 1828), pp. 57–58, 63–68.
P.R.O. S.P.1/83, fos. 161–162, S.P.1/84, fos. 68–69.
[8] B.A.O. Mayor's Audits 1557–1558, fos. 72, 74. I owe these references to the kindness of Miss D. Livock.
[9] B.A.O. 07831, 18th Century MS., copy of Adams' Chronicle of Bristol.
[10] Ledger fo. 278.
[11] Smythe was Constable of the Staple in 1548 and 1555.
C.P.R. 2 Edw. VI, Pt. I (Roll 808, m.13).
C.P.R. 1 and 2 P. & M., Pt. I (Roll 881, m.27).
C.P.R. 2 and 3 P. & M., Pt. I (Roll 897, m.3).
P.R.O. C152/23, Statute Staple Certificates 1 and 2 Edw. VI.
Sir G. SHERSTON BAKER, *The Office of Vice-Admiral of the Coast* (London 1884), pp. 17, 29–35, 117–119.

is shown in the ledger to have been the wise provision of £20 to two Bristol hauliers to purchase wood when it was cheap so that the poor could buy it at a reasonable price throughout the year and money would then be available to buy more each summer.[1]

He was concerned to retain as much of the Chantry land as possible for the city. Hardly had the Guildhall gutters been cleared of January's snow,[2] when pursuivants arrived with proclamations, including one 'abowte ceremonys' and leather and nails were purchased for posting up the proclamations 'at dyvers places'. Then the Mayor's Audits record the expenditure of £4 'for a dynner to convide the king's com*my*ssioners when they were here to suppresse Chauntryes whiche was don by master mayors and his brethrens commaundement'. This was followed by much energetic activity. The Chamberlain rode to Wells to consult Mr. Kelway, the Recorder, and saw him again in London when he fetched the patent for the Lord Lisle's lands. Messengers rode into Dorset and again to London and, eventually, the grant of the Chapel on Bristol Bridge was secured in September 1548 for £51 paid to the Court of Augmentations.[3] The Chamberlain reckoned the total cost as £87 18s 6d as well as a ton of wine for my Lord Protector and the entertainment of the Lord Protector's son.[4] At the same time, money and plate were still being collected from the churches to make up the £1,789 17s 10d needed for the earlier land purchases.[5]

For Smythe's second term as Mayor in 1554–1555 fewer records remain beyond the rentals of houses and lands owned by the city and repairs to this property.[6] The city continued jealously to guard its freedom of choice of officials and members of Parliament[7] and the Ordinances of Common Council for that year laid it down that no one not an 'utter barrister of some Inne of Courte' should be appointed Town Clerk or Steward of the Tolzey Court and no one appointed Recorder 'under the degree of a Bencher'.[8]

The small inner group of Sheriffs and Mayors may have been 'a self-perpetuating oligarchy' but there is little evidence of corruption at this time. On the contrary, they seem to have been energetic and public spirited. Not that the City Fathers always received praise for their efforts. After the imprisonment of the Protestant preacher, George Wishart, there in 1539, the Mayor received at least three abusive letters, addressed to 'Yow folys Mayer and that knave Thomas White, with the lyar Abynton, the prater Pacy, the flatering Hutton and dronkyn Tonell, folis Coke, dremy Smyth and the nigarde Thorne . . .'. Another letter threatens, 'if the poyntmakers do ryse some of yow will lese theyre eares and that shortly'.[9]

Continued from p. 23

F. R. SANBORN, *Origins of the Early English Maritime & Commercial Law* (New York 1930), p. 307.
H. A. CRONNE (ed.), *Bristol Charters 1378–1499*, *B.R.S.*, Vol. XI, pp. 122–127.
R. G. MARSDEN, 'The Vice Admirals of the Coast', *E.H.R.*, Vol. 22 (1907), p. 472.

[1] Ledger fo. 219.
[2] B.A.O. 04026(4), Mayor's Audits, fo. 43.
[3] C.P.R. 2 Edw. VI, Vol. II, pp. 69–70.
[4] B.A.O. 04026(4), Mayor's Audits, fos. 52–54, 98, 117–119.
R. H. WARREN, 'The Medieval Chapels of Bristol', *B. & G.A.S.*, Vol. XXX (1907), pp. 182–183.
A. E. HUDD, 'The Chapel of the Assumption on Old Bristol Bridge', *Proceedings of the Clifton Antiquarian Club*, Vol. IV, 1897–1899, pp. 1–11.
[5] B.A.O. 04026(4), Mayor's Audits, fos. 97–99.
D. M. LIVOCK, 'City Chamberlain's Accounts in the Sixteenth and Seventeenth Centuries', *B.R.S.*, Vol. XXIV (1966), pp. XVII–XVIII.
[6] B.A.O. 04026(5), Mayor's Audits, fos. 113–132.
[7] J. E. NEALE, *The Elizabethan House of Commons* (London 1949), p. 163.
P.R.O. S.P.1/95, fo. 170.
[8] B.A.O. 04273(2), Ordinances of Common Council, fo. 3.
[9] B. M. Cotton MS. Cleop. E. V, fo. 361.

8 Land, wealth and family

By 1539 Smythe had begun to invest his profits in land. A series of documents in the Ashton Court MSS.[1] records the purchase from Sir Nicholas Poyntz and John Poyntz for £660 of the manors of Stanshawes and Sturdon in South Gloucestershire. This estate was extended by the purchase of more lands in Winterbourne from Robert Bradston in the years 1552 to 1556,[2] and, with the house in Small Street, was settled on Smythe's younger son Matthew.[3] Smythe bought the Long Ashton estate in 1545 from Sir Thomas Arundel for £920.[4] This included the manor house, the Chantry of Long Ashton and extensive lands, a fine estate which Thomas Cromwell had earlier coveted.[5] In July 1546 Smythe bought from the King for £447 6s 0d the adjoining manor of Ashton Merriettes, the rectory of Long Ashton and the advowson of the parish church there, all formerly owned by Bath Priory and amounting to a clear annual value of £23 13s 4d.[6] In 1549 Edward VI granted him the Chocke Chantry in Ashton parish church with its lands in Huntspill, Stone Easton, Keynsham, Wookey and Wells, to the annual value of £13 10s 8d. For this Smythe paid £293 16s 8d. He also bought the chantry lands of Newnham in Gloucestershire for £112 14s 0d,[7] including the house in which his friend and partner John Spark lived. This house, for which Spark had been paying 8s a year rent, Smythe sold to him for £6.[8]

Negotiations for the purchase of these monastic lands were no doubt expedited by Smythe's friendship with another Bristolian, Dr. George Owen, the King's Physician,[9] whose servant William Martin actually filed the application for the Newnham lands. Smythe lent Owen £100, of which only £50 is recorded as having been repaid, and in 1546 he sent him a butt of sherry, 'which I gave hym for olde frendship'.[10]

By 1554 Smythe had purchased at least fifteen houses in Bristol, as well as the Small Street house to which he had moved, and another in Corn Street.[11] Six houses were bought from the King in July 1543, together with the manor of Durleigh in Somerset and two houses in Bridgwater, for £340 7s 6d.[12] These purchases at the peak period for monastic sales[13] were obtained for a price equal to about twenty years' annual income. By 1555,

---

[1] B.A.O. AC/D3/28-34 (1539-1541).
 P.R.O. Feet of fines. C.P. 25 (2) 14/82, fos. 21, 27, 44.
[2] B.A.O. AC/D3/35-52.
 P.R.O. Feet of fines. C.P. 25 (2) 57/426, fos. 40, 54.
[3] B.A.O. AC/D3/48a, settlement of 28 October 1555.
 C.P.R. 3 and 4 P. & M., Vol. III, p. 412 (Roll No. 913, m.4).
 AC/F7/3, Will of John Smythe.
 P.R.O. Inq. P.M., C142/107/52.
[4] B.A.O. AC/D1/143-149.
 P.R.O. Feet of fines. C.P. 25 (2) 36/242, fo. 46.
 Dr. Owen may have helped in this transaction—Ledger fo. 171.
[5] P.R.O. S.P.1, Vol. 85, fos. 232-233.
[6] B.A.O. AC/D1/148 a and b.
 P.R.O. S.P.1, Vol. 228, fo. 57.
 P.R.O. Aug. Office, Partic. for Grants, E318/1017.
[7] B.A.O. AC/D1/150.
 P.R.O. Aug. Office, Partic. for Grants, E318/1948, 1949.
 C.P.R. 3 Edw. VI, Vol. II, pp. 403-404.
[8] Ledger fo. 264 L; B.A.O. AC/C2/1.
 L. & P. H. VII, XVII, 882 (p. 499). Spark was Mayor of Newnham 1542.
 RUSSELL JAMES KERR, 'Notes on the Borough and Manor of Newnham', *B. & G.A.S.* XVIII (1893-1894), pp. 158-160.
[9] *D.N.B.*, Vol. XIV, p. 1301.
 L. & P. H. VIII, XX, pt. ii, 909 (55).
[10] Ledger fo. 171.
[11] B.A.O. AC/S1/2.
 B.A.O. 00567(14), 00566(14).
[12] P.R.O. Aug. Office, Partic. for Grants, E318/1016, also P.R.O. Ct. of Aug. Books, E315/214, fo. 130.
 Various properties are mentioned in the ledger, for example fos. 11, 209, 244.
[13] W. C. RICHARDSON, *History of the Court of Augmentations 1536-1554* (Baton Rouge 1961), p. 235.

when he was making his will, Smythe set aside £800 for the purchase of lands worth £30 a year, lands 'that be abroade, in the fealdes and contrye and not in candell rente onlye'.[1] This suggests a static or declining population in the city and probably a strong resistance to rising prices in such necessities as rent.

The house in Corn Street which he inherited from his mother was sold to John Cutt in September 1549 for 100 marks[2] and Smythe and his family moved to one of the larger and more fashionable houses in Small Street. There Smythe had several alterations made to the house, including 120 square feet of ceiling in his 'cownter', a trestle table for the shop and 'ij dayes wurck abow*t* my shop wyndos at 10d a daye', a coffer for an apprentice and 'a frame for my table in the p*ar*lar'.[3] The detail of the furnishings of hall and parlour, shop and kitchen and several chambers shows considerable attention to comfort while the inventory of plate in the ledger shows the wealth which a merchant was able to amass in the first half of the sixteenth century.[4] Until his death John Smythe continued to live in Small Street rather than at Ashton Court. He went sometimes to Long Ashton, for wine was sent there 'for my p*rovicion*' in March 1549[5] and his will understandably provides for money to 'be bestowed wyth all conveniente speade in dressyng the cawsey that ledeth from thende of Bedmyster towarde my mansyon house at Longe Ashton'.[6] After his death his wife, Joan, lived on in Small Street until she died in 1560 when Matthew sold the house to George Higgins for £280. Hugh sold most of the other town properties to Walter Standfaste in 1566.[7]

On 9th May, 1544, 'John Smythe of Bristowe, gent. of the Lordship of Long Aisheton' received a grant of arms.[8] His sons were to live as gentlemen. John and his wife had seven sons and two daughters,[9] but only three sons, Hugh, Matthew and Nicholas, and a daughter, Ann, were mentioned in their grandmother's will in 1546.[10] In the Bristol Apprentice Book there is a reference to John Smythe, son of John Smythe, merchant of Bristol, apprenticed to Thomas Williams, tailor, in 1541.[11] However, after 1546, only Hugh and Matthew are mentioned. Hugh was born in 1530 and Matthew in 1533.[12] By 1547 they were at Oxford,[13] but do not appear to have taken a degree. From there they went to London in 1550, Hugh to the Inner Temple[14] and Matthew to Middle Temple. Hugh probably did little more than 'hear the chimes at midnight'. In July 1552 he was reported to have been put out of commons for three months 'for giving Master Lawton, one of the outer barristers, a blow on the ear, because the said Lawton counselled someone to arrest the brother of the said Smythe for debt'.[15] As it was his first offence he was fined and readmitted, but in 1554 Dr. Owen had to rescue them both from the results of a fracas with a certain

---

[1] B.A.O. AC/F7/3.
Candle-rent: rent derived from house property subject to waste or deterioration, *N.E.D.*
H. J. HABAKKUK, 'The Market for Monastic Property', *Ec.H.R.*, 2nd series X (1958), pp. 362–380.
W. H. HOSKINS, *Provincial England* (London 1964), pp. 77–78.
[2] B.A.O. 38-00566(12).
[3] Ledger fos. 45, 280.
[4] B.A.O. AC/F8/1—the inventory of John Smythe. Ledger fo. 63.
[5] Ledger fo. 259.
[6] B.A.O. AC/F7/3.
[7] B.A.O. Miscellaneous Deeds of Bristol Property in AC/MSS.
L. U. WAY, 'Miscellaneous Bristol Deeds', in *B. & G.A.S.*, Vol. XLII (1920), pp. 108, 119–120.
[8] My thanks are due to Dr. Conrad Swan, York Herald, for permission to consult the record of this grant and for his help and advice. See App. I, p. 320
[9] W. BARRETT, *The History and Antiquities of the City of Bristol* (Bristol 1789), pp. 483–484.
[10] Ledger fo. 246 R. B.A.O. AC/F7/2.
[11] B.A.O. 04352(1), Apprentice Book, fo. 171.
[12] B.A.O. Family Album of Lewis J. U. Way, AC/F1/4.
[13] Ledger fos. 74, 267, 268.
[14] F. A. INDERWICK (ed.), *Register of Students Admitted to the Inner Temple 1547–1660* (London 1877), p. 10.
[15] F. A. INDERWICK (ed.), *A Calendar of the Inner Temple Records*, Vol. I, *1505–1603* (London 1896), p. 165.

Mr. Carew, which gave him a great deal of trouble and cost their father £40.[1] Possibly it was considered wise to have Hugh married and settled at Long Ashton as soon as possible.

The marriage settlement had already been made on 21st December, 1553,[2] between John Smythe and Hugh Byccombe of Crowcombe in Somerset. Hugh was to marry Maud Byccombe 'yf the same Mawde will thereunto assent and agree' before the feast of the Purification of the Virgin Mary next coming.[3] Ashton Merriettes, Long Ashton parsonage, lands in Somerset and a house in Corn Street were to be a jointure for Maud. The rest of the Long Ashton estate was settled on Hugh[4] and John also covenanted to purchase lands worth £30 a year, which, with the fifteen houses in Bristol would become Hugh's property when his father and mother died.[5] These lands were later entailed and, as Hugh died in 1581, leaving only a daughter, Matthew succeeded to the property. Matthew had made better use than his brother of his time in London. He remained at Middle Temple, becoming Treasurer from 1570 to 1573. It was during this time that the Middle Temple Hall was completed and his coat of arms may be seen at the top of the fine East window.[6] It was probably Matthew who began the systematic collection of the family papers in the muniment room at Ashton among which the ledger was found, for some of the earlier rolls are endorsed, 'my father's lands' and 'my brother's lands'.

Smythe's increasing wealth and his advance to high civic responsibility are shown clearly in the Lay Subsidy rolls. From 1545 onwards he was always one of the Commissioners for the assessment and collection of the subsidy. In the years 1545–1548 he appears in St. Leonard's parish in Corn Street paying subsidy on 100 marks in lands and £100 in goods. In the list of contributions to the benevolence of 1545 he and Nicholas Thorne head the list with £15 each. No one else in Bristol gave more than £5 or was given the title of 'Master'.[7]

By 1549 he was living in St. Werburgh's parish in Small Street and then and in 1550 he was still assessed at £100.[8] By 1552 this had dropped to £80, though this assessment was still the highest in the city.[9] In 1560 his widow was assessed at only £30.[10] When one compares these figures with the large sums he paid for lands during these years,[11] the value of the ship *Trinity*,[12] a trading profit he reckoned at £1,427 for the years 1539 to 1543[13] and the inventory which valued his goods at Small Street at £1,641 in 1556,[14] additional point is given to Sir Walter Raleigh's criticism of the Subsidy Books in the Parliament of 1601,[15] especially as the position probably worsened considerably in the intervening half century. Smythe was hardly charged to his 'best and utt*er*most substance . . . wythowt any conceylment favor affeccyon dread fear or malyce'—the oath which he himself took as a commissioner.[16]

---

[1] B.A.O. AC/C5.
[2] B.A.O. AC/S1/1a.
[3] 2nd February.
[4] B.A.O. AC/S1/2–4.
[5] B.A.O. AC/F7/3, Will of John Smythe.
P.R.O. Inq. P.M., C142/108–109.
[6] A. R. INGPEN (ed.), *The Middle Temple Bench Book* (London 1912), pp. 151, 438.
A. R. INGPEN (ed.), *Master Worsley's Book on the History and Constitution of the Honourable Society of the Middle Temple* (London 1910), p. 170.
C. H. HOPWOOD (ed.), *Middle Temple Records*, Vol. I, *1501–1603* (London 1904).
[7] P.R.O. Lay Subsidy, Bristol, E179/114/256, 269, 273, 274.
[8] P.R.O. Lay Subsidy, Bristol, E179/115/308, 317.
[9] P.R.O. Lay Subsidy, Bristol, E179/115/330.
[10] P.R.O. Lay Subsidy, Bristol, E179/115/355.
[11] See above p. 25.
[12] See above p. 16.
[13] Ledger fo. 92.
[14] B.A.O. AC/F8/1.
[15] J. E. NEALE, *Elizabeth I and her Parliaments 1584–1601* (London 1957), p. 415: 'Our estates are £30 or £40 in the Queen's books—not the hundredth part of our wealth'.
[16] P.R.O. Lay Subsidy, Bristol, E179/114/276.

9 Conclusion

'Dremy' or 'Vir dignus amari'—his epitaph in St. Werburgh's? It is difficult to determine. Ambitious and hard-working John Smythe must have been and proud of his wealth and lands and of his sons at Oxford. His friends remained loyal, men like Nicholas Thorne and Edward Pryn, while his apprentices, Giles White, Hugh Hamond and Robert Tyndall seem to have become life-long friends. Towards the end of his life he had a serious quarrel with Thomas Chester which even drew the attention of the Privy Council. A letter instructed the Mayor with Sir John St. Loo and John Welch 'texamyne a mattier in variaunce betwene' them.[1]

He seems not to have been a harsh man. Once or twice a debtor was thrown into prison[2] but he agreed to fix days of payment when sureties were given. When Thomas Turbot's house was 'brent this last sommer by myschawnce' he gave him time to pay[3] and in two very difficult cases debts were forgiven.[4] When he died the total of debts owing to him was £816,[5] some of which his widow was able to collect by actions in the Tolzey Court.[6]

No great sums of money were left to the city in John Smythe's will since he had two sons to succeed to his property. Small charities included £12 to be distributed to the poor at his funeral, £5 to the poorest of his tenants at Long Ashton and £5 to the poor at Sturdon. He also made provision for a dowry for an illegitimate daughter living in London 'whome my frende Hughe Hammon doo knowe'.[7]

His religious views are equally obscure. The part he played in the Latimer case is not clear:[8] his will is non-committal, showing his willingness to compromise in the uncertain years of Mary's reign, 'ffyrste I bequeathe my soule to Almighty god three persons in trynitie and my bodye to be buryed in Chrystian buryall with suche devyne servyce as for a good Christen man shulde apparteyne'.[9] It may be significant that in 1551 he received a licence for himself, his family and friends at his table to eat 'flesh and milk foods in Lent and other fasts'.[10] Also, when Paul Bush, Bishop of Bristol, was dispossessed in Mary's reign he obtained a living at Winterbourne where Smythe held lands and had purchased the Chantry in the Church of St. Michael and might be supposed to have some influence.[11] Finally, on 22nd June, 1556, about two months before his death, John and his elder son, Hugh, were summoned to appear before the Commissioners of Examinations.[12] This may have been a religious matter, but the State Papers of the year are very much concerned with the examination of suspects from the West Country as a result of the conspiracy of Sir Anthony Kingston.[13] It may be that, after the Latimer incident, his attitude became more radical in religion and that he was even under some suspicion in Mary's reign.

He died on 1st September, 1556 and was buried in St. Werburgh's Church. Joan, his wife, was buried there too at her death in 1560 and Hugh and Matthew placed there a fine arched monument.[14] This was demolished when the church was rebuilt in 1761 and its brass plate was removed and cleaned by William Barrett, the Bristol historian, who suggested that it should be set up in Long Ashton Church.[15] However, there is no record

---

[1] J. R. DASENT, *Acts of the Privy Council* (New Series), Vol. III, p. 485.
[2] For example Ledger fo. 75 L and see fos. 5 L, 6 L.
[3] Ledger fo. 23 R.
[4] Ledger fos. 39 R and 236 L.
[5] B.A.O. AC/F8/1, Inventory of John Smythe.
[6] B.A.O. Tolzey Court Book 1555–1557, 29v, 54v, 59v, 64v, 75v, 86r, 118r.
[7] Will of John Smythe, B.A.O. AC/F7/3, P.C.C. 14 Ketchyn.
[8] See above p. 22.
[9] Will of John Smythe, B.A.O. AC/F7/3, P.C.C. 14 Ketchyn.
[10] C.P.R. 5 Edw. VI, Vol. IV, p. 177.
[11] *Victoria County History of Gloucestershire*, Vol. II, p. 30.
[12] J. R. DASENT, *Acts of the Privy Council* (New Series), Vol. V, p. 290.
[13] P.R.O. S.P.11, Vols. 7 and 8 (1556). S.P.11/7, fos. 45–48 contain lists of suspects, including one 'Smyth'.
[14] W. BARRETT, *The History & Antiquities of the City of Bristol* (Bristol 1789), p. 484.
[15] B.A.O. AC/F9/4a, b. Letters from William Barrett to John Hugh Smith, Esq., 1765 and 1769.

that this was ever done. In the nineteenth century, St. Werburgh's Church was finally demolished and removed from its medieval site. Soon afterwards, Dr. Beddoe, M.D., F.R.S., reported to a meeting of the Bristol and Gloucestershire Archaeological Society on some studies he had made of skulls disinterred from the vaults and churchyard of St. Werburgh's. He found that the older ones taken from the vaults under the Church were 'short, broad, rounded, rather flat, with rather a small frontal region, but otherwise well-filled'.[1]

'Alas! poor Yorick.'

---

[1] J. BEDDOE, M.D., F.R.S., 'On certain Crania disinterred at St. Werburgh's Bristol', *B. & G.A.S.*, Vol. III, 1878–1879, pp. 77–82.

Text

1(L)[1]

1(R)   This boke of acowmpt*es* ap*er*teynith to J*oh*n Smythe m*ar*chant of Bristowe.

2(L)   anno 1539

John Gane the yon*ger* of Bristowe m*ar*chant owith the 10th daye of
October £21 15s for acowmpt in my old boke fo. 10 & it is £19 to paye
by 3 severall bills ffinyd & sealid with his hand datid the 28 daye of June
a*n*no 1533, £4 at Candellmas in a*n*no 1533, £7 10s at Seynt Jamystide 1534
& £7 10s at Seynt Jamystide 1535, & it is for £15 I pd. to Thomas Wottley of
Batc*om* yeoman for hym & £4 pd. the seid Wottley for hym in redy money,
& more I lent the seid Gane the 4th day of October
1533 a pipe of ire*n* in 55s to pay at Candelmas next after   £21 15s

         anno 1537

Watkyn Tayllo*r* of Tynby owith the 18 day of Decemb*er* a*n*no dicto 30s 9d
which is for 5 C 14 li. iren d'd for hym to Richard Vale his son in the lawe, to
be paid at all tymes requyrid   £1 10s 9d
Itm. the 27 day of Agost 1538 6s 3d which is for 3 qr. 21 li. iren of S.S. at
6s 8d the C d'd for hym to Will*ia*m Floyde m*aster* of his bote, to be pd. at all
tymes, mon*tith*   6s 3d

2(R)[2]

3(L)   anno 1535

Thomas Upgenckyng of Aburgeyne smythe owithe the 26 day of Novemb*er*
56s 8d, to pay hallf at Candellmas next & the other hallf at Seynt Jamistide
next after *that* which is for a pipe 4 li. iren after £5 13s 4d *the* ton, mon*tith*   £2 16s 8d
Itm. the 27 day of the same 28s 6d to pay 13s 4d in hand & 15s 2d at
Candellmas next which is for a h'd 4 li. iren at 5s 8d *the* C & at *the* seid tyme
he d'd to me in pledge a woma*n*s girdil   £1 8s 6d
M*em*orandum that Alice the wif of the seid Thomas Upgenckyn deceassyd
agreid with me at Bristowe the last day of July a*n*no 1539 to pay yerly
13s 4d tyll the dett of her husband war fully paide, *that* is 6s 8d at Candellmas
& 6s 8d at Seynt Jamystide.[3]

         anno 1540

Will*ia*m Sheward of Bedmister carrier owith the 18 day of Febryver a*n*no
dicto 20s 6d for 3 C 8 li. iren of S.S. at 6s 8d the C to pay it at Seynt
Jamistide next comyng   £1 6d

3(R)   anno 1535

     Thomas Upgenckyn p*er* contra is dewe to have the 27 day
     of Novemb*er* 13s 4d r. in hand for the h'd iren p*er* contra   13s 4d

---

[1] *Fo. 1L is blank in the MS.*
[2] *Fo. 2R is blank in the MS.*
[3] *Marginal note* Jo*h*n Thom*as.*

3(R) contd.

Itm. the first day of Marche anno 1538 r. from his wif Alice Watkyn by Edward Jones of Aburgeyne 6s 8d	6s	8d
Itm. the 28 day of July anno 1539 r. from his wif by Edward Jones 13s 4d	13s	4d
Itm. the 15 day of February 1539 r. by the handes of E. Jones	6s	8d
Itm. the 28 day of July 1540 6s 8d r. of Alice the late wif of Thomas Upgenkyne	6s	8d
1541 Itm. the 27 day of July r. of her in Bristowe 6s 8d	6s	8d
Itm. the 14 day of October r. by John Thomas	6s	8d

anno 1541

William Sheward per contra is dewe to have the 24 day of September 10s which my wif r. of hym	10s	
Itm. the 3d day of September 1542 r. 8s 8d	8s	8d

4(L)   **anno 1539**

Richard Smythe of Bramyerd in Harvartshire owith the 10th day of October 23s 4d which is for 2 barells herryng d'd for hym to Richard Barne his neighbur at 10s the barrel & more he owith for an old rest of his acowmpt 23s 3s 4d as it aperith in his cownt in my old boke fo.14	£1	3s	4d

anno 1538

William Buchar of Cowlley clothiar owith the 17 daye of Aprill £10 paide to hym for the first payement of my bill per contra	£10		
Itm. the 3d day of Agost 33s 3d that is for 1 ½-bale of Tullus wood conteynyng C 3 qr. 3 li. at 17s the C, montith	£1	10s	3d
1539 Itm. the 26 day of Marche 1539 £8 9s 9d that is for so myche redy money paide to hym	£8	9s	9d
1540 Itm. the 10th day of Aprell 1540 £10 pd. to his son in redy monney & r. my bill	£10		
S.	£30		

anno 1540

William Buchar of Cowlley owith the 18 day of Jenyver £12 15s paide to hym in redy money	£12	15s	
Itm. the same day 2 ½-bales wood conteynyng 3 C ½, 12 li. at 16s 8d the C, montith £3	£3		
Itm. the 16 day of February £5 for so myche pd. to hym in redy monney	£5		
1541 Itm. the 7 day of February 1541 £10 pd. to hym in parte of payement of his bill datyd the 18 day of Jenyver anno 1540	£10		
Itm. the 8 day of February pd. to hym £4 16s 8d	£4	16s	8d
1542 Itm. the 6 day of May 1542 my wif paid to hym £10 that is for a payment dewe at Ester last past & so r. on of my bills	£10		
Itm. the 27 day of Jenyver pd. for hym to John Buchar his brothers son 40s	£2		
Itm. the 3 day of February pd. to hymsellf £8 the which is with the 40s in this other itm. £10 & it is for the last & hole payment of my bill datyd the 18 day of Jenyver anno 1540 & I r. my bill	£8		
Itm. the 14 day of Marche pd. to hym £10 which was payable at Candellmas last past & so r. my bill putt it apon the backsyde of my bill	£10		
Itm. the seid day £10 for so myche I do make hym creditor of fo. 187 for the closyng up of this cowmpt	£10		
S.	£75	11s	8d

4(R)   anno 1541

Richard Smythe of Bra*m*yerd p*er* contra is dewe to have
the 25 day of July 23s 4d for so myche Richard Barns pd.   £1   3s   4d

anno 1538

Willi*am* Buchar of Cowley in Somersetshire clothiar is
dewe to have the 27 day of Marche £30, that is for the
rest of 10 clothes in collow*res*, 5 azars & 5 hewlyng*es*
whiche I bowght & r. of hym at 5 m*ar*k*es* the clothe, to
pay £10 in hand, £10 at M*ar*che next & £10 at M*ar*che
next after that as it ap*er*ith by my bill made *this* preasent
day, mon*tith*   S.   £30

Itm. the 10th day of Aprell 1540   [1]

anno 1540

Willi*am* Buchar of Cowlley in Som*er*zetshire clother is
dewe to have the 18 day of Jenyver £40 15s which is for
12 clothes r. & bowght of hym at £3 6s 8d the clothe & 15s
over & apo*n* all, to pay £15 15s in hand & £5 ten dayes after
Candellmas next com*m*yng & £10 at Cristmas next & £10
at Cristmas next after *that* as it may apere by my bills   ~~£40 15s~~
Itm. the 8 day of February £34 16s 8d & is for 10 clothes
r. of hym *that* is 5 blewes & 5 hewling*es* at £3 10s the
clo*the* less 3s 4d apo*n* all, to pay £4 16s 8d in hand,
~~£10 at Easter next commyng £10 at Candellmas in a*n*no 1542~~
& £10 at Candellmas in a*n*no 1543 as it may apere by 2
bills which I have made   £34   16s   8d
~~Itm. the 6 day of May~~

                                                                           S.   £75   11s   8d

5(L)   anno 1539

John Nappar of M*ar*tock in Som*er*setshire hussbandma*n* owith the 26
day of July £8, to pay 40s at Seynt Jamystide next and so ev*er*y Seynt
Jamistide next enshewyng on after a nother, other 40s, till the seid som of
£8 be ffully paide, as it may apere by an obligacio*n* made by John Sare
nottary of Bristowe and it is for the rest of an old cowmpt in my old boke
fo. 22   £8
This cownt is passed into my newe booke fo. 1 the 2de day of July a*nno* 1550.

anno 1532

Willi*am* Whelar of Bridgewater marchant owith the 5th day of July 16s 4d
by a bill fyrmyd with his hand. His wif *that* was & nowe Joan Lovell promezid
me at Seynt Jamistide 1539 to pay me the seid mon*n*ey at Cristmas next
after.   S.   16s   4d

anno 1543

Richard Master of Wesbery in the Forrest of Deane smythe owith the 26 day of
July £3 to be paide at Candellmas next com*m*yng & it is for ~~the rest of~~ a pipe
& 3 li. iren solld & delyverd to hym. I have a bond apo*n* hym & besyd*es* that
M*aster* Wynter is shewerty for hym   £3
Itm. the 28 of Jenyver £3 which is for a pipe of Rendry iren to be pd. at
Seynt Jamistide next com*m*yng. John Sparck is shew*er*ty   £3

---

[1] *Blank in MS.*

5(R)   anno 1540

John Nappar per contra is dewe to have 40s that is for so
myche monney r. of Hancot the fisshar   £2

anno 1541

William Whelar per contra is dewe to have the 26 day of
August 15s r. for hym of Geffrey Arnedells wif & 16d I
forgave hym. So amontith the hole   S.   16s   4d

anno 1543

Richard Master per contra is dewe to have the 27 daye
of Jenyver anno 1543 £3 which he pd. me in redy monny   £3
Itm. the 26 of July 1544 r. £3   £3

6(L)   anno 1539

Lawarence Hanckot of Barnsgrove owith the 28 day of June £12 2s that
is for 2 ton 1 qr. 9 li. iren d'd for hym to his uncle Symond Hanckot of
Bristowe tayllor, to be paide at Candellmas next and the seid Symond is
shewerty for the payement   £12   2s
Nottandum[1] and ffor becaws the seid 2 ton 1 qr. 9 li. iren was lost owt
of the trowe going throwgh the Shuttes the seid Lawrence dezirid me to be
content that he might pay it £3 every yere, the which I grawntyd hym & his seid
uncle restith shewerty for the performance thereof.
Itm. the 24 day of July £12 that is for 2 ton iren sold & d'd to hymseallf to
pay this tyme twell monthes & Symond Hanckot tayllor is shewerty for hit   £12
Itm. the 4 day of February £6 2d that is for 1 ton 4 li. of my best Rendry
iren to pay at all tymes, his foresseid uncle is shewerty   £6   2d
1540 Itm. the 7th day of Maye £11 19s 11d that is for 2 ton Rendry iren less
2 li. at £6 the ton sent to hym in Symond Astones trowe, to pay at Candelmas
next montith   £11 19s 11d
Itm. the 13 day of October 1540 £12 that is for 2 ton iren sent hym in
Thomas Afeltes trowe of Wursettor   £12
Itm. the 16 day of December £7 16s 5d that I pay in redy monney for
lether per contra & 6s 8d for C 3 qr. 8 li. rosyne at 11 grotes the C   £8   3s   1d
Itm. the 14 day of December £6 which is for 1 ton iren sold & delyverd to
hym   £6
1541 Itm. the 25 day of July £12 1d that is for 2 ton 2 li. iren delyverd to hym
at £6 the ton montith   £12   1d
Itm. the 6 day of October £18 which is for 3 ton iren at £6 the ton laden in
Thomas Afletes trowe   £18
1542 Itm. the 4 day of May 1542 £5 which I d'd to hym at Barnssgrove in
part of payement of 10 dicker lethir, cow & stere, at 43s 4d the dicker to be
d'd at Newnam the 19 day of this monthe   £5
Itm. the 23 day of Maye £12 that is for 2 ton of iren laden for hym in
Thomas Aflettes trowe   £12
Itm. the 24 day of July £36 that is for 6 ton of my better Rendry iren solld
& d'd to hym at £6 the ton   £36
Itm. the 26 day of September £17 6s 8d which he r. for me of Edward Rowley
of Kyngesnorton in part of payement of the 10 dicker & 1 hide & C dozen
skuyns per contra   £17 6s 8d
Itm. the 1 day of October £21 13s 4d pd. to hym at Bristowe in redy money
the which £21 13s 4d & the seid £17 6s 8d & £12 for the 2 ton iren d'd the 23
day of May last past as before may apere do make up the hole payment of £51
for the lether and skuyns per contra   £21 13s 4d
Itm. the 3 day of February £18 6s 8d & is ffor the rest of 3 ton 1 qr. 15 li.
iren solld & delyverd to hym att Bristowe to be[2] at all tymes by me requyrd
as in my shop boke may apere   £18 6s 8d

---

[1] Marginal note.
[2] pd. is omitted here.

6(L) contd.

Itm. the 25 day of May anno 1543 solld to hym 2 ton 1 qr. 2 li. Rendry iren & 1 to*n* 1 qr. 5 li. S.S. iren for the which he rest owyng £18 to be paide at all tymes — £18

S. £226 5s 1d

6(R)   **anno 1539**

Lawrence Hanckot p*er* contra is dewe to have the 15 day of Ma*r*che £16 11s 4d *that* is for 7 dicker lethir & 1 hide, cow & stere, r. in Thomas Aflet*es* trowe at 46s 8d p*er* dicker mon*tith* — £16 11s 4d

1540 Itm. the 25 day of July 1540 28s 8d r. of hym in redy money — £1 8s 8d

Itm. the same day £3 in p*a*rt of payement of the 2 ton p*er* contra d'd the 28 of June 1539 — £3

Itm. the 16 day of December 1540 for 44 dozens calve skuyns with the cost*es* delyv*er*d at Bristowe £13 19s 9d & for a dicker le*ther* 43s 4d whereof £8 is pd. toward iren p*er* contra — £16 3s 1d

1541 Itm. the 23 day of July 1541 r. of hym at Bristowe £4, the which £4 & the £8 mencyonyd in the item beffore is full payement of the 2 to*n* iren d'd the 7 day of May 1540 as p*er* contra apere — £4

Itm. more r. of hym the same day £3 in p*a*rt of payement of the 2 to*n* iren d'd the 28 day of June 1539 as p*er* contra ap*er*ith — £3

Itm. the same day r. of hym £6 which is for 1 to*n* ire*n* p*er* contra d'd the 14 day of December 1540 — £6

Itm. the 26 day of Septemb*er* r. of hym at Bristowe £12 — £12

Itm. the 18 day of May 1542 he d'd for me to John Sp*a*rk of Newna*m* 10 dicker 2 hid*es* at 43s 4d the dicker & 3 doze*n* calve skuyns at 6s the dozen, mon*tith* (ow*t* of this must be discowntyd 3s 8d *that* S*p*ark paide the troweman for carage)[1] — £23 16s

Itm. r. the 24 day of July r. of hym at Bristow in redy money £12 4s mon*tith* — £12 4s

Itm. the 25 day of July 1542 r. of hym at Bristow 50s & the 15 day of Jenyver 1542 r. for hym of his uncle Symon Hancott 10s, mon*tith* the hole — £3

Itm. the 1 daye of October 1542 £51 *that* is ffor won 100 doze*n* of calve skuyns at 6s *the* dozen & 10 dicker & 1 hide for £21 which war dischargid into John Sparck*es* howse of Newneham — £51

Itm. the 2d day of February r. of hym at Bristowe £12 in p*a*rt of payment of 6 ton iren d'd the 24 day of July last past as p*er* contra ap*er*ith — £12

Itm. the 25 day of Maye 1543 r. at Bristowe of hym £24 — £24

Itm. the 29 of Augost 1543 £24 & is for so myche my wif r. of hym at Bristowe in redy mon*n*ey — £24

Itm. the same day £15 2s & is for so myche I make hym detto*r* in a newe cowmpt fo. 191 — £15 2s

S. £226 5s 1d

7(L)   **anno 1539**

Willi*a*m Yerwith of Bristowe grocer owith the 2d day of June £12 13s 4d whiche is for 2 ton iren solld & d'd to hym at 19 nobles the ton, to be pd. at Allhaloutide next com*m*yng as it ap*er*ith by a byll which he & W*i*lliam

---

[1] *These words were inserted later.*

7(L) contd.

Ballard of Bristowe marchant ffyrmyd and sealid for to acomplische the seid payement	£12	13s	4d

anno 1532

Master William Shipman marchant of Bristowe owith the 28 day of November for dying 2 clothes wull in a settyng of myne at John Lawrence diar, which clothes conteynyd ech 88 li. & war died 2d every li. in wood & hallf a clothes wull conteynyng 44 li. made penny hewe & ½ a clothes wull a jobber. So amontith the seid dyeing besides the jobber 33s	£1	13s	
1533 Itm. the 26 day of September anno 1533 5 markes for a but seck rackid which Frances Codrynton chose for hym in my sellar	£3	6s	8d
1539 Itm. the last day of May anno 1539 £6 5s that is for the rest of 15 tons iren in the Trynte at 15s the ton	£6	5s	
Itm. the 12 day of June 26s 8d for 1 h'd claret wyne	£1	6s	8d
Itm. the 10 day of October £7 10s for 10 ton freight in my ship the Trynte this viage at 15s the ton	£7	10s	
Itm. for his part of 4 ton which came unladen as ded freight in the complyment of hym, William Car & Frances[1]			
Itm. the 3 day of December £6 10s which is for 1 ton of S.S. iren sold to hym to be pd. at all tymes	£6	10s	
Itm. the 22 day of Jenyver £5 for the freight of 5 ton wyne this vyntage from Burdes in the Trynte at 20s the ton, to pay hallf in hand & thother ½ at Owr Lady Day in March next	£5		
1540 Itm. the 14 day of Maye 1540 £8 that is £6 10s for 1 ton iren of S.S. & 30s for 1 h'd of my best Rendry iren	£8		
Itm. the 23 day of Agost £3 6s 8d for the freight of 5 ton iren in the Trynte from Spayne	£3	6s	8d
Itm. the 23 day of September £10 which I lent hym yn redy monney to pay at Mighellmas next commyng	£10		
Itm. the 15 day of November £12 for freight of 12 ton Gascon wyne in the Trynte from Burdes at 20s per ton, to pay ½ within 3 monthes & ½ 3 monthes next after that	£12		
Itm. the 4 day of Maye anno 1541 £6 13s 4d that is for the freight of 10 ton iren in the Trynte at 13s 4d per ton, to pay ½ in hand & ½ at the end of 3 monthes	£6	13s	4d
Itm. the 23 day of Jenuary 1545 £4 3s 4d for 1 but seck to pay at all tymes	£4	3s	4d

7(R)   anno 1539

William Yerwith per contra is dewe to have the 13 day of December £7 13s 4d r. by the handes of William Ballardes sarvant	£7	13s	4d
Itm. the 3 day of ~~December~~ Jenyver r. by the handes of William Ballardes sarvant £5	£5		
S.	£12	13s	4d

anno 1539

Master William Shipman per contra is dewe to have the 20 daye of October £6 which he pd. me in redy money	£6		
Itm. the 22 day of November r. of hym 25s & 20d I rebatyd to hym which all do amontith 26s 8d for the h'd wyne per contra	£1	6s	8d
Itm. the 7 day of Jenyver r. of hym £6 13s 4d	£6	13s	4d

---

[1] *The name is not completed and no amount is shown.*

7(R) contd.

Itm. the 5 day of February r. of hym 16s 8d	16s	8d
Itm. the 22 day of March r. by the handes of his sarvant £5 for the 5 ton freight in the Trynte in Jenyver last past *1540* Itm. the 26 day of Aprel 1540 r. of hym £3 for in part of payement of £6 10s dew for the ton iren per contra	£5 £3	
Itm. the 11 daye of May r. of hym £3 6s 8d in part of payement of the same ton iren per contra	£3 6s	8d
Itm. the 29 day of July r. of hym £7 16s 8d & 3s 4d he descowntyd in the price, which is for payement of the ton 1 h'd iren per contra	£8	
Itm. the 28 day of September r. of hym £10	£10	
Itm. the 15 day of December r. 55s & 11s 8d was rebatyd apon the 5 ton freight in Agost per contra	£3 6s	8d
Itm. the 7 day of Aprell 1541 r. by Hamond £6 in parte of payement of £12 conteynyd in the itm. of the 15 of November	£6	
Itm. the 24 day of September anno 1541 £12 13s 4d r. of his sarvant Raf Richemond	£12 13s	4d
~~Itm. the 7 day of February, r. by my sarvant Henry 20s~~		

8(L)   **anno 1537**

Humfrey Beare of Chepstowe marchant owith the 13 day of Agost £4 16s 6d which is for the rest of reckenynges as it apere by a lettor which he wrote me the seid day with his owne hand from Chepstowe, mon*tith*   £4 16s 6d
Itm. the same day for 1 h'd white wyne 30s the which h'd he make mencion of in his seid lettor   £1 10s
passed this cownt the 2de day of July 1550 to my newe boke fo. 1

                 anno 1537

Master Ris Moris Abowen of Kermerdyne gentillman owith the 3d day of May 24s 3d that is for 2 buttes bear with the caskes 20s, for 1 qr. Newland fische 3s 9d & for a seame of great wood 6d, the which stuff John Enyon purser of his ship the Mary Grace r. at Burdes in theyr greate nede of my sarvant Tyndall & purser of my ship the Trynte, as it may apere by a bill of the seid John Enyon   £1 4s 3d

                 anno 1539

Master John Popley preste chancellar of Seynt Davis owith the 25 day of Agost £3 13s 4d to be paide by a byll fyrmyd with his hand & sealid with his seale in this maner ffollowyng, that is at Cristmas next 13s 4d, at Owr Lady Day in Lent 10s, at Mydsomer 10s, at Mighellmas 10s, & so from quarter to quarter untill the som of £3 13s 4d be truly paide, and it is for so myche *that* he becom debtor to me for Thomas Whaley of Bristow surgon   £3 13s 4d

8(R)   **anno 1537**

Humfrey Beare per contra is dewe to have the 4th day of December 20s which she sent, I sey his wif sent me by my sarvant Humfrey Swift	£1	
Itm. the 18 day of Jenyver 20s r. of theyr maide Amee	£1	
Itm. the 23 day of December anno 1539 r. from hym by the handes of Margerit White of Seynt Stevyns parische in Bristo 6s 8d	6s	8d
Itm. the 13 day of June 1542 6s 8d for so myche r. at Chepstowe of his wif & Robert Pole of Glocester is wytnes to the same[1]	6s	8d

---

[1] *There is no credit entry for Abowen.*

8(R) contd.

anno 1539

M*aster* Popley *per* contra is dewe to have the 24 day of February 13s 4d r. in redy mon*n*ey & thereof I made hym aquyttance	13s	4d
Itm. the 10 day of November 1541 r. 30s	£1 10s	
Itm. the 18 day of Octob*er* 1542 r. of hym 30s & so d'd to hym his bill	£1 10s	
	£3 13s	4d

9(L)

anno 1538

Phelip Griffith baylif to thabbot of Seynt Agustyne by Bristowe ow*ith* the 29 day of Octob*er* £10 which I lent hym in redy money to be paide at all tymes & left in pledge for hit s*er*teyne plate as it ap*erith* by a bill   S. £10

anno 1538

David Harris of Bristow pottycary ow*ith* the 13 day of Aprell £21 17s 9d *that* is for 12 serons of white Sevyll sope *conteynyng* 20 C ½, 5 li. whereof was desductid for tare 6 li. for ev*er*y seron, so rest nete 19 C 3 qr. 17 li. at 22s the C to pay at Bartyllmewtide next, mo*ntith*	£21 17s	9d
Itm. the 9 day of May 1538 £11 19s 3d *that* is for 10 C 3 qr. 14 li. white Sevill sope which I sowld lowse with owt serons at 22s the C, to pay at the day foresseid	£11 19s	3d
Itm. he ow*ith* me for Willi*am* Sodebery 6s 8d which the seid Sodbery rest owing & the seid David became his shewerty	6s	8d
1539 Itm. the first day of October an*n*o 1539 £20 16s that is for 8 portugezis which I lent hym after 52s the pece & sent *them* hym by his wif acordyng to his owne lett*or* which I have & he promezid by *the* same lett*or* to repay hit within a moneth next after	£20 16s	
Itm. the 12th day of May 1542 22s 11d paide to hym for the rest & ffynischement of this & all other acowmpt*es* & reckenyng*es* untill this daye	£1 2s	11d
	S. £56 2s	11d

9(R)

anno 1539

Phelip Griffythe *per* contra is dewe to have the 25 of November £10 r. of hym in redy mon*n*ey & so I delyverd to hym the plate which I had in pledge   £10

anno 1538

Davyd Herrys *per* contra is dewe to have to have[1] the 26 day of Agost £20 which his s*ar*vant Mighell paide to me for hym in redy money	£20	
Itm. the 14 day of November a*n*no 1539 £20 16s that is for 8 portugezis whiche he paide to my wif	£20 16s	
Itm. 6s 8d which I pay hym for a Spanyart ffor who*m* I was shew*er*ty for a fforffett of turpentyne	6s	8d
Itm. £14 19s 11d for medycyns had of hym untyll this day the 12th day of Maye 1542	£14 19s	11d
	S. £56 2s	11d

[1] To have *is written twice.*

9A(L)[1]   anno 1533

Thomas Phelips of Montagew my bro*th*er in the lawe ow*ith* the   [2]   day
of October a*nno* dicto 33s 4d to be pd. at all tymes whiche is for so myche
he restith owyng to me for J*oh*n Nappar of M*a*rtock   £1   13s   4d
Itm. the 21 day of Octob*er* 1537 15s 8d which I fornysshid for fryze &
kerssy for hym   15s   8d
1539 Itm. the 21 day of Agost 1539 £10 which I lent hym in redy mon*n*ey &
sent hit hym by his s*a*rvant John Tayllor   £10
passed this cownt to my new boke fo. 1 the 2de day of July a*nno* 1550.

anno 1532

Sir Thomas Crane preste dwellyng at Bridgewater owithe the 19 day of
October £4 payable at all tymes whiche is for the rest of acowmpt of
Allexander Skelltons as it a*p*erith in my old boke fo. 167 & the seid S*i*r
Crane is his shewrty by his le*tt*or   £4
Itm. the 4th day of September a*nno* 1539 £12 which I lent hym in redy
mon*n*ey to pay at C*ris*t*m*as next as it a*p*erithe by his bill   £12

9A(R)   anno 1541

Thomas Phillips *per* contra is dewe to have the 22 day of
July 20 nobles which is for 5 smawle oxen which he sent
me by my s*a*rvant Robert Leight, skuins worth 4 nobles
the ox yet I put them at eich 30s   £6   10s

anno 1538

Sir Thomas Crane *per* contra is dewe to have the 18 day of
Decemb*er* 1538 46s 8d, which is for kepyng of an obbyt
this 7 yeres for M*aster* Thomas Hop*er* of Bridgewater
marchant at 6s 8d the yere   £2   6s   8d
Itm. the 7 day of Decemb*er* 1539 r. of hym at Bristo £6
for in p*a*rt of payement of the £12 *per* contra   £6
Itm. the 28 day of July 1540 r. by Watkyn Coyder £6   £6

10(L)   anno 1539

John Rokesby of Wells skynnar owith the 15 day of October £~~18 6s 8d~~ to be
paide at all tymes requyrid, whiche is for so myche that I pass the same day
to *this* boke for the rest of his cownt in my old boke fo. 167 I sey he ow*ith*   £16   13s   4d
for the rest of his seid acowmpt ~~£16 13s 4d~~ £17   ~~£18 - 6s - 8d~~
Itm. the 12th day of November £3 10s for a but of seck which my wif sold
& d'd to hym to pay at all tymes   £3   10s
Itm. the 10th day of December £8 that is ~~£4 6s 8d~~ for a pipe of muscadell &
£3 10s for a butt of seck as in my shop boke a*p*erithe £7 10s   £7   10s
Itm. the 17 day of Jenyver £15 3s 4d that is for 2 but*te*s seck at eich £3 10s
& 1 pipe teynt at £4 6s 8d & a pipe muscadell at £3 16s 8d to be paide at   £15   3s   4d
all tymes ~~£14 16s 8d~~   ~~£14 16s 8d~~
Itm. the 10 day of February £6 5s *that* is £4 for a p*i*pe ossey & 45s for 1 ton
Gascon wyne   £6   5s
Itm. the 14 day of the same £5 15s that is £3 10s for a but of seck & 40s for
2 h'd Gascon wyne, £5 10s   £5   10s
1540 Itm. the 2d day of June 1540 £22 13s 4d *that* is for 4 but*te*s seck at eich
11 nobles & 2 to*n* Gascon wyne at £4 the ton, mon*tith*   £22   13s   4d
[3]Itm. the 15 day of November £4 13s 4d[4] for 1 to*n* Gasco*n* wyne sent by
Sheward the carriar. I sey £4 13s 4d *the* ton[5]   £4   13s   4d

---

[1]*Two folios are numbered '9'.*
[2]*Blank in MS.*
[3]*Marginal note, 4. 13. 4.*
[4]*13s 4d inserted above, see credit entry.*
[5]*This amount inserted later.*

10(L) contd.

Itm. the 26 day of November £7 10s *that* is for 1 pipe bastard £4 & 1 butt seck £3 10s	£7	10s	
Itm. the 4th day of December £5 5s th*at* is 23s 4d[1] for 1 h'd red wyne & £4 3s 4d[1] for a pipe teynt sent by the seid carryer £5 6s 8d[1]	£5	6s	8d
Itm. the 11 day of December £5 for 1 to*n* Gasco*n* wyne sent by the seid carryer	£4	13s	4d
Itm. the 28 day of Jenyver £5 16s 8d that is for 1 but of seck £3 10s & for 2 h'd claret wyne 46s 8d to be paide at all tymes	£5	16s	8d
1541 Itm. the 17 day of Maye 1541 £13 6s 8d that is for 4 butt*es* seck at 5 m*ar*kes the butt, mo*ntith*	£13	6s	8d
Memorandum[2] Itm. the 6 day of Aprell for 2 butt*es* seck 20 nobles, for 1 pipe muscadell £4, for 1 h'd c*laret* wyne 23s 4d & for 1 h'd r*ed* wyne 26s 8d	£13	3s	4d
Itm. £4 13s 4d for 1 to*n* Gasco*n* wyne which he had for my acowmpt of my uncle Thomas Smythe the seid 6 day	£4	13s	4d
Itm. the 15 day of June £5 3s 4d for 1 to*n* Gascon wyne	£5	3s	4d
Itm. the 1 day of Julye £6 13s 4d for 2 butt*es* of seck sold at 5 m*ar*kes the butt	£6	13s	4d
Itm. the 17 day of November £5 6s 8d for 1 to*n* Gascon wyne at 16 nobles the ton	£5	6s	8d
Itm. the 26 day of November £6 13s 4d *that* is £4 for 1 pipe muscadell & 53s 4d for 2 h'd Gascon wyne	£6	13s	4d
Itm. the 3 day of December £8 for 2 p*ipes* muscadell	£8		
Itm. the 26 day of Jenyver £43 6s 8d that is ffor 4 tons of Gascon wyne at £5 6s 8d p*er* ton & 6 butt*es* of seck at 11 nobles the butt, mo*ntith*	£43	6s	8d
1542 Itm. the 6 of May 1542 for 1 butt seck 11 nobles	£3	13s	4d

S. £215 3s 4d

10(R)   **anno 1539**

John Rokesby p*er* contra is dewe to have the 12 day of December £13 for so myche redy mon*n*ey r. from hym by M*aster* Davyd Herris of Bristowe pottycary	£13		
Itm. the 15 day of Jenyver £7 3s 4d r. of hy*m*	£7	3s	4d
1540 Itm. the 9 day of Aprell 1540 r. of hym at Bristow £10 mo*ntith* I sey £10 3s 4d[3]	£10	3s	4d
Itm. the 2d day of June r. of hym at Bristowe £6	£6		
Itm. the 12 day of October r. £24 which he sent me from Wells by Master Sylk of Bristowe	£24		
Itm. the 28 day of November r. fr*om* hym by M*aster* W*illiam* Chester of Bristow poyntmaker £12	£12		
Itm. the 28 day of Jenyver r. of Jo*hn* Roxby at Bristowe £4 & 13s 4d I forgave hym in recompens of a pipe of muscadell which he sayde was fawty so *that* the hole is £4 13s 4d, which is full payement of o*wr* old cowmpt the last yere	£4	13s	4d
Itm. the same day £8 3s 4d r. of hym for payment of 1 to*n* Gasco*n* wyne & 1 but seck of *this* yeres wyne	£8	3s	4d
Itm. the 4 day of M*ar*ch r. of hym at Wells £10	£10		
1541 Itm. the 13 day of May 1541 r. of hym at Bristowe £6	£6		
Itm. the 14 day of June r. £3 10s & 6s 8d I geve hym apo*n* 2 butt*es* of seck, mo*ntith* the hole £3 16s 8d	£3	16s	8d
Itm. the 12 day of October r. by M*astres* Pick*es* son £17 19s 4d	£17	19s	4d
Itm. the 23 day of November r. of hym at Wells £10	£10		
Itm. the 3d day of December r. at Bristow of hy*m*	£5		
Itm. the 26 day of Jenyver r. of hym at Bristowe £10 for the rest & hole payement of all the last yeres reckeny*n*g	£10		

---

[1] *These amounts inserted later.*
[2] *Marginal note.*
[3] *I sey £10 3s 4d inserted later.*

10(R) contd.

Itm. the same day £5 for so myche r. for wynes d'd this yere	£5		
Itm. the 4 day of May 1542 my wif r. of hym £15	£15		
Itm. the 7 day of July r. of hym at Bristowe £10	£10		
Itm. 4s for so myche I allowe hym for horse mete		4s	
Itm. the seid 7 day of July 1542 £37 that is for so myche he owe for the rest & closyng up of this acowmpt whereof I make hym debitor fo. 162	£37		
	S. £215	3s	4d

11(L)   **anno 1539**

John Tizon of Alberton in Closetorshire yeman owith the 15 day of July £3 to be paide at Mighellmas next after, the which £3 I lent hym in redy monney apon a flat cup & a smawle standyng cup of sylver which rest pledges   £3

1541 Itm. the 17 day of Maye 1541 £5 2d that is for 3 h'd 2 li. ½ iren of S.S. after 20 nobles *the* ton whiche he wyllid me to delyver to John Smythe of Wollston   £5   2d

anno 1539

Antonyo Diez Portyngall dwelling in Bristowe owithe the 29 day of Agost £3 which I lent hym & sent hit by his son in redy monney, to be paide at all tymes I wulld requyre it   £3

anno 1539

John Wynter of Bristow marchant owith the last daye of May anno dicto £5 12s 6d that is for the ffreyght of 7 ton pipe iren in my ship the Trynte *this* viage at 15s the ton, to pay ½ in hand & thother ½ 3 months after her discharging   £5 12s 6d

Itm. the 4th day of August 1541 £36 *that* is for 3 ton wull oyle sold & d'd to hym, to be payde £18 at Candellmas next & £18 at Seynt Jamistide next after *that*, as by 2 bills obligatory sygned & sealid with his hand may apere   £36

Itm. for 5 great Bewdeley powlles 5s, for vytall for my shipp which I fornysshid she being in the Kinges wayges 8s, & for 2 yeres rent of his howse endyd at Owr Lady Day in Lent in anno 1545 £7, montith all £7 13s   £7 13s

     S. £49 5s 6d

11(R)   **anno 1540**

John Tizon hereageynst is dewe to have the 10th daye of July £3 r. of hym in redy money   £3

Itm. the 21 day of September 1541 r. of hym   £3

Itm. the 16 day of November 1541 r. by thandes of his son Jamys 40s & the 2d I geve hym   £2   2d

anno 1539

Antonio Diez per contra is dewe to have the 16 day of December £3 which his son browght & paide to me   £3

anno 1539

John Wynter is dewe to have the 12 day of November £5 r. of John Snyg for hym   £5

Itm. the 26 day of Aprell 1542 r. by the handes of John Wynters son Arture £10   £10

Itm. the 26 day of September r. by his son George   £8

11(R) contd.

Itm. for 1 pipe 1 h'd sallt 11s 4d		11s 4d
Itm. for 1 C 3 qr. 5 li. gunpowder £3 10s		£3 10s
Itm. for vytayles which I r. of his wif to fornische owt of Bristowe the ship that the Scott[1] went in for capteyn £14 13s 4d		£14 13s 4d
Itm. r. of hym in London the 2d day of Marche anno 1544 £6 18s 4d		£6 18s 4d
Itm. 12s 6d which I lost by this cowmpt		12s 6d
	S.	£49 5s 6d

(11 A)

Two small loose pages between Folios 11(L) and 11(R)[2]

I) To receave of Master Smythe for 13 caskes to (put) the bere yn after 18d every caske & 1 hoges hede 8d   19s 11d[3]
for whopyng of all the caskes   5s
for hawlyng of the bysket, bere & beffe to the crane   20d
for cranege   2s
to the lyghterman for bryngyng hyt downe to the shepe   3s
    Summa   31s 7d[3]

II) I, Wyllyam Logan capten has resavet fra Maister Smyth 31s 7d
for 7 caskes 7s

III) [4] To be payed to Mastres Wynter
of Master Smythe
for 20 C of bysket   £6 13s 4d
20 buttes of bere[5]   £8
    Summa   £14 13s 4d

12(L)   **anno 1539**

Richard Chamber of Kyngesnorton yeoman owithe the 29 daye of Agost £29 10s to be paide by his bill at Corpus Cristitide next commyng, which is for the rest of 9 ton iren that I sold and delyverd to hym	£29 10s
Itm. the 10 day of Jenyver £6 that is for a ton of iren laden for hym in Thomas Sevarns trowe to be pd. at all tymes requyrid	£6
1540 Itm. the 31 day of July £6 1d ob. for 1 ton 3 li. iren sent in Thomas Affletes trowe	£6 1d ob.
1543 Itm. the 12 day of Jenyver anno 1543 £12 & is for 2 ton Rendry iren of the better sort at £6 the ton to be paid at all tymes requyrid, the which iren I lade in Thomas Aflettes trowe	£12
1544 Itm. the 21 day of July laden in Thomas Aflettes trowe 3 tons 19 C 3 quarters 24 li. Rendry iren, more the 4th day of August in Thomas Asevarns trowe 3 tons Rendry iren, montith all 7 tons less 4 li. at £6 the ton to be paide at all tymes £41 19s 9d ob.	£41 19s 9d ob.
Itm. the 18 day of September £6 & is for 1 ton Rendry iren laden for hym in Thomas Asevarns trowe	£6
Itm. the 22 day of Awgost 1545 £24 & is for 4 ton Rendry iren solld to hym a £6 per ton to be paide at all tymes requyrid	£24
Itm. the 15 day of July 1546 £24 2d & is for 4 ton 3 li. Rendry iren at £6 the ton to be paide at all tymes. I d'd it for hym to his son T. Chamber	£24 2d
Itm. the 25 day of Maye 1547 £7 & is for 1 ton of Rendry iren to be paide at all tymes	£7

---

[1] *William Logan—see folio 11 A.*
[2] *Sections I and III are in the same hand, not that of Smythe.*
[3] *This should read £1 2d and the total £1 11s 10d.*
[4] *Sections I and II are on one page, section III on the other.*
[5] *Smythe's accounts of these purchases are on folio 11.*

12(L) contd.

Itm. the 12 of July £19 to pay £9 at Candellmas & £10 at Corpus Cristitide next after which is for the rest of 3 tons 1 qr. iren   £19

                                                                S. £185 10s 3d ob.

anno 1540

William Reynolldes of Kyngesnorton owith the 31 day of July £6 that is ffor 1 ton iren sent hym in Thomas Affletes trowe, montith to be pd. at all tymes   £6 £5 13s 4d

Itm. the 18 day of Marche £11 13s 4d for 2 ton iren sent hym in Thomas Sevarns trowe   £11 13s 4d

Itm. the 11th day of September 1541 £11 6s 8d and is for 2 ton Rendre iren, to paye the won halfe at Corpus Christy tyde and the other halfe at Seynt James tyde next, montith   £11 6s 8d

1543 Itm. the 12 day of Jenyver anno 1543 £12 which is for 2 ton of my better Rendry iren at £6 the ton, to be pd. at all tymes requyrid. It was laden in Thomas Afletes trow   £12

1544 Itm. the 18 day of September anno 1544 £12 & it is for 2 ton Rendry iren sent hym in Thomas Sevarns trowe   £12

Itm. the 9 day of December laden in Thomas Palmers trowe 2 ton Rendry iren at £6 the ton montith   £12

Itm. the 22 day of Awgost 1545 solld to hym 2 ton Rendry iren at £6 the ton to be paide at all tymes requyrid   £12

Itm. the 25 day of May 1547 £7 & is for 1 ton Rendry iren to be pd. at all tymes   £7

                                                                S. £83 6s 8d

12(R)   anno 1540

Richard Chamber per contra is dewe to have the 17 day of Julye £9 10s that my sarvant Robert Leight did bryng me from hym, I sey the 17 day of June   £9 10s

Itm. the 25 day of July r. of William Le Daiper of Kynges norton £20   £20

Itm. the 30 of Awgost r. of hym £6 whereof I gave hym ageyne to his costes 20d   £6 £5 16s 8d

Itm. the 24 day of July 1541 r. of John Lyndon   £12

Itm. r. from hym by John Lyndon the 24 of July 1544 £12

Itm. the 19 day of August anno 1545 r. at Bristow by thandes of his son Thomas Chamber £40   £40

Itm. r. of Thomas Harrys in December 1545 £8   £8

Itm. the 13 daye of July anno 1546 r. from hym by Thomas Harrys marchant of Bristowe ten powndes   £10

Itm. r. of his son Thomas Chamber the 13 daye of July 1546 £14   £14

Itm. the 16 day of June anno 1547 r. from hym by thandes of Thomas Harrys marchant of Bristowe £12   £12

Itm. the 11 day of Julye anno 1547 r. of hym at Bristowe £12 2d   £12 2d

Itm. the 6 day of November r. of Henry Borwyck northernman £7   £7

r. more £9   £9

Itm. the 7 day of June anno 1547 r. by thandes of Richard Langston Master Shrevys[1] man £10   £10

                                                                S. £185 10s 3d ob.

---

[1] *The Sheriffs in 1546–1547 were John a Welles and Thomas Joahim.*

12(R) contd. anno 1540

William Reynold per contra is dewe to have the 2 day of February of John Lynedon daiper £5 13s 4d	£5	13s	4d
Itm. the 1 day of September 1541 r. of hym in Bristowe £11 6s 8d	£11	6s	8d
Itm. the 20 day of Augost 1542 r. of hym at Bristowe £11 6s 8d	£11	6s	8d
Itm. the 21 day of Augost anno 1544 my sarvant Leyt r. £12	£12		
Itm. the ~~18~~ 19 day of Augost anno 1545 r. from hym by the handes of Thomas Chambers £18	£18		
Itm. r. by Thomas Harrys in December 1545 £6	£6		
Itm. r. the 24 day of Awgost 1546 by thandes of Grevys son £12	£12		
Itm. the 27 day of September 1547 r. from of Thomas Harrys marchant of Bristowe £7	£7		

S. £83 6s 8d

13(L) anno 1539

William Polloughan of Aburgeyne smythe owith the 26 day of July 30s for a hogshed of iren which I sold & d'd to hym to be paide at Candellmas next commyng £1 10s

Itm. the 14 day of February 33s 4d that is for 1 h'd 1 qr. 1 li. of the better Rendry iren at 19 nobles the ton to pay at Seynt Jamystide next £1 13s 4d

1540 Itm. the 29 day of July 1540 31s 8d that is ffor 1 h'd iren after 19 nobles the ton to pay at Candellmas next £1 11s 8d

Itm. the 21 day of February 31s 8d that is for 1 h'd of my best Rendry iren after 19 nobles the ton to be pd. at Seynt Jamistide next commyng £1 11s 8d

1541 Itm. the 26 day of July 1541 30s that is for 1 h'd iren sold & d'd to hym to pay at Candellmas next commyng £1 10s

anno 1539

John David of Kermerdyne marchant owith the 30 day of Agost anno dicto £6 to be paide by his bill at Seynt Androwstide next commyng, which is for a ton iren that I sold & d'd to hym £6

Itm. the 5th day of December £3 3s 4d that is for 1 pipe of my best Rendry iren d'd in & for his name to his sarvant Davith Griffith, to pay at Candelmas next £3 3s 4d

Itm. the 5th day of February £6 7s 6d for 1 ton 16 li. of the better Rendry iren payable at Phelips Norton fayer which wylbe in May next[1] £6 7s 6d

Itm.[2]

anno 1540

David Williams of Bristowe baker owith the 11 day of September 30s that is for 1 h'd iren to be pd. at Owr Lady Day in Marche next commyng.
Thomas Romessey tayllor is bownd with hym for the payement £1 10s

Itm. the 2 day of February my wif pd. to hym 6s 8d   6s 8d
Itm. more was paide to hym in redy money 20s   £1
1541 Itm. the 5th day of Maye 1541 30s that is for a h'd iren to be paide at all tymes   £1 10s
Itm. 33s 4d delyverd to hym in redy monney   £1 13s 4d
Itm. for 7 busshells whet at 13d the busshell   7s 7d
Itm. the 10 day of September my wif pd. hym 6s 8d   6s 8d
Itm. the 6 day of October pd. to hym 4s 5d   4s 5d
Itm. the 14 day of November £3 which is for a pipe of iren d'd for hym to Master Richard Abyngton
Itm. the 27 day of Jenyver pd. to hym in redy monny 7s 5d   £3 7s 5d[3]

---

[1] All John David's account is crossed through.
[2] This item is not completed in the MS.
[3] The entries for 14th November and 27th January are totalled together because Smythe was pressed for space at the bottom of the page.

13(L) contd.

Itm. the last day of Jenyver £3 13s 4d for a butt of seck	£3	13s	4d
Itm. in June 1542 the last day payd to hym in money 6s		6s	

13(R)   **anno 1539**

Willi*a*m Pollowghan p*er* contra is dewe to have the 14 day of February 30s which my wif r. of hym	£1	10s	
1540 Itm. the 29 day of July r. of hym 33s 4d	£1	13s	4d
Itm. the 21 day of February 1540 r. of hym 31s 8d	£1	11s	8d
Itm. the 26 day of July r. of hym 31s 8d	£1	11s	8d

anno 1539

John David p*er* contra is dewe to have the 5 day of December £6 r. of his s*a*rvant David Luyes	£6		
Itm. the 5th day of February r. of hym seallf £3 3s 4d	£3	3s	4d
1540 Itm. 37s 10d r. of hym the 12 of May 1540	£1	17s	10d
Itm. the 26 day of July Thom*m*as Shipma*n* r. of J*oh*n Gervis of Bristow groc*er* £4 6s 8d[1]	£4	6s	8d

anno 1540

David Willi*ams* p*er* contra is dewe to have the 21 day of Jenyver ffor 15 C ½, 8 li. bisquyt at 3s 6d *the* C	£2	14s	3d
Itm. the 11 day of Aprell r. of hym 2s 5d		2s	5d
Itm. the 25 day of Awgost 1541 £4 2s *that* is for 20 C ½, 4 li. bisquyt r. of hym at 4s the C, mo*ntith*	£4	2s	
Itm. the 21 day of Jenyver 1541 for 14 C 3 qr. 15 li. of bisquytt r. of hym for my ship at 14 grot*es* the C less apo*n* all 2s, mon*tith* £3 7s 5d	£3	7s	5d
Itm. r. in June 1542 for the p*ro*vision of my ship 17 C 14 li. bisquytt at 4s 8d the C, mon*tith* £3 19s 4d	£3	19s	4d

14(L)   **anno 1539**

Robert Bisshop of Bridgewater owith the 26 day of July £3 that is for so myche he owith for rest of reckenyng*es* untyll this daye & it is payable at my pleaz*er*	£3		
Itm. the 7 day of Agost £3 14s ob. that 11 nobles for a but of seck, 4d for a cocquet, 2d for halyng, 2d for cranage & ob. for spletyng	£3	14s	ob.
Itm. the 26 day of November £3 13s 4d for a butt of seck sent in Grawng*ers* bote, to pay the morow apo*n* Lent fayer	£3	13s	4d
Itm. the 21 day of Jenyver £8 that is 11 nobles for a but of seck & 13 nobles for a but of muscadel, at Ester	£8		
1540 Itm. the 11 day of Agost a*nno* 1540 22s 6d *that* is for 1 h'd claret wyne sent to her[2] as in my shop boke aperith	£1	2s	6d
Memorandum[3] Itm. the 2d day of June £3 13s 4d for 1 but seck sent in Davyd Luyes bote of Bristowe mon*tith*	£3	13s	4d
Itm. the 14 day of Jenyver £7 10s that is for 1 but of seck £3 10s & ffor 1 pipe of muscadell £4 which I sent her in J*oh*n Davys bote	£7	10s	
Itm. the 17 day of December £7 15s *that* is £3 15s for a butt of seck & £4 for a pipe of bastard sent her in Whit the coferars bote, to pay at Easter next com*m*yng	£7	15s	
S.	£37	13s	4d

---

[1] *All John David's account is crossed through.*
[2] *Presumably Robert Bisshop's wife.*
[3] *Marginal note.*

14(L) contd. anno 1538

Robert Hamond of Bridgewater owith the 22 day of February £3 10s for a
butt seck sent hym in Grawngers bote   £3 10s

anno 1540

John Laughton of Handeley troweman owith the 22 day of June £6 10s
that is for 1 pipe Rendry iren at £3 3s 4d d'd the 7 day of this present & for
1 pipe of S.S. iren at £3 6s 8d, to pay at all tymes   £6 6s 8d
Itm. the 17 day of February £3 6s 8d that is ffor 1 pipe of Seyn Sebastyans
iren to pay at Seynt Jamistide next   £3 6s 8d
1541 Itm. the 27 day of June 1541 £3 6s 8d that is for a pipe iren of S.S. to
be pd. at Cristmas next commyng   £3 6s 8d
Itm. the 25 of Jenyver £3 3s 4d for a pipe of my best Rendry iren to be pd.
at Seynt Jamistide next   £3 3s 4d

                            S. £16 3s 4d

14(R) anno 1539

Robert Bisshop per contra is dewe to have the 7 day of
November £4 13s 4d r. by Hanckotes the ffisshar   £4 13s 4d
Itm. the 19 day of Jenyver r. by Granger 40s   £2
Itm. the 6 day of Marche r. of Hancot the fisshar £3 13s 4d   £3 13s 4d
1540 Itm. the 21 day of May 1540 r. by Hamond £5 6s 8d   £5 6s 8d
Itm. r. the 26 day of July by Robert Thomas 53s 4d   £2 13s 4d
Itm. the 17 day of October r. of her in Bristow   £3 13s 4d
Itm. the 14 day of June anno 1541 r. from her by my
sarvant Hewgh Hamond 53s 4d   £2 13s 4d
Itm. pd. to Sir Thomas White preste 5 nobles   £1 13s 4d
Itm. the 24 day of July r. by Robert Thomas 4 markes   £2 13s 4d
Itm. the 16 day of December 1541 r. by Giles 5 nobles   £1 13s 4d
Itm. the 17 day of December £7 15s that is for so myche I
pass to a new cowmpt fo. 152 for the evenyng & closyng
up of this cownt   £7 15s

                            S. £37 13s 4d

anno 1539

r. for Robert Hamond per contra the 7 day of November
of Hanckotes the fisshar 35s   £1 15s

anno 1540

John Lawghton per contra is dewe to have the 22 day of
July 10s that is for bryngyng downe of serteyne wheat in his
trowe   10s
Itm. the 10th day of November £4 which he pd. to my wif   £4
Itm. r. the 17 day of February of hym 36s 8d   £1 16s 8d
Itm. the 26 day of June 1541 r. £3 6s 8d   £3 6s 8d
Itm. the 25 day of Jenyver 1541 r. £3 6s 8d   £3 6s 8d
Itm. the 24 day of July 1542 r. at Bristow of hym   £3 3s 4d

                            S. £16 3s 4d

15(L) anno 1538

Morgan David of Bristowe smythe owith the 18 day off February 23s 4d
which is for the rest of his reckenyng in my old boke fo. 55 & it is payable
at my pleazer   £1 3s 4d

45

15(L) contd.   anno 1539

John Coles of Tymby m*ar*chant ow*ith* the 13 day of October £6 to be paid at Cristmas next com*m*yng which is for the rest of a ton of my best Rendry iren	£6 ~~9s~~
Itm. the 10 day of Decembe*r* £12 6s 8d for 2 to*n* of my best Rendry iren to be pd. at Candellmas next	£12 6s 8d
1540 Itm. the 28 day of July 1540 £6 12s 6d *that* is for 1 ton C 1 qr. 6 li. iren after £6 *the* ton, mo*ntith* £6 7s 10d & 1 C 18 li. pitche after 4s the C, mo*ntith* 4s 8d, so mon*tith* the hole to be paide at all tymes	£6 12s 6d
Itm. the 18 day of October £12 11d that is for 2 to*n* 17 li. iren at £6 the ton to be paide at all tymes requyrid	£12 11d
Itm. the 7 day of February £6 that is for 1 to*n* of Rendry iren sold & d'd to hym to pay at all tymes	£6
1541 Itm. the 26 day of July a*n*no 1541 £6 6s 3d ob. which is ffor 1 ton C 5 li. iren of *the* Rendry at £6 the ton to be paide at all tymes	£6 6s 3d½
Itm. the 7 day of February £6 which is for 1 ton off iren sold to hym for to be pd. at Seynt Jamistide next	£6
1542 Itm. the 27 day of July 1542 £6 that is for 1 to*n* bett*er* Rendry iren to be paide at Candellmas next	£6
Itm. the 21 day of October £6 that is for 1 ton of my bett*er* Rendry iren d'd for hym to his son Henry at £6 the to*n*, to be pd. at all tymes	£6
1544 Itm. the 28 July a*n*no 1544 £6 & is for 1 ton of iren to be paide at Mighellmas next com*m*yng	£6
Itm. the 7 day of February for 1 ton less 4 li. Rendry iren at £6 the to*n* to pay at Seynt Jamistide next	£5 19s 10d
Itm. the 13 daye of October 1545 £6 12d *that* is for 1 ton 18 li. ire*n* to be paide at Seynt Andros tide next com*m*yng	£6 12d
Itm. the 4th day of February 1545 £6 15s which is for 1 ton 2 C ½ Rendry iren after £6 the ton to be pd. at Seynt Jamystide next com*m*yng	£6 15s
Itm. the 27 day of July 1546 £6 2d which is for 1 to*n* 3 li. ire*n* to be paide at Candellmas next com*m*yng	£6 2d
Itm. the 22 of February 1547 for 5 C 11 li. ire*n*	£1 15s
Itm. the 27 of July 1548 for a p*ip*e iren to pay at Mighellmas	£4 9s 10d

15(R)   anno 1540

Morgan David p*er* contra is dewe to have the 14 day of September 6s 8d which his wif pd. to my wif	6s 8d
~~Itm. more r. of hym 6s 8d~~	~~6s 8d~~
Itm. more r. of his wif the 14 day of February 1542	6s 8d

anno 1539

John Coles p*er* contra is dewe to have the 10 day of December £6 r. of hym at Bristowe in redy mon*n*ey	£6
1540 Itm. the 28 day of July r. of hym £12 6s 8d whereof I gave ageyne to his wif ffor a kerchoff clothe 3s 4d	£12 6s 8d
Itm. the 20 day of Jenyver r. of W*illiam* Cary of Bristo drap*er* £5 16s in redy money & a white kerse price 16s 6d & thereof made to the seid Cary a discharge, mon*tith* the hole	£6 12s 6d
Itm. the 7 day of February r. of hym £6	£6
Itm. the 26 day of July 1541 r. of hy*m* 12d[1] & the 11d I rebatyd to hym, so mo*ntith* all	£12 11d
Itm. the 4 day of February 1541 r. of hym at Bristow £6 6s 3d ob.	£6 6s 3½d
Itm. the 26 day of July 1542 r. of hym at Bristowe	£6
Itm. the 9 day of October r. of hym at Bristowe £6	£6
Itm. the 7 day of February r. of hym at Bristowe £3 in redy mon*n*ey	£3
Itm. the 24 day of July 1543 r. of hym at Bristowe £3	£3
Itm. the 26 day of Jenyver 1544 my wif r. for hym of W*illiam* Cary of Bristowe drap*er* £6	£6

---

[1] *This should read £12.*

15(R) contd.

Itm. the 10 day of October 1545 my wif r. of hym	£5 19s 10d
Itm. the 1 day of February 1545 £6 12d which my wif r.	£6 1s
1546 Itm. the 24 day of July r. of hym at Bristowe	£6 15s
Itm. the 7 day of December a*nno* 1546 my wif r. of hym	£4
Itm. the 25 day of July 1547 I r. of hym 40s 2d	£2 2d
Itm. my wif r. £1 15s	£1 15s
Itm. r. the 4 day of December 1548 of hym at Bristow	£4 9s 10d

16(L)   anno 1539

Edward Jones of Aburgeyne owith the 28 day of July £2 6s 8d to be paide at all tymes requyrid, whiche is for the rest of a but of mawmessey as in my shop boke may apere, mon*tith*   £2 6s 8d
1540 Itm. the 10 day of Agost 1540 £3 13s 4d for a but seck to be paide at Allhaloutide next com*m*yng   £3 13s 4d

         anno 1539

Nicholas Gay m*ar*chant of Bristowe owithe the last daye of May for the freight of 10 ton iren in my ship the Trynte £6 18s 4d, that is 3 to*n* at 15s & 7 to*n* at 13s 4d the ton   £6 18s 4d
Itm. the 22 day of September £3 3s 5d for 2 ½-bales wood *conteynyng* 3 C ½, 3 li. at 18s the C, to pay by his bill at Easter next com*m*yng   £3 3s 5d
Itm. the 8th day of October £12 for 2 to*n* iren at £6 the to*n*, to pay by his bill at Ow*r* Lady Day in Lent next   £12
Itm. £3 10s for 3 ton pipe freight *this* vyntage fro*m* Burd*es* in the Trynte at 20s the ton, to pay hallf in hand & tho*ther* hallf at Ow*r* Lady Day in M*ar*che next com*m*yng   £3 10s
1540 Itm. the 15 day of Novembe*r* 1540 £3 which is for the freight of 3 ton Gascon wyne in the Trynte, to pay at 3 monthes & 3 monthes   £3
Itm. the 18 day of February 1542 £3 that is for the freight of 3 tons wyne in my ship, to pay hallf in hand & tho*ther* hallf 3 monthes next after   £3

16(R)   anno 1539

Edward Jones p*er* contra is dewe to have the 5th day of December 46s 8d r. of hym at Bristowe   £2 6s 8d
1540 Itm. the 14 day of Nove*m*ber 1540 r. £3 13s 4d   £3 13s 4d

         anno 1539

Nicholas Gay p*er* contra is dewe to have the 23 day of October £7 that is for 28 d*ucatts* less 20d my s*ar*vant Giles White r. of his s*ar*vant in Andaluzia, mon*tith* 6. 18. 4.   £6 18s 4d
Itm. the 16 day of February r. in p*ar*t of payement of the 3 ton pipe wyne fro*m* Burd*es* *this* last vyntaige 35s   £1 15s
Itm. the 13 day of M*ar*che r. of hym the £12 p*er* contra payable at Ow*r* Lady Day in Lent & so d'd to hym his bill   £12
1540 Itm. the 14 day of July 1540 r. of hym £4 18s 5d   £4 18s 5d
Itm. the 19 day of M*ar*che r. of his wif by thand*es* of his dowghter 30s in p*ar*t of payement of the 3 to*n* freight p*er* contra   £1 10s
Itm. the 3 of M*ar*che 1542 r. of her 30s   £1 10s
Itm. for 4 butt*es* bere 6s, for C ½ wett hake 34s 6d, for 8 cople dry Newland fisshe 20d, more for the rest of C qr. wet hake 10s, mon*tith* all   £2 12s
Itm. the 18 day of October 1544 r. of her 8s   8s

17(L)   anno 1538

Thomas Cot*es* of Eyssam owithe the 24 day of M*ar*che a*nno* dicto £36 11s that is for 3 butt*es* of seck at £3 10s the butt and a but of mawmessey at £5 3s 4d and 2 h'd claret wyne p*r*ice 56s 8d and 12 ½-bales Tullus wood

17(L) contd.

conteynyng 21 C 27 li. at 17s the C, all which stuff I sent in W*illiam* Tayllers trowe of Twexbury & hit is payable at all tymes requyrid	£36	11s	
Itm. the 19 day of December £9 10s that is for 2 but*es* of seck at eiche £3 10s & 2 h'd Gasco*n* wyne p*r*ice 50s, which wy*nes* I lode in W*illiam* Taylers trowe of Twexbury, the Gasco*n* wyn*e* 43s 4d[1]	£9	3s	4d
Itm. the 6 day of February £14 10s for the rest of 1 to*n* Gasco*n* wyne at £4 10s, 2 butt*es* seck at eich £3 10s & 1 pipe ossey at £4 & 1 pipe bastard at £4, to be pd. at all tymes	£14	10s	
1540 Itm. the 25 day of November 1540 £6 *that* is £3 10s for a butt of seck & 50s for 2 h'd Gascon wyne sent to hym in Pulltons trowe	£6		
Itm. the 15 day of December 3s 6d which is for 12 li. of m*a*rmylado at 3d ob. the li. which I sent by Nycholas Stanley		3s	6d
Itm. the 12 day of M*a*rche £6 ~~6s 8d~~ 13s that is for 2 butt*es* of seck sold to hym at eich 5 m*a*rkes to be paide at all tymes requyride	£6	6s--8d	
1542 Itm. the 4 day of May 1542 £18 6s 8d & is for 5 butt*es* seck to be pd. by his byll at Allhaloutide next	£18	6s	8d

17(R) **anno 1539**

Thomas Cot*es per* contra is dewe to have the 27 day of Novemb*e*r £27 7s 7d ½ r. of hym at Brystowe in redy mon*n*ey	£27	7s	7d ob.
Itm. r. fro*m* hym by W*illiam* Tayllers trow of Twexbury 6 ½-bales of my wood bagk ageyne valent £9 3s 4d½	£9	3s	4d ob.
Itm. the 5th day of February r. of hy*m* at Bristow £9 3s 4d	£9	3s	4d
1540 Itm. the 8 day of November a*nn*o 1540[2] r. of his wif in Eyssam £10 10s & thereof made aquyttance	£10	10s	
Itm. the 11 day of Marche a*nn*o 1540 r. of hym in Bristowe £4 10s that is 5 m*a*rkes for 1 butt seck & 23s 4d for 1 h'd Gasco*n* wyne	£4	10s	
Itm. 3s 6d which I geve hym in the m*a*rmylade *per* contra		3s	6d
Itm. 6s 8d which I rebate to hym in *the* price of the wynes		6s	8d
Itm. the 21 day of Dece*m*ber 1541 £6 13s 4d r. at Eyssam of hym by my s*a*rvant Robert Leight	£6	13s	4d
Itm. the 1 day of February a*nn*o 1542 r. of hym £18 6s 8d	£18	6s	8d

18(L) **anno 1539**

Margery Northall wedo in Bristowe diar owith the 9 day of September £3 5s for 2 ½-bales of Tullus woode *conteynyng* 3 C ½, 13 li. at 18s the C sold & d'd to her, to be pd. at all tymes requyrid	£3	5s	
1540 Itm. the 9 day of December 1540 £3 10s that is for a butt of seck which I sold & delyverd to her	£3	6s	8d[3]
Itm. the 24 day of December 20s pd. to her in redy mon*n*ey	£1		
Itm. the 23 daye of February 58s 6d *that* is for 2 ½-bales wood *conteynyng* 3 C 1 qr. 21 li. at 17s the C, mon*tith*	£2	18s	6d
Itm. for ½ a C of madder after 14s the C mo*ntith*		7s	
	£10	17s	2d

anno 1541

Thomas Heward of Bristowe diar owith the 2d day of Aprel 4s 8d for the rest of the above seid acowmpt		4s	8d
Itm. the 5th day of Aprell £3 6s 8d for a but seck	£3	6s	8d
Itm. the 19 day of July £3 10s for a butt of seck	£3	10s	
1542 Itm. the 19 day of Aprill 1542 £3 13s 4d for a butt of seck to be pd. at all tymes	£3	13s	4d

---

[1] The Gasco*n* wyn*e* 43s 4d *inserted later*.
[2] a*nno* 1540 *is inserted above the line*.
[3] £3 10s *altered to* £3 6s 8d.

18(L) contd.

Itm. the 26 of Aprill 56s 10d for 2 bales wood[1] *conteynyng* 3 C ½, 10 li. at 16s p*er* C mon*tith*	£2 16s	10d
1543 Itm. the 30 of July £3 7d & is for 2 ½-bales wood waying 3 C ½, 7 li. at 17s the C mon*tith*	£3	7d
Itm. the 27 day of August £3 3d ob. which is for 2 ½-bales of Tullus wood *conteynyng* 3 C ½, 5 li. at 17s the C	£3	3d ob.
1544 Itm. the 26 of Maye 1544 £4 which is for a butt seck[2] sold to his wif to be pd. at all tymes requyrid[3]	£4	

anno 1539

Allsson Deane of Sherehampton wedo owi*th* the 30th day of May £6 6s 8d for a ton of my best Rendry iren sold & d'd to her in presence of John Darby, to be pd. the ffyve of November next £6 6s 8d

Itm. the 21 day of June 53s 4d for 2 h'd Gascon wyne sold & d'd to her in presence of *the* seid Darby, to pay at all tymes £2 13s 4d

S. £9

anno 1540

Antony Duttsson of Glocester diar owi*th* the 18 day of Octob*er* 59s 4d ob. which is for 2 ½-bales Tullus wood *conteynyng* 3 C ½, 7 li. at 16s 8d the C, to be pd. at all tymes requyrid £2 13s 5½d

anno 1542

Allson Smythe of Shirehampto*n* wyddo owi*th* the 7 day of Marche £8 which is for 2 butt*es* of seck solld & delyverd to her to be paide at all tymes £8

18(R)

anno 1539

Margery Northal p*er* contra is dewe to have the 6th day of Septemb*er* 9s 6d for the rest of acowmpt *this* p*res*ent day 9s 6d

Itm. the 7 day of Octob*er* 1540 reckenyd for grazyng of 7 grenes at 3s the clo*the* & of 12 at 4s the clothe, mon*tith* £3 9s £3 9s

Itm. the 2d day of Aprell a*nno* 1541 for the hand of 5 violet*es* 10s & for grazing of 23 grenes at 4s the clo*the* & for wodyng of 3 rewyd hewlyng*es* of Yerberys to be made violet*tes* 30s, mon*tith*, & 2s for reffresshyng of the collowrs of 2 old gownes 2s,[4] mon*tith* £6 14s £6 14s

Itm. the seid day 4s 8d for the rest & makyng evyn of this cowmpt whereof I make her husband Thom*as* Heyward dettor in a newe cowmpt p*er* contra 4s 8d

£10 17s 2d

anno 1541

Itm. the last day of February Thomas Heyward p*er* con*tra* is dewe to have for grazyng of 42 grenes sens the 2d day of Aprill hetherto at 3s the clothe & for wodyng of a clothe & for the hand of the same to be a vyolet 10s, mon*tith* all £6 16s

Itm. the 15 day of June 1542 for grazing of 16 clothes at 3s p*er* clothe mon*tith* 48s £2 8s

---

[1] *Marginal note*, 37. 9.
[2] *Marginal note*, £5 15s ob.
[3] *The whole of Thomas Heward's account is crossed through.*
[4] *The first* 2s *is written over an erasure and* 2s *is therefore repeated.*

18(R) contd.

Itm. the 27 day of December 1542 for grasyng of 15 clothes at 3s the clothe mon*tith*	£2	5s
Itm. the 23 of August 1543 £3 5s 4d & is for the hand & grass*yng* of 20 clothes at 3s p*er* clothe & of 5 whit lynyng*es* at 12d the clothe, mon*tith*[1]	£3 5s	4d

anno 1539

Allson Deane p*er* contra is dewe to have the 20 day of December £6 6s 8d which she paide to my wiff in redy money		£6 6s	8d
Itm. the 3d day of May r. fro*m* her by Hamond 53s 4d		£2 13s	4d
	S.	£9	

anno 1541

Antony Duttson hereageynst is dewe to have the 21 day of Aprell 53s 5d which I r. of hym in redy money for the hole payment p*er* contra[2]	£2 13s	5d

19(L)   **anno 1538**

Richard Woodwall of Warwyck otherwise of Bewdeley owith the 20 day of Jenyver £11 16s 8d *that* is for 2 butt*es* of seck at eiche £3 10s, a h'd of taynt price 40s & 2 h'd claret wyne price 56s 8d, payable at Seynt Jamystide next com*m*yng	£11 16s	8d
1540 Itm. the 15 day of December a*nno* 1540 £20 that is for 6 butt*es* seck*es* sold to hym at 5 m*arkes the* but to pay at Mydsomer next com*m*yng	£20	

anno 1539

Thomas Treheren of Kerm*er*dyne m*a*rchant owith the 5th day of February £6 6s 8d that is for the rest of 1 ton 1 qr. 16 li. of my bett*er* Rendry iren at 19 nobles *the* ton, to be payd in May next	£6 6s	8d
1540 Itm. the 3d day of May a*nno* 1540 £10 17s 2d that is £7 14s 2d for 1 ton 1 h'd 12 li. of the best Rendry ire*n*, & £3 3s for 2 ½-bales Tullus wood conteynyng 3 C ½ at 18s the C, to pay by his bill at Mighellmas next	£10 17s	2d
Itm. the 5th day of the same £3 5s that is for a pipe iren of S.S. to be pd. by his bill at Mighellmas next com*m*yng	£3 5s	
Itm. the 4th day of February £3 4s that is £3 for a pipe of my best Rendry iren & 4s for 1 C rozyne	£3 4s	
1541 Itm. the 2d day of Maye 1541 £14 12s that is for the rest of 2 to*n* 7 li. ire*n* & 1 C rozyne sold hym, to be pd. by his bill at Mighellmas next com*m*yng as it maye ap*ere* in my shop boke	£12 14s	
Itm. the 6 day of February £3 which is for a p*i*pe of the best Rendry iren sold to hym to be pd. at all tymes	£3	
1542 Itm. the 2d day of May 1542 £18 11s that is ffor 3 to*n* 4 li. iren as in my shop boke may apere, to be paide by his bill at Mighellmas next com*m*yng	£18 11s	
Itm. the 4 day of September £3 6s 2d ob. for 1 pipe less 6 li. iren of S.S. at 20 nobles *the* ton d'd for hym to his s*ar*vauntt Jenkyn up Yevan, to pay at Seynt Androwstide next	£3 6s	2d ob.
Itm. the 7 of ~~November~~ December d'd to his son 1 p*i*pe iren pr*i*ce £3 to pay at C*a*ndellma*s*	£3	
	S. £64 4s	ob.

---

[1] *The whole of Thomas Heyward's account is crossed through.*
[2] *There is no credit entry for Alison Smythe.*

19(R) anno 1538

Richard Woodwal *per* contra is dewe to have the 20 day of Jenyver 59s 2d *that* is for 11 doze*n* & 10 Bewdeley powles at 5s the dozen r. in p*art* of payement	£2	19s	2d
Itm. the 14 day of Septemb*er* r. by the hand*es* of Arture Smythe of Bristowe m*a*rchant £6 13s 4d	£6	13s	4d
Itm. the 22 day of November 1539 r. of hym at Bristowe 43s ~~10d~~ 4d	£2	3s	4d
1541 Itm. the 25 day of July 1541 r. of W*illiam* his bro*ther*	£20		

anno 1540

Thomas Treheryn p*er* contra is dewe to have the 29 day of Aprill £6 6s 8d r. at Bristow of hym	£6	6s	8d
Itm. the 13 day of October £10 r. of J*oh*n Thom*as* Treheren his son & thereof made aquyttance	£10		
Itm. the first day of February r. of hym at Bristowe £4 2s 2d	£4	2s	2d
Itm. the 26 day of Aprell 1541 r. £3 4s	£3	4s	
Itm. the 1 day of Decemb*er* r. of his son, J*oh*n Thomas Treheren £8, I sey £8, & so gave hym aquyttance of the seid £8	£8		
Itm. the 5 day of February r. of hym at Bristowe	£4	14s	
1542 Itm. the 26 day of Apr*ell* 1542 r. of hym at Bristo	£3		
Itm. the 29 day of November r. of his son J*oh*n Thomas Traharan £3 6s 2d ob. for the iren d'd the 4 day of September last past & £8 13s 9d ob. for in p*art* of payment of the iren d'd in May last past, mo*ntith* all	£12		
Itm. £12 17s 2d ob. that is for the rest & closyng up of this acowmpt whereof I make the seid Thomas debito*r* in fo. 175	£12	17s	2d ob.
S.	£64	4s	ob.

20(L) anno 1539

John Howlat of Ullarhampton drap*er* owith the 24 day of July £6 3s 6d that is for 1 ton 4 li. iren, p*ar*te of S.S. & p*ar*t of the Rendry, as in my shop boke ap*er*ith, to be paide at Ow*r* Lady Day next com*m*yng	£6	3s	6d
Itm. the 2d daye of December £45 for so myche redy money d'd & paide to hym for to by there*with* for me 20 dicker tand hid*es* to be d'd at Bristow the spryng next after this now being or com*m*yng, as it may apere by a bill which I have fyrmyd with his hand	£45		
Itm. the 2d day of February pd. hym in redy mon*n*y	£11	2s	4d
Itm. the 4 day of February £6 13s 4d for 1 ton of S.S. iren sold to hym to be paide at all tymes	£6	13s	4d
1545 Itm. the 5 day of February 1545 £7 6s 8d & is for 1 to*n* Gascon wyne to pay at Easter next	£7	6s	8d

anno 1535

John Bucland of Reding goodman of the George there owith the 13 day of May £3 6s 8d, to be pd. at Mighellmas next which is for a butt of seck sold & d'd & delyverd to hym	£3	6s	8d

20(R) anno 1539

John Howlat here ageynst is dewe to have the 3d day of December £6 r. in redy mon*n*ey & 3s 6d I geve hym in recompens of s*er*teyne calve skuyns, mo*ntith*	£6	3s	6d
Itm. the 30 day of Jenyver £55 10s 2d for 25 dicker lethir r. from hym at 2 tymes & it cost at the first penny *the* foresseid price, as by his le*tto*r & cow*n*t apere	£55	10s	2d
Itm. for carrage to Bewdeley 12s 2d mo*ntith*		12s	2d

20(R) contd.

1540 Itm. the 22 day of March r. £6 3s 4d & 3s 4d I gave hym for hors hire when he bowght *the* foresseid lethir & 6s 8d I abatid in *the* price	£6 13s	4d
Itm. the 12 day of October 1546 r. of hym £7 6s 8d	£7 6s	8d

anno 1537

John Buckland p*er* contra is dewe to have the 16 day of June 13s 4dy r. from hym by M*aster* Pic*ke*s son of Bristo	13s	4d
Itm. r. the 4 day of February 1538 being in the fayre at Bristowe of a man unknowen to me 6s 8d	6s	8d
Itm. the 13 day of Novemb*er* 1539 r. of hym at Reding 6s 8d	6s	8d
Itm. 6s 8d pd. to Hewgh Hamond the 1 day of Dece*m*ber 1540	6s	8d
Itm. the 25 day of M*ar*che 1542 I r. of hym at Reding 13s 4d	13s	4d
Itm. the 19 day of February 1543 r. of hym at Bristowe 13s 4d	13s	4d
Itm. more 6s 8d which is lekewise discowntyd fr*om* my reckenyng	6s	8d

21(L)   anno 1535

Robert Will*iam*s of Stowrewestover in Dorsetshere husbandma*n* owith the 25 day of October 15s which I lent hym in redy money apo*n* a bill payable at Mydsom*er* next com*m*yng   15s

1536 Itm. the 16 day of June a*nn*o 1536 £5 *that* is for so myche paide to hym in p*ar*t of payement of £10 which he must have of me for the old hows before M*aster* Joh*n* Shipma*n* if he recover the same of John Kemys of Oldebury with in 2 yeres next & so recov*er*yd to make to me & myne heyres a shewre state of fee sympull in the same hows or ells to repay me the seid £5, as more largely apere by an oblig*acion*   £5

anno 1535

Hewgh Carn of Bristowe marchant owith the 18 day of Agost £3 which is for a but of seck rackyd payable by his bill at *Crist*mas next mon*tith*   £3
Itm. the 16 day of November[1]

21(R)[2]

22(L)   anno 1538

Richard Tovy of Stoke clothiar owith the 15 day of July £3 6d which is for 2 ½-bales of Tullus wood *conteynyng* 3 C ½, 6 li. at 17s the C, to pay at Candellmas next com*m*yng

	S. £3	6d

anno 1539

John Caps of Bristowe marchant owith the 9 day of May 36s 8d that is for a pipe of egar cap*r*ick'& a h'd egar taynt to be pd. at *Crist*mas next	£1 16s	8d
Itm. the 3d day of February £13 6s 8d for so myche redy mo*n*ney d'd to hym for 8 pipes salmon which he must d'd to me acordyng to a byll of his hand datid the 16 day of M*ar*che, & more by the seid bill he ow*ith* £16 13s 4d in redy money & £3 in 3 ton salt & 40s in a to*n* of corrupt Gascon wyne, mon*tith* the hole	£35	
1540 Itm. the 17 day of Agost 1540 pd. to hym £11	£11	
Itm. the same day 20s for the hier of my guns	£1	
Itm. for 1 h'd of corrupt wyne d'd the 12 day of Augost		10s

---

[1] *This entry is incomplete.*
[2] *Fo. 21 R is blank in the MS.*

22(L) contd.

Itm. the last day of Augost 45s 6d sent hym by Giles White for the fynischement of *this* acowmpt		£2	5s	6d
Itm. the 20 day of Jenyver £7 that is for the hier of 6 Portyngall verssos of ire*n* with eich 2 chambers & they*r* firelock*es* 20s, & £6 that I have sold the seid guns ffor to hym, mo*ntith*, £7 to pay at all tymes		£7		
The seid Joh*n* Cappys have made a byll the 10th day of Septembe*r* 1541 for to pay the seid som of £7 the fyrst weke in Lent next followyng.				
Itm. the 11 day of M*a*rche a*n*no 1544 for 3 butt*es* 1 h'd of corrupt wyne at 40s the butt to pay at Ester next, mon*tith* £7		£7		
Itm. the 9 day of July 1546 £4 which is for 2 butt*es* of corrupt seck to be paide this tyme twell monthe		£4		
	S.	£69	12s	2d

22(R)   **anno 1539**

Richard Tovy p*er* contra is dewe to have the 18 day of Novembe*r* £3 6d for so myche J*o*h*n* Wellsche of B*r*istowe m*a*rch*a*nt paid me for hym		£3		6d

anno 1539

John Caps hereageynst is dewe to have the 3d day of Jenyver 36s 8d r. of hym		£1	16s	8d
Itm. the 10th day of Augost 1540 £47 6d *that* is for 27 pipes samon with the custom at 34s 10d the pipe, mon*tith*		£47		6d
Itm. the same tyme for 2 C 1 qr. sallt yellis at 6s 8d *the* C, mon*tith* 15s			15s	
Itm. for a tassell jentyll 40s		£2		
Itm. the 10 day of February 1541 £7 which I r. of hym in redy mon*n*ey & d'd to hym his bill obligatory		£7		
Itm. the 29 daye of Ap*r*ell 1546 £7 which I r. of hym in ready money & d'd to hym his byll		£7		
Itm. the 18 day of Ap*r*ell an*no* 1548 £4 for so myche he dyd allowe unto me toward the som*m* of £34 16s 8d which I paide unto hym for 20 p*e*ces of sallt salmon as it may apere fo. 281		£4		
	S.	£69	12s	2d

23(L)   **anno 1539**

Thomas Turbot of P*e*rciar marc*hant* o*with* the 26 day of July £10 3s 9d that is for a ton 7 li. ire*n* & a but of seck, payable by his bill at C*a*ndellmas next		£10	3s	9d
Itm. the 13 day of Octobe*r* £4 13s 4d whiche is for the rest of a but of seck at 11 nobles & a p*i*pe of iren at £3, to pay for it at Cristmas next by a bill		£4	13s	4d
Itm. the 19 day of December 50s for 2 h'd Gasco*n* wyne which I sent hym in Pepwells trowe to be pd. at all tymes		£2	3s	4d
Itm. the 21 day of Jenyver £6 that is for 1 but of seck at 11 nobles & 2 h'd Gascon wyne p*r*ice 7 nobles		£6		
Itm. the 19 day of M*a*rche £3 7s 6d that is for a p*i*pe 14 li. iren of S.S. at 20 nobles *the* ton to be pd. at all tymes		£3	7s	6d
Itm. the 28 day of July £6 3s 4d for 1 ton of my best Rendry iren to be paide at Candellmas next as it may apere by his bill		£6	3s	4d
	S.	£32	5s	

anno 1540

Thomas Turbot above namyd o*with* the 4 day off February £14 6s 8d, for the which he is bownden by obligac*ion* made by Joh*n* Sare nottary to pay

23(L) contd.

£7 3s 4d at Mighellmas next com*m*yng & £7 3s 4d at Mighellmas next after that which will be in a*nn*o 1542 & it is ffor so myche he restith owyng for the fynischement and clozing up of his old cowmpt above wryte*n* as p*er* contra may apere £14 6s 8d
1541 Itm. the 26 day of November a*nn*o 1541 sold & d'd to hym 1 butt of old seck & 2 h'd new Gasco*n* wyne, the butt at £3 10s & the 2 h'd at 4 m*a*rkes, so mo*ntith* £6 3s 4d
1542 Itm. the 25 day of July 1542 £7 6s 8d which is ffor 1 ton of iren & 1 h'd of Gascon wyne solld & delyv*er*d to hym to be paide at Candellmas next com*m*yng £7 6s 8d
Itm. the 17 day of M*a*rche £7 3s 1d that is £4 for a but of seck & £3 3s 1d for 1 pipe less 5 li. of my best Rendry iren after 19 nobles the ton, the which wyne & iren I delyv*er*d in his name to Richard Nasche his son in lawe[1], to be pd. at Mydsomer next com*m*yng £7 3s 1d

S. [2]

23(R)   anno 1539

Thomas Turbot p*er* contra is dewe to have the 4th daye of February £10 r. of hym in redy mon*n*ey & d'd to hym his byll I had for the same som*m* £10
Itm. the 27 day of July 1540 r. of hym £7 18s 4d £7 18s 4d
Itm. the 4 day of February anno 1540 £14 ~~13s~~ 6s 8d for so myche he restyth owyng for the clozing up of this acowmpt whereof I make hym debitor in a newe cowmpt as in thother syde may apere, & I geve hym dayes of payement for the seid som of £14 6s 8d becawse his hows was brent this last som*m*er by myschawnce, mo*ntith* £14 6s 8d

£32 5s

anno 1541

Thomas Turbot p*er* contra is dewe to have the 25 day of November £7 r. of hym at Bristowe £7
Itm. the 26 day of July 1542 r. of hym in Bristowe £2 13s 4d
Itm. the 15 day of Jenyver my s*a*rvant Robert Lett r. of hym at P*er*cyar £10 & made hym a byll for the receypt thereof, mo*ntith* £10
Itm. the   [2]   day of May 1544 r. of hy*m* at Londo*n* £5 6s 8d
Itm. the 19 day of October 1544 my s*a*rvant Leyt r. of hym at P*er*cyar £4 £4
Itm. the 18 day of September 1546 r. fro*m* hym by Lawrence Hanccott of Barnsgrove £6 £6

S. [3]

24(L)   anno 1539

Willi*a*m Northe of Bruton owith the 13 day of Agost a*nn*o dicto £5 6s 8d whiche is for a ton Gascon wyne sold to hym to be paide at all tymes requyrid £5 6s 8d
Itm. the 13 day of November £8 which my wif lent hym £8
Itm. the 3 day of Dece*m*ber pd. for hym to J*o*hn Mowllton 20s £1
Itm. the 10th day of Dece*m*ber £4 *that* my wif d'd to hym in redy money £4

---

[1] *Marginal note*, 9. 19. 1.
[2] *Blank in MS.*
[3] *Blank in MS.*

24(L) contd.

Itm. the same day £9 6s 8d for 2 to*n* Gascon wyne	£9	6s	8d
Itm. the 5th day of Jenuary £7 6s 8d for 2 butt*es* of seck sent by Lockiar at 11 nobles the butt	£7	6s	8d
anno 1540 Itm. the 6 day of Aprell a*nno* 1540 £12 10s that is for 2 ton ~~pipe~~ Gascon wyne at £4 the ton & 1 pipe corrupt ossey price 50s which I sold to hym to pay at Mighellmas next	£11	16s	8d
[1]Itm. the 1 day of July 50s for 1 pipe corrupt ossey[1]	£2	10s	
S.	£49	6s	8d

anno 1540

Willi*a*m Northe of Bruto*n* owith the 1 day of July £15 6s 8d that is for so myche he owith for the rest & clozing up of thaboveseid acowmpt	£15	6s	8d
Itm. the 15 day of October £4 which my wif delyv*er*d to hym in redy mon*n*ey	£4		
Itm. the 14 day of October £3 3s 1d which is for 1 pipe less 4 li. iren of S.S. at 19 nobles the ton	£3	3s	1d
Itm. the 12 day of Novemb*er* £4 16s 8d which is for 1 to*n* Gascon wyne at 7 m*ar*kes 3s 4d the ton	£4	16s	8d
Itm. the 16 day of November £24 3s 4d[2] that is for 4 ton (pipe 1 h'd)[3] Gascon which he bowght for hym sellf & M*aster* Bridges at £4 16s 8d *the* ton. (I sey 4, ½, ¼)[3]	£24	3s	4d[2]
Itm. the 27 day of November £6 18s 10d that is £7 for 2 butt*es* seck, 5s for a pece rezyng*es* & 6d for a busshell of sallt, water messure (£6 18s 10d)[3]	£6	18s	10d
Itm. the 19 day of Jenyver £13 6s 8d for 4 butt*es* seck sold to hym at 5 m*ar*kes the butt	£13	6s	8d
Itm. the same day £6 13s 4d *that* is for so myche pd. for hym to a Londenar for 2 pipes bastard	£6	13s	4d
Itm. the 9 day of M*ar*che 26s 8d that is for 1 h'd Gasco*n* wyne 23s 4d, for 1 gallo*n* mete oyle 22d & 6 li. almo*ndes* 18d	£1	6s	8d
1541 Itm. the 13 day of June 1541 £7 10s 6d that is £7 10s for 6 h'd Gasco*n* wyne & 6d for a busshell of sallt	£7	10s	6d
S.	£86	2s	5d

anno 1538

John Pavy of Bristowe wever owith the last day of December a*nno* 1538 30s to pay at Ester next, he & Robert Eyssham tayllor stondith bownd for hit. It is for 1 h'd ire*n* sold to the seid Pavy	£1	10s

24(R)   ### anno 1539

Willi*a*m Northe p*er* contra is dewe to have the 18 day of November £20 which he paide for me to J*oh*n Yerbery fo. 48	£20		
Itm. the 1 day of July he pd. to J*oh*n Yerbery £14	£14		
1540 Itm. the 1 day of July 1540 £15 6s 8d *that* is for so myche I make hym debitor of in a newe cowmpt as p*er* contra may apere	£15	6s	8d
	£49	6s	8d

---

[1] *Marginal note*, 15. 6. 8. the 10 of Sep. 1540.
[2] £1 3s 4d *erased*.
[3] *Inserted later*.

24(R) contd.   **anno 1540**

William Northe per contra is dewe to have the 5 day of November £20 which he pd. for me in redy monney to John Yerbery of Bruton clother as it aperith fo. 48	£20		
Itm. the 14 day of February £17 10s¹ paide to John Yerbery	£17	10s	
1541 Itm. the ² day of May 1541 £22 7s 11d pd. for me to John Yerbery fo. 125	£22	7s	11d
Itm. the 27 day of July £20 which he pay for me to John Yerbery fo. 125	£20		
Itm. the 8 day of November r. for hym of John Yerbery theldir 8s 4d		8s	4d
Itm. £3 10s for 1 butt seck he retornyd to me	£3	10s	
Itm. 46s 2d gevyn hym in the prices of my wyne per contra & other smawle thinges I sent hym	£2	6s	2d
S.	£86	2s	5d

anno 1539

John Pavy per contra is dewe to have the 17 daye of December 30s for so myche r. for hym of Water Robertz of Bristowe marchant   £1 10s

25(L)   **anno 1539**

William Jones of Kerdif motleymaker owith the 28 daye of July £4 5s 4d which is for 4 C ½, 27 li. Tullus wood at 18s the C, to pay hallf at Cawstons ffayer next commyng & the other hallf at Seynt Androwtistide next after that, montith   £4 5s 4d

anno 1539

William Tayllor of Twexbury thellder owith the 16 daye of September £8 6s 8d which is for a ton & a h'd iren of S.S. sold & d'd to hym at 20 nobles the ton, to be paide at Owr Lady Day in Lent next commyng   £8 6s 8d
1540 Itm. the 8 day of May 1540 £8 6s 8d that is for 1 ton 1 h'd iren of S.S. at £6 13s 4d the ton, to be paide in wheat d'd at Hungrode or the Key at 11d the busshell when I shall cawle for it. It is 145 busshells   £8 6s 8d
Itm. the 7 day of Agost £8 6s 8d³ that is for 1 ton 1 h'd of my best **Rendry** S.S. iren to pay at Candellmas next   £8 6s 8d
1543 Itm. the 24 day of July anno 1543 £6 & it is for 1 ton of iren solld & delyverd to hym to be paide at Allhaloutyde next commyng   £6
Itm. the 14 of November £6 13s 4d & is for 1 ton of S.S. iren solld & d'd to hym to pay at the Annunciacion of Owr Blessyd Lady next commyng   £6 13s 4d

25(R)   **anno 1539**

William Jones per contra is dewe to have the 27 day of February £3 4d⁴ r. of hym in reddy monney   £3   4d
Itm. the 4 day of February 1540 r. of hym 24s 4d & 8d he dyscowntyd for a gallon of metheglyn   £1 5s

anno 1540

William Taylor per contra is dewe to have the 13 daye of Aprell £6 13s 4d r. of hym in redy monneye   £6 13s 4d

---

¹ 10s *inserted above the line.*
² *Blank in MS.*
³ 8d *inserted above the line.*
⁴ 4d *inserted above the line.*

25(R) contd.

Itm. the last day of June r. of his sarvant Cockes 33s 4d	£1	13s	4d
Itm. the 25 day of Agost r. of hym in Bristow £8 6s 8d	£8	6s	8d
Itm. the 21 day of February r. of hym £6	£6		
Itm. the 17 day of Marche r. of hym 46s 8d	£2	6s	8d
Itm. the 14 of November 1543 r. of hym £6	£6		
Itm. the 21 day of Aprell anno 1544 r. of hym £6 13s 4d	£6	13s	4d

26(L)   **anno 1539**

John Sutton of Harvartwest marchant owith the 29 day of July £6 6s 8d
that is for a ton of iren sold & d'd to hym payable by his bill at
Synt Androstide next   £6 6s 8d
Itm. the 11 day of February £6 14s 5d that is for 1 ton 18 li. iren of S.S. at
£6 13s 4d the ton to be pd. at   [1]   Maye. It was laden in Davyd Smythes bote   £6 14s 5d
1540 Itm. the 27 day of July £6 that is for 1 ton of Rendry iren to be pd. at
Seynt Androwstide next commyng   £6
1541 Itm. the 26 day of July £6 2d that is for 1 ton 3 li. Rendry iren sold &
d'd to hym to be paide at Seynt Androwstide next   £6   2d
1542 Itm. the 26 day of July 1542 £6 1d that is for 1 ton 2 li. of my better
Rendry iren to be pd. at Candellmas next   £6   1d
1543 Itm. the 27 day of July anno 1543 £6 13s 4d & is for a ton of S.S. iren
delyverd for hym to his kynsman John Sutton to be pd. at Seynt Androwstide
next commyng   £6 13s 4d

                                  anno 1538

Roger William John of Aburgeyne owith the 27 day of Julye 33s 4d for a
h'd of S.S. iren to be paide at Candellmas next commyng. David Gowgh is his
shewerty.   £1 13s 4d

26(R)   **anno 1539**

John Sutton per contra is dewe to have the 7 day of February £6 6s 8d r. for hym of John Sutton the yonger his kynssman & d'd his bill	£6	6s	8d
Itm. the 27 day of July 1540 £6 14s 5d r. of hym	£6	14s	5d
Itm. the first day of February r. of his son John Sutton the yonger at Bristow	£6		
Itm. the 3 day of February 1541 r. from hym by the handes of John Keker £6 & 2d I allowyd, montith	£6		
Itm. the 16 day of February anno 1542 r. for hym of William Sutton of Bristowe ~~weyvar~~ shereman £6	£6		
Itm. the 6 day of February 1543 r. of his kynsman the ~~weyvar~~ sherman 20 nobles	£6	13s	4d

                                  anno 1540

Roger William John per contra is dewe to have the 4 day
of February 33s 4d which Davy Gowgh pd. me in too whit
Aburgeynes at 19s the pece whereof I pd. ageyne 4s 8d so
rest that he pd. as affore seid   £1 13s 4d

27(L)   **anno 1538**

Watkyn Pollowghan of Aburgeyne smythe owith the first day of Marche
anno 1538 8s 3d which is for the rest of his reckenyng in my old boke fo. 119.
Edward Jones of Aburgeyne is his shewerty

                                                                                                        S.   8s   3d

---

[1] *Blank in MS.*

27(L) contd. anno 1539

John Cutt of Bristowe marchant owith the 24 day of Julye for the sale of
40 peces Malaga rezynges which com to my parte of 66 peces ½ betwen
Giles White & me, sold on with a nother at 4s 10d ob. the pece & more
apon the seid 66 peces ½ 3s 7d, whereof com to my 40 peces 2s 2d. So
amontith the hole for my part £9 17s 2d   £9 17s 2d
1540 Itm. the 10 day of Maye 17s 9d ob. that is for the freight of 1 ton 1
tertian iren from Spayne in the Trynte at 13s 4d per ton, to pay it at thend
of 3 monthes next commyng   17s 9½d
Itm. the 23 day of Auguste 17s 9d ob. that is for the freight of 1 ton 1 tertian
iren in the Trynte from Spayne   17s 9½d
1542 Itm. the 23 day of August 1542 £3 6s. 8d for the freight of 5 tons iren
in the Trynte   £3 6s 8d
Itm. the 18 day of February £7 10s that is for freight of 5 ton wyne in my
ship at 30s per ton to pay hallf in hand & hallf 3 monthes next after   £7 10s
Itm. the first day of October 1544 for a ton wull oyle   £14
Itm. the 20 day of December anno 1549 for 2 h'd Gascon wyne £4 to be
paide at all tymes requyred   £4

anno 1539

Nicholas Webster of Brymyjam smythe owith the 26 day of July £6 13s 4d
for a ton iren of S.S. to pay at Candellmas next commyng. John Peasley &
Henry Hickman of Bristowe sadelers be his shewertes.   £6 13s 4d

27(R) anno 1541

R. of Edward Jones for Pollowghan per contra the 15 of
September   1s 8d
Itm. r. of the seid Edward the last of November   1s 8d
Itm. the 29 day of Jenyver 1542 r. of Edward Jones
fforesseid 4s 11d   4s 11d

                                                                        S.   8s 3d

anno 1539

John Cutt per contra is dewe to have the 24 day of July
that is 6s in a pece rezinges that I cawsid to be d'd to
William Northe & £3 14s r. in redy money by the handes
of Giles Whit   £4
Itm. the last day of February r. by the handes of Giles Whit   £4 12s 6d
Itm. for a cordovan skyn 4s 4d   4s 4d
1540 Itm. the 29 of July 1540 he pd. to my wif 13s 5d   13s 5d
Itm. the last of December E. Prin pay for hym fo. 89,
17s 9½d   17s 9d[1]
Itm. the 15 of November 1542 4s for 2 stone of orchill &
9s 4d for won C ocam & 53s 4d which my sarvant R. Lett
r. in redy money of hym, montith all £3 6s 8d for the hole
freight of the 5 ton iren per contra   £3 6s 8d
Itm. the 26 of February Hamond r. £3 15s   £3 15s
Itm. the 2 day of August 1543 r. in money £3 5s & 10s in a
C of ocam   £3 15s
Itm. the 7 of November 1544 r. £14 for the ton oyle   £14
Itm. the 5 of Aprell 1550 r. for the 2 h'd wyne per contra   £4

anno 1539

Nycholas Webster per contra is dewe to have the 17 day of
February £4 r. by the handes of John Peasley   £4
Itm. the 5 day of July 1540 r. of his shewertes 4 markes   £2 13s 4d

---

[1] ½d omitted in the total.

28(L)   anno 1539

Robert Davys of Harvartwest marchant owith the 2d day of September
£6 13s 4d that is for a ton of iren of S.S., to be paide £3 6s 8d at Candellmas
next commyng & £3 6s 8d at Easter then next after that, as it aperith by his
bill   £6 13s 4d
Itm. the 11 day of September £6 10s that is for 1 ton of S.S. iren to be paide
at Owr Lady Day in Marche next   £6 10s
1541 Itm. the 29 day of Marche 1541 £6 13s 9d that is for 1 ton 8 li. iren of
S.S. d'd for hym to Philip Cardif of Myllford, as in my shop boke may
apere   £6 13s 9d
~~passed this cownt to my newe boke fo. 1 the 2d day of July, 1550.~~

anno 1536

Master Richard Phelips of Dorsettshire esquyer owith the 11 day of October
1536 32s 1d which is for 55 yerdes frize d'd for hym to John Tayllor sarvant
to his son T. Phelips   £1 12s 1d
1538 Itm. the 19 day of October 1538 £3 10s which is for 3 peces ½ grey
frize conteynyng 135 yerdes at 20s the pece, which fryzes I d'd to Roger
Wyrreat sarvant to Master Sheward   £3 10s
Itm. the 13 day of Marche £4 11s 2d pd. for hym to Antony Payne of
Bristow grocer   £4 11s 2d
passed this cownt the 2 daye of July 1550 to my newe boke fo. 1

28(R)   anno 1540

Robert Davys per contra is dewe to have the 14 day of
Agost £6 13s 4d which he pd. to my wif   £6 13s 4d
1541 Itm. r. the 28 day of March 1541 r. from hym by the
handes of Phillip Cardif of Myllffort £6 13s 4d   £6 13s 4d
Itm. the 16 day of Marche my wif r. of hym   £4   5d
Itm. the 28 day of May 1542 r. from hym by John Maggott
of Bristowe cardemaker 4 markes   £2 13s 4d
[1]

29(L)   anno 1539

John Wells of Wursettor weyver owith the 25 day of July £5 4s 6d ob. that
is for so myche he restith dettor by his reckenyng in my old boke fo. 129   £5 4s 6d ob.
passed this reckenyng the 2 de day of July anno 1550 to my newe boke fo. 1

anno 1539

William Davyd Luys of Harvartwest owith the 30 day of Agost £6 13s 4d
which is for a ton of iren of S.S. at 20 nobles, to pay by his byll at
Candellmas next montith   £6 13s 4d
Itm. the 4 day of February £6 13s 4d that is for 1 ton of S.S. iren to be
paide at Bartyllmewetide next commyng, montith   £6 13s 4d
1540 Itm. the 31 day of Augost £5 7s 6d that is £4 17s 6d for 3 h'd iren of
S.S. & 10s for 2 C ½ of rosyne, to be pd. all at Candellmas   £5 7s 6d
Itm. the 9 day of February anno 1540 £3 2s 7d ob. which is ffor a pipe 1 qr.
21 li. iren of the better Rendry after £6 the ton, to be paide by his bill at
Bartillmewtide next   £3 2s 7d
1541 Itm. £6 3s 4d that is for 1 ton iren d'd to hym the 27 day of July anno
1541, to be paide by his bill at Candellmas next commyng   £6 3s 4d
1542 Itm. the 27 day of July 1542 £3 that is for a pipe of my better Rendry
iren, to be pd. at Candellmas next commyng   £3
Itm. the 6th day of February £3 & it is for a pipe of iren solld & d'd to hym,
to be paide at Seynt Jamistide next   £3
1543 Itm. the 24 of July anno 1543 £6 10s & is for 1 ton of iren solld &
delyverd to hym, to be pd. by his bill at Candellmas next commyng   £6 10s

---

[1] *There is no credit entry for Phelips.*

29(L) contd.

Itm. the 13 of February £6 14s 3d ob. & is for 1 ton 16 li. iren of S.S. to be pd. at Seynt Jamistide next com*m*yng, whereof Cristover Joachym tanner must pay £6 6s 8d & the seid W*illiam* Davy Luyes the rest[1]   £6 14s 3½d

29(R)   anno 1540

John Wells p*er* contra is dewe to have the 15 day of Decemb*er* 20s r. by the hand*es* of Thomas Palm*er* of Higley	£1
Itm. the 17 of Ap*r*ell 1543 r. by Thom*as* Asevarns so*n* 5s	5s
Itm. the 19 day of Octob*er* 1544 my s*a*rvant Leyt r. of hym 5s	5s
R. of Griffith Estwyck*es* at 2 tymes 4 nobles	£1 6s 8d
Itm. r. the 1 day of Augost a*nn*o 1548 of Griffith	7s 10d

anno 1539

William David Luyes p*er* contra is dewe to have the last day of Jenyver £6 13s 4d r. in redy mon*n*y	£6 13s 4d
1540 Itm. the 30 day of Augost 1540 r. £6 13s 4d	£6 13s 4d
Itm. the 9 day of February 1540 r. of hym at Bristow £5 7s 6d mon*tith*	£5 7s 6d
Itm. the 26 day of July £3 2s 7d ob. r. of hy*m* in Bristowe	£3 2s 7d ob.
Itm. the 27 day of July 1542 r. of hym at Bristo	£6 3s 4d
Itm. the 6 day of February r. of hym at Bristowe £3 mon*tith*	£3
Itm. the 24 of July a*nn*o 1543 £3 for so myche reddy mon*n*y r. of hym at Bristowe	£3
Itm. the 13 of February r. of hym £6 10s	£6 10s
1544 Itm. the 10th day of Decemb*er* r. of Willi*a*m Davy Luys 7s 7½d[2]	7s 7d ob.

30(L)   anno 1537

Jamys Baylif of Bristowe m*a*rchant owe the 20 day off Julye £6 which is for 10 C grene wood at 12s the C to be paide at all tymes requyrid	£6
The 18 day of February 1538 8s 4d for 5 trussis of old hey at 20d the truss mon*tith*	8s 4d
	£6 8s 4d

anno 1541

Jamys Baylif of Bristowe m*a*rchant owthe the 1 day of December 25s which is for the rest & ½ payement of the freight of 2 to*n* bastard in the Trynte at 25s p*er* ton, to be pd. at thend of 3 monthes next com*m*yng, mon*tith*	£1 5s
1544 Itm. the 1 day of Ap*r*ell 1544 £6 13s 4d & is for the freight of 5 tons iren in the Trynte my ship at 4 nobles the ton, to pay hallf in hand & ½ at thend of 3 monthes next com*m*yng	£6 13s 4d

anno 1539

Willi*a*m Sprat m*a*rchant of Bristowe owith the 15 daye of Ap*r*ell 13s 4d which is for a scuchyn of the Kyng*es* armes in tymb*er* gilltyd to putt afore apo*n* the Nichollas stern	13s 4d
Itm. the 19 day of the same 22s which he owith me for Jo*h*n Baynes by a byll	£1 2s
1540 Itm. the 10 day of Maye £10 *that* is for the freight of 15 tons iren in my ship at 13s 4d p*er* ton to pay at thend of 3 monthes next ffollowyng	£10

---

[1] *These items for 1543 are crossed through.*
[2] *William Luyes' account is crossed through.*

30(L) contd.

Itm. the 8 day of July £3 10d that is for freight & averes of 40 ½-bales Tullus wood in the Mawdelen of the Passaige, master John de Sala, at 18d qr. per ½-bale	£3	10d
Itm. the 17 day of Agost 9s for a dozen ores as in Jornal aperith	9s	
Itm. the 23 day of Agost £3 6s 8d that is for the freight of 5 ton iren from Spayne in the Trynte	~~£3 6s 8d~~	
Itm. the same day 15s 1d for the freight of 1 ton 2 kyntalls iren in my seid ship laden for Nicholas, his son £3 8s	~~8s~~ ~~15s 1d~~	
Itm. the 15 day of November 1540 £5 for the freight of 5 ton Gascon wyne in my ship the Trynte from Burdes this vyntaige, to pay at 3 monthes & 3 monthes in hallfes	£5	
Itm. the last day of December pd. for hym to Edward Pryn 44s 6d	£2 4s	6d
Itm. the 14 day of February £3 that is for 1 pipe iren d'd for hym to Richard Baker in Cristmas Street, to pay at Seynt Jamistide next commyng	£3	
Itm. the 30 day of August 4s that is for 3 ores of 7 alnes & 3 of 8 d'd to Richard Lacon	4s	
1541 Itm. the 1 day of December 1541 £6 5s which is for the freight 5 ton bastard at 25s per ton in the Trynte, to pay ½ in hand & ½ at thend of 3 monthes next commyng	£6 5s	
1542 Itm. the 24 of Aprell 1542 £4 that is for freight of 6 ton iren in the Trynte to pay at 3 monthes & 3 monthes	£4	
Itm. the 23 day of August £4 13s 4d for 7 ton freight in the Trynte	£4 13s	4d

30(R)

anno 1538

Jamys Baylif per contra is dewe to have for 22 stone orchill at 2s the stone £3 4s — £3 4s
For 3 quarters rent of a seller under his hows in Cornestret — 7s
Itm. the 22 day of December 57s 4d r. of hym in redy monney — £2 17s 4d

£6 8s 4d

anno 1542

Jamys Bayly per contra ys dewe to have the 4th day of Aprill 25s which he paide to my sarvant Hewgh Hamon, montith — £1 5s
Itm. the 11 day of May 1544 he pd. to my wif £3 — £3
Itm. the 28 of July 1544 r. 11 nobles — £3 13s 4d

anno 1540

William Sprat hereageynst is dewe to have the 19 day of June £7 9s 6d that is for the freight of 6 ton 3 h'd 1 C wood from the Yles of Surys in his ship the Jhesus, acowmptyng 22 C for 1 ton at 22s the ton, montith — £7 9s 6d
Itm. the 16 day of October r. by his sarvant Filld £7 6s 8d — £7 6s 8d
Itm. the 20 day of December £10 12s 6d that is for the freight of 8 ton pipe in the Jhesus from Andaluzia this vyntaige at 25s per ton, to pay ½ in hand & thother ½ at 3 monthes — £10 12s 6d
Itm. the last day of Jenyver anno 1541 £3 2s 6d r. of hym by my sarvant for the hallf freyght of the 5 tons bastardes per contra — £3 2s 6d
Itm. the 19 of Aprell 1542 r. £3 by thandes of Hamon for the pipe iren per contra d'd to Richard Baker — £3
Itm. the 9 day of September r. of hym £5 2s 6d — £5 2s 6d
Itm. the 7 day of February my sarvant Leytt r. £4 — £4

61

31(L)   anno 1538

Henry Wellsche of Wursettor gentillman o*with* the 6 daye of Awgost
£3 13s 11d that is for so myche he o*with* for the rest of his cowmpt in my
old boke fo. 138

                                                                                       S.   £3 13s 11d

anno 1540

Willi*a*m Bellshire of Wekewar weyn*er* owithe the 30 day of Aprell £4 15s
that is for a but seck 11 nobles & for 1 h'd claret wyne 21s 8d to be paide
at Seynt Jamistide next. Richard Collymore of Sodebury clothir is his
shew*er*ty, mon*tith*   £4 15s

anno 1539

Thomas Machet of Barckeley tannar owithe the 2d day of Awgost £14
which is for 2 pipes wull oyle, of the which the on was d'd to Hawle of
Barcley & th*other* to Jo*hn* Gervis of Wynterborn wayneman for the which
£14 he must d'd to me at *Crist*mas next 7 dicker le*ther* of large ox, cow &
stere after 40s the dicker   £14
Itm. the 10 day of Jenyver £34 pd. to hym in redy mon*n*y for the hole &
full payement of 5 dicker ox hid*es*, 9 dicker cow & stere & 36 doze*n* calve
skuyns to be d'd at all tymes requyrid, as it may apere by his bill. The
ox le*ther* is at £3 the dicker, cow & stere at 7 nobles *the* dicker & calve
skuyns at 6s 8d the dicker   £34
Itm. 10s which 5s for a daggar & 5s for the rest of 15s which I delyverd to hym
to ley ernes apo*n* Packers le*ther*   10s
Itm. the 13 day of Jenyver 50s to be pd. at all tymes which is for the rest
of a pipe wull oyle as in my shop boke apere   £2 10s
1540 Itm. the 16 day of Novemb*er* anno 1540 £20 *that* is for so myche
redy mon*n*ey pd. to hym in yernes & p*ar*t of payement of 30 dozens calve skuyns
at 6s the doze*n*, of 7 dicker ox le*ther* at 4 m*ar*kes the dicker & of 9 dicker
& 1 hide[1] cowe & stere at 43s 4d the dickar, which le*ther* he must delyver at
all tymes requyrid & the rest of his mon*n*ey must be paide at Candellmas
next com*m*yng   £20
Itm. the 4 day of February paide to hym in Bristowe £10   £10
Itm. the 9 day of M*ar*che pd. to hym in Bristowe £7 7s 8d   £7 7s 8d
1541 Itm. the 8 day of Aprell 1541 pd. to hym £9 6s 6d & more a quarter
of madder p*r*ice 3s 6d, mon*tith* all £9 10s   £9 10s

                                                                                £97 17s 8d

31(R)   anno 1539

Henry Wellsche p*er* contra is dewe to have the 29 day of
November a*nno* 1539 £3 13s 11d for so myche redy money
r. at Bristowe from his wif by Edward Krosby Kendallman
& thereof I made aquyttans   S.   £3 13s 11d

anno 1540

W*illi*am Bellshire p*er* contra is dewe to have the 8 day of
December £3 14s r. by the hand*es* of his neighb*ur* John
Collwell   £3 14s
Itm. the 14 day of November 1541 r. by the hand*es* of
Myles Greve of Bristow taylor 20s   £1
Itm. the 20 day of December a*nno* 1541 r. fro*m* hym of
Rycha*r*t Hawkyns smythe 12d   1s

---

[1] & 1 hide *inserted later*.

31(R) contd.　　　　　　　　　　**anno 1539**

Thomas Machet per contra is dewe to have the 7 day of Marche £48 that is for 5 dicker ox hides, 9 dicker cow & stere & 36 dozen calve skuyns r. of hym at the prices mencyonyd hereageynst	£48
1540 Itm. the 15 day of May 1540 r. of hym 50s for the rest of the pipe oyle per contra	£2　10s
Itm. the 15 day of February £47 7s 8d that is for 7 dicker ox lether at 4 markes the dickar & 9 dicker of cow & stere & 1 hide at 43s 4d the dickar & 30 dozens calve skuyns at 6s the dozen, all which lether I r. of hym the seid day, montith all	£47　7s　8d
Itm. the 8 day[1]	
S.	£97　17s　8d

32(L)　　　　　　　　　　**anno 1539**

Jone Lovell of Bridgewater wedo owith the 7 daye of Agost 53s 4d for 2 h'd claret wyne laden to her in Grawngeres bote to pay at all tymes requyrd　　　　　　　　　　　　　　　　　　　　　　　£2　13s　4d

anno 1540

David Hobs of Bristowe grocer owith the 15 day of Jenyver £2 that is for so myche redy monney lent hym, to pay it at Easter next commyng as by his obligacion aperith　　　　　　　　　　　　　　　　　　　　　£2

anno 1543

Davy Hobbs of Bristowe owith the 17 day of December £2 & is for so myche lent hym in redy monney, to be paide at Mydsomer next as may apere by his byll, montith　　　　　　　　　　　　　　　　　　　£2

anno 1538

William Lord of Bristow marchant owithe the 10 day of Agost 20s that is for the rest of his cownt in my old boke fo. 143　　　　　　　　　　　　　£1

32(R)　　　　　　　　　　**anno 1539**

Jone Lovell per contra is dewe to have the 7 day of November 53s 4d r. from her by William Spyring　　　　　　　£2　13s　4d

anno 1541

David Hobs per contra is dewe to have the 12 day of September 40s which my sarvant Leight r. & so I d'd to hym his obligacion　　　　　　　　　　　　　　　　　　　　　£2

1545

Davy Hobbs per contra is dewe to have 40s which Master Pekes paide to me for hym[2]　　　　　　　　　　　　　　　£2

---

[1] This entry is incomplete in MS.
[2] There is no credit entry for Lord.

33(L) anno 1539

John Smythe of Wynterborn my tenant owith the 24 day of September £4 that is for 12 C iren of S.S. to be paid at all tymes	£4	
Itm. the 13 day of December 40s which he owith for the rest of a pipe & 1 qr. iren as in my shop boke may apere	£2	
Itm. the last day of Jenyver £4 for 12 C S.S. iren at 6s 8d the C to be paide at Ester next commyng	£4	
1540 Itm. the 8th day of May £4 15s that is for 15 C iren, part of S.S. & part of the best Rendry iren at 6s 4d the C to be paide ffortnight after Midssomer	£4 15s	
Itm. the 23 day of August 40s which is for the rest of 12 C qr. 2 li. iren of S.S. at 19 grotes the C, montith	£2	
Itm. the 13 day of November 40s which is for the rest of 7 C 1 qr. 13 li. iren of S.S. at 6s 4d the C	£2	
Itm. the 15 day of Jenyver £6 6s 8d for 1 ton of S.S. iren to be pd at Midssomer next	£6 6s 8d
1541 Itm. the 21 day of Maye 1541 £4 which is for the rest of 12 C 3 qr. 6 li. iren as in the shop boke may apere	£4	
Itm. the 21 day of July £4 that is for the rest of 1 pipe 3 C 26 li. iren as in the shop boke may apere	£4	
Itm. the first day of October 30s which is for the rest of 1 h'd 8 li. iren of S.S. to be pd. at all tymes	£1 10s	
Itm. the 10 day of October 30s which is for 1 h'd Rendry iren to pay at all tymes	£1 10s	
Itm. the 10 day of December 30s which is for 1 h'd of Rendry iren montith	£1 10s	
1542 Itm. the 15 day of Aprell 1542 £6 & it is ffor the rest of 1 ton 3 qr. 21 li. iren to be pd. at Midsomer next	£6	
Itm. the 17 day of June £6 that is for 1 ton iren to be pd. at Seynt Jamistide next	£6	
Itm. the 19 day of Augost £6 which is for the rest of 1 ton iren after 19 nobles the ton	£6	
Itm. the 13 day of November 34s 10d that is ffor 1 h'd 1 qr. 13 li. iren of S.S. at 6s 6d the C to be paide at all tymes, montith	£1 14s 10d
Itm. the 28 day of November for 3 h'd less 1 qr. 6 li. of S.S. iren at 6s 6d the C, montith £4 15s 7d	£4 15s 7d
1543 Itm. the 18 of Maye 1543 £6 13s 4d & is for 1 ton of S.S. iren solld & d'd to hym to pay at Seynt Jamistide next	£6 13s 4d
Itm. the 28 day of June £6 13s 4d that is for 1 ton of S.S. iren sold to hym to be paide at all tymes	£6 13s 4d
S.	£75 8s 9d

anno 1538

David Americk of Kerdif yeoman owith the 22 day of February 56s 8d for 1 h'd claret wyne & 1 h'd white wyne sent hym in David Watkyns bote to be paide at Mydsomer next commyng   £2 16s 8d

33(R) anno 1539

John Smythe per contra is dewe to have the 26 day of October 40s for so myche r. of hym at Bristow in monny	£2	
Itm. the 22 day of November r. of hym in Bristowe 40s	£2	
Itm. r. the last day of Jenyver 40s	£2	
Itm. r. the 13 of Marche 4 markes which he hym self pd.	£2 13s 4d
1540 Itm. the 10 of Aprell 1540 r. of hym 26s 8d	£1 6s 8d
Itm. the 5th day of June r. £4 15s	£4 15s	
Itm. the 9 day of October r. 40s	£2	
Itm. the 15 day of Jenyver r. of hym 40s	£2	
1541 Itm. the 21 daye of Maye 1541 r. £6 6s 8d	£6 6s 8d
Itm. the 21 day of July r. of hym £4	£4	
Itm. the first day of October r. of hym £4	£4	
Itm. the 10 day of December r. of hym £3	£3	
Itm. the 10 day of February r. of hym at Bristowe 30s	£1 10s	

33(R) contd.

Itm. the 17 day of June my wif r. of hym £6	£6		
Itm. the 12 day of Augost 1542 r. £5	£5		
Itm. the 19 day of the same r. 20s	£1		
Itm. the 29 day of September r. by my wif £4	£4		
Itm. the 11 day of November r. of hym 40s	£2		
Itm. the 28 day of November r. 30s 5d	£1	10s	5d
Itm. the 18 day of May 1543, my wif r. £5	£5		
Itm. the 28 of June 20 nobles for so myche r. of hym for the ton of S.S. iren d'd the 18 of May last past	£6	13s	4d
Itm. the 18 of August r. of hym £6 13s 4d	£6	13s	4d
S.	£75	8s	9d

anno 1538

David Americk per contra is dewe to have the 27 day of July 40s r. of his wif in Bristowe	£2		
Itm. the 6 day of February r. of Water Jones his son in the lawe 13s 4d		13s	4d

34(L)   **anno 1539**

John Luys of Twexbury smythe owith the 26 day of July £13 that is for 2 ton iren of S.S. sold & d'd to hym at £6 10s the ton to be pd. at all tymes requyrid	£13		
Itm. the 7 day of October £6 10s for a ton of iren of S.S. which his wif wyllid me to send hym	£6	10s	
Itm. the 19 day of December £10 16s 8d that is for 1 but seck price £3 6s 8d & for 6 h'd Gascon wyne at £5 the ton, laden in William Tayllers trow	£10	16s	8d
Itm. the 8 day of Marche £11 5s which is for the rest of 1 ton pipe iren of S.S. after £6 10s the ton & 1 h'd C 1 qr. of my best Rendry iren at £6 the ton, as in my shop boke may apere	£11	5s	
Itm. the 8 of June £3 13s 4d for 1 but of seck sent in Pulltons trowe	£3	13s	4d
S.	£45	5s	

anno 1540

Richard Carrick of Twexbury owith the 31 day of August 11s 8d that is for 1 h'd claret wyne sent hym in Pulltons trowe to be paide at all tymes	£1	1s	8d
Itm. the 12 day of November £5 that is ffor 1 ton of Gascon wyne sentt in Lawghtons trowe	£5		
Itm. the 24 day of November £7 that is for 2 buttes of seck sent in Dymockes trow at £3 10s the butt	£7		
1541 Itm. the 27 day of Aprell 1541 £5 that is for 1 ton of Gascon wyne lade in T. Afletes trowe	£5		
Itm. the 25 day of Julye £10 that is for 3 buttes of seck sold to hym at £3 6s 8d the butt to be pd. at all tymes	£10		
Itm. the 9 day of February £7 6s 8d for 2 buttes of seck sent hym in Dymockes trowe to be paide at all tymes	£7	6s	8d
1542 Itm. the 8 day of Maye 1542 £12 13s 4d & is for 2 buttes seck at eich 11 nobles & 1 ton Gascon wyne at 16 nobles to pay at Seynt Jamistide next	£12	13s	4d
Itm. the 16 day of May 4 nobles for 1 h'd red wyne sent her in William Tayllers trowe of Twexbery	£1	6s	8d
Itm. the 19 day of February £8 for 2 buttes seck sent to hym in Pepwells trowe	£8		
1543 Itm. the 19 day of Aprill anno 1543 £16 & is for 4 buttes of seck at eich £4 sold & d'd to hym to be paide at all tymes in Tawlers trowe[1]	£16		
Itm. the 30 day of May laden in Pawllmers trowe of Higgley 4 buttes of seck at eich £4 to pay at all tymes	£16		

[1] In Tawlers trowe *inserted later*.

34(L) contd.

Itm. the 20 day of February £18 10s & is for 4 butt*es* of seck at ech 11 nobles & 1 pipe bastard at £3 16s 8d, mo*ntith*	£18	10s	
1544 Itm. the 25 of Julye 1544 £7 & is for 2 butt*es* seck*es* to be paide at all tymes	£7		
Itm. the 14 day of December 1545 £15 13s 4d which is for 6 h'd Gas*con* wyne after £7 6s 8d p*er* to*n* & 1 but seck at 14 nobles to be pd. at all tymes	£15	13s	4d
Itm. the 11 day of February for a butt seck 13 nobles	£4	6s	8d

34(R) anno 1539

John Luys p*er* contra is dewe to have the 2d daye of February £10 13s 4d r. of his wif & 3s 4d she rebatid in the price of the 6 h'd wyne p*er* contra, mo*ntith*	£10	16s	8d
Itm. the 6 day of M*ar*che r. of hym £19 7s 6d & 2s 6d allowyd hym toward horssmet, mo*ntith* the hole	£19	10s	
Itm. the 26 day of July 1540 r. of Richard Caryck £14 18s 4d in redy money	£14	18s	4d
S.	£45	5s	

anno 1541

Richard Carryck p*er* contra is dewe to have the 29 day of M*ar*che £11 6s 8d which he paide for me to Willi*am* Bullock, mo*ntith*	£11	6s	8d
Itm. the 24 day of July r. in Bristowe £5 15s	£5	15s	
Itm. 20s which she discownt in the pric*es* of wyne p*er* contra	£1		
Itm. the 21 of December £10 which my s*ar*vant Robert Leight r. of hym at Twexbury	£10		
Itm. the 2 day of May 1542 r. of Thomas Lamb £6 12s 6d	£6	12s	6d
Itm. the 2 day of May r. of his wif at Twexbury 6s 8d		6s	8d
Itm. more I geve her in the p*r*ice 6s 8d		6s	8d
Itm. the 24 day of July 1542 r. of his wif at Bristowe £13 6s 8d	£13	6s	8d
More 13s 4d which his wif rebate in the p*r*ice		13s	4d
Itm. the 28 day of M*ar*che a*nno* 1543 £8 which is for so myche r. fro*m* hym by my s*ar*vant Robert Leight	£8		
Itm. the 4th daye of September a*nno* 1543 my s*ar*vant Robert Leight r. of hym at Twexbury £32	£32		
Itm. the 21 day of Aprell a*nno* 1544 £7 which my s*ar*vant Lett r. at Twexbury in redy mo*n*ney	£7		
Itm. the 24 of July 1544 r. £11 6s 8d	£11	6s	8d
Itm. 3s 4d which is rebatyd in the p*r*ice of *the* wynes		3s	4d
Itm. the 20 day of October my sarvant Leyt r. £7	£7		
Itm. the 10 day of February 1545 r. fro*m* hym by Richard Cox £4 13s 4d	£4	13s	4d
Itm. r. by Leight £10 10s	£10	10s	
Itm. r. the 27 day of October by ~~Richard the carryer~~ William the Shrevis s*ar*vant[1] £4	£4		

35(L) anno 1539

Willi*am* Grawng*er* of Ullerhampto*n* smythe owith the 24 day of July £6 6s 8d for a ton of S.S. iren to be pd. by his bill at Allhaloutide next. John Howlat is shew*er*ty	£6	6s	8d
Itm. the 26 day of July £6 6s 8d that is for 1 ton iren of S.S. to be pd. at Candellmas next	£6	6s	8d

---

[1] *The Sheriffs in 1546–1547 were John a Wells and Thomas Joahim.*

35(L) contd.

Itm. the 22 day of Marche £6 6s 8d for 1 ton of S.S. iren to be paide by his obligacion at Mighellmas next commyng	£6	6s	8d
Itm. the 7 day of October £6 6s 8d which is for 1 ton of S.S. iren to be pd. by his obligacion at Ester next	£6	6s	8d
1542 Itm. the 20 day of June £6 10s which is for 1 ton of S.S. iren to pay by his obligacion made by John Sare at Allhaloutyde next	£6	10s	
Itm. the 3 daye of February £8 3s 4d that is for 1 ton of S.S. iren at 20 nobles & 1 h'd Rendry iren after £6 the ton solld & delyverd to hym, to be paide at Mydsomer next commyng as it may apere by his obligacion	£8	3s	4d

anno 1539

Master William Chester of Bristowe poyntmaker owith the 28 day of Jenyver £16 that is for 2 pipes wull oyle payable by his bill at Whitsontyde next commyng	£16
Itm. the ¹ day of May £2 *that* is for 2 gouns callid Portyngall verssos with theyr chambers at 20s *the* gun	£2

anno 1537

William Sawnders of Burton apon Trent vyntnar owith the 28 day of Agost £14 which is for the rest of 3 ton iren at £6 the ton, to be pd. by a bill at Candelmas next	£14

anno 1537

William Tayllor of Wursettor owith the 11 day of Marche £18 10s for £3 ton iren at £6 3s 4d the ton to be pd. by his bill at Bartyllmewetide next commyng	£18	10s

35(R)   **anno 1539**

William Grawnger per contra is dewe to have the 23 day of November £6 6s 8d r. of hym in Bristo	£6	6s	8d
Itm. the 22 day of Marche 1540 r. of hym £6 6s 8d	£6	6s	8d
Itm. the 7 day of October 1541 r. of hym £6 6s 8d	£6	6s	8d
Itm. the 20 day of June 1542 r. by my wif £6 6s 8d	£6	6s	8d
Itm. the 3 daye of February 1542 r. of hym at Bristowe £6 10s	£6	10s	
Itm. the 5 of Jenyver 1543 my sarvant Leytt r. of hym £3	£3		
Itm. the 20 of Augost 1544 my sarvant R. Leyt r.	£5	3s	4d

anno 1540

William Chester per contra is dewe to have the last day of June £16 for so myche redy money r. by thandes of Thomas Bewley, montith	£16
Itm. the 26 day of July r. by thandes of Thomas Tyzons sarvunt 40s²	£2

36(L)   **anno 1539**

William Ballard of Bristow marchant owith the 17 day of July 53s 4d for 2 h'd claret wyne to be paide at all tymes, montith	£2	13s	4d
Itm. the 12 day of December 20s that is for the hallf & hole rest of the freight of 2 ton Gascon wyne *this* vyntage in *the* Trynte, to be paide at Owr Lady Day in March next commyng	£1		
1540 Itm. the 2d day of October 1540 £12 which is for 2 ton iren that Robert Sexy draper r. of me for hym at £6 the ton, to be paide at Seynt Jamistide next commyng	£12		

---

¹ *Blank in MS.*
² *There are no credit entries for Sawnders and Tayllor.*

36(L) contd.

1541 Itm. the 1 day of December 1541 £3 2s 6d *that* is ffor the rest & hallf freight of 5 ton bastard in the Trynte at 25s *per* ton, to be pd. at the end of 3 mo*n*thes next com*m*yng   £3   2s   6d
1542 Itm. the last daye of M*a*rche 1542 54s 2d that is for so myche redy mo*n*ney paide to his s*a*rvant Richard Mos for the last payment of my freight in the Trynte of Carlyon & so broke of my seale   £2   14s   2d
Itm. the 24 day of Ap*r*ell 1542 13s 4d that is ffor the freight of 1 to*n* iren in the Trynte, to pay at 3 mo*n*thes & 3 mo*n*thes[1]   13s   4d
Itm. the 23 day of Augost £6 13s 4d for the freight of 10 to*n* iren in the Trynte from Spayne   £6   13s   4d

  £28

anno 1539

Thomas David of Lyswayne owith the 12 day of Septe*m*ber £3 6s 10d that is for a pipe 32 li. iren to be pd. by his bill at Candellmas next   £3   6s   10d
Itm. the 4 day of February £3 4s 6d that is for a pipe 21 li. of my best Rendry iren aft*e*r 19 nobles the ton to be paide at Whitsontide next com*m*yng   £3   4s   6d
1540 Itm. the 15 day of June £3 3s 6d for 1 pipe 4 li. iren of S.S. at 19 nobles *the* ton to pay at Mighellmas next   £3   3s   6d
Itm. the 3 day of February 1540 £3 3s 4d that is for a pipe of my best Rendry iren to pay for it by his byll at Whitsontyde next   £3   3s   4d
Itm. the 10 day of June 1541 £3 3s 4d that is for a pipe of my bett*er* Rendry iren to be pd. at Mighellmas next   £3   3s   4d
Itm. the 18 day of November £3 3s 4d for 1 p*ipe* of *the* best Rendry iren to be paide at Easter next   £3   3s   4d
1542 Itm. the 29 of Ap*r*ell 1542 £3 3s 4d for a p*ipe* iren to be pd. at thassumptio*n* of O*w*r Lady next com*m*yng   £3   3s   4d
Itm. the 27 day of October £3 3s 4d which is for a p*ipe* of the bett*er* Rendry iren to be paid at Ester next   £3   3s   4d
1543 Itm. the 20 of Ap*r*ell 1543 £4 15s for 3 h'd iren d'd to hym & Martyne Willi*a*ms to be pd. at thassumptio*n* of O*w*r Lady next   £4   15s

  S.   £30   6s   6d

anno 1539

Sir Edward Gorge knyght owith the 23 day of July 53s 4d for 2 h'd claret wyne d'd for hym to Willi*a*m Atwood his s*a*rvant, to be paide at Mighellmas next   £2   13s   4d
1540 Itm. the 20 day of December 1540 46s 8d for 2 h'd Gascon which I sold & his s*a*rvant r. the*m* of me for hym   £2   6s   8d
Itm. the 9 day of June 25s for 1 h'd cl*a*ret wyne   £1   5s
1541 Itm. the 18 day of February 1541 26s 8d *that* is for 1 h'd cl*a*ret wyne sold & d'd for hym to his s*a*rvunt   £1   6s   8d
Itm. the 12th day of May 1547 56s 8d that is for 2 h'd Gascon wyne to his s*a*rvant Cotto*n* to pay at Mydsomer next   £2   16s   8d

36(R)   **anno 1539**

Willi*a*m Ballart hereageynst is dewe to have the 3 daye of Jenyver 50s r. by the hand*es* of his s*a*rvant   £2   10s
Itm. the 14 day of Agost r. of hym 20s   £1
1541 Itm. the 4 day of August 1541 r. of hym £6   £6
Itm. the 12 day of September r. of hym £6   £6
Itm. the 8 day of November 1541 £5 16s 8d which is for so myche I rest for the hallf freight of 10 to*n* in the Trynte of Carlyon aft*er* 25s *per* to*n* to be pd. at thend of 3 mo*n*thes next com*m*yng   £5   16s   8d

---

[1] *This item is crossed through.*

36(R) contd.

Itm. the ¹ day of November 1542 r. of hym of Thomas Shipma*n* 40s	£2	
Itm. the 8 of Jenyver 1542 26s 8d r. by thand*es* of his waytingman Lanssdon	£1 6s 8d	
Itm. the 13 day of February £3 6s 8d *that* is for so myche redy mon*n*ey r. of hym by my s*a*rvant Leytt	£3 6s 8d	
	S. £28	

anno 1539

Thomas David of Lyswayne p*er* contra is dewe to have the 3d day of ~~Jenyver~~ February £3 6s 10d which he paide to my wif	£3 6s 10d
1540 Itm. the 15 day of June a*n*no 1540 r. of hym in Bristo	£3 4s 6d
Itm. the ~~fyfrst~~ day of February, I sey the p*r*imo day, r. of hy*m*	£3 3s 6d
Itm. the 9 day of June r. of hym £3 3s 4d	£3 3s 4d
Itm. the 17 day of November 1541 r. of hym at Bristowe £3 3s 4d	£3 3s 4d
1542 Itm. the 28 day of Aprell 1542 £3 3s 4d r. of hym at Bristowe in redy money	£3 3s 4d
Itm. the 27 day of Octob*er* r. of hym at Bristowe	£3 3s 4d
Itm. the 19 day of Aprill 1543 r. of hy*m* £3 3s 4d	£3 3s 4d
Itm. the 4th of Octob*er* r. by my wif £4 15s	£4 15s
	S. £30 6s 6d

anno 1540

Sir Edward Gorge p*er* contra is dewe to have the last day of June 53s 4d r. of W*illiam* Atwood & thereof I made aquyttance	£2 13s 4d
Itm. the 21 day of February 1541 r. fro*m* my Lady Gorge by the hand*es* of Mastres Catyssby £3 11s 8d	£3 11s 8d
Itm. the 15 of November 1544 Robert Leyt r. of hym 26s 8d	£1 6s 8d
Itm. the 23 day of June r. of his s*a*rvant Benett Cotton 56s 8d a*n*no 1547	£2 16s 8d

37(L)

anno 1539

Thomas Howel berebruar of Bristowe owi*t*he the 19 daye of Maye £6 for a to*n* of iren to be pd. by his bill at Seynt Jamystide next	£6
1540 Itm. the 9 day of October 1540 29s 11d that is for ½ a bale wood conteynyng C 3 qr. & 1 li. at 17s the C to be pd. at all tymes requyrid	£1 9s 11d
1546 Itm. the 6 day of Aprell a*n*no 1546 £6 13s 4d & is for 1 ton of S.S. iren to be paide at ~~Seynt Jamystide next~~ Mydsomer next com*m*yng	£6 13s 4d

anno 1539

John Gibs of Bridgewater dewllyng there at the Saserns Hed owith the last day of September £7 3s 4d for 2 butt*es* seck *that* rest unpd. of his reckenyng in my old boke fo. 157, the on at £3 10s & tho*ther* £3 13s 4d	£7 3s 4d
Itm. the 26 day of November £3 13s 4d for a butt of seck sent hym by Grawng*er*	£3 13s 4d
Itm. the 9 day of December £6 16s 8d *that* is for 1 pipe bastard p*r*ice £4 6s 8d & 2 hogshed*es* claret wyne p*r*ice 50s payable at all tymes which wynes I sent hym in Grawng*er*s bote	£6 16s 8d
Itm. the 7th day of February £6 5s that is for 1 pipe ossey £4 & 2 h'd Gascon wyne 45s sent in Grangers bote	£6 5s

---

¹ *Blank in MS.*

37(L) contd.

Itm. the 9 daye of March £5 18s 4d that is £3 13s 4d for a butt of seck & 45s for a pipe Gascon wyne	£5	18s	4d
1540 Itm. the 11 day of Agost 1540 £3 7s 6d which is for 2 h'd claret & 1 h'd white wyne as in my shop boke aperith	£3	7s	6d
Itm. the 14 day of Jenyver £17 6s 8d that is £4 for 1 pipe bastard, £4 for 1 pipe teynt, £7 for 2 buttes seck & 46s 8d for 2 h'd claret wyne which I sent in John Davys bote of Bristowe	£17	6s	8d
S.	£43	7s	6d

37(R)   anno 1539

Thomas Howel per contra is dewe to have the 12 day of July 48s for 6 buttes beare for my ship	£2	8s	
Itm. for 6 truss hey in the filld		6s	
1540 Itm. the 9 day of Maye 1540 r. of Thomas Howell £3	£3		
Itm. the 9 day of June 6s r. of hym in acownt of bere		6s	
Itm. the 20 day of Jenyver 1541 29s 11d r. of hym in Albristey herryng	£1	9s	11d
Itm. r. of hym the 1 day of September 1546	£6	13s	4d

anno 1539

John Gibs per contra is dewe to have the 7 day of November £4 pd. to my wif by William Spyring fisshar	£4		
Itm. the 2 day of February r. of his wif £3 3s 4d	£3	3s	4d
Itm. the 20 day of Marche r. by Giles White £3 13s 4d	£3	13s	4d
1540 Itm. the 21 day of May 1540 r. by Hewgh Hamond £6 6s 8d	£6	6s	8d
Itm. the 9 day of July r. by thandes of Giles White £4	£4		
Itm. the 3 day of September r. by the fisshar £4	£4		
Itm. the 29 October r. by Spyring £4	£4		
Itm. to Sir Thomas Whit the 11 day of Jenyver 5 nobles	£1	13s	4d
Itm. the 15 day of Marche r. by a beddar dwelling on Bristows bridge for the fenysche of owr old reckenyng of the last yere 46s 8d & 10d I geve her, montith the hole 47s 6d	£2	7s	6d
Itm. of the seid beddar the seid tyme £3 r. in part of payment of the £17 6s 8d per contra, which is for wynes sent to her sens her husbandes dethe in her pure wydohode	£3		
Itm. the seid 15 day of Marche 1540 £14 6s 8d that is for so myche rest owyng for the clozing up of this acowmpt, of the which I make Susan Gibs wedo late wif of John Gibs per contra debitor in fo. 126	£14	6s	8d
S.	£43	7s	6d

38(L)   anno 1538

Symond Astone of Bewdley owith the 4th day off December £18 to be paide at all tymes requyrid that is for 2 ton iren at £6 the ton & 1 ton Gascon wyne at £6 the ton, montith	£18		
Itm. 13s 4d for so myche he made me pay for 2 dozens of calve skuyns & I r. them not		13s	4d

anno 1539

Thomas Hasche[1] of Batcom clothiar owith the 3d daye & the 10th day of September £22 13s 10d, that is for 15 ½-bales Tullus wood conteynyng 26 C ½,

---

[1] *Smythe wrote* Nasche *then altered it to* Hasche.

38(L) contd.

22 li. at 17s the C, d'd at 2 tymes as in my shop boke aperith, & it is in
part of payement of 10 clothes penny hewes of his London sort to be d'd in
Bristowe at Cristmas next at £3 10s the clothe to be all pd. in Tullus
wood at *the* seid price, montith £22 13s 10d
Itm. the 23 day of December £13 11s 1d, that is ffor 9 ½-bales Tullus
woode conteynyng 15 C 3 qr. 12 li. which I d'd to hym at 17s the C to be pd. as
afforesseid £13 11s 1d
1540 Itm. the 3d day of Awgost 1540 £15 7s 11d, that is for 24 C ½, 2 li. ½
grene wood at 10s the C & 2 ½-bales Tullus wood conteynyng 3 C ½, 17 li. ½
at 17s the C, d'd at dyvers tymes senss the 13 day of June as in my shop
boke may apere £15 7s 11d
1541 Itm. the 14 day of July 1541 47s 1d for so mych pd. to hym at
Bristowe in redy monney £2 7s 1d
Itm. the 7 day of November 1541 £7 18s 4d for so myche redy monney pd.
to hym at Bristowe £7 18s 4d
1542 Itm. the 7 day of June 1542 £20 which I pay to hym in part of payment of
his bill datyd the 26 day of Aprill last past £20
Itm. the 21 day of June my wif pd. to hym £5 £5
Itm. the 26 day of July pd. to hym £17 18s 4d for a payment at this
Seynt Jamistide by a byll datyd the 25 of Awgust last past & £5 for a byll
of *the* 26 of Aprell last past 1542 £22 18s 4d
Itm. £53 15s which I past for the rest of *this* cownt to fo. 169 £53 15s

£163 11s 7d

38(R) anno 1539

Symond Astone per contra is dewe to have the 30 daye of
Awgost £4 17s 4d for so myche redy monny r. by the
handes of Thomas Astone of Shravell £4 17s 4d
Itm. the 21 day of November r. of hym in Bristow £7 16s
Itm. the 5 day of Jenyver r. of hym in Bristo £4 10s £4 10s
Itm. the 6 day of February r. by the handes of my wif 30s £1 10s

anno 1539

Thomas Hasche per contra is dewe to have the 20 day of
February £35 that is for 10 clothes penny hewes r. of hym
at £3 10s the clothe, amontith £35
Itm. the 3 day of July 1540 24s 11d which I r. of hym in
redy money £1 4s 11d
Itm. the monthe of October 1540 £17 15s which is for 5
clothes penny hewes I r. from hym £17 15s
Itm. the 25 day of Awgust anno 1541 £25 16s 8d, that is for
the rest of 10 penny hewes at 5 markes 5s the clothe, to pay
£7 18s 4d at Mighellmas next and £17 18s 4d at Seynt
Jamystide next after that as it may apere by my bill which
I made for *the* seid somm £25 16s 8d
Itm. the 26 day of Aprill 1542 £65 16s 8d that is ffor the rest
of 20 penny hewes which I bowght of hym at 5 markes &
5s the clothe, to pay £30 at Whitsontyde next & £17 18s 4d
at Allhaloutyde next after *that* & £17 18s 4d at Easter next
after *that* which wylbe in anno 1543, as may apere by my
bill £65 16s 8d
Itm. £17 18s 4d for the ½ payment of 10 clothes & it must
be paide at Candellmas 1542 by a bill datyd the 10th of
February 1541 £17 18s 4d

S. £163 11s 7d

39(L)   anno 1538

Edward Buttlar marchant of Bristowe ow*ith*e 3d day of Awgost 4 nobles
which is for a capuz that I sold to hym to be paide in freight [1]
1539 Itm. the last day of June 1539 for 2 C rozyne price   £1   6s   8d
1540 Itm. the 7 day of September a*nn*o 1540 £6 13s 4d which I lent hym in
redy money to pay at Mighellmas next com*m*yng   £6 13s   4d
Itm. for a pipe of beveraige 6 f*r*anks 46 a. mo*ntith* sterlyng   11s 3½d
Itm. the 17 day of Marche pd. to hym £3 17s 6d which Bess his mayde r. £3 17s   6d
1544 Itm. the 15 day of Octob*er* a*nn*o 1544 £3 & is for a pipe of Rendry iren
delyverd by his co*m*mawndement to Morys Smythe   £3

                              anno 1538

John Sumpter of Bristowe m*a*rchant owith the 12 day of Agost £3 for a pipe
iren d'd by his wyll to Jo*h*n Benet payable by his bill at *Crist*mas next[2]   £3

                              anno 1538

John Mayo of Brodefort diar owith the 5th day of July £12 17s 4d which is
for 8 ½-bales Tullus wood *conteynyng* 14 C 1 qr. 5 li. at 18s the C to pay
hallf at Allhaloutide next & tho*ther* ½ at Candellmas next after that,
mon*tith*   £12 17s   4d

39(R)   anno 1539

Edward Buttlar p*er* contra is dewe to have the 2d day of
October 2s 6d for 10 Yrische bord*es* for my bote at 3d the
borde mon*tith*   2s   6d
1540 Itm. the monthe of December 1540 £11 17s 6d which
is for the freight of 9 ton pipe wyne r. ow*t* of his ship the
M*a*rgr*e*t this vyntaige fro*m* Andaluzia at 25s the ton   £11 17s   6d
~~Itm. the 17 day of Marche pd. to hym £3 17s 6d which
Bess his mayde r.~~

                              anno 1545
                3

                              anno 1539

John Mayo p*er* contra deceasyd is dewe to have the 28 day
of July £6 r. of his wif Dorothe & his son Thomas executors
of his testament   £6
Itm. the 24 day of September 1540 r. of her in pr*e*senc*e* of
her neighbu*r* Nicholas Myllars 40s & more 22s which I
fforgave her, mo*ntith* £3 2s whereof I made her aquyttance   £3   2s
& she promess to pay 6s 8d at Ester next com*m*yng of the
which 6s 8d I r. of the seid Nycolas 6s 4d the 27 day of July
1541 & 4d I forgave hym   6s   8d

40(L)   anno 1539

Sir Jo*h*n Seyntlo knyght ow*ith* the first day of Agost 53s 4d for 2 h'd
Gascon wyne to be pd. at Mighellmas next com*m*yng, mon*tith*   £2 13s   4d
1540 Itm. the 15th day of Aprell 1540 £2 6s 8d for 1 h'd claret & 1 h'd
white sold & d'd for hym to Richart Uphall his s*a*rvant to be paide at all
tymes   £2   6s   8d
Itm. the 14 day of December 46s 8d for 2 h'd claret wyne which I sent hym £2   6s   8d
Itm. the 28 day of February £4 13s 4d that is for 1 to*n* Gascon wyne sent
hym by Myllward his carryar   £4 13s   4d
1541 Itm. the 9 of June 1541 £5 for 1 to*n* Gascon wyne sold & delyverd at
the seid price   £5

---
[1] *Blank in MS.*
[2] *This item is crossed through.*
[3] *There is no credit entry for Sumpter.*

40(L) contd.

Itm. the 29 day of November £5 6s 8d for a ton of Gascon wyne mon*tith*	£5 6s 8d
Itm. the 19 day of December £11 10s 10d that is for 2 ton Gascon wyner at 16 nobles the ton, 10 gallons muscadell at 10d the gallon, 11 gallons 1 quart at[1] ossy seck at 8d the gallon & for 2 smawle barells to fyll it yn 20d, so mo*ntith* the hole	£11 10s 10d
Itm. the last day of December for 10 gallons ½ seck at 8d *the* gallon & 10d the barell, mon*tith* all	7s 10d
ffor 2 chayers	~~10s~~

anno 1539

Joan Tizon of Bristow widdo owi*th* the 19 daye of Awgost £12 13s 4d payable by her obligacio*n* at the Ann*u*nciasion of O*w*r Blessid Lady next com*m*yng which is for 2 to*n* iren sold and delyverd to her	£12 13s 4d

40(R)   anno 1540

Sir *John* Seyntlo hereageynst is dewe to have the 15th daye of Aprel 46s 8d r. by thand*es* of Richard Uphall his s*a*rvant, mon*tith*	£2 6s 8d
Itm. the 26 day of June 1541 r. of Richart Uphall £14 6s 8d	£14 6s 8d
Itm. the 25 day of November 1542 r. of Richart Hawes £16 & gave aquyttance of the seid som	£16
Itm. the 1 day of December r. ~~by her sarvantt~~ Smythe 17s 4d	17s 4d

anno 1542
anno 1540

Johan Tizo*n* per contra is dewe to have the 1 day of Ap*re*ll £12 13s 4d r. of her in redy mon*n*ey & d'd her bill	£12 13s 4d

41(L)   anno 1539

John Tovy of Rogent owi*th* the 18 day of October 9s which is for the rest of a bale Tullus wood as it may apere in my old boke fo. 46	9s
Itm. the 28 day of October 30s 5d which is for won ½-bale wood *conteynyng* 3 qr. 4 li. at 17s the C to pay at Easter next	£1 10s 5d
1549 Itm. the 9 of October 1549 40s and is for 3 C Yland wood at 13s 4d p*er* C to be paide at all tymes requyrid	£2

anno 1538

*Ma*ster Clement Bays of Bristowe poyntmaker owi*th* the 14 day of Jenyver £3 9s 2d that is 5s 4d for *the* rest *that* was unpd. apo*n* 6 ½-bales wood d'd before this day & for 2 ½-bales Tullus wood *conteynyng* 3 C ½, less 4 li. at 17s *the* C & ½ a C grene wood after 10s the C, which 2 ½-bales & ½ C grene wood was d'd this p*r*esent day to his s*a*rvant John Sheppard all which is payable at all tymes requyrid	£3 9s 2d
Itm. the first day of July 1541 59s 8d *that* is for 2 hallf bales Tullus wood delyv*er*d to Joh*n* Shepward his s*a*rvant, to pay 12 dayes after Seynt Jamystide next. It *conteyn*ed 3 C ½, 1 li. wood at 17s the C	£2 19s 8d
Itm. the 27 day of August 59s 6d which is for 2 ½-bales Tullus wood *conteynyng* 3 C ½ at 17s the C d'd to *the* forseid *John* Shepward, to be pd. at all tymes	£2 19s 6d
Itm. the 13 day of February £2 19s 6d that is for 2 ½-bales of Tullus wood *conteynyng* 3 C ½ at 17s the C, to be paide at all tymes, mon*tith*	£2 19s 6d
1542 Itm. the 2 day of May 1542 £3 2s 2d that is ffor 2 ½-bales wood *conteynyng* 3 C ½, 16 li. at 17s the C d'd to *John* Shepard	£3 2s 2d

---

[1] *Smythe wrote* at *in error.*

41(L) contd.

Itm. the 10 day of Jenyver 1542 £3 3d that is for 2 ½-bales wood
conteynyng 3 C ½, 5 li. at 17s the C, to be pd. at all tymes & it is d'd to
John Shepward   £3   3d

                           S. £18 10s 3d

anno 1538

Sir Stevan Lions preste and curat of Stowremynster owith the 27 day of
September 30s to be paide at Cristmas next commyng, which is for 1 h'd iren d'd
by his lettor to his sister Mawde Jones of Bristowe wyddo   £1 10s

41(R)   **anno 1540**

John Tovy per contra is dewe to have the 12 day of
February 39s 5d which he paide to me in redy monney   £1 19s 5d
Itm. r. of John Tovy the 25 of Jenyver by thandes of my
wif 40s   £2

anno 1540

Master Bays per contra is dewe to have the 4 day of Agost
£3 8s r. by the handes of William Appowell grocer & 14d he
rebatyd of my hole sum, montith the hole   £3 9s 2d
Itm. the 5 day of July 1541 for 12 trusses of hey in the
fylld at 12d the truss, montith   12s
Itm. the 21 day of July r. by thandes of her sarvaunt John
Shepward 47s 8d   £2 7s 8d
Itm. the 10 day of Jenyver 1542 r. by the handes of his
sarvaunt John Shepward £5   £5
Itm. the 22 of September anno 1543 r. of his wif   £7 1s 5d

                          S. £18 10s 3d

anno 1542

Syr Stevan Lyons per contra is dewe to have the 22 daye
of November 30s which I r. of hym at Bristowe   £1 10s

42(L)   **anno 1539**

Giles White of Bristowe marchant owith the 29 day of Agost £12 10s
payable at all tymes requyrid, which is for the rest of a reckenyng past
betwen hym & me the same day as by the same wryten with his owne hand
may apere   £12 10s
Itm. the 10 day of October 46s 1d that is for freight of 2 ton pipe iren in
my ship the Trynte at 15s the ton, for averes 8d per ton, for costom 2s 6d per
ton & for halyng & weying 8d   £2 6s 11d
1540 Itm. in Aprell pd. to a messenger for London abowt a coccet 10s & £5 to
the shomamaker[1] whereof Giles must pay hallf   £2 15s
Memorandum[2] Itm. the 5 day of Aprell £8 15s which I paide to John Yerbery
for a payement exspyrid at Owr Lady Day in Lent last past   £8 15s
Itm. the 10 day of May 26s 8d that is for the freight of 2 ton iren in the
Trynte at 13s 4d per ton   £1 6s 8d

anno 1540

Giles White above namyd owith the 12 day of Augost £8 8s 5½d which is
for lycens & costes of serteyne lethir belongyng to hym & Thomas Smythe &

---

[1] *Probably an error for* shoemaker, *but see glossary.*
[2] *Marginal note.*

42(L) contd.

Robert Presy marchantes his compartenars, as by a cownt of the seid Giles may apere	£8	8s	5d ob.
Itm. the 26 day of the same 3s 6d for the costom of 3 clothes which he entryd apon me in the Jhesus		~~3s~~	~~6d~~
Itm. £3 d'd for hym in Aprell 1541 to Master Stanbank	£3		

anno 1541

Thomas Shipman & Giles White owith the 24 daye of December anno 1541 £5 14s 8d for the rest of acowmpt as it maye apere	£5	14s	8d
The[1] for the freight of 4 ton bastardes in the Trynte at 25s per ton to be pd. the 1 day of Marche next commyng	£5		
~~Itm. the 23 day of December 4s 8d for 7 ores d'd to the master of the Ship of London~~		4s	8d
1542 Itm. the 24 of Aprell 1542 £6 13s 4d that is for the freight of 10 tons iren in the Trynte to pay at 3 monthes & 3 monthes[2]	£6	13s	4d

anno 1546

Giles White marchant of Bristowe owith the 27 day of July £4 16s 8d & is for a pipe of muscadell rackyd d'd for hym to William Edwardes of Dunster, to be pd. at all tymes requyrid	£4	16s	8d
1549 Itm. the 24 day of December anno 1549 £5 that is for a but of seck delyverd unto hym to pay at all tymes requirid	£5		

42(R)   anno 1540

Giles White per contra is dewe to have the last day of Aprell £8 14s 6d r. of hym untill this day in his wayges & otherwise as by acowmpt past betwen hym & me may apere	£8	14s	6d
Itm. the 11 day of May £7 6s 8d r. of Master Bell of Glocester for 2 buttes seck of his	£7	6s	8d
Itm. for 11 C 2 li. iren, £3 6s 1d[3]	£3	6s	1d
This cownt is deschargid the 21 day of Agost thowgh it apere not here by partyculer items.			

1546

Giles White per contra is dewe to have the 25 of Jenyver £4 16s 8d which he pd. to my wif	£4	16s	8d
Itm. for my allmes off 29 Sundayes in Seynt Warberows parische at 13d every Sunday & for too quarters wayges to the clerk at 20d the quarter, montith	£1	14s	9d
Itm. the 6 of Maye 1550 r. of Giles White	£3	5s	3d

43(L) Dessperid dettes conteynyd in my old boke which began in anno 1533.

In primis Robert Grawnger of Bristowe yeman 4s 4d as it aperith fo. 10	10		4s	6d
Itm. Richard Kelly smythe of Kerdif 7s 10d fo. 12	12		7s	10d
John Combe of Brecknoc 30s	16	£1	10s	
Robert Fayrebarn 40s	20	£2		
William Diar of Kermerdyne £11 10s 9d	29	£11	10s	9d
John Ryve of Pethirton 15s	25		15s	
John Hutchyn of Martoc ~~£5 3s 2d~~ £3 4s 2d	26	£3	4s	2d
John Crickelet £4 6s 5d	26	£4	6s	5d
Watkyn Cuttlar of Kerdif 36s 8d	29	£1	16s	8d
John Browne of Yllchester 28s 4d fo.	31	£1	8s	4d
Richard Kyrby of Wedmore ~~£3 10s~~ 6s 8d	31		6s	8d

---

[1] A word is omitted in MS.
[2] All items before this are crossed through.
[3] These items are all crossed through.

43(L) contd.

William Wyllet of Bristowe marchant £3 10s fo.	31	£3	10s
Thomas Bewley 55s fo.	36	£2	15s
William Barn of Stowe the old £3 10s fo.	37	£3	10s
Robert Store of Bridgewater weyver 25s 10d fo.	37	£1 5s	10d
William Stile of Mells 9s	41		9s
Roger Walker sopemaker £6 3s 4d	38	£6 3s	4d
John Adeane of Ettlowe in the Forrest 6s 8d	38	6s	8d
Johannes Depontyra of the Rendry in Spayne 51s 9d ob.	40	£2 11s	9½d
John Husse of London the younger & marchant £13 1s 9d	41	£13 1s	9d
Marry Riddall of Brymyjam wedo 14s fo.	43		14s
Nota¹ Thomas Fels of Bryntniche owith the 13 day of May 1538 21s for 1 ton of sallt fo.	²	£1	1s
William Sutton of Barckeley 35s fo. r. for the hole 10s³	44	£1 15s	
Robert Samwest of Bruton 43s 4d	48	£2 3s	4d
Ris David Vaghan of Bristowe shomaker 30s fo.	49	£1	10s
John Grossgrene of Chepstowe carpynter 11s 4d	67	11s	4d
Thomas Keynssam of Bristowe shereman 7s 2d	71	7s	2d
Thomas Dyngley of Eyssam 3s 4d he wyll not pay it⁴	77	3s	4d
John Westen of Langffort 13s 4d	102	13s	4d
John Dowdyng fo. 39			⁵
Thomas Aflete of Wursettor 8s 9d		8s	9d
William Smythe of Laffordes Yate 6s 8d		6s	8d
William Ostriche for a daggar at his next chilld by his wif 6.13.4		£6 13s	4d
Water Robertz ffor a daggar 13s 4d to pay at his first chilld by his wif		13s	4d

43(R)⁶

44(L)   anno 1539

Gregory Showryng of Mylkssam smythe owith the 8th day of July £6 8s 7d that is for a ton 1 qr. 5 li. iren to pay £4 at Mighellmas next & 48s 7d at Allhaloutide next after that, montith	£6	8s	7d
Itm. the 14 day of November £3 13s 4d for 11 C iren of S.S. iren⁷ at 20 grotes the C & 10 C iren of the Rendry at 6s the C, montith £6 13s 4d, to pay hallf at Owr Lady Day in Lent & hallf at Allrode Day next after in May	£6	13s	4d
1540 Itm. the 16th day of Aprill 1540 £5 5s 5d that is for 6 C ½, 17 li. iren of S.S. & 10 C of Giles iren at 6s 4d the C, montith to be pd. £4 at Mydesomer & 25s 5d at Seynt Jamistide next	£5	5s	5d
Itm. the 22 of Maye £6 6s 8d for the rest of 1 ton iren, to pay hallf at Bartylmewtide next & thother hallf at Mighellmas next after that as in my shop boke maye apere	£6	6s	8d
Itm. the first day of October £6 13s 4d to pay 5 markes at Cristmas next & 5 markes at Shraftyde next after, which is for the rest of 20 C 3 qr. 9 li. iren as in my shop boke maye apere, montith	£6	13s	4d
Itm. the 11 day of February £8 7s that is for 26 C 1 qr. 12 li. iren, ½ of S.S. & ½ of the Rendry, to pay £4 3s 6d at Whitsontyde next & £4 3s 6d fornight after Mydsomer next after that followyng, montith	£8	7s	
Itm. the last day of June £3 19s 3d that is for 12 C ½, 2 li. iren to be pd. at Mighellmas next	£3	19s	3d
Somma	£43	13s	7d

---

¹*Marginal note.*
²*Blank in MS.*
³r. for the hole 10s *inserted later.*
⁴he wyll not pay it *inserted later.*
⁵*Blank in MS.*
⁶*Fo. 43R is blank in the MS.*
⁷*Smythe repeats* iren.

44(L) contd.   anno 1539

John Smythe of the Vise ow*ith the* 15 daye of October £3 5s that is for a
pipe iren of S.S. d'd for hym to his fa*ther* John Smythe of Shyne, to be
paide at Ow*r* Lady Day in M*a*rche next com*m*yng. His seid father is
shewerty for hym   £3   5s
Itm. the 9 day of M*a*rche £3 11s 4d which is for the rest of a ton ½ a C 10 li.
iren of S.S. at £6 10s the ton, to be paide at all tymes as in my shop boke
maye apere   £3   11s   4d
Itm. the 17 day of Octob*er* sold to J*o*hn Smythe of Shyne 1 to*n* 11 C 1 qr.
13 li. iren whereof I r. £6 5s 1d, rest £3 6s 8d to be pd. at Cristmas next
com*m*yng   £3   6s   8d
1542 Itm. the 5 day of May 1542 £3 which is for the rest of 1 ton 12 li. iren
to be paide at Seynt Jamistide next   £3
Itm. the 12 day of Octob*er* sold & d'd to hym 1 ton 6 li. iren for the rest
whereof he ow*ith* £3 6s 8d to be paide at all tymes   £3   6s   8d
1543 Itm. the 27 day of Apr*i*ll 1543 33s 4d & is for 1 h'd of S.S. iren d'd
for hym to Rog*er* Stovey to be paide at all tymes   £1   13s   4d
Itm. the 25 day of June 33s 4d which is for 1 h'd of S.S. iren to be paide at
Seynt Jamistide next com*m*yng   £1   13s   4d
Itm. the 17 of September 33s 4d ob. for 1 h'd of S.S. ire*n* d'd to his sons son
to be paide at all tymes   £1   13s   4d ob.

44(R)   anno 1539

Gregory Showlyng p*er* contra is dewe to have the 22 daye
of October £4 which I r. of his s*a*rvant Thom*as* Newma*n*   £4
Itm. the 14 day of November my wif r. 48s 7d   £2   8s   7d
1540 Itm. the 15th day of Ap*r*ell r. of hym in redy mon*n*ey
£4   £4
Itm. the same day 40s r. of hym in redy mon*n*ey   £2
Itm. the 22 day of May r. of hym 13s 4d   13s   4d
Itm. the 3 day of July r. of hym £4   £4
Itm. the 26 day of July r. of hym 25s 5d   £1   5s   5d
Itm. the 28 day of Augost r. by Thomas Watt*es* £3   £3
Itm. the 1 day of October r. of hym 4 m*a*rk*es*   £2   13s   4d
Itm. the 10 day of December r. of hym 13s 4d   13s   4d
Itm. the 11 day of February r. of hym £6 13s 4d   £6   13s   4d
Itm. the 29 day of June 1541 r. £5 6s 8d   £5   6s   8d
Itm. the 12 day of September my wif r. of hym   £6   19s   7d

                                                                   Som*m*a   £43 13s 7d

anno 1539

John Smythe p*er* contra is dewe to have the 9 daye of
M*a*rche £3 5s r. by the hand*es* of J*o*hn Smythe of Shyne   £3   5s
Itm. the 3 day of November 1540 r. of hym 11s 4d   11s   4d
Itm. the 28 day of June r. of hym in Bristowe £3   £3
1542 Itm. the 5 day of May 1542 my wif r. of hym 5
m*a*rkes   £3   6s   8d
Itm. the 12 day of October r. of hy*m* at Bristowe   £3
Itm. the 27 1543[1] day of Ap*r*ell r. fr*om* hym of Rog*er*
Stovey £3 6s 8d for payment of the iren d'd the 12 of
October last past as p*er* contra ap*er*ith   £3   6s   8d
Itm. the 25 of June r. for hym of Rog*er* Stovey 33s 4d   £1   13s   4d
Itm. the 17 day of September 1543 my wif r.   £1   13s   4d
Itm. the 21 of July 1544 r.   £1   13s   4d

---

[1] 1543 *inserted above.*

45(L) anno 1539

Robert Jacksson of Bristowe hallier owith the 11 day of October 30s which is for 1 h'd iren sold & d'd to hym to be paide at all tymes requyrid | £1 10s
1540 Itm. the 30 day of June 1540 30s 10d that is for 1 h'd 12 li. iren to be paide at Mighellmas next | £1 10s 10d
Itm. the 23 day of September £3 that is for a pipe of Rendry iren to be paide at all tymes | £3
1541 Itm. the 13 day of May 1541 £3 6s 8d for a pipe of S.S. iren to be paid at all tymes | £3 6s 8d
1542 Itm. the 20 day of October 1542 £3 6s 8d which is ffor 1 pipe of S.S. iren sold & d'd to hym to be paide at all tymes | £3 6s 8d
1543 Itm. the 21 day of December 1543 1 h'd 2 li. of the better Rendry iren at 19 nobles the ton 31s 9d | £1 11s 9d
Itm. the 11 day of Aprell anno 1544 £3 13s 4d for a but wyne | £3 13s 4d
Itm. 28s which he have r. of my wif at dyvers tymes in money untyll October 1544 | £1 8s

S. £6 13s 1d

anno 1539

Morgan Bade of Calicot in Wales smythe owith the 10th day of October 30s which is for a h'd iren sold & d'd to hym to be paide at Candellmas next commyng, Master Clement Bays is his shewertye, montith | £1 10s
Itm. the 11 day of February 30s that is for the rest of 3 C Rendry iren & 2 C S.S. iren to be pd. at Whitsontyd next. Master Bays is his shewerty | £1 10s
1540 Itm. the 2d day of July 30s for 1 h'd iren to pay at Myghellmas next commyng | £1 10s
Itm. the 30 day of November 1540 29s 11d that is for 1 h'd less 2 li. iren sold to hym to be pd. at Ester next commyng | £1 9s 11d
Itm. the 4 of February 1541 12s which is for the rest of 2 C 19 li. iren to be paide at Easter next | 12s
Itm. the 8 day of Marche 13s 6d that is for 2 C 1 qr. Rendry iren at 6s the C, montith | 13s 6d
1542 Itm. the 20 day of June 1542 13s 6d which is for 2 C 1 qr. iren to be pd. at Seynt Jamistide | 13s 6d
Itm. the 26 day of August 12s which is for 2 C iren to be paide at all tymes | 12s
Itm. the 21 day of November 12s ob. which is for the rest of 2 C 12 li. iren of S.S. to be pd. at Candellmas next as may apere in my shop boke | 12s ob.

45(R) anno 1539

Robert Jacksson per contra is dewe to have the 24 day of December 10s which he descownt to me in halyng | 10s
Itm. the 24 day of Marche 3s 4d which he descont in hallyng as it aperith in his owne boke wryten with my owne hand | 3s 4d
Itm. the last day of June 1540 13s 6d which he descownt in halyng as it aperith in his boke wryten with my owne hand | 13s 6d
Itm. the 17 day of September r. of hym in hawllyng home of my gudes 19s 8d as may apere in his bok | 19s 8d
Itm. the same day r. of hym in redy monney 13s 6d | 13s 6d
Itm. the 13 day of May 1541 r. in money 21s 1d & in hawlyng 38s 11d, montith all £3 | £3
[1]
Itm. the last day of February anno 1541 38s 6d ob. that is for so myche I owe hym for hallyng untill this daye as it may apere in his boke wrytten with my hand | £1 18s 6d
Itm. the 28 day of October 1542 r. in hawling 45s 10d I sey the 20 day of October 1542 | £2 5s 11d ob.

---

[1] *An item is completely erased in the MS.*

45(R) contd.

Itm the 21 of December 1543 48s 10d r. in haly*ng* & so quytt	£2 8s 10d ob.
Itm. reckenyd for halyng the 11 day of Ap*re*ll 1544 & it mo*ntith*	£2 11s ~~11d~~
Itm. the 8 day of November 1544 I reckenyd with hym for haling from my hous in Smawlestret of 364 vates of rubbell & for 5 vate of stone from Haynes & 55 vates of smawle stone from the same Hayenes & of 32 vates of frestone & 23 vates smawle stone from J*oh*nson, mo*ntith* all 43 dozens ½ at 8d p*er* dozen. More 50s for haling by his boke, montith the hole	£3 19s 5d
More for 14 drawght*es* of boord*es*	1s 2d
he pd. in money	1s 6d
	S. £6 13s 1d

anno 1539

Morgan Bade of Callycot *per* contra is dewe to have the 10 day of February 30s r. of hym at Bristowe	£1 10s
1540 Itm. the 1 day of July r. of hym 30s	£1 10s
Itm. the 29 day of November 1540 r. of hym 30s	£1 10s
Itm. the 14 day of Jenyver 1541 15s r. for so myche r. of Richard Bayes s*ar*vant to M*aster* C. Bayes	15s
Itm. the 3 day of February r. of hym 15s	15s
Itm. the 8 day of M*ar*che r. of hym at Bristowe 10s	10s
Itm. the 20 day of June 1542 my wif r. of hym	15s 6d
Itm. the 26 day of Augost r. of hym 13s 4d	13s 4d
Itm. the 21 day of November r. of hym 12s	12s
Itm. the 14 day of July 1543 r. of hym 12s	12s

46(L)   **anno 1539**

Thomas Glazynbe of Bristowe diar owithe the 25 day of Agost 16s 6d for the rest of on hallf bale wood as in my shop boke ap*er*ith	16s 6d
Itm. the 19 day of November 18s 2d which he rest owyng for a bale of Tullus wood as in my shop boke ap*er*ithe	18s 2d
Itm. the last day of February paide to his wif 7s 4d	7s 4d
	S. 42s

anno 1539

Robert Leighton of Bristowe m*a*rchant owithe the 10 daye of Octob*er* £13 6s 6d that is for 2 ton iren of S.S. sold & d'd to hym at 20 nobles the ton, to be pd. at Ester next com*m*yng, mo*ntith* 2 ton less 4 li.	£13 6s 6d
Itm. the 22 day of December 52s 11d that is for the ½ & hole rest for the freight of 5 to*n* wyne & 4 ½-bales wood *this* vyntage fro*m* Burd*es* in the Trynte at 20s the to*n*, to be pd. at O*w*r Lady Daye in Marche next com*m*yng	£2 12s 11d
	S. £15 19s 5d

anno 1540

Robert Leighton above namyd o*with* the 6 day of November £3 which is for freight of 3 to*n* wyne fro*m* Burd*es* in the Trynte at 20s the to*n*, to pay 30s at thend of 3 monthes next ffollowyng & 30s at thend of 3 monthes next after that	£3
1541 Itm. the 1 day of December 1541 £3 15s *that* is for the freight of 3 tons bastard in the Trynte at 25s p*er* ton, to pay ½ in hand & ½ at *the* end of 3 monthes next com*m*yng	£3 15s

46(L) contd.

1543 Itm. the 6 day of February 1543 £13 6s 8d & is for 2 tons iren of
S.S. to be paide at Seynt Jamistide next   £13   6s   8d
Itm. the 11 day of ~~August~~ December a*nn*o 1544 paid to his *sa*rvant Edward
Whelar £5 13s 4d   £5   13s   4d

46(R)   **anno 1539**

Thomas Glazynbe p*er* contra is dewe to have the last day
of February for grazing of 14 clo*the*s at 3s *the* clo*the*, I
fyndyng allem, mon*tith*   £2   2s
~~Itm. the same day 13s 4d in redy monney by his wif~~   ~~13s 4d~~
                                                                        _____
                                                                        S.   42s

anno 1540

Robert Leighton p*er* contra is dewe to have the 22 day of
Maye, £15 19s 5d r. of hym in mon*n*ey
                                                                        S. £15 19s   5d

anno 1540

Robert Leighton p*er* contra is dewe to have the 12 day of
February £3 r. of hym in redy mon*n*ey   £3
Itm. the 5th day of Ap*r*ell my *sa*rvant Hamon r. of hym   £3   15s
Itm. the 21 day July for 9 to*n* pipe freight of oyle in the
Mary James at 40s p*er* ton   £19

47(L)   **anno 1539**

Willi*a*m Trawnter of Langley yeoman owith the 10th daye of Octob*er*
29s 11d which is for a h'd less 2 li. iren d'd for hym to Thomas Gozelyng
of Langley, mon*tith*   £1   9s   11d
Itm. for a mare which I sold to hym for 10s   10s
Itm. the 23 day of December 29s 11d that is for 1 h'd less 2 li. ire*n* d'd for hym
to Robert Chew at 30s the h'd   £1   9s   11d
Itm. the 16 day of Jenyver £11 10s pd. to kynssma*n* Russell   £11 10s
Itm. the last day of the same 48s pd. by Russells wyll & com*m*yssion for
the freight of 31 weys beanes p*er* contra   £2   8s
Itm. 30s 2d that is for 1 h'd 3 li. of my best Rendry ire*n* laden the 20 day
of M*ar*ch in Davys bote of Langney   £1   10s   2d
1540 Itm. the 15 day of June 1540 d'd a h'd of S.S. iren to W*illia*m Bretherns
bote at £6 the to*n*, mon*tith*   ¹
Itm. the 26 day of July pd. to Russell £43   £43
Itm. the 5 day of November pd. to Russell 20s   £1
Itm. the 22 day of December 30s which is for 1 h'd iren sent to hym in
Thomas Jess*e*s bote   £1   10s
Itm. the 7 day of Marche 30s *that* is for 1 h'd iren sent hy*m* in John Dees bote £1   10s
1541 Itm. the 11 day of June 1541 30s 3d for 1 h'd 5 li. iren laden in
Fyld*es* bote   £1   10s   ~~3d~~
Itm. the 26 day of July for 3 to*n* 1 h'd iren d'd to hym & to Gibs for hym
after £6 the to*n*   £19 10s
Itm. the same day £22 8s 9d paide to hym in reddy mon*n*ey   £22   8s   9d
Itm. the 20 day of Octob*er* 30s which is for 1 h'd iren sent to hym in
Robert Chewes bote   £1   10s
1542 Itm. the 30 day of May 1542 £3 & it is for 1 pipe of ire*n* d'd for hym
to Robert Chew of Langley to be pd. at all tymes   £3
Itm. the 26 day of July £12 for 2 to*n* S.S. iren delyverd for hym to Richard
Gibbs   £12

---

¹*Blank in MS.*

47(L) contd.

Itm. the 8 day of November £6 that is for 1 ton less 2 li. of my best Rendry iren laden in Robert Chewes bote		£6		
	S.	£131	16s	9d

anno 1539

Stevyn Chick of Bruton owith the 13 day of February £3 6s 8d that is for a pipe iren of S.S. at £6 13s 4d the ton to be paide at Ester next	£3	6s	8d
1540 Itm. the 6th day of Aprell anno 1540 33s 4d that is for 1 h'd iren of S.S. to be pd. at all tymes requyrid	£1	13s	4d
1542 Itm. the 28 day of July 23s 4d that is for so myche money he must geve with a ton led for a pipe oyle	£1	3s	4d
Itm. the 17 of August £3 5d ob. which is for 1 pipe 8 li. Rendry iren at £6 the ton to be pd. at all tymes	£3		5d ob.

47(R)   **anno 1539**

William Trawnter of Langley yeoman is dewe to have the 10th day of July £4 which I owe hym for the rest of beanes		£4		
Itm. the last day of February £58 18s which is for 31 weyes benes r. of hym at 9d ob. the wey montith		£58	18s	
1540 Itm. the 26 day of July 1540 pd. to Russell[1]				
Itm. the 16 day of Marche 1540 £46 8s 9d that is for 30 weys 46 busshells benes r. from hym abord a Portyngall ship in Sharstons Poole at 30s the wey, montith		£46	8s	9d
Itm. 30s which I descowmpt the 12 day of December to John Russell in part of payement of a horss		£1	10s	
Itm. the 20 day of March anno 1543 £12 which my sarvant Robert Leight r. of John Goseling at Langney		£12		
Itm. the 27 day of October 1544 r. from John Goseling by his neighbur John Davy £9		£9		
	S.	£131	16s	9d

anno 1540

Itm. the 7 day of May £3 6s 8d which he pd. to John Yerbery of Bruton clothiar for me	£3	6s	8d
Itm. the 28 day of July my wif r. of hym 33s 4d	£1	13s	4d
Itm. the 22 day of August 25s that is for 10 sheff of arrowes with theyr girdilles & cassis at 2s 6d the sheff	£1	5s	
Itm. the 5 of February 30s which John Yerbery pd. for hym as it aperith fo. 163	£1	10s	
Itm. the 21 day of Aprell 1544 John Yerbery pay me for hym as it may apere fo. 201, 28s 9d	£1	8s	9d

48(L)   **anno 1539**

John Yerbery of Bruton clothiar owith the 9 day of October 12 clothes penny hewes callid truckers which is for the rest of 20 clothes of the same sorte which I have paide ffor in Tullus wood & he must delyver them to me of the best he make of that sorte at all tymes requyrid	2		
Itm. the 9 day of October £3 5s which he r. of William Peter of Bruton smythe, more William Northe pd. the 18 day of November £20 & I paide to John Yerbery his son the 28 day of November 55s, montith £26, payable by a byll at Bartyllmewtide last past	£26		
Itm. the 22 day of Jenyver £45 8s 4d that is £17 18s 4d for the hole payement of a byll endid at Bartillmewetide last past & £10 for the hole payment of a byll endid at Mighellmas last past & £17 10s for a payement dewe at Allhaloutide last past, so amontith all	£45	8s	4d

---

[1] Entered by Smythe on this side in error and transferred to the opposite folio.
[2] Blank in MS.

48(L) contd.

Itm. the 27 day of Jenyver 26s 3d for 4 C 2 li. ½ iren d'd for hym to his sarvant & more £3 6s 8d which Stevyn Chick payed, mon*tith*	£4 12s 11d
Itm. the 18 day of Marche £26 10s paide to hym for the payement payable the fyve of February & r. my bill	£26 10s
1540 Itm. the 7th daye of Maye a*n*no 1540 £43 15s for so myche redy money paide to hym seallf at Bristowe which is £8 15s payable at Candelmas last past & £17 10s payable the 17 day of February last past for the first payeme*n*t of a bill & £17 10s payable the 1 day of M*a*rche last past	£43 15s
Itm. the 1 day of July pd. £17 10s for the full payement of 1 bill payable at Candellmas last past, more pd. £17 10s for a payement dewe at Seynt Jamistide next com*m*yng, which payement*es* war made in £14 pd. by Northe & £4 12s 11d pd. by Chick & in iren as in the itm. foresseid of the 27 of Jenyver may apere & I pd. in mon*n*ey £16 7s 1d	£35
Itm. the same day £17 10s payable at Ester last past	£17 10s
Itm. the 29 day of July £53 15s pd. to hy*m* seallf	£53 15s
Itm. the 20 day of Agost pd. to J*o*hn Yerbery the yong*er* £26 5s ffor the last & ffull payement of 2 bills payable at Bartyllmewetyd next com*m*yng	£26 5s
Itm. the 31 day of August £1 *that* is for C k*yntalls* of grenewood d'd at dyvers tymes sens the 2d day of July at 10s the C to be pd. at all tymes in clothe callid truckers at 40s the clothe	£1
Itm. the 5 day of November £20 which William Northe paide to hym	£20
Itm. the 31 day of December £8 9s 8d *that* is for 16 C 3 qr. 24 li. Jean*er* wood at 10s the C d'd at dyv*ers* tymes sens the 28 day of November last past	£8 9s 8d
Itm. £17 10s which W*illiam* Northe pay for the full payment of a byll endyd at Candellmas 1540 as *per* contra may apere	£17 10s
Itm. the 15 day of February 1540 £17 10s which is for the payment payable at Candellmas last past by W*illiam* North & is for the first payment of 55 pen*n*y hewes bowght the 25 of September & 15 of February as *per* contra apere	£17 10s
the 15 day of February I past to fo. 125 £162 15s 10d for the rest & closyng up of this cowmpt	£162 15s 10d
	£512 18s 10d

48(R)   anno 1539

John Yerbery of Bruton clothiar is dewe the 8 daye of Octob*er* £202 18s 4d for the rest of his cowmpt in my old boke folio 170, which som is payable by dyvers of my bills at *the* days here after ffollowyng:

Itm. first £43 18s 4d payable by 2 bills at Bartyllmewetide last past	£43 18s 4d	
Itm. £10 payable at Mighellmas last past	£10	
Itm. £17 10s[1] payable at Allhaloutide next	£17 10s	
Itm. £26 10s[1] payable the fyve of February	£26 10s	
Itm. £26 5s payable by 2 bills at Candelmas	£26 5s	
Itm. £17 10s[1] payable the first day of M*a*rche	£17 10s	
Itm. £17 10s payable at Easter a*n*no 1540	£17 10s	
Itm. £17 10s payable at Seynt Jamystide	£17 10s	
Itm. £26 5s payable by 2 bills at Bartillmewtyde 1540	£26 5s	£202 18s 4d
Itm. the 17 day of February £35 to be paide by my bill £17 10s at all tymes requyrid & £17 10s at Candellmas next com*m*yng	£17 10s £17 10s	£35

Itm. the 17 day of Marche he is dewe to have 12 clo*thes* callid truckers which I have r. for the full payement of 12 clothes that restid unpaide the 9 day of Octob*er* as p*er* contra ap*er*ith [2]

1540 Itm. the 1 day of July 1540 £107 10s which is for

---

[1] 10s *inserted above the line.*
[2] *Blank in MS.*

48(R) contd.

30 clothes penny hewes r. of hym at 5 m*ark*es 5s the clothe to pay ~~£53 15s~~ at Seynt Jamistide next & £53 15s at Seynt Jamistide in a*nno* 1541, mon*tith* as afforesseid	~~£53 15s~~ £53 15s	} £107 ~~10s~~
Itm. the 29 day of November £89 11s 8d which is ffor 25 clothes penny hewes r. in Agost & September last past at 5 m*ark*es & 5s the clothe, to pay £44 15s 10d at all tymes requyrid & £44 15s 10d the first day of September next com*m*yng which wylbe in a*nno* 1541.[1]	~~£44 15s 10d~~ ~~£44 15s 10d~~	} £89 ~~11s~~ ~~8d~~
Itm. the 25 day of September £44 15s 10d to pay £22 7s 11d at Easter next & £22 7s 11d at Mighellmas next after *that* which is for 25 penny hewes at eich 5 m*ark*es & 5s the clothe, whereof I pd. hallf in hand & tho*ther* ½ to be pd. as aforesseid	£22 7s 11d £22 7s 11d	} £44 15s 10d
Itm. the 15 day of February £53 15s, to pay £26 17s 6d at Seynt Jamistide next & £26 17s 6d at Candellmas next after which is for 30 clothes penny hewes at 5 m*ark*es & 5s p*er* clothe, whereof I pd. the on hallf in hand & the other hallf must be paide as aforesseid	£26 17s 6d £26 17s 6d	} £53 15s
Itm. the same day £10 10s for 3 pe*n*ny hewes *that* be rewed, to pay it at Whitsontyde in a*nno* 1542		£10 10s
Itm. £54 that is for 27 truckers r. fro*m* hym at dyvers tymes untill this day after 40s the clo*the*		£54
Itm. £8 9s 8d which I pass to fo. 125 to be pd. in truckers at 40s the clothe		£8 9s 8d
	S.	£512 18s 10d

49(L)   **anno 15339**[2]

Thomas Shipman my s*a*rvant owith 569 d*u*cat*t*s 9 r*i*alles off plate for that he wryte me by his lett*er* datid the 2d day of Aprell that he had sold for my acowmp*t*[3]

anno 1539

John Wyll*iam*s of the Newe Yn in Bristowe owithe the 2 day of June 22s 6d which restith this day unpaide of 31s for 1 h'd iren sold to Luys Jones of Aburgeyne in Octob*er* 1538 & the seid Jo*hn* Wyll*iam*s being his shew*er*ty agreid with me the foreseid 2d day of June to paye 7s 6d at Mighellmas next & 7s 6d at Cristmas next after that & 7s 6d at O*w*r Lady Daye in Lent next followyng after *that*

                                                              S.   £1   2s   6d

anno 1538

Nicholas Hanckot of Wellyngton ffisshar ow*ith* the 14 day of February 20s for 2 C grene wood sold to hym

                                                              S.   £1

---

[1] *The whole entry for 29th November is crossed through.*
[2] *Smythe has written* 15339 *in error.*
[3] *This item is crossed through.*

49(L) contd.   **anno 1538**

John Clement of Ullaston smythe o*with* the 24 day of September 6s 5d for
C 8 li. ire*n*. His son yn lawe foreman to Thomas Howell berebruar is
shew*erty*

6s	5d

anno 1540

John White of Ullaston smythe owithe the 2 day of Octobe*r* 20s 7d which
is for 3 C 10 li. iren of S.S. which I sold & d'd to hym at 6s 8d the C, to be
paide at Cristmas next   £1   7d

49(R)   **anno 1539**

John Willi*ams* p*er* contra is dewe to have the 4 day of
October 7s 6d r. of hym at Bristow in redy mon*n*y   7s   6d
Itm. the 24 day of Jenyver 7s 6d   7s   6d
Itm. the 24 day of Aprill 1540 r. 7s 6d & made to hym
aquyttance for the hole 31s dewe to me for 1 h'd ire*n* as
p*er* contra ap*er*ith   7s   6d

                                                           £1   2s   6d

anno 1539

Nicholas Hanckot fishar p*er* contra ~~owith~~ is dew to have the
4 day of February 20s r. of hym

                                                    S.   £1

anno 1540

John Clement p*er* contra is dewe to have the 9 day of
June 6s 5d r. of ~~hym in desee~~ Thomas Howell in acowmpt
of bere

                                                    S.   5s   5d

anno 1541

John White p*er* contra is dewe to have the 25 day Of
Marche 20s 7d r. of hym   £1   7d

50(L) ·

Thomas Shipman owith for the rest of my reckenyng r. of hym in Bristowe
the monthe of June a*nn*o 1538 103 d*ucatts* 20 cha. amon*tith* in M.   038750 M.
Itm. for a turques in a ryng 22 d*ucatts* mon*tith*   008250 M.
Itm. for the rest of his reckenynge r. from hym ow*t* of the Mary Conception
the 7 day of February 1538 12530 M. in redy money & more 2 Aburgeynes
& 11 vares yelow lynard which war sold for 4685 M. & 28 dozens calve
skuyns which war sold for 16184 M., mon*tith* the hole   033399 M.
Itm. 536077 M. that is 205125 M. for the sale of 26 London clothes & 10
costom clothes and 32096 M. for the sale of 47 dozen calve skuy*n*s and
298856 M. for the nete sale of 21 weyes ½ wheate and of 22 weyes 44 busshells
beanes, all which good*es* he r. ow*t* of the Trynte in M*a*rche anno 1539   536077 M.
Itm. 120863 M. ½ for so myche he cawsyd my p*re*ntes Robert Tyndall pay
to hym in Spayne in Septe*m*ber a*n*no 1539   120863 M.
737339
680602

056737

50(R) anno 1539

Thomas Shipman here ageynst is dewe to have in Aprell anno dicto for costes don apon my clothe & calve skuyns r. owt of the Trynte my ship 958 M.	000958 M.
for 7 C kyntalls iren laden the same tyme in the seid Trynte	379300 M.
for wheate, sider & hake for her vytaylls 12554 M. for 3 C 28 li. cordaige 3750 M., for 2 knes for the dalehed 750 M. & for towyng her in & owt to the Passage the same viage 1445 M., montith all	018499 M.
for 421 ducatts which he charge for my hallf & last payement for wood to the Surryes	157875 M.
for 195 kyntalls iren in the ships of Anton de Asteacu & John Peres de Arana that cost abord 107614 M. & for for[1] assurance made apon part of the same 1990 M., montith	109604 M.
for my part of a cote clothe to Mynar de Burbo 750 M. & for costes in a plea ageynst Sebastyan de Myranda 391 M. ½, montith all	001141 M.
for his owne exspences untill the last day of Awgost 1539, 11250 M. & for Tyndalls tables 1975 M.	013225 M.

51(L) anno 1539

Richard Litell[2] smythe of Bristowe owith the 21 day of October 22s which is for the rest of all iren that he have had of me untyll this day, as it aperith in a paper which I d'd to hym wryten with my owne hand & payable all tymes requyrid   £1 2s

anno 1540

Thomas Dekyn of Bristowe yeoman owith the 19 daye of Aprell £6 that is for 1 ton of Rendry iren sold & d'd to hym to be paide at Bartylmewetid next commyng as it aperith by his bill   £6

51(R) anno 1539

Richart Lytell per contra is dewe to have the 6 day of February 8s which he paide to my wif   8s

anno 1540

Thomas Decon per contra is dewe to have the 29 daye of November £6 r. of hym in redy monney & so delyverd his bill   £6

52(L) anno 1539

37	Woode of Tullus owith for my acowmpt the 20 day of October anno dicto £55 10s that is for 37 ½-bales of 28 florynges of 8 capassos the carg which restith in my hows this day unsolld & I valure them at 30s the ½-bale	£55 10s
6	The 17 day of Jenyver £9 3s 4d ob that is for 6 ½-bales r. back ageyne from Thomas Cotes of Eyssam	£9 3s 4d ob
	S.	£64 13s 4d½

---

[1] Smythe repeats for.
[2] Litell is inserted above the line.

52(L) contd. anno 1540

16	Wood of Tullus of 8 capassos the cargg & of 28 florynges warantes owith the 16 day of June for my acowmpt proper £23 8s 3d ob that is for 16 ½-bales that restyd unssold of the abovesseid acowmpt	£23	8s 3d½
150	Itm. r. the first & second dayes of July owt of the Mawden of the Passaige, master Johannes de la Sala, 150 ½-bales wood of the abovesseid mesure & waranties, which cost at the first penny 632 ducatts, for costes at Burdes untyll abord the ship £3 10s sterlyng, for shewrance of 500 ducatts £3 15s, for freight, custom, lycens, averes & hawlyng £6 13s 4d, montith all	£171 18s	3d
13s 1d	Itm. r. the 13 day of November owt of the Trynte 5 bales wood that my horss was sold for which cost with all charges leyid in my hows	£5 10s	3d
5	1541 Itm. the month of November 1541 r. owt of the An off London 24 ballettes of woode which cost clere abord 104 Crowns of the Son ¼, 3s. 1a. more for freight 35s sterlyng, for costom 14s, for haling 8d, for averes of 1 ton pipe 1 h'd wood 17d ob, montith all £28 11s 1d ob.	£28 11s	1d½
24	Itm. the 7 day of December £22 03s 4d goten by this acownt as it aperithe to gayenes in credito fo. 92	4222 s	4d
		S. £251 11s	3d½

52(R) anno 1539

1	Wood per contra is dewe to have the 23 daye of October 29s 9d for 1 bale conteynyng C 3 qr. at 17s the C sold to Thomas Silk fo. 67	£1 9s	9d
1	Itm. the 28 day of October 30s 5d for 1 bale conteynyng C 3 qr. 4 li. at 17s the C sold to John Tovey fo. 41	£1 10s	5d
1	Itm. the 17 day of November 31s 6d for 1 bale conteynyng C 3 qr. at 18s the C sold to Thomas Glazynbe fo. 46	£1 11s	6d
9	Itm. the 23 day of December £13 11s 1d for 9 bales conteynyng 15 C 3 qr. 22 li. at 17s the C sold to T. Nasche fo. 38	£13 11s	1d
2	Itm. the 26 day of February r. of John Babor £3 for 2 bales conteynyng 3 C ½, 3 li. at 17s the C, montith	£3	
2	Itm. the 28 day of the same £3 4d for 2 bales conteynyng 3 C ½, 7 li. at 17s the C sold to William Babor of Cumsbery	£3	4d
4	1540 Itm. the 3 of Aprill 1540 £6 7s 9d for 4 bales conteynyng 7 C 11 li. at 17s the C to Thommas Keynssam 96	£6 7s	9d
1	Itm. the 13 of the same 31s 5d for 1 ½-bale conteynyng C 3 qr. 11 li. at 17s the C to Thomas Sylk fo. 67	£1 11s	5d
1	Itm. the 3 day of the same to the seid Silk 1 bale conteynyng C ½, 27 li. at 17s the C montith 29s 8d	£1 9s	8d
2	Itm. the 3 day of May £3 3s for 2 bales to T. Treheren fo. 19	£3 3s	
2	Itm. the 16 day of June £3 2d for 2 bales to R. Tippar	£3	2d
1	Itm. 30s r. for a bale wood	£1 10s	
	Itm. the same day £23 8s 3d½ for 16 ½-bales which I pass to a newe cownt per contra & to close up this acowmpt	£23 8s	3d½
		S. £64 13s	4d ob.

52(R) contd.   anno 1540

		Wood per contra is dewe to have the 20 day of Augost £6 19d for 4 bales sold to Thomas Nasche & Richard Tippar sens the 3 day of the same	£6	1s	9d
4					
1		Itm. the 9 day of October 29s 11d that is for ½ a bale sold to Thomas Howell fo. 37	£1	9s	11d
2		Itm. the 18 of the same 59s 4d for 2 bales to Antony Duttsson 18	£2	19s	4d
2		Itm. the 18 of Jenyver £3 2d ob for 2 bales to William Buchar	£3	s	2d ob
2		Itm. the 8 day of February £3 9d for 2 bales to John Awood 124	£3	s	9d
2		Itm. the 9 of February 57s 6d for 2 bales to R. Tippar fo. 57	£2	17s	6d
2		Itm. the 23 of February 58s 6d for 2 bales to T. Heyward 18	£2	18s	6d
~~3~~		Itm. the 16 day of Maye 1541 for 3 bales to John Yerbery conteynyng 5 C 1 qr. 14 li. at 15s per C.	~~£3~~	~~19s~~	~~11d~~
2		Itm. the 27 day of May for 2 bales to William Hazard fo. 132	£2	10s	
2		Itm. the 27 day of June £2 15s 6d for 2 bales to T. Silk fo. 67	£2	15s	6d
50		Itm. the 28 of June £67 3s 6d for 50 bales to William Bullock fo. 131	£67	3s	6d
2		Itm. the 1 day of July 59s 8d for 2 bales to Master Base fo. 41	£2	19s	8d
52		Itm. the 27 day of Julye 1541 £69 12s 9d that is for 52 bales conteynyng 92 C ¾, 11 li. sold to Robert Crosby in truck of nothern dozens at won C ½ per dozen. So I do cownt the price in money to be 15s per C, montith	£69	12s	9d
16		Itm. the 29 day of July £21 9s 4d that is for 13 bales conteynyng 28 C ½, 16 li. sold to John Yerbery after 3 C less 14 li. for a clothe callid truckers so every C may be in redy monney 15s	£21	9s	4d
2		Itm. the 5 day of Augost 57s 3d for 2 ½-bales conteynyng 3 C 1 qr. 13 li. at 17s per C to Master Bayse fo. [1]	£2	17s	3d
2		Itm. the 27 of Augost for 2 bales conteynyng 3 C ½ to Master Bayes fo. 41	£2	19s	6d
2		Itm. the 12 of October for 2 bales to G. Gogan fo. 140	£3		10d
2		Itm. the 7 day of December 54s for 2 ½-bales conteynyng 3 C ½, 9 li. to John Yerbery fo.[1]	£2	14s	
		Itm. the 7 day of December £60 that is for so myche I do valure 48 bales which I pass to a new cownt fo. 147	£60		
		S.	£251	11s	3d ob.

53(L)   anno 1539

Iren for my owne acowmpt owithe the 15 day of October £382 17d that is for so myche rest this day in my hows unsolld for the rest & clozinges up acownt of my iren in my old boke fo. 172. 6335 endes which iren is 63 tons 19 C 3 qr. 12 li. conteynyng 6335 endes   £382   1s   5d

1540 Itm. the 29 day of Aprell 1540 £36 18s 6d½ that is for so myche goten by this acowmpt as it aperith to gaynes in credito fo. 92   £36   18s   6d½

S.   £418   19s   11d½

---

[1] Blank in MS.

53(L) contd. anno 1540

Iren for my owne acowmpt owith the 29 day of Aprell £7 that is for 1 ton 5
C 19 li. iren conteynyng 74 endes which restith unsolld in my hows this
present daye as it aperith in the cowmpt above in credito £7
Itm. the same day £220 9s that is for 477 kyntalls iren of the Rendry & 244
kyntalls iren of S.S. which made by the weightes of my hows 52 tons 5 C
3 qr. 10 li. conteynyng 5193 endes & it cost clere abord my ship the Trynte
at the first penny & bryng abord with averes, vyndag & other costes in
Spayne £220 9s as aforesseid.
Itm. more for freight 13s 4d per ton, for costom 2s 6d per ton, for averes 9d
per ton, for hallyng & pyling 4d per ton, montith this costes £40 12s. So montith
the fforesseid iren with the first penny & costes don in Spayne & Yngland
£261 12d £261 1s
Itm. the 3d day of July bowght of Johannes de Sala master of the Mawdelen
of the Passaige 2 ton iren[1] of S.S. which made by my weightes 2 ton 4 C
14 li. conteynyng 203 endes & it cost £10 15s
Itm. the 19 day of Augost r. owt of my ship the Trynte 420 kyntalls iren of
S.S. which made by my weightes 30 ton 16 C 9 li. conteynyng 3024 endes &
it cost[2] putt in my hows £169 4s. More 435 kyntalls iren of the Rendry
which made by my weightes 31 ton 18 C ½, 4 li. conteynyng 2834 endes & it
cost putt in my hows £153 16s 10d £323 10d
Itm. £132 8s 3d ob that is for so myche goten by this acowmpt as it aperith
to gaynes in credito fo. 92 £132 8s 3d½

S. £734 5s 1d½

53(R) anno 1539

Iren per contra is dewe to have the 21 day of Jenyver
£182 9d that is for 29 tons iren 13 C 3 qr. 20 li.
conteynyng 2884 endes sold from the 23 day of October
untill this present day at dyvers tymes as by my shop
boke may largely apere montith £182 9d
Itm. the last day of February £158 19s 10d½ that is for
25 tons 5 C 5 li. iren conteynyng 2355 endes sold from
the 21 day of Jenyver last past unttyll this present daye
at dyvers tymes as by my shop boke may apere £158 19s 10d ob
1540 Itm. the 29 day of Aprell 1540 £70 19s 4d that is
for 11 ton, ½ a C, 21 li. iren conteynyng 969 endes sold
from the last day of February untill this present day at
dyvers tymes as by my shop boke may apere montith £70 19s 4d
Itm. the same 29 day of Aprell £7 that is for 1 ton 5 C 19 li.
iren conteynyng 74 endes whereof I make the newe cowmpt
per contra debitor for so myche iren which this day rest
unsolld in my hows of this acownt £7

S. £418 19s 11d½

anno 1540

Iren per contra is dewe to have the 28 day of July £286 10s 1d
that is for 47 tons 3 C 21 li. conteynyng 4625 endes sold
from the 29 day of Aprell last past for the foresseid som
as in my shop boke may apere £286 10s 1d
Itm. the 19 day of Jenyver £268 14s 2d½ that is for
43 tons 1 C ½, 26 li. iren conteynyng 4047 endes sold
from the 28 day of Aprell July last past for the foreseid
somm as in my shop boke may apere £268 14s 2d ob

---
[1] Marginal note, S.S. 5. 10s.
[2] Marginal note, Rendry 4. 18s.

53(R) contd.

Itm. the 26 day of Aprell anno 1541 £156 1s 10d that is for 24 tons 16 C 22 li. ½ iren conteynyng 2388 endes sold from the 19 day of Jenyver last past as by my shop boke may apere	£156	1s	10d
Itm. the same day £22 19s that is for 1 ton 15 li. iren of S.S. conteynyng 82 endes & 2 ton 15 C ½ of Rendry iren conteynyng 217 endes which iren I pass to a newe cowmpt fo. 127 for the clozing up of this acowmpt	£22	19s	
S.	£734	5s	1d ob.

54(L)   anno 1539

Sallt of Rochell for my acownpt 65 tons which rest in my hows this present day owith £65 for so myche it cost & standith me in, montith

£65

54(R)   anno 1540

Salt per contra is dewe to have the 9 day of Aprell £3 21d for 3 ton 3 busshells & hallf d'd to John Caps	£3	1s	9d
Itm. the 1 day of July £52 for 52 ton sold to John Wells of Bristowe sope maker as it may apere to hym in debito fo. 124	£52		
Itm. £3 for 3 ton that I have taken at dyvers tymes for my owne ocupying	£3		
Itm. £6 18s 3d for so myche lost by this acowmpt as it may apere to gaynes in debito fo. 92	£6	18s	3d
	£65		

55(L)   anno 1539

24L
6C
1 Tynby Frize
1 Manchester

Robert Tyndall my prentis resydent at S.S. in Spayne owe and owght to geve me acowmpt & payment of 24 London clothes & of 6 corse costom clothes & of a pece of grey Tynby fryse & of a Manchester which goodes he r. of myne at Bilbo owt of Domyngo de Lessos ship of the Rendry in June. It cost me all abord	£113	14s	2d
Itm. that he r. in Awgost owt of my ship the Trynte 10 London clothes & a grey Tynby frize that cost £40 & 20 dicker lether that cost £42 & 29 wey 43 busshells wheat that cost £87 4s 9d & 10 weyes 16 busshells beanes that cost £20 14s amontith the hole	£189	18s	9d
Itm. the same tyme he r. owt of Anton de Asteacus ship of the Passaige for my parte 10 dicker lethir, 16 calve skuyns, 2 weyes 4 busshells wheat & 1 wey 24 busshells ½ benes, all which cost me clere abord	£32	3s	4d
Itm. I sent hym in October in my ship the Trynte by my prentes Hewgh Hamond 2 great ox hides that cost 14s & a bay gellding that cost £3 13s 4d & more 196 ducatts & 97 crowns of the son. Montith all sterlyng	£76		
Itm. the same tyme 110 crowns of the son which I sent by land with Frances Codryngton whereof the seid Tyndall must geve accowmpt in leke case, montith sterlyng	£25	13s	4d
Itm. the 4th daye of December £3 13s 4d for so myche that my clothe per contra montith less then £153 14s 2d	£3	13s	4d

55(L) contd.

Itm. this present day the 4th day of December 1539 £161 14s 5d½ for the gaynes & clozing up of this acowmpt	£161	14s 5d½
	S. £602	17s 4d½

55(R) anno 1539

Robert Tyndal per contra is dewe to have the 4th day
of December £197 1d for so myche that all my wheat
& benes in the Trynte & de Asteacus ship was sold for
nete as it may apere by his cowmpt r. the same day
& it is in M., 2955068½ M. £197 1d
Itm. the same day by the same acowmpt £119 19s 3d
which is for 179942 M. that my lethir & calve skuyns
r. in Awgost owt of the aboveseid 2 shipps made clere
montith £119 19s 3d
Itm. 14s 8d for 2 hides sold at Burdes 14s 8d
Itm. £4 that my horss was sold for, pd. in 2 ton pipe wyne £4
Itm. £8 9s 4d which Tyndal let rest in Hamondes powar
& the same Hamond must geve me acownt of hit & it is
for 18 ducatts & 17 crowns £8 9s 4d
Itm. £84 16s 8d that is for 178 ducatts & 190 crowns he
bestoweth for me at Burdes this vyntage 1539 £84 16s 8d
Itm. £153 14s 2d that is for 34 London clothes, 5 costom
clothes, 1 Tynby frize & 1 Manchester cotton which rest
unsolld & I pass it to viages fo. 69. I sey 5 costom clothes £153 14s 2d
Itm. £34 3s 2d½ which is for 51241 M. that Tyndall rest
owyng this day in redy money & thereof I make hym
debitor in fo. 70 £34 3s 2d½
Itm. thes day the 4th of December 1539 £161 14s 5d½ for
the gaynes & clozing up of this acowmpt, montith. This
item shuld aben sett in the other syde as it aperith therefore I somm it not at this end.
  S. £602 17s 4d½

56(L) anno 1539

Viages besowthe, that is to sey to the parties of Luxbron
and Andaluzia for my owne acowmpt (Giles White of
Bristowe marchant & my sarvant being factor ffor the
31 L same) owithe the 29 day of Agost £191 18s 6d that is
1 fyne ffor 31 London clothes in collores hewlynges and light
azar grenes & 1 fyne azar & 25 truckers in collores light grenes
25 truckers & hewlynges & 1 northen cotton all the which war
1 northern packyd in 6 fardells & laden in the Mary Cristofor, Mary
cotton Conception & Mary Bride as by Giles remenbrans
  playnlier aperithe £191 18s 6d
Itm. the seid Giles must be cowntable to me for
126 ducatts ¼ which he left for my acownpt in the handes of
Ruyfrero marchant of Luxbron, to be pd. at all tymes £31 12s 6d

  £223 11s

anno 1539

Viages besowthe for my owne acowmpt owith the 8 day
10 London of Marche £46 19s 1d that is for 10 London clothes of
clothes Yerberys better sorte at £4 the clothe clere abord & 2 weys
  20 busshells beanes, I sey wheate, that cost £6 19s 1d,
2 weys all which was laden in the Jhesus of Bristowe under God

56(L) contd.

20 busshells wheat	m*aster* Robert Thomas & yn the goverance of Frances Fowlar my factor for to employ it in wood at the Ylls of Surrys	£46	19s	1d
10L 15 truckers	Itm. the 16 day of the same £80 that is for 10 clo*thes* penny hewes & light grenes of Thomas Hasshes makyng which cost abord £4 the clothe & 15 truckers of Yerberys makyng which cost abord 53s 4d *the* clothe, all which is laden in the Mary *Cristof*or & Giles White my factor to employ it in wull oyles & other thing*es* acordyng to my remenbrance	£80		
3 truckars	*1540* Itm. the 6 day of Aprill 1540 £8 that is for 3 truckers which I lode in the Trynte of Wales M*aster* Jones ship in a fardell of Arthure Smythes, mon*tith*	£8		
		S. £134	19s	1d

56(R)

anno 1539

31L 1 azar 1 cotton	Viag*es* p*er* contra be dewe to have the 19 day of Jenyver £114 2s 6d *that* is for 186 V. 189 M. which he geve me in cownt for the nete sale of the 31 London clothes p*er* contra, mon*tith*, & won sad blew & a northen cotton	£114	2s	6d
9 truckers	Itm. the same tyme £23 17s 1d that is for the net sale of 9 truckers as by the same cowmpt ap*er*ithe	£23	17s	1d
	Itm. the same tyme £29 15d for 116 d*ucatts* 1 q*uarter* which he r. of Ruyfrero & employed it for me	£29	1s	3d
	Itm. 10 d*ucatts* which war lost *that* Ruyfrero wuld not paye	£2	10s	
	Itm. the seid 19 day of Jenyver £40 that is for 16 clothes truckers which Giles left unsold of this cowmp*t* & rest in the hand*es* of W*illiam* Ostriche, m*a*rchant of London, resydyng & abydyng at *this* pr*e*sent at Seynt Lucar in Andaluzia for to sell & employ the money of it for my acowmpt in wull oyle fo. 91	£40		
	Itm. the same day £14 2d lost by this cowmpt of viag*es* as it ap*er*ith to gaynes in debito fo. 92	£14		2d
		S. £223	11s	

anno 1540

Viag*es* p*er* contra be dewe to have the 4 day of June £53 1s 2d that is for 84893 r*es* that Franc*es* Fowlar geve me by acowmpt *this* pr*e*sent day, that is for the nete sale of 10 clothes 68053 r*es* & for the nete sale of 2 weyes 20 busshells wheate 16840 at in d*u*catts 213 d*u*catts 93 r*es* mon*tith* sterlyng	£53	1s	2d
Itm. the 12 day of June Giles Whit geve me in cowmpt for the sales of 10 London clothes & 18 truckers sold at Luxbro*n* in Aprell last past 134448 r*es* whereof descownt 4000 r*es* for his cost*es*. Rest clere 130448 r*es*	£81	10s	
Itm. the seid 12 day of June 7s 11d lost by			

91

56(R) contd.

this cownt of viages as it aperithe to gaynes in debito fo. 92		7s	11d
	S. £134	19s	1d

57(L)   anno 1539

Richard Tippar of Bristowe tucker owith the 4 day of September £6 12s 6d payable by his obligacion at the Anunciasion of Owr Blessid Lady next comyng	£6	12s	6d
Itm. the 23 day of Marche 6s 8d pd. to hym in monney		6s	8d
1540 Itm. the 5 day of June 1540 6s 8d pd. to hym		6s	8d
Itm. the 16 day of June £3 2d that is ffor 2 ½-bales wood conteynyng 3 C ½ 4 li. at 17s the C, montith	£3		2d
Itm. the 20 day of August 58s 11d that is ffor 2 ½-bales Tullus wood conteynyng 3 C 1 qr. 24 li. ½ at 17s the C, to be paide at all tymes requyrid	£2	18s	11d
Itm. the 24 day of December 30s 9d that is for 1 h'd 14 li. iren at 6s the C, to be pd. at all tymes	£1	10s	9d
Itm. the 15 of Jenyver 13s 4d payd to hym in redy		13s	4d
Itm. 23d for brawne he had of my wif		1s	11d
Itm. the 9 day of February 1540 pd. to hym in monney 3s 9d		3s	9d
Itm. the 9 day of February 1540 £6 4s 2d that is £3 6s 8d for a pipe of S.S. iren & 57s 6d for 2 bales wood weying 3 C 1 qr. 15 li. at 17s the C, montith	£6	4s	2d
1541 Itm. the 25 day of June 1541 pd. to hym 20s	£1		
Itm. the 26 day of September 12s 6d pd. to hym in redy money & so quyte untill this day		12s	6d
	S. £23	12s	4d

           anno 1539

David Hart of Bristowe shereman owithe the 1 daye of September 57s that is for the rest of his reckenyng in my old boke fo. 169 payable at all tymes	£2	17s	
1540 Itm. the 26 day of Marche anno 1540 6s 8d for so mych paide to his wif in redy monney		6s	8d
Itm. the 12 day of June pd. to his wif 9s montith		9s	
Itm. the 14 day of December £3 10s that is for 1 butt seck sold & d'd to his wif	£3	10s	
Itm. the 24 day of December d'd to his wif in monney 13s 4d		13s	4d
Itm. the 28 day of Jenyver £6 that is ffor 1 ton Rendry iren solld & d'd to hym, to pay at all tymes	£6		
1541 Itm. the 8 day of July 1541 paide to hym 4s		4s	
Itm. the 18 day of July £3 10s for a butt of seck d'd to his wif	£3	10s	
Itm. the last day of Augost 6s 4d d'd to hym in redy monney		6s	4d
Itm. the last daye of Jenyver £7 6s 8d that is for 2 buttes of seck sold to hym, to pay at Seynt Jamistide next	£7	6s	8d
	S. £25	3s	

57(R)   anno 1539

Richard Tippar per contra is dewe to have the 6 day of Marche £3 that is for the rowyng of 15 truckers at 16d the clothe & 10 clothes of Nasches & 10 clothes of Yerberys of the better sort at 2s the clothe, which clothes he have dreassyd sens the 4th day of September untill this present day, montith	£3		
1540 Itm. 8 day of Aprell 1540 4s for rowyng of 3 truckers		4s	

57(R) contd.

Itm. for rowyng of 21 clothes of Yerberys better sort the 7 day of June at 2s the clothe montith	£2	2s
Itm. the 18 day of Agost 56s that is for rowing of 24 clothes of Yerberys better sorte at 2s the clothe & 6 of his truckers at 16d the clothe, montith	£2	16s
Itm. the 15 of September 30s for rowyng 10 clothes of Yerberis better sort & 5 of Nasches at 2s per clothe	£1	10s
Itm. the 9 day of February £6 2s 8d that is for rowyng of 10 fyne clothes of Jamys Bissis at 4s the clothe & of 17 clothes of Yerberys & 3 clothes of Buchars at 2s the clothe & of 17 truckers of Yerberys at 16d the clothe, montith the hole as is aforesseid	£6	2s 8d
Itm. for musteryng of 3 clothes of Buchars 12d		1s
Itm. the 12 day of Marche 14s 8d that is for rowyng of 6 penny hewes of John Yerberys of the which 3 of them war made violettes at 2s the clothe & of 2 truckers 16d per clothe		14s 8d
1541 Itm. the 28 day of June 1541 for rowyng of 26 clothes of John Yerberys penny hewes at 2s the clothe & 4 truckers at 16d the clothe, montith 57s 4d	£2	17s 4d
Itm. for rowyng of 27 clothes of Yerberys & 10 of Naschis at 2s the clothe & 3 truckers at 16d the clothe & bryngyng up of 80 northens 6s 8d montith £4 4s 8d	£4	4s 8d
S.	£23	12s 4d

anno 1539

David Hart per contra is dewe to have the 6 day of Marche 41s 8d that is for barbyng & sheryng of 15 clothes of Yerberys corse sorte at 12d the clothe & of 10 clothes of his better sorte at 16d per clothe & of 10 clothes of Thomas Asshis at 16d the clothe, which clothes he have shorn sens the 1 day of September last past	£2	1s 8d
Itm. the 7 day of June 31s that is for sheryng of 21 clothes of Yerberis better sort & 3 of his truckers	£1	11s
1541 Itm. the 14 day of Aprell anno 1541 for sheryng of 1 clothe of Thomas Hasshes penny hewes & 6 of William Buchars clothes & 39 clothes of John Yerberys penny hewes at 16d the clothe & for sheryng of the seid Asshis clothe & 3 of the seid Yerberys clothes after the dyeing at 16d the clothe & sheryng of 10 clothes of Jamys Bisses at 3s 4d per clothe & for sheryng 19 truckers of John Yerberys at 12d the clothe montith all £5 19s	£5	19s
Itm. for barbyng & sheryng the 8 day of July 1541 of 20 clothes of Yerberys penny hewes at 16d the clothe & 4 truckers at 12d the clothe montith 30s 8d	£1	10s 8d
Itm. the last day of Augost £3 4s that is for barbyng & sheryng of 44 penny hewes of Yerberys & Naschis at 16d per clothe & of 2 truckers at 12d the clothe & of a ffyne blewe at 3s 4d per clothe	£3	4s
Itm. the 20 day of Jenyver £3 which is for barbyng & shering of 35 clothes of Yerberys & 10 of Hasshis	£3	
Itm. the last day of Jenyver £7 6s 8d for the rest of this cownt whereof I make hym debitor fo. 160	£7	6s 8d
S.	£25	3s

58(L) anno 1539

Master Robert Pole marchant of Glocester owithe the 10 day of September £3 18s 4d that is for the freight of 5 ton iren in my ship this viage at 15s the ton & for averes 8d per ton montith   £3 18s 4d

58(L) contd.

Itm. the same tyme 12s 6d for costom of the seid iren		12s	6d
Itm. the 27 day of Jenyver £12 8s that is for 2 ton 23 li. iren whereof 1 ton ys of S.S. which I d'd for hym to his sarvant Henry Browne, to be pd. at all tymes		£12	8s
Itm. the last day of February 53s 4d for the lycens of 4 dicker lethir whiche I sold to hym at 13s 4d the dickar		£2 13s	4d
Itm. the same tyme pd. for costom of the same lether 16s 6d & for costom of 10 clothes 11s 8d, montith the hole		£1 8s	2d
1540 Itm. the 10 day of May for freight of 5 ton iren in my ship at 13s 4d per ton & averes 9d per ton & for the freight of his clothe & lether this viage to Spayne valurid 19 clothes ½ at 2 rialles per clothe, montith all		£4 8s	1d
Itm. for the costom of the seid 5 ton iren at 2s 6d per ton		12s	6d
Itm. for freight of 2 ton 2 kyntalls iren in the Trynte from Spayne the 23 day of Agost at 13s 4d per ton		£1 8s	7d
	S.	£27 9s	5d

anno 1539

Robert Durban of Bristowe marchant owith the 10 daye of October £3 15s for 5 ton iren in my ship this vyage at 15s the ton montith		£3	15s
Itm. the 13 day of December 25s pd. to hym by the handes of my sarvant Hewgh Hamond		£1	5s
	S.	£5	

anno 1539

Robert Durban above namyd owith the 16 day of December £3 6s 8d which is for a butt seck I sold hym, to be paide in the Cristmas holydayes next commyng		£3 6s	8d
Itm. the 3d day of Jenyver £3 10s for a but of seck sold & d'd to hym, to be pd. at Shraftyde next		£3	10s
Itm. the 4 day of February £3 6s 8d for a pipe iren of S.S. to be paide at Ester next commyng		£3 6s	8d
1541 Itm. the 1 day of December £6 5s which is for the freight of 5 tons bastardes in the Trynte at 25s per ton, to pay ½ in hand & ½ at the end of 3 monthes next commyng		£6	5s

58(R) anno 1539

Master Robert Pole per contra is dewe to have the 24 day of November £4 10s 10d r. from hym by my sarvant Robert Leyte, montith		£4 10s	10d
1540 Itm. the 11 day of Maye 1540 £6 which my sarvant Let r. of his wif		£6	
Itm. the 27 day of May r. by Leight my sarvant		£8 9s	7d
Itm. the 28 day of September my sarvant Robert Leight r. of hym in Glocester £8 9s		£8	9s
	S.	£27 9s	5d

anno 1539

Robert Durban per contra is dewe to have the 13 daye of December £5 that is for 2 pipes of corrupt bastard montith			
	S.	£5	

anno 1539

Robert Durban per contra is dewe to have the 3 daye of Jenyver £3 6s 8d r. of hym		£3 6s	8d

58(R) contd.

Itm. the same day £3 10s for a but seck which I sold & d'd to hym to pay at Shraftyde next	£3 10s
Itm. the 18 day of Marche r. of his wif £4	£4
Itm. the 24 day of Aprill 1540 r. of his wif	£1
Itm. the 28 day of Aprell 10s which his wif pd.	10s
Itm. the 1 day of July r. of hym 26s 8d	£1 6s 8d
Itm. the last day of Jenyver 1541 r. £3 2s 6d	£3 2s 6d
Itm. the 1 day of Marche lent to his wif 40s	£2 it is pd.
Itm. the 9 day of September 1542 Lett my sarvant r. of hym 40s	£2
Itm. the 19 of October r. by his lad 22s 6d	£1 2s 6d

59(L)   **anno 1539**

Thomas Hart marchant of Bristowe owith the 10 daye of October £3 15s that is for freight of 5 ton iren in my ship this preasent viage at 15s the ton — £3 15s

Itm. the 22 day of December £6 that is for the freight of 6 ton wyne from Burdes this vyntage in the Trynte — £6

Itm. the first day of Marche 6s that is for 6 ores d'd to John Chawnceller purser of the Mary Bride — 6s

1540 Itm. the 15 day of November 1540 £4 which is for the freight of 4 ton in the Trynte at 20s per ton to pay at 3 monthes & 3 monthes — £4

Itm. the 18 daye of February 1542 £7 10s that is for the freight of 5 tons wyne laden in my ship at 30s the ton, to pay halff in hand & thother halff at 3 monthes next commyng — £7 10s

anno 1539

Thomas Tizon of Bristowe marchant owith the 10 daye of October £3 15s for the freight of 5 ton iren this preasent viage in my ship at 15s the ton — £3 15s

Itm. £4 10s for the freight of 4 ton pipe Gascon wyne this vyntage in the Trynte, at 20s the ton to pay halff in hand & thother ½ at Owr Lady Day in Marche next commyng — £4 10s

1540 Itm. the 10 day of May 53s 4d that is for the freight of 4 ton iren in the Trynte my ship at 13s 4d per ton to pay at thend of 3 monthes next commyng — £2 13s 4d

Itm. the 29 day of Agost 8s 10d that is for the freight of 10 kyntalls in the Trynte from Spayne at 13s 4d per ton, montith — 8s 10d

Itm. the 15 day of November 20s for the freight of 1 ton rozyn in the Trynte to pay at 3 monthes & 3 monthes — 15s

Itm. the 22 day of Marche £3 6s 8d which is for a pipe of S.S. iren d'd for hym to Morgan Davy of Kermerdyne, to be paide at Seynt Jamistide next commyng — £3 6s 8d

1541 Itm. the 1 day of December anno 1541 £6 5s that is for the freight of 5 tons bastard yn the Trynte at 25s per ton, to pay ½ in hand & ½ at the end of 3 monthes next commyng — £6 5s

1542 Itm. the 3 day of Aprell 1542 39s which I pd. to Thomas Tysons sarvant, & so r. & broke my seale from the Mary Bonaventures charter — £1 19s

Itm. the 18 day of February 1542 £7 10s for the freight of 5 ton wyn in my ship at 30s the ton to pay halff in hand & halff 3 monthes next after — £7 10s

59(R)   **anno 1539**

Thomas Hart marchant of Bristowe is dewe to have the 25 day of November £6 5s to pay hallf in hand & thother hallf which is for 5 ton seck laden for me this vyntage at Andaluzia in the Mary Bride — £6 5s

1540 Itm. the 7 day of Aprell anno 1540 r. by the handes of his maide £3 10s montith — £3 10s

Itm. the 14 day of February 8s for a yeres rent of a storehows endid at Cristmas last past & 32s r. in redy monney, montith bothe parcells 40s, which is for his ½ freight of the 4 ton wyne per contra — £2

1541 Itm. the 3 day of Augost r. by Hamond 40s — £2

59(R) contd.   anno 1539

Thomas Tizon *per* contra is dewe to have the 3d day of Jenyver £3 6s 8d r. of his s*ar*vant Hemmyng, & 8s 4d I rebatyd to hym for as myche he lode no corn at *the* viage *per* co*n*tra in my ship	£3	15s
Itm. the 20 day of February 45s which he pd. to my wife	£2	5s
1540 Itm. the 15 day of Aprell 1540 r. of hym 6s 8d in a pece of rezyns & 38s in redy mon*n*ey	£2	5s
Itm. the 29 day of July r. 1 bag of allem *conteynyng* C. 3 qr. 8 li. at 20s the C, whereof must be discowntyd for the bagg. [1] So mo*ntith* the hole	£1 16s	5d
Itm. the 12 day of September r. by the hand*es* of my s*ar*vant Leight 16s 8d	16s	8d
Itm. the 19 day of February 23s 10d r. of hy*m* in redy mon*n*ey	£1 3s	10d
Itm. the 27 day of July 1541 r. by Hem*m*yng his s*ar*vant	£3 6s	8d
Itm. the 8 day of February £3 2s 6d *that* is 5s for 1 qr. of allem, & 57s 6d r. by Herry in redy mon*n*y	£3 2s	6d
Itm. £5 which I must pay hym for my hallf freight of 8 tons this last vyntaige in *the* M*a*ry Bonaventure	£5	
Itm. 18d for 8 lbs of allem	1s	6d
Itm. the 21 day of M*a*rche my wif r. of his s*ar*vant	£3	15s
Itm. the 18 of July 1543 I r. of his s*ar*vant £3 15s	£3	15s

60(L)   anno 1538

Frances Codryngton and W*illiam* Car of Bristowe m*a*rchant*es* owe the 2d daye of February for lycens of 8 weyes of beanes entryd apo*n* my lycens for them in my ship	[1]
Itm. £5 5s 8d pd. to France*s* toward my q*u*arter p*a*rte of a lycens of 58 weyes wheat & beanes obteynyd[2] by Edward Stonebagg	[1]
Itm. for my part of the lycens & freight *that* Robert Du*r*ban paide for his 8 wey beanes in Anto*n* Deasteacu at 8s *per* wey	[1]
Itm. the 10 day of October £30 for the freight of 40 ton iren *this* pr*e*sent viage in my ship at 15s *the* to*n*	£30
Itm. for theyr p*a*rtes of 4 ton that came ded freight in they*res* & M*a*ster Willi*a*m Shipmans complyment	[1]
Itm. the 22 day of December £14 5s 8d to pay ½ in hand & th*o*ther ½ at the end of 3 monthes next com*m*yng which is for the freight of 200 ½-bales wood laden in my ship the Trynte at Burd*es this* present vyntaige, acow*m*ptyng 14 ½-bales for a to*n* at 20s the to*n* as may apere by the charterp*a*rtie	£14 5s 8d

anno 1540

Itm. the 14 day of June £6 13s 4d for a to*n* iren of S.S. at 20 nobles the to*n* d'd for hym to W*illiam* Darck to pay at Mighellmas next	£6	13s	4d
Itm. the 23 day of Augost £13 6s 8d which is for the freight of 20 to*n* iren in *the* Trynte fro*m* Spayne	£13	6s	8d
Itm. the 15 daye of Jenyver £2 7s 11d paide for the complyment of my hallf freight *per* contra to Thom*a*s Robertz pu*r*ser of the Harry	£2	7s	11d
Itm. the 10 day of February £14 9s 10d that is for the cost*es* of 30 weyes whet laden in the Trynte at 8s *per* wey & more 15s 2d for hallf Hamond*es* cost*es* & 33s 4d for ½ of £3 6s 8d to Stonebagg & 16d for 4 matt*es*, mo*ntith*[3]	£14	9s	10d
1541 Itm. the 10 day of Maye 1541 £9 15d which he owith me for Thomas Hick*es* as it ap*er*ith to hym in credito fo. 100	£9	1s	3d
Itm. the 4 day of Maye £26 13s 4d that is for the freight of 40 ton iren in the Trynte at 13s 4d the ton to pay ½ in hand & ½ at the end of 3 monthes next com*m*yng[3]	£26	13s	4d

---

[1] *Blank in MS.*
[2] *Marginal note 9. 7.*
[3] *The entries for 1540 and 1541 are crossed through.*

60(R)
anno 1539

Frances Codryngton & William Car per contra is dewe to have the monthe of July for the licens of 10 weyes wheat & 5 weyes beanes which com to my hallf part of 20 weyes wheat & 10 weyes beanes entryd in my ship the Trynte
Itm. the same tyme for my quarter part of 8 weyes wheate & 3 weyes beanes entryd in Anton Deasteacu is ship of the Passaige at 9s 7d per wey   £8 10s 1d
Itm. the 22 day of December £18 2s 6d that is for the freight of 27 buttes seck & 2 pipes taynt which I had laden this vyntaige in the John Baptist at 25s per ton   £18 2s 6d
Itm. the same tyme for 1 but seck laden more in her   12s 6d
Itm. the 15 day of Jenyver £25 10s 8d for so myche redy monney my sarvant Hamond r. of hym   £25 10s 8d

anno 1540

Frances Codryngton per contra is dewe to have the 18 day of November £13 6s 8d r. of hym in monney for payement of 20 ton freight per contra   £13 6s 8d
Itm. the   ¹   day of Jenyver £18 2s 6d that is for the freight of 14 ton pipe wyne from Andaluzia in the Harry, master Antony Picket, to pay   £18 2s 6d
Itm. the   ¹   day of Jenyver £18 2s 6d that is for the freight of 14 ton pipe wyne from Andalyzia in the Harry, 7s 2d¼ per wey, montith   £11 2s 10d
Itm. the same day 8s for 2 qr. wheat I had of his corn to make up my complyment of the seid 31 weyes   8s
Itm. the monthe of August 1541 £40 for the freight of 40 tons oyle in the Harry at 20s the ton²   £40
All this forseid countes betwen William Car, Frances Codryngton & me John Smythe be fynischid, past & fully pd. & contentyd so that all the above wrytten is voyde³

61(L)
anno 1539

The Trynte my Ship (God save her) owith £250 that is for so myche her hull, mastes, takle, sayles, 4 ankers, 4 cables, brazyn shevers, 2 gret gouns callid port peces with eich 2 chambers, 2 gret slynges with eich 2 chambers, 4 guns callid basys with eich 2 chambers & 11 peces iren callyd Portyngall verssos with eich 2 chambers & many pelletes of iren & stone belongyng to the same, with bowes, arrowes, bills, morys pikes & dartes & other monycions & abyllymentes belongyng to the same ship. It all cost as foresseid⁴   £250

61(R)⁵

62(L)
anno 1539

Thomas Bell of Glocester the yonger owithe the 29 day of Agost £3 13s 4d that is for so myche that Giles White d'd to me in hym for a but of seck which he sold hym   £3 13s 4d
Itm. the 21 day of February £4 for a pipe ossey   £4
Itm. the 25 day of the same £4 10s for 1 ton Gascon wyne   £4 10s
1540 Itm. the 7 day of May 1540 £7 6s 8d for 2 buttes seck sent to hym in Sparckes bote at 11 nobles the butt, to be paide at all tymes   £7 6s 8d
Itm. the 13 day of November £9 11s 8d which is for 7 h'd 1 tierce Gascon wyne at £5 the ton which he r. at Glocester owt of John Sparkes bote   £9 11s 8d

---

¹ Blank in MS.
² All the entries for 1540 and 1541 are crossed through.
³ This is written across the double folio.
⁴ The whole account is crossed through.
⁵ Fo. 61 R is blank in the MS.

62(L) contd.

Itm. the 24 day of November £7 which is ffor 2 butt*es* of seck laden for hym in Dymock*es* trowe — £7

£36 1s 8d

anno 1542

Thomas Web marynar & m*aster* of my ship the Trynte owithe the 13 day of Octob*er* for 3 wayes of wheat laden for hym in my saide ship this p*res*ent viage, which cost at the first penny 16d the busshell & more for lisence, costo*m* & matt*es* & other costes, 9s 4d p*er* wey. So mon*tith* the hole £11 — £11 [1]

anno 1543

Thomas Bell the yong*er* dwelling in Glocester owith the 10 day of M*ar*che £16 & is for 3 butt*es* of seck & 1 pipe of bastard at £4 the pece — £16

62(R)   **anno 1539**

Thomas Bell p*er* contra is dewe to have the 24 day of November £3 13s 4d r. from hym by my sarvant Robert Leyte mon*tith* — £3 13s 4d

1540 Itm. the 12 day of Agost £14 13s 4d r. at Glocester by Thomas Shipma*n* — £14 13s 4d

Itm. the 28 day of September my s*a*rvant Robert Leight r. of hym at Glocester 20s — £1

Itm. the 9 day of February 1540 £7 which he paid for me to Thomas Shipma*n* — £7

Itm. the 30 day of July a*n*no 1541 r. at Glocester £6 — £6

Itm. the 11 day of M*ar*che 1541 r. fro*m* hym by George Snyg £3 — £3

Itm. the same day 11s 8d which is 6s 8d rebatyd to hym in the price of 2 butt*es* seck & 5s more I rebate for one of the same butt*es* which he seythe was ffawty — 11s 8d

£36 1s 8d

anno 1542

Thomas Web p*er* contra is dewe to have the 15 daye of February 4s 5d for so myche corn did cost less than I chargyd hym p*er* contra, & more I r. of hym in mon*n*ey this day £10 15s 7d, mon*tith* — £11 15s

£11

anno 1544

Thomas Bell p*er* contra is dewe to have 20 of Aprell 40s which Lett r. of his wif at Glocester — £2

Itm. the 22 of August 1544 my s*a*rvant Leyt r. of his wif £8 — £8

Itm. the 20 of October my s*a*rvant Lett r. of hym £6 — £6

63(L)   **anno 1539**

Plate for my owne ocowmpt. That is to sey 2 gilt salt*es* with a cover weying 47 oz., 1 smawle gilt sallt with a coffer weying 13 oz., 3 gilt standyng cupp*es* withe a cover weying 74 oz. ½, 3 gilt goblet*es* with a cov*er* weying 80 oz. ½,

---

[1] *There is a curious symbol here which may be Thomas Web's mark.*

63(L) contd.

3 gilt gobletes with a cover weying 64 oz. ½, 1 goblet gilt withowt a cover weying 21 oz. ½, 3 gilt ale pottes with a cover weying 37 oz. ½, a spice dische giltyd weying 16 oz. ½. So montith all the foreseid 355 oz. ½ of gilt plate valeut at 5s the oz., 88.17.6   £88 17s 6d

Itm. more won bazyne & laver parcell gilt weying 68 oz., won salt sellar with a cover parcell gilt weying 21 oz. ½, won flat pece swaygid parcell gillt weying 12 oz., 12 syllver spones knoppid with lyons gilt weying 14 oz. ½, 6 spones with square gilt knops weying 9 oz. ½, 6 spones knoppid with ymages of Owr Lady gilt weying 6 oz. ½, 6 spones of 2 sortes that gothe abowt the hous every day weying 5 oz., 3 ale potes with a cover parcell gilt weying 26 oz. ½, a tastar that weyith 4 oz. So amontith all this parcell gilt plate 167 oz. ½, valeut at 4s 4d the oz. £36 5s 10d   £36 5s 10d

Itm. £10 2s 6d that is for a gilt goblet with a coffer conteynyng 40 oz. ½   £10

Itm. the 10 day of August 1542 pd. to a Portyngall for a spice dische gillt weying 14 oz. ¾ at 14 grotes the oz.   £3 8s 10d

Itm. 30s 6d that is for so myche that 2 covers of sylver weing 5 oz. ½ which serve to too great erthen crusys & cost with the makyng & guylldyng as aforesseid   £1 10s 6d

Itm. £6 12s 7d ob which is for 13 spones of the which 12 spones be knoppyd with the postills gyllt & the thirtyne spone is all gyllt & knoppid with Jhesus, montith (the 13 spones wey 29 oz. ¼)[1]   £6 12s 7d

Itm. a playne flat white pece which Tyndall r. in Spayne of a debtor of myne for 40s 4d. It weyth 8 oz. ¼ at 3s 8d per oz.   £1 10s 3d

Itm. 1 dozen & 1 pece of sylver spones of the which 12 of them be knoppid with the apostelles gyllt & 1 spone with Jhesus gyllt which weyethe 23 oz which after 13 grotes per oz. montith £4 19s 8d   £4 19s 8d

Itm. 2 white tasters weying 6 oz. at 3s 8d the oz. montith   £1 2s

Itm. 2 greate pottes of sylver wayng 101 oz. ½ & 2 less pottes of sylver wayng 79 oz. ½ & a basyne & a hewer of sylver weying 82 oz. at 4s 6d the oz.   £59 3s 6d

Itm. of my mothers plate 1 standyng cupp with a cover, parcell gyllt weying 31 oz. ½, 2 salltes with a cover parcell gyllt conteynyng 30 oz., 2 ale pottes parcell gyllt conteynyng 16 oz., a litell sylver cup made hornelike conteynyng 5 oz., 2 flat peces parcell gyllt conteynyng 24 oz., a flat pece with Seynt Androws cross waying 7 oz. 1 qr., 12 spones knoppyd with lyons gyllted conteynyng 18 oz ½. Montith all 132 oz. ¼ at 4s 6d the oz. More 3 gyllt ale pottes with a cover conteynyng 36 oz at 5s the oz. Montith the hole £38 15s 1d ob   £38 15s 1d½

63(R)   anno 1549

plate gyllt for my owne acowmpt that is to sey the parcells folowyng being in my powar the 22 day of October, owith

ffor on nest of goblettes waying	102 oz
ffor a nest of goblettes waying	083 oz ½
ffor one nest of goblettes waying	064 oz ½
ffor 2 goblettes with a cover waying	060 oz
ffor one goblet waying 17 oz 1 qr. ⅛	017 oz ¼⅛
Itm. for one nest of standyng cupps with a cover waying 74 oz ½	074 oz ½
for one standyng cup with a cover waying	020 oz
Itm. a peyre of guyllt sawlltes with a cover waying	047 oz
for 2 salltes with a cover waying	023 oz
Itm. one nest of ale pottes waying	037 oz ½
for one nest of ale pottes waying	036 oz
for one nest of ale pottes waying	028 oz
for 2 ale pottes with a cover waying	023 oz
Itm. a spice dische waying 15 oz 3 qrs.	15 oz ¾
Itm. a spice dische waying	16 oz ½
for a spice dische waying	14 oz ¾
for a pix waying with the glass	19 oz ½
parcell guyllt plate	
Itm. a basyne with a ewar waying	068 oz

---

[1] The 13 spones wey 29 oz. ¼ inserted later.

63(R) contd.

for a basyne & a laver waying	082 oz
Itm. 2 salltes with a cover waying	030 oz
for a salt with a cover waying	021 oz ½
for a salt with a cover, 17 oz ¾ ⅛	017 oz ¾ ⅛
for a sallt with a cover waying	019 oz
Itm. a cup coveryd & swaygid waying	024 oz ¾
for a swaygid cup coveryd waying	031 oz ½
Itm. ffor a flat pece waying	012 oz
for a flat pece waying	007 oz ¾
for a flat pece waying 7 oz ¼, myne,	007 oz ¼
for a flat pece waying	011 oz
for a flat pece waying	012 oz ¼
Itm. 13 spones, of the which the one spone knoppid with Jhesus is all guyll & all the other knoppyd with the postell waying	029 oz ¼
for 12 spones knoppid with the apostells, savyng one of them is knoppyd with Jhesus waying	023 oz
for 12 spones knoppyd with lyons	014 oz ½
for 12 spones knoppyd with lyons	018 oz ½
for 6 spones with square knopps	009 oz ½
for 6 spones knoppyd with Owr Lady	006 oz ½
Itm. for 2 present pottes waying	101 oz
for 2 present pottes waying	079 oz ½
Itm. one ale potte uncoveryd waying	008 oz

64(L)   anno 1539

Brode clothes for my owne acowmpt owith the 22 daye of October £14 14s that is for 6 clothes light plonckettes callid truckers whiche I bowght of John Yerbery of Bruton clothiar for 3 C Tullus wood every clothe which do amont acowmptyng every C wood at 16s 8d   £14 14s

64(R)   anno 1539

Brode clothes per contra is dewe to have the 16 day of Marche £14 14s that is for so myche I make viages to Andaluzia fo. 56 debitor of   £14 14s

65(L)   anno 1539

Moris Apowell of Bristowe smythe owithe the 24 daye of October 20s 5d ob. which is for the rest of iren which he have r. of me untill this day as it may apere in his owne boke of my owne hand wryting. It is payable at all tymes requyrid, montith   £1   5d ob.
Itm. the 12 day of Marche 9s 2d that is for 1 C 1 qr. 14 li. iren of S. S. at 6s 8d the C, montith   9s   2d
Itm. the 17 day of the same 30s which is for 1 h'd Rendry iren to be paide at Crismas next commyng   £1 10s
1541 Itm. the 27 day of February 15141[1] 3s 7d that is for the rest of 2 C 3 qr. 8 li. iren   3s   7d
1542 Itm. the 16 of June 1542 10s that is for C ½ iren of S. S. at 6s 8d the C, montith   10s
Itm. the 21 day of November pd. to hym in iren 3s 9d   3s   9d
Itm. the 22 day of November d'd to hym 2 C. 12 li. iren of S. S. at 20 grotes the C, montith 14s 1d whereof is discowntyd the 3s 9d in the next itm. before this, so rest he owith 10s 4d   10s   4d
Itm. 17s 11d for 2 C ½, 20 li. iren of S. S. at 6s 8d the C   17s 11d
Itm. 9d ob. pade the 21 day of March in monney   9d ob.
[2]Itm. the seid 21 day 13s 4d for 2 C S. S. iren   13s 4d
Itm. the 6 of July 1543 6s 6d for 3 qr. 25 li. iren of S. S.   6s   6d

---

[1] Smythe writes 15141.
[2] Marginal note, 3s 4d rest.

65(L) contd.

Itm the 7 of Augost 31s 6d & is for 10s 3d d'd in redy money & 21s 3d in 3 C 1 qr. 6 li. iren	£1 11s 6d
Itm. the 10 day of December 1543 £3 6s 11d ob. & is for 1 pipe 5 li. iren of S. S. d'd to hym	£3 6s 11d ob.
1544 Itm. the 21 day of Maye 1544 32s 1d & is for 5 C 1 qr. 7 li. iren as it may apere in my shop boke. (2 C 2 qr. S. S., 2 C ½, 7 li. Rendry)[1]	£1 15s 5d
Itm. the 8 of June 2 C ½, 10 li. S. S. iren 17s 4d	
Itm. the 30 day of June 2 C ½, 12 li. Rendry iren, 16s 5d. Itm. the 28 of July 1 C 14 li. S. S. iren & 1 C ½, 17 li. Rendry iren for the which he rest owyng 7s 4d ob.	£1 14s 7d ob 7s 4d ob
Itm 10s paide to hym in monney	10s
Itm. the 13 day of September 17s pd. in redy monney[2]	17s

anno 1540

John Darby m*aster* of my ship the Trynte owithe the 10 day of February 24s that is for the lisence, costo*m* & other cost*es* of 3 weyes wheat he lode in the Trynte at 8s p*er* wey	£1 4s

65(R)   ### anno 1539

Moris Appowell p*er* contra is dewe to have the 12 daye of Ma*r*che 5s 6d for s*er*teyne stuff he made for my ship	5s 6d
Itm. the seid day r. 14s 10d & 1d ob I gave mo*ntith*	14s 11d ob.
Itm. the 14 day of August 1541 14s that is for so myche r. of hym in iren warck for my Ship untill this daye	14s
Itm. the 16 day of December 1541 reckenyd with Morys smythe for iren warck for my ship the Trynte, so mo*ntith* I do owe hym till this daye 16s	16s
Itm. the 27 day of February 1541 r. in worck for my ship 9s 2d as it may apere in his boke wryte*n* with my owne hand	9s 2d
Itm. the first day of June he bryng a reckenyng of 6s 6d for spek*es*, bollt*es*, a hatchett, a botehooke, mendyng a candell barrell & for a fyreiren sens the 26 day of Ap*r*ell last past	6s 6d
~~Itm. paide to hym in iren 3s 9d ob the 24 daye of November 1542~~	~~3s 9d~~
Itm. the 21 day of November 1542 10s 10d which is for iren worck to my ship	10s 10d
Itm. the 21 day of M*a*rch 1542 39s ob which is for iren warck for my ship	£1 19s ob
Itm. the 7 of August 1543 41s 8d which is for mendyng of guns, dressyng of an ancker, makyng of a grap*er* & sherehokes & other iren warck belongyng to my ship, as in his boke the p*ar*cells may apere	£2 1s 8d
Itm. the 13 day of September 1544 for iren work which Hamon fet 2 tymes for my ship 35s 4d ob & more for the new dressyng of my ship £6 15s 11d ob mo*ntith*[2]	£8 11s 4d

anno 1539

John Darby p*er* contra is dewe to have the 14 day of Maye 10s which he pd. to me in redy mon*n*ey	10s
Itm. 14s the which geve & remyt hym for this cowmp*t*	14s

66(L)   ### anno 1539

Thomas Scales other wise callid Thomas a London dwellyng at the yn of the George in Bristowe owith the 24 day of October £24 which is for 6 ton iren sold & d'd to hym at £6 the to*n*, to be paide by his bill at Ester next	£24

---

[1] *Inserted later.*
[2] *All Moris Apowell's account is crossed through.*

66(L) contd.

1540 Itm. the 31 day of Augost 1540 £24 *that* is for 4 tons Rendry iren at
£6 *the* ton, to be pd. by his obligacio*n* at *the* Annunciasion of O*w*r Lady next
com*m*yng   £24
Itm. the same day £13 6s 8d that is for 2 to*n* iren of S. S. at £6 13s 4d the
to*n*, to be pd. by his oblygacio*n* at Bartyllmewtide next com*m*yng   £13   6s   8d
1541 Itm. the 4th day of June 1541 £12 6s 8d for 2 to*n* of my bett*er* Rendry
iren to be pd. the first day of Dece*m*ber next com*m*yng. I sey at Candellmass
next com*m*yng   £12   6s   8d
1542 Itm. the 24 of May 1542 £25 6s 8d & is for 4 tons iren at 19 nobles the
ton, to pay £12 13s 4d at Cristmas next com*m*yng & £12 13s 4d at
Candellmass next after that   £25   6s   8d
M*em*orandum that the 20 day of Augost a*n*no 1544 I cawsyd the fore namyd
Thomas Scales to be arestyd for the foreseid £25 & thereupon we agreed in
this man*er*: that is to saye that M*aster* Dudgyne chanter of Wells must pay
me for hy*m* at all tymes requyrid £10, & further the seid Thom*as* is bownd
in a newe obligacion of £15 6s 8d & with hym Robert Crosby & Myles
Wyllsson of Kendall in the cownty*e* of Westmorland chapmen, to pay
£7 13s 4d at Seynt Jamistyd in a*n*no 1545 & £7 13s 4d at Seynt Jamistide
in an*n*o 1546.

66(R)   **anno 1540**

Thomas Scales p*er* contra is dewe to have the 13 day of
July £16 r. of hym by thand*es* of my wif   £16
Itm. the 31 day of July r. £8 & d'd his bill   £8
1541 Itm. the 27 day of Maye 1541 £14 r. of hym in redy
mon*n*ey   £14
Itm. the 7 day of Julye r. of hym £5   £5
Itm. the 18 day of August r. of hym £5   £5
Itm. the 8 day of October r. of hy*m* £13 6s 8d   £13   6s   8d
1542 Itm. the 6 of May 1542 my wif r. of hym £4   £4
Itm. the 16 day of May r. of hym £8 6s 8d   £8   6s   8d
Itm. the 13 day of Novembe*r* a*n*no 1544 r. at Bristow fro*m*
M*aster* Dudgyne by my s*a*rvant Robert Lett £10 as it may
apere by my quyttance made to M*aster* Dudgyne for the
same   £10
Itm. the 25 day of November 1545 r. by the hand*es* of
Robert Crosby & Myles Willson £7 13s 4d   £7   13s   4d
Itm. r. of the seid Crosby £7 13s 4d   £7   13s   4d

67(L)   **anno 1539**

Thomas Silk of Bristowe fryzemaker owith the 23 day of October 29s 9d
that is for a hallf bale of Tullus wood *co*nteynyng C 3 qr. at 17s the C, to be
paide at all tymes   £1   9s   9d
anno 1540 Itm. the 3d day of Aprell 29s 8d that is for 1 hallf bale wood
*co*nteynyng C. 3 qr. less 1 li. at 17s the C   £1   9s   8d
Itm. the 13 day of Aprell 31s 5d that is for ½ a bale Tullus wood *co*nteynyng
C 3 qr. 11 li. mon*tith* at 17s the C   £1   11s   5d
Itm. the 1 day of June 11s 4d for 2 rawe hid*es*   11s   4d
Itm. the 27 day of June 1541 55s 6d that is for 3 C 1 qr. 25 li. in 2 ½-bales
at 16s the C   £2   15s   6d

anno 1549

Georg Wynter of Bristowe m*a*rchant owith the 28 day of December £20
which I paide for hy*m* to his pu*r*ser callyd W*illi*am Farnalls   £20
Itm. more for Hewgh Hamond £17 10s   £17 10s
Itm. for a but of wyne taken to *the* prize the freight & custo*m* abatyd £4   8s 6d[1]
Itm. for a butt of wyne which he & his company dranck at see
Itm. the 16 of Jenyver paide to his sarvant & purs*er* of his ship the Hart,
which s*a*rvant is name is W*illiam* Farnalls, £23 10s 9d   £23 10s 9d

---

[1] *Blank in MS.*

67(L) contd. anno 1539

William Yong grocer of Bristowe owith the 15 day of March £6 13s 4d which is for a ton of iren of S. S. to be pd. at Seynt Jamystide next commyng montith | £6 13s 4d

1541 Itm. the 24 day of Jenyver anno 1541 £46 17s 6d that is ffor 1 C 25 peces, I say 125 peces of Malaga rezyns sold to hym at 7s 6d the pece, to pay £23 8s 9d the 10th day of February next commyng & £23 8s 9d 10 dayes next after the feaste of Easter next commyng as it may apere by his bill | £46 17s 6d

£53 10s 10d

67(R) anno 1539

Thomas Silk per contra is dewe to have the 9 day of December 40s for an old bay amblyng geldyng which he sold to me | £2

Itm. the 26 day of February 5s that is for the tannyng of 3 ox hides of my owne slawghter | 5s

Itm. the 3d day of Agost r. of hym 56s 11d | £2 16s 11d

Itm. the last day of November 1541 r. of hym 55s & 6d I dyscowntyd in the price | £2 15s 6d

anno 1549

Georg Wynter per contra is dewe to have for the freight of 33 ton pipe of sackes at 35s per ton | £58 12s 6d

Itm. for averes of the same layde the 9th of Jenyver at 4s 1d per ton | £6 16s 9d ob

anno 1540

William Yong grocer is dewe to have the 22 day of Jenyver £6 6s 8d r. of his sarvant in redy monney & 6s 8d for a pece rezynges of Mallaga | £6 13s 4d

Itm. the 28 day of February 1541 r. by the handes of his son | £10

Itm. the 3 day of Aprell 1542 r. by his son William £6 13s 4d | £6 13s 4d

Itm. the 14 day of June 1542 r. for hym of John Spark of Newham £10 & gave John Spark a discharge in wryting for the same | £10

Itm. the 11 day of Augost r. by his son William £8 | £8

Itm. the 28 of the same £6 13s 4d r. by his son | £6 13s 4d

Itm. the 3 day of October r. by his son William 40s | £2

Itm. the 20 day of November r. by the handes of his dawghter Clementes Hoper 40s | £2

Itm. the last day of July 1543 my sarvant Leight r. of hym 30s 10d | £1 10s 10d

£53 10s 10d

68(L) anno 1539

Alexander Bosgrove of Wells owith the 19 day of November £3 10s that is for a butt of seck that I sold and delyverd to hym to be paide at all tymes | £3 13s 4d

Itm. the 20 day of December £5 for a ton of Gascon wyne which I sent hym by Sheward the carriar, 3.13.4[1] | £4 13s 4d

Itm. the 2d day of Marche £11 16s 8d that is for 4 h'd claret wyne, 1 h'd white & 1 h'd red after £4 6s 8d the ton, & 1 pipe taynt price £4 6s 8d, to be paide at all tymes | £11 16s 8d

---

[1] 3.13.4 *inserted later.*

68(L) contd.

1540 Itm. the 17 day of June 1540 £3 17s 4d that is 11 nobles for 1 but seck
& 4s for a C rozyn
    3 17s 4d

Itm. the 15 day of November £4 16s 8d ffor 1 ton Gascon wyne sent hym by
Sheward the carriar
    £4 16s 8d

Itm. the 11 day of December £7 *that* is for 2 but*tes* seck sent hym by the seid
carriar
    £7

Itm. the 17 day of the same £4 16s 8d for 1 ton Gascon wyne sent by the
seid carriar
    £4 16s 8d

1541 Itm. the 5th day of Maye 1541 £7 5s that is for 6 h'd of Gascon wyne
after 7 m*ar*kes 40d the ton
    £7 5s

Itm. the 27 day of June £6 3s 4d that is 53s 4d for 2 h'd of wyne & £3 10s
for a butt of seck
    £6 3s 4d

Itm. the 21 day of November £5 10s for 1 ton of Gascon wyne
    £5 10s

Itm. the 26 day of the same 55s for 2 h'd Gasco*n* wyne
    £2 15s

Itm. the 16 day of December £6 6s 8d that is 11 nobles for 1 butt of seck &
8 nobles for 2 h'd Gasco*n* wyne
    £6 6s 8d

1542 Itm. the 25 day of Aprell 1542 £12 13s 4d & is for 2 but*tes* seck at
11 nobles the butt and 1 ton Gascon wyne at 16 nobles the ton, mon*tith*
    £12 13s 4d

Itm. the 18 day of July £3 13s 4d that is ffor a butt of seck sold & delyverd
to hym
    £3 13s 4d

Itm. the 19 of February £4 for a butt of seck sent hym by W*illiam* Sheward
the carryar
    £4

Itm. the 26 day of the same £8 6s 8d that is £4 for a butt of seck &
£4 6s 8d for a pipe of bastard
    £8 6s 8d

1543 Itm. the 29 of May 1543 £8 for 2 but*tes* seck solld to hym to be paide
at all tymes
    £8

Itm. the 1 day of M*a*rche £16 & is for 3 but*tes* of seck & 1 pipe teynt at
eich £4, mon*tith*
    £16

1544 Itm. the 28 of Aprell 1544 £8 which is for 2 but*tes* of seck at eich £4
    £8

1545 Itm. the 26 day of Jenyver 1545 £8 6s 8d & is for 2 but*tes* seck to be pd.
at all tymes
    £8 6s 8d

1546 Itm. the 24 day of May 1546 £9 6s 8d & is for 2 but*tes* of seck to be
paide at all tymes[1]
    £9 6s 8d

68(R)   anno 1539

Alexander Bosgrove p*er* contra is dewe to have the 20 day
of February £3 13s 4d r. by my wif
    £3 13s 4d

Itm. the 2d day of M*a*rche 40s r. of hym in p*a*rt of
payeme*n*t of the to*n* Gascon wyne d'd the 20 day of
Dece*m*ber p*er* contra
    £2

Itm. the 11 day of June r. of hy*m* in Bristow £8
    £8

Itm. the 28 day of July 1540 r. 5 of hym, £5 4s
    £5 4s

Itm. the 9 day of Decembe*r* r. of hym in Bristow
    £4

Itm. 3s 4d which I rebate hym in *the* price of his wynes the
last yere
    3s 4d

Itm. the 4 day of M*a*rche r. of hym at Wells £4
    £4

1541 Itm. the 27 day of Aprell 1541 £6 r. of hym at
Bristowe
    £6

Itm. the 21 day of June r. of his wif in Wells £6 13s 4d
    £6 13s 4d

Itm. the 26 day of September my wif r. £5 10s
    £5 10s

Itm. the 17 day of November r. £5 10s of hy*m*sellf
    £5 10s

Itm. 20s which I rebate hym in the p*r*ice of 2 h'd wyne
p*er* contra sold the 27 of June last past
    £1

Itm. the 24 of Ap*r*ell 1542 r. of hym at Bristow
    £6

Itm. the 17 day of July r. of hym at Bristowe £7 6s 8d
    £7 6s 8d

Itm. the 12 day of October r. fro*m* hym by Jo*hn* Cutt £5
    £6 13s 4d

Itm. the 7 of February r. at Bristowe of hymseall £10
    £10

Itm. the seid day r. of hymseallf 13s 4d
    13s 4d

Itm. more I rebate in the p*r*ice of wynes *this* yere 5s
    5s

Itm. the 29 of M*a*ye r. at Bristowe of hym £4
    £4

---

[1] *The whole of Bosgrove's account is crossed through.*

68(R) contd.

1543 Itm. the 15 of Augost r. of hym at Wells £8	£8		
Itm. the 28 of November r. by Symond Taylor £7 6s 8d	£7	6s	8d
Itm. the 22 of February 1543 r. of hym at Bristowe 20s & so quyt untyll this day	£1		
Itm. the 16 of June 1544 r. of hym at Bristo	£8		
Itm. r. the 15 of Octob*er* by thand*es* of my neghbur J*oh*n Cutt £8	£8		
Itm. the 22 of Jenyver r. from hym by Robert Docquett tayll*er* £7 6s 8d	£7	6s	8d
Itm. the 17 day of May 1546 r. at Bristowe of hym £6 mon*tith*	£6		
Itm. the 3 day of September 1546 r. by John Cutt 40s	£2		
Itm. r. the ¹ day Jenyv*er* 1546 by J*oh*n Cutt £4	£4		
Itm. the 4 of M*ar*che r. by Leight £4²	£4		

69(L)   anno 1539

34 L 5 costoms won Tynby frize won Manchester	Viag*es* to Biscay in este Spayne (Robert Tyndal my prent*es* being my ffactor there) owithe the 4th day of December £150 10d that is for 34 London clothes, 5 corse costom clothes, won Tymby fryze, 1 Mawnchester which do rest in his powar to sell as it may ap*ere* by his reckenyng r. *this day in my ship the Trynte from Burdes*	£150	10d
39 dicker cow & stere 6 dicker, 3 ox hid*es* 73 doz*en* calve s*kuyns* 31 weys benes	Itm. the 8th day of M*ar*che lode in my ship the Trynte, under God m*aste*r J*oh*n Darby, 39 dicker le*ther* cow & stere & 6 dicker 3 hid*es* ox le*ther* which cost at the first penny £109 6s 8d & 73 doz*en* calve skuyns which cost at the first penny £21 17s 4d & for lycens, costo*m* & fardellyng of the same le*ther* £20. More in the seid ship 31 weyes beanes *that* cost at the first penny £58 18s & for lycens & costo*m* of the same £10. So mo*ntith* this hole ladyng £220 2s	£220	2s
5 dicker cow & stere	Itm. the same monthe £16 3s 4d for 5 dicker lethir cow & stere laden in the Mary Co*n*ception, m*aste*r Antony Picket, which cost with the cost*es* as afforesseid	£16	3s 4d
21 London clo*thes* 1 yelo lynard conteynyng 17 yerdes ½ doble 71 hid*es* 30 wey benes 16 b 11 wey ½ wheat 4 b	*anno 1540* Itm. the 9 day of June a*nno* 1540 laden in my ship the Trynte, m*as*t*er* J*oh*n Darby, 31 London clothes of Yerberis makyng in collor*es*, 14 hewlyng*es* & 6 light grenes *that* cost clere aborde £80, 1 yelo lynard *that* cost 17s. 7 dicker & 1 hide tand le*ther* of cow & stere that cost £19 17s, 30 weyes of beanes that cost £57 10s & 11 wey & ½ wheat *that* cost £32. Mo*ntith* the hole £194 4s	£194	4s
14 weyes whet 44 ells canvas	Itm. the 23 day of July 1540 laden by *the* grace of God in the Mawdelen of *the* Passaige 14 weyes wheat which cost clere abord £34. More 44 ells canvas which made 65 vares *that* cost 4d the ell. So mo*ntith* all. The m*asters* name is J*oh*n de Sala. £31 16s 4d	£31	16s 4d
48 weys whet 70 ox hid*es* 101 hid*es* cow & s*tere* 127 doze*ns* skuy*n*s 6 corse clo*thes* 2 whit Aburgeynes	Itm. the 15 day of February *anno* 1540 lode in my ship the Trynte, m*aster* under God J*oh*n Darby, 48 weyes of wheat which cost clere abord £134 13s 8d as it may apere folio 119. More 7 dicker ox le*ther* & 10 dicker & 1 hide cow & stere which cost clere abord £41 1s 8d as it may apere fo. 119. More 127 dozens of calve skuyns which cost clere abord £41 4s 9d as it may apere fo. 119. More 6 of J*oh*n Yerberys corse clothes *that* cost abord £15, & 2 whit Aburgeynes which cost abord 40s. Mo*ntith* all £234 1d	£234	1d
	Itm. the same tyme lode abord *the* Prymros, m*aste*r T. Web		

---

¹ *Blank in MS.*
² *The whole of Bosgrove's account is crossed through.*

69(L) contd.

11 corse clo*thes* 1 white kersy 11 wey whet	11 corse clothes of J*o*hn Yerbeyrs *that* cost clere abord £27 10s & 1 fyne whit kerssy which cost 20s, mon*tith*	£28	10s
31 wey benes	Itm. the 20 day of M*a*rche lode in the Antony of the Porte of Portyngal, m*aster* Antony Ferna*n*dez, 11 wey wheat which cost clere abord £29 14s & 31 weyes of beanes which cost abord £54 10s. Mon*tith* the hole £81 10s	£84	4s
20 L 2 kerssis	Itm the 28 day of June 1541 £81 15s that is for 20 clothes London sorte & 2 white kerssys packyd in 2 fardells & laden in the Mawdelen of the Rendry, m*aster* M*a*rtyne de Alsegar	£81	15s
	Itm. in Agost 1541 I pass to geynes fo. 92	£133 1s	1d
		£1,173 16s	8d

69(R)   anno 1540

Viag*es* p*er* contra is dewe to have the 22 day of May £144 13s 7d for so myche that the 34 London clo*thes* & 5 corse costom clothes, won Tymby frise & won Manchester cotton made clere, as by Tyndalls cowmpt r. the last day of June a*nno* 1540 of Thom*as* Shipma*n* may apere	£144 13s	7d
Itm. more £262 1d for so myche *that* 39 44 dicker lethir cow & stere, I sey 44 dicker, & 6 dicker 3 ox hid*es* & 73 doze*n* calve skuyns & 31 weys benes made clere as by the foresseid acowmpt may apere for it made in M. 393005	£262	1d
Itm. more £210 14d that is for 315086 M. ½ that was made clere of the sale of 21 London clothes, 17 yerd*es* ½ yelo Aburgeyne, 71 hid*es*, 30 weyes 16 busshells benes & 11 wey 28 busshells wheat, as it may apere in acowmpt of Robert Tyndalls reckenyng r. the 26 day of Ap*r*ell 1541	£210 1s	2d
Itm. 53579 M. which is for the nete sale of 14 weyes wheat & 44 ells canvas as by the seid cownt ap*erith*	£35 14s	5d
Itm. for the nete sale of 59 weys wheat & 31 wayes benes which came in my ship & the Antony of the Porte of Portyngall, 382854 M. ½. More for the nete sale of a 101 hid*es* cowe & stere & 70 ox hid*es* & 127 dozens calve skuyns 202204 M. and more for the nete sale of 17 truckers, 3 kersys, 2 whit Aborgeynes & 20 London clo*thes* 196998 M., the which clothe was laden my ship & in the Primros & in Allsegas pynas. So mon*tith* all	£521 7s	5d
	£1,173 16s	8d

70(L)   anno 1539   5.2.6½[1]

Robert Tyndall owith the 4th day of Decembe*r* £34 3s 2d ob. which is for 51241 M that he owith redy money for the rest of his reckenyng he sent me in my ship from Burd*es* & I r. it this daye, mon*tith*[2]	£34 3s 2d½

anno 1544

8 buttes S. 1 pipe T 3 pipes B	Wynes of Andaluzia for the acowmpt of Robert Tyndall r. the monthe of Jenyver ow*t* of a hulk callid the Sampsson of Ankewis, under God m*aster* William Jonsson, that is to say 8 buttes of seck, 1 pipe of taynt & 3 pipes bastards owithe for ffreight 26s 3d p*er* t*on*, for the pillot*es* wayges 15d p*er* ton,

---

[1] 5. 2. 6½ *was added in different ink.*
[2] *This item is crossed through.*

70(L) contd.

	for costom at Chepstowe 3d per ton, bote hier from the Forrest 12d per ton, wyndage 1d ob per ton, averes[1] per ton, the Kynges custom of 5 ton pipe at 3s per ton, for halyng & stowyng 4d per ton. Montith the hole £9 11s 9d	£9 11s 9d
9 buttes S. 2 pipes T. 3 pipes B	Itm. r. in Marche owt of the Trynte of the Rendry, master John Huar de Amassa, 9 buttes of seck, 2 pipes taynt & 3 pipes bastards which owith for costom of 5 ton pipe at 3s per ton, for freight 33s 9d per ton, for averes 5s 9d per ton, for halyng & stowyng 4d per ton, for 20 dozens & 8 hopes sett apon all his wynes with a newe hed & 2 chymes & for rackyng & pylyng of 2 pipes 1 h'd bastard, 16s 4d	£13 18s 10d
	1545 Itm. the 10 day of June £16 & is for so myche his brother William Tyndall r. of John Wylles, chamberleyne for this acowmpt	£16
	Itm. the last day of June 1545 £7 which I d'd to his brother in Thomas Machyne of Barckeley	£7
	Itm. the [1] day of Augost pd. to hym in redy monny	£17
	Itm. the [1] day of October 1545 £6 13s 4d which he r. for me of Thomas Machyne	£6 13s 4d

70(R) [2]   **anno 1544**

	Wynes here ageynst be dewe to have the 27 of	
2 b	Jenyver £13 6s 8d & is for 2 buttes seck at eich	
1 p	£4 & 1 pipe bastard at 13 nobles sold to John Wellsche	£13 6s 8d
2 b	Itm. to Jamys Rogers the 28 of Jenyver 2 buttes seck for	£8
1 p	Itm. the 29 of Jenyver to T. Wheteley 1 pipe bastard for	£4
1 h'd	Itm. the same day to Richard Vere 1 h'd taynt for 40s	£2
1 h'd	Itm. the 11 of February to John Roxby 1 h'd taynt for	£2
1 b	Itm. the 12 of February for 1 but seck to A. Stanbanck for	£3 13s 4d
2 b	Itm. the 28 day of Marche for 2 butes seck to John Wyllis for—1545	£8
2 b	Itm. the same day to Antony Stanbanck for 2 buttes seck for	£8
1 b	Itm. the 13 day of Aprell to John Roxby 1 butt seck for	£4
1 p	Itm. the 29 day of May to William Northe 1 pipe bastard reckyd for	£4 13s 4d
1 p	Itm. the 1 day of June to John Genynges 1 pipe bastard reckyd for	£4 13s 4d
3 b	Itm. drawen owt to ylladge 3 buttes seck & 2 pipes bastard	[3]
2 p 2 b	Itm. 1 but seck I toke for my howse & 1 but was taken to prize, montith £8	£8

71(L)   **anno 1539**

John Sprat, John Russell and Ris up Yevan maryners dewlling at the Mummylls in Wales owith the 12th day of December £6 which they owe for a ton of iren to be paide at Whitssontide next as it aperith by theyr bill   £6

---

[1] Blank in MS.
[2] There is no credit entry for Tyndall.
[3] Blank in MS.

71(L) contd.   anno 1539

Lycens for le*ther* owith the 19 daye of Jenyver £31 5s for so myche I send
by Thomas Sawll to Antonyo de Manuelo Spanyart for the payement of 50
dickar le*ther* at 12s 6d *the* dickar, avyding of the which lycens he must send
by the seid Sawll or the first o*ther* messeng*er*   £31   5s
Itm. the same day 17s spent by Giles to go for the same   17s
Itm. 24s 8d goten by this acowmpt as it a*peri*the to gaynes in credito fo. 92   £1   4s 8d

                                                                                S. £33   6s 8d

anno 1540

Lycens for wheat owith the the[1] 12 day of December £25 paide for the lycens of
won C qr. to Alvaro de Astodillo Spanyard at 5s the quarter for horse hire   £25
& Hamond*es* cost*es* 2 tymes to London 30s 4d   £1 10s 4d
for £3 6s 8d to Stanebanck for a gowne of damaskyn   £3   6s 8d
for a Cordavan skuyn to the *ser*cher of Glocester 4s   4s
for £3 pd. the 4 day of February to Tristan & his fellow   £3
for 7 doze*n* ½ matt*es* to J*oh*n Methwey 30s   £1 10s
for 2 bulkhed*es* 4s & fagott*es* 2s 8d   6s 8d
for costom & the cocquett 17s 4d   17s 4d

                                                                                    £35 15s

71(R)   anno 1540

John Sprat & his fellows p*er* contra be dewe to have the
28 day of July £6 which my wif r. of the*m* & d'd the*m*
theyr bill   £6

anno 1539

lycens p*er* contra is dewe to have the 26 day of February
£18 13s 4d that is for 20 dicker entryd in the Trynte for &
M*ari*a Conception for my seallf, 4 dicker for M*as*ter
Robert Poole of Glocester & 4 dicker for Edward Pryn,
mon*tith* 28 dicker at 13s 4d the dicker   £18 13s 4d
Itm. £10 for 15 dicker entryd in the Trynte the monthe of
June 1540 for me, Thom*as* Smythe & Giles White   £10
Itm. sold to Franc*es* Codryng*ton* 7 dicker for 7 m*ar*kes   £4 13s 4d

                                                                            S. £33   6s 8d

anno 1540

lysence p*er* contra is dewe to have the 10 of February
£20 8s for so myche I make 51 weyes laden in the Trynte
for my accowmpt debitor of   £20   8s
Itm. the same dey £14 9s 10d that is for so myche I do
make Frances Codryngto*n* debitor fo. 60 for the lycens
costo*m* & cost*es* of 30 weyes wheat in the Trynte at 8s p*er*
wey & of 15s 2d for Hamond*es* cost*es* & of 33s 4d to
Stonebagg & of 16d for 4 matt*es* d'd to the Harry   £14   9s 10d
Itm. 17s 2d for the lycens & cost*es* of 3 weyes which the
m*aster* lade at   [2]   the wey as it may apere to hym
in debito fo. 65   17s 2d

                                                                                    £35 15s

---
[1] *Smythe repeats* the.
[2] *Blank in MS.*

anno 1539

William Smothing of Harvarteste owith the 13 day of Decembrr £11 13s 4d
that is for 2 butes of seck at £3 10s the butt & 1 ton Gascon wyne price
£4 13s 4d payable at all tymes. It is laden in Sparkes bote | £11 | 13s | 4d
Itm. the 23 day of February £11 6s 8d that is £4 6s 8d for 1 ton Gascon
wyne & £7 for 2 buttes seck payable at all tymes | £11 | 6s | 8d
Itm. the 16 day of November £4 13s 4d that is for 1 ton Gascon wyne sold
& delyverd to hym | £4 | 14s | 4d
Itm. the 14 day of Jenyver £11 6s 8d that is 7 markes for 1 ton of Gascon
wyne & 20 nobles for 2 buttes of seck sent hym in John Sparkes bote | £11 | 6s | 8d
Itm. the 4 day of February £11 6s 8d that is £4 13s 4d for 1 ton Gascon
wyne & £6 13s 4d for 2 buttes of seck to pay at all tymes requyrid | £11 | 6s | 8d
1541 Itm. the 3 day of December anno 1541 £13 6s 8d that is for 1 ton
Gascon wyne at £5 6s 8d per ton & 2 buttes of seck. I sey 2 pipes swete wyne
at eich £4, montith | £13 | 6s | 8d
Itm. the 3 day of February £7 6s 8d for 2 buttes seck | £7 | 6s | 8d
1542 Itm. the 3 day of July 1542 £7 6s 8d that is ffor 2 buttes of seck sent
to hym by John Spark at 11 nobles the butt | £7 | 6s | 8d
Itm. the 28 day of July £7 6s 8d for 1 buttes seck | £3 | 13s | 4d
Itm. the 20 day of February £16 for 2 buttes seck & 2 pipes bastard at eich
£4 | £16
1543 Itm. the 3 of Aprell 1543 £8 which is for 2 buttes of seck solld &
delyverd to hym | £8
Itm. the first day of September £8 13s 4d & is for 2 buttes seck lode & sent
to hym in John Sparkes bote | £8 | 13s | 4d

S. £32 13s 4d

anno 1539

Jamys Nycolls of Allveley troweman owith the 25 day of February £7 11s
which is for 1 ton 2 C 1 qr. of the better Rendry iren after 19 nobles the ton
to be pd. by his bill at Seynt Jamystide next | £7 | | 11d

anno 1539

William Smothing per contra is dewe to have the 22 daye
of February £4 6s 8d & 6s 8d I abatyd to hym & it is for
the ton Gascon wyne per contra laden the 13 daye of
December in Sparkes bote, amontith the hole £4 13s 4d | £4 | 13s | 4d
1540 Itm. the 8 day of June 1540 r. of hym in Bristo
£14 | £14
Itm. the 15 day of November of hym £4 6s 8d | £4 | 6s | 8d
Itm. the 3 day of February r. of hym at Bristowe
£4 13s 4d for the full payement of 1 ton Gascon wyne sold
to hym the 16 day of November as per contra maye apere | £4 | 13s | 4d
1541 Itm. the 27 day of July 1541 r. of Jamys Webster | £13 | 6s | 8d
Itm. the 25 day of October 1541 r. from hym by Jamys
Webster £5 | £5
Itm. the 18 day of November 1541 r. of hym £4 6s 8d | £4 | 6s | 8d
Itm. the 3 day of February £10 r. of hym in 30 dozens
calve skuyns & 18s 8d in monny | £10
Itm. the 24 day of July 1542 r. of hym at Bristow £10 | £10
Itm. the 13 day of November r. by Jamys Webster £6 | £6
Itm. the 2d day of February r. of hym at Bristowe in redy
monney £4 | £4
Itm. the 19 day of February r. of hym 33s 4d | £1 | 13s | 4d
Itm. the 3 of Aprell 1543 my wif r. of hym £8 | £8
Itm. the 23 day of Aprell r. from hym by Nycolas Kelly
8 markes montith | £5 | 6s | 8d
Itm. the 24 of July r. of hym at Bristowe £8 | £8
Itm. £4 6s 8d which John Spark pay to me for hym for on
of the 2 later buttes of seck per contra as may apere fo. 186 | £4 | 6s | 8d
Itm. the 11 day of December 1543 r. by Jamys Webster £5 | £5

72(R) contd.

Itm. the 4 day of February r. of hym at Bristowe 40s	£2		
	S. £32	13s	4d

anno 1541

Jamys Nycolls per contra is dewe to have the 3 daye of February £4 11d which he pd. me at Bristowe	£4	11d
Itm. the 8 day of February r. £3 & d'd to hym his byll	£3	

73(L)   anno 1539

John Wyllys of Bristowe vyntnar owith the 18 day of December £10 which is for 2 ton Gascon wyne I sold to hym to be paide at all tymes	£10		
anno 1540 Itm. the 5th day of Aprell anno 1540 £4 that is for a pipe of ossey to be paide at Seynt Jamistide next	£4		
1541 Itm. the 6 day of July 1541 £3 6s 8d which is for the rest of 1 h'd taynt & 1 h'd claret wyne which I sold & d'd to hym to be paide at all tymes as in my shop boke may apere	£3	6s	8d
1542 Itm. the 6 of May 1542 £3 13s 4d for 1 pipe of bastard to be paide at all tymes	£3	13s	4d
1543 Itm. the 15 day of February anno 1543 £4 13s 4d[1] which is for a pipe of bastard d'd to his wif. I sey 11 nobles	£3	13s	4d
Itm. the 11 day of Marche £44 & is for 10 buttes of seck & 2 pipes bastard at 11 nobles the pece	£44		
1544 Itm. the 14 of June for 3 ton Gascon wyne £24	£24		
Itm. the 16 daye of July anno 1544 £20 & is for so myche redy money delyverd to hym & William Tyndall, Chamberlaynes of Bristowe, in lone for to hellp pay to the Kyng for the landes that the Lqrd Lisle had in Bristowe & thereabowt, which monney I lent at the request & desyre of Master Pacy then mayer & of Master Coke & others of the mayers.[2] The which money must be pd. at Midsomer next commyng as it may apere by an obligacion wherein the seid John Wylly & his successors chamberleynes stand bownd	£20		
Itm. the 28 day of February 1544 £16 & is for 4 buttes seck at £4 the but	£16		
Itm. the 12 day of Marche £8 which is for 1 ton of Gascon wyne, the 14 of Marche 1 ton 3 h'd Gascon wyne montith £14, montith 11 h'd at £8 the ton, montith	£22		
1545 Itm. the 28 day of Marche 1545 for 2 buttes of Tyndalls & 6 buttes seck of myne at £4 the butt, montith £32	£32		
Itm. £56 & is for 14 buttes seck at eich £4 to be paide at all tymes requyrid which buttes war d'd the 15 day, the 20 day, the 23 day & 28 day of Jenyver as by my shop boke may apere	£56		
Itm. the 24 day of Marche £8 for 2 buttes of seck	£8		
Itm. the 24 of Aprell 1546 £9 that is £5 for a but of hullock & £4 for a but of seck to be pd. at all tymes	£9		
Itm. for a pipe of muscadell rackyd 7 markes d'd the 25 day of September 1546 it lackyd of full 3 gallons 3 quartes	£4	13s	4d
Itm. the 29 day of Jenyver for 4 loves of shewgar weying 46 li. ½ at 10d the li. montith 38s 9d	£1	18s	9d

73(R)   anno 1539

John Wylles per contra is dewe to have the 16 daye of Marche £9 6s 8d for so myche redy money r. of hym & more he abatyd of the price of the wyne per contra 13s 4d, so amontith all £10	£10
Itm. the 1 day of September 1540 r. 45s & 35s was rebatyd becawse the pipe ossey per contra was corruptyd, so montith the hole £4	£4

---

[1] 13s 4d is inserted above the line.
[2] The former mayors who formed a close-knit group.

73(R) contd.

Itm. the 9 day of Augost £3 5s r. in redy money & 20d I rebatyd in *the* price of a h'd Gascon wyne mo*ntith*	£3	6s	8d
Itm. the 5 day of August 1542 r. of hy*m* 4 m*arkes*	£2	13s	4d
Itm. the same day 20s which I do geve hym toward the dressing of the kaye of Bristowe	£1		
Itm. the last day of July a*nno* 1544 r. £31 13s 4d	£31	13s	4d
Itm. the 4 day of October r. of hym £40	£40		

1545

Itm. the 25 day of Ap*r*ell 1545 ne*x*t my s*a*rva*n*t Henry r. of hym £20	£20		
Itm. the 10 day of June £16 which W*illia*m Tyndall r. of hym for his brother Robert Tyndall	£16		
Itm. the 5 daye of August 1545 r. of hym £34	£34		
Itm. the 3 day of Marche a*nno* 1545 my wif r. of hym £20	£20		
Itm. the 14 day of June Robert Leight r. of hym £20	£20		
Itm. the 11 day of Septemb*e*r 1546 r. of hym in redy mon*n*ey £33	£33		
Itm. the ¹ day of November 1546 r. at London of M*aster* Whit drap*er* & allderman £20 in payment of the £20 that I lent Jo*h*n Wyllis the 16 day of July 1544	£20		
Itm. r. of her for the 4 loves shew*ga*r *per* contra	£1	18s	9d

74(L)   anno 1539

John Wellsche m*a*rchant of Bristowe o*w*ith the 20 day of Decemb*e*r £5 which is for on ton of Gascon wyne which I sold to hym to be paide at all tymes	£5		
Itm. the 26 day of November 50s for 2 h'd Gascon wyne sold to hym to be paide at all tymes requyrid	£2	10s	
1541 Itm. the 24 day of October 1541 £24 which is for 2 to*n* wull oyle sold & d'd to hym at £12 *the* ton, to be pd. in Andaluz*i*a the next som*e*r viage or ells in Bristowe at Seynt Jamistide next com*m*yng	£24		
Itm. the 1 day of Decemb*e*r £6 5s which is for the freight of 5 tons bastard*es* in the Trynte at 25s *per* ton, to paye ½ in hand & ½ at thend of 3 monthes next com*m*yng	£6	5s	
1542 Itm. the 19 day of June 1542 £11 which is for 3 butt*es* of seck which my wif sold & d'd to hym at 11 nobles the butt	£11		
Itm. the 30 day of Octob*e*r £4 6s 8d which is ffor a butt of mawmessey ssold & d'd to hym, to be paide at myddell Lent next com*m*yng	£4	6s	8d
Itm. the 17 daye of February £4 6s 8d to be pd. at Seynt Jamistide next, which is for a but of mawmesey which he had of me	£4	6s	8d
1543 Itm. the 4 of February 1543 £6 13s 4d & is for 1 ton of S. S. iren after £6 13s 4d the ton, d'd for hym by his wiff*es* byddyng to Jamys Dison northenma*n* to be paide at Seynt Jamistide next	£6	13s	4d
Itm. the 28 of June 1544 for 1 h'd Gascon wyn*e* 40s	£2		
S.	£66	1s	8d

anno 1540

Willi*a*m Jones of Carlion gentleman owith the 16 day of October £11 for so myche pd. for 5 weyes wheat which was laden for hym in his ship the Trynte	£11		

anno 1544

John Wellsche of Bristowe m*a*rchant o*with* the 26 day of Jenyver £12 6s 8d & is for 2 butt*es* seck of Tyndalls at eich £4 & 1 pipe of bastard of myne at 13 nobles	£12	6s	8d

¹*Blank in MS.*

74(L) contd.

1545 Itm. the 2d day of Aprell 1545 13 nobles for 1 pipe bastard	£4	6s	8d
1546 Itm. the 30 day of March 1546 27s 6d	£1	7s	6d
Itm. the 26 day of May £4 for the rest of 5 h'd claret wyne. More he ow*ith* the 18 day of June for ~~the rest of~~ 2 h'd wyne which W*illiam* Abyam of Bathe had, to be paide at Seynt Jamistide next past, mo*ntith*	~~£6~~		
Itm. the 30 day of Marche a*nno* 1547 £6 & is for 1 ton Gascon wyne solld & d'd to hym to be pd. at all tymes requyrid	£6		

74(R) anno 1540

John Wellsche p*er* contra is dewe to have the monthe of November £5 that is for 20 du*catt*s which Giles Whit r. for me in Andaluzia of his s*a*rvant mo*ntith*	£5		
1541 Itm. the 2d day of Julye 1541 £2 6s 8d r. of J*ohn* Wellsshe & 3s 4d I abate to hym in the price toward a kerchow clo*the* for his wif	£2	10s	
Itm. the 24 day of Jenyver £3 2s 6d r. for ½ the freight of the 5 tons bastard p*er* contra	£3	2s	6d
Itm. the 27 day of Maye 1542 £3 2s. 6d for so myche reddy mon*n*ey r. of his wif & so she breke her husband*es* seale fro*m* the charterp*a*rtie	£3	2s	6d
Itm. the 26 day of July 1542 r. of hym £12	£12		
Itm. the 8 day of Augost £10 10s which is ffor 1 to*n* of wull oyle which he sold & delyv*er*d to me at *the* same pr*i*ce	£10	10s	
Itm. the 29 day of Augost r. of his wif in redy mon*n*y 20s & for 6 berebutt*es* 10s, mo*ntith*	£1	10s	
Itm. the 9 day of February a*nno* 1542 r. of his wif £11	£11		
Itm. the 30 day of July 1543 r. of his wif £4 6s 8d	£4	6s	8d
Itm. the 6 day of November r. of his wif in mon*n*ey, seck, resyns & won berebutt £4 6s 8d	£4	6s	8d
Itm. r. the 14 day of August 1544 of his wif 40s	£2		
Itm. the 27 day of September 1544 his wif pd. to my wif	£6	13s	4d
S.	£66	1s	8d

anno 1540

Will*ia*m Jones of Carlion in Wales gentleman is dewe to have the 11 day of September £3 2s 6d which is for the rest & full payement of the hallf freight of 6 to*n* ton[1] 1 h'd oyle *that* I had fro*m* Andaluzia in his ship the Trynte this reck wyntaige & for the other hallf freight I pd. *this* present day £3 2s 6d to his p*u*rser Jo*h*n Apowell so rest	£3	2s	6d
Itm. the [2] day of [2] £7 17s 6d	£7	17s	6d
			[2]

anno 1545

John Wellsche p*er* contra is dewe to have £8 for so myche money which my wif r. of his wif at 3 tymes	£8		
Itm. more my wif r. of his wif at 2 tymes	£4		
Itm. the 1 day of February a*nno* 1545 my wif r. of his wif	£4	13s	4d
Itm. the 26 day of Maye 1546 r. by my wif	£1	7s	6d
Itm. r. of his wif at dyvers tymes £8	£8		
Itm. the 30 day of July a*nno* 1547 r. of M*a*rgery Wellsshe £5 10s & 10s which Lett r. before of her in gold for to send unto my sons at Oxford	£6		

---

[1] *Smythe repeats* 'ton'.
[2] *Blank in MS.*

75(L)   anno 1539

John Williams of Bristowe skuynnar owith the 22 daye of December £18 13s 4d that is ffor 3 ton iren which I sold & d'd to hym to be paide the on hallf at Seynt Jamystide next commyng and the other hallf at Mighellmas next after that, as by his obligacion made by John Sare maye apere	£18	13s	4d
Itm. the 19 day of Jenyver 1540 £15 6s 8d which is for the rest of 3 ton iren & 1 butt of seck as in my shop boke may apere, for to pay £7 13s 4d at Mighellmas next commyng & £7 13s 4d at Cristmas next after that following	£15	6s	8d
Itm. the 11th day of September anno 1541 £18 13s 4d that is for won ton iren of S. S. and 2 ton of the Rendre iren, montith, to pay 6s 8d in hand, £9 3s 4d at Mighellmas in anno 1542 & £9 3s 4d at Cristmas next after that, as it may apere by his obligacion	£18	13s	4d
1542 Itm. the 25 day of September anno 1542 £19 16s that is for 2 ton & 3 qr. of a C of S. S. iren at 20 nobles the ton & 1 ton less 2 li. of the better Rendry iren at 19 nobles the ton, montith all 3 ton, ½ a C 26 li. which I solld & delyverd to hym, to pay hallf at Mighellmas com twellmonthes & thother hallf at Cristmas next after that, as it may apere by his obligacions	£19	16s	

Memorandum I had the seide John Wylliams in Newgat & for to have hym owt of prison this men followyng war bownd to pay the somms followyng, as by theyr severall obligacions may apere

William Pottell of Bristowe ropemaker	£1	6s	8d
Phillip Griffithe	£1		
Robert Guyttons	£2	13s	4d
William Serche	£1	6s	8d
Nicholas Shee	£1	6s	8d
Thomas Dekyn	£1		
Henry Sandyfford	£1	6s	8d
Philip Dawkyn dyar	£1		
Robert Newborn	£1	6s	8d
John Sessyll	£1		

75(R)   anno 1540

John Williams per contra is dewe to have the 4th day of Agost £5 which he paid to my wif	£5		
Itm. the 29 day of September r. 16 angells	£6		
Itm. the 17 day of November r. of hym £4 10s	£4	10s	
Itm. the 21 day of December he pd. to my wif	£3	3s	4d
1541 Itm. r. the 1 day of September 1541 35 angelotes ½, 6 crownes of 5s, 1 doble ducatt & 1 grote montith £15 6s 7d & 1d that I rebatyd, montith the hole	£15	6s	8d
Itm. the 12 day of October r. 6s 8d		6s	8d
Itm. the 25 day of September 1542 r. of John Williams in my hows in gold £18 6s 8d	£18	6s	8d
Itm. the last day of Jenyver 1543 r. of John Skynar 22s 8d & made aquyttance of 4 nobles	£1	2s	8d
Itm. the 10 day of Jenyver 1544 r. of John Wyllams 20s	£1		
Itm. the 20 day of Aprell 1546 r. of hym 20s	£1		
Itm. the 13 of October 1547 r. of Thomas Pacy 10s		10s	

75(A)   A small loose sheet between fo. 75(L) and fo. 75(R)

Memorandum that the 1 day of October 1543 & anno Regni Regis Henrici VIII 35, Richard Lane of Bristowe bruer is bownd by obligacion to pay unto me for John Wylliams skuynnar £6 13s 4d, to be pd. 26s 8d at Cristmas next & so to pay at every Cristmas ymmedyattly folowyng 26s 8d till the hole £6 13s 4d be fully paide.

Memorandum the same day & yere the seid John Wylliams & Tristan Lecknor serchor be bownd by obligacion in 20 markes to pay thereof at Mighellmas next 4 markes & so at every Mighellmas ymmedyattly followyng to pay 4 markes tyll the hole 20 markes be fully paide.

76(L)   anno 1539

Jamys Rogers of Coventry marchant owithe the 8th day of Jenyver £9 to be paide at all tymes, whiche is for the rest of 3 buttes seck, a pipe taynt & a ton Gascon wyne as it may apere by my shop boke & by a cowmpt of his owne hand	£9
Itm. the 4 day of February £8 for 2 pipes ossey d'd for hym to his sarvant payable at all tymes	£8
1541 Itm. the 29 day of November 1541 £38 which is for 3 ton of Gascon wyne at £5 the ton and 6 ~~buttes~~ pipes of muscadell at £3 16s 8d the pipe, to pay £8 at Twellstide next & £15 at Easter next after *that* & £15 at Seynt Jamystide next after *that* followyng	£38
1544 Itm. the 21 day of Aprell 1544 £40 & is for the rest of 10 ton 1 qr. 25 li. iren, to pay £20 at Mighellmas next commyng & £20 at Cristmas next after that	£40

anno 1544

Itm. the 29 day of February £8 & is for 1 butt of seck at £4 & 2 h'd taynt at eich 40s	£8		
Itm. the 14 day of the same £7 16s 8d & is for 2 pipes of bastard	£7	16s	8d
Itm. the 25 day of Jenyver £10 which is for the rest of 5 buttes seck which he bowght of me at £4 the but, which £10 he promises to pay at all tymes	£10		
1546 Itm. the last day of Aprell 1546 £22 10s & is for 3 pipes wull oyle, to pay hallf at Seynt Jamystide next & the other hallf at Bartyllmewtide tide[1] next after, mon*tith*	£22	10s	
Itm. the 18 day of Jenyver £38 6s 8d & is for ~~8~~ 10 buttes seck sold to his son Harry in his name at 11 nobles 40d the butt to pay at all tymes	£38	6s	8d
Itm. the 5 day of Marche sold & d'd to his seid son Henry Rogers 4 buttes seck at eiche 11 nobles 40d	£15	6s	8d
Itm. the 20 day of Aprell 1547 sold & delyverd to his son Henry Rogers 5 tons Gascon wyne at £5 10s per ton mon*tith*	£27	10s	
Jamys Rogers ow*ith* the 6th day of August anno 1549 £11 6s 8d & is for 17 C grene wood sent to hym in Richard Barns trowe in 2 buttes at 13s 4d the C ~~& for~~	£11	6s	8d
Itm. for the 2 caskes 2s 8d		2s	8d
Itm. the 17 day of September £40 & is for 60 C grene wood delyverd for hym to his sarvant Jamys Myddelltton at 13s 4d per C to pay £20 in hand & the rest at Easter next com*myng*	£40		
Itm. the 2 de & 4th day of Jenyver d'd for hym to his son Henry Rogers 44 C 1 qr. 13 li. ½ wood at 13s 4d per C, mon*tith*	£29	11s	8d
Itm. ffor 4 buttes at 20d the butt		6s	8d

76(R)   anno 1540

Jamys Rogers per contra is dewe to have the 24 day of July £10 r. by a neighbur of his	£10		
Itm. the 15 day of November r. at Bristow of hym seallf £7	£7		
Itm. the [2] day of Jenyver 1541 r. of his sarvant £8	£8		
Itm. the 17 day of Aprell 1542 r. of his sarvant Dyton	£15		
Itm. the 27 day of July r. of his sarvant Richart Vere	£15		
Itm. the 6 daye of October 1544 r. of Cristofor Dyton £20	£20		
Itm. the 27 of Jenyver 1544 my wif r. of hym £20	£20		
Itm. the 14 day of February 1544 my wif r.		13s	4d
Itm. £15 r. of hym the 20 day of July 1545	£15		
Itm. 3s 4d which I do rebate hym		3s	4d
Itm. the 29 day of Aprell 1546 r. of his sarvant Cristofor Dyton £10 in redy money	£10		
Itm. r. of his sarvant & of his son	£22	10s	
Itm. the 20 day of Aprell 1547 r. of his son Henry Rogers in part of payment of the seckes per contra	£20		
Itm. the same day r. in part of payment of the Gascon wynes per contra £21	£21		

---

[1] *Smythe repeats* tide.
[2] *Blank in MS.*

76(R) contd.

Itm. the 16 day of June r. by Thomas Harrys of Bristowe marchant £20	£20	
Itm. more r. £20 & 40d I gave in the cowmpt, mo*ntith* all	£20 3s 4d	
Itm. the 17 of Septemb*er* 1549 r. of his s*a*rvant Jamys Myddellton £20	£20	
Itm. the 22 of February r. at Bristowe of M*aster* Rogers £20 & more for 6 cask*es* 9s 4d	£20 9s 4d	
Itm. the last day of Apr*e*ll a*nn*o 1550 r. by the hand*es* of his son Henry Rogers £11 6s 8d	£11 6s 8d	
passed this cownt the 2 de day of July 1550 to my newe boke in fo. 3		

77(L)   **anno 1539**

John Hamonde marchant of Bridgewater owithe the 9th day of Jenyver £3 13s 4d for a butt of seck which I sent hym with Grawng*er*, to be pd. at all tymes	£3 13s 4d	
Itm. the 2d day of June 1540 £3 13s 4d that is ffor a but seck sent in David Luyes bote of Bristowe	£3 6s 8d	
1541 Itm. the 29 day of July 1541 £5 15s that is for a p*ip*e of oyle sent in Thomas Davys bote, to be paide at all tymes	£5 15s	
Itm. the 3 day of February £3 13s 4d for 1 butt of seck sold to hym to be pd. at Seynt Jamistide next com*m*yng	£3 13s 4d	
1542 Itm. the 28 day of July 1542 £6 which is for 1 pipe of wull oyle sent in Luyes up Richard*es* bote, to pay at all tymes	£6	
Itm. the 19 day of February £4 for a but of seck sent hym in Frees bote	£4	
1543 Itm. the 27 of July a*n*no 1543 £4 6s 8d & is for a butt of seck sent hym in Nycolas Lanesmans bote	£4 6s 8d	
Itm. the 28 day of February £4 6d which is for a butt of seck at £4 & 6d for cost*es*	£4 6d	
Itm. the 26 day of M*a*rche for a but seck 11 nobles & for the cost*es* 6d mo*ntith*	£3 13s 10d	
1544 Itm. the 28 day of July a*n*no 1544 £7 6s 8d & is for 2 butt*es* seck to be paide at all tymes	£7 6s 8d	
Itm. the last day of Jenyver £12 6s 8d & is for 2 butt*es* seck at eche £4 & 1 pipe of bastard at £4 6s 8d	£12 6s 8d	
Itm. the 30 day of M*a*rche 1546 £4 for a butt of seck to be pd. at all tymes	£4	
1547 Itm. the 26 day of September 1547 for a butt seck £4	£4	
Itm. the 26 of Novemb*er* for a p*ip*e bastard 13 nobles	£4 6s 8d	

anno 1540

Will*ia*m Peter of Bruto*n* smythe owithe the 10 day of June £6 10s that is for 1 to*n* iren of S. S. to be paide at all tymes. Jo*h*n Yerbery of Bruto*n* clothiar is shewerty	£6 10s	
Itm. £6 13s 4d that is for 1 ton of S. S. iren solld & delyverd to hym at 2 tymes, that is to sey the 15 & 16 day of February, as in my shop boke may apere. Jo*h*n Yerbery of Bruto*n* clothiar is shewerty to se it payde at al tyms requ*i*rid	£6 13s 4d	
Itm. the 18 day of May 1546 for a p*ip*e of S. S. iren £3 6s 8d to be paide at Mighellmas next. Jo*h*n Yerbery is his shewerty	£3 6s 8d	
Itm. the 20 day of June a*n*no 1547 £7 10s & is for 1 ton of iren of S. S. to pay £3 15s at Mighellmas next com*m*yng and £3 15s at Allhaloutide next after that	~~£7 10s~~	

77(R)   **anno 1540**

John Hamond p*er* contra is dewe to have the 14 daye of Aprell £3 13s 4d r. at Bristowe of his wif	£3 13s 4d	
Itm. r. the [1] day of [1] £3 6s 8d	£3 6s 8d	
Itm. the 3 day of February a*n*no 1541 r. of hym at Bristowe £5 15s in redy mo*n*ney	£5 15s	

---

[1] *Blank in MS.*

77(R) contd.

Itm. the 24 daye of July r. from hym by the handes of Geffrey Shorcom £3 13s 4d	£3	13s	4d
Itm. the last day of Jenyver anno 1542 r. of his son John £6	£6		
Itm. the 24 of July 1543 r. by his son in the lawe £4	£4		
Itm. the 13 of February r. of John Hamon his son	£4	6s	8d
Itm. r. by Tyndall from John Hamon the 24 of July 1544 £7 13s 4d	£7	13s	4d
Itm. 16d which he wyll not allowe for the costes		1s	4d
Itm. the 31 of Jenyver 1544 my wif r. of hym by the handes of John Pollton £7 6s 8d	£7	6s	8d
Itm. the [1] day of August 1545 r. of William Northe for Hamons acowmpt £10 6s 8d & more r. of Hew Hamon 20d in money & 1 h'd Gascon wyne in 38s 4d, montith all £12 6s 8d	£12	6s	8d
Itm. £4 which his son Hewgh pd. me in acowmpt	£4		
Itm. r. £7 6s 8d	£7	6s	8d

anno 1540

William Peter per contra is dewe to have the 15 day of February £6 10s r. of John Yerbery in acowmpt betwen hym & me	£6	10s	
Itm. the 27 day of July 1541 £6 10s which John Yerbery pay for hym, to Yerbery in debito fo. 125	£6	10s	
Itm. the 29 day of July 1546 £3 6s 8d for so myche John Yerbery pay to me for hym as it may apper 233	£3	6s	8d

78(L)   **anno 1539**

Richard Packer of Barcley tanner owith the 10 day of Jenyver £25 13s 4d which I paide to hym in redy monny for the hole & ffull payement of 11 dicker lether cow & stere at 7 nobles the dickar, to be d'd at all tymes as by his bill may apere	£25	13s	4d

anno 1540

Thomas Heynes of Bristowe berebruar owith the 14 day of June £6 that is for a ton of iren payable at Myghellmas next commyng		£6		
Itm. the 4th day of February £6 that is for 1 ton of iren sold & d'd to hym to be pd. at all tymes requyrid		£6		
Itm. the 15 day of September 1541 pd. to hym in redy money 51s 6d		£2	11s	6d
Itm. the 13 day of October £6 that is for a pipe of wull oyle to be paide at Owr Lady Day in Lent next commyng		£6		
1542 Itm. 12d which I pay in redy monney the 8 of May 1542			1s	
Itm. the 10th day of Maye 1542 £24 2d½ that is for 4 tons 4 li. iren at £6 the ton, to be pd. at Candellmas next or ells before if I take bere	£24		2d	ob
Itm. the 8 day of December 7s 6d which he allowe for 2 buttes of bere which I retornyd to hym after my ship came from Spaygne			7s	6d
Itm. the 5 day of December anno 1543 £13 7s 8d which is for 2 tons [1] li. of S.S. iren solld & delyverd to hym to be paide at all tymes requyrid		£13	7s	8d
Itm. the 10th day of Jenyver pd. to his wif in reddy monney £8 3s 3d½ [2]		£8	3s	3d½

78(R)   **anno 1539**

Richard Packar per contra is dewe to have the 7 day of Marche £25 13s 4d for 11 dicker lethir cow & stere r. of hym at the prises mencyoned per contra	£25	13s	4d

---

[1] Blank in MS.
[2] All Thomas Heynes' account is crossed through.

78(R) contd.

anno 1540

Thomas Heynes per contra is dewe to have the 16 day of
February £5 7s that is for 14 buttes & 1 barell a beare r. of
hym for my ship at 7s 6d the butt, montith £5 7s
Itm. the 15 day of September 1541 he browght by
reckenyng that he had d'd at soundry tymes for my ship
the Trynte 20 buttes & 1 h'd bere at 9s the butt, montith £9 4s 6d
Itm. the 8 day of ~~Jenyver~~ Maye 1542 for 15 butes, I sey 15
buttes 1 kynterkyn at 8s the butt £6 1s
Itm. the monthe of June 1542 for 13 buttes bere at 7s 6d
the butt for my ship the Trynte provisyon to Biscaye £4 17s 6d
Itm. the same viage 3 barells 5s 3d
Itm. the monthes of September & October for 19 buttes 1
h'd at 8s the butt, montith £7 16s, & I sett this itm. apon
my boke the 8 day of December 1542 £7 16s
Itm. he reckenyd with me the 19 of November 1543 that
I owe hym for beare r. of hym for my ship & my hows
that is for 20 buttes, 11 barells, 2 kynterkyns £10 5s, the
which is putt in the backside of his obligacion £10 5s
Itm. the 10 day of Jenyver 1543 r. 16 buttes bere at 9s the
butt & 4 pipes bere at 8s the pipe & 5 barells bere at 2s 3d
the barell montith £9 7s 3d[1]
This cownt is determynyd so the effect that Thomas
Haynes owith me yow shall fynde in fo. 262

79(L)

anno 1539

Seckes for my owne acownt owith the monthes of November, of
53 December & Jenyver, that is to sey 10 buttes r. owt of the Mary
Bride, 12 buttes owt of the Mary Cristofor, 28 buttes whereof on
butt was left for freight owt of the John Baptist & 4 buttes owt of the
Savior, which owith for freight 25s per ton, for costom 43 buttes at
18d the butt, ffor hallyng & stowyng of every ton 4d, for the first
penny 133064 M. & for Giles costes 5250 M. for averes
in the Mary Bride 3s 10d per ton & in the Mary Cristofor 4s 4d per
ton & in the John Baptist 4s 4d ob per ton & in the Savior 3s 6d per
ton, amontith the hole in sterlyng monny £133 10s 3d £133 10s 3d
Itm. £3 for 1 pipe of bastard for to dreass them £3
10 Itm. the monthe of February r. owt of the Kateryn of Barstable 9
buttes seck & 1 but hullock that cost clere abord 24553 M., for
freight 21s per ton, averes 4s 5d per ton, for costom 3s per ton, for
hallyng & stowyng 4d per ton, montith all £23 11s 1d £23 11s 1d
Itm. the 10 day of Augost 28s 8d which is for so myche rebatyd in
my prices to serteyne of my customers £1 8s 8d
Itm. the same day £26 goten by this acowmpt as it aperith to gaynes
in credito fo. 92 £26

£187 10s

anno 1543

Richard Androws of Banwell smythe owith the 24 day of July
41s 8d which is for the rest of a pipe 2 li. of iren solld & d'd to hym
to be paide at Cristmas next commyng. Richard Narcote of Shepton
Mallard is his shewerty for the same £2 1s 8d

79(R)

anno 1539

Seckes hereagaynst be dewe to have the 12 day of
November
1 £3 10s for 1 but sold to John Rokesby fo. 10 £3 10s
Itm. the 17 day of November £6 13s 4d r. of

---

[1] All Thomas Heynes' account is crossed through.

79(R) contd.

2	John Luys wif for 2 bute*s* seck at 5 marck*es* the butt	£6 13s	4d
1	Itm. the 19 day of November £3 10s for a butt of seck sold to Alexander Bosgrove fo. 68	£3 10s	
1	Itm. the 26 day of November £3 10s r. of W*illia*m Smothing for a butt of seck	£3 10s	
1	Itm. the same day £3 13s 4d for a but seck sold to J*oh*n Gibs of Bridgewater fo. 37	£3 13s	4d
1	Itm. the same day £3 13s 4d for 1 but to R. Bishop, fo. 14	£3 13s	4d
1	Itm. the 10 of Dece*m*ber £3 10s for 1 but to John Rokesby fo. 10	£3 10s	
2	Itm. the 13 of Dece*m*ber £7 for 2 bute*s* to W*illiam* Smothing fo. 72	£7	
1	Itm. the 16 of December £3 6s 8d for 1 but to R. Du*r*ban, 58	£3 6s	8d
1	Itm. the 19 of December £3 10s for 1 butt to J*oh*n Luys 34	£3 10s	
2	Itm. the same day £7 for 2 butt*es* to Thom*as* Cote*s* fo. 17	£7	
3	Itm. the 22 day of December £10 13s 4d for 3 bute*s* to J. Skuyn*n*ar	£10 13s	4d
1	Itm. the 3 day of Jenyver £3 10s for 1 but to R. Durban 58	£3 10s	
2	Itm. the 5 day of Jenyver £7 for 2 buttes to W*illia*m Northe fo. 24	£7	
3	Itm. the 8 of Jenyver £10 10s for 3 bute*s* to J. Rogers 76	£10 10s	
1	Itm. the 9 of Jenyver £3 10s for 1 but to J*oh*n Hamond	£3 10s	
2	Itm. the 17 day of Jenyve*r* £7 for 2 butt*es* to J. Rokesby fo. 10	£7	
1	Itm. the 21 day of Jenyver £3 13s 4d for 1 but to T. Tu*r*bot 23	£3 13s	4d
1	Itm. the same day £3 13s 4d for 1 butt seck to R. Bisshop 14	£3 13s	4d
1	Itm. the 4 day of February £3 10s for a but to J*oh*n Pignall 93	£3 10s	
1	Itm. the same day £3 10s for a but to Thomas Dyngley fo. 94	£3 10s	
3	Itm. the 6 day of February £10 6s 8d r. for 3 bute*s* of J*oh*n Luye*s* wif	£10 6s	8d
2	Itm. the same day £7 for 2 butt*es* to Thomas Cote*s* fo. 17	£7	
1	Itm. the 14 day of February £3 10s for a but to J*oh*n Rokesby fo. 10	£3 10s	
2	Itm. the 23 day of February £7 for 2 butt*es* to W*illia*m Smothing 72	£7	
1	Itm. £3 6s 8d r. for a but taken to p*r*ize in the Kateryn	£3 6s	8d
1	Itm. the 9 of M*a*rche £3 13s 4d for 1 but to J*oh*n Gibs fo. 37	£3 13s	4d
13	Itm. the 10 day of Augost £47 6s 8d *that* is for the sale of 13 butt*es* secke*s* to dyvers p*er*ssons from the 30 day of Aprell last past as by my shop boke may apere	£47 6s	8d
	S.	£187 10s	

anno 1544

Richard Andros of Banwell p*er* contra is dewe to have the 18 of Augost 20s r. by the hande*s* of Symon Hanckot tayllor £1

79(R) contd.

Itm. the 4th day of February 1545 Symon tayler pd. to me in a reckenyng for the seid Andros	£1	1s	8d

80(L)   **anno 1539**

Thomas Asevarn troweman dwelling at Shrawle owith the 20 day of Jenyver £6 3s 4d that is for 1 ton of my best Rendry iren which I d'd for hym to his son, to be pd. before Ester next   £6 3s 4d
1544 Itm. the 4 day of Augost anno 1544 £3 & is for 1 pipe of iren to be paide at all tymes   £3
Itm. the 17 day of Maye anno 1546 £3 & is for so myche rest to be paide at all tymes of 3 tons Rendry iren d'd to his son John Sevarn, montith   £3

80(R)   **anno 1540**

Thomas Asevarn is dewe to have the 25 day of July £6 r. of Gryffith Estwyck	£6	3s	4d
Itm. the 3 day of November 1544 r. by his sarvant John Yong £3	£3		
Itm. the 26 day of September 1546 r. by thandes of his son John Sevarn £3	£3		

81(L)   **anno 1539**

Richard Hickman of Ullarhampton arrowedmaker owith the 20 day of Jenyver £6 6s 8d which is for 1 ton of S.S. iren to be paide at Midsomer next commyng   £6 6s 8d

anno 1539

Patrick Gowgh of Bristowe hopar owithe the 26 daye of February £7 12s 6d which is for the rest of a pipe wull oyle sold to hym at £8, to pay by his obligacion £4 at Whitsontide next & £3 12s 6d at Seynt Jamistide next after   £7 12s 6d

81(R)   **anno 1540**

Richard Hickman per contra is dewe to have the 27 day of July £6 6s 8d r. by my wif of John Boner, Kendallman	£6	6s	8d

anno 1540

Patrick Gowgh is dewe to have the 28 day of July £4 12s 6d r. of hym in redy monney	£4	12s	6d
Itm. the 22 day of February r. of hym £3	£3		

82(L)   **anno 1539**

Nicholas Thorn marchant of Bristowe owith the 22 day of December £3 5s that is for the freight of 3 ton 1 h'd wyne from Burdes in my ship the Trynte this vyntage at 20s the ton   £3 5s
Itm. for 9 buge skuyns he had of me for Master Huntley at 16d the skuyn   12s
Itm. 23s pd. to his sarvant Harvest the 21 day of Jenyver for the clozing up of this accowmpt   £1 3s

            S. £5

anno 1540

Nicolas Thorn above namyd owith the 15 day of November £6 which is for the freight of 6 ton Gascon wyne in the Trynte to pay at 3 monthes & 3 monthes   £6

82(L) contd.

Itm. the 1 day of December a*nno* 1541 £7 10s that is for 6 ton bastard in the
Trynte at 25s p*er* ton, to pay ½ in hand & ½ at the ende of 3 monthes next
com*m*yng £7 10s

1542 Itm. the 24 day of Ap*re*ll 1542 £6 13s 4d that is ffor the freight of
10 ton iren in the Trynte, to pay at 3 monthes & 3 monthes £6 13s 4d

Itm. the 23 daye of Augost £5 9s 4d *that* is for 8 tons 3 k*yntalls* iren freight
in the Trynte at 13s 4d p*er* ton £5 9s 4d

Itm. the 18 day of February £6 15s that is ffor the freight of 4 ton pipe at 30s
the ton from Andaluzia in the Trynte my ship, to pay hallf in hand &
tho*ther* hallf 3 monthes next enshewing £6 15s

Itm. the 1 day of August 1543 £8 8s 8d for so myche redy money that I pd.
to hymseallf in his hows apo*n* his cubberd in the hawle £8 8s 8d

S. £27 6s 4d

82(R)   **anno 1539**

Nicholas Thorm p*er* contra is dewe to have the 19 day of
Jenyver £5 *that* is for the freight of 2 to*n* oyle & 2 ton
seck*es* from Andaluzia *this* vyntage in his ship the Savior
at 25s the ton, mo*ntith*   S. £5

anno 1540

Nicholas Thorn p*er* contra is dewe to have the 7 daye of
February £3 r. by Hamond £3

Itm. the 7 day of Ap*re*ll 1540 r. by Hamond £3 £3

Itm. the 8 day of February 1541 £3 15s r. for the hallf
freight p*er* contra by the hand*es* of my s*a*rvant Henry £3 15s

Itm. the 13 of Marche £3 15s which Hamond r. of hy*m* £3 15s

Itm. the last day of July a*nno* 1542 £3 *that* is for the freight
of 3 tons oyle in the Mary Conceptio*n* at 20s p*er* ton £3

Itm. the last day of October £6 8s which my s*a*rvant
Robert Lett r. of Nycolas Wosley in mon*n*ey £6 8s

Itm. the 26 day of February 1542 £14 5s & is for the
freight of 9 ton pipe in the Mary Conceptio*n* fro*m*
Andaluzia at 30s the to*n*, to paye hallf in hand & thother
hallf at 3 monthes £14 5s

Itm. for a mayne yerd to my shipp 11 nobles £3 13s 4d

S. £27 6s 4d

83(L)   **anno 1539**

29 ton 3 h'd

Wynes of Gascon for my owne acowmpt, that is to sey
24 ton 3 h'd in my ship the Trynte & 5 ton in the Primros
r. the monthes of December & Jenyver owith 97367 M.
that it cost at Burd*es* clereabord, for freight 20s p*er* ton,
for costom of 26 to*n* pipe 3s p*er* ton, for hallyng &
stowyng 4d p*er* ton, for av*er*es in the Trynte 2s 9d p*er* ton
& in the P*r*imros with the grose av*er*ies 4s 4d p*er* to*n* £103 8s 11d

Itm. 50s for a pipe muscadel to dreass & yllaige it £2 10s

1540 Itm. the 31 day of Augost 1540 £13 11s 1d for so myche
goten by this acowmpt as it ap*er*ith to gaynes in credito fo. 92 £13 11s 1d

S. £119 10s

anno 1540

Richard Peryman of Westerley smythe owithe the 27 daye
of September £5 17s 7d ob to be paide at the Annu*n*ciaco*n*

83(L) contd.

of Owr Lady next commyng, which is for the rest of 25 C 1 qr. 3 li. iren of S.S. which I sold & d'd to hym at 19 grotes 2d the C, as in my shop boke it maye apere	£5 17s 7d½
1541 Itm. the 13 day of December 1541 33s 4d that is for 1 h'd iren of S.S. d'd to hym to pay at Owr Lady Day in Marche next commyng	£1 13s 4d
1542 Itm. the 21 day of July 1542 40s that is for 6 C iren of S.S. to be paide at Candellmas next commyng	£2
1543 Itm. the 5 day of June anno 1543 40s & is for 6 C of S.S. iren sold & d'd to hym to be pd. at Mighellmas next	£2
Itm. the 24 day of September £3 6s 8d & is for a pipe of S.S. iren solld & d'd to hym to be paide at Owr Lady Day in Marche next commyng	£3 6s 8d
1545 Itm. the 26 day of Marche anno 1545 39s 6d & is for the rest of 6 C 18 li. iren to be paide at Mydsomer next as in my shop boke may apere	£1 19s 6d
Itm. the 24 day of Marche for the rest of a h'd 19 li. S.S. iren 33s 4d to be pd. at Midsomer next	£1 13s 4d

83(R)   **anno 1539**

2	Wynes per contra be dewe to have the 9 daye of December 46s 8d for 2 h'd sold to John Gibs 37	£2 6s 8d
8	Itm. the 10 day of December £9 6s 8d for 2 ton to North 24	£9 6s 8d
4	Itm. the 13 day of December £4 13s 4d for 1 ton to William Smothing fo. 72	£4 13s 4d
8	Itm. the 18 of December £10 for 2 ton to John Wylles fo. 73	£10
6	Itm. the 19 of December £7 for 6 h'd to John Luys fo. 34	£7
2	Itm. the same day 46s 8d for 2 h'd to T. Cotes fo. 17	£2 6s 8d
2	Itm. the same day 16s 8d for 2 h'd to T. Turbot 23	£2 6s 8d
4	Itm. the 20 of December £4 13s 4d for 1 ton to Bosgrove 68	£4 13s 4d
4	Itm. the same day £4 13s 4d for 1 ton to John Welsche 74	£4 13s 4d
4	Itm. the 8 of Jenyver £4 10s for 1 ton to Jamys Rogers 76	£4 10s
4	Itm. the 17 day of Jenyver £5 for 1 ton r. of Master Poyntz in the first quarter rent of Sturdon	£5
2	Itm. the 21 of Jenyver 46s 8d for 2 h'd to T. Turbot 23	£2 6s 8d
2	Itm. the 24 of Jenyver 45s for 2 h'd which I gave to Master Wekes	£2 5s
2	Itm. the 4 of February 45s for 2 h'd to T. Dyngley 94	£2 5s
4	Itm. the 6 day of February £4 10s for 1 ton to T. Cotes 17	£4 10s
2	Itm. the 7 day of February 45s for 2 h'd to John Gibs fo. 37	£2 5s
2	Itm. the 10th day of February 45s for 2 h'd to John Rokesby 10	£2 5s
2	Itm. the 14 of the same to the seid Rokesby 2 h'd price 45s	£2 5s
4	Itm. the 23 of February £4 6s 8d for 1 ton to William Smotheng 72	£4 6s 8d
4	Itm. the 26th day of February £4 10s for 1 ton to T. Bell 62	£4 10s

83(R) contd.

6	Itm. the 2 daye of Marche £6 15s for 6 h'd to A Bosgrove 68	£6 15s
2	Itm. the 9 of Marche 45s for 2 h'd to John Gibs fo. 37	£2 5s
8	1540 Itm. the 6 day of Aprell 1540 £10 for 10 h'd to William Northe 24	£8
18	Itm. the 31 day of August £18 5s for 4 ton pipe sold at dyvers tymes to dyvers perssons sens the 6 day of Aprell last past as by my shop boke may apere	£18 5s
		S. £119 10s

anno 1541

Richard Peryman per contra is dew to have the 25 day of Marche £3 6s 8d r. of hym by the handes of his brother Robert Peryman, montith — £3 6s 8d
Itm. the 28 day of May r. of hym at Bristow 50s 11d½ — £2 10s 11d ob
Itm. the 25 day of Marche anno 1542 r. by the handes of his brother Robert 5 nobles — £1 13s 4d
Itm. the 16 day of February r. at Bristow of hym 40s — £2
Itm. the 24 day of September 1543 r. of hym 40s — £2
Itm. the 22 of Marche 1543 r. at Bristow of hym — £3 6s 8d
Itm. the 3d day of July 1545 r. of hym 39s 6d — £1 19s 6d
Itm. the ¹ day of October 1546 r. 33s 4d — £1 13s 4d

84(L)

anno 1539

5 ton

Oylles for my owne acownt, that is to sey 2 ton in the Savior of Bristowe & 3 ton in the Jhesus of Bastable r. the monthe of Jenyver owith for the freight in the Savior 25s per ton, & for freight in the Jhesus 20s per ton & 3s per ton for the brynging of the seid 3 ton from Bastable to Bristowe, for averes in the Savur 11d ob per ton & in the Jhesus 2d per ton & for costom 4s per ton, & for hallyng & stowyng 4d per ton, for rebating 16d per ton & it cost at the first penny 81000 M. montith £61 9s 9d — £61 9s 9d
Itm. the 24 of Marche £15 5s 3d goten by this acownt as it aperith to gaynes in credito fo. 92 — £15 5s 3d

S. £76 15s

anno 1540

12 ton 1 h'd

Oylles for my owne acowmpt owith the monthe of August £108 18s 4d½, that is for 6 ton r. owt of the Mary Cristofor of Bristowe & 6 ton 1 h'd owt of the Trynte of Newport which cost clere abord as by William Harvest reckenyng may apere 163 V 378 M.
Itm. more for custom 4s per ton, for hawling & rebatyng 20d per ton, for freight 20s per ton, & averes 12d per ton, montith the costes £16 8s 4d — £125 6s 8d

1 pipe

Itm. the 1 day of September £6 that is for a pipe oyle r. of John Caps in the seid price for corrupt wyne — £6

80 pipes

1541 Itm. the 3d daye of August anno 1541 r. owt of a gud ship callyd the Harry of Bristowe, under God master Antony Pickett, 40 ton of wull oyle in 80 pipes which cost abord the ship with all costes 546 V. 640 M. & for Giles

---

¹ Blank in MS.

84(L) contd.

	costes 10 ducatts, for freight £40, for costom of 37 tons pipe at 4s the ton, for halyng 13s 4d, rebatyng 16d per ton, for 2 new pipes 3s, for nayles 15d, averes 14d per ton, sellarage 30s, ullaige, montith all	£422	19s	5d
6 pipes	Itm. the ¹ day of July 1542 r. owt of the Mary Conception of Bristowe 6 pipes wull oyle which cost clere abord 38 M, for freight £3, for costom 12s, for haling 8d, for rebatyng 4s 6d, for averes 3s, montith £29 5s 10d	£29	5s	10d
	Itm. the 8 day of Augost bowght of John Wellsche 1 ton for £10 10s	£10	10s	
2 pipes	Itm. the 27 day of Jenyver anno 1542 £76 11s 5d that is ffor so myche I make gaynes fo. 92 creditor of for the closyng up of this acowmpt	£76	11s	5d
	S.	£670	13.	4d

84(R)   **anno 1539**

1	Oylles per contra is dewe to have the 13 day of Jenyver £7 10s for a pipe sold to Thomas Machyne in fo. 31	£7	10s
1	Itm. the 22 day of Jenyver r. of Stevyn Chick for 2 h'd	£7	15s
2	Itm. the same day £15 for 2 pipes to William Beryn fo. 85	£15	
1	Itm. the 27 day of Jenyver of John Aschemore of Wursettor for 1 pipe oyle £7 10s	£7	10s
2	Itm. the 24 day of Marche £15 that is for 1 ton wull oylle sold to William Pickes fo.¹	£15	
1	Itm. the 26 of February £8 for 1 pipe to Patrick Gowgh fo.¹	£8	
2	Itm. the 16 day of February £16 for 1 ton oyle to Master Chester fo. 35	£16	
	S.	£76	15s

anno 1540

12 ton 1 h'd	Oyles per contra is dewe to have the 21 day of October £147 that is for 12 ton h'd at £12 the ton sold to William Pickes fo. 97	£147		
1	1541 Itm. the 29 day of July anno 1541 £5 15s for a pipe oyle sold to John Hamond fo. 77	£5	15s	
6	Itm. the 3d day of Augost £36 for 3 ton to John Wynter 11	£36		
10	Itm. the 6 of August £56 13s 4d for 5 ton to T. Machyn 128	£56	13s	4d
2	Itm. the 20 of Augost £12 for 1 ton to R. Guytton fo. 129	£12		
1	Itm. the 17 of October £6 for a pipe to T. Heynes fo. 78	£6		
6	Itm. the 19 of October £36 for 3 ton to John Huntley fo. 137	£36		
4	Itm. the 24 of October £24 for 2 ton to John Wellsche fo. 74	£24		
2	Itm. the 27 of October £12 for 1 ton to Artur Smyth fo. 116	£12		
2	Itm. the 4 of Jenyver £12 for 1 ton to Allen Hill fo. 117	£12		

¹ Blank in MS.

84(R) contd.

4	Itm. the 30 of Jenyver £25 for 2 tons to J*oh*n Huntley fo. 137	£25	
1	Itm. the 4 of February £6 r. for a pipe of Edward Parssons	£6	
3	Itm. the 17 of Ap*r*ell 1542 for 3 pipes to J*oh*n Wells fo. 129	£18	
2	Itm. the 30 of Ap*r*ell £12 10s for 1 ton to T. Machyne fo. 154	£12 10s	
2	Itm. the 3 of Aprill £13 for 1 to*n* to Nycolas Tizo*n* fo. 156	£13	
4	Itm. the same day £26 for 2 to*n* to Richard Pryn fo. 156	£26	
8	Itm. the 22 of May £52 for 4 tons to W*illiam* Pik*es* fo. 97	£52	
1	Itm. the 6 of June £6 10s for a pipe to Antony Payne fo. 159	£6 10s	
2	Itm. the 26 day of June £12 for a ton to J*oh*n a Wells fo. 129	£12	
1	Itm. the 27 of June £6 for a pipe to Richard Mors 161	£6	
1	Itm. the 28 of June £6 5s for a pipe to John Braghyng 109	£6 5s	
1	Itm. the 30 of June £6 for a pipe oyle to T. Aflete 161	£6	
1	Itm. the 5 day of July r. of Thomas Thuston £6 for a pipe oyle	£6	
4	Itm. the 6 of July £24 for 2 tons to J*oh*n a Wells fo. 129	£24	
1	Itm. the 19 of July solld to Thom*as* Thurston fo. 164 1 p*ipe* for £6	£6	
4	Itm. the 20 of July 2 tons to Robert Guytten fo 129 for £24	£24	
1	Itm. the 28 of July £6 for a pipe to J*oh*n Hamon fo. 77	£6	
1	Itm. the same day £6 for a pipe to Stevyn Chick fo. 47	£6	
1	Itm. the 3 of Augost £6 for a pipe to Gilbart Cogan fo. 140	£6	
1	Itm. the 15 of Septemb*er* for a p*i*pe to J*oh*n Snyg fo. 130	£6 13s 4d	
1	Itm. the 25 of Novemb*er* for 1 p*i*pe M*a*ster Hunteley fo. 137	£6 13s 4d	
2	Itm. the 3 of Jenyver for 1 ton to Richard Pryn fo. 156	£12	
4	Itm. the 27 of Jenyver for 2 to*n* to J*oh*n Pick*es* fo. 177	£24	
2	Itm. 2 pipes whereof the one is hallf ow*t* mont*ith* as I valew *them*	£6 13s 4d[1]	
2	Itm. 2 pipes to ylladge		
		£670 13s 4d	

85(L)   **anno 1539**

Will*a*m Beryn of Bristowe sopemaker owithe the 22 day of Jenyver £15 *that* is for 2 pipes wull oyle sold & delyverd to hym to be paide at Ester next   £15

anno 1539

Will*a*m Nawle of Brom*m*yche ow*ith* the 16 day of February £12 6s 8d that is for 1 to*n* of the bett*er* Rendry iren at £6 *the* ton & 1 ton of S.S. ire*n* at 19 nobles the ton, laden in Symond Astones trowe to pay at all tymes   £12 6s 8d

---

[1] *Blank in MS.*

85(R)   **anno 1539**

William Beryn per contra is dewe to have the 22 daye of
Marche £15 for so myche r. of his wif   £15

anno 1540

William Nawle per contra is dewe to have the 18 day of
September £12 r. from hym by William Sprat   £12

86(L)   **anno 1539**

Master John Shipman thelder marchant of Bristowe owith the 22 day of
December £4 for the freight of 4 ton wyn laden this vyntage from Burdes
in my ship the Trynte at 20s the ton, montith   £4
Itm. the 5th day of February pd. to John Wattes purser of the Mary
Cristofor 35s   £1 15s
Itm. the 2 day of Marche 35s pd. to his purser John Wattes in redy money
& so broke my seale from the Mary Cristofor is charter party, montith   £1 15s
1540 Itm. the 10 day of May 1540 £3 6s 8d *that* is for the freight of 5 ton
iren in my ship at 13s 4d the ton payable at thend of 3 monthes next
foloing   £3 6s 8d
Itm. the 23 day of Agost 46s 8d for the freight of 3 ton pipe iren in the
Trynte from Spayne   £2 6s 8d
Itm. the 20 day of October 13s 4d which I pd. for hym to John Snygg   13s 4d
Itm. the 8 day of Marche pd. to the purser John Watkyns 50s & broke my
seale from the Mary Cristofor is charter   £2 10s
1541 Itm. the 4th day of Maye 1541 £6 that is for the ½ freight of 18 ton
iren laden in the Trynte at 13s 4d the ton, to pay at thend of 3 monthes next
commyng   £6

       S. £22 06s 8d

anno 1539

Thomas Lawnston of Bristow grocer owith the 7th day of February
31s 2d ob *that* is for 1 h'd 23 li. iren at £6 the ton, to be paide at all tymes
requyrid   £1 11s 2d ob
Itm. the 21 day of Maye anno 1544 45s & is ffor 1 h'd Gascon wyne to be
paide at all tymes   £2 5s
1546 Itm. the 12 day of December 1546 £17 19s 4d that is for 49 peces
Malaga rezynges at 7s 4d the pece, to be paide at Mighellmas next   £17 19s 4d

86(R)   **anno 1539**

Jhon Shipman per contra is dewe to have the 23 day of
December £7 10s for the freight of 12 buttes of seck in his
ship the Mary Cristofor this vyntaige from Andaluzia at
25s the ton   £7 10s
1540 Itm. the 17 day of July 1540 £6 *that* is for the freight
of 6 ton oyle in the Mary Cristofor at 20s per ton, to pay
½ in hand & thother ½ 3 monthes after   £6
Itm. the 2 day of Agost r. of John Wattes purser   6s 8d
Itm. the 20 day of December 50s which is for 2 ton freight
in the Mary Cristofor, to pay at thend of 3 monthes next
commyng   £2 10s
Itm. the last day of Agost anno 1541 r. £6   £6

       S. £22 06s 8d

anno 1540

Thomas Lawnsdon per contra is dewe to have the 4th day
of Jenyver 31s which my wif. r. of his sarvant   £1 11s 2d ob

86(R) contd.

Itm. the 19 day of February Henry my sarvant r. of hym 40s	£2	
R. of hym by my sarvant £7 the 8 day of December 1547, more the 8 day of February Hamon r. £7, more r. £3 19s 4d	£17 19s 4d	

87(L)   **anno 1539**

Williαm Rowley marchant of Bristowe owith the 22 day of December 50s which is for the hallf & hole rest of 5 ton wyne freight *this* vyntaige from Burdes in my ship the Trynte at 20s the ton, which 50s is payable at Owr Lady Day in Marche next commyng   £2 10s

1540 Itm. the 15 day of November anno 1540 £5 which is for the freight of 5 ton Gascon wyne in the Trynte to pay at 3 monthes & 3 monthes   £5

Itm. the 28 day of November £3 13s 4d that is for 1 pipe of muscadell sold to hym to be paide at Mighellmas next commyng   £3 13s 4d

Itm. the 18 day of February anno 1542 £6 that is for 4 ton the freight thereof in my ship the Trynte from Andaluzia at 30s the ton, to pay hallf in hand & thother hallf 3 monthes after, montith   £6

1544 Itm. the 5 day of June 1544 £8 which is for 1 ton Gascon wyne to be paide at Mighellmas next   £8

Itm. the 27 day of November 1545 for 2 h'd Gascon wyne £3 13s 4d to be pd. at all tymes requyrid   £3 13s 4d

anno 1540

William Bullock of the parisshe of Elmore in Glocestershire yeoman owith the 11 day of May £13 6s 8d which my sarvant Robert Leight paid hym at his howse   £13 6s 8d

Itm. the 9 day of June paide to hym Bristowe £70 11s 4d montith   £70 11s 4d

                                                                                   S. £83 18s

anno 1540

William Bullock above namyd owe the 9 day of November £19 10s that is ffor 3 ton iren of S.S. d'd to hym at £6 10s the ton in yernes & part of payement of 40 wey wheat which he must d'd to me abord my ship or eny other ship at Hungrode or Kyngrode at eny tym I shall requyre hym, at 12d the busshell   £19 10s

Itm. the 14 day of the same £10 d'd hym in monney   £10

Itm. the 1 day of February pd. to hym at Bristowe £52   £52

Itm. £3 5s for a pipe of S.S. iren   £3 5s

Itm. the 16 day of February £10 pd. hym in redy monney, I sey £10   £10

Itm. the last day of February £24 paide for hym to his neighbur Robert Chewe   £24

Itm. the 8 day of Marche pd. to hym in Bristowe £10 1s   £10 1s

Itm. the 29 day of Marche £11 6s 8d which he r. at Twexbury of Richard Carrick, montith   £11 6s 8d

Itm. 10s for 10 busshells wheat that I pd. to myche for in the lading of the Trynte   10s

Itm. the 21 day of Aprell 1541 46s 4d pd. to hym in redy money   £2 6s 4d

                                                                                   S. £142 19s

87(R)   **anno 1540**

William Rowley per contra is dewe to have the 8 day of May 50s r. of hym by thandes of my sarvant Hamon   £2 10s

Itm. the 16 day of February 50s for so myche r. of hym   £2 10s

Itm. the 4 day of May 1541 r. by Hamond 50s   £2 10s

Itm. the 9 day of November 1542 r. of hym 11 nobles   £3 13s 4d

87(R) contd.

Itm. the 3 day of ~~February~~ Marche 1542 r. by Hamon £3	£3
Itm. the 19 of June 1543 £3 r. of hym	£3
Itm. the 8 of October 1544 r. £4	£4
Itm. the 29 day of November r. of hym £4	£4
Itm. r. £3 13s 4d	£3 13s 4d

anno 1540

William Bullock per contra is dewe to have the 9 day of June £85 4s that is for 30 wey benes at 36s the wey & 11 wey ½ wheat at 52s the wey, montith £83 18s

£83 18s

£83 18s

anno 1540

William Bullock per contra is dewe to have the first day of February £104 16s that is for 43 weys, 32 busshells wheat r. of hym into my ship at 48s the wey, montith   £104 16s
Itm. the 26 day of February £24 that is for 10 wey wheat r. of hym abord the Harry, Master A. Pyket   £24
Itm. the 19 day of Marche 1541 for 5 weys 43 busshells wheat browght abord a Portyngal ship at 12d the busshell, montith £14 3s   £14 3s

£142 19s

88(L)   anno 1539

John Gorney marchant of Bristowe owith the the[1] 22 day of December £5 that is for the freight of 5 ton wyne this vyntage from Burdes in the Trynte at 20s the ton, to pay hallf in hand & the other ½ at Owr Lady in March next commyng, montith   £5
Itm. the 6 day of November 1540 £5 which is for the freight of 5 ton wyne from Burdes in the Trynte at 20s the ton, to pay it in hallfes at 3 monthes & 3 monthes   £5
1542 Itm. the 18 day of February 1542 £4 10s which is for the freight of 3 ton wyne in my ship the Trynte, to paye hallf in hand & thother hallf 3 monthes next after, montith   £4 10s
1544 Itm. the 5th day of June anno 1544 £6 13s 4d & is for 1 ton S.S. iren delyverd for hym to William Egerton gunmaker, to be pd. at Seynt Jamistide next commyng, montith   £6 13s 4d
Itm. the 10th day of November 1546 lent hym at London 20s   £1
Itm. the 20 day of August anno 1547 £20 which I sent hym by Hewgh Hamon for ernes & part of payement of 3 goblettes with a cover, all gyllt   £20
Itm. the 25 daye of August £10 12s which I paide to hym in ready monney   £10 12s
Itm. the 28 of Marche anno 1548 for 20 ton freight of iren in his ship the Mary Georg from Spayne at 20s the ton montith[2]   £20
Itm. the 28 day of Marche anno 1548 36s & for 6 ducatts of gold which Henry Setterfort my sarvant lent to his purser Thomas Morrys in Spayne at 6s the ducatt, montith   £1 16s
Itm. the same day paide to his seid purser £15 10s 4d in ready monney & broke my seale from the charter partie consernyng the freight of the 20 ton iren per contra   £15 10s 4d
Itm. 53s 4d which he owith for the rest of his foresseid cowmpt   £2 13s 4d
1548 Itm. the 10th day of Aprell 1548 £5 & is for 2 oxen which he had of my wif, to be pd. at all tymes requyrid   £5
Itm. the 4th day of June £4 10s & is for the rest of 1 butt seck & 2 h'd Gascon wyne as by my shop boke maye apere   £4 10s
Itm. the 13 day of September 1548 £15 pd. to hym in redy monney   £15
Itm. the 12 of July £5 10s for a butt of mawmesey   £5 10s

---

[1] Smythe repeats the.
[2] This item is erased and almost illegible in MS.

88(R)   anno 1539

John ap Gornay per contra is dewe to have the 20 day of February 50s which my wif r. of hym	£2 10s
1540 Itm. the 7 day of February 1540 50s r. by Hamond for the rest of his 5 ton freight of the vyntaige in anno 1539	£2 10s
Itm. the first day of Aprell r. 40s	£2
Itm. the 18 day of December for 1 tierce of Gascon wyne after 7 markes the ton, montith 15s 7d	15 7d
Itm. the 10 day of Aprill 1542 r. by Hamon	£2 4s 5d
Itm. the 3 day of ~~February~~ March r. by Hamon 45s	45s
Itm. the 1 day of Augost 1543 my sarvant Leyght r. of hym 45s	£2 5s
Itm. the 9 of Augost 1544 £4 r. of his wif	£4
Itm. r. of hym the 1 day of Marche 1546 20s	£1
Itm. the 22 day of Augost 1547 for 4 gillt goblettes with a cover waying 102 oz at 6s the oz, montith £30 12s	£30 12s
So rest by this above seide cowmpt ffynisshid between Master Gorney & me the 25 day of Augost anno 1547 53s 4d to be paide at all tymes requyrid	~~£2 13s 4d~~

       per me   per me
     John Smythe[1]   John Gorney[1]

Itm. the 28 day of Marche 1548 £20 which is for the freight of 20 tons iren laden in Spayne in the Mary George his ship at 20s per ton, montith	£20
Master Gorney is dewe to have the 13 daye of September anno 1548 £20 & is for the freight of 20 ton iren from Spayne in his ship the Mary George	£20
Itm. 8 day of July my wif r. of hym £4 10s	£4 10s
Itm. the 18 day of February 1548 r. of hym £5 10s	£5 10s

89(L)   anno 1538

Edward Pryn of Bristowe marchant owith the last day of Jenyver £4 13s 11d[2] for so myche he r. of me to delyver Thomas Dowding of Bridgewater for to by beanes to be laden for me in the Prymros. It is £5 5s. The cowmpt is 43s 4d	£4 13s 11d
1539 Itm. the 22 day of December anno 1539 50s that is for the ½ & hole rest of the freight of 5 ton Gascon wyne this wyntage in the Trynte at 20s the ton, payable at Owr Lady Day in March next	£2 10s
	£7 3s 11d

1540

Edward Pryn owith the 10 day of Maye £10 that is for 15 tons iren in my ship at 15s per ton to pay at thend of 3 monthes next commyng	£11 5s

anno 1540

Edward Pryn above namyd owith the 23 day of Augost £3 19s 1d that is for the freight of 5 ton 14 kyntalls iren laden from Spayne in my ship the Trynte at 13s 4d per ton, montith, 14 kyntalls of it at 10s the ton	£3 16s 1d
Itm. the 6 day of December 40s which he owith for 3 ton freight of iren for Robert Sexy at the foreseid tyme in my seid ship as it aperith to the seid Sexy in credito fo. 97. 1 ton of it at 10s the ton	£1 16s 8d

---

[1] Smythe and Gorney have both signed here.
[2] 13s 11d is inserted above the line.

89(L) contd.

Itm. the same day 50s which he ow*ith* me for the freight of shuche iren as Jo*h*n Pryn, Jo*h*n Cutt & Luyes Robyns had in my ship fro*m* Spayne the same viage	£2	10s	
Itm. the 15 day of Novembe*r* £9 8s 4d which is for the freight of 9 ton 1 h'd 1 t*ierce* of Gascon wyne in the Trynte for hym & Jo*h*n Cutt, to pay at 3 monthes & 3 monthes	£9	8s	4d
1541 Itm. the 1 day of December a*nno* 1541 £5 12s 6d *that* is for the rest & ½ freight of 9 tons bastard*es* in the Trynte at 25s *per* ton, to be paide at *the* end of 3 monthes next enshewyng	£5	12s	6d
1542 Itm. the 24 day of Ap*r*ell 1542 £6 13s 4d £4 *that* is ffor the freight of 6 to*n* iren in the Trynte to pay ½ at 3 monthes next com*m*yng & tho*ther* ½ 3 monthes next after that	£4 £6 13s 4d		
Itm. the 23 day of Augost 53s 4d for the freight of 4 tons iren in the Trynte	£2	13s	4d
Itm. the 18 daye of February £3 that is for the freight of 2 tons wyne laden in my ship at 30s the ton, to pay hallf in hand & hallf 3 monthes next after, mon*tith*	£3		
Itm. the 6th day of October 1545 £20 that is for so myche redy mon*n*ey lent hym to pay the Portyngalls freight which browght o*w*r wood, which £20 he promises to pay at all tymes requyrid	£20		
1547 Itm. the 9 of Jenyver 1547 for 3 C wood at 14s p*er* C, the 21 day of Jenyver 3 C and on other tyme 2 C 3 qr. 2 li. I sey the 18 of Jenyver £6 2s 9d	£6	2s 13s	9d 4d

89(R)   **anno 1539**

Edward P*r*yn *per* contra is dewe to have the 26 daye of M*a*rche 50s 7d which I r. of hym for in *part* of payement of the £5 *per* contra for as myche the beanes war not laden	£2	10s	7d
Itm. the 26 day of M*a*rche 50s for my hallf freight in the P*r*imros	£2	10s	
Itm. the 7 day of May 43s 4d for so myche r. of Edward Pryn	£2	3s	4d
S.	£7	3s	11d

anno 1540

Edward P*r*yn *per* contra is dewe to have the 14 day of Agost £5 r. of hym in redy mon*n*ey	£5	
Itm. the 17 day of Septemb*er* £5 r. of hym	£5	
Itm. 25s which I geve hym & for the same he p*r*omezith me to laide at eny tyme in the P*r*imros 12 weys of corne to Spayne, freight free, as he have don with me in this seid viage	£1	5s
	£11	5s

anno 1540

Edward P*r*yn per contra is dewe to have the 6 day of Decemb*er* £5 r. of hym in p*a*rt payeme*nt* of my freight*es* per contra in 20 crusados	£5		
Itm. the last day of Decemb*er* £3 2s 8d r. of hy*m* in redy money	£3	2s	8d
Itm. the 15 day of Novemb*er* £5 which I owe for the freight of 5 to*n* Gasco*n* wyne in the P*r*imros, to pay at 3 monthes & 3 monthes	£5		
It*m*. the 2d day of M*a*rche r. of hym 44s 2d	£2	4s	2d

89(R) contd.

1541 Itm. the 19 day of May a*n*no 1541 44s 2d r. of hy*m* by Hamond	£2	4s 2d
Itm. the 5 of Ap*r*ell 1542 r. by Hamond £5 12s 6d	£5	12s 6d
Itm. the 19 day of May 1542 £5. 7s 6d½ that is for the freight of 8 tons & 2 kyntall iren in the P*r*imros at 13s 4d the ton, mo*ntith*	£5	7s 6d ob
Itm. the 16 day of Novembe*r* R. Lett my s*a*rvant r. of hym 25s 9d ob	£1	5s 9d ob
Itm. the 26 day of February 30s which Hamond r.	£1	10s
Itm. the last day of June 1543 r. of hy*m* 30s	£1	10s
Itm. the 5 day of Jenyver 1545 r. £20	£20	

90(L)   **anno 1539**

Mathewe Kent of Bristowe m*a*rchant ow*i*the the 22 day off Decembe*r* £6 5s 8d that is for the freight of 6 ton Gascon wyne & 4 ½-bales woode laden *this* vyntage in the Try*n*te at 20s the ton, to pay hallf in hand & tho*ther* hallf at O*w*r Lady Daye in M*a*rche next com*m*yng   S.   £6   5s   8d

anno 1540

Mathewe Kent above namyd ow*i*the the 15 day of Novembe*r* £3 which is for the freight of 3 ton Gascon wyne in the Try*n*te, to pay at 3 monthes & 3 monthes   £3

1541 Itm. the 1 day of Decembe*r* 1541 12s 6d which is for the freight of 1 pipe bastard in the Try*n*te after 25s the ton, to pay ½ in hand & ½ at *the* end of 3 monthes next com*m*yng   12s 6d

Itm. the 18 day of February a*n*no 1542 £7 10s that is for the freight of 5 tons wyne in my ship at 30s the to*n*, to pay hallf in hand & hallf 3 monthes next after   £7 10s

Itm. 21s 8d for so myche pd. to Hamon for the ave*r*es of his seid 5 tons wine at 4s 4d p*er* to*n*   £1 1s 8d

Itm. 30s for so myche he r. of Robert Lawrence my hoste at London, the [1]   1542   £1 10s

Itm. the monthe of July a*n*no 1544 r. ow*t* of *t*he Margret, m*a*ster John Wyll*ia*ms, 2 butt*es* seck, pd. for freight 40s, for custo*m* 2s 3d, for ave*r*es 6s 7d, for halying & stowyng 4d, for yllage 50 gallons & 1 pottell seck at 8d p*er* gallo*n*, for 3 dozen 4 hopes 2s 3d, mo*ntith* all the cost*es*   £4 10s   ob

For 2 yeres rent of his howse   £6

D'd to Langston his s*a*rvant £5   £5

anno 1539

Lawrence Vyne of Bristowe m*a*rchant ow*i*th the 22 day of Decembe*r* 40s for the freight of 1 to*n* pipe wyne & 7 ½-bales wood this vyntage fro*m* Burd*es* in the Try*n*te at 20s *the* ton, to pay hallf in hand & ½ at O*w*r Lady Day in M*a*rch next   S.   £2

anno 1546

Mathewe Kent the Kyng*es* s*a*rvant ow*ith* 11s which I pd. for the transscript[2]   11s

Itm. £3 paide to M*aster* Woodhows for hows rent   £3

Itm. the [1] day of Novembe*r* 1546 paide to hym at London £9 7s 2d   £9 7s 2d

Itm. the [1] day of Dece*m*ber 1546 pd. for hym to Edward Pryn £31   £31

Itm. the 8 day of Ap*r*ell a*n*no 1547 pd. to E. Pryn in redy mon*n*ey £34 16s 2d   £34 16s 2d

    S.   £78 14s 4d

---

[1] *Blank in MS.*
[2] *A document probably concerning the purchase of the Long Ashton estate or the sale of the 'Trinity' to the King.*

90(R)

anno 1539

Mathewe Kent per contra is dewe to have the 4th day of Marche 40s for so myche he pd. me by the handes of his sarvant		£2	
1540 Itm. the 25 day of Maye 1540 £4 5s 8d r. of hym in redy money		£4 5s	4d
	S.	£6 5s	4d

anno 1540

Mathewe Kent per contra is dewe to have the 23 day of February 30s r. of hym in redy monney	£1	10s
Itm. the 12 day of August 1541 30s r. of hym in monny	£1	10s
Itm. the ¹ of ¹ £8 6s 8d for 2 buttes seck delyverd at London in my name to Robert Lawrence my hoste	£8 6s	8d
Itm. £30 which his wif left with my wif	£30	

anno 1540

Lawrence Vyne per contra is dewe to have the 4 day of Maye 39s 8d which I r. of hym & 4d I allowyd hym for corteyn, montith all 40s		
	S.	£2

anno 1545

Mathewe Kent the Kynges sarvant is dewe to have the 7 day of Marche anno 1545, £78 14s 4d & is for 12 last & 8 dickers lether at 6s 8d the dicker, to pay £39 7s 2d the fyrst day of September next commyng & £39 7s 2d the fyrst day of Marche next after that			
	£78	14s	4d

91(L)

anno 1539

William Ostriche marchant of London owith the 19 day of Jenyver £40 that is for 16 clothes of John Yerberys 16 truckers, the which my sarvant Giles White left with hym this last vyntage at Seynt Lucar to sell & employ them for my acowmpt in oyles to my moste advantage, which clothes cost me the foreseid sum & they restyd unssold a viage to Andaluzia, as it may apere fo. 56	S.	£40

anno 1540

Luyes Robyns of Bristowe skuynnar owith the 23 day of Augost 13s 4d which is for the freight of a ton iren in my ship the Trynte from Spayne	13s	4d
Itm. the 24 day of Aprell 1542 53s 4d that is for the freight of 4 tons iren in the Trynte, to pay at 3 monthes & 3 monthes	£2 13s	4d

anno 1540

Master Thomas White marchant of Bristowe owith the 23 day of Agost £7 6s 8d for the freight of 11 tons iren in the Trynte from Spayne	S. £7 6s	8d

---

¹ Blank in MS.

91(L) contd.   anno 1543

Water Griffith of Homelacy owith the 25 day of July 20s & it is for the rest
of 1 ton 5 li. iren, to be paide at Candellmas next. John Sparck is shewerty   £1

91(R)   anno 1540

William Ostriche per contra is dewe to have 136 ducatts
that he awnswerith me for the nete of the 16 clothes per
contra, montith   £34
Itm. the same day the 7 of July 24 ducatts lost by *this* sale
of my principall to gaynes in debyto fo. 92   £6

                                                                                      £40

anno 1540

Luyes Robyns per contra is dewe to have the last daye of
December 1540 13s 4d r. for hym of E. Pryn fo. 89   13s 4d
Itm. the 23 day of February 1542 r. of hym in redy monney
4 markes   £2 13s 4d

anno 1540

R, per contra of Master Thomas White the 17 day of
September   S.   £7 6s 8d

anno 1544

Water Griffith per contra is dewe to have the   ¹   day
of Augost 20s which John Spark pay for hym in a
reckenyng   £1

92(L)   anno 1539

Gaynes for my owne acownt owith the 19 day of Jenyver £14 2d for so
myche lost by viages fo. 56.   £14   2d
1540 Itm. the 12 day of June 1540 7s 11d lost by viages fo. 56.   7s
Itm. the 7 day of July £6 lost by 16 truckers at thandes of William Ostriche
as it aperith fo. 91   £6
1541 Itm. the 1 day of July 1541 £6 18s 3d lost by acowmpt of sallt fo. 54 £6 18s 3d
Itm. the monthe of November 34s 4d lost by viages to Burdes fo. 104   £1 14s 4d
Itm. the 20 day of November £22 13s 4d for 12 buttes wyne seck lost in the
Jhesus as it aperith to seckes in credito fo. 145   £22 13s 4d
Itm. £60 lost by dettors & otherwise till the 30 day of Jenyver 1543   £60
Itm. £1427 16s ob. which is for the rest & nete gaynes of this acowmpt   £1427 16s ob

                                                                  S. £1539   9s 1d ob

92(R)   anno 1539

Gaynes is dewe to have the 24 of Marche £15 5s 3d for so
myche goten by acowmpt of oyles fo. 84   £15 5s 3d
1540 Itm. the 29 day of Aprell 1540 £36 18s 6d½ for so
myche goten by acowmpt of iren fo. 53   £36 18s 6d ob
Itm. the last day of June £7 8s 1d goten by acowmpt of
osseys fo. 96   £7   8s 1d
Itm. the 18 day of September £15 goten by 27 pipes
samon sold to my unckle Thomas Smythe   £15
Itm. the 10 day of Augost £26 goten by acowmpt of seckes
fo. 79   £26

---
¹ *Blank in MS.*

92(R) contd.

Itm. the 31 day of Augost £13 11s 1d goten by acowmpt of Gascon wyne fo. 83	£13	11s	1d
Itm. the 17 day of December £7 6s 8d goten by viages to Burdes fo. 104	£7	6s	8d
Itm. the 31 day of December £21 14s 4d½ goten by Yland wood fo. 101	£21	14s	4d½
Itm. the 14 day of Jenyver £5 15s 10d for so myche goten by bastardes fo. 118	£5	15s	10d
Itm. the 18 day of the same £92 1s 10d for so myche goten by viages to Andaluzia as it may apere fo. 103	£92	1s	10d
1541 Itm. the 6 day of Aprell 1541 £24 7s 10d goten by Gascon wynes fo. 108	£24	7s	10d
Itm. the 26 day of Aprell £132 8s 3d½ *that* is for so myche goten by iren fo. 53	£132	8s	3d ob
Itm. the 6 day of Aprell 26s 8d goten by 2 pipes of bastard fo. 118	£1	6s	8d
Itm. the 6 day of July 1541 £3 17s 9d goten by tayntes fo. 118	£3	17s	9d
Itm. the 21 day of July £85 11s 2d goten by viages to Andaluzia fo. 103	£85	11s	2d
Itm. 24s 8d goten by a lisence of lether fo. 71	£1	4s	8d
Itm. the 26 day of November 1541 £48 12s goten by seckes fo. 114	£48	12s	
Itm. in December 1541 £69 15s 5d goten by viages to Andaluzia as it may apere fo. 136	£69	15s	5d
Itm. the 17 of December £31 2s 4d goten by acownt of bastardes fo. 118	£31	2s	4d
Itm. the 7 day of December £22 3s 4d½ goten by acowmpt of wood fo. 52	£22	3s	4d½
Itm. the 14 day of Jenyver £3 5s 9d goten by rezinges fo. 146	£3	5s	9d
Itm. the 15 of Aprell 1542 £64 6s 2d½ goten by iren fo. 127	£64	6s	2d½
Itm. the 14 of Augost £37 11s 2d goten by seck fo. 145	£37	11s	2d
Itm. the same monthe £133 1s 1d goten by viages to Biscay fo. 69	£133	1s	1d
Itm. £91 2s goten by viages fo. 173	£91	2s	
Itm. the 3 day of Jenyver 1542 £151 10s 11d for so myche goten by acowmpt of iren fo. 153	£151	10s	11d
Itm. the 29 of Jenyver £17 2s 6d goten by Gascon wynes fo. 144	£17	2s	6d
Itm. the 27 day of Jenyver anno 1542 £76 11s 5d goten by oyles fo. 84	£76	11s	5d
Itm. in Dezember 1542 £30 9s 10d goten by viages to Andaluzia fo. 136	£30	9s	10d
Itm. £77 12s goten by viages to Spayne fo. 174	£77	12s	
Itm. £96 8s 8d goten by acowmpt of iren fo. 176	£96	8s	8d
Itm. £25 19s 7d goten oyles fo. 179	£25	19s	7d
Itm. £72 16s 10d goten by wynes fo. 180	£72	16s	10d
S.	£1539	9s	1d ob

93(L)   **anno 1539**

John Pignall of Kerdif smythe owithe the 4 daye of February £6 13s 8d that is for a butt seck price £3 13s 4d & 1 pipe 6 li. of my best Rendry iren price £3 4d, laden in Davyd Watkyns bote & it is payable at all tymes   £6 13s 8d

1540 Itm. the 16 day of June 1540 £6 11s 3d that is for 1 ton 21 li. iren of S.S. after £6 10s the ton, d'd for hym to Davyd Watkyns & it is payable at all tymes   £6 11s 3d

1541 Itm. the 27 day of Aprell anno 1541 £3 *that* is for 1 pipe of my better Rendry iren, laden in D. Watkyns bote   £3

133

93(L) contd.

Itm. the 12 day of May lade*n* in the seid Davy Watkyns bote 1 h'd claret wyne price 25s	£1 5s
Itm. the 12 day of June 50s *that* is for 2 h'd of claret wyne laden in Davyd Watkyns bote	£2 10s
Itm. the 2 day of July £6 *that* is for 1 to*n* 1 li. iren lade*n* in Davyd Watkyns bote, to be pd. at all tymes requyrid	£6
Itm. the 15 day of Septemb*er* £6 10s 10d that is for 1 ton 14 li. iren of S.S. at £6 10s the ton d'd for hym to Davy Watkyns boteman	£6 10s 10d
Itm. the 24 day of Novemb*er* 30s 2d that is ffor a ton 3 li. ire*n* d'd for hym to Davy Watkyns	£1 10s 2d
Itm. the 19 day of Decemb*er* £6 13d ob for 1 to*n* 21 li. iren d'd for hym to Davy Watkyns	£6 1s 1d½
1542 Itm. the 26 day of June 1542 £6 12d which is for 1 ton 18 li. of the bet*ter* Rendry iren d'd to Davy Watkyns, to be paide at all tymes	£6 1s
Itm. the 27 day of July £12 that is ffor 2 ton of my bet*ter* Rendry iren to be pd. at Candellmas next	£12
Itm. the 17 of October 13d *that* rest unpd. of 1 h'd 22 li. ire*n*	1s 1d
Itm. the 11 day of November £12 12d that is for 2 tons 18 li. of my best Rendry iren, d'd for hym to his s*ar*vant Stevan Cogan & it must be pd. at all tymes requyrid	£12 1s
1543 Itm. the 4 of Ap*r*ell 1543 solld & delyverd to hym 2 to*n* 1 qr. of the bet*ter* Rendry iren at £6 the ton & a pipe 10 li. iren of S.S. at 20 nobles the to*n*, mon*tith* all £15 8s 9d, to be pd. at all tymes	£15 8s 9d
Itm. the 29 of August £12 & is for 2 ton iren sold & delyverd to hym at £6 the ton, to be pd. at all tymes requyrid	£12
1544 Itm. the 26 day of July a*n*no 1544 £6 13s 11d & is for 1 to*n* & 10 li. iren of S.S. at 20 nobles the ton, to be pd. at all tymes	£6 13s 11d

93(R)   **anno 1540**

John Pignal p*er* contra is dewe to have the 15 day of July £6 13s 8d for so myche r. from hym of D. Watkyns	£6 13s 8d
Itm. the 3 day of Jenyver r. of Davy Watkyn £6 11s 3d	£6 11s 3d
1541 Itm. the 11 day of June r. of Davyd Watkyn 50s *that* is 25s for a h'd wyne sent *the* 12 of May & 25s for 1 h'd the 12 day of June	£2 10s
Itm. the 23 of June r. of Davyd Watkyns 25s	£1 5s
Itm. the 2d day of July r. of the seid Davy £3	£3
Itm. the 15 day of September r. of David Watkyne £6	£6
Itm. the 19 day of December r. of D*a*vid Watkyng*es*	£8 1s
Itm. the 24 day of June 1542 my wif r. of Davy Watkyns £6 13d	£6 1s 1d
Itm. the 26 day of July r. at Bristowe of hym	£6 1s
Itm. the 10 day of November r. by Davyd Watkyng*es* & of his boye £12 1s 1d	£12 1s 1d
Itm. the 3 of Ap*r*ell 1543 my wif r. of hym	£12 1s
Itm. the 29 of August my wif r. of hym at Bristow £15 8s 9d	£15 8s 9d
Itm. the 25 of July 1544 r. of his wif £12	£12
Itm. r. fro*m* his wyff at Seynt Jamystide 1545	£6 13s 11d

94(L)   **anno 1539**

Thomas Dyngley of Eyssam owith the 4 day of February £5 18s 4d that is for a but of seck p*r*ice £3 13s 4d & 2 h'd Gascon wyne p*r*ice 45s, to be pd. at all tymes	£5 18s 4d
1540 Itm. the 14 day of Maye 1540 £5 18s 4d which is for 1 but seck & 2 h'd Gascon wyne at the bove seid p*r*ices which I sent in Will*iam* Dymock*es* trowe	£5 18s 4d
Itm. the 30 day of June 22s 6d for 1 h'd wyne	£1 2s 6d

94(L) contd.   anno 1539

Luys Hopkyns of Kermerdyne owith the 5th day of February £6 14s that is for 1 ton 2 C 1 qr. 4 li. Rendry iren, to be pd. at Ester next. Henry Leke of Bristo tayler have made a byll for the payement

£6 14s

94(R)   anno 1540

Thomas Dyngley per contra is dewe to have the 25 day of June £10 which he paide me in Bristowe   £10
Itm. the same day r. of hym 30s   £1 10s
Itm. the same day 6s 8d which he rebate to me in the price of the 2 buttes seck hereageynst   6s 8d
Itm. the last day of Augost r. 20s 4d & 2s 2d which he rebate me in the price   £1 2s 6d

anno 1540

Luys Hopkynges hereageynst is dewe to have the 10 day of Aprell £6 14s r. by the handes of Henry Leke & d'd the seid Henry his bill   £6 14s

95(L)   anno 1539

John Kekar of Harvartwest owith the 4th day of February 30s payable at all tymes & it is for the rest of 2 h'd 1 qr. 13 li. iren, as it may apere in my shop boke, montith   £1 15s
Itm. the 27 day of July 30s that is for the rest of 3 h'd 22 li. iren to be paide at all tymes   £1 10s
Itm. the 8 day of February £3 that is for a pipe of my better Rendry iren to be pd. at Seynt Jamistide next   £3
1541 Itm. the 26 day of July anno 1541 £3 6s 7d that is for 1 pipe less 2 li. iren of S.S. sold & d'd to hym after £6 13s 4d the ton to be pd. at all tymes   £3 6s 7d
1542 Itm. the 26 day of July 1542 £3 6s 8d for 10 C iren of S.S. to be pd. at Candellmas next   £3 6s

anno 1539

Morgan Dave of Kermerdyne owith the 5th day of February £3 that is for the rest of 1 ton 22 li. iren to be payd at May next commyng. N. Gay is shewerty   £3

95(R)   anno 1540

John Kekar per contra is dewe to have the 26 day of July 35s that he paide to my wif   £1 15s
Itm. the first day of February r. of hym at Bristowe   £1 10s
1541 Itm. the 26 day of July 1541 r. of hym in Bristow   £3
Itm. the 3 day of February r. of hym £3 6s 8d   £3 6s 8d

anno 1540

Morgan David per contra is dewe to have the first day of Augost £3 r. of hym by my wif   £3

96(L)   anno 1539

10   Osses for my own acowmpt, 10 pipes r. in February owt of Margret of Mynnet, Master Thomas Web owith 66 ducatts 17 M. that it cost clereabord, for freight 22s per ton, for averes 4s per ton, for costom 3s per ton, for halyng & stowyng 4d per ton, amontith all £23 16s 11d   £23 16s 11d
Itm. £7 8s 1d goten by this acownt as it aperith to gaynes in credito fo. 92   £7 8s 1d

£31 5s

96(L) contd.   anno 1540

Thomas Keynssam of Bristowe shereman owith the 3d day of Aprell £6 7s 9d that is for 4 ½-bales of Tullus wood at 17s the C, to pay £3 3s 10d ob at Bartillmewetide next followyng & £3 3s 10d ob at Allhaloutyde next after that as by his bill ap*erith* £6 7s 9d

96(R)   anno 1539

2	Osseys p*er* contra is dewe to have the 4th day of February £8 for 2 pipes sold to Jamys Rog*er*s fo. 76	£8
1	Itm. the 6 day of the same £4 for a pipe to T. Cot*es* 17	£4
1	Itm. the 7 day of the same £4 for a p*ipe* to J*oh*n Gibs fo. 37	£4
1	Itm. the 10 day of February £4 for a p*ipe* to J*oh*n Rokesby 10	£4
1	Itm. the 21 day of February £4 for a p*ipe* to T. Bell fo. 62	£4
1	Itm. the 5 day of Aprell £4 for a pipe ossey to J*oh*n Wylles fo. 73	£2 5s
1	Itm. the 6 day of Ap*re*ll 50s for a corrupt pipe to W*illiam* North fo. 24	£2 10s
1	Itm. the last day of June 1540 50s for a corrupt pipe to W*illiam* Northe fo. 24	£2 10s[1]
1	Itm. 1 pipe to yllaidge	

£31 5s

anno 1540

Thomas Keynssam p*er* contra is dewe to have the 4th day of Octob*er* 40s which he paide me in presence of Willi*am* Wyllet £2
Itm. the 23 day of Dece*mber* r. of his wif £3 £3
Itm. the [1] day of Jenyver for sheryng of [1] corse clo*thes* [1]
Itm. the 16 day of Marche r. of his wif 20s £1

97(L)   anno 1537

Francisco de Subieta of the Rendry maryner owith the 29 day of September £12 for so myche I paide for hym to Thomas Fasshyn of Hampton £12

anno 1540

Robert Sexy of Bristowe drap*er* owith the 23 day of Augost 40s *that* is for the freight of 3 to*n* iren in *the* Trynte fro*m* Spayne at 13s 4d *the* ton £2
1542 Itm. the 23 day of August 1542 £4 13s 4d that is for the freight of 7 tons iren in the Trynte £4 13s 4d
1549 Itm. the 25 of October a*nn*o 1549 £14 13s 4d and ys ffor 22 C of Iland woode sold & delyverd unto hym this p*re*sent day & yesterday at 13s 4d the C, to be paide at Candellmas next, as by my shop booke may apere £14 13s 4d
Itm. the 11 day of December for 30 C woode at 13s 4d the C to be paide the 24 daye of Maye next co*mm*yng £20
    passed this cownt to my new booke fo. 4

---

[1] *Blank in MS.*

97(L) contd. anno 1539

William Pick*es* of Bristow marc*er* owithe the 24 day of M*a*rch £15 *that* is for a ton oyle sold to hym to be paide at Mydsomer next com*m*yng £15
1540 Itm. the 8 day of June a*nno* 1540 £60 16s 8d that is for 5 to*n* iren of S.S. at 19 nobles the ton & 5 ton of my best Rendry iren at 17 nobles 40d the to*n*, to be paide at Candellmas next £60 16s 8d
Itm. the 21 day of October £147 that is for 12 ton 1 h'd of wull oyle at £12 the to*n* sold & d'd to hym, for to pay on hallf at Seynt Jamistide next & thother ½ at Mighellmas next after, mon*tith* £147
1542 Itm. the 22 day of May 1542 £52 & is for 4 tons wull oyle sold & delyverd to hym £52
1543 Itm. the 13 day of July a*nno* 1543 £30 18s 9d & it is for 13 serons of Sevill sope weying 22 C 3 qr. 23 li. whereof must be taken ow*t* for the serons 3 qr. 12 li. rest 22 C 11 li. at 28s the C, to be paide at all tymes. So amon*tith* as is befforeseid ~~£30 18s 9d~~
more for the tare of the ynner serons ½ a C 10 li., rest neate 21 C 2 qr. 1 li. at 28s the C, mon*tith* £30 2s £30 2s
1544 Itm. the 11 day of December 1544 £3 which is for a pipe of Rendry iren d'd for hym to his s*a*rvant John Lasye, to be pd. at Candellmas next £3
1546 Itm. the 8th day of Aprill a*nno* 1546 £22 & is for 22 h'd of corrupt Gascon wyne, to be pd. at Mighellmas next £22
1547 Itm. the 30 day of Jenyver 1547 £84 and is for 6 ton wull oyle at £14 the ton, to pay at Seynt Jamystide next com*m*yng £84
Itm. the last day of January a*nno* 1548 £130 & is for 6 tons pipe of wull oyle sold & d'd to hym at £20 p*er* ton, to be paide at Bartyllmewetide next com*m*yng, as by his byll may appere £130
Itm. the 29 of M*a*rche £5 for a but seck & the 23 of May for 1 h'd claret wyne price 40s, mo*ntith* all £7 £7

97(R) anno 1539

Francisco p*er* contra is dewe to have the 4th day of M*a*rch, £4 10s r. of Edward Pr*y*n for hym £4 10s
Itm. the 13 day of Aprill 1540 £7 10s which he pd. in Spayne to my s*a*rvant Tyndall £7 10s

S. £12

anno 1540

Robert Sexy p*er* contra is dewe to have the 6 day of December 1540 40s for so myche I make E. Pryn debitor for hym as it may apere fo. 89 £2
Itm. the 15 of November 1542 my s*a*rvant R. Lett r. of hym 46s 8d for the hallf freight p*er* contra £2 6s 8d
Itm. the 10 of February 1542 Leyt r. of hym 46s 8d £2 6s 8d
Itm. for 2 yelow lynard*es* 54s & for 3 yerd*es* of white kerssey 8s mon*tith*[1] £3 2s
Itm. the 21 day of M*a*rche 1549 r. of his s*a*rvant Richard Harrys £11 11s 4d

anno 1540

Will*i*am Pick*es* p*er* contra is dewe to have the 9 day of June £15 *that* is for £14 r. of his wif & 20s for tallow & bytakle to my ship this viage £15
Itm. the 14 day of February £40 for so myche r. of hym in redy mon*n*ey £40 16s 8d
Itm. the 23 day of February r. of hy*m* £20 £20
Itm. the 24 day of October 1541 r. of hym £60 £60

---

[1] *See Sexy's account fo. 97 A.*

97(R) contd.

Itm. the 17 day of November r. of hym £40	£40		
Itm. the 24 day of December r. by the handes of his sarvant John Lasye £40	£40		
Itm. the last day of December £7 that is for so myche redy money r. of hym	£7		
Itm. the 9 day of February 1542 r. of hym in redy money £30 7s, more I owe hym 33s for 2 C talowe at 12s the C & 6 dozen bytakle at 18d the dozen, montith the hole £32	£32		
Itm. the 10 day of Marche r. of hym in redy monney £18 11s, more for 16 dozen of bytakle 24s & for 12 ells of canvas 5s, montith the hole	£20		
Itm. for 2 ollrowns for sayles at 12s the pece	£1	4s	
Itm. for ellmyne bordes which Hamon r. of hym for my shipp 20d		1s	8d
Itm. the 7 day of February 1543 r. of hym in redy money £28 16s 4d	£28	16s	4d
Itm. the 16 day of June 1545 he pd. to my wif £3	£3		
Itm. the 20 day of December 1546 Robert Sternall r. of hym for me £22	£22		
Itm. the last of July 1548 r. £84	£84		
Itm. the 6th day of Augost 1549 r. by Henry Setterford my sarvant £165, I sey £135	£135		
Itm. 40s which he do apoynt me to r. of John Wylly chamberlayne for the h'd wyne per contra	£2		

Small loose sheet with fo. 97 written by Robert Sexy.

97(A)

Master Sexy is cownt r. the 21 of Marche 1549

Master Smithe marchante owith me the 25 day of Jenuary anno 1549 for 36 yardes off yelow lyner	£1	7s
Item for 3 yardes of white kersy		8s
Item the 13th of February for 36 yardes of yelow lyning	£1	7s
S.	£3	2s

98(L)   **anno 1540**

John Bawle of Bristowe yeoman owith me the 13 day of May £3 which is for 1 pipe Rendry iren payable by his bill at Seynt Jamystide next commyng	£3
Itm. the 16 day of Agost £6, to pay £3 the 13 day of October next comyng & £3 the 15 day of November next after that which is for 1 ton Rendry iren as in my shop boke may apere	£6
The 20 day of July anno 1541 the seid John Bawle & Robert Guyttons marchant of Bristowe & William Bawle poyntmaker of the seid town be bownd in a obligacion made by William Nasche nottary to pay 13s 4d at Seynt Jamystide in anno 1542, & from yere to yere at the seid feste 13s 4d untyll the som of £6 be paide	
passed the rest of this cowmpt to my newe booke fo. 4	

anno 1540

Henry Dave of Bristowe tayllor owith me the 15 daye of May £3 which is for a pipe Rendry iren, to be paide 10 dayes after Mighellmas next. Thomas Carpynter marchant of Bristowe is shewerty for it	£3		
Itm. the 1 day of December £3 6s 8d that is for a pipe iren of S.S. sold & d'd to hym at 6s. 8d the C, to be pd. at Seynt Jamistide next. Thomas Carpynter is shewerty	£3	6s	8d
S.	£6	6s	8d

98(L) contd.   **anno 1547**

Thomas Updavithe of Cowebridge in Wales owithe the 30 day of Jenyver anno dicto 5 nobles to be paide at all tymes & is for a h'd of Gascon wyne sold & delyverd to hym. Master Bassett is shewerty   £1 13s 4d

98(R)   **anno 1540**

John Bawle per contra is dewe to have the 5 day of Agost £3 which he paide to my wif in monney   £3

Itm. the 28 day of July r. of William Bawle 13s 4d   13s 4d

Itm. the last day of the same month r. of Robert Guytton   £1 6s 8d

Itm. the 27 day of July 1543 r. of William Bawle poyntmaker 13s 4d   13s 4d

Itm. the 13 day of October anno 1544 r. of William Bawle 13s 4d   13s 4d

Itm. the 24 day of December 1545 being Cristmas Eve of William Bawle 13s 4d   13s 4d

anno 1540

Henry David per contra is dewe to have the 29 day of November £3 r. of hym in redy money   £3

Itm. the 15 day of September 1541 my sarvant Robert Leight r. 26s 8d   £1 6s 8d

Itm. the last day of Awgost 1542 r. 2 fryses for   £2

                              S. £6 6s 8d

Thomas Updavith is dewe to have the 27 of July anno 1548 5 nobles r. of hym at Bristow   £1 13s 4d

99(L)   **anno 1540**

William Cockes of Bristowe marchant owith the 10 day of May £6 that is for the freight of 9 ton iren in the Trynte my ship, to be paid at thend of 3 monthes next commyng, as it may apere by the charterparty   £6

Itm. the 6 day of November £3 15s that is for the freight of 3 ton 3 h'd Gascon wyne in the Trynte at 20s per ton, to pay at 3 monthes & 3 monthes   £3 15s

1541 Itm. the 4th day of May 1541 46s 8d that is for the hallf freight of 7 ton iren in the Trynte at 13s 4d the ton, to paye yt at thend of 3 monthes next commyng   £2 6s 8d

Itm. the 1 day of December 50s that is for the freight of 2 ton bastard in the Trynte at 25s per ton, to paye hallf in hand & hallf at the end of 3 monthes next   £2 10s

1542 Itm. the 24 day of Aprell 1542 £3 6s 8d that is for the freight of 5 ton iren in the Trynte, to pay at 3 monthes & 3 monthes, as by the charterparty may apere   £3 6s 8d

Itm. the 18 day of February £7 10s which is for the freight of 5 ton wyne in my ship at 30s per ton, to pay hallf in hand & hallf 3 monthes next after   £7 10s

anno 1540

John Pryn marchant of Bristowe owith the 10 day of May £6 13s 4d for the freight of 10 ton iren in my ship the Trynte, to pay at thend of 3 monthes next commyng   £6 13s 4d

Itm. the 23 day of Augost 44s 6d for the freght of 3 tons 5 kyntalls iren in the Trynte at 13s 4d per ton   £2 4s 6d

Itm. the 1 day of December 37s 6d which is for the rest & hallf freight of 3 tons bastard in the Trynte at 25s per ton, to paye at the end of 3 monthes next commyng   £1 17s 6d

1542 Itm. the 23 daye of Augost anno 1542 26s 8d that is for the freight of 2 tons iren at 13s 4d per ton   £1 6s 8d

99(L) contd.   anno 1540

Thomas Robertz sarvant to Master William Shipman marchant of Bristowe owith the 10 day of May 36s 1d that is for the freight of 2 ton iren 11 kyntalls at 13s 4d per ton, to pay at thend of 3 monthes next commyng | £1 16s 1d
Itm. the 23 day of August 3s 7d which is for the freight of 4 kyntalls iren in the Trynte at 13s 4d per ton | 3s 7d

99(R)   anno 1540

William Cockes per contra is dewe to have the 18 day of Agost £6 r. of hym in redy monney	£6		
Itm. the 15 day of February 37s 6d r. of hym for the hallf freight of 3 ton 3 h'd wyne per contra	£1	17s	6d
1541 Itm. the 7 day of May r. by Hamond 27s 6d	£1	7s	6d
Itm. the 30 day of Augost r. 46s 8d	£2	6s	8d
Itm. the last day of Jenyver 25s r. for the on hallf of his 2 ton freight per contra by thandes of Harry my sarvant	£1	5s	
Itm. the last day of Marche 1542 Hamon r. 25s	£1	5s	
Itm. the 19 day of August r. of hym £3 6s 8d	£3	6s	8d
Itm. the 3 day of Marche r. by Hamon £3 15s	£3	15s	
Itm. the 14 of June 1543 r. of hym £3 15s	£3	15s	

anno 1540

John Pryn per contra is dewe to have the 4th day of Agost £5 r. of hym in redy monney	£5		
Itm. the last day of December 44s 6d r. of Edward Pryn for hym in acowmpt fo. 89	£2	4s	6d
Itm. the 29 day of Jenyver r. of hym 5s 10d in 12 ores which my boteswayne ocupyed in the ship of the seid Pryns ores		5s	10d
Itm. the same day 27s 6d of hym in redy monney	£1	7s	6d
Itm. the 15 day of Maye 1542 37s 6d that is ffor so myche r. of his wif by thandes of Hewgh Hamon	£1	17s	6d
Itm. the 8 day of February 13s 4d that is for so myche my sarvant Leight r. of his wif		13s	4d
Itm. the 9 day of Marche 1542 my sarvant Leyt r. of hym		13s	4d

anno 1540

Thomas Robertz per contra is dewe to have the 21 day of [1] 36s 1d by thandes of Thomas Shipman	£1	16s	1d
Itm. the 15 day of Jenyver r. 3s 7d		3s	7d

100(L)   anno 1540

Richard Williams of Bristowe ropemaker owith the 10 day of Maye 13s 4d that is for the freight of 1 ton iren from Spayne in my ship at 13s 4d per ton, to pay at thend of 3 monthes next commyng | 13s 4d
1546 Itm. the 28 day of August £4 17s 1d ob & is for the rest of acowmpt ffynishid the same day as may apere | £4 17s 1d½

anno 1540

Thomas Hickes of Bristowe marchant owith the 11 day of June £3 3s 4d that is for 1 h'd iren of S.S. at 20 nobles the ton & 1 h'd of the Rendry at £6 the ton, d'd ffor hym to Morys Smythe, to pay at Easter next | £3 3s 4d
Itm. the 22 day of September £6 that is ffor 1 ton of iren d'd for hym to Thomas Howell berebruar, to be paide at Easter next commyng | £6
1541 Itm. the 27 day of May 1541 30s that is for 1 h'd iren d'd for hym to Morys Smythe | £1 10s

---

[1] Blank in MS.

100(L) contd.

Itm. the 18 day of February 30s for the freight of a ton wyne in my ship, to pay hallf in hand & hallf at 3 monthes £1 10s
1543 Itm. the 14 day of Jenyver 1543 £6 & is for 1 to*n* Rendry iren d'd for hym to T. Howell berebruar, to be pd. at Seynt Jamistide next com*m*yng £6

100(R)   **anno 1540**

Richard Willi*a*ms p*er* contra is dewe to have for s*e*rteyne ratlyne, m*a*rlyne & twyne *that* Hamond r. of hym for my ship 4s
Itm. 6d for a newe string to my crossbowe 6d
Itm. the 5th day of February 8s 10d which he pd. in redy money to my s*a*rvant Hewgh Hamond 8s 10d
Itm. the last day of Jenyver 1546 my wif r. of Richard Willi*a*ms wif 57s £2 17s
Itm. the 14 day of May 1547 I r. of Richard Wylli*a*ms wif 40s £2

anno 1541

Thomas Hick*es* p*er* contra is dewe to have the 10th day of May,[1] £9 15d *that* is for so myche Franc*es* Codryngton pay me for hym in the hallf freight of 14 to*n* pipe wyne *that* I lode in the Harry, m*a*ster Antony Picket, this last vintaage, as it may apere to the seid Franc*es* in debito fo. 60 £9 1s 3d
Itm. the 19 day of Maye 2s 1d r. of hym 2s 1d
Itm. the 24 day of December 30s which he paith for me to Franc*es* Codryngton, as by acowmpt may apere £1 10s
Itm. 30s which I owe for 1 to*n* freight of oyle in his ship this vyntage 1542 £1 10s
Itm. 29 of July 1544 he pd. me at my doore £4 £4
Itm. the 29 of August r. 40s & d'd to hy*m* his byll £4

101(L)   **anno 1540**

Wood of the Yles of Surrys 149 C ½ r. for my owne acowmpt the 19 day of June ow*t* of the Jh*e*sus of Bristowe, m*a*ster under God Phellip Thomas, ow*ith* 66842 r*es* of Portyngall for so myche *that* 143 qrs. weight of the Yland cost ~~at~~ there clere abord, as by Franc*es* Fowlers acowmpt may apere: for freight of the same valurid 6 ton 3 h'd 1 C at 22s the ton, for the costom, averes, hawllyng & all other cost*es* *that* growe apon hit after it ca*m* to the Key at 6s 8d the ton, mo*n*tith all £51 10s 3d½ £51 10s 3d½
Itm. the 31 day of December £21 14s 4d½ goten by this cownt of wood as it ap*er*ith to gaynes in credito fo. 92 £21 14s 4d½

                                                                                              £73 4s 8d

anno 1549

1 qr. 14 li.   Wood of the Yellis of Surrys, that is to sey 433 kyntalls of ollde wood & 439 k*y*ntall*s* 3 qr. 12 li. of newe woode, mo*n*tith both p*ar*cells 873 hundred*es*, 26 li. of Englische weyte, r. ow*t* of the Hart of Bristowe, under God m*a*ster Thomas Boyse the 29th, I sey the 29 day of July a*n*no dicto, ow*ith*e for my owne acowmpt 504 V 30 ryalls[2] of

---

[1] the 10th day of May *is inserted above.*
[2] *Smythe uses V here for Milres (1,000 res) as for 1,000 maravedis. Ryalls seems to be an error for res.*

101(L) contd.

	Portyngall, for so myche hit cost clere abord the ship.			
	More 6 V 400 res for Hewgh Hamondes costes, montith			
873 ks.	all 510 V 30 res which tyrnyd into crusados after 400 res			
26 li.	per crusado & the crusado valurid at 6s sterlyng montith	£382	10s	
	Itm. for freight acowntyng 22 kyntalls wood for a ton at			
	26s 8d per ton & for averes after 1d ob per kyntall,			
	montith all £59 6s	£59	6s	
873 ks.	Itm. the 28 day of Marche £143 6s 6d goten by this			
26 li.	cowmpt of woode	£143	6s	6d
		S. £575	2s	6d

101(R)   anno 1540

	Wood per contra is dewe to have the 31 day of			
	Augost £64 15s that is for 129 kyntalls ½ of			
	wood sold at dyvers tymes sens the 2d day of			
129½	July last past to John Yerbery, Thomas Nasche			
	& John Plumley clothiars as in my shop boke &			
	in every of theyr acowmptes in this boke may			
	apere	£64	15s	
	Itm. the 31 day of December £8 9s 8d which is for			
	16 C ¾, 24 li. sold sens the 28 day of October			
	last past at dyvers tymes to John Yerbery of			
	Bruton at 10s the C, montith	£8	9s	8d
		£73	4s	8d

Anno 1549

	Woode per contra is dewe to have the 20ti day			
	of November anno dicto £260 18s 4d & is for			
391 ks.[1]	150 kyntalls of old woode & 241 kyntalls of newe			
1 qr.	woode at 13s 4d per kyntall, solld & delyverd at			
14 li.	dyvers tymes sethens the 29 day of July last past to			
	William Cockes of Shepton, Jamys Rogers of			
	Coventry, William Brydges of Weston, Robert			
	Sallsbury of Bristowe dyar, Thomas Asche of Batcom.			
	John Hamon of Bridgewater, Edmond Guar of			
	Costom, Arllnolld of Wells, John Strovit,			
	Richard Edmondes tucker, John Yerbery,			
	William Buchar, William Appowell grocer, Robert			
	Nasche serchor, Thomas Harrys of Wells, John			
	Tovy, Robert Sexy, William Prell of Lytton, John			
	Wynschecom,[2] John Tucker of Bruton & John			
	Web of Shepton, as it dothe apere more at large &			
	partyculerly in my shop boke, montith	£260	18s	4d
157 ks.	Itm. the 4th day of December £105 5s 7d & is for			
3 qr.	86 hundreth 3 qr. 27 li. of the old woode & 70			
19 li.	hundreth 3 qr. 20 li. of the newe woode sold to			
	dyvers perssons, as to Cristofor Warren &			
	William Enderby of Coventre & to Henry			
	Wyeth of Hawxbury & others at 13s 4d the C sens			
	the 20 day of November last past, as by my shop			
	boke it dothe apere pertyculerly	£105	5s	7d
	Itm. the 11 day of December sold & delyverd to John			
	Buchar of of[3] West Hartrye & to others sens the			

---

[1] ks. *is the abbreviation of kyntalls in the marginal notes.*
[2] John Wynschecom *is written above the line.*
[3] *Smythe repeats* of.

101(R) contd.

054 ks. ½ 21 li.	5th of the same December, 40 C ½, 21 li. of the newe woode & 24 C of tholld woode, mon*tith* all 54 C, ½ a C, 21 li. at 13s 4d the C, mon*tith*	£36 9s 2d
086 ks. ¾ 21 li.	Itm. the 30 of December solld to Thomas Buchar of Sherolld, to *Cristofo*r Warren & others sens the 11 day of December, 45 k*yntalls* 10 li. of newe woode & 41 k*yntalls* 3 qr. 11 li. of olde wood, mon*tith* all 86 k*yntalls* 3 qr. 21 li. at 13s 4d the C, mon*tith*	£57 19s 2d
098 ks. 1 qr. 8 li. ½	Itm. the 11 of February £65 11s & is for 37 C 3 qr. 4 li. ½ of the newe wood & for 60 C ½, 4 li. of the olde woode, mon*tith* all 98 C 1 qr. 8 li. ½ wood solld sens the 30 of December & delyverd at 13s p*er* C to Thomas Burges & Robert Harrys of Wells & to others as in my shop boke may apere	£65 11s
73 ks. 1 qr. 22 li.	Itm. the 28 of Marche a*nno* 1550 £48 19s 3d & ys for 73 k*yntalls* 1 qr. 22 li. of tholde woode solld sens the 11 day of February last past to W*illiam* Brydg*es* & Henrye Wyeth & to others at 13s 4d the C	£48 19s 3d
10 ks. ½ 4 li. ½	Itm. 10 C ½, 4 li. ½ which is broken & wastyd of the 873 k*yntalls* 26 li. p*er* contra lying in my hows 9 monthes	[1]
873 ks. 26 li.		S. £575 2s 6d

102(L) **anno 1540**

Thomas Smythe of Bristowe m*a*rchant owithe the 23 day of Augost £3 19s 1d that is for the freight of 5 ton 14 k*yntall*s iren in the Try*n*te at 13s 4d p*er* ton £3 19s 1d
Itm. the 15 day of November £3 which is for the freight of 3 ton Gascon wyne in my ship the Try*n*te, to paye at 3 monthes & 3 monthes £3
Itm. the first day of December £3 2s 6d is for the rest & hallff freight of 5 tons bastard in the Try*n*te at 25s the ton, to be pd. at thend of 3 monthes next com*m*yng £3 2s 6d

anno 1540

Thomas Smythe hop*er* my unckle owith the 18 day of September £63 that is for 27 pipe samon which I sold & delyverd to hym at 46s 8d the pipe, to pay at Easter next com*m*yng £63
1542 Itm. the 12 day of August 1542 18s that is ffor 3 C of S.S. iren to be paide at all tymes 18s

102(R) **anno 1540**

	Thomas Smythe p*er* contra is dewe to have the 25 day of February £3 16s 4d r. of hy*m* in redy mon*n*ey	£3 16s 4d
	Itm. the 17 day*e* of May*e* r. by thand*es* of Hamond	£2
	Itm. the 7 of Ap*re*ll 1542 r. of Thomas Smythes s*a*rvant	£1 6s 8d
	Itm. the 1 day of December 1542 my s*a*rvant Robert Leight r. of his wif 35s 10d	£1 15s 10d

anno 1541

	Thomas Smythe p*er* contra is dewe to have the 4 day of Ap*re*ll £40 r. of hym by the hand*es* of his wif	£40
	Itm. the 11 day of May £4 13s 4d for 1 to*n* Gasco*n* wyne which he delyverd for me to J*oh*n Roxby	£4 13s 4d
	Itm. the 13 day of August r. £15 6s 8d	£15 6s 8d

---

[1] *Blank in MS.*

102(R) contd.

	Itm. the 1 day of Augost 1542 r. 55s 6d in redy money & 4s 6d for rebatyng of 3 tons of oyle, mon*tith* the hole £3	£3

103(L)   **anno 1540**

38 clothes

Viages to Andaluzia owith for my prop*er* acowmpt in Augost owith £152 that is for 38 clo*thes* of J*oh*n Yerberis better sorte in coll*ores* hewlyng*es* and light grenes, which cost clere abord £4 p*er* clothe, of the which 38 clothes war laden in the Jh*esu*s of Bristo, m*aster* Phillip Thomas, 29 cloth*es* in 4 fardells & 9 clo*thes* in won fardell in the M*a*rgeret of Bristo, m*aster* John Wyll*i*ams, mon*tith*   £152

Itm. the same tyme £40 *that* is for 7 weyes ½ wheat laden in the foresseid M*a*rket¹ & 9 weyes wheat laden yn the Harry of Bristowe, m*aster* Antony Picket, mon*tith*   £40

Itm. £10 *that* is for 40 d*u*catts which J*oh*n Wellshis attorney must pay in Andaluzia to my factor Giles White, mon*tith*   £10

Itm. the   ²   day of Octob*er* laden in the Trynte of Wales, m*aster* Bastian Millior, 10 weyes wheat which cost clere abord £24   £24

Itm. the 2d day of December £4 which is for 16 d*u*catts pd. & allowyd to Giles Whit ffor his cost*es*, as by his acowmpt maye apere   £4

Itm. the 18 day of Jenyver £92 1s 10d goten by this viages as it ap*er*ith to gaynes in credito fo. 92   £92   1s 10d

          S.   £322   1s 10d

anno 1540

Viag*es* to Andaluzia for my owne acowmpt owith the 20 day of February £83 that is for 10 clothes of J*oh*n Yerberys pen*n*y hewes which cost with grazing & all other cost*es* clere abord £40 & 11 clothes of W*illiam* Buchars makyng which cost with the grazing & other cost*es* clere abord £43 the which 21 clothes war laden in my owne sarplars made in 2 fardells in the Jh*esu*s of Bristowe, m*aster* Philip Thom*as*   £83

Itm. the 2d day of M*a*rche lade in the Harry of Bristow, under God m*aster* Antony Picket, 10 clothes of Jamys Bysses which cost clere abord £49 10s & 20 clothes of J*oh*n Yerberys penny hewes which cost with dying clere aborde £80 & 1 violet of Thom*as* Nasches which cost clere abord £5 & 1 clothe of W*illiam* Buchars £3 15s & 2 truckers of J*oh*n Yerberys £5 & 31 weyes of wheat which cost clereabord £85 10s 10d, amo*ntith* all £228 16s 10d   £228 16s 10d

Itm. 10 d*u*catts for the hallf of Giles cost*es this* viage   £2 10s

Itm. the 21 day of July 1541 £85 11s 2d which is for so myche goten by this viage as it may apere to gaynes in credito fo. 92   £85 11s 2d

          S.   £399 18s

103(R)   **anno 1540**

38

Viag*es* p*er* contra is dewe to have the 22 day of Decemb*er* £162 12s 5d *that* is for 243 V. 937 M. which Giles Whit geve me in cowmpt for the nete sale in Luxborn of the 38 cloth*es* p*er* contra   £162 12s 5d

---

¹i.e. *Margaret*.
²*Blank in MS*.

103(R) contd.

Itm. the same day, 149 V. 209 M. which the seid Giles r. at Luxborn for the nete sale of my wheat in the Marget & Henry per contra & as by the seid Giles cownt may apere, montith	£99	9s	5d
Itm. the same day £10 which is for 40 ducatts the seid Giles r. of John Wellshis attorney mencionyd per contra & made me payement of the same	£10		
Itm. the 18 day of Jenyver £50 that is for 200 ducatts which Nicholas Tizon marchant of Bristowe r. for my acowmpt of John Apowell pursser of the Trynte of Wales for the nete sale of the 10 weys wheat laden in her as per contra may apere, of the which 200 ducatts I do make Nicholas Tizon debitor in fo. 126	£50		
	£322	1s	10d

anno 1541

Viages per contra is dewe to have the 21 day of July £399 18s that is for 379 V. 206 M. which the 55 clothes per contra made clere & 220 V. 641 M. which the 31 weyes wheat per contra made clere, as it maye playnlyer apere by Giles Whitz acowmmpt, montith sterlyng as afore reherssyd	£399	18s	

104(L)

anno 1540

Viages to Burdes in Agost owith the 28 of the same for my owne acowmpt £15 that is for 6 clothes truckers laden in my ship the Trynte, master John Derby—15			
Itm. the same tyme in the seid ship, a bay gellding that cost me 50s —02. 10			
Itm. the same tyme to Thomas Shipman 216 ducatts & 79 crowns of the sun, montith sterlyng £72 8s 6d, 921 ffranckes,[1] 72.08.6. So montith the hole which goth consygnyd with & to Thomas Shipman	£89	18s	6d
Itm. 9s 4d that is for 6 ffranckes lost in the weight of the foresseid gold as by Thomas Shipmans cownt may apere		9s	4d
Itm. the 17 day of December £7 6s 8d goten by this acowmpt as it aperith to gaynes in credito 92	£7	6s	8d
S.	£97	14s	6d

anno 1541

Viages to Burdes for my acownt the 7 day of September owith £66 3s 4d that is for 40 northen dozens & 6 clothes truckers laden in the Marget, which cost £62 13s 4d & more a gelldyng laden in the An of London, master John Gawle, which cost £3 10s. So montith the hole	£66	3s	4d
Itm. more won C crowns of the son montith	£23	6s	8d
Itm. 4s 4d which Thomas Shipman r. in loss & thexchange of the seid C crowns		4s	4d
S.	£89	14s	4d

---

[1] £72 8s 6d, 921 ffranckes *inserted later*.

104(L) contd.   anno 1540

John Vele of Bristowe kerver owith the 23 day of October 30s which is for
1 h'd iren which I solld & d'd to hym, to be paide at Candellmas next
com*m*yng   £1   10s
Itm. the 19 day of February 30s that is for 1 h'd Rendry iren to be paide at
Seynt Jamistide next   £1   10s
1541 Itm. the last day of February a*nno* 1541 30s which is for 1 h'd iren to be
paide at Seynt Jamistide next com*m*yng   £1   10s
1542 Itm. the 11 day of November 1542 £6 that is for 1 to*n* Rendry iren less
2 li. to be paide by his obligacio*n* at O*w*r Lady Day in Lent next com*m*yng   £6

104(R)   anno 1540

Viag*es* p*er* contra is dewe to have £20 6s for 87 *crowns* of the
son which war made of the nete sale of the 6 truckers *per*
contra   £20   6s
Itm. £5 for so myche my horss was sold ffor & pd. in 5
½-bales wood at 4 d*ucatts* the ½-bale   £5
Itm. £72 8s 6d for so myche Thomas Shipman geve me
acowmpt of in won with all the afforesseid as it may apere
by the reckenyng r. of hym   £72   8s   6d

                                                                                                   £97 14s   6d

                                      anno 1541

Viag*es* p*er* contra is dewe to have the monthe of Nove*m*ber
£59 13s 4d that is for the nete sale of 40 northe*n*s & 6
truckers p*er* contra sold at Burd*es* for 255 *crowns* ½ of the
son & 6 K. ¼, mon*tith* after 14 grot*es* the *crown*   £59 13s   4d
Itm. £4 10s which 5 balett*es* of woode might be wu*r*the at
Burd*es* that Thomas Shipma*n* sold my gellding for & more
2 *crowns* that he had for hym in redy money, mo*ntith*
all £5   £5
Itm. £23 6s 8d which Thomas Shipma*n* pay me at Burd*es* in
his cownt corrent   £23   6s   8d
Itm. the monthe of Nove*m*ber 34s 4d lost by this viage as
it ap*er*ith to gayn*es* in debito fo. 92   £1   14s   4d

                                                                                            S.   £89 14s   4d

                                      anno 1540

John Vele p*er* contra is dewe to have the 17 day of February
30s for so myche r. of hym in redy mon*n*ey   £1   10s
Itm. the 30 day of July 1541 my wif r. 30s   £1   10s
Itm. the 11 day of Augost 1542 r. of hym 30s   £1   10s
Itm. the 28 day of July 1543 r. of hym £3   £3
Itm. r. of his wif 4 nobles   £1   6s   8d
Itm. the 3 day of Augost 1544 his wif pd. 20s   £1

105(L)   anno 1540

John Plumley of Bruton clothiar owith the 3d day of August 50s to pay at all
tymes which is for 5 C of Ylland wood sold & d'd to hym at 10s the C   £2   10s

                                      anno 1540

Charles Lowe m*a*rchant of Bristowe owith the 24 day of July 30s 5d that is
for 1 h'd 8 li. iren d'd for hym to Jo*h*n Jones of Chepston at £6 *the* ton, to pay
at Mighellmas next   £1   10s   5d
1542 Itm. the 10 day of June a*nno* 1542 £6 *that* is for 1 ton iren solld &
delyverd to hym to be pd. by his byll at *Crist*mas next com*m*yng   £6

146

105(R)

anno 1540

John Plumley per contra is dewe to have the 15 day of February 50s for so myche John Yerbery of Bruton r. of me in a payement I make hym	£2 10s

anno 1540

Charles Lowe per contra is dewe to have the 13 day of November 30s 5d r. of hym in monney	£1 10s 5d
Itm. the 4th day of August 1542 r. of hym £3	£3
Itm. the 26 day of Jenyver 1543 r. from hym by Thomas Peryngton 40s in monney	£2
Itm. the 27 day of November he sent me by my sarvant Leyt 10s	10s
Itm. the 14 of Jenyver 1544 r. by Lett from Charles Lowe 5s, more he r. the 16 day of the same monthe 5s montith 10s	10s

106(L)

anno 1540

Nicholas Mawrewood of Bristowe poyntmaker owithe the 27 day of July £3 that is for a pipe of iren d'd in his name to John Hwet of Cornewall to be paide at all tymes	£3	
1543 Itm. the 11 day of August 1543 £3 9d & is for 2 ½-bales Tullus wood conteynyng 3 C ½, 9 li. at 17s the C, sold & d'd to hym to be paide at all tymes requyrid	£3	9d
Itm. the 24 of Aprell 1544 £12 13s 4d & is for 2 ton iren to be paide by his byll at Mighellmas next	£12 13s	4d
Itm. the 18 day of December 1545 for 1 ton Gascon wyne £7 10s to be pd. the first day of Marche next commyng	£7 6s	8d
Itm. the 12 day of Aprell 1546 £7 10s which is ffor 1 pipe wull oyle to be paide at Sturbridge fayer next	£7 10s	
Solmd.	£33 10s	9d

anno 1540

Water Robertz of Bristowe marchant owithe the 15 day of October £12 13s 4d which is for 2 ton iren d'd for hym to Martyne Davith of Kermerdyne, to be pd. by his bill at Easter next commyng, montith	£12 5s	4d
1541 Itm. the 17 day of December anno 1541 £6 13s 4d that is £4 for a pipe of bastard & 4 markes for 2 h'd claret wyne, to pay at Mydsomer next	£6 13s	4d
1544 Itm. the 1 day of Aprell 1544 40s & is for the ½ freight of 3 tons iren which he had in my ship the Trynte, to be paid at thend of 3 monthes next commyng	£2	

106(R)

anno 1540

Nicholas Mawrewood per contra is dewe to have the 15 day of November 40s pd. by his mayde	£2	
the 18 day of December r. 20s	£1	
Itm. the 4 day of Aprell anno 1544 r. £3 9s	£3 9s	
Itm. 22 day of November my wif r.	£6 13s	4d
Itm. the 10th day of December I r. of hym £4	£4	
Itm. the 8 day of Jenyver 40s which he paide to my wif	£2	
Itm. the 5 day of ~~Marche~~ Aprell 1546 r. of hym £7 6s 8d	£7 6s	8d
Itm. r. by his son the 22 of Jenyver £7 10s	£7 10s	
Solmd.	£33 10s	9d

anno 1541

Water Robertz per contra is dewe to have the 19 daye of May £4 which I r. of hym in redy monney	£4

106(R) contd.

Itm. the 2d day of Augost r. of hym £8 13s 4d	£8	13s 4d
1542 Itm. the 2d day of Augost r. of hym £3	£3	
Itm. the 4 day of October r. of hym £3 13s 4d	£3	13s 4d

Itm. the 12 day of June 1545 he sent me a reckenyng by my sarvant Henry Setterfford of 25 seme Wellsche bord*es* at 6d *the* seame & of a brode yerd 3 qrs. of muster clo*the* at 4s the yerd & of a yerd of white kersy at 20d & 2 yerd*es* ½ Bristowe frise at 12d the yerd & of a yerd & 1 qr. russett kersy at 14d the yerd & for 4 yerd*es* 3 qr. grey frize at 6d the yerd. Mon*tith* the hole 27s 6d½   £1 7s 6d ob.

106(A)

A small loose page between fos. 106(L) and fo. 106(R) probably written by Henry Setterford, Smythe's apprentice.

My m*aster* Jhon Smyth o*with* to Water Robert*es*

Inp*rimis* for 3 seme of bordes mon*tith*	1s	6d
Itm. for 2 seme of bordes mon*tith*	1s	
Itm. for 18 seme of bordes mon*tith*	9s	
Itm. more for 2 seme mon*tith*	1s	
Itm. for a brod yard 3 qrs. of must*er* at 4s the yard mon*tith*	7s	
Itm. for a yard of whyt kersye	1s	8d
Itm. for 2 yard*es* ½ of Brystow fryze	2s	6d
Itm. for a yard 1 qr. ruset kersye	1s	6d
Itm. for 4 yard*es* 3 qr. grey fryze at 6d the yard mon*tith*	2s	4d ob.
	27s	6d ob.

107(L)   anno 1540

Diego de Bermy o*with* £157 18s that is for 631 d*ucatts* & 6 r*ialls* of plate which my sarvant Robert Tyndall have pd. to hym at 2 tymes in a*nno* 1540 & in a*nno* 1541, as by his acowmpt may apere, mon*tith*   £157 18s

107(R)   anno 1540

Diego de Bermy m*archant* of Burgos in Spayne is dew to have the monthe of June £157 18s *that* is for 150 hallf ballett*es* of Tullus wood of 8 capassos the cargg & of 28 floryng*es* warantiez, the which my sarvant*z* Thom*as* Shipma*n* & Robert Tyndall r. of hym at Burdes & lode it in the Mawdelen of the Passaige, Master J*oh*n de la Sala, for the which £157 18s which be in d*ucatts* 631 d*ucatts* 6 rialls of plate. The seid Thom*as* & Robert & I in won with them by bertewe of my powar gevyn to *the* seid Robert stond bownd in Spayne by obligacio*n* & allso I have conffyrmyd the seid obligacio*n* here in Yngland by me l*ettores* to Antonyo Jaymes ffactor for the seid Diego here in London, to pay 315 d*ucatts* 8 rialls ½ at Cristmas next com*m*yng & 315 d*ucatts* 8 rialls ½ at Cristmas next after *that*, mon*titih*   £157 18s

108(L)   anno 1540

33 ton
1 h'd

Wynes of Gascon for my owne acowmpt r. the monthes of November & December, *that* is to sey 11 ton ow*t* of my ship the Trynte, m*aster* Jo*hn* Derby, 5 ton ow*t* of the Prymros, m*aster* Thomas Web, 7 ton ow*t* of the Jh*es*us of Tor, m*aster* Robert Marchant, & 10 ton 1 h'd ow*t* of the

108(L) contd.

1 ton	*Cristo*for of Darckmowthe, m*aster* Nicholas Huchyn, ow*ith* 998 ffranckes 50 a. Burdalez, for so myche as the seid 33 ton 1 h'd wyne cost clere abord at Burd*es*, as by Thomas Shipmans cowmpt may apere, mon*tith* sterlyng acowmptyng the ffranck for 20d sterlyng £83 5s	£83 5s
	Itm. for freight of 16 to*n* in the Trynte & Pr*y*mros at 20s p*er* ton, of 7 ton in the Jh*esu*s of Tor at 13s p*er* ton & of 10 to*n* 1 h'd in the *Cristo*for of Darckmowthe at 13s 4d p*er* ton, for aver*e*s in the Trynte 2s 8d p*er* ton, in the Pr*y*mros 3s 3d p*er* to*n*, in the Jh*esu*s of Tor 3s 9d p*er* ton & in the *Cristo*for of Darckmowthe 2s 7d ob p*er* ton, for costom of 30 ton at 3s p*er* ton & ffor halyng & stowyng 3d p*er* ton. So mon*tith* all	£37 4s 11d
	Itm. 26s 7d for 1 t*ier*ce of taynt to fill the red wynes	£1 6s 8d
	Itm. £4 13s 4d paide to Thom*as* Shipm*an* for 1 ton of white wyne	£4 13s 4d
	anno 1541 Itm. the 6 day of Aprell 1541 £24 7s 10d *that* is for the gaynes had by the sale of the wynes of this p*artido* as it apere to geynes in credito fo. 92	£24 7s 10d
		£150 17s 9d

108(R)   anno 1540

	Wynes p*er* contra be dewe to have the 11 day of	
6	November £7 *that* is for 6 h'd sold to John Braughyng fo. 109	£7
4	Itm. the 12 day of November £4 16s 8d for 1 to*n* to W*illiam* North fo. 24	£4 16s 8d
4	Itm. the seid day £4 13s 4d for 1 to*n* to Richard Carrick 34	£4 13s 4d
7⅓	Itm. the 13 day of the same 1 ton 3 h'd 1 t*ier*ce to Robert Pole 111	£9 11s 8d
7⅓	Itm. the same day 1 ton 3 h'd 1 t*ier*ce to Thom*as* Bell fo. 62	£9 11s 8d
4	Itm. the 15 of November 1 to*n* Gasco*n* wyne to Jo*h*n Roxby 10	£4 16s 8d
4	Itm. the same day 1 to*n* to Alexander Bosgrove 68	£4 16s 8d
4	Itm. the 16 day of Nove*m*ber 1 to*n* to W*illiam* Smothing 72	£4 13s 4d
4	Itm. the 18 day of the same 1 ton to Jo*h*n Coves fo. 110	£4 13s 4d
19	Itm. the 23 day of November 5 to*n* to W*illiam* North*e* fo. 24 less 1 h'd	£23
2	Itm. the 25 day of November 2 h'd Thom*as* Cotes 17	£2 6s 8d
2	Itm. the 26 of November 2 h'd to Jo*h*n Wellsche fo. 74	£2 6s 8d
1	Itm. the 4 of Dece*m*ber 1 h'd to Jo*h*n Roxby fo. 10	£1 3s 4d
2	Itm. the 6 of December 2 h'd to M*aster* N. Wekes fo. 112	£2 6s 8d
4	Itm. the 11 of December 4 h'd to M*aster* Doctor Fitzjamys 112	£4 13s 4d
4	Itm. the seid day 1 to*n* to Jo*h*n Roxby of Wells fo. 10	£4 16s 8d
2	Itm. the 14 day of Decem*b*er 2 h'd to M*aster* Sentlo fo. 40	£2 6s 8d
4	Itm. the seid day 1 ton to M*aster* Fitzjamys & M*aster* Gilbert fo. 112	£4 13s 4d
6	Itm. the 15 day of Dece*m*ber £7 for 6 h'd to W*illiam* Goldsmythe 113	£7
4	Itm. the same day r. of Jo*h*n Wyllis for 1 to*n* £4 15s	£4 15s

108(R) contd.

6	Itm. the 17 of December £7 for 6 h'd to John Braughyng 109	£7
4	Itm. the same day 1 ton to Alexander Bosgrove fo. 68	£4 16s 8d
2	Itm. the 20 of the same 2 h'd to Master Gorge fo. 36	£2 6s 8d
2	Itm. the 14 of Jenyver 2 h'd to John Gibs fo. 37	£2 6s 8d
4	Itm. the same day 4 h'd to William Smothing fo. 72	£4 13s 4d
2	Itm. the 28 of Jenyvery 2 h'd to John Roxby fo. 10	£2 6s 8d
4	Itm. the 4 of February 4 h'd to William Smothing fo. 72	£4 13s 4d
1	Itm. the same day r. for 1 h'd of a man of Carlyon 23s 4d	£1 3s 4d
3	Itm. the 28 day of February for 3 h'd to Sir John Sentlo fo. 40	£3 10s
2	Itm. the 24 of Marche for 2 h'd to John Brawghyng fo. 109	£2 6s 8d
2	Itm. the 6 day of Aprell 1541 for 2 h'd to John Roxby fo. 10	£2 6s 8d
7½	Itm. 1 ton 2 h'd 1 tierce de pipe which went to yllaidge	[1]
	S.	£150 17s 9d

109(L)   **anno 1540**

John Braughyng of Wursettor vyntener owith the 11 day of November £7 10s
that is ffor 6 h'd of Gascon wyne laden for hym in John Lawghtons trowe
of Handeley at £5 the ton   £7 10s
Itm. the 17 day of December £15 that is for 6 h'd Gascon wyne at £5 the ton
& 2 buttes seck at £3 10s the butt laden ffor hym in the abovesseid trow   £14 10s
Itm. the 22 day of February £8 5s that is for a pipe of taynt £4 5s & for a
pipe of bastard £4, which wynes I sent hym in Thomas Fletes trowe, montith   £8 7s 8d
Itm. the 21 day of Marche sent hym in Thomas Sevarns trowe 4 buttes seck
at eich 5 markes & the 24 day of the seid monthe in the seid trowe lode 2 h'd
Gascon wyne price 50s, montith all £15 16s 8d   £15 16s 8d
1541 Itm. the 27 day of Aprell anno 1541 laden & sent hym in Thomas
Afletes trowe 3 ton 14 li. of my better Rendry iren at £6 the ton & 2 tons of
Gascon wyne at £5 the ton, a jar of oyle berys price 16d & a jar of mete oyle
price 16d, montith the hole £28 3s 5d   £28 3s 5d
Itm. the 29 day of November £13 6s 8d that is for 2 pipes bastard & ossey at
eich £4 & 1 ton Gascon wyne at £5 6s 8d, montith the hole   £13 6s 8d
Itm. the seid tyme 2 h'd Gascon wyne price 4 markes   £2 13s 4d
Itm. the 13 day of Jenyver £7 6s 8d for 2 buttes of seck sent hym in Thomas
Afflettes trowe   £7 6s 8d
Itm. the 28 day of February £14 6s 8d which is for 2 tons Gascon wyne at 16
nobles the ton & 1 butt of seck at 11 nobles the butt sent in T. Afletes trowe   £14 6s 8d
1542 Itm. the 28 day of June anno 1542 £18 18s 4d that is £7 6s 8d for 2
buttes seck £5 6s 8d for 1 ton Gascon wyne & £6 5s for 1 pipe of wull [2] oyle,
all which goodes I sent hym in Thomas Aflettes trowe   £18 18s 4d

                                                                                S. £130 19s 5d

109(R)   **anno 1541**

John Brawghyng per contra is dewe to have the 11 daye of
Aprell £20 for so myche r. of Myles Willsson of Kendale,
montith   £20
Itm. the 28 day of July r. by Myles Willsson £20   £20

---

[1] *Blank in MS.*
[2] *Marginal note,* 36.19.1.

109(R) contd.

Itm. the 18 day of November r. of Mylles Wyllsson £14 & more 54s 4d mon*tith* all		£16	14s	4d
Itm. the 1 day of Ap*r*ell 1542 r. by the seid Myles		£10		
Itm. the 3 day of May r. of hym at W*u*rsett*or* £9 12s 8d. So there is r. ap*o*n & for the wynes of this yere £20		£9	12s	8d
Itm. the first day of Augost r. of Myles Willsson £17 13s 4d		£17	13s	4d
Itm. the 3d day of September my s*a*rvant Robert Leight r. of hym at Wursettor £14		£14		
Itm. the 7 day of February 1543 r. from hym by Myles Willsson £10		£10		
Itm. the 29 day of September 1544 r. for hym of Myles Willsson £12 19s 1d		£12	19s	1d
	S.	£130	19s	5d

110(L) anno 1540

Richard Browne of Bristowe groc*er* owith the 12 day of November £6 which is for 1 to*n* iren sold to hym to be paide the 12 day of May next com*m*yng, as it ap*eri*th by a byll ffyrmyd & sealid by hym & Water Robertz   £6

1541 Itm. the 2 day of June 1541 £6 for 1 to*n* iren to be pd. the 1 day of December next com*m*yng. Water Robert*es* before reherssyd is bownd for hym   £6

Itm. the 21 day of December 1541 £6 13s 4d payable by his & Water Robertz bill at Midssomer next com*m*yng & is for the rest of 2 butt*es* seck sold & d'd to hym at £3 13s 4d *the* butt   £6 13s 4d

anno 1540

Robert Coves of Mawnsbury yeoma*n* owith the 18 day of November £4 13s 4d which is for 1 ton of Gascon wyne sold & d'd to hym, to pay at Candellmas next & Thomas Smythe of Bristowe hop*er* my uncle is shew*er*ty   £4 13s 4d

110(R) anno 1541

Richart Browne p*er* contra is dewe to have the 16 day of Maye £5 r. of hym in redy money	£5		
Itm. the 30 day of Maye r. 20s	£1		
Itm. the 12 day of Decemb*er* 1541 r. £4	£4		
Itm. the 15 day of December r. of hym 40s	£2		
1542 Itm. the 25 day of Augost r. by his wif £3	£3		
Itm. the 26 day of Octob*er* 20s r. by Lett	£1		
Itm. the 14 of June 1543 r. of hym by Henry	£1		
Itm. the 27th of October anno d*om*ini 1556 by the hand*es* of Water Robart*es* and Rychard Browne for the cleare of this acowmpt[1]	£1	13s	4d

anno 1540

Robert Coves p*er* contra is dewe to have the 16 day of Marche 53s 4d r. for hym by thand*es* of Thomas Smythe my unckle mon*tith*	£2	13s	4d
Itm. the last day of M*a*rche 1541 r. from hym by thand*es* of my unckle Thom*as* Smythe 40s	£2		

111(L) anno 1540

Robert Pole m*a*rchant of Glocester owith the 13 day of November £9 11s 8d that is for 7 h'd 1 t*ier*ce Gasco*n* wyne which he r. at Glocester ow*t* of John Sp*a*rkes bote at £5 *the* ton, mon*tith*   £9 11s 8d

---

[1] *The item of 27th October 1556 is not in Smythe's handwriting.*

111(L) contd.

Itm. the 25 day of Jenyver 8s that is for 12 ores d'd for hym to his sarvant John Davys at 8d the ore		8s	
1541 Itm. the 6 day of Maye anno 1541 £12 which is for 2 ton of my better iren of the Rendry at £6 the ton	£12		
Itm. 6s 8d for the freight of 2 anckers in my ship the Trynte owt of Spayne		6s	8d
Itm. the 13 day of June £12 that is for 2 ton iren sold to hym to be paide at all tymes requyrid	£12		
Itm. 41s 10d which is for 2 h'd wyne which his purser r. in December of his averes for 2 h'd red wyne which was taken of mine to the prize, montith	£2	1s	10d
Itm. the 10 day of December 1541 £35 that is ffor £20 d'd to hym in redy money & £15 for a lysence of 60 qrs. wheat which I delyverd to hym at 5s the qr. & I must enjoye hallf the ladyng of all the corne which shalbe laden in his ship this present viaige	£35		
Itm. the 21 day of December 1541 £10 for so myche my sarvant Robert Leight pd. for hym at Twexbury to Giles Gest, montith	£10		
Itm. the 6 daye of Jenyver £20 for so myche redy money paide to hym at Bristowe	£20		
Itm. the 11 day of February anno 1541 £13 6s 8d ffor so myche I sent hym by my sarvant Henry Setterfford & the seid Master Poole r. it of hym at Chepstow	£13	6s	8d
S.	£114	14s	10d

anno 1542

Robert Pole of Glocester forenamyd owith the 2d day of Maye £17 3s 5d & is for so myche he rest owyng for the rest & closing up of his aforeseid cowmpt, as per contra maye apere, montith	£17	3s	5d
Itm. the 14 day of June 291 ducatts 234 M. the which he owith me for 109356 M. that restith for 20 weys ½ wheat sold at Luxbron by his sarvant Henry Browne. It amontith sterling £72 18s 2d	£72	18s	2d
Itm. the same day 36s 3d which is for so myche I have pd. hym for hallf a wey wheat more than his seid sarvant geve me acownt of, as may apere to viages fo. 136	£1	16s	3d
Itm. the same day 56s 7d & it is for so myche gaynes he geve me for 80 cahisses sallt laden this viage for my acowmpt by his seid sarvant Henry Brune, the which sallt the seid Robert is content & agreed to take & r. for his owne acowmpt & do stond to the freight, averes & other costes dewe for the same hymseallf & clerely & fully discharge me thereof & more do allowe me for the same the 56s 7d of gaynes as aforesseid, montith	£2	16s	7d
S.	£94	14s	5d

111(R)   **anno 1541**

Robert Pole per contra is dewe to have the 12 day of June £9 11s 8d r. of hym in redy monney	£9	11s	8d
Itm. the 5th day of December £10 which is for the freight of 10 ton Gascon wyne laden at Burdes this vyntage in his ship the Mary Fortune, master John Derby	£10		
Itm. 36s 8d for averes of the same 10 ton at 3s 8d per ton	£1	16s	8d
Itm. the 23 day of December 5s 2d r. of his pursser for the rest of my 2 h'd wyne taken to prize		5s	2d
Itm. ffor 20 weys & ½ 29 bushell[1] of wheat which he lode for me in February in his ship the Mary, which cost clereabord with all costes, lysence & charges £75 17s 11d I sey it is 21 weys less 1 busshell	£75	17s	11d

---

[1] 29 bushell *is inserted above the line.*

111(R) contd.

Itm. the 2 day of May 1542 £17 3s 5d that is for the rest & makyng evyn of this cowmpt as it may apere to hym in debito hereageynst in a newe cow*n*t	£17	3s	5d
S. £114	14s	10d

anno 1542

Robert Pole p*er* contra is dewe to have the 14 day of June £30 which is for 60 doble d*ucatts* which his s*a*rvant Henry Browne delyverd & paide for me to my s*a*rvant Robert Lett   £30

Itm. £10 that I my seallf r. of the seid Robert Pole in Chepsto the seid day   £10

Itm. the same day my s*a*rvant Robert Lett r. of M*a*stres Pole his wif at Glocester £22 & thereof made her a byll for the discharge of the same   £22

Itm. the same day £32 14s 5d which is for the rest & clozing up of this cowmpt, for the which he have delyverd me a byll obligatory sealyd & sygnyd with his owne hand of £30 to pay £10 at Seynt Jamistide next & £20 at C*ris*tmas next after *that* & for the 54s 5d I have no byll but this cowmpt & his feythefull promes to pay it at at[1] all tymes as it may apere to hym in debito fo. 159   £32   14s   5d

  S.   £94   14s   5d

112(L)   **anno 1540**

M*aster* Nicholas Wekes of Dodyngto*n* in Glocestershire esquyer o*with* the 11 day of December 46s 8d whiche is for 2 h'd wyne d'd to hym *this* day & the 6 day of this p*r*esent as in my shop boke may apere   £2   6s   8d

Itm. the 16 day of Aprill 1547 £3 & is for 2 h'd Gascon wyne at £3 mon*tith* passed to my newe boke fo. 32 the 2de day of July A*n*no 1550   £3

anno 1540

M*aster* Nicholas Fitzjamys esquyer o*with* the 14 day of Decemb*er* £3 10s that is for 3 h'd Gascon wyne sold to hym & sent hym by Rog*er* Parssons of Litellto*n* carrier   £3   10s

anno 1540

M*aster* Doctor Fitzjamys of Wells o*with* the 11 day of December £4 13s 4d which is for 1 ton of Gasco*n* wyne which I sent hym W*illiam* Sheward carriar passed this cownt the 2de day of July 1550 to my newe boke fo. 32   £4   13s   4d

112(R)[2]

113(L)   **anno 1540**

Will*iam* Thom*as*[3] goldsmythe of Harvardeaste o*with* the 15 day of Decemb*er* £17 that is for 3 butt*es* of seck at 5 m*a*rkes the butt & 6 h'd Gascon wyne at 7 m*a*rk*es* the ton, which I sold for hym & in his name to his s*a*rvant W*illiam* Bridg*es*, mon*tith*   £17

Itm. the 1 day of February £6 13s 4d that is for 2 butt*es* seck sold to the seid Will*ia*m goldsmythe   £6   13s   4d

---

[1] *Smythe repeats* at.
[2] *Fo. 112(R) is blank in the MS.*
[3] Thom*as is inserted above the line.*

113(L) contd.

1541 Itm. the 3 day of December a*nno* 1541 £14 13s 4d *that* is ffor 4 butt*es* of seck at eich £3 13s 4d d'd for hym to his s*ar*vant W*illi*am Brydg*es*   £14 13s 4d

1542 Itm. the 5th daye of June 1542 £11 *that* is for 2 butt*es* seck & 1 pipe bastard at each 11 nobles d'd to W*illi*am Brydg*es* for hym to be paide at all tymes   £11

Itm. the 20 day of February 20s which is for the rest of 1 but seck & 1 pipe bastard which I solld & d'd to ~~theyre~~ his s*ar*vant Brydges in his name   £8

Itm. the 22 of February £8 which is for a but of seck & a pipe of bastard at £4 the pece, mon*tith*   £8

113(R)   anno 1540

W*illi*am goldsmythe p*er* contra is dewe to have the 15 day of Decemb*er* £3 for so myche W*illi*am Brydg*es* pd. me   £3

Itm. the 26 day of February £10 for so myche r. fr*om* hym by J*oh*n Sparck of Newneham   £10

Itm. the last day of June 1541 r. of his wif   £10 13s 4d

Itm. the 28 day of M*ar*che 1542 £5 r. of his wif at Bristowe, mon*tith*   £5

Itm. the 4 day of June r. by Bridg*es* £5   £5

Itm. the 3 of July r. by Bryan Carter Kendallman £5 in whit mon*n*ey   £5

Itm. the 26 day of Augost 1542 r. of Bryddg*es* £5   £5

Itm. the 15 day of September he pd. to my s*ar*vant Robert Leight at Harvart £5   £5

Itm. the last daye of Maye 1543 r. of his wif at Bristowe 5 nobles, mon*tith*   £1 13s 4d

Itm. 8 which J*oh*n Sp*ar*k r. the ¹ day of 1544   £8

114(L)   anno 1540

72

Seck*es* of Sherys for my owne acowmpt r. the monthes of November & December, that is to sey 20 butt*es* in the M*ar*get, master J*oh*n Willi*am*s, 1 butt in the Jh*es*us of Bydeffort, 6 butt*es* in the Jh*es*us, m*aster* Phelip Thomas, 8 butt*es* in the Mary Cristo*f*or, m*aster* Richard White, 7 butt*es* in the Brytton & 30 buttes in the Harry, m*aster* Antony Pickett, owith 145 V. 167 M. which they cost clere abord the ship in Andaluzia, as by Giles White cowmpt may apere, mon*tith* sterlyng £96 15s 8d   £96 15s 8d

Itm. for freight of 19 butt*es* in the M*ar*get, 1 butt in the Jh*es*us of Bydefort, 6 but*es* in the Jh*es*us of Bristowe, 8 but*es* in the Mary Cristo*f*or & 29 butt*es* in the Harry at 25s the ton, & of 7 butt*es* in the Brytten at 15s the ton, for averes in the M*ar*get 4s 4d ob p*er* ton, in the Jh*es*us of Bristowe 3s 10d p*er* ton, in the Mary Cristo*f*or 4s 2d p*er* ton, in the Brytten 3s 11d p*er* ton & in the Harry 3s 3d p*er* ton, for costom of 30 ton at 3s p*er* ton & hallyng & strekyng of 35 ton at 4d p*er* ton, so mon*tith* the hole cost*es* £53 12s 3d   £53 12s 3d

Itm. £3 ~~10s~~ for 1 pipe muscadell to fyll them   £3 ~~10s~~

2

Itm. the 27 day of June 1541 £7 that is for 2 butt*es* bowght of Johan Carpynter weddo   £7

Itm. the 26 day of November £48 12s goten by this acowmpt to geynes in credito fo. 92   £48 12s

     S. £209

---

¹ *Blank in MS.*

9	Seckes per contra be dewe to have [1] which be for 1 but owt in the Marget & 1 but owt in the Harry & 7 buttes to make yllaidge	[1]
2	Itm. the 24 day of November £7 for 2 butes to T. Bel 62	£7
2	Itm. the same day £6 13s 4d for 2 buttes to Richard Carick fo. 34	£6 13s 4d
1	Itm. the 25 of the same 1 butt to Thomas Cotes fo. 17	£3 6s 8d
1	Itm. the 26 of the same 1 butt to John Roxby fo. 10	£3 10s
2	Itm. the 27 day of the same 2 buttes to William North 24	£6 13s 4d
1	Itm. the 10 day of December 1 butt to Margery Northol 18	£3 6s 8d
2	Itm. the 11 day of December £7 for 2 butes to A. Bosgro 68	£7
1	Itm. the 14 day of December £3 6s 8d for 1 but to David Hart fo. 57	£3 6s 8d
3	Itm. the 15 of December 3 buttes to William Goldsmythe 113	£10
6	Itm. the same day 6 buttes to Richard Woodoll fo. 19	£20
2	Itm. the 17 day of the same £7 for 2 butes to Braghyng 109	£7
2	Itm. the 14 day of Jenyver 2 buttes to William Smothing fo. 72	£6 13s 4d
2	Itm. the same day 2 buttes to John Gibs fo. 37	£7
1	Itm. the same day 1 butt to Allson Bisshop fo. 14	£3 10s
1	Itm. the 19 day of Jenyver 1 but to John Skynnar fo. 75	£3 6s 8d
4	Itm. the same day for 4 buttes to William Northe fo. 24	£13 6s 8d
1	Itm. the 28 day of Jenyver for 1 butt to John Roxby fo. 10	£3 6s 8d
2	Itm. the first day of February for 2 buttes to William Goldsmythe 113	£6 13s 4d
2	Itm. the 4 of February for 2 buttes to William Smothing fo. 72	£6 13s 4d
2	Itm. the 12 of Marche for 2 buttes to Thomas Cotes fo. 17	£6 13s 4d
4	Itm. the 21 day of Marche for 4 buttes to John Braghyng fo. 109	£13 6s 8d
2	Itm. the 5th day of Aprell anno 1541 for 1 but seck to Thomas Heyward fo. 18	£3 6s 8d
2	Itm. the 6 day of Aprell for 2 buttes to John Roxby fo. 10	£6 13s 4d
4	Itm. the 11 day of May for 4 buttes to John Roxby fo. 10	£13 6s 8d
1	Itm. the 27 day of June £3 6s 8d for 1 butt to Alexander Bosgrove fo. 68	£3 6s 8d
2	Itm. the 2d day of July for 2 buttes to John Roxby fo. 10	£6 13s 4d
1	Itm. the 15 day of July £3 10s for 1 butt to Davy Hart 57	£3 10s
1	Itm. the 19 of July to Thomas Hewart fo. 18 1 but price	£3 10s
3	Itm. the 25 day of July £10 for 3 buttes to R. Caryck 34	£10
1	Itm. the 31 day of October £3 10s for 1 but to John Wade fo.[1]	£3 10s

[1] Blank in MS.

114(R) contd.

1	Itm. the 5 day of November £3 6s 8d r. of Thomas Davyds wif of Uske in Wales, mon*tith*	£3	6s	8d
1	Itm. the 26 day of November £3 10s to Thomas Turbot for a butt seck fo.[1]	£3	10s	

Som*ma* £209

115(L)   anno 1541

Jamys Biss of Stokelane clothiar owith the 27 day of Maye £23 10s paide to hym at Bristowe by my wif in redy mon*n*ey & so r. my bill   £23 10s

115(R)   anno 1540

Jamys Biss of Stokelane in Some*r*zetshire clothiar is dewe to have the 6 day of Jenyver £23 10s payable by my bill at Easter next com*m*yng which is for the rest & full payement of 7 clothes hewlyng*es* & of 2 clothes aza*rs* at £4 5s the clothe & of a sadblewe clothe at £5 5s, mo*ntith* the hole £43 10s, whereof I pd. to hym in hand £20 of mon*n*ey. So rest as it is beforeseid   £23 10s

116(L)   anno 1540

Thomas Carpynter of Bristowe m*a*rchant owith the 15 day of November £5 which is for the freight of 5 to*n* Gascon wyne in the Trynte at 20s the ton to pay at 3 monthes & 3 mo*n*thes

Som*ma* £5

anno 1541

Johan Carpynter of Bristowe wedo o*with* the 13 day of October £6 which is for a to*n* iren d'd for her to Thom*as* Heynes berebruar, to be paide at O*wr* Lady Day in Lent next com*m*yng   £6
Itm. the 1 day of Decembe*r* £3 15s *that* is for the freight of 3 tons bastard*es* in the Trynte at 25s the ton, to pay hallf in hand & hallf at the end of 3 mo*n*thes next com*m*yng   £3 15s
1542 Itm. the 24 day of Ap*r*ell 1542 40s that is ffor freight of 3 tons iren in the Trynte at 13s 4d p*er* to*n*, to pay at 3 monthes & 3 monthes, as by *the* charterp*a*rtie may apere   £2

S. £11 15s

anno 1540

Arture Smythe m*a*rchant of Bristowe owith the 15 day of Novembe*r* £5 10s which is for the freight of 5 to*n* Gascon p*i*pe wyne in the Trynte, to pay at 3 monthes & 3 monthes   £5 10s
1541 Itm. the 25 day of Octobe*r* 1541 £12 that is for a ton of wull oyle sold & delyverd to hym, to be paide at Ester next com*m*yng   £12
Itm. the first day of Decembe*r* 37s 6d that is for the rest & hallf freight of 3 tons bastard*es* in the Trynte at 25s p*er* ton, to be paide at the end of 3 mo*n*thes next com*m*yng   £1 17s 6d
1542 Itm. the 23 day of Augost 1542 53s 4d for the freight of 4 tons iren in the Trynte   £2 13s 4d
Itm. the 18 day of February £4 10s that is for the freight of 3 ton wyne in the Trynte at 30s p*er* ton, to pay hallf in hand & hallf 3 monthes next after   £4 10s

---

[1]*Blank in MS.*

116(R)
anno 1541

Thomas Carpynter per contra is dewe to have the 11 day of July £5 which his wif paide & discowntyd to me in the payement of 2 buttes of seck which she sold to me at £3 10s the butt

Somma £5

anno 1541

Johan Carpynter per contra is dewe to have the 10 daye of February 37s 6d r. by my sarvant of her for the hallf payement of the £3 15s per contra £1 17s 6d
Itm. the 23 day of Augost 1542 r. from her by the handes of her sarvantt Phillip Grene £4
Itm. the 19 day of November 1542 my sarvant Robert Lett r. of her in presence of Thomas Copar her husband £5 17s 6d £5 17s 6d

S. £11 15s

anno 1541

Itm. the 13 day of May r. of his wif by Hamond £3
Itm. the 16 day of July r. by Hamond 30s £1 10s
Itm. the 3 day of Augost r. by Hamond 20s £1
Itm. the 19 of Aprell 1542 r. of Arture Smythe £1 17s 6d
Itm. the 1 day of Augost r. of his wif £6 £6
Itm. the 5 of Augost r. of hymseallf £6 £6
Itm. the 23 of February r. by Hamond my sarvant 4 markes, montith £2 13s 4d
Itm. the 26 of February Hamond r. 45s £2 5s

117(L)
anno 1540

William Jones of Bristowe marchant owithe the 15 day of November 40s whiche is ffor the freight of 2 ton Gascon wyne in the Trynte, to pay at 3 monthes & 3 monthes, montith £2

anno 1540

Allen Hill of Bristowe marchant owith the 21 day of February 30s 10d ob that is ffor 1 h'd 16 li. iren at £6 the ton, to be paide at all tymes, montith £1 10s 10d½
1541 Itm. the 1 day of December 1541 50s for so myche he rest owyng for the hallf freight of 4 ton bastardes in the Trynte after 25s the ton, montith £2 10s
Itm. the 4 day of Jenyver £12 which is for 1 ton wull oyle to be paide at Seynt Jamistide next £12
Itm. the 18 day of February £4 10s which is for the freight of 3 ton wyne in my ship at 30s per ton, to pay hallf in hand & hallf 3 monthes next after £4 10s
more 45s for the freight of a ton pipe oyle the same viage £2 5s
1543 Itm. the 23 day of Julye anno 1543 £12 & it is for 2 tons of Rendry iren solld & d'd to hym to be paide by his byll at Cristmas next commyng £12
Itm. the 14 day of February £12 & is for 2 ton iren at £6 the ton to be paide at Seynt Jamystide next commyng £12
Itm. the first day of Aprell 1544 £6 13s 4d for the ½ of 10 ton freight of iren in my ship the Trynte, to pay at thend of 3 monthes next commyng £6 13s 4d
Itm. the 22 of Augost 1544 £14 for 1 ton oyle to be pd. at Candellmas next £14
Itm. the 16 of Marche for 3 pipes oyle £24 to pay at Seynt Jamistide £24

117(R)
anno 1540

William Jones per contra is dewe to have the 7 day of February 20s which Hewgh Hamond my sarvant r. of hym £1
Itm. the 7 day of May 1541 r. 20s by Hamond £1

117(R) contd.

anno 1541

Allen Hill per contra is dewe to have the 30 day of Augost 30s 10d ob which my wif r.	£1	10s	10d	ob
Itm. the 29 of Marche 1542 r. of hym by Hamon	£2	10s		
Itm. the 7 of Augost r. of his wif £12	£12			
Itm. the 26 day of February £3 which Hamon r.	£3	7s	6d	
Itm. the 3 of July 1543 r. of his wif	£3	7s	6d	
Itm. the 11 day of February 1543 r. of his wif	£12			
Itm. the 8 of August 1544 £12 which his wif pd. to me for the 2 ton iren d'd in February last past	£12			
Itm. the 3 day of Marche 1544 my wif r. 20 nobles for the freight of 10 tons iren per contra	£6	13s	4d	
Itm. the 3 day of Marche 1544 my wif r. of his wif £10	£10			
Itm. my wif r. £4	£4			
Itm. £16 r. the 30 of July of his wif	£16			
Itm. my wif r. of his wif in October 1545	£8			

118(L)

anno 1540

Bastardes 4 pipes for my acowmpt r. in December owt of the Jhesus of Bristowe, master Phillip Thomas, £5 19s 10d that is for 8 V. 986 M. that 4 pipes cost putt clere aborde the ship	£5	19s	10d
Itm. for costom 3s per ton, for averes 3s 10d per ton, for freight 25s per ton, for halyng & strekyng 4d per ton, montith the hole £3 4s 4d	£3	4s	4d
Itm. the 14 day of Jenyver £5 15s 10d for so myche goten by this acownt as it aperith to gaynes in credito fo. 92	£5	15s	10d
	£15		

anno 1540

Bastardes 2 pipes owith the 27 day of Jenyver £6 13s 4d for so myche paide to a man of London for them		£6	13s	4d
Itm. the 6 day of Aprell 26s 8d goten by this acowmpt as it may apere to gaynes fo. 92		£1	6s	8d
	S.	£8		

anno 1541

33	Bastardes owith for my acowmpt that is 33 pipes r. the monthe of December November owt of my ship the Trynte, which cost at the Condado clereabord the ship 86 V. 675 M. ½, for costom of 28 pipes at 3s per ton, for averes 3s 4d per ton, for freight 25s per ton, for hawlyng & stowyng 4d per ton, montith all	£83	2s	8d
	Itm. the 17 day of December £31 2s 4d for so myche goten by this acowmpt as it aperith to gaynes in credito fo. 92	£31	2s	4d
	S.	£114	5s	

anno 1540

Tayntz 3 pipes & 1 butt for my acowmpt r. in December owt of the Jhesus of Bristowe master Phillip Thomas owith £8 12s 11d that is for 12 V. 842 M. that they cost put clere abord the ship as by Giles cowmpt may apere	£8	12s	11d
Itm. for costom, averes, freight, halyng & strekyng downe into my sellars £3 4s 4d	£3	4s	4d

118(L) contd.

    Itm. the 6 day of July 1541 £3 17s 9d for so myche I make gaynes creditor of in fo. 92 for the clozing up of this acowmpt   £3 17s 9d

                                                                                £15 15s

118(R)

anno 1540

Bastard*es* p*er* contra is dewe to have the 26 day of Dece*m*ber £4 that is for 1 pipe sold to J*oh*n Roxby fo. 10   £4

Itm. the 14 day of Jenyver £4 for 1 pipe sold to J*oh*n Gybs fo. 37   £4

Itm. the same day £4 for 1 pipe to Alis Bishop 14   £4

Itm. the same day £3 which I do allowe for 1 pipe *that* lackyd & was not ffull which I toke to fyll my seck*es* as it ap*er*ith fo. 114   £3

                                                          £15

anno 1540

Bastard*es* p*er* contra is dewe to have the 22 day of February £4 for a pipe sold to J*oh*n Braghy*n*g fo. 109   £4

Itm. the 6 day of Aprell 1541 £4 for a pipe of bastard sold to J*oh*n Roxby fo. 10   £4

                                                          £8

anno 1541

1	more r. of J*oh*n Americk*es* wif for 1 p*ip*e bastard £3 13s 4d	£3 13s 4d
1	Bastard*es* p*er* contra is dewe to have the £4 for 1 pipe bastard sold the 26 day of November to John Roxby fo. 10	£4
1	Itm. the 28 day of Novembe*r* £3 13s 4d for a p*ip*e to W*illia*m Rowly fo. 87	£3 13s 4d
6	Itm. the 29 day for 6 pipes to Jamys Rogers fo. 76 ffor	£22
2	Itm. the same day for 2 pipes at eich £4 to J*oh*n Brawghy*n*g fo. 109	£8
1	Itm. the secon day of Dece*m*ber r. for a p*ip*e taken to p*r*ize £3 16s 8d	£3 16s 8d
2	Itm. the 3 day £8 for 2 pipes to W*illia*m Smothing fo. 72	£8
2	Itm. the same day £8 for 2 pipes to J*oh*n Roxby fo. 10	£8
2	Itm. the 6 day of December £7 6s 8d for 2 p*ip*es to W*illia*m Northe fo. 141	£7 6s 8d
1	Itm. the same day r. of M*aste*r Hamlyng £3 13s 4d for a p*ip*e	£3 13s 4d
2	Itm. the 17 of December £4 for a p*ip*e to Alis Bisshop & £4 for a p*ip*e to W. Robert*es* & 8s 4d for 10 gallons to M*aste*r Seyntlo, mo*ntith*	£8 8s 4d
7	Itm. 3 pipes ½ to yllage & 3 corrupt pipe ½ for Gascon wyne & 2 pipes for seck*es*, mo*ntith* in mon*n*ey	£15 6s 8d

159

118(R) contd.

5	Itm. £18 6s 8d for 5 pipes which I pass to fo. 146	£18	6s	8d
	S.	£114	5s	

anno 1540

Tayntz per contra is dewe to have the 4 day of December £4 which is for 1 pipe sold to John Roxby fo. 10	£4		
Itm. the 14 day of Jenyver £4 for 1 pipe to Gibs 37	£4		
Itm. 26s 8d which I dowe allowe for 40 gallons that I toke to ffill up my red wynes as it apere fo. 108	£1	6s	8d
Itm. the 22 day of February £4 5s for a pipe sold to John Braghyng of Wursettor fo. 109	£4	5s	
Itm. the 6 day of July 1541 43s 4d for 1 h'd sold to John Wyllis	£2	3s	4d
	£15	15s	

119(L)　　　　　　　　　　　anno 1540

53	Calve skuyns for my owne acowmpt owith the 10 daye of November £16 16s 8d that is for 6 dozens bowght at Wursettor of Thomas Aberley for 43s 4d & at Glocester for 15 dozens bowght of Luyes tanner & 20 dozens of Edmond Allen at 6s 8d the dozen & ffor 12 dozens bowght of Richard Allen at 5s the dozen, montith	£16	16s	8d
44	Itm. the 16 day of December £13 19s 9d for 44 dozens bowght of Lawrence Hanckot for the same somm	£13	19s	9d
30	Itm. the seid day £9 which is for 30 dozens calve skuyns r. of Thomas Machyn at 6s the dozen, montith	£9		
	Itm. for costes & charges to ride for to by them & to lade them		13s	4d
	Itm. for bryngyng them abord the Trynte 15s		15s	
127		£41	4s	9d

anno 1540

Wheat for my owne acowmpt owith the 10 day of November £104 16s that is for 43 weyes 32 busshells bowght of William Bullock at 48s the wey	£104	16s	
Itm. £12 pd. to Thomas Hawle for 5 weyes	£12		
Itm. £5 12s for 2 weyes 16 busshells r. of Frances Codryngton owt of Lawghtons trowe at 12d the busshell	£5	12s	
Itm. £19 8s for for[1] lycens of 51 weyes in the Trynte & other costes as it may apere fo. 71	£20	8s	
Itm. the 5 day of Marche £79 4s that is for 17 wey bowght of Russell, 6 wey of Hawle & 10 wey of William Bullock, montith 33 weyes at 48s per wey, montith	£79	4s	
Itm. £11 2s 10d for the costes of the seid wheat	£11	2s	10d
S.	£233	2s	10d

---

[1] *Smythe repeats* for.

119(L) contd.	anno 1540			
1	Hides owith for my owne acowmpt the 16 day of December 43s 4d for so myche pd. to Lawrence Hancot for won dickar of cow & stere, montith	£2	3s	4d
16.1.	Itm. the same day 9 dicker & 1 hide cowe & stere bowght of Machyn at 40s 40d the dicker & 7 dicker ox lether at 53s 4d the dicker, montith £38 3s 4d	£38	3s	4d
	Itm. for bryngyng it abord the Trynte 15s	15s		
		£41	1s	8d

119(R) anno 1540

Calve skuyns per contra is dewe to have the 15 day of February £41 4s 9d that is for so myche I have made viages to Biscay debitor of for 127 dozens laden in my ship the Trynte as it may apere fo. 69

S. £41 4s 9d

anno 1540

Wheat per contra is dewe to have the 25 day of February £8 2s 4d r. of William Tyndall for his brother Robert my sarvant for 3 wey wheat with the costes in my ship, montith	£8	2s	4d
Itm. £14 9s 10d which I make Frances Codryngton debitor of for the lysence & costes of 30 weyes wheat as it may apere fo. 60	£14 –	9s–	10d
Itm. 23s for the costes of 3 weyes of John Derby fo. 65	£1–	–3s	
Itm. £134 8s for 48 weyes with the costes laden in the Trynte, as it may apere to viages fo.[1]	£134	13s	8d
Itm. the [1] day of Marche £5 12s for 2 wey 1 tierce pd. to Frances Codryngton for so myche I borowid of hym for the Trynte	£5	12s	
Itm. £84 14s 10d for 30 wey ⅔ laden in the Herry for my acowmpt	£84	14s	10d
S.	£233	2s	10d

anno 1540

Hides per contra is dewe to have the 15 day of February £41 1s 8d that is for 7 dicker ox hides & 10 dicker 1 hide cow & stere which I lode for Byscaye abord the Trynte my ship, as it may apere to viages in debito fo. 69

S. £41 1s 8d

120(L) anno 1540

John Russell of Langney in Glocestershire hussbandman owithe the 5th day of February £6 13s 4d which I delyverd to hym in redy money, in yernes & part of payement of 20 weyes of good & sownd wheat at 48s the wey d'd at Hungrode or Kyngrode abord shuche ship or ships as I shall apoynt hym, a thisside the end of the spryng which shalbe next after the spryng that is now commyng	£6	13s	4d
Itm. the 5 day of Marche £34 2s 8d for so myche redy monney paide to hym in Bristowe	£34	2s	8d

---

[1] Blank in MS.

120(L) contd.

Itm. the last day of Maye 1541 £13 8s *that* is for so myche paide in redy monney to John Russell	£14	8s
Itm. the 12 day of December £10 8s paide to hym in redy monney	£10	8s
1548 Itm. the 13 day of February Anno 1548 £12 & is for so myche ready monney delyverd unto hym in part of payment of 10 weyes beanes, to be d'd aborde the ship in Hungrode or Kyngrode at enny time requyrid at 12d ob the busshell[1]	£12	

120(R) anno 1541

John Russell hereageynst is dewe to have the 5 day of Marche £40 16s *that* is for 17 weyes wheat r. of hym at 48s the wey	£40	16s
Itm. the 16 day of Marche £14 8s that is for 6 weyes wheat at 48s the wey which he browght to Sharschestone Poole abord a Portyngall ship	£14	8s
Itm. the first day of September £10 8s for 4 weyes wheat at 13d the busshell to pay at all tymes	£10	8s
John Russell of Langley is dewe to have in Marche 1548 £25 & is for 10 weys benes r. for my acownt into Bastyan de Sanscistes ship at 12d ob the busshell, that is to sey in John Sparkes bote 6 wayes		

121(L) anno 1540

John Yong of Hannam gentleman owithe the 27 day of Jenyver £6 13s 4d that is ffor 1 ton of S.S. iren sold & d'd to hym for the which he & Stevan Cole of Bristow lawyer stond bownd in a obligacion to pay it at Mighellmas next commyng, montith	£6	13s	4d

anno 1540

William Pepwell of Bristowe grocer owe the 31 day of Jenyver £3 that is for a pipe of Rendry iren d'd by his wyll & comawndement to Richard Willshire broker, to be paide at Mydsomer next commyng	£3

anno 1544

John White of Kerdif marchant owe the 28 day of Augost 33s 9d which is for 1 h'd 7 li. S.S. iren to be paide 14 dayes next after Allhaloutyde next commyng	£1	13s	9d

anno 1540

Martyne William of Carffile smythe in Wales owith the 3 daye of February 31s 8d which is for 1 h'd of my best Rendry iren at 19 nobles the ton. He & Thomas Davy of Lyswayn be bownd in a obligacion to pay it at Whitsontide next	£1	11s	8d
1541 Itm. the 10 day of June 1541 31s 8d for 1 h'd of my better Rendry iren to pay at Mighellmas next comyng. The foreseid T. Davyd is his shewerty	£1	11s	8d
Itm. the 18 day of November 32s that is for 1 h'd 6 li. iren at 6s 4d the C, to be paide at Ester next & the seid Thomas David is shewerty	£1	12s	
1542 Itm. the 29 day of Aprell 1542 32s that is for 1 h'd 6 li. iren at 19 grotes per C, to be pd. at thassumption of Owr Lady next	£1	12s	
Itm. the 27 daye of October 32s that is for 1 h'd 6 li. iren to be pd. at Ester next & Thomas Davyd is bownd for hym	£1	12s	

---

[1] *The item of 13th February is crossed through.*

121(R)

anno 1542

John Yong per contra is dewe to have the 19 daye of
October £4 which Stevan Cole his shewerty pay me in redy
monney, as it aperith in the baksyde of thobligacion £4
Itm. the 22 day of March r. of Stevan Cole £1 13s 4d

anno 1541

William Pepwell per contra is dewe to have the 30 day of
July £3 which my wif r. from hym £3

1545

John White per contra is dewe to have the 20 ti day of
Aprell 33s 9d which my wif r. £1 13s 9d

anno 1541

Martyne William per contra is dewe to have the 9 daye of
June 31s 8d r. of hym at Bristowe £1 11s 8d
Itm. the 17 day of November r. of hym £1 11s 8d
Itm. the 28 day of Aprell 1542 32s for so myche r. of hym at
Bristowe £1 12s
Itm. the 28 day of October r. of hym at Bristo £1 12s
Itm. the 19 of Aprell 1543 r. of hym 32s £1 12s

122(L)

anno 1540

Thomas Suffell of Harvarteste smythe owith the 3 daye of February £4 13s 4d
for the rest of 1 ton of S.S. iren sold after 20 nobles the ton. Henry Tayler of
Hervorteste draper have made a byll & is bownd to pay it 46s 8d at
Whitsontide next & 46s 8d at Seynt Jamystide next after *that* £4 13s 4d
1541 Itm. the 25 day of Julye anno 1541 £6 15s *that* is for 1 ton 1 qr. iren of
S.S. at 20 nobles the ton, to paye £4 at Candellmas next & £2 15s at Easter
next after that. The above namyd Henry Tayllor is his shewertie £6 15s

anno 1542

Henry Tayllor of Harvarteste draper owith the 27 day of July £3 which is for
so myche he is bownd by his byll obligatory to pay at Mighellmas next
commyng for Thomas Suffell, as in the other syde may apere £3

anno 1540

Henry Duttson of Hervarteste owith the 3 day of February 20s which is for
the rest of 1 h'd 11 li. iren of S.S. which I sold to hym after 20 nobles the
ton, to pay it at Easter next commyng. William Smothing is his shewerty £1

anno 1547

Master John Goodman Deane of Wells owith the 18 of February anno
dicto 20 nobles for a ton of Gascon wyne, to be pd. at Seynt Jamistide next
commyng £6 13s 4d

122(R)

anno 1541

Thomas Suffell per contra is dewe to have the 25 daye of
July £4 13s 4d r. of hym at Bristow £4 13s 4d
Itm. the 18 day of February r. of hym at Bristo £2
Itm. the 26 day of July r. at Bristow of Henry Taylor £1 15s
Itm. the 27 day of July £3 for so myche that Henry Tayllor
per contra is bownd by his bill to paye unto me at
Mighellmas next as it may apere to hym in debito
hereagaynst £3

122(R) contd.   anno 1542

Henry Tallor per contra is dewe to have the 5 day of
February 40s for so myche r. of hym at Bristo   £2
Itm. the 25 of July 1543 r. of hym at Bristo   £1

anno 1541

Henry Duttson per contra is dewe to have the 25 day of
Julye 20s r. of hym in Bristowe   £1

anno 1548

Master John Goodman per contra is dewe to have the
27 day of July anno dicto £6 13s 4d & is for so myche ready
monney r. for hym of Master Brampston   £6 13s 4d

123(L)   anno 1540

Davy Gowgh of Aburgeyne daiper owe the 5th day of February £3 which is
for a pipe iren d'd by his comawndement to Robert Smythe of Aburgeyne, to
be pd. at Seynt Jamistide next commyng   £3
1541 Itm. the 26 day of July anno 1541 £3 that is for a pipe of Rendry iren
d'd by his comawndement in presence of John Coles of Tymby to Robert
Smythe of Aburgeyne & to William Pollowghan of the same Aburgeyne
smythes, to be pd. at Candellmas next commyng   £3
Memorandum the 29 day of November 1543 & in presens of Master Fitzjamys
Esquyer Towne Clerck & Mary Kent, won John Thomas of Aburgeyne &
Symond Hanckot of Bristow taylor became shewertes to me for the forenamyd
Davy Gowgh for the above namyd £3, for to pay 20s at Candellmas next,
20s at Philips Norton fayer next after that & 20s at Seynt Jamystide next
following after that, whereupon I delyverd in presence of the foreseid
wytnesses to the afore namyd Symon & John Thomas the obligacion wherein
the seid Davyd stode bownded to me in & for the seid thre powndes
                                                        S.   £6

anno 1540

Henry Leke of Bristowe draper owith the 5th day of February £3 3s 4d[1]
which is for a pipe of S.S. iren d'd for hym to Luyes Hopkyns after £6 6s 8d
the ton, to be paide at Easter next commyng. £3 3s 4d[1]   £3 3s 4d
Itm. the 18 day of October anno 1543 £5 which is for 15 C S.S. iren sold &
delyverd to hym at 6s 8d the C, to pay at thannunciasion of Owr Blessyd Lady
next commyng   £5
1544 Itm. the 21 daye of Aprell 1544 for 2 ton iren at £6 the ton, to pay at
Mighellmas next[2]   £12
Itm. the 2 day of May £3 13s 4d & is for 1 butt seck to be paide at Cristmas
next   £3 13s 4d

123(R)   anno 1541

David Gowgh per contra is dewe to have the 26 daye of
Julye £3 that is for 30s r. of Robert Smythe of Aburgeyne
& 30s of Watkyn Polloghan of Aburgeyne smythe,
montith all   £3
Itm. the 9 of February 1543 r. of John Thomas of
Aburgeyne 20s   £1
Itm. the 18 of August 1544 r. of Symond Hanckot 20s   £1
Itm. the 4th day of February 1545 r. of Symon tayler in a
reckenyng 20s   £1
                                                        S.   £6

---

[1] 4d and £3 3s 4d were inserted later.
[2] to pay at Mighellmas next was inserted later.

123(R) contd.

anno 1541

Henry Leke per contra is dewe to have the 14 day of Maye £3 3s 4d which he paide to my wif	£3	3s 4d
Itm. the 11 day of Aprell 1544 r. of hym	£5	
Itm. the 22 day of October 1544 my wif r. of hym £3 montith	£3	
Itm. the 19 day of November 1544 r. of hym £3	£3	
Itm. the 17 of Jenyver 1544 r. of hym £6	£6	
Itm. the 4 day of Aprell 1545 his sarvaunt pd. to my wif 46s 8d	£2	6s 8d
Itm. my wif r. of hym seallf the 2d day of May 26s 8d	£1	6s 8d

124(L)

anno 1540

John Awood of Bridgewater tuckar owith the 8th day of February £3 9d that is for 2 ½-bales of Tullus wood d'd for hym to his neighbur William Cley, which wood conteynyd 3 C ½, 9 li. at 17s the C, to be paide at all tymes   £3   9d
1542 Itm. the 12 day of June 1542 £3 18d that is for 2 ½-bales wood conteynyng 3 C ½, 13 li. at 17s the C, d'd to Byddell for him, to be paide at all tymes   £3   1s 6d

anno 1548

John Coles of Tynbye owith the 6th daye of December £9 11s 2d which is for a ton 14 li. iren of the Rendry at £9 10s per ton, to be paide at all tymes, montith   £9 11s 2d
Itm. the 27 day of July anno 1549 £10 & is for 1 ton of Rendry iren to be paide at Seynt Androwstide next commyng   £10

anno 1540

Richard Record of Tynby marchant owith the 10 day of February £3 6s 8d which is for a pipe iren of S.S. sold & d'd to hym, to be paide by his bill at Seynt Jamistide next   £3 6s 8d

anno 1549

David Vicarye of Penbrooke owith the 29 of July anno dicto £5 & is for the rest of 15 C 1 qr. 25 li. ½ Rendry iren after £10 per ton, to be paide at Seynt Androwstide next. John Coles of Tynby is shewerty for hym   £5

124(R)

anno 1541

John Awood per contra is dewe to have the 25 day of July 59s r. in monney & 21d I gave hym in the price	£3	9d
1543 Itm. the 26 day of July r. of hym at Bristow £3 & more 18d which I do geve hym	£3	1s 6d

anno 1549

John Coles per contra is dewe to have the 26 of July £9 11s 2d which my wif r. of hym	£9	11s 2d
Itm. the 21 day of February 1549 r. of hym	£10	

anno 1541

Richard Record per contra is dewe to have the 26 day of July £3 6s 8d r. of hym in reddy monney	£3	6s 8d
David Vicary per contra is dewe to have the 21 daye of Jenyver 1549 £5 r. from hym by John Coles of Tymby	£5	

125(L) anno 1540

John Yerbery of Bruton clothiar owith the 15 day of February £8 9s 8d to be paide in clothes callid truckers at 40s the clothe, as it apere fo. 48 in credito   £8 9s 8d

1541 Itm. the 27 day of July a*nno* 1541 £120 12s 6d,[1] that is £80 12s 6d for paymen*tes* dewe at *this* p*re*sent Sey*nt* Jamistide & £35 16s 8d[2] dewe for the first payement of a bill datyd the 17 day of June last past & £4 3s 4d toward the first payement of a bill datyd the 22 day of this p*re*sent monthe of July, mon*tith*   £120 12s 6d

Itm. the 22 day of May 1541 £22 7s 11d pd. for me by W*illiam* Northe for the payement dewe at Ester last past   £22 7s 11d

Itm. the foreseid 27 day of July 1541 £31 13s 4d that is for £20 I geve hym in W*illiam* Northe fo. 124 & £6 10s in W*illiam* Peter fo. 77 & £5 3s 4d I pay in redy mon*n*ey, the which is to make up full £35 16s 8d for the first payment of the bill datyd the 22 day of July   £31 13s 4d

Itm. the first day of Augost he ow*ith* 10 clo*thes* truckers to be pd. at all tymes, which is for 3 bales wood d'd *the* 16 day of May & 13 bales *this* p*re*sent day, mo*ntith* 16 ½-bales *conteynyng* 28 C ½, 16 li. to be pd. in the seid truckers after 2 C 3 qr. 14 li. for a truckar   [3]

Itm. the 8 day of November pd. to hym at Bristowe £22 7s 11d for the later & full payment of a byll payable at Mighellmas last past   £22 7s 11d

Itm. the 7 day of December £7 pd. to his s*ar*vant for the blewe p*er* contra   £7

Itm. the 2d of ~~February~~ Jenyver 1541 £20 which W*illiam* Northe fo. 141 paide to hym & more the 6 day of February he is co*n*tent to r. of the seid Northe £20 & more I pay hym the same 6 day £31 13s 4d, mon*tith* £71 13s 4d which is for the first payemen*tes* to be pd. in hand of my too bills p*er* contra, of the which won bill is datyd the 20 day of December 1541 & thother the 17 day of Jenyver a*nno* 1541 as in the backsyde of *the* same bills maye apere   £71 13s 4d

1542 Itm. the 2 day of May 1542 pd. to his son *John* Yerbery £44 15s 10d that is £26 17s 6d for the later payement of a byll dewe at Candellmas a*nno* 1541 & £17 18s 4d for p*ar*t of payement of a byll datyd the 22 of July last past & payable at Candellmas 1541   £44 15s 10d

Itm. the 20 day of June pd. to hym by the hand*es* of my wif £55 which is for the first payement of 2 bills, one datyd the 10 of May 1542 & the other the 1 day of June, as p*er* contra ap*er*ithe   £55

Itm. the 13 day of July W*illiam* Northe paide to hym £17 18s 4d, more paide by the seid North the 24 of July £14 9s 5d & more I paide the 28 day of July £3 8s 11d, mo*ntith* all £35 16s 8d & it is for the hole payement of a byll datyd *the* 17 of June 1541   £35 16s 8d

Itm. the 28 day of July 1542 I pass to fo. 163 £155 1s 8d   £155 1s 8d

S. £574 18s 10d

125(R) anno 1540

John Yerbery of Bruton clothiar is dewe to have the 15 day of February for clozing up of his acowmpt fo. 48 £162 15s 10d to be paide in man*er* folowyng, that is ~~£22 7s 11d~~ at Ester next, ~~£80 12s 6d~~ at Seynt Jamistide next, ~~£22 7s 11d~~ at Mighellmas next, ~~£26 17s 6d~~ at Candellmas next and £10 10s at Whitsontyde in a*nno* 1542, as it may ap*ere* by my sev*er*all bills made of the seid som*m*s, amo*ntith* all   £162 15s 10d

1541 Itm. the 17 day of June a*nno* 1541 £71 13s 4d to paye in hand ~~£35 16s 8d~~ & ~~£17 18s 4d~~ at C*ris*tmas next com*m*yng, & ~~£17 18s 4d~~ at Mydsomer next after that which wylbe in the yere of O*w*r Lorde God 1542, and it is for 20 clo*thes* penny hewes r. of hym at £3 11s 8d the clothe, as it may apere by my bill   ~~£71 13s 4d~~

---

[1] 12s 6d *inserted later*.
[2] 8d *inserted later*.
[3] *Blank in MS*.

125(R) contd.

Itm. more for freight of 50 tons Spanische weight at 13s 4d £35 16s 8d & £17 18s 4d at Candellmas next com*m*yng & £17 18s 4d at Seynt Jamystide next after *that* which wilbe in a*n*no 1542, and it is for 20 clothes penny hewes r. of hym at £3 11s 8d the clothe, as it may apere by my bill	£71	13s	4d
Itm. r. 4 truckers at eich 40s in *p*art of payement of £8 9s 8d *conte*ynyd in the item of the 15 day of February a*n*no 1540 *p*er contra	£8	9s	8d
Itm. £7 for 1 blewe clo*the* r. the 15 of August	£7		
Itm. the 20 day of Decemb*e*r 1541 £71 13s 4d that is for 20 clothes penny hewes, to pay £35 16s 8d in hand & £17 18s 4d at Mydsomer next & £17 18s 4d at Cristmas in a*n*no 1542, as it may apere by my bill	£71	13s	4d
Itm. the 17 day of Jenyver a*n*no 1541 £71 13s 4d that is for 20 penny hewes to pay in hand £35 16s 8d & at Seynt Jamystide next £17 18s 4d & at Candellmas after *that* which wylbe in a*n*no 1542 £17 18s 4d, as by my bill it may apere	£71	13s	4d
Itm. the 10 day of Maye a*n*no 1542 £73 6s 8d & is for 20 clothes penny hewes at 11 nobles the clothe, to pay £36 13s 4d in hand & £18 6s 8d at Allhaloutyde next com*m*yng & £18 6s 8d at Whitssontyde next after that which wylbe in a*n*no 1543	£73	6s	8d
Itm. the 1 day of June £36 13s 4d, to pay £18 6s 8d in hand, £9 3s 4d the first day of Decemb*e*r next com*m*yng & £9 3s 4d at Mydsomer next after *that*, which is for 10 penny hewes at 11 nobles the clothe	£36	13s	4d
Itm. I have r. of the seid Yerbery 10 clothes truckers for the full payment *conte*ynyd in a itm. *p*er contra of the first daye of August 1541			
S.	£574	18s	10d

126(L)   **anno 1540**

Sussan Gibs of Bridgewater wedo owith the 15 day of Marche £14 6s 8d payable at all tymes requyrid for the rest of acowmpt fo. 37 and it is ffor s*er*teyne wynes which I sent her the 14 day of Jenyver last past, she being then weddo	£14	6s	8d
1541 Itm. the 17 daye of Decemb*e*r £3 15s which is for a butt of seck sent her in White the coferars bote	£3	15s	
Itm. the 21 day of February £4 which is for a pipe of bastard laden in Luyes bote	£4		
S.	£22	1s	8d

anno 1542

Sussan Gibbs above namyd owe the 16 day of February £8 7s 4d & is for a but seck *p*rice £4 & 1 pipe bastard *p*rice £4 6s 8d & more 8d for haling, cranage & cocquett, laden in Heynes bote of Chepstowe & m*a*rkyd apo*n* the buldge ⌇ & it must be paide at Easter next com*m*yng	£8	7s	4d
1543 Itm. the 4 of June 1543 £4 13s 4d & is for a butt of seck sent to hym in her in Lanemans bote	£4	13s	4d
Itm. the 28 day of February £8 12d & is for a but seck & 1 *p*ipe bastard at eich £4 & 12d for cost*e*s, mon*tith*	£8	1s	
Itm. the 17 of M*a*rche £12 & is for 3 butt*e*s seck at ech £4, mon*tith*	£12		

anno 1540

Nicholas Tizo*n* m*a*rchant of Bristowe owith the 18 day of Jenyver £1 that is for 200 d*u*cat*t*s he r. for my acowmpt at *San Lucar* of J*o*hn Apowell *p*urser of the Trynte of Wales, as by a bill which I have of the seid Nicholas conser*n*yng the receypt of the seid 200 d*u*cat*t*s more playnlier maye apere, mon*tith*	£1		

126(L) contd. anno 1541

Robert Gowghe of Bristowe hop*er* owith the 6th day of Aprell 30s 7d *that* is for the rest of 1 h'd 9 li. ire*n* of S.S. after 20 nobles the ton, to be pd. at Allhalouday next, W*illiam* Benet hop*er* is bownd with hym £1 10s 7d
Itm. the 24 day of Decemb*er* £3 13s 4d that is for 1 butt of seck sold & d'd to hym, to be paide at Mydssomer next, as it may apere by a byll sealid by hym & W*illiam* Benett hop*er* as his shewerty £3 13s 4d

126(R) anno 1541

Susan Gibs p*er* contra is dewe to have the 14 day of Maye £4 r. fro*m* her by W*illiam* Spyring £4
Itm. the 24 day of July r. fro*m* her by Robert Cross of Mertyllcom £4 £4
Itm. the 12 day of Augost r. by thand*es* of Giles White 40s £2
Itm. the 16 day of December r. by Giles Whit £3 £3
1542 Itm. the 8 day of Ap*re*ll 1542 r. fro*m* her by Thomas Shipma*n* £5 £5
Itm. the 25 day of July r. of her at Bristowe £4 £4
Itm. 20d rebatyd in the price of wynes 1s 8d

S. £22 1s 8d

anno 1543

Sussan Gibs p*er* contra is dewe to have the 21 day of May £8 6s 8d r. fro*m* her by Giles Whit £8 6s 8d
Itm. the 16 of Augost r. of her at Bridgewater 4 nobles £1 6s 8d
Itm. the 2 day of Octob*er* r. of Geffrey Shorco*m* £3 £3
Itm. r. 25 of July 1544 by Tyndall £10
Itm. the 4 of October r. from her by Philip Gryffyth baylif to *the* Bisshop of Bristowe £6 £6
Itm. the 24 of Jenyver 1544 my wif r. of her son Richard Gibbs £4 £4

anno 1541

Nicholas Tizo*n* p*er* contra is dewe to have 200 d*u*ca*tts* for so myche he paide in May to Giles Whit at Andaluzia

£50

anno 1541

Robert Gowgh p*er* contra is dewe to have the 23 day of December 30s 7d r. of hym in redy mon*n*y £1 10s 7d
Itm. the 8 day of Jenyver 1542 r. for W*illiam* Benet & Robert Gowgh of M*aster* Ballard Sherif of Bristowe by thand*es* of his waytingma*n* Lanssdon £3 13s 4d £3 13s 4d

127(L) anno 1541

Iren for my owne acowmpt owith the 26 day of Aprell
3 to*n* £22 19s that is for 1 ton 15 li. of S.S. *conteynyng* 82 end*es*
15 C ¼ & 2 ton 15 C ½ Rendry iren *conteynyng* 217 end*es*, that is for so
15 li. myche rest in my howss this preasent day unsold for the rest & clozing up of acowmpt of iren fo. 53 £22 19s
54 to*n*, Itm. the seid day r. ow*t* of my ship the Trynte m*aster* under
8 C ½ God John Derby 525 kyntalls 75 li. Rendry iren which
26 li. made by my weight*es* at home 38 ton 3 qr. 26 li. *conteynyng* 3700 end*es* and 225 k*y*ntalls 40 li. iren of S.S. which made by my weight*es* 16 ton 7 C ¾ *conteynyng* 1643 end*es*, all the which foresseid 750 k*y*ntalls 115 li. cost in Spayne clere abord 970 d*u*ca*tts* 92 M.

168

127(L) contd.

10 ton, 17 C 3 qr.	Itm. more for freight of 50 tons Spanische weight at 13s 4d the ton, costom of 48 tons at 2s 6d per ton, averes of 50 tons at 11d per ton, hawlyng & weying 3d per ton, montith the costes £42 5s. So amontith the pryncipall & costes £284 16s 3d	£284 16s 3d
	Itm. the 4 day of October r. owt of the John Baptist of the Rendry master Johannes Deyrancu, 10 ton iren Rendry & Fontraby weight which made by my weightes 10 ton 17 C 3 qr. conteynyng 1070 endes, which cost clere abord in Spayne £45 10s, for costom 25s, for halyng & weying 6s 8d, for freight & averes £5 9s 2d	£52 10s 10d
	Itm. the 15 day of Aprell 1542 £64 6s 2d½ that is ffor so mych goten by this acowmpt, as it may apere to gayenes in credito fo. 92	£64 6s 2d½
	S.	£424 6s 2d ob

anno 1542

John Satchefilld marchant of Bristowe owith the 13 day of February £31 13s 4d & is for won C ducatts of gold & weight delyverd by Giles Whit to hym for my acowmpt in Andaluzia after 19 grotes the ducatt, to be paide 20 days next after tharryvall of the Kateryn of Bastable at Bristowe, which ship arryvid the forseid 13 day of February, so that it must be paide the 5th day of Marche next commyng £31 13s 4d

Itm. the 1 day of Aprell 1544 £6 13s 4d & is for the freight of 5 tons iren in my ship the Trynte at 4 nobles the ton, to pay hallf in hand & hallf at thend of 3 monthes next commyng £6 13s 4d

127(R)   **anno 1541**

Iren per contra is dewe to have the 5 day of Augost £257 17s 2d½ that is for 41 tons 17 C 1 qr. 26 li. conteynyng 4079 endes sold from the 26 day of Aprell last past, as in my shop boke may apere £257 17s 2d ob

Itm. the 27 day of February £162 1s 8d½ that is for 27 tons, 10 C ½, & ½ a li. iren conteynyng 2537 endes sold from the 5 day of Augost last past untyll this daye, as in my shop boke may apere, montith £162 1s 8d ob

Itm. the 5 day of Aprell 1542 33s 4d½ that is for 5 C ½, 6 li. conteynyng 24 endes sold from the 27 of February last past untill this daye £1 13s 4d ob

Itm. the 15 day of Aprell 1542 £3 that is for 10 C 14 li. conteynyng 29 endes which rest to selling of this cowmpt & I pass it to fo. 153 £3

S. £424 6s 2d ob

anno 1543

John Satchefilld per contra is dewe to have the 4th day of June £25 6s 8d that is for 7 buttes of seck r. of his master John Wellsche for hym at 11 nobles the butt, less a noble apon all £25 6s 8d

Itm. the 10 of November 1543 r. for hym of the good wif Wellsche £6 £6

More the 13 of the same r. of hym 6s 8d 6s 8d

128(L)   **anno 1541**

Thomas Machyne of Barckeley owithe the 30 day of March for ¼ a C madder, I sey 1 qr. madder   3s 3d

128(L) contd.

Itm. the 9 day of May 26s 8d for 1 h'd Gascon wyne	£1	6s	8d
Itm. the 18 of Maye 1 qr. madder after 14s the C		3s– 6d	

Itm. the 11 day of Julye £19 that is £13 for 2 ton iren of S.S. & £6 redy monney which iren & money I d'd to hym in yernes & part of payement of 60 dicker of cowe & stere of a large sort & of his owne tannyng in sufficient wise, at 43s 4d the dicker d'd abord my ship or eny other ship at Hungrode, Kyngrode or Chepstowe & allso more 60 dozens of large calve skuyns of his owne tannyng at 6s the dozen browght aborde the ship as aforeseid. The seid Thomas Machyne must d'd 30 dicker lether & 20 dozen calve skuyns with in this 3 wekes & 10 dicker lethir & 20 dozen calve skuyns at Mighellmas & 20 dozens skuyns at Allhaloutyde & 20 dicker lether at Cristmas next & for payement of the rest of the foreseid lether & skuyns I must pay 5 ton wull oyle at £11 6s 8d the ton & £20 of monney 15 dayes after Seynt Jamistyde & £30 at Allhaloutyde & £22 6s 8d at Seynt Katerynstyde next after. So amontith that which is payde in yernes as aforesseid

	£19		
Itm. the 6 day of August anno 1541 £10 pd. to hym at Bristowe in redy money	£10		
Itm. the 27 day of August £10 pd. to hym in redy money	£10		
Itm. the 23 day of September £56 13s 4d that is for 5 ton wull oyle at £11 6s 8d d'd to hym at dyvers tymes sens the 6 day of August untill this day, as in my shop boke may apere	£56	13s	4d
Itm. the 4th day of November anno 1541 paide to hym at Bristowe in redy monney £20	£20		
Itm. the 12 day of December paide to hym £30	£30		
Itm. the 17 day of Jenyver £20 pd. to hym in monney	£20		
Itm. the 3 day of February £8 4s 8d that is 4 markes paide for hym to my mother for a pipe of samon £5 11s 4d paide to hym in redy monney, montith	£8	4s	8d
Itm. 37s 6d which I pd. the 25 of February to Hawle for hym for bryngyng the lether	£1	17s	6d
Itm. the 21 day of Marche pd. by my wif to his sarvant Thomas Martyne £5	£5		
Itm. the 22 day of Aprell 1542 £3 15s 10d which I pay hym in redy money	£3	15s	10d
S.	£185	18s	4d

128(R)   **anno 1541**

Thomas Machet per contra is dewe to have the 27 day of Augost £65 for 30 dicker lether laden abord Robert Pooles ship at 43s 4d the dicker	£65		
Itm. the 16 day of Jenyver r. from hym 10 dicker of ox lether at 4 markes the dicker & 5 dicker less 1 hide cowe & stere at 43s 4d the dicker, montith	£37	5s	8d
Itm. the 1 day of February r. 25 dicker & 1 hide cow & stere at 43s 4d per dicker & 58 dozens calve skuyns at 6s the dozen & 20 dozens at 5s 4d the dozen & 20 dozens at 5s 10d the dozen, montith all £82 19s	£82	19s	
Itm. the 22 day of Aprill 1542 13s 4d which I owe for the freight of 10 dicker from Glocester in Hawles bote		13s	4d
S.	£185	18s	4d

129(L)   **anno 1541**

Robert Guytton of Bristowe marchant owith the 5th day of Maye £6 which is for a ton of iren to be pd. at Seynt Jamistide next commyng	£6	
Itm. the 19 day of August £12 to pay by his bill £6 at Candellmas next & £6 att Easter next after that, which is for a ton wull oyle sold & d'd to hym at the seid price	£12	
1541 Itm. the 1 day of December 1541 50s which is for the rest & hallf freight of 4 tons bastard in the Trynte at 25s per ton, to pay it at the end of 3 monthes next commyng	£2	10s

129(L) contd.

1542 Itm. the 24 day of Aprill 1542 £4 that is for the freight of 6 tons iren
in the Trynte, to pay at 3 monthes & 3 monthes, as by the charterp*artie* may
apere   £4
Itm. the 20 day of July £24 that is for 4 pipes of wull oyle sold & d'd to hym
at £6 the pipe, to be paide at Candellmas next com*m*yng   £24
Itm. the 23 day of Augost £4 for the freight of 6 tons iren fro*m* Spayne in
my ship the Trynte   £4
Itm. the 18 day of February £9 that is for the freight of 5 ton wyne & 1 to*n*
oyle in my ship at 30s p*er* ton, to pay hallf in hand & hallf 3 monthes next
after   £9

                       S.   £61   10s

1541

John Wells of Bristowe sopemaker o*with* the 2d day of July £52 for 52
to*n* salt sold & delyverd to hym, to pay £17 6s 8d at Mydsomer next com*m*yng &
£17 6s 8d at Midsomer in a*n*no 1543 & £17 6s 8d at Midsomer in a*n*no 1544,
as it may apere by an obligacio*n* wryten by Jo*h*n Sare & subscribyd & sealid
by the seid J*oh*n Wells, mon*tith*   £52
1542 Itm. the 17 day of Aprill £18 for 3 pipes of oyle to be pd. at Whitssontide
next   £18
Itm. the 26 day of June 1542 £12 for 1 to*n* oyle to be paide at Mighellmas
next   £12
Itm. the 6 day of July £24 for 2 pipes of wull oyle sold & d'd to hym, to
pay at Allhaloutyde next   £24
Itm. the 18 day of June for 1 h'd Gasco*n* wyne   £2
1547 Itm. the 23 day of Jenyver a*n*no 1547 £28 & is for 2 tons wull oyle at
eich £14, to be pd. at Seynt Jamystide next com*m*yng   £28
1548 Itm. the 18 day of Jenyver a*n*no 1548 £36 & is for 2 tons wull oyle at
£14 p*er* ton, to pay at Ester next, as by his byll may apere[1]   £36

129(R)   **anno 1541**

Robert Guytton p*er* contra is dewe to have the 4 daye of
Augost £6 r. of hym in redy mon*n*ey   £6
Itm. the 10th day of February r. of hym £6 & putt it in the
backsyde of his byll   £6
Itm. the 7 of June a*n*no 1542 r. of hym £6 & d'd to hym
his bill of £12 p*er* contra   £6
Itm. the last day of July 1542 r. of hym £3 10s   £3   10s
Itm. the 8 day of Augost r. of hym 2 doble d*ucatts*   £1
Itm. the 25 day of November Lett r. of hym 40s for the
last payement of 6 tons iren in Ap*r*ell last past   £2
Itm. the 5 of Jenyver 40s r. of hym for the hallf freight of
6 tons ire*n* which came home in my ship the 23 of Agost   £2
Itm. the 13 day of February 1542 my s*a*rvant Leyt r. of hym
in redy money 40s   £2
Itm. the 2d day of M*a*rche, r. of hym £16   £16
Itm. more r. the 24 of M*a*rche £6   £6
Itm. the 4 of Aprill 1543 r. of hym 40s   £2
Itm. the 21 day of Aprill r. of hym 40s   £2
Itm. the 2d day of July 1543 26s 8d that is 8s for 4 Bewdeley
powles & 4s for 3 Bewdeley powles & 14s 2d for 1 C 1 qr.
19 li. tallow at 10s p*er* C & 6d r. in mon*n*ey   £1   6s   8d
Itm. the 17 of Octob*er* 1543 r. of hym £5 13s 4d   £5   13s   4d

                       S.   £61   10s

---

[1] *The whole of the last item is crossed through.*

129(R) contd.   **anno 1542**

John Wells sope maker per contra is dewe to have the 27 day of May £12 for so myche reddy monney r. of hym	£12
Itm. the 15 day of June r. of hym in monney £6	£6
Itm. the 5 day of July r. of hym £17 6s 8d for the first payment of the sallt per contra	£17 6s 8d
Itm. the last day of September r. of hym £12	£12
Itm. the 18 day of November r. of hym	£20
Itm. the 9 day of December r. of hym £4	£4
Itm. the 27 day of July 1543 £17 6s 8d r. of hym in part of payement of the sallt per contra	£17 6s 8d
Itm. the 22 day of November anno 1544 John Wells d'd unto me acowmpt of £3 3s 3d that I owed to hym, that is for 10 dozen ½ betakle candells at at[1] 1d ob the li, for 2 C ½ molton tallo at 14s the C & for 241 fote of planckes at 5s the C, montith the hole as afforeseid	£3 3s 3d
Itm. the same day r. of hym in redy monney £16 3s 5d	£16 3s 5d
r. the 27 of July 1548 £28	£28

130(L)   **anno 1541**

John Snygg marchant of Bristowe owith the 2d day of July £3 that is for a pipe of iren delyverd for hym to Richard Willshire broker, to pay 30s at Mighellmas next & 30s at Cristmas next after that	£3
1542 Itm. the 15 day of September 1542 £6 13s 4d that is for 1 pipe wull oyle to be paide by his byll at Mydsomer next commyng	£6 13s 4d
1544 Itm. the 27 day of Marche anno 1544 £3 & is for 1 pipe of iren to be paide at Mighellmas next commyng as by his byll may apere	£3

                               anno 1541

Thomas Smythe of Soodbery owith the 28 day of May £6 6s 8d which is for 1 ton iren to be pd. at Mighellmas next commyng. Sir Thomas Sergant of Sodbery vicar is shewerty for hym	£6 6s 8d
Itm. the first day of October £6 that is for 1 ton iren sold & d'd to hym to be pd. at Allrode Day in Maye next commyng. Sir Thomas Sergant foreseid is his shewerty	£6
Itm. the 28 day of February anno 1542 £6 10s which is for the rest of 1 ton 25 li. iren, to be paide at Lammas Day next commyng. The foreseid Sir Thomas Serjent is his shewerty, as it may apere by his lettor	£6 10s
1543 Itm. the 28 day of Julye anno 1543 £6 13s 4d & is for 1 ton of S.S. iren sold & delyverd to hym, to be paide at Candellmas next & the foresseid Sir Thomas Serjant is his shewerty	£6 13s 4d
Itm. the 21 day of May anno 1547 for the rest of a ton 23 li. Rendry iren which I d'd to his son Edward after £7 the ton, 41s 5d to be paide the weke after Mydsomer next commyng	£2 1s 5d

130(R)   **anno 1541**

John Snygg per contra is dewe to have the 19 daye of December 30s r. of hym in redy monney	£1 10s
Itm. the 7 day of February r. of hym 30s	£1 10s
~~Itm. the 18 day of May £3 which Robert Lett r. at Sodbery of hym in redy monney~~	~~£3~~
Itm. the 3 day of September 1543 my wif r. of hym £6 6s 8d	£6 6s 8d
Itm. the 19 day of October r. 6s 8d & d'd the byll	6s 8d
Itm. the 22 day of November 1544 r. of George Snygg his son £3	£3

---

[1] *Smythe repeats* at.

130(R) contd.   **anno 1541**

Thomas Smythe per contra is dewe to have the first day
of October £6 6s 8d r. of hym at Bristowe in redy monney   £6   6s   8d
Itm. the 18 day of May 1542 Robert Lett r. of hym at
Sodbery £3 of monney   £3
Itm. r. of hym at Bristowe the 22 of Julye £3   £3
Itm. the 28 day of July 1543 r. of hym at Bristowe £6 10s   £6 10s
Itm. the 6 of February 1543 r. of hym at Bristowe £6 13s 4d   £6 13s   4d
Itm. the 12 of July 1547 r. of hym   £2   1s   5d

131(L)   **anno 1541**

William Bullock of the parische of Ellmore in Glocester shere yeoman
owithe the 28 day of June £67 3s 6d that is for 50 hallf bales Tullus wood
weying 89 C ½, 7 li. sold & delyverd to hym at 15s the C, to be paide at
Mighellmas next commyng, as by his bill may apere   £67   3s   6d
Itm. the 27 day of Augost £40 paide to hym in reddy monney   £40
Itm. the 17 day of September £20 for so myche redy money pd. to hym in
Bristowe   £20
Itm. 26s which is for hallf a wey whet r. less then 51 weyes which be
mencionyd per contra   £1   6s
Itm. 6s which he owith for a dozen mattes & cocquettes for serteyne wheat
he sent to Cornwale   6s
Itm. the 8 day of October £4 11s 6d pd. to hym in monny   £4 11s   6d

                                                               S. £133   7s

                                                anno 1542

William Bullock of Ellmore above reherssyd owith the 28 daye of June
£6 10s which is for 1 ton iren of S.S. solld & delyverd to hym at £6 10s,
to be paide at all tymes requyrid   £6 10s
Itm. the 7 of November pd. to hym in redy monny £20 sterling   £20
Itm. 38s 8d that is ffor 29 busshells wheat at 16d the busshell which lackyd
of the 23 wayes per contra, montith   £1 18s   8d
Itm. the 30 day of December £11 11s 4d which is for so myche redy monney
pd. to hym at Bristo by my wif & I r. my bill   £11 11s   4d

                                                               S.   £40

                                                anno 1543

William Bullock of Ellmoore above reherssyd owith the 8 day of Augost
£10 3d ob & is for 1 ton pipe 5 li. of S.S. iren at 20 nobles the ton, to be
paide at all tymes requyrid, montith   £10   3d ob
Itm. the 22 of Jenyver 1543 44s 10d & is for 29 gallons 3 quartes & 1 pynt
wull oyle solld to hym at 18d the gallon, montith   £2   4s 10d
Itm. the 25 day of Jenyver d'd to hym in redy monney £13 15s   £13 15s

131(R)   **anno 1541**

William Bullock per contra is dewe to have the 27 day of
Augost £132 12s that is for 51 weys whet r. of hym at 13d
the busshell, montith   £132 12s
Itm. 15s which I allowe hym for lack of weight in the
wood per contra   15s

                                                               S. £133   7s

173

131(R) contd.   **anno 1542**

   William Bullock of Ellmore is dewe to have the 2d day of
   October £40 which is for the rest of 23 weyes wheat at 16d
   the busshell, for the which £40 restyng I have made hym a byll
   to pay at Allhaloutyde next

                    £40

anno 1544

   William Bullock per contra is dewe to have the 18 day of
   October £20 which Lett r. of hym   £20
   Itm. the 8 day of May 1545 r. of hym   £6

132(L)   **anno 1541**

William Hazard of Glocester diar owith the 27 day of May 58s 2d that is
for 2 ½-bales Tullus wood conteynyng 3 C ½, 9 li. at 16s the C which he r.
from me owt of Thomas Filldes bote of Glocester   £2 18s 2d

anno 1543

Jamys Gowgh of Waterford marchant owith the 23 day of Marche £10
which I lent hym in redy money to be paide of the first messenger as do
com from Waterfford, as by his bill may apere   £10

anno 1541

Mawrice Shepward of Amesbery in Glocestershire gentleman owith the 5th day
of Aprell £9 to be paide at Mighellmas next commyng, which I lent hym in redy
money apon serteyne plate weying 62 owynces. The peces be 2 gillt nuttes
with theyr covers & 1 goblet passell gillt with his cover, as it may apere
by a byll I indentyd, which the seid Mawrice have of my hand   £9

132(R)   **anno 1541**

   William Hazard per contra is dewe to have the 26 day of
   July by thandes of William Hazard his kynssman 50s &
   the rest I rebate   £2 18s 2d

anno 1544

   Jamys Gowgh per contra is dewe to have the 5 daye of
   November £10 which I r. of Edmond Slattery of Waterford
   & d'd to hym his bill   £10

   Itm. the 28 day of July 1546 r. of Morys Shepward per
   contra £9 & d'd to hym the plate in the other side
   mencyoned   £9

133(L)   **anno 1541**

Lysence for wheat 60 wey bowght for my acowmpt owith the last day of
June £50 17s that is for £50 pd. for it by Thomas Shipman to Master Paget
the Kynges Secrettary & 17s for the seid T. Shipmans costes to London for
to fetche it   £50 17s

anno 1541

John Wade of Bristowe coverlet maker owith the 31 day of October
£3 10s which is for a butt of seck sold & d'd to hym to paye at Cristmas
next   £3 10s
1542 Itm. the 14 day of Augost anno 1542 £4 which is for a butt of seck to
be paide by his bill at Cristmas next   £4

133(L) contd.

Itm. the 23 day of February £4 for a butt of seck d'd to John Williams of Castilenethe, to be pd. by theyr obligacion at Seynt Jamistide next commyng	£4
1544 Itm. the 16 of September anno 1544 £4 which is for a butt of seck to be paide at Candyllmas next, montith	£4

133(R)   anno 1541

Lysence per contra is dewe to have the 1 day of September £25 8s 6d which is for 30 weyes entryd in my ship the Trynte	£25	8s	6d
Itm. the 10 day of December £15 for 60 qrs. solld to Robert Pole of Glocester, as it aperith to hym in debito fo. 111	£15		
Itm. the first day of June 1542 40s which is for 2 weyes ocupyed between T. Web & me in my ship the Trynte	£2		
Itm. the 1 day of October 1542 £8 for 8 weyes entryd in the Trynte my shipp	£8		
Itm. the last day of Marche anno 1543 £5 that is for lysence of 5 wey wheat entryd for my acowmpt in the Clement of Fromyland	£5		

anno 1541

John Wade per contra is dewe to have the 23 day of December £3 10s r. of hym in redy monny	£3	10s
Itm. the 12 day of Jenyver 1542 r. for hym of his brother in the lawe John Williams coverlett maker £4 & d'd to hym his bill	£4	
Itm. the 27 day of July 1543 r. of John Wyllyams £4	£4	
Itm. the 4 of Aprell 1545 r. of John Wade £4	£4	

134(L)   anno 1541

Thomas Web of West Hartry owith the 9 day of November £3 13s 4d pd. to hym in monny	£3	13s	4d
Itm. the 6 day of December paide to hym £16 10s	£16	10s	
1542 Itm. the 19 day of Aprell 1542 £40 which I paye to hym in redy monney & r. my bill	£40		
Itm. the 21 day of October pd. to hym at Bristow in redy monney £20 & putt it apon the byll	£20		
Itm. the 11 day of November paide to hym in Bristowe £20 for the full payement of £40 conteynyd in a byll datid the 2d day of June last past, as per contra aperithe & broke the byll	£20		
1543 Itm. the 7 day of Aprell 1543 pd. to Thomas Web £28 & r. my bill	£28		
1544 Itm. the 20 day of September 1544 £40 which my wif paide to hym in redy monney & so r. my byll	£40		
1549 Itm. the 26 of Jenyver anno 1549 £10 & is for so myche paide & delyverd for hym to his son	£10		
Itm. the last day of Jenyver pd. to hymseallf at Bristowe[1]	£14		

134(R)   anno 1541

Thomas Web of West Hartry in Somerzetshire yeoman is dewe to have the 1 day of Augost £20 3s 4d to be payd at Cristmas next commyng & it is for the rest of 10 ton pipe led which I r. of hym at £3 13s 4d the ton & more 2s for every tons carrige. It make by my weightes 10 ton 11 C 21 li. 186 peces	£20	3s	4d

---

[1] All items on this folio are crossed through.

134(R) contd.

1541 Itm. the 14 day of Jenyver a*nn*o 1541 £40 which is for 10 ton led *conteynyng* 212 pec*es* bowght of hym at £4 the to*n*, to be pd. by me bill at East*er* next, & the same led make by my weight*es* 12 ton 3 C ½, 7 li.	£40
Itm. the 2d day of June 1542 £40 which is for 10 ton led *conteynyng* 172 peces bowght at £4 the ton, to be paide by my bill at Mighellmas next & the same led make by my weight*es* 10 to*n* 2 C ½	£40
Itm. the 24 day of Augost £28 that is for 6 ton led *conteynyng* ¹ peces at 7 m*arkes* the ton, to pay by my bill at Candellmas next com*m*yng	£28 ¹
Itm. the 2⫽ day of October 1542 Itm. the 22 day of M*a*rche 1543 £40 & is for 10 ton led in a 175 pec*es*. It made by my weight*es* ¹ , & it is payable by my bill at Seynt Jamistide next	£40
Itm. the 26 of Jenyver for 2 tons led, the last day of Jenyver 2 tons led, the first day of February 2 tons led, the 3d day of February 3 tons led ²	

135(L)   **anno 1541**

Benet Jaye of Bristowe m*ar*chant otherwise of Mawnsbery in Wilschere m*ar*chant owith the 9 day of Augost £5 19s 10d, to be pd. by his bill at Cristmas next com*m*yng & it is for a to*n* less 3 li. of Rendry ire*n* d'd for hym to W*illiam* Yevers at £6 the to*n*	£5 19s 10d
1542 Itm. the 27 day of July a*nn*o 1542 £12 that is ffor 2 to*n* Rendry iren sold & delyverd to hym, to be paide at Candellmas next	£12

135(R)   **anno 1541**

Benet Jaye p*er* contra is dewe to have the 6 day of February £5 19s 10d for so myche redy money r. of hym at Bristowe & I d'd to hym his byll obligatory	£5 19s 10d
Itm. the 9 day of February a*nn*o 1542 £12 that is for so myche redy mon*n*ey r. of hym at Bristowe	£12

136(L)   **anno 1541**

Viages for my acowmpt to Luxbron the 17 day of Augost owith £87 8s 4d that is for 10 clothes of Yerberys bet*ter* sort £40 & 40 northen dozens £46 13s 4d & 2 northen cottons 15s, the which clothes went in 5 fardells & laden in the Savior of Bastable whereof Richard Chapell is ownar. This good*es* gothe under the rule & governance of my prent*es* Hewgh Hamond	£87	8s 4d
Itm. d'd to the seid Hamond in his purss for his cost*es*	£1	
Itm. £251 that is £80 for 20 clothes of Jo*h*n Yerberys & Thomas Nasches & £171 that 53 weys 41 busshells whet cost clereabord, the which good*es* be laden in my ship the Trynte, m*aster* Thomas Webb, & gothe under the rule & governance of Giles Whit my late s*ar*vant	£251	
Itm. the same tyme £7 10s that is for a fyne blewe of Jo*h*n Yerberys lode in my seid ship	£7	10s
Itm. 6 d*ucatts* for Hamon*des* hallf cost*es* & 8 d*ucatts* for Giles & Tizons hallf cost*es*, mon*tith*	£3	10s
Itm. £69 15s 5d for so myche goten by this acowmt, as it may apere to gayns in credito fo. 92	£69	15s 5d
S.	£420	3s 9d

---

¹ *Blank in MS.*
² *All items on this folio are crossed through.*

136(L) contd. anno 1541

Viages to Luxbron the 1 day of February owith £75 17s 11d that is for 20 weyes & a hallf, 27 busshells¹ of wheat laden for my acowmpt in the Mary Fortune of Glocester under God master Lawrence Nunny, the which foreseid som of monney I allowe to Robert Poole of Glocester in acowmpt, as it may apere to hym in credito fo. 111. I sey 21 weys less 1 busshell £75 17s 11d

Itm. I have more in Andaluzia won 100 ducatts which Giles White left for my acowmpt the last vyntaige in the powar & custodye of Master Thomas Harrys in Sevyll £25

Itm. more I have at Gibralltar in the handes of a correo callyd Alexander Rodryguez 45 ducatts, & won Diego de Bollona marchant & Diego Mollynez corredor be shewrtes to my sarvant Hamond for the trewthe of the seid correo £11 5s

Itm. the 15 day of October 1542 laden in the Trynte, master Thomas Web, 119 peces led conteynyng 7 ton 1 C which cost clereabord £33 17s 6d & 23 weyes wheat which cost abord £81, montith £114 17s 6d

Itm. the same tyme in the Mary James, master Richard White, 2 fardells clothe conteynyng 10 clothes, 1 Bristow frize & 34 Manchesters, montith £66 10s

Itm. the same tyme in the Mary Conception 2 fardells of Manchesters conteynyng 64 Manchesters which cost clere abord £48

Itm. in Dezember £30 9s 10d goten by this cownpt of viages, as may apere in credito to geynes fo. 92 £30 9s 10d

£372 3d

136(R) anno 1541

Viages per contra is dewe to have the monthe of December for the sales of 20 London clothes sold by Giles at Luxbron & for a fyne blewe nete the costes deductyd 120 V. 840 M. as by his acowmpt may apere, which amontith sterlyng £80 11s 3d

Itm. more sold by the seid Giles 53 weyes & 41 busshells wheate which made at Luxbron clere of all costes 405 V. 955 M. as by his cowmpt may apere & it montith sterling £270 12s 9d. Montith the foreseid clothe & corn in won som £351 4s

Itm. the seid tyme r. acowmpt of my sarvant Hewgh Hamond by the which it apere that he made clere of the sale of 40 northen dozens & of 2 cottons & of 10 clothes of John Yerberys penny hewes 104 V. 232 M. which montith sterlyng £68 19s 9d

S. £420 3s 9d

anno 1542

Viages per contra is dewe to have the 14 daye of June £72 18s 2d sterling which is for 109356 M. which Henry Brune by his reckenyng geve me for the rest & nete of 20 weys ½ corn per contra. It montith in ducatts 291 ducatts 234 M. Of the £72 18s 2d I do make his Master Robert Pole debitor fo. 111 £72 18s 2d

Itm. 36s 3d which I make the seid Pole debitor of fo. 111 for hallf a wey of the corn per contra which I pd. for to hym & his sarvant Brune geve me no cowmpt of it, as may apere, for he geve me in reckenyng but for 20 wey ½, where I pd. for 21 wey less 1 busshell £1 16s 3d

Itm. in July last Giles r. the 100 ducatts left in Thomas Harrys handes & lode it for me in oyles in the Conception £25

Itm. in Dezember 45 ducatts which Giles r. of Hamon for that in Gibralltar £10 5s

---

¹27 busshells *is inserted above the line.*

136(R) contd.

Itm. £123 which is for the nete sale of 10 clothes & 98 Manchesters & 1 Bristowe frise, as ap*er*ith by Giles cowmpt	£123	
Itm. £38 15s for the sale of 7 to*n* 1 C led	£38 15s	
Itm. £100 5s 10d for the nete sale of 23 wey of whete	£100 5s 10d	
S.	£372 3d	

137(L) anno **1541**

Thomas Abowen of Kerdif gentlema*n* owith the 25 day of Augost 33s 1d *that* is for 1 h'd less 4 li. iren of S.S. at 20 nobles *the* ton, which was delyverd for hym to Ris his son, to be pd. at all tymes £1 13s 1d

anno 1541

John Hunteley in Glocestershire esquyer ow*ith* the 19 day of Octob*er*, £36 *that* is for 3 to*n* wull oyle sold to hym, to pay £18 with in a monethe next com*m*yng & £18 at Seynt Jamistide next £36

Itm. the 30 day of Jenyver £25 *that* is for 2 tons of wull oyle sold to hym, to be pd. at Seynt Jamystide next com*m*yng, mon*tith* £25

S. £61

anno 1542

John Untely esquyer before reherssid owith the 25 day of Novemb*er* £6 13s 4d whiche is for a pipe of wull oyle sold & d'd to hym, to be paide at all tymes £6 13s 4d

137(R)[1] anno **1541**

John Huntley p*er* contra is dewe to have the 6 daye of December £18 r. from nym by his s*ar*vu*n*t Jo*h*n Holder £18

Itm. the 7 day of Augost 1542 r. fro*m* hym by his sarvant Jo*h*n Hollder £37 mon*tith* £37

Itm. the 27 day of October 1542 £6 for so myche redy mon*n*ey r. of hym by the hand*es* of his s*ar*vau*n*tt Thomas Le £6

S. £61

anno 1543

John Huntely p*er* contra is dewe to have the 10 of July £6 13s 4d r. in mon*n*y by his s*ar*vant John Coke £6 13s 4d

138(L) anno **1541**

Gregory Shewryng of Mylksam smythe ow*ith* the 19 day of Septemb*er* £6 6s 1d ob that is for for[2] 1 to*n* 1 qr. 10 li. ½ iren to be paide at all tymes £6 6s 1d½

Itm. the 11 day of Jenyver for 12 C 2 li. of my best Rendry iren at 6s the C & 5 C ½ 22 li. of my wiff*es* iren at 6s 4d the C, mon*tith* all £5 8s 2d, to be paide at Whitssontyde next £5 8s 2d

1542 Itm. the 8 day of Maye 1542 £6 13s 4d that is for the rest of 1 to*n* 1 C 26 li. iren, to be pd. at Mighellmas next £6 13s 4d

Itm. the 7 day of November £6 10s that is for 1 pipe S.S. iren & 1 pipe of the bett*er* Rendry iren sold & d'd to hym, to pay £3 10s at Owr Lady Day in Lent next com*m*yng & £3 at Whitsontyde next after that, mon*tith* the hole £6 10s

---

[1] *There is no credit entry for Thomas Abowen.*
[2] *Smythe repeats* for.

138(L) contd.

1543 Itm. the 8 day of June £6 10s that is for 1 pipe of S.S. iren at 20 nobles the ton & 1 pipe of the best Rendry iren at 19 nobles the ton, to pay £3 10s at Mighellmas next & £3 at Cristmas next after that £6 10s

Itm. the 14 day of Jenyver 1543 £6 13s 4d which is for 10 C Rendry iren at 19 grotes the C & 10 C ½ of S.S. iren at 20 grotes the C, to pay hallf at Midssomer next commyng & the other hallf at Seynt Jamystide next after that £6 13s 4d

1544 Itm. the 4 of of¹ August anno 1544 £4 3s & is for the rest of 12 C 3 qr. 17 li. iren, to be paide at Cristmas next as in my shop boke may apere £4 3s

Itm. the 9 day of Jenyver for 13 C iren £4 3s 4d to be paide at Whitsontide next £4 3s 4d

Itm. the 13 day of July 1545 £4 & is for the rest of 12 C 20 li. iren to be paide at Mighellmas next as it may apere by my shop boke £4

Itm. the 13 day of November 1545 for 9 C 25 li. iren £3 to be paide at Owr Lady in Marche next commyng, as it may apere in my shopp booke £3

Itm. the 15 day of Marche anno 1545 £4 10s 1d for 14 C iren to be paide at Mighellmas next commyng £4 10s

Itm. the 19 day of February 1546 13s 4d for 2 C iren to be paide at all tymes. More lent to hym the same day in redy monney 14s, montith al £1 7s 4d

Itm. the 21 day of May 1547 £3 2s 6d & is for 3 C S.S. iren at 8s per C & for 5 C ½ Rendry iren at 7s per C, to be paide at Seynt Jamystide next commyng £3 2s 6d

S. £62 7s 1d ob

138(R)   anno 1541

Gregory Shewring per contra is dewe to have the 11 daye of Jenyver 5 markes r. of hym at Bristowe in redy monny, montith £3 6s 8d

Itm. the last day of Marche 1542² r. from hym by his neighbur Thomas Wattes £3 6s 8d £3 6s 8d

Itm. the 14 day of July r. for hym of Thomas Wattes 7 markes £4 13s 4d

The 25 of October r. for hym by Thomas Wattes 8 markes £5 6s 8d

Itm. the 9 day of Jenyver 1542 r. for hym by Thomas Wattes 34s 3d ob. £1 13s 3d ob

Itm. the 8 of June 1543 r. of hym £6 10s £6 10s

Itm. the 14 of Jenyver r. of hym £6 10s £6 10s

Itm. the 4 of August 1544 £6 13s 4d r. of hym for iren d'd the 14 day of Jenyver last past £6 13s 4d

Itm. the 9 day r. by my wif £4 3s £4 3s

Itm. the 13 day of July 1545 r. of hym £4 3s 4d

Itm. the 12 day of November r. £4 £4

Itm. the 15 day of Marche anno 1545 r. of hym £3 £3

Itm. my wif r. in November 1546 £4 10s £4 10s

Itm. the 21 day of May 1547 r. of hym 27s 4d £1 7s 4d

Itm. the 13 day of Augost r. of hym £3 2s 6d £3 2s 6d

S. £62 7s 1d ob

139(L)   anno 1541

Tristan Lecknor won of the serchors at Bristowe owith the 27 day of October £6 13s 4d which I lent hym in redy monney to be paide by his bill the 12th day of ~~September~~ December next commyng £6 13s 4d

1542 Itm. the 9 day of Augost anno 1542 £11 6s 8d that is for 2 tons Rendry iren, to be paide at Seynt Jamystide next commyng, montith £11 6s 8d

---

¹ *Smythe repeats* of.
² *1542 is inserted above the line.*

179

139(L) contd.   anno 1543

Thomas Kemys of Bedmyster gentleman owith the 14 day of February £5
& is for so mych reddy monney lent to hym, to be paide at Mydsomer next,
as by his bill may apere

	S.	£5	

anno 1548

Gregory Shewring of Mylksam smythe owithe the 6 day of Augost anno
dicto 47s & is for 5 C iren, to be pd. within 3 monthes next followyng — £2 7s
Itm. the 11th day of Jenyver 44s & is for the rest of 4 C 1 qr. 10 li. iren of the
Rendry & part of S.S. to be paide at Easter next, as in my shop boke may
apere — £2 4s
Itm. the 3d day of Maye 22s 1d & for 2 C 9 li. S.S. iren at 10s 8d per ton to be
paide at Whitsontyde next, montith — £1 2s 1d
Itm. the 14 day of August 1549 35s & is for the rest of 3 C 1 qr. 11 li. iren
to be paide a thissyde Allhaloutyde next commyng — £1 15s
Itm. the 4th day of October 1549 43s which is for the rest of 4 C 8 li. iren to
be paide at Cristmas next comyng — £2 3s

139(R)   anno 1541

Tristan here ageynst is dewe to have 50s which is for lysence
of 5 dickers lether which he sold to me the last day of
November at 10s the dicker — £2 10s
Itm. the 3 day of June 1542 17s that is for a powledavy r. of
his wiff — 17s
Itm. the last day of September for a burden lyng — 18s
Itm. the 14 of September 1543 r. 2 ton led in 34 peces
at £4 6s 8d the ton — £8 13s 4d

anno 1546

Thomas Kemys per contra is dewe to have the 12 day of
February 20s for his dett per contra of William Wyllet of
Bristowe — £1
Itm. the 14 of May 1547 r. of William Wyllett — £1
Itm. the 8 day of Augost 1547 r. of William Wyllett 20s — £1
Itm. the 26 day of Jenyver 1547 r. by thandes of William
Wyllet 40s & so quyte — £2

	S.	£5	

1548

Gregory Shewryng per contra is dewe to have the 26 day of
October 47s r. of hym at Bristowe — £2 7s
1549 Itm. the 3d day of May anno 1549 my wif r. 44s — £2 4s
Itm. r. 22s 1d — £1 2s 1d
Itm. the 4th of October 1549, r. of hym 35s — £1 15s
Itm. my wif r. of hym the 12 of Jenyver 23s — £1 3s
Itm. r. by my wif the 14 of Marche 1549 20s — £1

140(L)   anno 1547

Gilbart Cogan of Bristowe marchant owithe the 12 day of October £3 10d which
is for 2 ½-bales of Tullus wood conteynyng 3 C ½, 9 li. at 17s the C, to be pad
at all tymes — £3 10d
1542 Itm. the 3 day of August anno 1542 £6 that is for a pipe of wull oyle to
be pd. at Cristmas next — £6

180

140(L) contd.

Itm. the 8 day of the same £6 6d that is ffor 4 ½-bales Tullus wood weying 7 C 9 li. at 17s the C, to be pd. at Cristmas next com*m*yng		£6	6d
	S.	£15 1s	4d

anno 1548

John Aston of Harvardeast owith the 15 day of Jenyver £5 and is for a p*ip*e of bastard sold & d'd to hym, to be paide at all tymes requyrid £5

Itm. the 25 of Feburary £8 & is for 1 ton Gasco*n* wyne sent to hym in J*ohn* Sp*arkes* bote £8

140(R) anno 1542

Gilbart Cogan p*er* contra is dewe to have the 4 daye of
July 6s 3d which I owyd hym for the rest of 4 M tile
stones of 2 yeres past & 27s 11d r. of his wif in reddy
mon*n*ey   6s 3d
   £1 7s 11d
Itm. for a yeres rent of a sellar 4 nobles   £1 6s 8d
Itm. the 7 day of February 1542 r. by the hand*es* of his wif £6   £6
Itm. the 10 of February £3 1s 9d which is for 2 ½-bales wood
conte*y*nyng 3 C ½, 15 li. after 17s the C, which he retornyd
to me ageyne of the 4 bales p*er* contra d'd the 8 of Augost   £3 1s 9d
Itm. the 27 of February r. of his wif   £2 18s 9d

  S. £15 1s 4d

anno 1548

John Aston p*er* contra is dewe to have the 14 daye of
Februarye £5 which Henry Setterford r. of hym at Herfort
for to pay unto Philip Symons tanner   £5
Itm. the 11 day of June 1549 r. £8   £8

141(L) anno 1541

Itm. the 21 day of November Willi*am* Northe of Bruton owithe £27 3s 4d *that* is for 5 ton Gascon wyne, whereof 3 to*n* was at £5 10s p*er* ton & 2 to*n* at £5 6s 8d p*er* ton, mo*n*t*ith*	£27 3s	4d
Itm. the 6 day of December £30 13s 4d *that* is for 2 pipes of muscadell at £3 13s 4d the pipe & 2 butt*es* of seck at £3 13s 4d the butt & 3 tons of Gascon wyne at £5 6s 8d the to*n*, mo*n*t*ith*	£30 13s	4d
Itm. the same tyme £5 6s 8d for a to*n* red wyne which I bowght for hym of Thomas Shipma*n*	£5 6s	8d
Itm. the 26 day of Jenyver £12 6s 8d that is for 3 butt*es* of seck at eich 11 nobles & 1 h'd of clare*t*t wyne at 26s 8d, mo*n*t*ith*	£12 6s	8d
1542 Itm. the 19 day of July sold to hym a butt of hulok price 11 nobles	£3 13s	4d
Itm. the 20 day of the same £11 16s 8d that is for £6 6s 8d paide to Thomas Blake & £5 10s paide to Thomas Tizon	£11 16s	8d
Itm. the same day £3 3s which is for 10 C ½ of my wiff*es* iren at 6s the C	£3 3s	
Itm. the 29 day of Jenyver £8 which I pd. for hym to J*ohn* Gorney in redy mon*n*ey	£8	
Itm. the same day £4 6s 5d & is ffor 1 h'd cla*ret* wyne at 4 nobles & for a pipe iren less 6 li. of the Rendry after £6 the to*n*. So mo*n*t*ith* the hole	£4 6s	5d
Itm. the 20 day of February £8 that is £4 for a butt of seck & £4 for a pipe bastard which I sent hym by his carryer callid Cox	£8	
Itm. the 6 day of M*a*rche £16 that is for 4 butt*es* of seck sold & delyv*erd* to hym at £4 the butt	£16	
1543 Itm. the 18 day of February a*n*no 1543 £7 16s 8d & is for 2 butt*es* seck at £4 less 20d the pece, mo*n*t*ith* 11 nobles 40d[1]	£7 16s	8d

---

[1] 11 nobles 40d *inserted later*.

141(L) contd.

Itm. the 20 day of February £31 6s 8d & is for 5 butt*es* seck & 3 pipes bastard at 11 nobles 5s the pece, mon*tith* ~~buttes & pipes at 11 nobles~~ 40d ... £31 6s 8d
Itm. the first day of Marche ~~7s 6d for a pece resy*n*ges~~ ... ~~7s 6d~~
1544 Itm. the 22 of Aprell 1544 £3 16s 8d & is for a pipe tay*n*t solld & d'd to hym ... £3 16s 8d
Itm. the 27 of May £8 which is for 1 to*n* Gasco*n* wyne ... £7 10s [1]
Itm. the 10 of September £7 6s 8d & is for 1 but seck & 1 butt of hullock at 11 nobles the butt, mon*tith* ... £7 6s 8d
1545 Itm. the 29 day of May a*nno* 1545 for 1 pi*pe* tay*n*t of myne £4 & for 1 pi*pe* bastard of Tyndalls £4 13s 4d, mon*tith* ... £8 13s 4d
Itm. the 20 of July 1545 for 22 C ire*n* less 4 li. ½ of S.S. at £6 11s 8d *the* ton, £7 4s 10d ... £7 4s 10d
Itm. for 2 to*n* wyne *that* I pd. to Hewgh Hamo*n* £15 6s 8d ... £15 6s 8d

S. [2]

141(R)   anno 1541

Willi*a*m Northe of Bruto*n* vyntenar is dewe to have the 23 day of November, 10s which I r. of his wif at Bruton ... 10s
Itm. the 2d day of Jenyver £20 pd. by W*illiam* Northe ffor me to John Yerbery fo. 125 ... £20
Itm. the 6 day of February £20 which he must pay to *the* seid Yerbery which John Yerbery is co*n*tent to r. hytt of hy*m* ... £20
Itm. the 13 day of July 1542 pd. by W*illiam* Northe for me to Jo*hn* Yerbery of Bruton thellder £17 18s 3d ... £17 18s 3d
Itm. 15s 7d pd. for caraige of a to*n* wyne to M*aster* Arnedell ... 15s 7d
Itm. 10s which I rebate hym in the price of 3 tons Gascon wyne ... 10s
Itm. the 24 day of July he paide to Jo*hn* Yerbery fo. 125 £14 9s 5d ... £14 9s 5d
Itm. the 28 daye of July £14 19s 8d which he must paye for me to Jo*hn* Yerbery for as miche I have dischargyd my bill of the 17 day of Jenyver 1541 of so myche mon*n*ey to be r. of hy*m*, as it may apere fo. 163 ... £14 19s 8d
Itm. 26s 4d that is for the h'd wyne co*n*teynyd in the itm. of the 26 day of Jenyver, as p*er* contra may apere & he r. not the seid h'd ... £1 6s 8d
Itm. the 21 day of February 1542 he paide for me to Jo*hn* Yerbery thelder, that is to sey £3 13s 4d for the but of hullock p*er* contra & 8 which I paide for hym to Jo*hn* Gorney & 26s 8d for the h'd c*l*aret wyne sold the 29 of Jenyv*er* last past ... £13
1543 Itm. the 17 day of July £10 which he paide for me to Jo*hn* Yerbery as it may apere fo. 163 ... £10
Itm. the 5th of Septemb*er* a*nno* 1543 £17 which he paide for me to Jo*hn* Yerbery as it may apere fo. 163 ... £17
Itm. the 21 day of Aprell a*nno* 1544 £10 which is for so myche he pay for me to Jo*hn* Yerbery fo. 201 ... £10
Itm. the 27 day of Maye r. of hy*m* ... £3
Itm. £10 which he paide to Jo*hn* Yerbery fo. 201 ... £10
Itm. the 10 day of Augost he pd. to Jo*hn* Yerbery £4 ... £4
Itm. the 18 of Augost £6 which he pd. to Jo*hn* Yerbery fo. 201 ... £6
Itm. the 29 of September a*nno* 1544 he pd. to Jo*hn* Yerbery fo. [2] £16 13s 4d ... £16 13s 4d
Itm. the 9 day of December £7 6s 8d which he paide to Jo*hn* Yerbery for me ... £7 6s 8d
Itm. 16s 8d which I do rebate in *the* prices of my wynes ... 16s 8d

---

[1] *£8 erased.*
[2] *Blank in MS.*

141(R) contd.

Itm. the 27 day of July 1545 £31 4s 10d & is for so myche he paide to John Yerbery for my acowmpt in 3 payment*es*, as apo*n* Yerberys byll may apere	£31	4s	10d

142(L)   anno 1541

Richard Tipp*ar* tucker of Bristowe ow*ith* the 25 day of Decemb*er* 6s 8d pd. to hym in redy mon*n*ey		6s	8d
Itm. the 5 day of December pd. to hym in mon*n*y 25s 4d	£1	5s	4d
Itm. the 24 day of December 6s 8d pd. to hy*m* in redy mon*n*ey		6s	8d
Itm. the 7 day of Jenyver pd. to hym 6s 8d		6s	8d
Itm. the 14 day of the same by his son 6s 8d		6s	8d
Itm. 13s 4d delyv*er*d to his boye		13s	4d
Itm. to his boy 6s 8d		6s	8d
Itm. the 10th day of February £3 pd. to Thomas Shipman	£3		
1542 Itm. the 30 day of M*ar*che a*n*no 1542 £5 14s 9d & is ffor 4 ½-bales wood conteynyng 7 C 19 li. at 16s the C, to be pd. at all tymes	£5	14s	9d
Itm. the 20 day of May 6s 8d d'd in mon*n*ey to his s*ar*vant		6s	8d
Itm. the 27 day of May 6s 8d d'd to his s*ar*vant Nicholas Rede		6s	8d
Itm. the 7 day of June pd. to hym seallf		6s	8d
Itm. the 30 day of June £3 13s 4d for 1 butt of seck solld & delyverd to hym at the seid price	£3	13s	4d
Itm. the 12 day of Augost my wif paide to hym 6s 8d		6s	8d
Itm. the 2 day of Augost my wif paide to hy*m* 6s 8d		6s	8d
Itm. 26s 8d for so myche paide to hym in redy mon*n*ey	£1	6s	8d
Itm. the 13 day of M*ar*che £4 which is for a butt of seck solld to hym to be pd. at all tymes requyrid	£4		
Itm. the 4 daye of Julye 1543, pd. to hym in mon*n*ey 20s	£1		
[1] Itm. more in money 10s	~~£1~~	10s	
Itm. the 1 day of M*ar*che a*n*no 1543 10s paide to hym in reddy mon*n*ey		10s	
Itm. the 14 day of M*ar*che a*n*no 1543 11 nobles which is for a butt of seck	£3	13s	4d
[2] Itm. d'd to hym at 2 tymes 13s 4d		13s	4d
Itm. the 9 day of Augost *anno* 1544 paide to hym 14s 7d		14s	7d
1545 Itm. the 14 of June 1545 my wi*m* pd. hy*m* a noble		6s	8d

142(R)   anno 1541

Richard Tippar is dewe to have the 5th day of Decemb*er* for rowyng of 10 penny hewes of John Yerberys at 2s the clo*the* & 9 of his truckers at 16d the clothe, mo*ntith* 32s	£1	12s	
Itm. the 10th day of February for rowyng of 20 penny hewes of John Yerberys & 10 of Thomas Hasshis & 10 of W*illiam* Buchars at 2s p*er* clothe, mo*ntith*	£5		
1542 Itm. the 7 day of June a*n*no 1542 for rowing of 30 clothes of John Yerberys & 10 of Hasshis at 2s p*er* clo*the*	£5		
Itm. the 3d day of October for rowyng of 30 clothes of John Yerberys & 10 of Hasshis at 2s p*er* clo*the*	£4		
Itm. the 21 day of February for rowyng of 30 clothes of John Yerberys at 2s p*er* clothe, mo*ntith*	£3		
Itm. the 25 day of Augost 1543 for rowyng of 36 clothes of Yerberys & 14 of Buchars at 2s per clothe, mo*ntith*	£5		
Itm. for evenyng of 5 yelowes		1s	4d
Itm. the 15 day of Marche a*n*no 1543 for rowyng of 30 clothes of John Yerberys at 2s the clothe	£3		
Itm. the 9 day of Augost a*n*no 1544 for rowyng 20 clothes of Yerberys & 10 of Buchars at 2s p*er* clothe & of 6 truckers of Yerberys at 16d p*er* clothe, mo*ntith*	£3	8s	

---

[1] *Marginal note*, 16s 9d.
[2] *Marginal note*, 40s. 1d.

143(L)

John Towsan of Plymowthe maryner owith the 9 day of February £4 which
I pd. in presence of Thomas Shipman to John Knyght of Bristowe poyntemaker
& sarvant to Master Chester of the same towne & r. of the same Knyght my
bill which I made to the seid Towssan

                S. £4

anno 1549

Robert Nasche of Bristowe serchor owith the 5th day of October 40s & is for
3 C Yland wood at 13s 4d the C, d'd by his wyll & commawndement to his
brother John Nasche of Northe Petherton, to be pd. at all tymes requyrid   £2
Itm. the 12 of Jenyver 40s for 3 C Yland wood to be paide with one moneth next   £2

anno 1541

Thomas Lyncoll of London owith the 23 daye off December for my part of
5 sakes of Spanysche woll which his ship fownd at Sylly [1]
Itm. the [1] day of [1] pd. to Thomas Lockyar £5 14s 11d &
broke my seale from the charter   £5 14s 11d

143(R)   anno 1541

John Towsan per contra is dewe to have the first day of
December £4 that is for so myche I owe to hym for the
hallf of the freight of 10 ton pipe, 1 tierce de pipe from
Burdes this present vyntaige, to be pd. at Candellmas next

                S. £4

anno 1549

Robert Nasche per contra is dewe to have the 12 of Jenyver
40s for so myche ready monney which he paide to my wif   £2

anno 1541

Thomas Lyncoll of London is dewe to have the 23 daye of
December £5 14s 11d ob which is for the hallf freight from
Burdes in his ship the An, master John Hawle, this vyntage at
20s the ton, to be paide at the end of 3 monthes next
commyng, amontith. It is for the hallf freight of 9 ton 3 h'd
wyne & 24 ballettes woode   £5 14s 11d

144(L)   anno 1541

Wynes of Gascon r. for my proper acowmpt the monthe of November owt
of dyvers ships owith 1418 ffranckes 32 a, Burdalez, that is for 334 ffranckes
34 a, ½ that 10 ton 2 h'd 1 tierce laden in the Marget Bonaventure of
Plymowthe cost clere abord, & for 10 ton, 1 h'd wyne laden in the
Marget of Bristowe which cost clere aborde 367 ffranckes 52 a, ½ and for 10
ton wyne laden in the Mary Fortune of Glocester which cost clere abord 374
ffranckes 50 a. and for 9 ton 3 h'd wyne laden in the An of London which cost
clere abord 341 ffranckes 15 a. Som the hole wyne, 40 ton pipe & ⅓ de pipe
which cost as aforeseid 1,418 ffranckes 32 a. Burdalez, which do amont
sterlyng after 20d the franck, £118 3s   £118 3s
Itm. for Thomas & Tyndalls costes 20 ducatts   £5
Itm. for freight in the Marget of Bristowe, the Mary Bonaventure of
Glocester & the An of London at 20s per ton & in the Margett Fortune of
Plymowthe at 15s per ton. So montith the hole freight of 40 ton ½ ⅓   £38

---

[1] Blank in MS.

144(L) contd.

Itm. for costom of 35 tons at 3s per ton & for haling of 40 ton ½ and stowing 3d per ton, mon*tith* £5 15s 2d	£5	15s	2d
Itm. for av*er*es in the M*ar*get of Bristowe 34s 2d and in the M*ar*get of Plymmowthe 28s 5d¼ and in the Mary Bonaventure of Glocester 36s 8d and in the An of London 37s 4d ob. So mon*tith* the hole	£6	16s	8d
Itm. for 2 pipes ½ corrupt muscadell to wlladge the*m*	£7	10s	
1542 Itm. the 29 of Jenyver £17 2s 6d for so myche that I make gaynes creditor of fo. 92 for the closing up of this cowmpt	£17	2s	6d
	£198	6s	8d

144(R)   anno 1541

6	Wynes of Gascon p*er* contra is dewe to have the 17 day of November £8 that is for 6 h'd sold the 17 & 26 day of the seid monthe to Jo*h*n Roxby fo. 10	£8		
½	Itm. the 19 day of Nove*m*ber 17s 9d for 1 h'd geven to M*aster* Vowell			[1]
32	Itm. the 21 day of November & so furthe till the 6 daye of December £42 13s 4d which is for 8 tons to W*illiam* North 141	£42	13s	4d
8	Itm. the 21 & 26 of November & the 16 of Decem*ber* £10 13s 4d for 2 to*n* to Alexander Bosgrove fo. 68	£10	13s	4d
2	Itm. the 26 of Nove*m*ber £2 13s 4d for 2 h'd to T. Turbot 23	£2	13s	4d
4	Itm. the 28 day of Nove*m*ber geven to S*i*r Thom*as* Arnedell 1 to*n* p*r*ice	£5	6s	8d
12	Itm. the 29 day of November & the 19 day of December £16 for 3 tons to S*i*r J*oh*n Seyntlo fo. 40	£16		
12	Itm. the 29 of Nove*m*ber £15 10s for 3 ton to Jamys Rog*er*es 76	£15	10s	
6	Itm. the same day £8 for 6 h'd to J*oh*n Braghyng fo. 109	£8		
4	Itm. the 3 day of Decem*ber* £5 6s 8d for 1 to*n* to W*illiam* Smothing 72	£5	6s	8d
2	Itm. the 17 of Decem*ber* £2 13s 4d for 2 h'd to Wa*ter* Robertz 106	£2	13s	4d
4	Itm. £5 6s 8d for 1 ton taken to p*r*ize	£5	6s	8d
2	Itm. the 3 day of Jenyver 50s which is for 2 h'd I gave to his M*aster* J*oh*n Poyntz for to confess a fyne	£2	10s	
16	Itm. the 26 day of Jenyver £21 6s 8d for 4 tons to J*oh*n Roxby of Wells fo. 10	£21	6s	8d
1	Itm. *the* same day 26s 8d for 1 h'd to W*illiam* Northe	£1	6s	8d
4	Itm. the 30 day of Jenyver £5 6s 8d for 1 ton sold to the Bisshop of W*ur*sett*or* fo. 151	£5	6s	8d
1	Itm. the 18 of February for 1 h'd to M*aster* Gorge fo. 36	£1	6s	8d
8	Itm. the 28 of the same for 2 tons to Braghyng fo. 109	£10	13s	4d
4	Itm. the 25 of Ap*r*ell for 1 ton to Alexander Bosgrove 68	£5	6s	8d
4	Itm. the 8 of May for 1 to*n* to R. Carryck fo. 34	£5	6s	8d
1	Itm. the 18 of Maye for 1 h'd to W*illiam* Reynold fo. 157	£1	6s	8d
2	Itm. the 5 of June for 2 h'd to Richard Aprise fo. 158	£2	13s	4d

[1] *Blank in MS.*

144(R) contd.

4	Itm. the 28 day of June for 1 to*n* to J*oh*n Braghyng fo. 109	£5	6s	8d
1	Itm. the 25 of July for 1 h'd to T. Turbot fo. 23	£1	6s	8d
1	Itm. the 28 of July for 1 h'd to Alson Bisshop fo. 152	£1	6s	8d
1	Itm. the 3 day of Augost 1 h'd to M*aste*r Bulkeley			[1]
4	Itm. the 7 of July to Roxby 1 to*n* fo. 162	£5	6s	8d
~~1~~	~~Itm. the 25 of July 26s 8d for 1 h'd to T. Turbot fo. 23~~	~~£1~~	~~6s~~	~~8d~~
~~1~~	~~Itm. the 28 of July to Allson Bisshop fo. 152 1 h'd for 26s 8d~~	~~£1~~	~~6s~~	~~8d~~
1	Itm. the 29 day of Jenyver to W*illiam* Northe fo. 141, 1 h'd p*r*ice 4 nobles	£1	6s	8d
3	Itm. to Richard Smy*the* of Coventry the 6 of February 3 h'd p*r*ice	£4	6s	8d
	Itm.	£198	6s	8d

145(L)   anno 1541

94	Seck*es* for my owne acowmpt 94 butt*es* cost clere aborde in Andaluzia, as by Giles acowmpt maye apere 265 V. 303 M. which the same butt*es* cost putt clere aborde the ships, that is to sey in the Jh*es*us of Brystowe, m*aster* Phelip Thomas 12 butt*es*, in the Trynte of Carlyon m*aster* Bastyan Myllyor 20 butt*es*, in the Mary Bonaventure m*aster* Richard White 16 butt*es*, in J*oh*n Gorneys Brytton 16 butt*es*, in the Mary of Penmark 8 butt*es*, in the Harry m*aster* Antony Pigott 20 butt*es*, & in George Thorntons ship of London 2 butt*es*. So mon*tith* the hole aforesseid in sterling mon*n*ey £175 17s 4d	£175	17s	4d
	Itm. for freight of 10 to*n* in the Trynte of Carlion & of 8 ton in the Mary Bonaventure & of 10 ton in the Henry at 25s the ton, & of 4 ton in the Brytton, the Mary of Penmarck at 15s the ton, mon*tith* all	£38		
	Itm. for averes in the Trynte of Carlon 30s 10d & in the Mary Bonaventure 32s & in the Mary of Penmerck 21s & in the Harry 34s 2d. So mon*tith* all £5 18s	£5	18s	
3	Itm. the monthe of December r. owt of the Savyor of Northam, m*aster* J*oh*n Auger, 3 butt*es* wyne of Gibralta*r* which cost clere abord 7 V. 979 M. ½, as by Hamond*es* cownt apere. For freight & ded freight 48s, for costom 4s 6d, for averes ¹, ffor halyng & stowy*n*g 6d, mon*tith* £7 19s 5d	£7	19s	5d
64	Itm. for the costom of 25 ton at 3s p*er* ton & haly*n*g & stowyng of 64 butt*es* at 2d p*er* butt, mon*tith* £4 5s 8d	£4	5s	8d
	Itm. £7 6s 8d for 2 pipes bastard to ulledge the*m*	£7	6s	8d
	Itm. for hallf of Giles & Hamond*es* cost*es* 14 d*u*cat*t*s	£3	10s	
2	Itm. the 12 day of Jenyver £5 13s 4d for 2 butt*es* seck of Gybrawlltar bowght of Richard Chappell of Northam	£5	13s	4d
12	Itm. the same tyme r. fro*m* Bastable of the 16 butt*es* wyne lost in the Brytton 12 butt*es* which owe for cost*es* don at Bastable £3 3s 11d & for freight 26s 6d, mon*tith* £4 10s 5d	£4	10s	5d
	Itm. the 23 day of M*a*rche 19s which Thomas Shipman r. of my wif for to pay J*oh*n Gorney for the Brytton for the ffreight of my wynes lost at Bastable		19s	
	Itm. the 14 day of August 1542 £37 11s 2d that is for the closyng up of this cowmpt & gaynes had by the same, as it may apere to gaynes in credito fo. 92	£37	11s	2d
	S.	£291	10s	

---

[1] *Blank in MS.*

145(R) anno 1541

12	Seck*es per* contra is dewe to have the 20 day of November £22 13s 4d which is for 12 butt*es* seck lost in the Jh*esus*, master Philip Thomas at Byttbay & they cost abord 90 d*ucatts* ⅔. So mo*ntith* as it a*perith* to gaynes in debito fo. 92	£22	13s	4d
4	Itm. the 3 day of December £14 13s 4d for 4 butt*es* to W*illiam* Golldesmythe fo. 113	£14	13s	4d
2	Itm. the 6 day £7 6s 8d for 2 butt*es* to W*illiam* Northe fo. 141	£7	6s	8d
1	Itm. the 16 day £3 13s 4d for 1 butt to Alexa*nder* Bosgrove fo. 68	£3	13s	4d
1	Itm. the 17 day £3 15s for 1 butt to Alis Bishop fo. 14	£3	15s	
1	Itm. the same day for 1 butt seck to Susan Gibs fo. 126	£3	15s	
2	Itm. the 21 day of December £7 6s 8d for 2 but*es* to R. Browne 110	£7	6s	8d
5	Itm. 4 butt*es* to ylladge & 1 but ow*t* in the Harry			[1]
1	Itm. *the* 24 of Dec*ember* for 1 but seck to Robert Gowgh fo. 126	£3	13s	4d
	Itm. 14s 4d for 21 gallons seck ½ at 2 tymes to M*aster* Seyntlo		14s	4d
2	Itm. the 13 day of Jenyver £7 6s 8d for 2 butt*es* to Jo*h*n Brawghyng fo. 109	£7	6s	8d
6	Itm. the 26 day of Jenyver £22 for 6 but*es* to Jo*h*n Roxby fo. 10	£22		
3	Itm. the same day to W*illiam* Northe fo. 141 3 butt*es* for £11	£11		
2	Itm. the last day of Jenyver for 2 butt*es* to Davy Hart £7 6s 8d, 57	£7	6s	8d
1	Itm. *the* same day for a butt to Davy Willi*ams* baker fo. 13, £3 13s 4d	£3	13s	4d
2	Itm. the 3 day of February £7 6s 8d for 2 butt*es* to Smothe 72	£7	6s	8d
1	Itm. the same day £3 13s 4d for a butt to Jo*h*n Hamond fo. 77	£3	13s	4d
2	Itm. the 9 day of February £7 6s 8d for 2 butt*es* to Richard Carrick fo. 34	£7	6s	8d
2	Itm. r. from M*aster* Lawrence of London for 2 butt*es*	£4		
1	Itm. the 28 of February £3 13s 4d for 1 but to Allso*n* Bisshop 152	£3	13s	4d
1	Itm. the 28 of February for 1 butt to Jo*h*n Brawghyng fo. 109	£3	13s	4d
1	Itm. the 20 of Ap*r*ell 1542 1 but to T. Heyward fo. 18	£3	13s	4d
2	Itm. the 25 of *the* same for 2 butt*es* to Alexander Bosgrove 68	£7	6s	8d
1	Itm. the 30 of Ap*r*ell for 1 butt to Jo*h*n Sp*ar*k of Newnham 155	£3	13s	4d
5	Itm. the 4 of May for 5 butt*es* to Thom*as* Cotes fo. 17	£18	6s	8d
1	Itm. the 6 of Maye for 1 butt to Jo*h*n Roxby fo. 10	£3	13s	4d
2	Itm. the 8 day of May for 2 butt*es* to Richard Carryck 34	£7	6s	8d
2	Itm. the 20 of May 2 but to Water Rumney fo. 157 for	£7	6s	8d
2	Itm. the 5 of June 2 butt*es* to W*illiam* Goldsmythe fo. fo.[2] 113 for	£7	6s	8d
1	Itm. the same day 1 butt to Richard Ap*ri*se fo. 158 for	£3	13s	4d

---

[1] *Blank in MS.*
[2] *Smythe repeats* fo.

145(R) contd.

3	Itm. the 19 of June £11 for 3 butt*es* to J*oh*n Wellsche fo. 74	£11		
2	Itm. the 28 of June £7 6s 8d for 2 butt*es* to Braghyng 109	£7	6s	8d
1	Itm. the 30 of June £3 13s 4d for 1 butt to Tipp*ar* 142	£3	13s	4d
2	Itm. the 3 of July £7 6s 8d for 2 butt*es* to Smothing	£7	6s	8d
1	Itm. the 11 day of July £3 13s 4d for a but to J*oh*n Gryffith 164	£3	13s	4d
1	Itm. the 12 of July £3 13s 4d for 1 but to Davy Baker 165	£3	13s	4d
1	Itm. the 15 of July £3 12s 8d r. of M*aster* Hamlyn for 1 butt	£3	12s	8d
1	Itm. the 18 of July £3 13s 4d for a butt to J*oh*n Sp*ar*k 155	£3	13s	4d
1	It*m*. the same day £3 13s 4d for a butt to Bosgrove fo. 68	£3	13s	4d
1	Itm. the 20 of July £3 13s 4d for a but hullok to Northe fo. 141	£3	13s	4d
3	Itm. the 24 of July £11 *that* is for 2 butt*es* to Roxby fo. 162 & a butt to T. Hasbery fo. 165	£11		
2	Itm. the 26 day of July r. of R. Carryck £7 for 2 butt*es*	£7		
1	Itm. the 28 of July £3 13s 4d for a butt to A. Bishop 152	£3	13s	4d
1	Itm. the 28 of July £3 13s 4d for a butt to Smothing fo. 72	£3	13s	4d
	Itm. the 14 of August £4 for a butt to J*oh*n Wade fo. 133	£4		
		£291	10s	

146(L) **anno 1541**

5	Bastard*es* 5 pipes which I pass for the rest of acowmpt fo. 118 o*with* the 17 day of December £18 6s 8d for so myche I do valure the*m* at after 11 nobles the pipe	£18	6s	8d

anno 1541

129	Rezing*es* of Mallaga o*with* the monthe of Dece*m*ber for my owne acowmpt, that is to sey 90 pec*es* r. at Bristowe ow*t* of the Savyor of Northam, M*aster* John Auger, which coste clere aborde 38 V. 472 M. which mo*ntith* sterly*ng*	£25	13s	
	Itm. for costom 1d p*er* pece, for haly*ng* 18d, for freight & ded freight £6, mo*ntith* £6 9s	£6	9s	
	Itm. £11 3d for 33 pec*es* which I bowght of the m*aster*	£11		3d
	Itm. 42s for 6 pec*es* bowght of the maryners	£2	2s	
	Itm. the 14 day of Jenyver £3 5s 8d for so myche proffett had by this acowmpt, as it may apere to gaynes in credito fo. 92	£3	5s	8d
	S.	£48	10s	

anno 1542

14	Sope of Sevyll for my owne acowmpt 14 serons r. the 14 of February ow*t* of my ship the Trynte & laden in Andaluzia for 26 k*yntalls* £14 and made by my weight*es* 23 k*yntalls* 6 li. owithe 36 V. 944 M. which it cost at the

146(L) contd.

first penny clere abord, more for freight 30s, for halyng 4d, for averes 12d, for costom of every seron at 7d ob the seron, montith £26 12s 9d   £26 12s 9d

146(R)   **anno 1542**

	Bastardes per contra be dewe to have the 21 day	
1	of February £4 for a pipe to Sussan Gibs fo. 126	£4
1	Itm. the 6 of May 1542 for 1 but to John Wylles fo. 73	£3 13s 4d
1	1542 Itm. the 5 day of June £3 13s 4d for a pipe to William Goldsmythe fo. 113	£3 13s 4d
1	Itm. the same for a pipe to Richard Aprise fo. 158	£3 13s 4d

anno 1541

	Rezinges per contra be dewe to have the 5 day of	
1	Jenyver 6s 8d for a pece of rezinges to John Rede	6s 8d
1	Itm. 6s 8d for a pece sold to T. Smythe my uncle	6s 8d
1	Itm. 7s 6d for a pece that Thomas Shipman sold	7s 6d
1	Itm. 6s 8d for a pece taken for the provicion of my hows	6s 8d
125	Itm. the 14 day of Jenyver £46 17s 6d that is for 125 peces sold to hym¹ at eich 7s 6d & more he gave me over all 5s. So montith the hole	£47 2s 6d
		£48 10s

anno 1543

	Sope per contra is dewe to have the 14 daye of Aprell	
1	46s for a seron conteynyng of clene sope C ½ 16 li solld to William Hyll serchor at 28s per C	£2 6s
13	Itm. the 13 of July £29 19s 6d & is for 13 serons Sevyll sope which wayed, the serons abatyd, 21 C 1 qr. 18 li. at 28s per C, montith	£29 19s 6d

147(L)   **anno 1541**

	Woode of Tullus owith the 7 day of December for my owne	
48	acowmpt £60 which is for 48 hallf bales that I pass to this lesses for the rest of acowmpt of wood fo. 52	£60
2	1542 Itm. the 10 day of February £3 1s 9d that is for 2 ½-bales conteynyng 3 C ½, 15 li. which Gilbart retornyd to me ageyne after 17s the C, as I made hym pay	£3 1s 9d
	Itm. the 5 day of February 1543 £11 19s 10d ob which I make gaynes fo. 200 creditor of for so myche avatonsyd by this acowmpt	£11 19s 10d½
	S.	£75 1s 7d ob

147(R)   **anno 1541**

	Wood per contra is dewe to have the 13 day of	
2	February 1541 59s 6d & is for 2 bales wood conteynyng 3 C ½ at 17s the C sold to Clement Bayss fo. 41	£2 19s 6d
4	Itm. the 30 of Marche 1542 £5 14s 9d for 4 bales conteynyng 7 C 19 li. at 16s the C to Richard Tippar fo. 142	£5 14s 9d

---

¹ William Yong fo. 67.

189

147(R) contd.

2	Itm. the 28 of Aprell for 2 bales *conteynyng* 3 C ½ 10 li. at 16s the C to Thomas Heyward fo. 18	£2 16s 10d
2	Itm. the 2d day of May for 2 bales *conteynyng* 3 C ½, 16 li. at 17s the C to Clement Bayss fo. 41	£3 2s 2d
2	Itm. the 2d day of June r. of Shepward M*aster* Bases s*ar*vant for 2 ½-bales *conteynyng* 3 C ½, 12 li. £3 15d	£3 1s 3d
2	Itm. the 12 day of June for 2 bales *conteynyng* 3 C ½, 13 li. at 17s the C to J*ohn* Awood of Bridgewater tucker fo. 124	£3 1s 6d
4	Itm. the 8 of August 1542 £6 6d for 4 bales to Gilbart Cogan fo. 140	£6 6d
2	Itm. the 10 day of Jenyver £3 3d for 2 bales *conteynyng* 3 C ½, 5 li at 17s the C to Clement Bays fo. 41	£3 3d
1	Itm. the 2d day of June 1543 30s 6d r. for ½ a bale of Jamys Symons *conteynyng* C 3 qr. 5 li. at 17s the C	£1 10s 5d
2	Itm. the 3d day of July for 2 bales *conteynyng* 3 C ½, 5 li at 17s the C. sold to Jamys Symons fo. 188	£3 3d
5	Itm. the 21 day of July for 5 bales *conteynyng* 9 C 1 li. for the which I r. £7 10s 2d of W*illiam* Buchar of Cowley & of J*ohn* his son in clothe after 16s 8d the C	£7 10s 2d
2	Itm. the 30 day of July for 2 bales *conteynyng* 3 C ½, 7 li. at 17s the C to Thomas Heyward fo. 18 mon*tith* £3 7d	£3 7d
2	Itm. the 11 day of Augost for 2 bales *conteynyng* 3 C ½, 9 li. at 17s the C, mo*ntith* £3 9d to Nycolas Mawrewood fo. 106	£3 9d
2	Itm. the 27 day of Awgost for 2 bales *conteynyng* 3 C ½, 5 li. at 17s the C, mon*tith* fo. 18	£3 3d ob
2	Itm. the 10 of September for 2 bales to my mother fo. 183	£3 8d
4	Itm. the 22 day of September for 4 bales to Clement Bays 193	£6 1s 9d
10	Itm. the 5th day of February 1543 solld to J*ohn* Yerbery thellder 10 bales *conteynyng* 17 C 3 qr. 3 li. to be paide in 6 clothes truckers & more he must pay in mon*n*ey for 1 qr. 3 li. So that I acowmpt it to be solld for redy mon*n*y in £15[1]	£15
	S.	£75 1s 7d ob

148(L) anno 1541

Robert Buttler of Bristowe m*ar*chant owithe the 1 daye of Decemb*er* 25s which is for the rest & hallf freight of 2 to*n* bastard in the Trynte at 25s p*er* ton, to be pd. at thend of 3 monthes next com*m*yng   £1 5s

148(R) anno 1542

Robert Buttlar p*er* contra is dewe to have the 19 day of Ap*r*ell 25s which Hamon r. for me of hym   £1 5s

---

[1] *The* 'bales' *in this account are ballettes or* ½-*bales.*

149(L)	**anno 1540**	**23 Agustij 1540**

Aventure in company to the Ylles of Surrys ffor woode, that is to sey with
Nycholas Thorne which putt yn to the same company 650 d*ucatts*, Willi*am*
Spratt 650 d*ucatts*, Edward Pryn & Robert Buttler 650 d*ucatts*, France*s*
Codryngton & Willi*am* Car 650 d*ucatts*, W*illiam* Ballard & Frances
Fowlar 650 d*ucatts*, & Frances Blanckeley & Pedro Goncalez 1300 d*ucatts*,
ow*ith* the 20 day of July 500 d*ucatts* ffor so myche paide for me at Luxbron
by my ffactor Giles White to France*s* Blanckeley ffor to be ocupyed for 6 yeres
in won with the foresseid soms of mon*n*ey as more playnely may apere by a
co*n*tratacion datyd the 23 day off Augost a*n*no 1540 & ffyrmyd by me & the
foresseid m*a*rchantz. And for to trate & ocupy the foressed moneyes as allso
to geve a good & true acowmpt thereof with payement at thend of the seid
6 yeres, the seid Edward Pryn is admyttyd for mynes*ter* here in Ynglande
& the seid France*s* Blanckeley & Pedro Goncalez for mynesters beyend the
see   £125

Itm. more the 23 day of October £37 10s *that* is ffor 150 d*ucatts* paide at
Luxbron by the foreseid Giles White to the foresseid France*s* Blanckeley to be
usyd & ocupyed in leke man*er* before reherssyd   £37 10s

149(R)[1]

150(L)	**anno 1542**	

Richard Chappell ow*ith* the 16 day of May £4 4s which I pay hym in redy
mon*n*ey at Bristowe for the rest & hole payement of 7 tons freight *per* co*n*tra   £4   4s
Itm. the 24 daye of July paide to hym at Bristowe £16 & r. my byll   £16

                                                                       S.   £20   4s

150(R)	**anno 1541**	

Richard Chapell of Northeham in the cownty of Deveshire
m*a*rchant is dewe to have the 2d daye of Jenyver £4 4s *that*
is for the rest of 7 tons freight fro*m* Malaga, to be pd. at the
fyve of M*a*rche next com*m*yng   £4   4s
Itm. the 11 day of the same £16 that is for so myche I must
pay by a bill of my hand apo*n* Sent Jamys day next com*m*yng
for 33 pec*es* rezyng*es* & 2 butt*es* of seck   £16

                                                                       S.   £20   4s

151(L)	**a*n*no 1541**	

The Bisshop of W*ur*sett*or* owthe the 30 day of Jenyver £5 6s 8d which is for
1 ton Gascon wyne sold & delyv*er*d for hym to my uncle Thom*a*s Smythe &
to the steward of the seid Bisshop, mon*tith*   £5   6s   8d

	a*n*no 1548

John Russell of Mum*m*ells owith the 12 day of Decembe*r* a*n*no dicto 52s 6d
& is for the rest of a pipe 27 li. iren of S.S. to be paide the fyrst weke of
Lent next. John Stone dyar is[2] his shewerty[3]   £2 12s 6d

151(R)	**anno 1542**	

The Bisshop p*er* contra is dewe to have the 2 day of May
£5 3s 4d which my uncle Thomas Smythe paide me   £5   3s   4d
Itm. 3s 4d which my seid uncle cawsyd me rebate in the
price   3s   4d
[4]

---

[1] *Fo. 149 R is blank in the MS.*
[2] is *is inserted above the line.*
[3] *The whole of the item for John Russell is crossed through.*
[4] *There is no credit entry for Russell.*

152(L) anno 1541

Allsson Bisshop wedo the late wif of Robert Bisshop of Bridgewater owithe the 17 day of December £7 15s *that* is £3 15s for a but of seck & £4 for a p*ipe* of muscadell sent her in Whit the cofferars bote and it is for the rest & clozing up of acowmp*t* fo. 14	£7	15s
Itm. the 18 day of February £3 15s for a butt of seck sent her in Luyes bote	£3	15s
1542 Itm. the 28 day of July 1542 £5 20d that is £3 15s for 1 but seck & 26s 8d for 1 h'd c*lar*et wyne which wynes I lode in Luyes Uprichar*des* bote	£5 1s	8d
Itm. the 16 day of February laden for her in Luyes Hayenes bote of Chepstowe 1 butt of seck price £4 & 1 pipe of bastard price £4 6s 8d, more for haling, cranage & the cocquet 8d, mon*tith* the hole £8 7s 4d	£8 7s	4d
1543 Itm. the 4 day of June 1543 £4 6s 8d & is for a butt of seck sent her in N*i*chalas Lanesmans bote	£4 6s	8d
Itm. the 28 day of February £12 18d & is for 2 butt*es* seck & 1 p*ipe* muscadell at ech £4 & 18d for cost*es* mon*tith*, to pay £8 at Est*er* & £4 18d at Seynt Jamistide	£12 1s	6d
1544 Itm. the 28 day of July a*nno* 1544 £8 & is for 2 butt*es* seck sent her in John Robbyns vote of the Mum*m*ylls to be paide at all tymes	£8	

anno 1542

Will*i*am Brydg*es* of Wanhope in Harvartshire carryar o*with* the 15 day of June 30s that is for 1 h'd iren sent hym in J*oh*n Sparck*es* bote, to be pd. at all tymes	£1	10s

152(R) anno 1542

Allson Bisshop p*er* contra is dewe to have the 8 daye of Ap*r*ell £6 r. fro*m* her *this* daye of Thomas Shipma*n*	£6	
Itm. the 13 daye of Julye r. fro*m* her by Thomas Shipma*n*	£4	
Itm. the 24 day of July r. fro*m* her by Robert Thomas	£1 6s	8d
Itm. the 25 day of October r. fro*m* her by T. Shipma*n*	£2 13s	4d
Itm. the 22 day of Jenyver r. fro*m* her by J*oh*n Kelly of Petherton 51s 8d	£2 11s	8d
1543 Itm. the 21 day of May r. fro*m* her by Giles Whit £7	£7	
Itm. the 24 day of July r. by Robert Thom*as*	£3	
Itm. the 16 day of August r. of her at Bridgewater 4 nobles	£1 6s	8d
Itm. r. by Symon Tayler	£1 6s	8d
Itm. the 25 of July 1544 r. by Tyndall £10	£10	
Itm. the 13 day of Oct*obe*r 1544 r. from her by her son in the lawe John Parcar 7 m*ar*k*es*	£4 13s	4d
Itm. the 14 of February 1544 my wif r. of her by the hand*es* of Giles White £3	£3	
Itm. the 24 day of July 1545 r. fro*m* her by her neighbur Robert Thomas 46s 8d	£2 6s	8d

anno 1543

Will*i*am Bridges p*er* contra is dewe to have the 30 daye of May 30s r. of hym in Bristowe	£1	10s

153(L) anno 1542

10 C 14 li. Iren o*with* for my prop*er* acowmpt the 15 day of Ap*r*ell anno dicto £3 which is for 10 C 14 li. *conteynyng* 24 end*es* which I pass to *this* less for the rest of acowmpt of iren fo. 127	£3
Itm. the 20 day of the same r. by God*es* grace ow*t* of my ship the Trynte, m*aster* under God Thomas Web, 450 k*ynt*alls iren of the Rendry which made by my weight*es* 32 tons 13 C 1 qr. 1 li. *conteynyng* 3156 end*es*, more 300 k*y*nt*alls* iren of Vryn & Fontraby which made by my weight*es* 21 tons	

153(L) contd.

86 ton 3 C 1 qr. 10 li.	11 C ½, 25 li. *conteynyng* 2066 end*es*, more 435 k*y*ntalls of S.S. which made 31 to*n* 18 C 1 qr. 12 li. *conteynyng* 3006 end*es*, mon*tith* the hole 86 tons 3 C 1 qr. 10 li. *conteynyng* 8228 end*es* & it cost clereaborde the ship in Spayne 574166 M. ½, ffor freight 13s 4d p*er* ton of 79 tons & for costom of 74 tons at 2s 6d p*er* ton, for hallyng home & pyllyng 21s & for av*er*es 10d p*er* ton, mon*tith*	£449	6d
16 ton 8 C 18 li.	Itm. the same tyme, r. ow*t* of a good ship callyd the Androwe of Plym*m*owthe, under God m*aster* John Androwe, 10 to*n* Rendry iren & weight which made by my my[1] weight*es* 10 tons 17 C *conteynyng* 1032 end*es* & 75 k*y*ntalls iren of S.S. which made 5 ton 11 C 18 li. *conteynyng* 524 end*es*, mon*tith* the hole 16 tons 8 C 18 li. iren *conteynyng* 1556 end*es* & it cost clereabord the ship in Spayne 107688 M. ½, for freight 10s p*er* ton, for av*er*es 12d ob p*er* ton, for costom 2s 6d p*er* ton, for halling & pyllyng 4s, mon*tith*	£82	2s 4d
8 ton 15 C 3 qr. 14	Itm. the 19 day of May r. ow*t* of the P*r*imros of Bristowe, master Thomas Latche, 121 k*y*ntalls 103 li. iren of the Rendry & Vryn which made by my weyght*es* 8 tons 15 C 3 qr. 14 li. *conteynyng* 211 end*es* which cost clere abord my ship in Spayne 56811 M. ½, for freight 13s 4d p*er* ton, for costom 2s 6d p*er* ton, for hallyng 2d p*er* ton, & for av*er*es 8d p*er* ton, mon*tith* the hole 811 endes[2]	£44	11s 7d
68 tons 3 h'd ½ a C, 8 li.	Itm. the 19 day of Augost, r. ow*t* of my ship the Trynte, m*aster* Thomas Web, 150 k*y*ntalls ½, 48 li. Rendry iren, 450 k*y*ntalls 20 li. iren of Vryn, 345 k*y*ntalls ½, 58 li. iren of S.S., all the which made by my weight*es* 68 tons xv C ½, 8 li. *conteynyng* 6352 end*es*, which iren cost clere abord the ship 463020 M., for costom of 55 tons £6 17s 6d, for freght of 63 tons £42, for haling home & pyling 16s, for averes after 10d p*er* to*n* mon*tith* 52s 6d, mon*tith* all	£360	19s 7d
	Itm. the 3 day of Jenyver a*n*no 1542 £151 10s 11d that is for so myche goten by this acownt of iren as may apere to gaynes in credito fo. 92	£151	10s 11d
	S.	£1,091	4s 11d

153(R)   anno 1542

Iren p*er* contra is dewe to have the 19 day of Augost, £405 7s that is ffor 67 tons 7 C 1 qr. 11 li. iren *con*teynyng 6451 end*es* solld from the 7 day of Aprill last past untyll *this* day at dyvers pr*i*ses as by my shop boke more largely may apere, mon*tith* as aforesseid	£405	7s
Itm. the 3d day of Jenyver £152 17s 11d that is for 24 tons 8 C 3 qr. ½ a li. iren *conteynyng* 2328 end*es* sold sens the 19 day of Augost last past at dyvers prices, as by my shop boke mor largely ape*r*ithe, mon*tith* as aforesseid	£152	17s 11d
Itm. the same day, £533 that is for 88 tons 16 C 3 qr. 17 li. iren *conteynyng* 8192 end*es* which is for so myche iren that restith this day to sell for this acowmpt the which iren I do make dett*or* of the seid £533 in a newe acow*m*mpt fo. 176 after the respect & price of £6 the ton	£533	
Itm. S.	£1,091	4s 11d

---

[1] *Smythe repeats* my.
[2] 811 endes *inserted later.*

154(L)   anno 1542

Thomas Machyn of Barckeley tanner o*with* the 14 day of M*arche* 7s that is for hallf a C madder d'd by his comawndement to Thomas Bowyer of Barkeley, this 7s is pd.[1]   ~~7s~~

Itm. the 30 day of Aprell £12 10s that is for 1 ton wull oyle to pay at Mighellmas next or ells descownt it before if I by eny lethir of hym   £12 10s

Itm. the 26 day of July pd. to hym yn Bristowe £15 of mon*ney*   £15

Itm. the same day £6 13s 4d *that* is for 1 ton 3 li. iren of S.S. sold to hym   £6 13s 4d

1543 Itm. the 7 daye of M*arche* anno 1543 £7 10s & is for 1 butt seck & 1 *pipe* bastard solld & d'd to hy*m*   £7 10s

Itm. the 22 of February £3 13s 4d for 1 but seck   £3 13s 4d

1544 Itm. the 8 of July a*nno* 1544 £6 which is for 1 ton Rendy iren to be paide at all tymes   £6

Itm. the 28 of July £20 which he r. of my wif in redy money   £20

Itm. the 23 of July £28 & is for 2 to*n* oyle to be pd. at all tymes   £28

Itm. the 6 of August £14 for 1 to*n* wull oyle to be paide at all tymes, mon*tith*   £14

Itm. the 15 day of Septem*ber* £12 3s 4d which I pd. to hym in redy mon*ney*   £12 3s 4d

Itm. the 16 day of September £6 & is for 1 to*n* iren lade*n* in Hawles bote to be paide at *Cris*tmas next com*m*yng   £6

154(R)   anno 1542

Thomas Machyn p*er* contra is dewe to have the 7 day of June £30 13s 4d that is for 3 dicker ox leth*er* at £3 the dicker & 10 cow & stere at 43s 4d the dicker, mon*tith*   £30 13s 4d

Itm. the last day of September r. in mon*ney*   £3 10s

Itm. the 8 of August a*nno* 1544 £76 3s 4d & is for 7 dicker ox lethir at £3[2] p*er* dicker & 26 dicker cow & stere at 43s 4d p*er* dicker to pay ~~£20 in han~~ at all tymes   £77 6s 8d

Itm. the last day of June 1545 £17 which he d'd me in W*illiam* Tyndall   £17

Itm. £3 which Robert Tyndall r. of hym   £3

155(L)   anno 1542

Richard Goodwyne Goodyng[3] of P*er*ciar smythe o*with* the 24 day of Ap*r*ell 59s 11d for 1 pipe less 2 li. iren after £6 *the* ton sent by Dymock of Twexbury, to be pd. at all tymes   £2 19s 11d

Itm. the 24 day of July £5 13s 4d which is for 1 to*n* iren to be paide at Mydsomer next com*m*yng   £5 13s 4d

anno 1542

John Sparck of Newneham o*withe* the 30 day of Ap*r*ell £3 13s 4d that is ffor a butt of seck to be paide at all tymes   £3 13s 4d

Itm. the 18 day of July £3 13s 4d that is ffor 1 butt of seck delyverd for hym to Thomas Laffan of Gatco*m* for to d'd to John M*a*rkes wif of Gatco*m*, to pay at Allhaloutide next   £3 13s 4d

Itm. the 12 day of September £13 6s 8d d'd & paide to hym in redy mon*ney* for to by for me calve skuyns & le*ther*   £13 6s 8d

Itm. the 26 day of the same £6 13s 4d pd. to hym in redy money for to by le*ther* as aforesseid   £6 13s 4d

Itm. the 24 day of October £20 pd. to hym for the forsseid *p*urpose of le*ther*   £20

Itm. the 24 day of Jenyver a*nno* 1542 £20 that is for so myche redy mon*ney* delyverd to hym in p*ar*t of payment of 15 weys wheat which he must d'd to me aborde my shipp at eny tyme athissyde Ester next at 12d the busshell putt aborde the bote, & more I must pay the charg*es* to bryng it aborde my shipp   £20

Itm. £4 which my wif pd. to hym   £4

---

[1] this 7s is pd. *inserted later.*
[2] 4 mark*es* 3s 4d *is erased and* £3 *written over it.*
[3] Goodyng *is inserted above the line.*

155(L) contd.

Itm. 45s pd. to hym for the bying of my wheat & for *con*veying of my whetes, skuyns & lethir to Bullock*es* bote	£2 5s
Itm. paide the 4 of June 1543 £3 9s 4d	£3 9s 4d
Itm. I make hym creditor in fo. 186 of £20	£20
	£97 1s

155(R)

anno 1542

Richard Goodyng p*er* contra is dewe to have the 24 daye of July £2 16s 8d r. of hym & 3s 3d I rebatyd to hym in the price
Itm. the 2d day of Julye 1543 r. by Robert Pepwell of Twexbury £5 13s 4d

19s 11d
£2 ~~16s 8d~~
£5 13s 4d

anno 1542

John Sparck here ageynst is dewe to have the 24 daye of October £48 8s ~~4d~~ that is for 12 dicker le*ther* cow & stere at 40s the dickar & 143 dozens calve skuyns at 5s 4d the dozen, & 20 doze*n*s at 4s 8d the dozen, the which lethir & skuyns he have bowght abrode in the Forest & other plac*es* ffor me & he saythe all is in his howse at *this* present & shalbe delyverd at all tymes *that* I wyll.
More 5 dicker of ox lethir at 50s the dicker, so the hole is 163 dozens calve skuyns & 12 dicker lethir, all the which amon*tith* to £69 6s
Itm. more for 5 dozens of old at 6s the doze*n*
Itm. for *con*veying my wheat & a 100 doze*n* calve skuyns & 17 dicker lethir to Bullock*es* bote 45s
Itm. for 10 weyes wheat at 12d the busshell
~~Itm. the 4 day of Maye 1543 £20 which is for so myche I rest owyng to hym by this acowmpt as it may apere to hym in credito fo. 186~~

~~£48 8s~~

£69 6s
£1 10s

£2 5s
£24

~~£20~~
£97 1s

156(L)

anno 1542

Richard Pryn m*ar*chant of Bristowe o*with* the 20 daye of Maye £26 to be paide at Cristmas next com*m*yng, which is ffor 2 tons of wull oyle which I sold & d'd to hym at £13 the ton
Itm. the 3 day of Jenyver £12 that is for 1 ton of wull oyle sold & d'd to hym to be paide at thend of 4 monthes next com*m*yng
1543 Itm. the 23 day of July £15 & is for 2 pipes wull oyle solld & d'd to hym to be paide by his bill at Candillmas next com*m*yng
1546 Itm. the 24 day of October 1546 £26 13s 4d & is for 2 ton wull oyle to pay the on hallf at Easter next com*m*yng & tho*ther* hallf at Seynt Jamistide next after that

£26

£12

£15

£26 13s 4d

anno 1542

Nicholas Tizon of Bristowe m*ar*chant o*with* the 3 day of May £13 that is ffor 1 ton wull oyle which I sold & d'd to hym, to be paide at Candellmas next
Itm. the 18 day of February 30s for 1 to*n* freight in my ship, to pay hallf in hand & hallf 3 monthes next after
Itm. the 28 day of June 1543 paide to hym 10s

£13

£1 10s
10s

156(R)

anno 1542

Richard Pryn per contra is dewe to have the 20 day of December £26 for so myche r. of hym in redy money & I delyverd to hym his bill £26
Itm. the 3 day of Marche £12 r. of hym in monney £12
Itm. the 6 day of February 1543 £15 which he pd. in redy monney & so I d'd to hym his bill £15
Itm. the 24 day of Marche 1546 r. of hym £13 6s 8d
Itm. the 17 day of June 1547 r. of hym £13 6s 8d

anno 1543

Nicholas Tizon per contra is dewe to have the 11 daye of Aprill £11 10s that is for 3 buttes of seck r. of his brother Jamys for hym, with condicion that if Nicholas wulld nedes have for the seid 3 butes 10s more, I must allowe it & pay it £11 10s
Itm. £3 which he do pay for me to Thomas Hickes, Frances Codryngton & William Car for 2 ton freight at this last vyntaige in theyr shipp, & for thother ton which I had in the seid ship at the same tyme Thomas Hickes do pay, as it may apere to hym in credito fo. 100 £3
Itm. 10s which I pay above £11 10s for the 3 buttes seck 10s

157(L)

anno 1542

William Reynoldes of Newneham in the Forest of Deane yeoman owith the 16 day of May 26s 8d which is for a h'd of clarett wyne which I sent hym in John Sparckes bote, to be paide at all tymes £1 6s 8d
1544 Itm. the 4 of Aprill 1544 £3 13s 4d and is for a butt seck to be paide at Seynt Jamystyde next £3 13s 4d

anno 1542

Water Rumney of Tedbery owith the 20 day of May £7 6s 8d & is for 2 buttes of seck at 11 nobles the butt to be pd. at Allhaloutyde next commyng & my uncle Thomas Smythe is shewertye £7 6s 8d
Itm. the 10th day of Marche £8 that is for 2 buttes of seck solld & d'd to hym to pay £4 at Mydsomer next commyng & £4 at Seynt Jamistide next after that £8
1544 Itm. the 5th of Aprell 1544 £7 13s 4d and is for 1 butt seck & 1 pipe bastard to be paide at Bartyllmewetide next £7 13s 4d

157(R)

anno 1542

William Reynoldes per contra is dewe to have the 26 day of August 25s r. of hym in money & 20d I rebate to hym in the price, montith 26s 8d £1 6s 8d
Itm. the 30 day of August 1544 40s r. in redy monny £2
Itm. r. of hym at Seynt Jamistide 1545 £1 13s 4d

anno 1542

Water Rumney per contra is dewe to have the 19 day of November £4 6s 8d which my sarvant Lett r. of hym at Tedbury £4 6s 8d
Itm. the 27 day of Jenyver r. of hym at Bristowe £3, montith £3
Itm. the last day of July 1543 r. of hym at Bristowe £8, I sey £8 £8
Itm. the 22 day of November Robert Leyght r. of hym at Tedbery £7 13s 4d £7 13s 4d

158(L) anno 1542

John Smythe of Hyntyne in the parische of Barckeley owith the 25 day of May
£6 15s ob & is for 1 ton 1 qr. & 1 li. iren of S.S. at 20 nobles the ton, to be pd.
at Mighellmas next. Thomas Machyne is his shewerty   £6 15s ob
1543 Itm. the 24 day of Jenyver 1543 £3 6s 2d which is for a pipe less 8 li.
S.S. iren to be pd. at Mydsomer next. T. Machyn shewerty   £3 6s 2d

anno 1542

Richard Apris of Harvarteste owith the 5th day of May £10 that is for a but
seck & a pipe bastard at eiche 11 nobles & 2 h'd Gascon wyne at 4 markes,
to be pd. by his bill obligatory £3 at Seynt Jamistide, £3 at Mighellmas next
commyng & £4 at Allhaloutyde next after that, montith, William Ballard
marchant of Bristow is shewrty   £10

158(R) anno 1542

John Smythe of Hynton per contra is dewe to have the 14
day of October £4 which my wif r. of hym   £4
Itm. the 30 day of Marche anno 1543 55s ob for so myche
redy monney which I my seallf r. of hym at Bristowe   £2 15s ob
Itm. the 29 day of October 1544 r. of hym at Bristowe   £2 3s 4d
Itm. r. by the handes of Thomas Machyne   £1 3s 4d

anno 1542

Richard Apris here ageynst is dewe to have the 24 day of
July £3 r. of hym at Bristowe   £3
Itm. the 17 day of September r. by Richard Mors William
Ballardes sarvant £3   £3
Itm. the 13 day of November r. of hym at Bristow   £4

159(L) anno 1542

Robert Poole marchant of Glocester owith the 14 day of
June £32 14s 5d for the rest of his cowmpt fo. 111, whereof
he have made me a byll to pay £10 at Seynt Jamistide next
& £20 at Cristmas next after that and for 54s 5d I have no
byll, howbeit by his promes & fydelyte it is payable at all
tymes requyryd   £32 14s 5d

36s 3d   the foreseid 54s 5d is for ½ a wey wheat with the costes &
17s 2d   for 3 ducatts 234 M for rest of acownt.
1543 Itm. the 22 day of October 1543 £3 5s 7d & is for so
myche paide to hym at Bristowe in redy money   £3 5s 7d
Itm. the 23 day of Jenyver 1543 £12 13s 2d & is for 1 ton
Rendry iren at £6 & 1 ton less 3 li. S.S. iren at £6 13s 4d,
to be pd. at all tymes requyryd. It was delyverd to his
sarvant John Davys   £12 13s 2d
1544 Itm. the 18 of December 1544 £12 & is for 2 ton
6s 7d ob & is for 2 ton less 1 li. Rendry iren at £6 3s 4d
the ton, to be paide at Cristmas next commyng   £12 6s 7d½

anno 1542

Antony Payne of Bristowe grocer owith the 6 daye of June
£6 10s which is for a pipe of wull oyle solld & d'd to hym
to be pd. by his bill at Seynt Jamistide next   £6 10s

anno 1543

William Byttun of Cawllme smythe owith the 13 day of
June £3 3s 4d & is for 1 h'd of my better Rendry iren, to
pay 5 nobles at Mighellmas next commyng & 30s at
Cristmas next after that, Master William Snowe Deane of
Bristowe is shewerty for the payment of the same   £3 3s 4d

159(L) contd.

Itm. the 9 day of Jenyver anno 1543 £3 3s 4d & is for a pipe of my better Rendry iren conteynyng 50 endes, to pay 33s 4d at Owr Lady Day in Lent next commyng & 30s at Mydsomer next after that	£3	3s	4d

159(R)   **anno 1542**

Robert Poole per contra is dewe to have the 29 daye of October £10 r. for hym of Miles Willsson Kendallman & I made the seid Miles a byll of my hand conffessing the receyt of the same £10 for the seid Poole	£10		
Itm. the 28 day of Marche r. from hym by my sarvant Robert Leight £10	£10		
1543 Itm. the 2d day of July r. by the seid Leight	£10		
Itm. the 22 day of October £6 & is for 2 C of dry hake & 2 C wett hake at 30s the C, montith	£6		
Itm. the 22 of August 1544 my sarvant Leyt r. £12 13s 2d	£12	13s	2d
Itm. the 13 day of Aprell anno 1545 r. from hym by John Raven serchor £10 of monney	£10		
Itm. r. from her by her sarvant 46s 8d	£2	6s	8d

anno 1542

Antony Payne per contra is dewe to have the 23 daye of October £4 for so myche redy monney r. of hym	£4		
Itm. the 6 day of December r. by his sarvant 50s	£2	10s	
~~Itm. the 15 of October anno 1543 33s 4d which his wif paide at Bristowe in redy monney~~	~~£1~~	~~13s~~	~~4d~~

anno 1543

William Byttun per contra is dewe to have the 16 of October 5 nobles which his wif pd. at Bristowe in monny	£1	13s	4d
Itm. the 19 day of Jenyver 1543 r. 30s	£1	10s	
Itm. the 3 day of November anno 1545 r. of Master Snowe by thandes of Water Phillips £3 3s 4d	£3	3s	4d

160(L)   **anno 1541**

Davy Hart of Bristowe shereman owith the last daye of Jenyver £7 6s 8d & is for 2 buttes seck which rest unpayde for the clozing up of his cownt fo. 57	£7	6s	8d
Itm. the 3d day of February 1542 13s 4d that is ffor so myche redy monney paide to hym		13s	4d
1543 Itm. the 7 day of Aprell 1543 £4 which is for a butt of seck sold & d'd to hym to pay at all tymes	£4		
Itm. the 28 day of February £8 which is for 1 but seck & 1 pipe bastard at £4 the pece, to pay £4 at Whitsontyde & £4 at Seynt Jamystide next commyng	£8		
anno 1544 Itm. the 12 day of Aprell anno 1544 10s paide to hym in redy monney		10s	
Itm. the 13 of December 1544 pd. & d'd to Richert Tippar for hym 6s[1]		6s	

anno 1547

Thomas Williams & Stevyn Bragdon of Bristowe grocers owith the 20 day of February anno dicto for 149 peces of resynges of Malaga at 7s the pece, montith £52 3s, to be paide by theyr obligacion at Mighellmas next commyng	£52	3s

160(R)   **anno 1542**

Davy Hert per contra is dewe to have the 15 day of June £3 6s 8d & is for sheryng of 30 clothes of Yerberys & 20 clothes of Thomas Hasshis at 16d per clothe, montith	£3	6s	8d

---

[1] *The whole of Hart's account is crossed through.*

160(R) contd.

Itm. the 7 day of October 53s 4d *that* is for barbyng & shering of 30 clothes of Yerberys & 10 of Hasshis at 16d p*er* clothe, mon*tith*	£2	13s	4d
Itm. the 3d day of M*ar*che 40s that is for barbing & shering of 30 clothes of Yerberys at 16d p*er* clothe, mon*tith*	£2		
Itm. the 18 of Septemb*er* for barbing & shering of 46 clothes of J*oh*n Yerberys & 14 clothes of Willi*am* Buchars at 16d the clothe, mon*tith* £4	£4		
Itm. the 15 of M*ar*che 1543 40s & is for ~~rowyng~~ shering & barbyng of 30 clothes of J*oh*n Yerberys at 16d the clothe	£2		
Itm. he pd. to my wif the 23 of June 1544	£2	10s	
Itm. the 13 day of Decemb*er* 1544 £8 16s & is for barbyng & sheryng of 80 clothes of J*oh*n Yerberys & 10 clothes of W*illia*m Buchars at 16d p*er* clo*the* & of 6 truckers of J*oh*n Yerberys at 12d p*er* clothe, mon*tith*.[1] This itm. is not so myche[2]	~~£8 16s~~		

anno 1548

Thomas Willi*ams* & Stevyne Bragdon hereageynst ar dewe to have the 6th daye of Octob*er* a*n*no dicto £52 r. of them all in testons & 3s in grottes & pens of too pens, & so delyverd unto the*m* they*r* obligacion, mon*tith*	S. £52	3s	

161(L)   anno 1542

Richard Mors of Bristowe baker owith the 22 day of June £6 which is for a pipe of wull oyle sold & d'd to his wif, to be paide at Seynt Jamistide next com*m*yng	£6		

anno 1542

Thomas Aflete of W*ur*sett*or* troweman owith the 30 daye of June £6 which is for a pipe of wull oyle solld & d'd to hym, to be paide at Seynt An day next com*m*yng	£6		
Itm. the 6 day of December £6 13s 6d that is for 1 ton 4 li. iren of S.S. at 20 nobles the ton to be paide at Seynt Jamistide next com*m*yng	£6	13s	6d
1543 Itm. the 27 of July 1543 £6 & is for 1 to*n* iren solld & d'd to hym to be paide at O*w*r Lady Day in Lent next com*m*yng	£6		

161(R)   anno 1542

Richard Mors p*er* contra is dewe to have the 5 day of August r. by his s*ar*vant Ellnor Willi*a*ms	£3	13s	4d
Itm. the 28 of the same my wif r. 7 nobles	£2	6s	8d

anno 1542

Thomas Aflete p*er* contra is dewe to have the 28 day £6 for so myche mon*n*ey he paide to my wif	£6		
Itm. the 26 day of July 1543 £6 13s 6d for so myche redy money r. of hym at Bristow	£6	13s	6d
Itm. the 24 of May 1544 r. £5	£5		

162(L)   anno 1542

John Roxby of Wells skuynnar owthe the 7 daye of Julye £37 which is for the rest & clozing up of his cowmpt fo. 10 & it is payable at all tymes r*e*quyrid	£37		
Itm. the same day £5 6s 8d for 2 h'd c*l*aret wyne & 2 h'd white wyne sold to hym	£5	6s	8d

---

[1] *The whole of Hart's account is crossed through.*
[2] This itm. is not so myche *inserted later.*

162(L) contd.

Itm. the 24 day of July £7 6s 8d that is ffor 2 buttes of seck sold & d'd to hym	£7 6s 8d	
Itm. the 25 day of Jenyver £4 which is for a butt of seck sent hym by William Sheward the carryer	£4	
Itm. the 19 day of February £8 which is for a but of seck & 1 pipe of bastard sent by William Sheward carryer	£8	
Itm. the 20 day of the same £24 13s 4d which is for 2 buttes seck at eich £4, 3 pipes bastard at eich £4 & 1 pipe taynt at 7 markes	£24 13s 4d	
Itm. the 8 day of Marche £28 which is for 7 buttes of seck solld to hym at £4 the butt, to be pd. at all tymes	£28	
1543 Itm. the 8 day of May 1543 £4 which is for a butt of seck solld & delyverd to hym to pay at all tymes	£4	
Itm. the 14 day of February £16 & is for 2 buttes of seck & 2 pipes of bastard at £4 the pece	£16	
Itm. the 13 of Marche £8 & is for a butt seck & 1 pipe of taynt at £4 the pece	£8	
1544 Itm. the 28 of Aprell £30 & is for 6 buttes seck at 11 nobles the but & for 1 pipe of teynt & 1 pipe of muscadell at eich £4, montith	£30	
Itm. the 14 of Maye for 2 tons Gascon wyne at £8 the ton montith	£16	
Itm. the 14 of June 1544 for 1 ton Gascon wyne	£8	
Itm. the 2d day of September £7 6s 8d which is for 2 buttes seck solld to hym	£7 6s 8d	
Itm. £11 which he owith for 3 buttes of my mothers seck	£11	
Itm. the 11 day of February for 1 pipe bastard at 13 nobles & 1 h'd taynt at £2. The 16 day of the same for 1 butt seck price £4, montith the	£10 6s 8d	
Itm. the 16 of Marche anno 1544 3 tons Gascon wyne at £8 the ton, montith £24	£24	
Itm. the 13 of Aprell for 5 buttes seck at £4 the butt, for 2 pipes bastard at 13 nobles the pipe & 1 pipe taynt at £4, montith all	£32 13s 4d	
Itm. the 25 of August 1545 solld to hym 11 h'd Gascon wyne & 1 h'd teynt at 40s the h'd	£24	
	S.	£91

162(R)   anno 1542

John Roxby per contra is dewe to have the 12 daye of October £9 17s 11d for so myche r. from hym by John Cutt	£9 17s 11d
Itm. the 28 day of November r. of hym at Bristowe £20 2s 1d in redy monney	£20 2s 1d
Itm. the 3 day of Jenyver r. of hym at Bristo £14	£14
Itm. the 15 day of Jenyver r. of hym at Bristowe £5 13s 4d	£5 13s 4d
Itm. the 20 day of February r. at Bristowe of hym	£4
1543 Itm. the 11 day of June anno 1543 r. of hym in Wells	£11
Itm. the 1 day of August r. of hym at Bristowe £10, montith	£10
Itm. the 2d daye of November r. of hym at Bristowe £20	£20
Itm. the 28 of November r. by Symon Taylor £8	£8
Itm. the 13 day of Jenyver 1543 r. of hym at Bristo	£15 13s 4d
1544 Itm. the 28 of Aprell 1544 £12 which he paide to my wif at Bristowe	£12
Itm. the 14 of June 1544 r. of hym at Bristow	£8
Itm. the 2d day of September r. of hym at Bristowe	£10
Itm. the 15 day of October r. by thandes of my neighbur John Cutt £16	£16
Itm. the last daye of November r. by John Cutt £16	£16
Itm. the 20 day of Jenyver anno 1544 r. of hym at Bristowe £18	£18
Itm. the 25 day of February he pd. to me at Bristowe £12	£12
Itm. the 17 day of Marche r. £4 6s 8d	£4 6s 8d
Itm. r. the 15 of Marche £8	£8
Itm. the 8 day of June 1545 r. from hym by my neighbur Symon Taylor £16	£16
Itm. the 29 of July 1545 £10	£10
Itm. the 17 day of August r. of hym at Bristowe £6	£6
Itm. the 25 of August r. of hym 40s	£2

162(R) contd.

Itm. r. £16 which he pd. me after Cawstons feyer		£16
Itm. the 2d day of December r. of hym		£18
Itm. the same day £15 whereof I make hym debitor for the rest of this acowmpt fo. 236		£15
	S.	£91

163(L)   anno 1542

John Yerbery of Bruton clothiar owith the 28 daye of July £64 5s that is for £49 5s 4d which I have paide hym in monney this present day & more £14 19s 8d which he is content to r. for my acowmpt of William Northe fo. 141, & hit is for £10 10s payable at Whitsontyde last past & £17 18s 4d payable at Mydsomer last past & £35 16s 8d payable by 2 bills at Seynt Jamistide now last past, montith   £64   5s

Itm. the 23 day of Augost £15 for so myche pd. to John Yerbery the yonger in part of payment of a byll datyd this present day, more the 2 day of October paide to hym seallf £15, more the 16 day of November pd. to John Yerbery hymseallf £6 13s 4d, so montith the hole conteynyd in this itm. £36 13s 4d, which I have sett on the backside of my byll datyd the 23 day of Augost   £36   13s   4d

Itm. the 16 day of Augost pd. to John Yerbery hymseallf £8 in part of payement of a byll datyd the 2d day of October last past, more pd. the 7 day of December for hym to Richard Copar of Amfford £10 6s 8d. So montith this bothe parcells £18 6s 8d which is for the first payement of my bill datyd the 2d day of October last past   £18   6s   8d

Itm. the 21 day of February £13 which William Northe pd. to hym for me, more paide by me to hym at Bristow the 7 day of Marche 1542 £68 13s 4d, montith the hole £81 13s 4d, and it is for £18 6s 8d payable at Allhaloutyd last past & £9 3s 4d payable the first day of December last past & £17 18s 4d at Cristmas last past & £17 18s 4d payable at Candellmas last past & £18 6s 8d payable the first day of this present monethe of Marche, montith the hole   £81   13s   4d

1543 Itm. the 22 day of June anno 1543 £36 13s 4d that is for £9 3s 4d payable at Owr Lady Day in Lent last past & £18 6s 8d payable at Whitsontide last past & £9 3s 4d at Mydsomer now next commyng   £36   13s   4d

Itm. the 17 day of July William Northe paide £10 & the last day of the same I paide £45, montith the hole £55 which is for the fyrst payment of the bargeyne made the 7 day of Marche last past   £55

Itm. the 5th day of September William Northe paide to hym £17, more I paide the 10 day of the same £10 10s, which £27 10s is payable the first day of this monthe by a byll datid the 7 of Marche last past, more I pd. £18 6s 8d for the last payment of a byll datyd the 23 of August 1543   £45   16s   8d

Itm. the 10th day of September £30 paide at Bristowe to John Yerbery in parte of payment of £82 8s 4d, the fyrst payment of my byll made & datyd this present day, more pd. to his son John Yerbery the 23 day of November £21, more paide the 28 day of Jenyver to John Penny £10, of Chack 30s & more pd. the 5 of February £20 18s 4d   £82   8s   4d

Itm. the 26 day of October anno 1543 £9 3s 4d which I paide to his son William Yerbery for the hole & later payment of my byll datid the 2 day of October anno 1542, as per contra aperith   £9   3s   4d

Itm. the 5 of February 1543 £109 18s 4d which I pass to fo. 201 for closyng up of this cowmpt   £109   18s   4d

                                                                                                                            £539   18s   4d

163(R)   anno 1542

John Yerbery of Bruton clothiar is dewe to have the 28 daye of July £155 1s 8d which is for the rest & closyng up of his acowmpt fo. 125, & it must be paide in maner followyng, that is to sey £10 10s at Whitsontide last past & £17 18s 4d at Mydsomer last past, & £35 16s 8d at Seynt Jamistide now last past & £18 6s 8d at Allhaloutyde next

201

163(R) contd.

com~~m~~yng & ~~£9 3s 4d the first day of December next~~
~~com~~myng & ~~£17 18s 4d at~~ Cris~~t~~mas next com~~m~~yng &
~~£17 18s 4d at Candellmas next~~ com~~m~~yng & ~~£18 6s 8d at~~
Whitsontide in a~~nno 1543 & £9 3s~~ 4d at Mydsomer in a~~nno~~
1543. ~~So~~ mon*tith* £155 ~~1s 8d~~

Itm. the 23 day of Augost £73 6s 8d that is ffor 20 clothes
pen*n*y hewes bowght of hym at 11 nobles the clothe, to pay
£36 13s 4d in hand £18 6s 8d ~~the first day of M~~*a*~~rche next~~
~~com~~myng & ~~£18 6s 8d the first day of September next after~~
~~that,~~ mon*tith* ~~£73 6s 8d~~

Itm. the 2d day of October £36 13s 4d to pay ~~£18 6s 8d in~~
~~hand £9 3s 4d at O~~wr ~~Lady Day in Lent next~~ com~~m~~yng &
~~£9 3s 4d at~~ Migellmas in a*n*no 1543 & it is for 10 clothes at 11
nobles the clothe £36 ~~13s 4d~~

Itm. the 7 day of M*a*rche a*n*no 1542 £110 which is for 30
penny hewes at 11 nobles the clothe, to pay ~~£55~~ in hand,
~~£27 10s~~ the first day of September next com*m*yng & £27 10s
the first day of M*a*rche next after *that* which wylbe in a*n*no
1543 £110

Itm. the 10 day of September £164 16s 8d which is for 46
clothes of his penny hewes at 5 m*a*rkes 5s the clothe, to pay
~~£80 8s 4d in hand~~, £41 4s 2d at O*w*r Lady Day in Marche
next com*m*yng & £41 4s 2d at Mighellmas next after that
which wylbe in a*n*no 1544, as it may ap*e*re by my bill datyd
the seid tenthe day £164 16s 8d

S. £539 18s 4d

164(L) anno 1542

John Griffithe of Bristowe rop*er* owithe the 11 day of Julye £3 13s 4d that is
for a butt of seck sollde & delyverd to hym, to be paide at Cris*t*mas next
com*m*yng £3 13s 4d

1543 Itm. the 18 of June 1543 £3 that is for a p*i*pe Rendry iren sold & d'd to
hym to be pd. at Cris*t*mas next £3

Itm. the 30 day of May 1544 £6 8s 4d which is for 1 ton iren to be pd. at
Cristmas next £6 8s 4d

Itm. the 16 day of June 1545 for a pipe 2 li. Rendry iren at 19 nobles the ton
& 1 pipe 3 li. S.S. iren at 20 nobles the ton, mon*tith* £6 10s 3d, to be pd. at
Allhaloutyde next com*m*yng, mon*tith* £6 10s 3d

Itm. the 30 day of June 1546 £6 13s 4d & is for 1 ton of S.S. iren which I d'd
for hym to his wif, to be paide at Allhaloutyde next com*m*yng £6 13s 4d

anno 1542

Thomas Thurston of Bristowe sopemaker owe the 19 daye of Julye £6 *that* is
for a pipe of wull oyle solld & delyverd to hym, to be pd. at Cris*t*mas next
com*m*yng £6

1543 Itm. the 10th day of Augost 1543 £15 that is for 2 pipes of wull oyle
sold & d'd to hym, to be paide at Cristmas next com*m*yng £15

1550 Itm. the 10th day of May 1550 £58 & is for 2 tons of wull oyle solld to
hym in 4 pipes at £29 the ton, to be pd. £29 at Mighellmas next com*m*yng &
£29 at Cris*t*mas next after that £58
passed the rest of this cowmpt to my newe boke fo. 5

164(R) anno 1542

John Griffithe of Bristowe rop*er per* contra is dewe to have
the 15 day of December £3 13s 4d for so myche r. of his
wif to who*m* I d'd his obligacio*n* £3 13s 4d

Itm. the 19 of Jenyver 1543 r. in ropes 24s & in mon*n*ey 36s,
mon*tith* £3 £3

Itm. the 7 day of Jenyver 1544 r. of hym £5

164(R) contd.

Itm. the 28 day of Marche anno 1545 my wif r. of hym 28s 4d	£1	8s	4d
Itm. the 8 day of February r. of his wif £3 6s 8d	£3	6s	8d
Itm. the 3 day of Aprell 1545 £3 3s 7d r. of his wif	£3	3s	7d
Itm. the 10 day of November 1546 my wif r. of hym £5	£5		
Itm. the 9 day of Aprell 1547 r. of hym	£1	13s	4d

anno 1542

Thomas Thurstone per contra is dewe to have the 10 daye of December £6 for so myche r. of hym in redy money	£6		
Itm. the 9 day of February 1543 r. of hym £15	£15		

165(L)   **anno 1542**

Davy Williams of Bristowe baker owithe the 12 day of July £3 13s 4d that is for 1 butt of seck solld & delyverd to hym to be paide at all tymes requyrid	£3	13s	4d
Itm. the 20 day of September he r. of my wif 4 nobles	£1	6s	8d
Itm. the 19 day of October pd. to hym 3s 5d ob		3s	5d½
Itm. the 21 day of October £3 that is for a pipe iren sold & d'd to hym to be paide at all tymes requyrid	£3		
Itm. 22s 4d that is for 8 busshells wheat at 16d the busshell & 11s 8d in money which was pd. & d'd to hym	£1	2s	4d
Itm. the 27 day of October 1543 pd. to hym in monny 21s 8d	£1	1s	8d

anno 1550

Nicholas Shee of Bristowe sopemaker owith the 19 day of May anno dicto £112 & is for 4 tons of wull oyle sold & delyverd to hym in 8 pipes at £28 the ton, to be paide at Seynt Androwstide next commyng   £112
passed this cowmpt to my newe boke fo. 6

anno 1542

Thomas Hasbery of Barnsgrove owithe the 24 daye of July 4 markes which is for the rest of a butt of seck which I delyverd for hym to Lawrence Hanckot, & it must be paide at Candellmas next   £2 13s 4d

165(R)   **anno 1542**

Davy Williams per contra is dewe to have the 26 day of September for 24 C less 14 li. bisquytt at 13 grotes the C, which I had of hym for my ship the Trynte	£5	3s	5d ob
Itm. the 27 of October 1543 r. of hym 19 C ½ bisquytt at 5s 4d the C, montith £5 04s[1]	£5	4s	

anno 1542

Thomas Hasbery per contra is dewe to have the 2d day of February 53s 4d r. at Bristowe for hym of Lawrence Hanckot his neighbur   £2 13s 4d

166(L)   **anno 1542**

John Lawghton of Handeley troweman owith the 24 daye of Julye £3 7s 8d that is for 1 pipe 17 li. iren of S.S. sold & d'd to hym, to be pd. at Candellmas next commyng   £3 7s 8d

---

[1] There is no credit entry for Shee.

166(L) contd. anno 1548

Robert Kemp of Wynschecom in Wissetorshire draper owithe the 25 day of Jenyver 1548 £3 10s & is for the rest of a but of seck sold & d'd to hym after £5 the but, to pay the same £3 10s at Easter next commyng as by his byll may apere[1]   £3 10s

anno 1550

Hughe Hamon owithe the 28 of Aprell anno dicto 13 V. 122 M. for the rest of his acowmpt of Andaluzia this last vyntage as may apere   013 V. 122 M.

Itm. the 21 of Maye £4 2s 8d that is for the freight of 2 tons oyle in the Mary Conceptyon at 40s per ton & for averes of the same at 16d per ton, montith   £4 2s 8d

Itm. the 28 of May £28 & is for 1 ton of oyle d'd for hym to Slake the northenman, to be pd. at Seynt Jamistide next commyng   £28

Itm. 10s paide to the Kyng for his subsedy   10s

Itm. 3s that is for custom of one ton of seckes which I pd. the 26 of June, entryd in the San John of the Rendry   3s

passed this cowmpt to my newe booke fo. 7

anno 1542

John Robbyns of Cropthorne in Wursettorshire smythe owith £3 19s 7d that is ffor the rest of 1 ton less 9 li. iren of my better Rendry sorte at ~~19~~ 17 nobles the ton & of this must be pd. 40s at Candellmas next commyng & 39s 7d at Mydsomer next after that. Richard Goodwyne of Perciar is his shewerty   £3 19s 7d

1543 Itm. the 18 day of June 1543 £3 which is for a pipe of Rendry iren after £6 the ton which I solld & delyverd to hym to be paide at Cristmas next commyng[2]   £3

166(R) anno 1543

John Lawghton per contra is dewe to have the 19 daye of June 53s 4d r. for hym of his neighbur Richard Bane   £2 13s 4d

Itm. the 6 day of August r. of hym 13s 4d   13s 4d

Itm. the same day 12d which he pay not for the od weightes   1s

[3]

Anno 1550

more for a Cordavan skyn   000 V. 375 M.

3928 M.   Hugh Hamon per contra is due to have the 28 of Aprell anno dicto for 2 portugesis which he d'd unto my wif after 11 ducatts ½ per portuges   008 V. 819 M.

Itm. for a pece of black lynyng for a wrapper 9s   9s

Itm. 16d which he paide for lymons   1s 4d

Itm. 18d which he paide for 18 mylk pans   1s 6d

anno 1542

John Robbyns per contra is dewe to have the 9 daye of February £3 19s 7d that I r. from hym of Thomas Coke of Twexbury in redy money   £3 19s 7d

167(L) anno 1542

Edward Rowley of Kyngesnorton owith the 24 day of July £17 13s 4d that is ffor 1 ton iren of S.S. at 19 nobles the ton & 2 ton of my better Rendry iren at 17 nobles the ton, to be paide at Mighellmas next commyng   £17 13s 4d

---

[1] *The whole item for Robert Kemp is crossed through.*
[2] *The whole item for 18th June is crossed through.*
[3] *There is no credit account for Kemp.*

167(L) contd.

Itm. the 5 day of February £23 6s 8d & is for 4 ton Rendry iren sent to hym in Thomas Aservarns trowe at £5 16s 8d the to*n*, to be paid at Whitssontide next, mon*tith*	£23	6s	8d
1543 Itm. the last day of June a*nno* 1543 £19 9s 6d & it is for 3 ton less 9 li. of S.S. iren at £6 10s the ton, to be paide at Seynt Jamistide next com*m*yng	£19	9s	6d
Itm. the 19 of July £23 19s 7d ob & is for 4 ton less 7 li. iren of the bet*ter* Rendry at £6 the ton laden in Penssons trowe	£23	19s	7d
Itm. the 24 day of July £54 10s 5d and is for 8 tons Rendry iren at £6 the ton & 1 to*n* 7 li. iren of S.S. at £6 10s the ton solld & d'd to hym, to be paide at all tymes	£54	10s	5d
Itm. the 11 day of Jenyver 1543 £42 10s & is for 6 ton of my bet*ter* Rendry iren at £6 the ton & for 1 ton of S.S. iren at £6 10s the ton, to be pd. at all tymes requyrid, the which iren I lode in Thomas Flet*es* trowe, mon*tith*	£42	10s	
1544 Itm. the 22 day of July a*nno* 1544 £48 & is for 8 ton Rendry at £6 *per* ton, to be pd. at all tymes as in my shop boke may apere	£48		
Itm. the 25 of July laden in Flet*es* trowe 2 to*n* 3 li. of S.S. iren at 20 nobles the ton, mon*tith*	£13	6s 10d	
Itm. the 4 of August laden in Thomas Asevarns trowe 4 tons Rendry iren at £6 the ton	£24		
1545 Itm. the 22 day of Ap*rell* a*nno* 1545 laden for hym in Thomas Palmers trowe of Higgley 1 ton 4 li. S.S. iren at £6 10s *per* ton & 1 ton Rendry iren les 6 li. at £6 the ton, more the 26 day of May for 3 ton 2 li. Rendry iren in Thomas Palmers trowe at £6 the ton, more the same tyme in Thomas Asevarns trowe 2 tons Rendry iren at £6 the ton & 2 ton 3 li. S.S. iren at 19 nobles the ton, mon*tith* all 10 tons 6 li. & in mon*ney* £60 10s 4d £61 10s 7d	£61	10s	7d
Itm. the 22 day of Awgost for 8 ton, ½ a C, 18 li. ire*n* £48 17s 4d to be pd. at all tymes requyrid, which ire*n* do apere largely in my shop boke	£48	17s	4d
Itm. the 15 day of February for 4 tons Rendry iren & 2 tons at £6 *per* ton & 2 tons S.S. ire*n* at 19 nobles *per* ton, mon*tith* the hole 6 tons	£36	13s	4d
1546 Itm. the 17 day of May 1546 £18 2d ob & is for 3 tons Rendry iren to be pd. at all tymes	£18	2d ob	
S.	£431	6s	3d ob

167(R)   **anno 1542**

Edward Rowley p*er* contra is dewe to have the 26 daye of September £17 6s 8d which he paide for me to Lawrence Hancott of Barnsgrove as may apere fo. 6	£17	6s	8d
Itm. the 4 day of February 6s 8d r. of *John* Lyndon		6s	8d
Itm. the 26 day of June 1543 r. of *William* Gest his son in the lawe at Bristowe £23 6s 8d	£23	6s	8d
Itm. the 24 of July r. of hym at Bristow	£43	9s	1d
Itm. the 6 day of Jenyver 1543 my s*arvant* Leyt r. of hym £40	£40		
Itm. the 3 day of July by his neighbur John Lett £22 10s	£22	10s	
Itm. to Lawrence Hanckot	£14	10s	
Itm. r. the 24 of July by *John* Lyndon £20	£20		
Itm. the 20 of August 1544, my s*arvant* R. Leyt r. £5	£5		
Itm. the 22 day of Ap*rell* 1545 r. by *John* Lett £50	£50		
Itm. the 19 daye of August a*nno* 1545 r. of hym at Bristowe £30	£30		
Itm. the 19 day of August a*nno* 1545 r. of hym at Bristowe in p*art* of payment of the 10 tons 6 li. iren menceonyd in the itm. of the 22 day of Ap*rell* last past, mon*tith*	£30		
Itm. the 13 day of February r. fro*m* hym by his s*arvant* Joh*n* Hosyer	£31	10s	
Itm. the 13 day of this monthe July 1546 r. at Bristowe of hym £53	£53		
Itm. more r. of hym the 14 day of the same monthe in redy money £16 17s 3d	£16	17s	3d
Itm. more the same day £15 9s 9d & is for so myche that I must r. for hym of George Knight of the Mynte for 3 oz.			

167(R) contd.

3 qr. & ½ qr. angell golld & 12d corrant & for 26 oz. sylver as by his byll may apere	£15	9s	9d
Itm. the 14 daye of Julye 1546 £18 2d ob & is for so myche I make hym debitor in fo. 248 for the rest & closyng up of this acowmpt	£18	2d ob	
	S. £431	6s	3d½

168(L)   **anno 1543**

Thomas Abeck of Manchester owithe the 27 daye of Julye £60 that is for so myche redy money pd. for hym to his sarvant Thomas Higgyn & he delyverd to me my bill, mon*tith*   £60
1544 Itm. the 26 daye of M*a*rche a*nno* 1544 £14 13s 4d & is for 3 pipes muscadell & 1 butt seck at ech 11 nobles solld & d'd for hym to his s*a*rvant Thomas Higgyn   £14 13s 4d
Itm. the 30 day of Augost a*nno* 1544 £70 6s 8d & is for so myche redy money paide to his s*a*rvant Thomas Higgyns & so r. my byll *that* I was bownd yn   £70 6s 8d
Itm. the 30 day of August 1544 £105 and is for 150 Manchester cottons at 14s the pece, to pay 2 tons of wull oyle in hand for the price of £30 & the rest being £75 must be paide at Bartyllmewtide next com*m*yng, as it shall apere by my byll[1]   I arryd in settyng this itm. & therefore wryte it discowntid in a newe cow*nt* £105

anno 1544

Thomas Abeck of Manchester owith the 1 day of September £30 & is for 2 tons wull oyle d'd to his s*a*rvant Thom*as* Higgyns in p*a*rte of payment of the 150 Manchesters p*er* contra   £30
Itm. the ~~12~~ 9 day of December delyverd to his s*a*rvant John Higgyns 3 tons wull oyle at £15 the to*n*   £45
Itm. the 29 of Jenyver £8 6s 8d which is for 1 but seck at £4 & 1 p*i*pe bastard at £4 6s 8d d'd for hy*m* to his s*a*rvant T. Higgyns   £8 6s 8d
Itm. the last day of August 1545 £66 13s 4d & is for the hole & last payment dewe at Bartyllmewtide ~~next~~ last past as may apere in the itm. p*er* contra datyd the 30 day of August 1544 & so I r. my byll. It is pd. to Thomas Higgyns   £66 13s 4d
Itm. the 6 day of February 1545 pd. to his s*a*rvant Thomas Higgyns £30 in p*a*rt of my byll datyd *the* 12 day of Dece*m*ber 1544   £30
Itm. the 5 day of Marche a*nno* 1545 £30 which he r. of my wif for the full payment of my byll datyd the 12 day of December 1544 & so he delyverd to her my seid byll   £30
Itm. the 13 of Ap*r*ell 1546 for 3 ½-bales Tullus woode *conteynyng* 5 C 12 li. at 16s ~~8d~~ p*er* C, mon*tith* £4 5s 2d
Itm. the 24 day of July an*no* 1546 for 7 ½-bales of Tullus woode *conteynyng* 12 C 3 li. at 16s ~~8d~~ p*er* C, mon*tith* £10 5d ob, mon*tith* this bo*the* itms. £13 14s 2d   £13 14s 2d
Itm. the 26 day of July 1546 pd. to Thomas Higgyns 10d   10d
Itm. the same day, paid to the seid Thomas £33 for the payment dewe at Bartyllmewtyde next & r. of hym a quyttance for the same   £33
Itm. the 12 day of October 1546 pd. to his s*a*rvant John Abeck £50   £50
Itm. the 19 day of Nove*m*ber pd. apo*n* my bill to Thomas Higgyns   £30
Itm. the 4 day of February 1546 my wif pd. Higgyns £20   £20
Itm. the 28 of July 1547 pd. to Higgyns £95[2]   £95

168(R)   **anno 1542**

Thomas Abeck of Manchester is dewe to have the 18 day of Augost £60 to be paide by my bill at Seynt Jamistide next com*m*yng & it is for the rest of won C Manchesters of

---

[1] *The item for 30th August 1544 is crossed through.*
[2] *All the items from 1st Sept. 1544 are crossed through.*

168(R) contd.

dyvers collors which I bowght of his sarvaunt Thomas Higgyn at 14s 6d the pece, mon*tith*	£60
Itm. the 29 daye of September a*nno* 1543 £85 that is for won 150 pec*es* of Manchester of dyvers collow*res* at 14s the pece whereof I paide in hand £20. So rest £85 to be paide by my bill at Bartyllmewtide next com*m*yng, mon*tith*	£85
Itm. the 30 day of Augost a*nno* 1544 £71 6s 8d & is for so myche redy money paide to his sarvant Thomas Higgyns & so r. my byll that I was bownd in	[1]
Itm. the 1 day of September a*nno* 1544 £30 & is for 2 tons wull oyle d'd to his sarvant Thomas Higgyns in p*ar*t of payment of the 150 Ma*n*chesters p*er* co*n*tra	~~£30~~

anno 1544

Thomas Abeck of Manchester is dewe to have the 30 daye of Augost £105 & is for 150 Manchester cottons at 14s the pece, to pay in hand 2 tons wull oyle for the price of £30 & the rest being £75 at Bartyllmewtide next com*m*yng as it shall apere by my byll	~~£105~~
Itm. the 12 day of December £105 to pay in hand £45 in 3 tons wull oyle & £60 at Cristmas co*m* twellmonthes which wylbe in *anno* 1545	~~£105~~
Itm. the 1 day of September 1545 £133 that is for a 190 Manchester cottons, to be payde £33 at Bartyllmewetide next com*m*yng & £100 at Mighellmas next after *that* which wylbe in a*nno* 1546	~~£133~~
Itm. the 26 day of July 1546 ~~£95~~ £108 15s & is for a 150 Manchester cottons at eich 14s 6d, to pay ~~£13 14s 2d~~ in hand & £95 at Seynt Jamystide next which wylbe in a*nno* 1547[2]	~~£108 15s~~
Itm. the[1]	

169(L)   **anno 1542**

Thomas Hasche of Batco*m* clothiar ~~is dewe~~ owithe to have the 28 day of October £10 pd. to hym in redy money apo*n* ~~his~~ my byll datyd the 21 day of September last past	£10		
Itm. the 8th daye of February £17 18s 4d that is for so myche paide to hym in redy money dewe at Allhaloutide last past & it is sett apo*n* the backside of my bill	£17	18s	4d
Itm. the 14 daye of M*ar*che a*nno* 1542 paide to hym £17 18s 4d payable at Candellmas last past & so I r. my bill	£17	18s	4d
Itm. the 21 day of June 1543 £10 for so myche pd. to hym at Bristowe & putt it apon the backsyde of my bill datyd the 26 day of Ap*r*ell a*nno* 1542 Itm. the 26 of July £7 18s 4d pd. to hym in Bristowe & r. my byll of the 26 day of Ap*r*ell before specyfied. So amo*ntith the* monney of this 2 items £17 18s 4d	£17	18s	4d
Itm. the 29 daye of Octob*er* a*nno* 1543 £17 18s 4d which I paide to hym at Bristowe in reddy mon*n*ey for the full & last payment of my byll datyd the 21 day of September a*nno* 1542 & so r. my byll	£17	18s	4d
1549 Itm. the 11 day of September 1549 for 5 C Yland woode at 13s 4d the C, more the 17 of December 1 C ½, 14 li. mo*ntith* all 6 C ½, 14 li. at 13s 4d p*er* C	£4	8s	4d
Itm. the 23 day of Jenyver for 17 C	£11	6s	8d

passed this cowmpt to fo. 8 in my newe booke

169(R)   **anno 1542**

Thomas Hasche of Batco*m* clothiar is dewe to have the 26 day of Julye £53 15s which is for the rest and closyng up

---

[1] *Blank in MS.*
[2] *All the items from 30th August 1544 are crossed through.*

169(R) contd.

of his acowmpt fo. 38, and it must be paide in maner followyng. That is to sey £17 18s 4d at Allhaloutyde next com*m*yng & £17 18s 4d at Candellmas next com*m*yng & £17 18s 4d at Easter next com*m*yng, as may apere by my bills	£53 15s
Itm. the 21 day of September £27 18s 4d which is for the rest of 10 clothes at 5 m*ar*kes 5s the clothe, to be paide £10 at all tymes requyrid & £17 18s 4d at Bartyllmewtide next com*m*yng	£27 18s 4d
Itm. the 24 day of September 1549 £30 & is for the rest of 10 clothes bowght of hym at 17 nobles the clothe, to pay £15 at Owr Lady Day in Lent & halff £15 at Cristmas next after that	£30

170(L)   anno 1542

Robert Tayllo*r* otherwise Cator of Bristowe yeoman ow*ith* the 26 day of Augost £6 13s 4d & is for 1 to*n* iren of S.S. to be paide the 26 day of February next com*m*yng, for the which payment he & Morys Smythe stand bounden by obligacio*n*, mon*tith*	£6 13s 4d

anno 1542

Will*i*am Spyllman s*a*rvant to M*a*ster Nycolas Thorn ow*ith* the 23 day of Augoste 26s 8d which is for the freight of 2 ton iren in my ship the Trynte fro*m* Spayne	£1 6s 8d

a*n*no 1549

John Nervol of Bruto*n* ow*ith* the 5th day of December a*n*no dicto £9 6s 8d & is for 14 C Yland woode delyverd for hym to Thomas Burge of Batco*m* carryar	£9 6s 8d
Itm. the 30 day of December for 2 C woode delyverd for hym to M*aster* Jo*h*n Yerberys son at 13s 4d the C. The last day of December 10 C	£8
	S. £17 6s 8d

170(R)   anno 1543

Robert Cator p*er* contra is dewe to have the 5 daye of Aprill 10s which was dewe to hym for a quarters rent endid at Owr Lady Day last past of a hows I toke of hym in Seynt Awstens Grene for M*aster* Wallsche which hows I have gevyn up to hym ageyne	10s
Itm. the same day £6 3s 4d paide by hym to my wif in redy mon*n*ey	£6 3s 4d

anno 1542

Will*i*am Spillma*n* p*er* contra is dewe to have the last daye of Jenyver 26s 8d that is for so myche my s*a*rvant Robert Leyght r. of hym in mon*n*ey	£1 6s 8d

an*n*o 1549

John Nervol of Bruton is dewe to have the 12 day of November £12 10s & is for so myche my wif r. of John Penny for hym in yernes & p*a*rt of payement of 30 C Yland wood at 13s 4d p*er* C	£12 10s
Itm. the 16 day of Maye 1550 r. from hym by my s*a*rvant W*illi*am Clerck £4 16s 8d	£4 16s 8d
	S. £17 6s 8d

171(L)   **anno 1542**

M*aster* George Owen of London, doctor of phisyck & physision to the Pryn*ces* Grace of Yngland, owith the 9 daye of November an*no* dicto won hundred pown*des* of gold which I lent to hym in 225 angell nobles, 10 ryalls of gold, 30 crusados, 1 doble ducatt & 8 sengle d*ucatt*s of gold, the which mon*n*ey I delyverd for hym & in his name to his s*ar*vaunt Bartillmewe Redhed & the seid Bartyllmewe delyv*er*d to me an obligacio*n* with a condycio*n* sealyd & subscrybyd by his seid M*aster* to pay the seid mon*n*ey. That is to sey £50 at the Anu*n*cyasyon of O*w*r Lady next com*m*yng or won mon*n*eth after & £50 at Mighellmas next after that or won mon*th* after. So mon*tith* as aforeseid £100   £100
Itm. the 22ti day of Jenyver a*n*no 1546 £4 & is for a but of seck which I sent hym to Londo*n*   £4
passed this to my newe[1] booke fo. 9 the 2de day of July 1550

171(R)   **anno 1545**

     M*aster* George Owen p*er* contra ~~owe~~ is dewe to have £50 which he paide to M*aster* Arundell the Quenes Chancellor for me in May   £50
     Itm. £4 which I gave hym for olde frendship   £4

172(L)   **anno 1542**

Thomas Uprichard[2] smythe of Seynt Fagans in Wales owithe the 28 day of October 29s 10d that is ffor 1 h'd less 3 li. of the best Rendry iren at £6 the ton to be paide at all tymes. It was lade*n* in Davy Watkyns bote of Kerdiff, mon*tith*   £1   9s   10d
Itm. the 5 daye of February 29s 5d which is for h'd less 10 li. iren d'd for hym to Davy Watkyns to be paide at all tymes   £1   9s   5d
1543 Itm. the 3 day of July 1543 35s which is for 1 h'd 1 qr. S.S. iren at 20 gro*tes* the C d'd for hym to his brother to be paide at all tymes   £1   15s
Itm. the 10 day of Decemb*er* 13s 7d½ & is for 2 C 5 li. iren of S.S. d'd for his brother to Davy Luyes to be paide at all tymes   13s   7d½
Itm. the 4 of February 12s 7d & is for C 3 qr. & 16 li. S.S. iren d'd for hym to his bro*ther* at 20 gro*tes* the C, to be paide at Mydsomer next com*m*yng   12s   7d

           anno 1542

John Raven of Bristowe s*er*chor owithe the 30 day of Octob*er* £6 which is ffor 1 to*n* of Rendry iren solld & d'd to hym to be paide by his byll obligatory at Bartyllmewetide next com*m*yng   £6
1543 Itm. the 7th daye of Septemb*er* 1543 £6 13s 10d ob & is for 1 ton 9 li. iren of S.S.   £6   13s   10d
Itm. the 19 of June a*n*no 1550 £6 & is for so myche I lent hym in ready mon*n*ey apo*n* a p*ar*cell gyllt goblett waying 20 own*ces* & 1 qr. of an ownce to be paide at all tymes requyred   £6
passyd to my newe boke fo. 9

172(R)   **anno 1542**

     Thomas Smythe of Seynt Fagans p*er* contra is dewe to have the 3 day of February 29s 8d r. for hym of D*avi*d Watkyns   £1   9s   8d
     R. of Davy Watkyns the 6 of June 1543 29s 4d   £1   9s   4d
     R. the 3 day of July 1543 of his brother Thom*as* Smythe 3d   3d
     Itm. the 20 day of October r. of hym at Bristowe   £1   15s
     Itm. the 4 of February 1543 r. of Thomas Uprichard of Kerdif 13s 7d ob   13s   7d ob
     Itm. the 25 of July 1544 my wif r. 12s 7d   12s   7d

---

[1] newe *is inserted above the line.*
[2] Uprichard *is inserted above the line.*

172(R) contd.

anno 1543

John Raven per contra is dewe to have the 27 of Augost
£6 which I r. by thandes of his wif £6
Itm. r. a hewlyng clothe at the price of, r. a clothe valent £6 13s 4d

173(L)

anno 1541

Viages to Biscay into thandes of my prentes Robert
3 truckers   Tyndall for my owne acowmpt owith the 15 day of October
£9 which is for 3 truckers laden in the John Baptist, master
Johannes de Yrancu   £9

10 tons
12 C led
300 hides
cow & stere

Itm. I shulld have wryten first £115 9s 8d for 10 tons 12 C
led in 186 peces & 30 dicker lethir cow & stere, all the
which was laden in Robert Pooles ship of Glocester callid
the Mary Fortune, master John Darby   £115 9s 8d

10 L clothes
7 truckers
2 kerssys

Itm. the 2d day of December £59 10s that is ffor 10 clothes
of John Yerberys better sorte & 7 of his truckers & 2 fyne
white kersys laden in the Primros of Bristowe   £59 10s

40 L
4 kerses
12 ton 4 C led
100 ox hydes
300 cow & stere
152 dozens skuyns
3 wey 9 b grene pezon

Itm. the last day of Jenyver £375 12s 8d that is ffor 40
clothes penny hewes, that be 30 of John Yerberys & 10 of
Hasshes & 4 white kerssis & 12 tons 4 C led in 212 peces
& 10 dicker ox lether & 30 dicker cow & stere & 152 dozens
calve skuyns & 3 weyes 9 busshells grene peson, all which
godes be laden in the Trynte my ship, under God master
Thomas Web   £375 12s 8d

10 L
5 kersses

Itm. the 14 day of February £45 that is for 10 clothes of
William Buchars & 2 fyne black kerses & 2 fyne white
kerses & a white kersy of a corser sorte, all the which goodes
was laden in the Mary Bride   £45

50 L
2 kerses
10 ton 3 C led
2 w. whete
200 cow & stere and 2 hides
30 ox
67 dozen skuyns

Itm. the 20 day of June anno 1542 lode in my ship the
Trynte, under God master Thomas Web, 50 clothes
penny hewes of the which 30 war of John Yerbery & 20
of Hasshes & 1 whit kerssy & 8 yerdes of another & 10 tons
3 C ledd in 172 peces & 2 wayes of wheat & 20 dicker & 2
hides cow & stere & 3 dicker ox lether & 67 dozens of calve
skuyns, all the which cost clere aborde £319 5s   £319 5s

Itm. £91 2s that is for so myche goten by this acowmpt as it
aperith to gaynes in credito fo. 92   £91 2s

S. £1,014 19s 4d

anno 1542

Allom for my owne acowmpt, 4 bagges laden in my ship at
Andaluzia for 8 kyntalls 4 li. & made by my weightes 7 C
1 qr. 17 li., owith 9 V. 361 M. which it cost athe first penny,
for halling 2d, for costom of 4 bagges, 3s, for freight 10s,
montith   [1]

173(R)

anno 1541

Viages per contra is dewe to have the monthes of October,
November & December 196534 M. which is for the nete sale
of 3 truckers, 10 tons 12 C led & 300 hides cow & stere, as it
may apere by Robert Tyndalls acowmpt r. the 4 day of
Aprell anno 1542, all the which goodes war laden in the
John Baptist & Robert Poles ship, as per contra may apere,
montith sterling I sey it is M. 196534   £131 11d

Itm. 729676 M. & it is for the nete sale of 60 London
clothes & of 7 truckers & of 11 whit kerssys & 1 blacke
kerssy   £486 9s

---

[1] Blank in MS.

173(R) contd.

Itm. 20s that is for a blacke kerssy which do rest to sell in Spayne the 2d day of October 1542 of the which kerssy I do make viages debitor fo. 174 — £1

Itm. 157439 M. ½ & is for the sale of 22 ton 7 C led, montith sterling £104 19s 2d — £104 19s 2d

Itm. 390401 M. ½ & it is for the nete sale of 502 hides cow & stere & 130 ox hides & of 219 dozen calve skuyns. Owt of this I must discownt 19 ducatts for 19 hides. So rest clere sterlyng £255 10s 4d — £255 10s 4d

Itm. £21 5s sterlyng, that is for 41 hydes & 27 dozens calve skuyns which rest to selling in Spayne the 18 day of November 1542 whereof I make viages dettor fo. 174 — £20 5s

Itm. 12182 M. & is for the nete sale of 2 weys wheate montith — £8 2s 5d

Itm. £7 13s that is for 3 weys 9 busshells of grene pesson which rest in Spayne to selling & I make viages debitor thereof fo. 174 — £7 13s

[1]

S. £1,014 19s 4d

174(L)   anno 1542

Viages to Biscay into the handes of my prentes Robert Tyndall owith for my owne acowmpt the 20 day of December 235054 M ½ the which he owith to me in redy money for the rest of his acowmpt r. from hym this present day, montith sterling — £156 13s 1d

Itm. more 1 ducatt which he r. of the purser of the Primros & gave me no cowmpt of hit — 5s

95 fanegas ¼

Itm. 11s 4d for 2 kyntalls iren which he r. for me of Pedro Delisardy pillott — 11s 4d

3 ways
9 b of grene pezon
1 black kerssy
41 hides
27 dozen skuyns

Itm. £29 18s that is for 3 wey & 9 busshells grene peson £7 13s & for a black kersy 20s & for 41 hydes & 27 dozen calve skuyns £21 5s, all the which pezon, kersy & lether rest in Spayne unsolld, as it may apere fo. 173 — £29 18s

30 L clothes
1 Bristow frise
2 Manchester cottons

Itm. the 11 day of Aprill anno 1543 lode by Goodes grace in the good ships, the one of them callyd the San John of the Rendry, under God master Johannes de Camon, 2 fardells clothe & in thother ship callyd the John of the Passaige, master Thomas de Naviejas, 1 fardell clothe, the which 3 fardells conteyn 23 clothes of Yerberys & 7 of Hasshis in collores, 11 light grenes & 19 hewlynges, which cost clere abord £120, more for wrappers 1 Bristowe frize valent 20s & 2 Manchesters valent 30s. God send it saff. Montith — £122 10s

20 weys whet
90 hides cow & stere
a C dozen calve skuyns

Itm. the same tyme laden in the Clement of Fromyland, under God master Nicholas Weysford, 20 weyes of whet which cost clere abord £67 15s, more 9 dicker lether cow & stere which I bowght of Lawrence Hanckot & it cost clere abord £22 3s, more a C dozens calve skuyns bowght of the seid Lawrence which cost clere abord £30 15s 10d. So montith the hole laden in this balyngar — £120 13s 10d

80 hides cowe & stere

more in the same balinger lode 8 dickar lether cow & stere wiche cost clere abord £19 13s 4d — £19 13s 4d

30 L clothes
5 hewlow lynardes conteynyng 167 yardes ¼
5 dicker ox
3 dicker cow & stere
210 dozens calve skuyns

Itm. the 30 day of July laden in the Sancta Maria of the Rendry, under God master Domyngo de Lesso, 20 clothes of John Yerberis which cost abord £80 & 3 yelow lynardes conteynyng 107 yerdes ¾ which cost 48s, 5 dicker ox & 3 of cow & stere & a C dozens skuyns cost £56 5s 2d. So montith — £138 13s 2d

Itm. the same tyme, in the San John of the Passaige, master Stevan de Sancta Clara, 10 clothes which cost £40, 2 yelow

---

[1] *There is no credit entry for alum.*

174(L) contd

	lynardes conteynyng 59 yerdes ¾ that cost 32s & 110 dozens skuyns £32 12s	£74 4s
20 clothes 2 Manchesters	Itm. the first day of October anno 1543 lode in the John of the Rendry, master Myghell de Arisavalo, in 2 fardells 20 clothes London sorte & 2 Manchester cottons which cost £81 10s	£81 10s
	Itm. for costes of all the seid goodes & his truble at Bilbo 9 V. 474 M. and for his costes till the 28 day of October 1543, 19 V. 728 M.	£19 9s 4d
	Itm. £77 12s goten by this cowmpt as apere fo. 92	£77 12s
		£841 14s 1d

174(R) anno 1543

3 wayes & 9 bushells grene pesson 1 black kersy 41 hides 25 dozen calve skuyns	Viages per contra is dewe to have for the sale of 3 wayes & 9 busshells grene pezon 19 V. 939 M. & of 1 black kerssy 2 V. 210 M. & of 41 hides & 25 dozens calve skuyns 35 V. 972 M. whiche Tyndall my sarvant have solld at the seid prices, as by his acowmpt r. of Hewgh Guytten the 26 day of November anno dicto may apere, montith sterling	£38 14s 7d
30 L clothes 1 Bristo frise 2 Manchesters	Itm. for the sale of 30 clothes, 1 Bristowe frise & 2 Manchester cottons which I lode in Aprill last past in the San John of the Rendry & the John of the Passage 207 V. 387 M. ½, montith sterling	£138 5s 2d
197 hides cow & stere 170 dozens calve skuyns	Itm. for the sale of a 197 hides cow & stere & of a 170 dozens calve skuyns 220 V. 796 M. as it may apere by his seid reckenyng, montith sterling	3s 11d £147 ~~17s 3d~~
50 L clothes 5 yelow lynardes 2 Manchester cottons 598 fanegas ½ whet 140 dozens calve skuyns 50 ox hides	Itm. 236 V. 312 M. ½ & is for so myche that Tyndall make me creditor of in his seid cowmpt for the £156 14s 1d rest of acowmpt per contra & for 5s r. of the purser of the Prymros & 11s 4d r. of Johannes Delisardy in 2 kyntalls iren, montith sterling	£157 10s 5d
	Itm. more the rest this present 26 day of November anno 1543 in Spayne to selling of my goodes per contra 598 fanegas ½ wheate, 50 London clothes 5 yelow lynardes conteynyng 167 yerdes, 2 Manchester cottons, 140 dozens calve skuyns & 50 ox hides, all the which goodes restyng there unssolld standithe me in £360, as it may apere in debito to viages fo. 196	£360
	S.	£841 14s 1d

175(L) anno 1542

Thomas Traherine of Kermerdyne marchant owithe the 29 daye of November, I sey the first day of December £12 17s 2d½ which is for the rest of his cowmpt fo. 19 & it is payable £6 11s at Mighellmas last past & £3 6s 2d ob at Seynt Androstide last past & £3 at Candellmas next commyng	£12 17s 2d ob
Itm. the 6 day of February £3 that is for so myche redy monney lend to hym to be pd. the myddell of Lent now commyng	£3
Itm. the 8 day of February £3 which is for a pipe of iren sold & delyverd to hym to be pd. in May next commyng	£3

212

175(L) contd.

Itm. the 26 day of February £6 4d for 1 ton 5 li. iren after £6 the ton d'd for hym to his neighbur Thomas Abynon to be paide at all tymes requyrid, at Seynt Jamistide next[1]	£6	4d
1543 Itm. the 30 day of Aprill 1543 £12 11s 8d & is for 2 ton iren & 16 li. to be paide at Mighellmas next as may apere by his bill	£12 11s	8d
Itm. the 5 of February £6 3s 4d & is for 1 ton of iren to be paide at Seynt Jamistide next	£6 3s	4d
1544 Itm. the 30 day of Aprell 1544 £3 7s 1d & is for 1 pipe 7 li. iren of S.S. to be paide at Mighellmas next commyng. It was d'd to his son	£3 7s	1d

anno 1549

Myles Willson of Chepstowe marchant owith the 21 day of Marche £25 which I lent to hym in ready monney to be paide att all tymes requyred	£25

175(R)   anno 1542

Thomas Treharen per contra is dewe to have the 2d day of February £9 17s 2d½ for so myche r. of hym at Bristowe in redy money	£9 17s	2d ob
Itm. the 23 day of February r. from hym by his neighbur Thomas Abynon £3 lent hym as per contra aperith	£3	
Itm. the 26 day of Aprill 1543 he paide to my wif £6 montith	£6	
Itm. the 25 of November 1543 r. of his son John Thomas £12	£12	
Itm. the 3 day of February r. of hym £6 12s	£6 12s	
Itm. the 25 day of November 1544 r. of his son John	£6	
Itm. the 6 day of February 1544 my wif r. of hym £3 10s 5d	£3 10s	5d

Anno 1550

Myles Willson per contra is dewe to have the 23 day of June anno dicto £25 for so myche r. in ready monny for hym of his brother George Willsson	£25

176(L)   anno 1542

88 tons 16 C 3 qr. 17 li.	Iren owith for my proper acowmpt the 3 day of Jenyver £533 which is ffor 88 tons 16 C 3 qr. 17 li. iren *conteynyng* 8192 endes which is for so myche iren that restith this day to sell of acowmpt of iren fo. 153	£533
33 tons 14 C 3 qr. 3 li.	Itm. the 4 day of July 1543 r. owt of the Clement of Fromyland 390 kyntalls more 106 li. of Rendry iren which made by my weightes 28 tons 5 C ½, 21 li. *conteynyng* 2740 endes & it cost clere abord ~~215 V.~~ more 75 kyntalls iren of S.S. which made by my weightes 5 tons 9 C 10 li. *conteynyng* 508 endes, all the which iren cost clere abord 215 V. 220 M. ½, more for freight £30, for costom £3 17s 6d, for hallyng & weying 10s 4d. So montith the hole £177 17s 5d	£177 17s 5d
21 tons pipe, ½ a C, 17 li.	Itm. the 10 day of July r. owt of the good ship callid the Sancta Maria of the Rendry, under God master Domyngo de Lesso, 180 kyntalls more 86 li. Rendry iren & owt of the San John of the Rendry, master Estevan de Sancta Clara, 120 kyntalls more 40 li. Rendry iren, all the which made by my weightes 21 ton, pipe, ½ a C, 17 li. *conteynyng* 2100 endes, all the which iren cost clere aborde 135 V. 608 M., more for freight £20, for costom of 17 tons 42s 6d, for hawllyng & weying 6s 8d, for averes 8d per ton, montith the hole £113 10s 7d	£113 10s 7d

---

[1] at Seynt Jamistide next *inserted later*.

176(L) contd.

21 tons 14 C 27 li.	Itm. the 15 day of December a*nno* 1543 r. ow*t* of the Trynte of the Rendry under God m*aster* Guyllem de Lesso, 255 k*yntall*s 20 li. iren, Rendry weight & ow*t* of the Trynte of Develing 45 k*yntall*s ½, 42 li. iren Rendry weight, the which 300 k*yntall*s 137 li. iren made by my weigh*tes* 21 tons 14 C 27 li. *conteynyng* 2200 end*es*, all the which iren cost clere abord 135 V 148 M, for the freight of 17 tons £17, & for the freight of 3 tons 35s, & for the ~~freight~~ averes of 17 tons at 13d *per* ton, mo*ntith* 18s 5d, for costom of 20 tons 50s, for hawling & waying 6s 8d, mo*ntith* the hole £112 12s 1d	£112	12s 1d
3 tons	Itm. the 22 day of December bowght of Richard Wyllshire broker ow*t* of M*aster* Thorns hows 3 tons iren of S.S. *conteynyng* 283 end*es* for £16 10s & more 12d paide to the broker	£16	11s
	Itm. the 24 day of Jenyver a*nno* 1543 £96 8s 8d which I pass to the cowmpt of gayenes fo. 92	£96	8s 8d
		S. £1,049	19s 9d

176(R)   **anno 1542**

Iren p*er* contra is dewe to have the 8 day of February £85 5s 10d that is for the sale of 14 ton, 1 C 3 qr. 22 li. ½ iren *conteynyng* 1347 end*es* sold sens the 3 day of Jenyver last past at dyvers p*rices*, as by my shop bok may apere	£85	5s 10d
Itm. the 13 day of June a*nno* 1543 £127 17s 4d½ & is for the sale of 20 tons 7 C 13 li. ½ iren *conteynyng* 1903 end*es* solld sens the 8 day of February last past at dyvers tymes & pric*es*, as by my shop booke may apere, mo*ntith*	£127	17s 4d ob
Itm. the last of July £350 4s 5d½ and is for the sale of 56 tons 14 C 1 qr. 1 li. iren *conteynyng* 5360 end*es* solld sens the 13 day of June last past at dyvers tymes & pric*es* as by my shop boke may apere, mo*ntith*	£350	4s 5d ob
Itm. the 24 of Jenyver a*nno* 1543 £386 17s 9d and is for the sale of 61 tons, ½ a C, 25 li. iren *conteynyng* 5690 end*es* solld sens the first daye of Augost last past at dyvers tymes & pric*es* as by my shop boke maye apere	£386	17s
Itm. the seid day £99 15s 1d & is for 16 tons 12 C ½, more 2 li. iren *conteynyng* 1440 end*es* which rest to sell of this acowmpt, the which iren I do pass to a new acowmpt of iren fo. 198 after the price of £6 the ton, mo*ntith*	£99	15s 1d
	S. £1,049	19s 9d

177(L)   **anno 1542**

John Lyndon of Kyngsnorton drap*er* o*with* the 5th daye of February £5 16s 8d that is ffor 1 ton of the Rendry iren laden for hym in Thomas Asevarns trowe, to be paide at Seynt Jamistide next com*m*yng   £5 16s 8d

anno 1542

John Pick*er* of Bristowe groc*er* o*with* the 27 daye of Jenyv*er* ~~12~~ £24 & it is for 2 tons wull oyle solld & delyverd to hym for to be paide at all tymes by me requyrid   ~~12~~ £24

177(R)   **anno 1543**

John Lyndon p*er* contra is dewe to have the 24 of July £5 16s 8d r. of hym at Bristow   £5 16s 8d

177(R) contd.

anno 1543

John Pick*es per* contra is dewe to have the 30 day of July £24 & it is for so myche redy money *that* my wif r. of hym	£24

178(L)   **anno 1542**

Jamys Webster of Mawnchester owithe the 5th daye of February £11 19s 11d & is for 2 to*n* iren solld & delyv*er*d to hym at £6 the ton to be paide at Mydsomer next com*m*yng, or 10 days next after, & his byll for payement is datyd the 7 day of M*ar*ch 1542   £11 19s 11d
1543 Itm. the 28 of July 1543 £12 & is for 2 ton iren solld & delyverd to hym to be paide at Cristmas next com*m*yng   £12
Itm. the 5th day of February £12 & is for 2 ton of Rendry iren after £6 the ton d'd for hym to his s*ar*vant Evan Garlick, to be paide at all tymes requyrid   £12
1544 Itm. the 26 day of M*ar*che 1544 for 2 butt*es* seck at ech 11 nobles & 2 pipes bastard at eche £3 16s 8d, to be paide at all tymes requyrid, mo*ntith* £15   £15
1544 Itm. the 4 day of Augost a*nno* 1544 £12 2d ob & is for 2 ton iren more 4 li, to be at C*a*ndellmas next   £12   2d½

anno 1542

~~William~~ Richard Smythe of Coventry m*a*rchant owith the 5th day of February 33s 4d that is for so myche he rest owing for 3 h'd claret wyne to be paide at all tymes by me requyrid   £1 13s 4d
Itm. the 26 day of February £4 which is for the rest of 5 butt*es* of seck & 1 p*i*pe bastard solld to hym at £4 the pece as in my shop boke may apere   £4

178(R)   **anno 1543**

Jamys Webster p*er* contra is dewe to have the 24 day of July £11 19s 11d r. of hym at Bristowe in redy mo*nn*ey   £11 19s 11d
Itm. the 4 day of February r. of his s*ar*vau*nt* £12   £12
Itm. the 26 of July 1544 r. by Garlick £12   £12
Itm. the 13 of Octob*er* r. of hym £7 6s 8d   £7 6s 8d
Itm. £7 13s 4d for 2 pipes bastard which I solld forbecawse he fott not the*m* at his day apoyntyd, yet I gave hym 3s 4d for amend*es*   £7 13s 4d
Itm. my wif r. from hym by Myles Willson ~~son to Rowland Will~~ £4   £4
Itm. the last day of Octob*er* £8 which W*illia*m Smothyng pd. to J*oh*n Sp*ar*k for me as may apere   £8

anno 1542

Richard Smythe p*er* contra is dewe to have the 26 day of February 5 nobles r. of hym in redy mo*nn*ey   £1 13s 4d
Itm. the 9 day of Maye a*nno* 1543 £4 for so myche he paide at Bristowe to my wif   £4

179(L)   **anno 1542**

1 p*ipe* ½   Oylles for my prop*er* acowmpt owith the 27 daye of Jenyver £6 13s 4d that is for a pipe of oyle & hallf a pipe & forbecawse the pipe is corruptyd by reason it ffell ow*t* into the lighter & was ge*ther*d up ageyn I do valure it but at the seid price   £6 13s 4d
4 p*i*pes   Itm. the 14 day of February r. ow*t* of my ship the Try*n*te, under God m*a*ster Thomas Web, 4 pipes wull oyle which cost clere abord 25242 M., for freight 30s p*er* ton, for custom 4s p*er* ton, for averes 12d p*er* ton, for haling & stowyng 4d p*er* ton, for rebating 16d p*er* ton, mo*ntith* all   £20 9s 11d
6 p*i*pes   Itm. the 27 day of the same r. ow*t* of the Harry, m*a*ster

179(L) contd.

Antony Pickett, 6 pipes oyle which cost clere aborde 37 V. 881 M., for freight 30s p*er* ton, for costom 4s p*er* ton, for av*er*es 13d p*er* ton, for haling & stowing 4d p*er* to*n*, for rebating 16d p*er* ton, mo*ntith* all	£30	15s	4d
It*m*. the 22 of Jenyver 1543 £25 19s 7d goten by this cowmpt as it may apere to gaynes in credito fo. 92	£25	19s	7d
S.	£83	18s	2d

anno 1544

37 p*ipe*s

Oyles for wull & for my acowmpt prop*er* 37 pipes of the which 7 p*ipe*s war laden in the Mary Bulleyne, 20 pipes in the Mary Jamys & 10 pipes in the Mary Co*n*ception, which cost clere abord 220 V. 462 M., for freight in the Mary Bulleyn 28s p*er* to*n* & 12d p*er* ton of av*er*es, for freight of 19 pipes in the Mary James at 40s p*er* ton & 11d the av*er*es p*er* ton, & for freight in the Mary Conception of 5 tons at 40s p*er* ton & av*er*es 10d p*er* ton, for costom 4s p*er* ton, for halyng & stowyng 4d p*er* ton, for rebating 16d p*er* ton, mo*ntith* all	£186	15s	10d
It*m*. the 16 day of M*a*rche £52 4s 2d & is for so myche gaynes had in this oyle as it may apere to gaynes in credito fo. 200	£52	4s	2d
S.	£239		

179(R)

anno 1542

1	Oyles p*er* contra is dewe to have the 28 daye of February £6 13s 4d r. of Richard Smythe of Coventry for a pipe of oyle		£6	13s	4d
1	*1543* It*m*. the 23 day of June 1543 £7 10s & is for a p*ipe* oyle solld & d'd to Richard Syms fo. 182		£7	10s	
2	It*m*. the 23 of July £15 for 1 to*n* oyle to R. Pryn fo. 156		£15		
2	It*m*. th*e* 10 day of *A*ugost £15 for a ton to Thom*as* Thurston fo. 164		£15		
4	It*m*. the 8 of Octobe*r* £30 r. in calve skuyns of Jo*h*n Wells & Lueys Skuynnar for 2 to*n* oyle at £15 the ton		£30		
1	It*m*. the 12 of Octobe*r* £7 10s for a pipe to W*illiam* Baylis fo. 194		£7	10s	
	It*m*. the 22 day of Jenyver 44s 10d & is ffor 29 gallons, 3 quart*es*, 1 pynt of oyle solld to W*illiam* Bulloc 131		£2	4s	10d
		S.	£83	18s	2d

anno 1544

2	Oyles p*er* contra be dewe to have the 17 day of July £14 which is for 2 pipes solld to ~~hym~~ Jo*h*n Yerbery fo. 201	£14	
4	It*m*. the 23 of July for 4 p*ipe*s to T. Machyn fo. 154	£28	
2	It*m*. the 26 of July for 2 pipes to T. Byck fo. 208	£14	
2	It*m*. the 6 of Augost for 2 p*ipe*s to T. Machyn fo. 154	£14	

179(R) contd.

1	Itm. the 9 of Augost for 1 p*ipe* to R. Justice fo. [1]	£7
2	Itm. the 22 of Augost for 2 pipes to Allen Hill 117	£14
4	Itm. the 1 day of September for 4 p*ipe*r to T. Abeck 168	£30
4	Itm. 1 p*ipe* clene ow*t* in the Mary Bride & 3 p*ipe*s to yllage	[1]
2	Itm. the first day of Octo*ber* for a to*n* to J*oh*n Cut 27	£14
2	Itm. the 11 day of Octo*ber* for a ton to J*oh*n Walker 225	£14
2	Itm. the 25 of October for 1 to*n* to J*oh*n Yerbery 201	£14
6	Itm. the 9 of Decem*ber* for 3 tons to T. Abeck	£45
1	Itm. the 12 of Decem*ber* for 1 pipe to J*oh*n Yerbery which he pd.	£7
3	Itm. the 16th day of March for 3 p*ipe*s to Allen Hill 117	£24
37 pipes		S. £239

180(L)   anno 1542

20 b. sek
17 p*ipe*s b.
2 pipes
taynt

Wynes of Andaluzia for my owne acowmpt, that is to sey 20 butt*es* of seck, 17 pipes of bastard & 2 pipes of taynt r. the 14 day of February ow*t* of my ship the Trynte, under God m*a*ster Thomas Web, owithe for freight 30s *per* ton & for the pryncypall *that* it all cost clere aborde the ship 113 V. 920 M., ffor coston of 17 tons at 3s *per* ton, hallyng & strykyng 6s 4d, for hoping 3s 4d, for av*e*res 4s 4d *per* ton, mo*ntith* the hole £112 9s 1d   £112   9s   1d

20 b seck

Itm. the 26 day of February, 58 V. 713 M. for so myche 20 butt*es* seck r. owt of the Mary Con*ception did cost clere abord the ship, for custo*m* of 9 ton at 3s *per* ton, hallyng & strekyng 3s 4d, hopyng 20d, av*e*res 4s 2d *per* ton, mon*tith* all   £42   8s
more for freight of 9 ton pipe at 30s *per* ton   £14   5s

20 b

Itm. the 7 day of M*a*rche r. owt of the Portyngall ship which J*oh*n Gorney freightyd 19 butt*es* of seck & 1 butt of hulloc which cost clere abord 61 V. 581 M. for the freight of 10 to*n* at 21s, I sey 21s 3d *per* ton, for costo*m* of 9 to*n* at 3s *per* ton, & haling strekyng & hopyng 6s 8d, for av*e*res 4s 8d ob *per* ton, £41 13d   £41   1s   1d

03 b

Itm. the 11 day of Ap*re*ll 1543, £12 which is for 3 butt*es* at £4 the butt which Jamys Tizo*n* paide unto me for a det of his brother Nicholas   £12

07 b

Itm. the 4 of June 1543 £25 6s 8d & is for 7 butt*es* seck bowght of J*oh*n Sachefylld   £25   6s   8d

Itm. the 27 of September 1543 £72 16s 10d & is for so myche goten by this acowmpt, as it may apere to gaynes in credito fo. 92   £72   16s   10d

                                                         S.   £320   6s   8d

180(R)   anno 1542

1 but seck
3 p*ipe*s b

Wynes hereageynst owithe the 15 daye of February [1] that is for 1 butt of seck & 3 pipes bastard which war drawen to ylladge for to fyll all the wynes in the Trynte *per* contra   [1]

---

[1] *Blank in MS.*

180(R) contd.

2 butt*es* ½	Itm. for 1 but seck & ½ *that* went to yllage in the Conception & 1 butt ow*t*			[1]
1 pipe b	Itm. the 15 of February £4 for 1 p*ipe* bastard to *the* prise ow*t* of the Trynte	£4		
½ a but	Itm. to yllaige of the 20 butt*es* in the Portyngall			
½ a pipe	½ a butt of seck & ½ a pipe bastard			[1]
2 b	Itm. the 16 of February £16 13s 4d for 2 butt*es*			
2 pipes	seck & 2 pipes bastard to Susan Gibs & Allson Bisshop of Bridgewater as in my shop boke may apere	£16	13s	4d
2 b	Itm. the 19 of the same £8 for 2 butt*es* seck to R. Caryck, 34	£8		
1 b	Itm. £4 for a but seck to Alexander Bosgrove 68	£4		
1 b	Itm. £8 6s 8d for a but seck & 1 p*ipe* bastard to			
1 pipe	*Joh*n Roxby fo. 162	£8		
1 b	Itm. £4 for a but seck to *Joh*n Hamo*n* fo. 77	£4		
2 b	Itm. the 20 of February £16 for 2 butt*es* seck & 2			
2 pipes	pipes bastard to W*illiam* Smothing fol. 72	£16		
2 butt*es*	Itm. £24 13s 4d for 2 butt*es* seck, 3 pipes bastard			
4 pipes	& 1 pipe taynt to *Joh*n Roxby fo. 162	£24	13s	4d
1 butt	Itm. £8 for 1 but seck & 1 p*ipe* bastard to			
1 pipe	W*illiam* Goldsmythe 113	£8		
1 b	Itm. £8 for 1 but seck & 1 p*ipe* bastard to			
1 pipe	W*illiam* Northe fo. 141	£8		
2 b	Itm. the 23 of February £8 for 2 buttes seck to *Joh*n W*illiam*s of Castellnethe fo. 133	£8		
1 pipe	Itm. the 26 of February £24 for 5 butt*es* seck &			
5 butt*es*	1 pipe bastard to Richard Smythe fo. 178	£24		
1 b	Itm. £8 6s 8d for 1 butt seck & 1 pipe bastard to			
1 pipe	Alexander Bosgrove fo. 68	£8	6s	8d
4 butt*es*	Itm. the 6 of M*a*rche £16 for 4 butt*es* to W*illiam* Northe 141	£16		
2 butt*es*	Itm. the 7 of M*a*rche £8 for 2 butt*es* to Alice Smythe 18	£8		
7 butt*es*	Itm. the 8 day of M*a*rche £28 for 7 butt*es* to *Joh*n Roxby fo. 162	£28		
1 pipe	Itm. the 10 day r. of W*illiam* Jonys for a p*ipe* taynt £4 10s	£4	10s	
2 b	Itm. £8 for 2 butt*es* to Water Ru*m*ney fo. 157	£8		
1 b	Itm. the 13 of M*a*rche £4 for a butt to Tippar fo. 142	£4		
1 b	Itm. the 17 of M*a*rche £4 for 1 butt to T. Turbot 23	£4		
2 b	Itm. the 3 of Aprill 1543 £8 for 2 but*es* to W*illiam* Smothing fo. 72	£8		
1 b	Itm. the 7 day Ap*ri*lis £4 for a but to Davy Hart 160	£4		
1 b	Itm. the 12 day £4 for a but to R. Prynce fo. 184	£4		
1 b	Itm. the same day r. £4 of *Joh*n Hamo*n* for 1 butt	£4		
4 b	Itm. the 19 day for 4 butt*es* to R. Carryck fo. 34	£16		
1 b	Itm. the 8 day of May £4 for 1 but to Roxby fo. 162	£4		
2 b	Itm. the 29 day £8 for 2 butt*es* to Bosgrove fo. 68	£8		
4 b	Itm. the 30 of May £16 for 4 butt*es* to R. Carryck 34	£16		
1 b	Itm. the 4 of June £4 6s 8d for 1 butt to Also*n* Bisshop 152	£4	6s	8d
1 b	Itm. the same day for 1 butt to Susan Gibs fo. 126	£4	6s	8d
1 b	Itm. the 8 of June for 1 butt to W*illiam* Nasche fo. 185	£4	6s	8d
1 b	Itm. the 18 of July £4 ~~6s 8d~~ for 1 but to Sp*a*rk fo. 186	£4		

---

[1] *Blank in MS.*

180(R) contd.

2 b	Itm. the 26 of July r. for 2 butt*es* £8 6s 8d	£8	6s	8d
1 b	Itm. the 27 of July sold to J*oh*n Hamond 1 butt fo. 77 for	£4	6s	8d
2 b	Itm. the 1 of September for 2 butt*es* to W*illiam* Smothing 72	£8		
	Itm. the 22 of September for 1 butt to W*illiam* Nasche fo. [1]	£4	10s	
	S.	£320	6s	8d

181(L) anno 1542

Will*ia*m Sprat m*a*rchant of Bristowe o*with* the 7 daye of February 53s 3d which is for the rest of freight for 7 to*n* iren laden my ship the Trynte in Augost last past £2 13s 4d

Itm. the 18 day of the same £3 15s which is for the freight of 2 to*n* pipe wyne laden fro*m* Andaluzia in my ship the Trynte, to paye hallf in hand & hallf at the end of 3 monthes next £3 15s

a*nno* 1549

Nicholas Kellway of Bristowe hop*er* o*with* the 5th day of Dece*m*b*er* £5 & is for a ton of corrupt Gasco*n* wyne & 1 p*ipe* of corrupt bastard to be paide at Whitsontyde next com*m*yng £5
passed this cownt to my newe booke fo. 9

anno 1542

Robert P*re*ssy of Bristowe m*a*rchant o*with*e the 18 day of February £6 that is for the freight of 4 ton wyne in my ship at 30s the ton, to pay hallf in hand & the other hallf 3 monthes next after £6

181(R) anno 1543

Will*ia*m Sprat p*er* contra is dewe to have the 13 daye of Aprill 4 m*a*rkes which my s*ar*vaunt Lett r. of his wif £2 13s 4d
Itm. the 27 of July 1543 r. of hym £3 15s £3 15s
[2]

anno 1542

Robert P*re*ssy p*er* contra is dewe to have the 28 daye of February £3 r. of hym in redy mon*n*ey £3
Itm. the 23 day of June a*nno* 1543 r. of hym £3 £3

182(L) anno 1542

Thomas Harrys m*a*rchant of Bristowe o*with* the 18 day of February £7 10s which is for the freight of 5 tons oyle in my ship at 30*s* p*er* ton, to pay hallf in hand & hallf 3 monthes next com*m*yng £7 10s
1543 Itm. the 15 of June a*nno* 1543 £18 4d ob & is for 3 to*n* 7 li. Rendry iren d'd in his name to M*a*rtyne Grevys at £6 the ton to be paide at Seynt Jamistide next £18 4d ob
Itm. the last day of Augost £50 13s 8d whiche is for 4 tons of S.S. iren at 20 nobles the ton & 4 ton more 6 li. Rendry iren at £6 the ton solld & delyverd to hym to be pd. at all tymes £50 13s 8d

---

[1] *Blank in MS.*
[2] *There is no credit entry for Kellway.*

182(L) contd.

Itm. the 5th day of March £74 13s 4d & is for 16 buttes of seck at 11 nobles the butt & 4 pipes of bastard at £4 the pipe to be paide at Seynt Jamystide next commyng	£74 13s 4d
1544 Itm. the fyrst day of Aprell anno 1544 £13 6s 8d & is for the freight of 10 tons iren in the Trynte my ship from Spayne this present viage, to pay hallf in hand & the other ½ at thend of 3 monthes next commyng	£13 6s 8d
Itm. the 5 of Maye 1544 £25 13s 4d & is for 7 buttes seck solld & d'd to hym at eiche 11 nobles	£25 13s 4d
Itm. the 14 day of February for 1 dozen ores d'd to John Richardes purser of the Conception 16s	16s
Itm. the 30 day of August anno 1546 for 3 C 35 li. gownpoder at ¹ d ob per li. & ffor 6 lere h'd at 10d per hogshed, montith²	1

anno 1542

Richard Sawnders marchant of Bristowe owith the 18 daye of February £9 that is for the freight of 6 ton wyne in the Trynte at 30s per ton, to pay hallf in hand & thother hallf 3 monthes next after	£9

anno 1543

William Syms of Bristowe sopemaker owith the 23 daye of June £7 10s & is for a pipe of wull oyle sold & d'd to hym, to be paide at Cristmas next	£7 10s

182(R)

anno 1542

Thomas Harrys per contra is dewe to have the 26 day of February £3 15s which Hewgh Hamon r. of hym	£3 15s
Itm. the 14 of June 1543 r. of hym £3 15s	£3 15s
Itm. the 11 day of August r. of Thomas Harrys £18 & 4d ob I allowyd hym for the wyne	£18 4d ob
Itm. the last day of August £50 13s 4d for so myche past to Mastres Cristyan Whites cowunt fo. 212	£50 13s 4d
Itm. the 5 day of March £74 13s 4d for so myche past to Mastress Whites cowmpt fo. 212	£74 13s 4d
Itm. the 23 day of July 1544 for the freight of 5 ton oyle in the Mary Conception	£10
Itm. the 12 day of July	³
Itm. the 20 day of June 1545 r. by the handes of Lawrence Vyne £12	£12
Itm. for averes of 30 Manchesters & 10 clothes valurid 16 clothes at 85 M. per clothe, montith sterlyng	18s
Itm. for averis of 5 tons oyle at 204 M. per ton	13s 7d ob
Itm. the 7 day of May 1546 r. of hym £10⁴	£10

anno 1542

Richard Sawnders per contra is dewe to have the 26 of February £4 10s which Hamon r. of hym	£4 10s
Itm. the 27 of July 1543 £4 r. of hym	£4

anno 1543

William Syms per contra is dewe to have the 2d daye of Jenyver 1543 £7 10s for so mych r. of hym in redy monney	£7 10s

---

[1] Blank in MS.
[2] The whole of Thomas Harris' account is crossed through.
[3] An item here is crossed through and is illegible in the MS.
[4] The whole of Thomas Harris' account is crossed through.

183(L)

anno 1542

	Alice Smythe[1] my mother owithe the 18 day of February 30s that is for the freight of 1 ton oyle in my ship the Trynte this viage from Andaluzia	£1	10s
	1543 Itm. the 30 day of Julye a*nno* 1543 £6 & is for 1 ton iren d'd to her to be pd. at Cristmas next	£6	
	Itm. the 10th day of Septemb*er* £3 8d & is for 2 hallf bales of Tullus wood weying 3 C ½, 8 li. at 17s the C, which I delyverd & sold to her	£3	8d

anno 1548

17 p*ipe*s wull oyle	Oylles for wull for my *p*roper acowmpt owith the 3de day of Jenyver a*nno* dicto 129 V. 058 M. & is for so myche that 17 pipes oyle r. ow*t* of the Hart cost clere aborde at the fyrst pen*n*y, which amo*ntith* sterlyng at 6s p*er* d*u*catt £106 5s, more for ffreight at 35s p*er* ton, for averes 14d p*er* ton, for custom 4s p*er* ton, for hallyng 4d p*er* ton, for rebatyng 20d p*er* ton, mon*tith* all £124 5s 5d	£124 5s	5d
1 p*ipe* oyle	Itm. the 29 of Jenyver r. ow*t* of the Savyor of Bristowe 1 p*ipe* of wull oyle which cost clere abord 20 d*u*catts 95 M., valeut at 6s p*er* d*u*catt £6 1s 4d, for freight 16s 8d, for custom 2s, for averes 3d ob, for hawlyng 2d, for rebatyng 10d, mon*tith* £7 15d ob	£7 1s	3d ob
	Itm. the last day of Jenyver £44 13s 3d ob & is for so myche gaynes had at the closyng up of this acowmpt	£44 13s	3d ob
	S.	£176	

anno 1549

20 p*ipe*s	Oyles, I sey wull oyles, 20 pipes for my acowmpt r. the [2] day of Septemb*er* ow*t* of the Savy*o*r of Bristowe owith 186 V. 832 M. which is 491 d*u*catts 12 M. whiche it did cost clere abord as by Hewgh Tiptons acowmpt may apere, mo*ntith* sterlyng valuryng the d*u*catt at 6s £147 6s 2d	£147 6s	2d
	for freight 30s p*er* ton	£15	
	for costom 4s p*er* ton	£2	
	for halyng 4d p*er* ton	3s	4d
	for hopyng & rebatyng 18d p*er* ton	15s	
	for generall averes with the gage 17d p*er* ton	14s	2d
	for grose averes of ev*er*y ton oyle valuryd in £12 2d ob p*er* libra	£1 5s	
	Itm. the 28 of November £44 16d & is for the gayenes had by the sale of this 20 p*ipe*s wull oyle	£44 1s	4d
	S.	£211 5s	

183(R)

[3]

anno 1548

4 p*ipe*s	Oyles p*er* contra is dewe to have the 19th day of Jenyver £36 & is for 4 p*ipe*s solld & d'd to J*o*hn Wells of Bristowe sopemaker fo. 129	£36	

---

[1] Smythe *is inserted above the line.*
[2] *Blank in MS.*
[3] *There is no credit entry for Alice Smythe.*

13 pipes	Itm. the last day of Jenyver £130 & is for 6 tons 1 pipe of oyle solld & d'd to Master William Pikes Mayer of Bristowe at £20 the ton as it maye appere in fo. 97		£130	
1 pipe	Itm. the 25 of Jenyver £10 & is for one pipe oyle to N. Mawrewood as it may apere fo. 260		£10	
		S.	£176	

anno 1549

02	Oyles per contra is dewe to have the 4th day of September £22 for 2 pipes sold to William Mathews fo. 294		£22	
06	Itm. the 10th of September for 6 pipes to William Beryne fo. 294		£63	
02	Itm. the same day for 2 pipes to Thomas Cowper fo. 218		£22	
02	Itm. the 12 of September for 2 pipes to William Ayre fo. 239		£22	
01	Itm. the 15 of September £10 10s for 1 pipe to John Strowd fo. 295		£10	10s
04	Itm. the 18 of September for 4 pipes to Master Pikes fo. 296		£44	
02	Itm. the same day for 2 pipes to William Brydges fo. 293		£22	
½ a pipe	Itm. the 28 of November my wif r. for ½ a pipe oyle		£5	15s
½ a pipe	Itm. drawen to ylladge ½ a pipe oyle			
20 pipes		S.	£211	5s

[1]

184(L)   anno 1543

Richard Prynce clarck of the churche of Allhallows in Bristowe owith the 12 day of Aprell £4 which is for a butt of seck sold & d'd to hym to be pd. at Seynt Jamistide next	£4
1544 Itm. the 18 day of September anno 1544 £6 which is for 1 ton of iren solld & d'd to hym to be pd. at Candellmas next	£6

anno 1549

John Tucker of Bruton owith the 12 day of November for 4 C Yland woode d'd for hym to John Penny at 13s 4d the C	£2	13s	4d
Itm. the 10th of December d'd for hym to Thomas Jamys 2 C woode	£1	6s	8d

anno 1543

Nicolas Kelly of Bristowe hoper owithe the 24 day of Aprell £3 6s 8d which is for a pipe of S.S. iren solld & d'd to hym to be paide at Mighellmas next commyng	£3	6s	8d
Itm. the 26 day of July £3 6s 8d & is for a pipe of S.S. iren sold & d'd for hym to John Turlo of Rancom to be paide at Mighellmas next	£3	6s	8d
Itm. the 30 day of the same monthe £6 & is for 1 ton iren sold & d'd to hymseallf to be paide at Cristmas next commyng	£6		
Itm. the 15 of December 25s 8d to be pd. at Ester next that he is shewerty for the rest of 8 C 4 li. iren d'd to William Pyncket of Tedbery	£1	5s	8d

---

[1] *Blank in MS.*

184(L) contd.

Itm. the 22 of July £6 & is for 1 ton Rendry iren to be paide at Cristmas next com*m*yng	£6
Itm. the 23 day of July 1545 for 2 to*n* ire*n* at 19 nobles p*er* ton & for 1 C 3 qr. 15 li. allem at 23s *per* C, mon*tith* all £14 16s 8d ob	£14 16s 8d ob
Itm. the 28 of Ap*r*ell 1547 £16 & is for 2 tons ire*n* of S.S. to be paide at *Cris*tmas next com*m*yng as it may apere by his obligac*i*on	£16
Itm. the 6 of Augost for 1 pipe & a hallf corrupt bastard	£2 10s
Itm. £6 13s 4d which I lent hym in redy mon*n*ey	£6 13s 4d

184(R)   **anno 1543**

Richard Prince p*er* contra is dewe to have the 22 daye of Augost 40s for so myche r. of hym in mon*n*y	£2
Itm. the 14 daye of Novem*b*er r. of hym 40s	£2
Itm. the 18 of February a*nn*o 1544 my wif r. of hym £6	£6

a*n*no 1550

Jo*h*n Tucker p*er* contra is due to have the 20 of June £4 r. for hym in Bristowe of Thomas Yerbery son to Jo*h*n Yerbery of Bruton	£4

anno 1543

Nicholas Kelly p*er* contra is dewe to have the 25 of July £3 6s 8d r. of Jo*h*n Turlo of Rancum	£3 6s 8d
Itm. the 12 of Decem*b*er r. of hym £6	£6
Itm. r. of Nycolas Kelly the 19 of Jenyver for Jo*h*n Turlo 3 barrells herryng in 50s & in money 16s 8d, mo*ntith* the hole	£3 6s 8d
Itm. the 23 of June 1544 my wif r. of hym 25s 8d	£1 5s 8d
Itm. for 2 h'd claret wyne £3 13s 4d	£3 13s 4d
Itm. 46s 8d r. the 19 day of Jenyver 1544	£2 6s 8d
Itm. the 3 day of M*a*rche a*n*no 1545 r. £6 ~~6s 8d~~ 13s 4d	£6 13s 4d
Itm. the 13 day of M*a*rche r. of hym £8 3s 4d	£8 3s 4d
Itm. the 17 day of February a*n*no 1547 r. of hym in mon*n*ey £16 all in gold	£16
1549 Itm. the fyrst day of June he geve me acownt of 59s which I owe hym for 2 barells herryng & other fische which I had of hym	£2 19s
Itm. r. by thand*es* of my wif the seide day in ready mon*n*ey £6 4s 4d	£6 4s 4d

185(L)   **anno 1543**

Thomas Whaley of Bristowe tanner owith the 5 daye of June £6 6s 8d & is f*or* 1 ton of my bett*er* Rendry iren iren[1] solld & d'd to hym to be paide by his bill at Allhaloutide next, mon*tith*	£6 6s 8d

anno 1550

36 Oylles I sey wull oyles for my owne acowmpt 36 pip*es* whereof r. ow*t* of the Savy*or* of Bristowe 24 pipes, ow*t* of the Mary Conception of Bristowe 8 pipes & ow*t* of the Sant Espirit*us* of the Port of Portyngall 4 pipes owithe the monthe of May a*nno* dicto 384 V. 025 M. for so myche it

---

[1] *Smythe repeats* iren.

185(L) contd.

cost clere aboorde as by Hugh Hamons acowmpt may apere & hit amon*tith* sterlyng acowntyn*g* 6s 8d for ev*ery* dockett, being 1024 d*ucatts* 25 M., £341 7s	£341	7s
Itm. for Leight & Hamon*des* cost*es* 30 d*ucatts*	£10	
Itm. for freight of 12 tons in the Savyo*r* at 40s p*er* ton & for av*eres* of the same 15d p*er* ton & for freight in the Mary Conception of 4 tons at 40s p*er* ton & for av*eres* of the same 16d p*er* ton & for freight in the Sant Espyritu*s* of 2 tons at 26s 3d p*er* to*n* & for av*eres* of the same 19d p*er* ton, mon*tith* the whole £35 16s	£35	16s
Itm. for custom of 18 tons at 4s p*er* ton for hawlyng 4d p*er* to*n* & for rebatyng 2s p*er* ton, mon*tith* the whole £5 14s	£5	14s
Itm. £101 13s goten by this cowmpt the 2de day of July 1550	£101	13s
	S. £493	10s

anno 1543

Will*iam* Nasche of Bristowe nottary owith the 8 daye of June £4 6s 8d & is for a butt of seck sollnd & delyv*erd* to hym to be paide at Mighellmas next	£4	6s	8d
Itm. the 22 day of Septemb*er* £4 10s & is for 1 butt of seck sollnd & delyv*erd* to hym to be paide at Candellmas next comyng	£4	10s	
Itm. the first day of M*arche* £8 & is for a butt of seck & a pipe bastard at ech £4 to be paid at Seynt Jamistide next com*m*yng	£8		

185(R)

anno 1544

Thomas Whaley p*er* contra is dewe to have £5 which he pd. to my wif the 29 of July	£5		
Itm. the 13 of Septemb*er* I r. of T. Whaly 26s 8d	£1	6s	8d

a*nno* 1550

10	Oyles p*er* contra is due to have the 2de day of May £140 & is for 10 pipes oyle sollnd & d'd to W*illiam* Pik*es* fo. 296 at £28 the ton, mon*tith*	£140	
2	Itm. the 7 of May £29 10s for 2 p*ipes* to Rog*er* Taylor fo. 275	£29	10s
4	Itm. the 10 of Maye £58 for 4 p*ipes* to T. Thu*rston* fo. 164	£58	
1	Itm. the 14 of Maye r. of Thomas Trayguss of Mells for 1 p*ipe* £14	£14	
8	Itm. the 19 of Maye £112 for 4 tons to Nycolas Shee fo. 165	£112	
2	Itm. the 28 of Maye £28 for 2 p*ipes* to Thomas Clark for H. Hamo*n* fo. 166	£28	
2	Itm. the 31 of Maye £29 for 2 p*ipes* to Henry Wyeth fo. 211	£29	
2	Itm. the 2de daye of June £28 for 2 p*ipes* to W*illiam* Beryn fo. 294	£28	
1	Itm. the 13 of Maye £15 for a p*ipe* of mete oyle to J*ohn* Sprynt fo. 288	£15	
1	Itm. the 18 of June for 1 p*ipe* to Edmond Hanckott fo. 279	£14	
1	Itm. the 2de day of July £4 I sey £4 for the t*ierce* of a p*ipe* oyle lost of a pipe broken to		

185(R) contd.

	ylladge which I pass to my newe booke in debito fo. 34	£4
2	Itm. the same day £44 £22 & is for 2 pipes which I pass to my seid newe boke into fo. 34 for to make evyn this cownt	£22
		£493 10s

anno 1543

William Nasche per contra is dewe to have the
14 daye of September £4 6s 8d r. of hym in redy
monny   £4 6s 8d
Itm. the last day of February r. of hym £4 10s   £4 10s
Itm. the 11 day of October 1544 r. by Robert Cator   £4
Itm. the 21 day of Jenyver r. of hym 40s   £2
Itm. r. of Edward Jones for hym   £1
Itm. the 10 day of Awgost r. of E. Jones 20s   £1

186(L)   **anno 1543**

John Sparke of Newenham yeoman owith the 4 day of July £20 which I
paide to hym at Bristowe in redy money   £20
Itm. the 18 of July £4 that is for a but of seck to be paide at all tymes   £4 13s 4d
Itm. the 31 day of the same £19 10s 8d that I pay to hym in redy money   £19 10s 8d
Itm. the last day of August £20 for so myche d'd to hym in redy monney for
to by lether & calve skuyns for me   £20
Itm. the 14 day of September 1543 paide to hym in redy money £20   £20
Itm. the 3 day of October £20 which my wif delyverd to hym in redy monney   £20
Itm. the 17 day of October £21 16s pd. to hym at Bristowe this present day
in redy money   £21 16s
Itm. 13 nobles which he must pay for William Smothing, as it apere to
William Smothing in credito fo. 72   £4 6s 8d
Itm. the 14 of November paide to hym at Bristowe in redy monney £17 13s 4d   £17 13s 4d
Itm. the 13 day of June 1545 pd. to hym in redy money 24s 8d   £1 4s 8d

             Solmd.   £148 4s 8d

anno 1549

Robert Wyeth of Lughburn in the cowmpty of Lysetter gentleman owithe the
19 of Marche £21 16s 8d & is for 20 C woode at 13s 4d the C & 1 butt of
seck price £5 & 2 h'd of claret Gascon wyne at £3 10s, to pay 20 markes
the 1 day of May next commyng & £8 10s the at Mydsomer next after that   £21 16s 8d
1550 Itm. the 30 day of May anno 1550 £80 10s 9d ob & is for 3 tons more
7 li. iren of S.S. at £12 10s per ton & for 1 ton of wull oyle price £29 & for
2 tons of Gascon wyne at £7 the ton, to pay £40 5s 9d ob at Bartyllmewetide
next commyng & £40 5s at Mighellmas next after that, all which goodes
war laden in Hugh Skelars trowe & Richard Pawllmers trowe of Bewdeley
passed this cowmpt to my newe booke fo. 10   £80 10s 9d ob

186(R)   **anno 1543**

John Spark of Newenham in the Forrest of Deane yeoman
is dewe to have the 4 day of May £20 which is for so
myche I owe hym to be paide at all tymes for the rest of
acowmpt fo. 155, & there rest this present day for my
acowmpt at Newenham in the seid Sparkes howse & in his
kepyng 5 dicker of ox lethir, won hide of a stere or cow &
163 dozens of calve skuyns to be d'd to me or to my assygnes

186(R) contd.

at all tymes requyrid & I have pd. hym for all the seid le*ther* & skyns saving the foreseid £20	£20		
Itm. the 30 day of July £18 10s 8d which is for 47 dozens calve skuyns at 5s 4d p*er* dozen & 3 dicker of hid*es* cow & stere at 40s the ~~dozen~~ dicker, the which lether & skuyns was laden abord the Sancta Maria of the Rendry & the San J*oh*n of the Passage with won with all the le*ther* & skuyns above mencynyd in the itm. before this	£18	10s	8d
Itm. more 20s for carrying of all my saide le*ther* to Kyttells wood aborde the seid shipps	£1		
Itm. the 14 day of September for 2 long pec*es* of chestnutt tymb*er* at 10s the pece & for won hundred bord*es* for my bote ~~20~~ 40s & for 1 kelle & stem & stern post for my bote ~~12d~~, for 3 C beche boord at 2s p*er* C, 7 knees 12s	£3	18s	
Itm. the 17 day of Octob*er* £81 16s which is for 18 dicker & ½ lether cowe & stere, 6 dicker ox le*ther* & 113 dozens calve skuyns which he bowght for me & all do rest & remayne to kepe in the seid Sparck*es* howse, to be d'd to me or to myne assygne at all tymes requyrid, as by a byll indentyd more largely do apere	£81	16s	
Itm. the 14 day of Novemb*er* £22 16d & is for 6 dicker ox at 4 m*ar*kes 3s 4d the dicker & 19 dozens calve skuyns at 5s 4d p*er* dozen, the which he have bowght for me & the seid le*ther* & skuyns remaynith in his keping at his hows in won with the foreseid le*ther* to be d'd to me or to myne assygnes at all tymes	£22	1s	4d
Itm. 20s for 1 botes ladyng to my ship	£1		
S.	£148	4s	8d

anno 1550

Robert Wyeth p*er* contra is due to have the 29 of Aprell £13 6s 8d & is for so myche r. from hym by the hand*es* of his brother Henry Wyethe	£13	6s	8d

187(L)   **anno 1542**

Will*ia*m Buchar ~~is dewe to have~~ ow*ith* the 13 day of February a*n*no 1543 £10 which I pd. to hym in redy mon*n*ey	£10		
1544 Itm. the 28 of July 1544 £14 10s for so myche paide to hym in redy mon*n*ey	£14	10s	
1545 Itm. the 29 day of July 1545 £14 10s which I paide to hym for the full paym*en*t of the £29 p*er* contra & r. my byll	£14	10s	
Itm. the 21 day of Augost paide to his son J*oh*n Buchar £5, more pd. to hymseallf the 2d day of September £5, mon*tith* bothe p*ar*cells £10 & it is for ther payment of £10 dewe at Seynt Jamystide last past as p*er* contra may apere	£10		
Itm. the 2d day of October 1545 paide to W*illia*m Bucher £6 13s 4d, more the 15 day of October £6 13s 4d, mon*tith* £13 6s 8d & is for the fyrst payment of his byll datid the 2 day of ~~this present~~ September, as p*er* contra may apere, mon*tith*	£13	6s	8d
1546 Itm. the last day of ~~Augost~~ July pd. to hym in Bristowe £20	£20		
1547 Itm. the 7 day of Augost 1547 paide to hym £10 & r. my byll datyd the 2d day of September 1545	£10		
1549 Itm. the 2de day of October an*n*o 1549 33s 4d & is for 2 C ½ Yland woode d'd to hym at ~~19~~ 13s 4d per C, the 21 of October ½ a C woode, so mon*tith* all 40s	£2		
Itm. the same day £8 13s 4d paide unto hym in redy money	£8	13s	4d
Itm. the 11 of Novemb*er* 53s 4d & is for 4 C of Yland woode at 13s 4d the C, mon*tith*	£2	13s	4d

187(L) contd.

Itm. the 20 of November for 1 C woode, the 26 of November for 5 C, the
29 of November for 1 C, the 6 day of December for 4 C, mon*tith* all   [1]   C at
13s 4d p*er* clothe, I sey 11 C   £7   6s   8d
Itm. the 6 day of December paide to hym in ready mon*n*ey   £6
Itm. the 11 daye of December for 1 C Yland wood   13s   4d
Itm. the 30 day of Jenyver for 2 C woode   £1   6s   8d
Itm. the same day pd. to hym £11 20d   £11   1s   8d
Itm. to his s*ar*vant W*illia*m Grey 40s   £2
Itm. the 5 day of February 1549 pd. for hym to *the* seid Grey £12   £12
Itm. the 16 of Ap*r*ell 1550 my wif paide to hym in ready money £7   £7

187(R)   **anno 1542**

William Buchar of Cowlley p*er* contra is dewe to have the
14 day of M*ar*che £10 which is for the rest and clozing up of
his acowmpt fo. 4, to be paid at Candellmas next   ~~£10~~
Itm. the 24 day of July 1543 £29 & it is for the rest of 12
clothes at 5 m*ar*kes the clothe, to pay ~~£14 10s~~ at Seynt
Jamistide 1544 & ~~£14 10s~~ at Seynt Jamistide in a*nn*o 1545   ~~£29~~
Itm. the 19 day of July 1544 £20 & is for the rest of 50 m*ar*kes
for 10 clothes bowght of hym at 5 m*ar*kes the clothe, ~~to pay~~
~~£10 at~~ Seynt Jamistide in a*nn*o 1545 ~~& £10~~ at Seynt
Jamistide in a*nn*o 1546   ~~£20~~
Itm. the 2d day of September a*nn*o 1545 £33 6s 8d & is for
10 clothes r. of hym at 5 m*ar*kes the clothe, to pay ~~£13 6s 8d~~
at Mighellmas next com*m*yng & ~~£10 at~~ Seynt Jamistide in
a*nn*o 1546 & ~~£10~~ at Seynt Jamystide in a*nn*o 1547, as it may
apere by my bill   £33   6s   8d
Itm. the 21 day of October a*nn*o 1549 £10 13s 4d & is ffor
2 plonckett*es* sortyng clo*thes* bowght & r. of hym *the* same
daye   £10   13s   4d
Itm. the 6 day of December for 3 sortyng clo*thes* culler
plonket*es*   £16
Itm. the 30 day of Jenyver for 5 clothes at 16 nobles 20d
the clothe, mon*tith*   £27   1s   8d
Itm. the 13 of M*ar*che £7 to be paide at Ester next & is for
the rest of 4 clothes bowght of hym as in my shop booke
may apere   £7

188(L)   **anno 1543**

Jamys Symons of Bristowe tuckar owith the 3d daye of July £3 3d that is for
2 ½-bales Tullus wood weying 3 C ½, 5 li. at 17s the C solld & d'd to hym
to be paide at Cristmas next com*m*yng   £3   3d

                      a*n*no 1549

John Buchar of West Hartry owithe the 7th day of December for 1 C of the
newe wood at 13s 4d the C, more the 11 day of December for 2 C woode,
mon*tith* all 3 C & in mon*n*ey 40s, to be paide at all tymes requyryd[2]   £2
Itm.

                      anno 1543

John Willi*am*s of Castill[3] Neathe owith the 30 day of July £3 7s 6d & is for
a pipe 14 li. iren of S.S., to be pd. at Candellmas next com*m*yng   £3   7s   6d
Itm. the 10 day of M*ar*che £3 16s 8d & is for 1 butt seck solld & d'd to hym to
be paide at Seynt Jamistide next com*m*yng   £3   16s   8d

---

[1] *Figure erased and illegible in MS.*
[2] *All John Buchar's account is crossed through.*
[3] Castill *is inserted above the line.*

188(R) anno 1544

Jamys Symons p*er* contra is dewe to have the 18 day of Augost 20s which he paide to my s*a*rvant R. Leytt	£1		
Itm. the 24 of December r. of his wif 40s 3d[1]	£2		3d

anno 1543

John Willi*a*ms p*er* contra is dewe to have the 13 of February 53s 4d & is for 4 m*a*rkes r. of hym in redy money at Bristowe,	£2	13s	4d
more 10d[2]			10d
Itm. the 7 day of M*a*rche r. of hym 13s 4d		13s	4d
Itm. the 28 of July 1544 my wif r. of hym £3 16s 8d	£3	16s	8d

189(L) anno 1543

Will*a*m Lawrence of Stapillton owith the 8 day of Augost £3 6s 8d to be paide at Candellmas next com*m*yng. Robert Arden of Maginsfilld & Robert Gun*n*yng of Barten Hundred & ev*e*ry of them for the hole be shew*ertes* for the payment

£3 6s 8d

anno 1545

Thomas Harrys m*a*rchant of Bristowe owithe the 4th day of February for the rest of acowmp*t* subscribyd with his name £16 4s 4d ob	£16	4s	4d ob
Itm. the 30 day of Augost a*nno* 1546 delyverd for hym to J*o*hn Richard*es* thre barrells of gunpowdr waying neate the barells dysductyd 3 C 35 li. of gunpowdr at 7d the li. mon*tith*	£9	17s	5d
Itm. the last of Augost d'd to J*o*hn Richard*es* 6 lery h'd at 10d the h'd, mon*tith* 5s		5s	
Itm. the 3d day of February for a but of seck a p*i*pe bastard taken to the prise in the Mary Co*n*ception	£3	8s	6d
Itm. for lisence of 8 dicker le*ther* at 10s per dicker	£4		
	S. £33	15s	3d ob

anno 1547

Thom*as* Harrys m*a*rchant of Bristowe & nowe sherif of the same owithe the 2d day of Jenyver a*nno* dicto 5 nobles & is for 1 h'd claret wyne solld & delyv*e*rd to hym	£1	13s	4d
Itm. the 11 day of M*a*rche £10 which I lent to hym in redy mon*n*ey	£10		
Itm. he owith £4 16s for chese which J*o*hn Richard*es* his purser had of my wif & the seide Master Harrys have p*ro*mesyde to pay hit	£4	16s	
Itm. the 16 day of Jenyver 1548, pd. to his p*u*rss*e*r J*o*hn Richard*es* £6 5s 8d ffor the hole payment of my ffreight p*er* contra, & so broke my seale from the charter p*a*rtye	£6	5s	8d
	S. £22	15s	

189(R) anno 1543

Will*a*m Lawrence p*er* contra is dewe to have the 5 day of February £3 6s 8d r. for hym of John Gunwyn of Eston in Barkyn Hundred

£3 6s 8d

---

[1] *There is no credit entry for Buchar.*
[2] more 10d *inserted later.*

189(R) contd.   **anno 1546**

Thomas Harrys per contra is dewe to have the 7th day of Maye £10 which I r. of hym in redy monney	£10
Itm. more for a C of Frensche pruyenes	5s
Itm. the 3d day of February £15 10s £14 5s & is for the freight of 9 ton, pipe wyne in the Mary Conception at 30s per ton	£14 5s
Itm. for averes of the same at 4s 10d per ton	£2 5s 11d
Itm. for 1 h'd of claret wyne r. the 8th day of December 30s	£1 10s
Itm. for the rest of stones from the Fryers	£1 12s 8d
Itm. for 2 yeres rent of my gardeyne at the Fryers endyd at Mighellmas anno 1546	13s 4d
Itm. the 25 day of February I r. of hym in his hows £3 3s 4d ob	£3 3s 4d ob
Solmd	£33 15s 3d ob

anno 1548

Thomas Harrys per contra is dewe to have the 16 day of Jenyver anno dicto for the freight of 29 buttes seck from Andaluzia this vyntage in his shipp the Mary Conception at 30s per ton	£21 15s
Itm. for 2 yeres rent of my gardeyne by the Whit Fryers endyd at Mighellmas last past	13s 4d
Itm. for 32 bundells lathes at 2d ob the bundell	6s 8d
	£22 15s

189(A)

A separate small account with fo. 189.

owith ffor 2 yeres rent ffor a gardyn	13s 4d
ffor 32 bundylles layttes at 2d ob per bundyll, montith	6s 8d

per me Thomas
Hares

190(L)   **anno 1543**

John Smythe of Wynterborn smythe owithe the 18 day of Awgost £5 & is for 3 h'd of S.S. iren solld & d'd to hym to be paide at all tymes	£5
Itm. the 19 day of Jenyver £6 12s 3d & is for 3 h'd of S.S. iren at 20 nobles the ton & 1 h'd 1 qr. 14 li. of the better Rendry iren at £6 the ton, montith	£6 12s 3d
1544 Itm. the 16 day of Maye anno 1544 33s 4d which rest unpaide for 10 C 5 li. iren as it may apere in my shop boke wrytten the 4 day of Aprell last past	£1 13s 4d
1550 Itm. the 30 day of May Anno 1550 £7 to be paide at all tymes & is for the rest of 1 ton of S.S. iren	£7

190(R)   **anno 1543**

John Smythe per contra is dewe to have the 6 daye of October £5 for so myche r. of hym at Bristowe	£5
Itm. the 25 of Jenyver r. 32s 3d	£1 12s 3d
1544 Itm. the 4 day of Aprell r. £5 anno 1544	£5
Itm. the 14 day of June r. of hym 5 nobles	£1 13s 4d
Itm. the 28 day of June 1550 r. of hym at Bristowe £7	£7

191(L)   **anno 1543**

Lawrence Hanckot of Barnsgrove owithe the 29 daye of Augost £15 2s for
the rest of his acowmpt fo. 6 and it is for £3 2s that rest for 2 ton 1 qr. 9 li. iren

191(L) contd.

sold the 28 of June a*nno* 1539 & £12 for 2 ton iren delyverd the 25 day of Maye last past	£15	2s	
Itm. the last daye of Augost £37 6s 8d & is for 4 tons Rendry iren at £6 the ton & 2 ton S.S. iren at 20 nobles the ton to be paide at all tymes	£37	6s	8d
Itm. the 4th day of February solld & d'd to hym 2 ton 4 li. Rendry iren at £6 the ton to be paide at all tymes requyrid	£12		2d
Itm. the 23 day of M*arche* 40s which I pay to hym in a butt of seck which he had for Thomas Hassbery after 11 nobles the ton	£2		
Itm. the same day £14 10s which I apoynt hym to r. of Edward Rowley, fo.[1]	£14	10s	
1544 Itm. the 26 of M*arche* 1544 5 nobles which he ow*ith* for the rest of a but seck d'd to hym for Thomas Hassbery to pay at Bartyllmewtide next comyng	£1	13s	4d
Itm. the 29 day of May laden for hym in Thom*as* Aflet*tes* trowe 5 ton Rendry iren at £6 *the* ton	£30		
Itm. the 3 day of Novemb*er* a*nno* 1544 £30 13s 8d & is for 4 ton 21 li. of my Uncle chilldrens iren *that* was in my kytchin after £6 the ton & for 1 ton, ½ a C, 7 li. S.S. iren at £6 10s the ton d'd to hym to be paide at all tymes	£30	13s	8d
Itm. the 11 day of Decemb*er*, for 1 ton pipe iren less 3 li. of the Rendry at £6 the ton, mon*tith*	£8	19s	10d
Itm. the 26 day of June anno 1545 £12 *that* is for 2 tons iren of the Rendry at £6 the ton to be paide at all tymes, sent in Pawlmers trowe	£12		
Itm. the 8 day of October 1545 £48 & for 8 to*n* Rendry iren solld & d'd to hym at £6 the ton, to be paide at all tymes	£48		
1548 Itm. the 11 day of Ap*r*ell 1548 £9 9s 10d & is for 1 ton less 2 li. of S.S. ire*n* at £9 10s the ton to be paide at all tymes requyred	£9	9s	10d
Itm. the 7 day of September 1548 £9 10s & is for 1 ton Rendry iren to pay at all tymes	£9	10s	
Itm. the fyrst day of February a*nno* 1548 £9 12s 10d & is for 1 ton 1 qr. 5 li. iren of the Rendry to be paide at all tymes requyred	£9	12s	10d
Itm. the 23 daye of July a*nno* 1549 £21 5s 3d & is for 1 ton 1 qr. 8 li. ire*n* of the Rendry at £10 the ton & for 1 ton 20 li. of S.S. ire*n* at £11 to be pd. at all tymes	£21	5s	3d

191(R) anno 1543

Lawrence Hanckot p*er* contra is dewe to have the 12 daye of September £12 that is for 40 doze*n* calve skuyns at 6s the doze*n* which he sent for me in Thomas Aflet*es* trowe & d'd the*m* at Newneham to J*ohn* Sparck	£12		
Itm. the 6 day of Jenyv*er* my s*a*rvant Leyt r. of hym	£10		
Itm. the 4 day of ~~Jenyver~~ February 1543 r. of hym at Bristowe £14	£14		
Itm. £13 16s for 46 dozens calve skuyns r. the 23 of M*arche* after 6s the dozen	£13	16s	
Itm. the same tyme £21 13s 4d for 10 dicker of lether which lether & skuyns he browght to J*ohn* Sparck	£21	13s	4d
Itm. the 1 day of Novemb*er* 1544 r. of hym at Bristow £38, mon*tith*	£38		
Itm. r. of hym 40 dozens calve skuyns at 6s the dozen, mon*tith*	£12		
Itm. the 6 daye of October 1545 £39 11s 2d r. of hym in redy mon*n*ey	£39	11s	2d
Itm. the last day of July 1546 r. of hym £28 & more r. the 18 day of September £20, mon*tith* the hole	£48		
Itm. the 7 of September 1548 r. of hym £7 9s 10d	£7	9s	10d
Itm. the last day of Jenyver a*nno* 1548 r. of hym at Bristowe	£9	10s	
Itm. the 22 of July 1549 r. by my wif of hym £9 12s 10d	£9	12s	10d
Itm. the fyrst of February r. at Bristow of hym £21 5s 3d	£21	5s	3d

---

[1] *Blank in MS.*

192(L) anno 1543

William Tyndall one of the Chamberleyns of Bristowe owithe the 29 daye
of Augost £6 20d that is for 1 ton 1 qr. 3 li. Rendry iren at £6 the ton to
be paide at all tymes requyrid   £6   1s   8d
Itm. the 1 day of Aprell 1544 £8 & is for the freight of 6 tons iren in my ship
the Trynte at 4 nobles per ton & to pay ½ in hand & ½ at thend of 3 monthes
next commyng   £8

192(R) anno 1544

William Tyndall per contra is dewe to have the 29 day of
Marche £6 20d which my sarvant Robert Leight r. of hym in
redy money   £6   1s   8d
Itm. the [1] day of Aprell 5 markes which he fornysshid
for me to the Kynges subsedy   £3   6s   8d

193(L) anno 1543

Clement Bayse of Bristowe poyntmaker owith the 22 daye of September
£6 21d & is for 4 ½-bales Tullus wood waying 7 C 19 li. at 17s the C, to be
paide at all tymes, montith   £6   1s   9d

anno 1550

John Sowche & William Barret be dewe to have the last day of Marche anno
dicto £20 for so myche r. of the seide Shuche in gold & I delyverd unto hym
the £20 of white money which he left with me in gaige for the same as per
contra aperithe   £20

anno 1543

Thomas Davy of Lyswayne in Wales smythe owith the 4th day of October
£3 3s 4d & is for a pipe of my best Rendry iren solld & d'd to hym & to
Martyne William of Carffyll, to be pd. at Candellmas next commyng   £3   3s   4d
Itm. the last day of February 33s 4d & is for 5 C S.S. iren at 20 grotes per C,
to pay at Mydsomer next commyng   £1   13s   4d
Itm. the 4 of July 1544 31s 8d and for 5 C iren to be paide at Mighellmas
next   £1   11s   8d
Itm. the 12 day of September 34s 10d which is for 1 h'd 25 li. S.S. iren to be
pd. at Candellmas next   £1   14s   10d
Itm. the 18 day of November 1544 37s 6d & is for 5 C ½, 14 li. S.S. iren solld &
d'd to hym after 20 nobles the ton, to pay at Ester next as it may apere by his
byll   £1   17s   6d

193(R) anno 1544

Clement Bayse per contra is dewe to have the 18 daye of
October £6 21d r. for hym of Agnes Grey   £6   1s   9d

anno 1549

John Sowche marchant of Bristowe owithe the 10 of Marche
£20 to be in golld at Easter next or sone apon, & is for
so myche lent in gold apon £20 in white money r. of hym &
William Barret   £20

anno 1543

R. of Thomas Davy per contra the 29 day of February at
Bristowe £3 3s 4d in redy monney for hym & Martyne
Williams is payment & d'd theyer byll   £3   3s   4d
Itm. the 4 of July 33s 4d r. for the iren d'd the last of
February last past   £1   13s   4d

---

[1] Blank in MS.

193(R) contd.

Itm. my wif r. the 12 day of September 1544 31s 8d	£1	11s	8d
Itm. the 18 day of November 1544 r. 34s 10d	£1	14s	10d
Itm. the 10 of February 1544 my wif r. of hym 37s 6d	£1	17s	6d

194(L)   anno 1543

William Baylif of Whitnest in the countye of Glocester weyvar owith the 12 daye of October £7 10s & is for 1 pipe of wull oyle solld & d'd to hym, to be pd. at the Anunciacion of Owr Blessyd Lady next commyng. Master John Huntely squyer is his shewertye   £7 10s

anno 1543

Thomas Uprichard of Kerdif smythe owithe the 20 daye of October 33s 4d which is for a h'd of S.S. iren sold & d'd to hym, to pay at Candelmas next	£1	13s	4d
Itm. the 4 of February 46s 8d & is for 7 C S.S. iren at 20 grotes the C to be pd. at Mydsomer next commyng	£2	6s	8d
Itm. the 25 day of Julye anno 1544 £3 6s 8d & is for 10 C S.S. iren to be pd. at Candellmas next	£3	6s	8d
Itm. the 17 day of February, for a pipe of S.S. iren at 5 markes to pay at Easter next	£3	6s	8d
Itm. the 7 day of Jenyver 1545 for 11 C 3 qr. iren of S.S. at 20 grotes the C, montith £3 18s 4d to be paide at Mydsomer next	£3	18s	4d
Itm. the 26 day of July anno 1546 £3 6s 8d & is for 1 pipe of S.S. iren to be pd. at Cristmas next	£3	6s	8d

194(R)   anno 1544

William Baylif per contra is dewe to have the 15 day of May £7 10s which my wif r. of hym   £7 10s

anno 1543

Thomas Uprichard per contra is dewe to have the 4 day of February 5 nobles r. of hym in redy monny	£1	13s	4d
Itm. the 25 of July 1544 r. of hym 46s 8d	£2	6s	8d
Itm. the 17 of February anno 1544 my wif r. of hym £3 6s 8d	£3	6s	8d
Itm. the 25 day of July 1545 r. £3 6s 8d	£3	6s	8d
Itm. the 26 day of July 1546 my sarvant son Hewgh Smythe r. at Bristowe of hym	£3	18s	4d
r. of hym £3 6s 8d	£3	6s	8d

195(L)   anno 1543

30 clothes
111 Manchesters

Viages besowthe for my owne acowmpt owith the 15 day of Jenyver £203 9s 6d & is for 30 clothes of John Yerberys & William Buchars which cost clere abord £4 the clothe and for 111 Manchester cottons which cost clere abord 14s 6d the pece, of the which ware laden in the Mary Conception 10 clothes & 37 Manchesters in 2 fardells & in the Margett 10 clothes & 37 Manchesters in 2 fardells & in the Mary Jamys 10 clothes & 37 Manchesters in 2 fardells, all the which goodes I have dyrectid to Luxborn to my prentes Henry Setterford & in his absence I have comyttyd the same to William Harvest, he to do by it acording to my letters   £203 9s 6d

Itm. the monthe of February £4 10d goten by the venture of this viage, as may apere to gaynes in credito fo. 200   £4 10d

S. £207 10s 10d

195(L) contd.

anno 1543

Figes & rezynges for my owne acowmpt, that is to sey, 50 cargges conteynyng 100 peces Malaga rezyns which cost clere abord, after 595 M per carg, montith 29 V. 750 M., & 80 quarterons figges which cost clere abord, after 108 M. per quarteron, 8 V. 655 M., which godes I r. owt of a hulk of Hansardam namyd the Swan, master under God Garet Coster. More for the egchange of 30 doble & 10 olld crownes 355 M., for the freight of the seid rezynges valurid 4 tons & of the figges valuryd 1 ton at 28s per ton, for averes 2s per ton, for halyng 20d, for costom of the resynges 1d per pece & of the figges 2s per ton, montith all   £33 18s 10d

Itm. the 20 of Marche £8 17s 10d & is for so myche goten by this acownt as may apere to gaynes in credito fo. 200   £8 17s 10d

S.   £42 16s 8d

195(R)

anno 1543

Viages per contra be dewe to have the monthe of February, 311 V. 279 M. that is 189 V. 716 M. for the neat sale of the 30 clothes per contra, & 121 V. 563 M. for the neate sale of 111 Manchesters per contra, as by Henry Setterfordes acownt may apere, amontith sterlyng £207 10s 4d   £207 10s 4d

anno 1544

Figges & resynges per contra is dewe to have the 23 of February £8 2s 8d, which is for the sale of 76 quarterons to Roger Abyngton, William Yong & Thomas Pacy at 2s 2d per quarteron   £8 2s 8d

Itm. r. of Master Ely for 1 quarteron 2s   2s

Itm. I gave to the Towne Clerck 1 quarteron & to William Northe 1 quarteron & for my hows 1 quarteron [1]

Itm. the 13 day of Marche £33 5s which is for the sale of 95 peces resynges to William Yong fo. 205 at 7s the pece, montith   £33 5s

Itm. r. of John Spark for 3 pesys resynges 20s   £1

Itm. r. of William Northe for 1 pece resynges 7s   7s

Itm. ocupyed in my hows 1 pece [1]

S.   £42 16s 8d

196(L)

50 London clothes
5 yelow lynardes conteynyng 167 yerdes
2 Manchester cottons
598 fanegas ½ whet
140 dozens calve skuyns
50 ox hides
2 dozen calve S
3 hides
10 L clothes
37 Manchesters

1543

Viages to Este Spayne owith for my proper acowmpt £360 which is for 50 clothes London sorte, 5 yelowe lynardes conteynyng 167 yerdes, 2 Manchester cottons, 598 fanegas ½ whet, 140 dozens of calve skuyns & 50 ox hides, all which goodes rest in the powar of my prentes Robert Tyndall for the rest of his acowmpt r. the 26 day of November anno dicto, as it may apere in acowmpt of viages fo. 174   £360

Itm. more for 2 dozen calve skuyns & 3 hides cow & stere which my seid sarvant geve me in cowmpt less then he r. valent   £1 6s 8d

Itm. the 8 day of Jenyver lode by Godes grace in the Trynte of the Rendry, master under God Guyllem de Lesso, 2 fardells conteynyng 10 clothes London sorte and 37 Manchester cottons which cost clere abord £66 16s 8d,

---

[1] Blank in MS.

196(L) contd.

130 dozens of calve skuyns	more 5 fardells calve skuyns *conteynyng* 130 dozens which cost clere abord £58, more 6 gret ox hid*es* of my owne			
6 gret ox hid*es*	slawgh*ter* valent 40s, mon*tith* all	£126	16s	8d
2 tons 1 C led	Itm. the same tyme laden in my ship the Trynte, under God m*aster* John Darby, 2 tons 1 C of led in 34 pec*es* which cost clere abord £10, more 38 dicker 6 hid*es* whereof			
12 dicker ox 26 dicker 6 hid*es* cow & stere	12 dycker was ox le*ther*, more 168 dozens of calve skuyns, the which le*ther* & skuyns cost clere abord £150 10s, more in a pipe 3 C ½, 24 li. tallow valent 44s 6d, so amon*tith* the			
168 dozens of calve skuyns 3 C ½, 24 li. of tallow	hole lading in my shipp	£162	14s	6d
10 tons 2 C led	Itm. the 4 day of Aprell a*nno* 1544 I lode in the John Baptist of the Rendry, m*aster* Joha*nn*es de Yrancu, 175 pec*es* ledd *conteynyng* 10 tons 2 C which cost £45, 3 fard*ells* clothe *conteynyng* 30 of Yerberys clothes which cost clere abord £120 & 3 northe*n* cottons for the			
30 clothes	wrapp*ers that* cost 20s, all which good*es* gothe under governau*nc*e of my pren*tes* Hewgh Hamon, so mon*tith*			
3 north*ern* cotto*ns*	the hole £166	£166		[1]
	Itm. 1 butt of syder valent			
116 pec*es* led *conteynyng* 6 ton 3 C	Itm. the 12 of Ap*re*ll 1544 lode in the Peter of the Passage, m*aster* Anton de Altamyra 116 pec*es* ledd *conteynyng* 6 tons 3 C *that* cost clere abord £26 10s	£26	10s	
	Itm. 15 V. 641 M. which my s*ar*vant have spent & paide for abatemen*tes* for sale of clothes, mon*tith*	£10	8s	7d
	Itm. £4 9s goten by this acowmpt to gaynes in credito fo. 200	£4	9s	
		S. £858	5s	5d

196(R)   **anno 1544**

60 L clo*th*es 39 Ma*n*chesters 5 yelow lynard*es*	Viag*es* p*er* contra is dewe to have the monthes of December, February & Marche 422 V. 516 M. and is for the nete p*ro*cedewe of 60 clothes, 39 Manchester cottons & 5 yelow lynard*es*, as it may apere by Tyndalls acowmpt geven in June 1544, mon*tith* sterlyng £281 13s 7d	£281	13s	7d
2 tons 1 C led	Itm. 13 V. 838 M. which is for the sale of 2 tons 1 C led, as may apere by Tyndalls acowmpt beforesseid, mo*ntith*	£9	4s	6d
176 hid*es* ox 254 hid*es* cow & 225 do*zen*s calve	Itm. 336 V. 550 M. & is for the sale of 176 ox hid*es*, 254 hid*es* cow & stere & of 225 dozens calve skuyns, mon*tith* sterlyng, as by Tyndalls seid cownt apere	£224	7s	4d
582 f*anega*s whet 12 hid*es* cow & 213 do*zens* calve	Itm. £150 10s & is for 582 f*anega*s wheat, 12 hid*es* cow & stere & 213 dozens calve skuyns, the which good*es* the seid Tyndall left in Spayne the 19 of June 1544 with my p*re*ntes Hewgh Hamon for the rest of his seid cownt that war unsolld, which good*es* cost me as before is seyd & it ap*er*ith in debito to viag*es* fo. 221	£150	10s	
30 clo*thes* L 16 ton 5 C led 3 northe*n* cotto*ns*	Itm. the 25 day of July £192 10s and is for 16 tons 5 C led, 30 clothes & 3 northen cottons the which I pass from this cownt to a newe cowmpt fo. 221	£192	10s	
		S. £858	5s	5d

[1] *Blank in MS.*

197(L)   anno 1543

Henry Setterford my prentes owith the 28 day of September 237 V. 500 M. which is for so myche d'd to hym in Biscay by my sarvant Tyndall for to carry to Andaluzia & there to employ it for my acowmpt acording to my remenbrance, 900 ducatts   £225

Itm. £5 which I pd. to Thomas Yong of Bristow grocer the 28 of February for 20 ducatts which he borowyd of hym at Andaluzia   £5

Itm. 22 ducatts which Tyndall paide for hym to Martyn Grevys   £5 10s

Itm. £207 10s 4d for the neat procedewe of 30 clothes & 111 Manchesters, as it aperith to viages in credito fo. 195   £207 10s 4d

197(R)   anno 1543

Henry Setterford per contra is dewe to have 328 V. 95 M. & is for so myche that 104 buttes seck & 20 pipes bastard & 8 pipes taynt & 50 carges of resynges & 80 quarterons of figges did cost clere aborde a good ship namyd the Swan of Hanserdame, under God master Garet Coster, as by the seid Henrys acowmpt may apere, montith sterlyng   £218 14s 7d

Itm. for 9 buttes seck laden to my oste of London, 4358 M.   £2 18s 2d

Itm. for 30 buttes seck laden in the Mary Bulleyn, the Jelyan & in a Portyngall ship which cost clere abord 71 V. 759 M. as by his seid cowmpt r. in July 1544 may apere, montith sterlyng   £47 15s 9d

Itm. for 37 pipes oyle laden in the Mary Jamys, the Mary Conception & in the Mary Bulleyn, which cost clere abord 220 V. 462 M. as by his seid acownt may apere, montith sterlyng   £146 19s 6d

Itm. 1500 M. pd. to John Keynes in part of payment of my averes in the Mary Jamys in Andaluzia   £1

Itm. for shewger, spices & other tryffylls 7739 M.   £5 3s 2d

Itm. 29 V. 179 M. which the same Henry have spent, montith   £19 9s 3d

198(L)   anno 1543

16 tons 12 C ½ 2 li.   Iren for my owne acowmpt the 24 daye of Jenyver £99 15s 1d & is for 16 tons 12 C ½, 2 li. iren conteynyng 1440 endes which restith of acowmpt fo. 176   £99 15s 1d

Itm. the 26 day of Marche anno 1544 £11 5s for so myche goten by this acowmpt as it may apere to gaynes in credito fo. 200   £11 5s

                                                                S. £111 1d

                             anno 1544

3 tons 11 C 1 qr. 21 li.   Iren for my owne acowmpt owith the 26 day of Marche £21, & is for 3 tons 11 C 1 qr. 21 li. conteynyng 314 endes which rest in my howse of the olld cowmpt here before as per contra may apere   £21

54 ton 8 C 1 qr. 13 li.   Itm. the same day r. owt of my ship the Trynte under God master John Darby, 600 kyntalls Rendry iren which made by my weightes 43 tons 8 C 13 li. conteynyng 4432 endes, more 150 kyntalls of S.S. iren which made by my weightes 11 tons 28 li. conteynyng 1160 endes, all the which 750 kyntalls cost clere abord 348 V. 516 M., for freight 26s 8d per ton, for averes 8d per ton, for custom 2s 6d per ton, ffor hallyng & pylling 4d per ton, montith   £306 15s 3d

04 ton 7 C 1 qr.   1544 Itm. the 13 of May anno 1544 r. owt of the Sancta Maria of S.S. 4 ton Rendry iren which made by my weightes 4 ton 7 C 1 qr. conteynyng 526 endes which cost at Spayne clere abord the shipp 27 V. 046 M., for freight

198(L) contd.

	15s per ton, for costom 2s 6d per ton, for averes 10d per ton, for halyng, weying & pyling 4d per ton	£21 15s 3d
	Itm. the 17 daye of July anno 1544 r. owt of the San John of the Rendry, under God master Johannes de Beroby, 225 kyntalls more 13 li. iren of S.S. which made by my weightes 16 ton 10 C ½, conteynyng 1615 endes & more owt of the same ship 150 kyntalls Rendry iren more 75 li. which made by my	
49 ton 4½ C 15 li.	weightes 10 tons 16 C 3 qr. 8 li. conteynyng 1091 endes. Itm. more r. the same tym owt of the San John of the Rendry, master under God Myghell de Aerysavalo, 303 kyntalls iren of the Rendry which made by my weightes 21 tons 17 C 1 qr. 7 li. conteynyng 2190 endes, all the which 678 kyntalls 88 li. iren cost clere abord in Spayne 325 V. 031 M. ½, for freight £45, for costom £5 12s 6d, for halyng & pyling 4d per ton, for averis in John de Berobys ship 8d ob per ton & in the other ship 6d per ton, montith	£269 8s 11d
02 ton 4 C 14 li.	Itm. the foreseid 17 day of July paide to Tyndall for 2 ton 4 C 14 li. flat iren conteynyng 112 endes £10 16s & 45s for freight & costom, for halyng 8d, montith all	£12 7s
	Itm. the 22 of August anno 1544 £58 4s 5d goten by this cowmpt of iren to gaynes in credito folio 200	£58 4s 5d
	S.	£689 10s 10d

198(R)   **anno 1544**

Iren per contra is dewe to have the 26 day of Marche £90 1d & is for 14 tons 4 C 2 qr. 27 li. iren conteynyng 1367 endes solld at dyvers tyms sens the 24 day of Jenyver last past at dyvers prices, as by my shop boke may apere, montith	£90	1d
Itm. the same day £21 & is for 3 tons 11 C 1 qr. 21 li. iren conteynyng 314 endes that rest unsolld of my olld iren per contra of the which I make the newe cowmpt per contra crediter as maye apere	£21	
S.	£111	1d

anno 1544

Iren per contra is dewe to have the 22 daye of Augost £511 12s and is for 82 tons iren 13 C 1 qr. 18 li. conteynyng 8217 endes solld at dyvers tymes & at dyvers prices as by my shop boke may apere sens the 26 day of Marche last past	£511 12s	
Itm. 1 ton 12 C which I do fynde lackyng by this cownt whether it be stolen or forgoten to be sett apon my shop boke when it was solld I can not well say. Valent after £6 the ton £9 12s to gaynes in debito, fo. [1]		[1]
Itm. the foreseid 22 day of Augost 29 ton 10 C 1 qr. 17 li. which I pass to iren in debito fo. 234 after £6 the ton, montith £177 18s 10d	£177 18s 10d	
S.	£689 10s 10d	

199(L)   **anno 1543**

Thomas Moore of Bristowe bruar owith the 14 daye of December £6 13s 4d & is for a ton of S.S. iren solld & d'd to hym, to pay at Seynt Jamistide next commyng   £6 13s 4d

---

[1] *Blank in MS.*

199(R) anno 1544

    Thomas More per contra is dewe to have the 8 day of
Augost £6 13s 4d r. of hym in redy monney   £6 13s 4d

200(L)

Gaynes for my owne acowmpt owithe   [1]

200(R) anno 1543

Gaynes for my owne acowmpt is dewe to have the 5th daye
of February £11 19s 10d ob goten by acowmpt of Tullus
wood, fo. 147   £11 19s 10d ob
Itm. the 26 day of Marche anno 1544 £11 5s goten by
acowmpt of iren, fo. 198   £11 5s
Itm. the 26 of July anno 1544 £58 3s 8d for acowmpt of
seckes, fo. 202   £58 3s 4d
Itm. £11 9s 8d goten by acownt of tayntz, fo. 213   £11 9s 8d
Itm. £23 2s 6d goten by bastardes, fo. 203   £23 2s 6d
Itm. £4 10d goten by viages fo. 195   £4 10d
Itm. £8 17s 10d goten by figges & resynges, fo. 195   £8 17s 10d
Itm. £4 9s goten by viages, fo. 196   £4 9s
Itm. the 16 of Marche 1544 £52 4s 2d goten in oyles 179   £52 4s 2d
Itm. the 4 day of Maye 1547 £38 16s 4d goten by viages
to Andaluzia fo. 254   £38 16s 4d

201(L) anno 1543

John Yerbery of Bruton clother owith the 5th day of February 1543 6 clothes
truckers of good lenghthes & of the best makyng & more 4s 9d in monney for
1 qr. 3 li. wood & it is for 10 ½-bales & 1 C of Lowse wood which conteyn in
all 17 C 3 qr. 3 li. as in my shop boke may apere   [1]
Itm. the 21 day of Aprell 1544 £34 whereof he r. of Stevyn Chick 28s 9d &
6s 8d of Stevan Rodwey & his son r. of my wif 40s & more he is content to r.
of William Northe £10 & more he r. of me this present day at Bristowe
£20 4s 7d, so montith as aforesseid £34 whereof £27 10s is pd. for the hole
& last payment of a byll dewe the fyrst day of Marche last past & £6 10s is
putt in the backsyde of a byll datyd the 10 of September 1543   £34
Itm. the 6 of May my wif pd. £10, more he r. of William Northe of Master
Elys money £20, more payde to his son William the 6 of June anno 1544
£4 14s 2d & so ys the £41 4s 2d dewe at Owr Lady Day in Marche last past
fully payde   £34 14s 2d
Itm. the 6 of June 1544 paide to his son William £20 in part of payement of
his byll datyd the 18 of Marche last past, more paide the 3d day of July to his
son William £20 in part of payment of the same byll, more William Northe
paide to hym £10 as it aperith to Northe in credito 141 & so is the £50 fully
pd. for the fyrst payment of his byll datyd the 18 of Marche   £50
   ⎧ Itm. the 17 of July £14 which is for 1 ton of wull oyle   £14
   ⎪ Itm. the 18 of August 1544 William Northe payde £6 as it may apere to hym
   ⎨ in credito 141 & the 10 day of August I paide hym in Bristowe £5
   ⎪ montith £11 & so with the 1 ton oyle foreseid the £25 payable at
   ⎩ Bartyllmewetyde last past is fully paide & content montith   £11
Itm. the 26 day of September 1544 pd. £10 in parte of payment of the
£41 4s 2d payable at Mighellmas next, more William Northe paide to hym
the 29 day of September £16 13s 4d, more I paide to hym at Bristowe the
24 day of October £14 10s 10d, montith the hole of this item   £41 4s 2d
~~Itm. the 30 day of October 1544 for 1 ton of wull oyle~~
Itm. the 9 day of December 1544 paide to his son Stevy Yerbery £23 15s that
is for £7 6s 8d which his father r. of William Northe & 26s 8d which he r. of
the smythe of Wanstrowe & my wif paide to hym in redy monney £15 20d
montith all £23 15s which is for the fyrst payment of my byll datyd the 15
day of November 1544   £23 15s

---

[1] Blank in MS.

201(L) contd.

1545 Itm. the 15 of May pd. £15 & the 2d of June £16 10s & he r. of Stevyn Rodwey 20s & is for the payment at O*w*r Lady Day £32 10s
Itm. pd. by Northe & my wif £10 & is for 1 p*i*pe oyle in £7 mo*ntith* £17 18s 4d £17 18s 4d
Itm. I make hym creditor in fo. 233 for £71 13s 4d £71 13s 4d

£331

201(R)   anno 1543

John Yerbery of Bruton clothiar ~~owithe~~ is dewe to have the 5 day of February for the rest of his cowmpt fo. 163 £109 18s 4d & it must be paide in maner followyng, that is to saye ~~£27 10s~~ the fyrst day of M*a*rche next com*m*yng £4̶1̶ 4̶s̶ 2̶d̶ at the Annu*n*ciacion of O*w*r Blessyd Lady next after *that* & £4̶1̶ 4̶s̶ 2̶d̶ at Mighellmas next after that which wylbe in a*nno* 1544 as by bylls may apere £109 18s 4d
Itm. the 18 day of M*a*rche £107 10s which is for 30 clothes pen*n*y hewes at 5 mark*es* 5s the clothe to pay ~~£50~~ in hand ~~£25~~ at Bartyllmewetide next com*m*yng & ~~£32 10s~~ at O*w*r Lady Day in Lent next followyng after that which may apere by my bill made for the same £107 10s
Itm. the 14 of Augost a*nno* 1544 £35 16s 8d & is for the hallf & last payment of 20 clothes at 5 m*a*rk*es* 5s p*e*r clothe to pay ~~£17 18s 4d~~ at Candellmas next & £17 18s 4d at Seynt Jamystide next after that as by my byll may apere £35 16s 8d
Itm. the 15 day of November a*nno* 1544 £77 10s & is for the rest of 30 clothes pen*n*y hewes at 5 m*a*rk*es* 5s the clothe to pay £23 15s at all tymes requyrid & £26 17s 6d the last day of May next com*m*yng & £26 17s 6d at Seynt Androwstyde in November in a*nno* 1545 as by my byll may apere £77 15s

S. £331

202(L)   1543

25 butt*es*   Seck*es* for my owne acowmpt 25 buttes [1] owith the 14 day of February £84 7s 6d & is for 5 m*a*rkes 10d paide for ev*e*ry of the same butt*es* to Henry Ev*e*rson of London & his fellows £84 7s 6d
Itm. the 1 day of M*a*rche r. ow*t* of a hulk callid the Swan
104 butt*es*   of Hansardam, m*a*st*er* under God Garet Coster, 104 butt*es* seck which cost clere abord 226 V. 704 M., for freight 28s p*er* ton, for aver*es* 3s 4d p*er* ton, for costom of 42 tons 3s p*er* ton, for hawlyng & stowyng 4d p*er* ton, for hopy*n*g 14d p*er* ton, mo*ntith* all £242 16s £242 16s
1544 Itm. the monthe of July a*nno* 1544 r. 30 butt*es* seck*es*, which cost clere abord the ship 71 V. 754 M. which is
030 butt*es*   sterlyng £47 16s 8d, for the costom £4 10s, for hallyng & stowyng 5s, for freight of 6 butt*es* in the Mary Bulleyn,
So*m* all   m*a*st*er* Robert Whitsson, 28s p*er* ton & av*e*res 5s 1d p*er* ton,
159 butt*es*   mo*ntith* the freight & av*e*res £4 19s 4d, for freight of 18 butt*es* in the Sancta Maria de Misericordia of Villa de Conde, m*a*st*er* Alvers Fernandez 25s p*er* to*n* & for av*e*res 4s 5d p*er* to*n*, mo*ntith* the freight & av*e*res £12 15s 9d, for freight of 2 ton in the Jelyan, m*a*st*er* Thom*as* Davys, wherein I pd. but the Mary Bulleyns freight after 28s p*er* ton, & for av*e*res 7s 7d p*er* ton, mo*ntith* the freight & av*e*res £3 11s 4d, for hopy*n*g 20d, mo*ntith* the hole £79 12s 2d

---

[1] *Words erased and illegible in MS.*

202(L) contd.

Itm. £20 which my sarvant Henry spentt		£20		
Itm. the 26 of July £58 3s 8d & is for so myche goten by this acowmpt as it aperith to gaynes fo. 200		£58	3s	8d
	S.	£484	19s	4d

202(R) anno 1543

2	Seckes per contra is dewe to have the 14 of February £8 for 2 buttes to John Roxby, fo. 162	£8		
7	Itm. the 18 & 23 day of the same 7 butes to Northe 141	£26	16s	8d
1	Itm. the 18 day of February for 1 but to Gosselet 204	£4		
1	Itm. the 19 of February r. of Master Pacy for 1 butt	£3	7s	6d
2	Itm. r. of Dissom of Wynscheton for 2 buttes £8 10s	£8	10s	
4	Itm. the 20 day of February 4 buttes to Carryck, 34 for	£14	13s	4d
3	Itm. the 21 day of February & the 11 of Marche 3 butes to William Yong 205	£11	5s	
2	Itm. the 22 of February 2 buttes to Smothing 207 for	£7	10s	
1	Itm. the same day 1 butt to William Golldsmythe 113 for	£3	13s	4d
1	Itm. the same day 1 butt to T. Machyne 113 for	£3	16s	8d
1	Itm. r. of Margery Wellsche for 1 but	£3	7s	6d
1	Itm. the 27 of February r. of Henry Wyot for 1 butt	£3	7s	6d
1	Itm. the 28 of February for 1 butt to D. Hart 160	£4		
1	Itm. the same day to John Hamon 77 1 butt	£4		
2	Itm. the same day for 2 buttes to A. Bisshop 152	£8		
1	Itm. the same day to Susan Gibs fo. 126 1 but for	£4		
1	Itm. the 1 day of Marche to William Nasche 185 1 butt for	£4		
3	Itm. the same day for 3 buttes to A. Bosgrove 68 for	£11	10s	
16	Itm. the 5 of Marche for 16 buttes to Cristyan Whit 212 for	£58	13s	4d
1	Itm. the 7 of the same for 1 butt to T. Machyn 154 for	£3	15s	
1	Itm. the 8 of Marche for 1 but to T. Hawle 209 for	£3	10s	
3	Itm. the 10 of Marche for 3 buttes to T. Bell 62 for	£11	10s	
1	Itm. the same day for 1 butt to John Williams of Castilneth 188	£3	16s	8d
10	Itm. the 11 of Marche for 10 buttes to J. Willis 73 for	£36	13s	4d
1	Itm. the 12 of Marche r. of Henry Wyatt for 1 butt	£3	7s	6d
1	Itm. the 13 of Marche for 1 but to John Roxby for fo. 162	£3	16s	8d
1	Itm. the same day for 1 but to William Smothyng 207 for	£3	16s	8d
1	Itm. the 14 of Marche for 1 butt to Giles Dane 209 for	£3	13s	4d
1	Itm. the same day for 1 butt to R. Tippar 142 for	£3	13s	4d
3	Itm. the 17 of Marche for 3 buttes to Susan Gibs 126	£12		
1	Itm. the same day for 1 butt to Jeffrey Arndell 210	£3	13s	4d

202 (R) contd.

1	*anno 1544* Itm. the 26 of M*ar*che a*nno* 1544 for 1 butt to L. Hanckot 191	£3	13s	4d
1	Itm. the same day for 1 butt to T. Abeck 168 for	£3	13s	4d
1	Itm. the same day for 1 butt to J*oh*n Hamo*n* 77 for	£3	13s	4d
2	Itm. the same day for 2 butt*es* to Jamys Webster 178	£7	6s	8d
1	Itm. the 4 of Ap*r*ell for 1 butt to W*illi*am Reynolld 157 for	£3	13s	4d
1	Itm. the 5 of Ap*r*ell for 1 but to Wat*er* Ro*m*ney 157 for	£3	13s	4d
1	Itm. the same day for 1 butt to T. Whetley 214 for	£3	13s	4d
1	Itm. the 9 of Ap*r*ell for 1 butt*es* to M. Murton 214 for	£3	13s	4d
10	Itm. drawen to ylladge 10 butt*es*			[1]
1	Itm. the 11 of Ap*r*ell £3 13s 4d for 1 but to R. Jackso*n* 45	£3	13s	4d
6	Itm. the 28 of Ap*r*ell 6 butt*es* to J*oh*n Roxby, fo. 162, for	£22		
2	Itm. the same day, for 2 butt*es* to A. Bosgrove fo. 68 for	£7	6s	8d
1	Itm. the 2d day of May 1 but to Henry Leke 123 for	£3	13s	4d
7	Itm. the 5 day of the same 7 butt*es* to T. Harrys 182 for	£25	13s	4d
2	Itm. the 16 of the same r. for 2 butt*es* £7 6s 8d	£7	6s	8d
1	Itm. the 26 of the same 1 butt seck to Heyward 18 for	£4		
2	Itm. the 24 of July, r. of J*oh*n Browne of P*er*cyar for 2 butt*es*	£7	6s	8d
5	Itm. solld to Richard Caryck fo. 34 5 butt*es* for	£17		
2	Itm. 25 of July for 2 butt*es* to Will*iam* Smothing for	£7	6s	8d
1	Itm. the 26 of July for 1 butt to Jeffrey Arndell fo. 210 for	£3	13s	4d
7	Itm. sold from the 26 of May tyll the 13 of July to a man of Brodeford, W*illiam* Smothing, J*oh*n Goselet, J*oh*n Genyng*es*, W*illi*am Kemer 7 butt*es* for £26 2s 8d, as in the shop boke do apere	£26	2s	8d
7	Itm. 2 butt*es* ow*t*, 2 butt*es* to yllage & 3 butt*es* drounck & wast			[1]
20	Itm. £31 w*hich* I pass to fo. 220 for 20 butt*es that* rest to sell	£31		
159				
		S. £484	19s	4d

203(L)   anno 1543

36 pipes	Bastard*es* for my owne acowmpt owith the 14 day of February £121 10s & is for 36 pipes bowght of W*illi*am Cheyne & his co*m*panyons of London at 5 m*ar*kes 10d the pipe, for the which I paide the*m* redy money ow*t* of hand	£121	10s	
20 pipes 56	Itm. the 1 day of M*ar*che r. ow*t* of a hulk calld the Swan 20 pipes bastard which cost clere abord 43 V. 551 M., for freight 28s p*er* ton & aver*es* 3s 4d p*er* ton & for costom of 8 to*n* pipe at 3s p*er* ton, for hallyng & stowy*n*g 4d p*er* ton, & for hopyng 14d p*er* ton	£46	13s	4d

---

[1] *Blank in MS.*

203(L) contd.

Itm. the 26 of Augost a*nno* 1544 £23 7s 6d & is for so myche goten by this acowmpt as it may apere to gaynes in credito fo. 200 £23 7s 6d

S. £191 10s 10d

203(R) **a*nno* 1543**

2	Bastard*es* p*er* contra is dewe to have the 14 day of February £8 which is for 2 p*ipes* sold to Roxby 162	£8	
3	Itm. the 15 of the same & *the* 11 of M*a*rche 3 p*ipes* to J*o*hn Wyllis 73	£11	
1	Itm. *the* 18 of February to J*o*hn Goselet fo. 204 1 p*ipe* for	£4 3s 4d	
1	Itm. the 19 of February to R. Carick 34 1 p*ipe* for	£3 13s 4d	
2	Itm. the same day r. of W*illiam* Jaye for 2 pipes	£7 6s 8d	
3	Itm. the same day, to W*illiam* Northe fo. 141 3 pipes for	£11 10s	
2	Itm. the 21 of February for 2 p*ipes* to W*illiam* Yong 205	£7 10s	
2	Itm. the 22 of February for 2 p*ipes* to W*illiam* Smothing 207	£8	
1	Itm. *the* same day, to W*illiam* Goldsmythe fo. 113 1 pipe for	£4	
1	Itm. the 23 of February r. of M. Wellsche for 1 p*ipe*	£3 7s 6d	
4	Itm. the 27 of February to A. Stanbank 206 4 p*ipes*	£16	
2	Itm. the same day & the 12 of M*a*rche r. of H. Wyot for 2 p*ipes*	£6 15s	
1	Itm. the 28 of February to Davy Hart 165 1 pipe for	£4	
1	Itm. the same day to Allson Bisshop fo. 152 1 p*ipe* for		[1]
1	Itm. the same day to Susan Gibs fo. 126 1 pipe for	£4	
1	Itm. the 1 day of M*a*rche to W*illiam* Nasche 185 1 pipe for	£4	
1	Itm. the 5 of M*a*rche to Jamys Chester fo. 208 1 p*ipe* for	£3 16s 8d	
4	Itm. the 6 of M*a*rche to Cristyan White 212 4 p*ipes* for	£16	
1	Itm. the 7 of M*a*rche to Thom*as* Machyn fo. 154 1 p*ipe* for	£3 15s	
1	Itm. the 10 of M*a*rche to T. Bell 62 1 p*ipe* for	£4	
3	*anno 1544* Itm. the 26 of Marche 1544 to T. Abeck fo. 168 3 p*ipes* for	£11	
2	Itm. the same day to Jamys Webster 178 2 p*ipes* for	£7 6s 8d	
1	Itm. the 5 day of Ap*re*ll to Wat*er* Romney 157 1 p*ipe* for	£4	
5	Itm. to ylladge 5 pipes		[1]
1	Itm. the 28 of Aprell for 1 p*ipe* to Roxby 162 for	£4	
1	Itm. the 2 of May 1 pipe to W*illiam* Yong for £4 6s 8d 205	£4 6s 8d	
1	Itm. the 26 of May r. for 1 p*ipe* of a man of Brodefort £4	£4	
	Itm. for a barell bastard 20s	£1	

[1] *Blank in MS.*

203(R) contd.

1	Itm. r. of William Preston for a pipe rackyd £4 6s 8d	£4	6s	8d
1	Itm. r. of John Cutt for 1 pipe £4 6s 8d	£4	6s	8d
2	Itm. the 5 of Awgost for 2 pipes to Antony Stanbank 206	£8	13s	4d
1	Itm. the 26 of Augost r. of a man of Warmyster for a pipe	£4	13s	4d
2	Itm. 1 corrupt pipe to fyll Gascon wynes & 1 pipe was wastyd in reckyng of 7 other pipes so I do cowmpt for the corrupt pipe £3	£3		
—— 56				
	S.	£191	10s	10d

204(L)   **anno 1543**

John Gunnyng of Bartyne Hundred owith the 8 day of February £3 6s 8d & is for a pipe of S.S. iren to be paide at Bartyllmewtide next. Robert Ardeyn of Mangunffilld is shewerty   £3   6s   8d

anno 1543

John Goselett of Marshefilld owith the 18 day of February £4 6s 8d which is for the rest of a butt of seck & 1 pipe of bastard which he r. of me as in my shop boke may apere   £4   6s   8d
Itm. the 5th day of June £3 16s 8d & is for 1 butt seck solld & d'd to hym to pay at all tymes   £3   16s   8d

204(R)   **anno 1544**

John Gunnyng per contra is dewe to have the 25 day of Augost 53s 4d for so myche he pd. me at Bristowe   £2   13s   4d
Itm. the 29 day of November r. of hym   13s   4d

anno 1544

John Goselett per contra is dewe to have the 15 of May 1544 £4 r. of hym at Marschefilld   £4
Itm. more my wif r. 3s 4d   3s   4d
Itm. the 1 day of July r. of his wif 3s 4d   3s   4d
Itm. the 19 day of Jenyver r. by his son £3   £3
Itm. r. of his wif in December 1545 16s 8d   16s   8d

205(L)   **anno 1543**

Master Richard Suche son & heyre to the Lord Suche owith the 21 daye of February £3 6s 8d which I lent & d'd to William Weylland his sarvant in redy monney to be paide at Whitsontyde next & I r. for pledge a tablett of golld with a yello silkyn[1] lase waying 2 owncess   £3   6s   8d
passed this acowmpt to my newe booke fo. 1 the 2de day of July anno 1550

anno 1543

William Yong of Bristowe grocer owith the 21 day of February £7 10s for the rest of 2 buttes seck & 2 pipes bastard, to be paide at Easter next commyng, as in my shop boke may apere   £7   10s
Itm. the 23 day of February 54s 2d & is for 25 quarterons of figges at 2s 2d the quarteron   £2   14s   2d
Itm. the 13 day of Marche £33 5s & is for 95 peces of reasynges at 7s the pece, to be paide at Mighellmas next commyng, montith   £33   5s
Memorandum Itm. the 11 day of Marche £3 13s 4d for a but seck   £3   13s   4d

---

[1] sylkyn *is inserted above the line.*

205(L) contd.

1544 Itm. the 2 day of Maye a*nno* 1544 13 nobles & is for 1 pipe of muscadell rackyd, d'd for hym to Thomas Wale of Harvarteste	£4	6s 8d
Itm. the 15 day of Decem*ber* 1545 40s for 1 h'd of white wyne to be paide at Candellmas next	£2	
Itm. the 15 day of October 1546 £29 & is for 81 pec*es* of Malaga resyng*es* at 6s 8d the pece & for 10 pec*es* at 4s the pece, mon*tith*, to be pd. at Ester next com*m*yng, as it may apere by his byll	£29	

205(R)

[1]

anno 1544

Willi*a*m Yong p*er* contra is dewe to have the [2] of Ap*r*ell 54s 2d which I r. of hym for the figg*es*	£2	14s	2d
Itm. the 16 of June 1544 r. £4 10s	£4	10s	
Itm. the [2] of July 1544 Leight r. £3	£3		
Itm. r. the 6 day of Septe*m*ber by his s*a*rvant Jamy Doule £5	£5		
Itm. the 23 day of September r. of hym by his boy £3	£3		
Itm. the 19 day of November 1544 r. of his son £20	£20		
Itm. the 14 Jenyver r. by his boy	£10		
Itm. the 12 day of July 1545 r. by the hand*es* of his boy 40s	£2		
Itm. r. of hym 25s the 15 day of Dece*m*ber 1545	£1	5s	
Itm. r. 40s	£2		
Itm. the 18 daye of June a*nno* 1547 r. of hym by thand*es* of his s*a*rvant W*illi*am Sherwood £20	£20		
R. of hym £9	£9		

206(L)   **anno 1543**

Antony Stanbanck of Bristowe sarcher owithe the 27 daye of February £16 which is for 4 pipes of bastard at £4 the pipe, mon*tith* £16	£16		
Itm. the 1 day of Marche £4 which is for a p*ipe* teynt	£4		
1544 Itm. the 19 of Maye 1544 £8 & is for 1 to*n* Gascon wyne solld & d'd to hym	£8		
Itm. the 14 of June for 2 h'd Gasco*n* wyne £4	£4		
Itm. the 5 day of August £9 6s 8d & is for 2 pipes of bastard rackyd to be paide at all tymes	£9	6s	8d
1545 Itm. the 28 day of M*a*rche a*nno* 1545 for 2 butt*es* of seck at £4 the butt, more the 2d day of Ap*r*ell for 2 butt*es* seck at £4 the butt mon*tith* £16	£16		
Itm. the 13 day & 15 daye & 23 day of Jenyver for 10 butt*es* seck d'd to hym as may apere in my shop boke at £4 the butt, to pay at all tymes, mon*tith* £40	£40		
Itm. the 24 day of M*a*rche £25 for 4 butt*es* of seck at eich £4 to be paide at all tymes	£16		
Itm. the 24 last day of M*a*rche 1546 £16 for 4 butt*es* seck	£16		
Itm. the 29 day of Jenyver for 6 butt*es* of seck at eiche £4 & the 11 day of February for 9 butt*es* seck & 5 pipes bastard at eich £4, more the same day for a p*ipe* of taynt £4 13s 4d, mon*tith* al £84 13s 4d, to pay the on hallf at Seynt Jamystide next com*m*yng & the other hallf at Mighellmas next after that, as it [2]	£84	13s	4d
1547 Itm. the 2d day of Jenyver a*nno* 1547 £6 13s 4d & is for 1 ton Gascon wyne sold & delyverd to hym to be paide at all tymes requyride	£6	13s	4d
Itm. the same day 10 h'd Gascon wyne at the same p*r*ice	£16	13s	4d
Itm. the 7 of Jenyver for 2 h'd Gascon wyne at *the* seid p*r*ice	£3	6s	8d
Itm. the 12 of Jenyver for 4 h'd Gascon wyne at *the* same p*r*ice	£6	13s	4d
Itm. the 24 of Jenyver for 14 h'd at the seide p*r*ice	£23	6s	8d
Itm. the 28 of Jenyver for 6 h'd Gasco*n* wyne at *the* same p*r*ice	£10		
Itm. the 31 of Jenyver for 10 butt*es* seck at eich £4	£40		
1548 Itm. the 5th day of Jenyver a*nno* 1548 £20 & is for 4 pipes of bastard at £5 the pipe, I sey 4 p*i*pes	£20		

---

[1] *There is no credit entry for Suche.*
[2] *Blank in MS.*

206(L) contd.

Itm. the 8 day of Jenyver £35 & is for 7 butt*es* seck at £5 the but	£35
Itm. the 9th of Jenyver £10 & is for 2 butt*es* seck	£10
Itm. the fyrst day of February £28 & is for 3 ton pipe of Gasco*n* wyne at £8 the ton	£28
Itm. the 7 day of February £55 & is for 11 butt*es* of seck solld & delyverd to hym	£55
Itm. the 27 of February £40 & is for 5 tons Gascon wyn*e* sold & delyverd to hym at £8 the ton	£40
Itm. the 8 of M*a*rche £12 & is for 6 h'd Gascon wyne	£12
Itm. the 30 of December 1549 for 10 butt*es* seck at eich £4 16s 8d & the 8 of Jenyver for 4 butt*es*, the 17 of Jenyv*er* for 3 butt*es*, the 22 of Jenyv*er* 3 butt*es*, mo*n*tith all 20 butt*es* at £4 16s 8d p*er* butt	£96 13s 4d

206(R)   anno 1544

Antony Stanbanck p*er* contra is dewe to have the 16 day of May £10 which his wif *pd.*[1] unto me	£10
Itm. the 2d day of Awgost r. of hym £22	£22
Itm. the 7 day of November r. of hym £9 6s 8d	£9 6s 8
Itm. r. of hym in Awgost 1545 £16	£16
Itm. the 3 day of Marche 1545 r. of hym £10	£10
Itm. the last day of July 1546 r. of hym by the hand*es* of his wif £62 & made aquyttans thereof	£62
Itm. the 1 day of July 1547 r. of hym £44 13s 4d	£44 13s 4d
Itm. the 14 day of September 6s 8d which I do rebate in the p*i*pe of the p*i*pe taynt p*er* contra	6s 8d
Itm. more 5s which I geve for a kercho to his wif	5s
Itm. r. the same day of hym £39 8s 4d	£39 8s 4d
Itm. the last day of Jenyver r. of hym 40 m*a*rk*es*	£24 13s 4d
Itm. the last day of M*a*rche r. of hym £20	£20
Itm. the 18 day of July a*n*no 1548 r. of hym £60	£60
Itm. the 19 day of Ap*r*ell a*n*no 1549 r. of hym £40	£40
Itm. the 27 day of May[2] a*n*no 1549 r. of hym £80	£80
Itm. the fyrst day of Awgost r. of hym £80	£80
Itm. the 24 day of M*a*rche 1549 my wif r. of hym £60	£60
Itm. the 6 day of May a*n*no 1550 r. of hym £20	£20
Itm. the 3de day of June r. of hym £16 13s 4d	£16 13s 4d

207(L)   anno 1543

Willi*a*m Smothing of Harvarteast owith the 22 daye of February £16 & is for butt*es* of seck & 2 pipes bastard at eche £4	£16
Itm. the 13 day of M*a*rche £8 & is for a butt of seck & a pipe of taynt	£8
1544 Itm. the 5th day of June 1544 £7 13s 4d & is for a butt of seck at 11 nobles & 2 h'd of Gasco*n* wyne for £4, mo*n*tith the hole	£7 13s 4d
Itm. the 25 of July £9 6s 8d & is for 1 h'd Gascon wyne at 40s & 2 butt*es* seck at eich 11 nobles to be paide at all tymes	£9 6s 8d
Itm. the 14 day of February for 1 butt seck £4 & 1 pipe bastard 13 nobles mo*n*tith	£8 6s 8d
Itm. the 19 day of February 1545 for a pipe of teynt £5 & for 3 terssis of Gascon wyne £3 15s, mo*n*tith all	£8 15s
Itm. the 26 day of July 1546 for 1 h'd muscadell 7 nobles	£2 6s 8d
Itm. the 24 day of Jenyver a*n*no 1546 £12 13s 4d & is for a but seck & 1 pipe bastard at eiche £4 & for 1 p*i*p*e* of taynt price 7 m*a*rk*es*	£12 13s 4d
Itm. the 7 day of Marche for 3 butt*es* of seck at £4 the butt to be paide at all tymes	£12
Itm. the 6th day of Ap*r*ell 1547 £6 & is for 1 ton of Gascon wyne to be paide at all tymes	£6
Itm. the 22 day of Ap*r*ell £7 & is for a butt of seck at £4 & 2 h'd Gasco*n* wyne at £3 mo*n*tith	£7
Itm. the 16 day of June £6 for 1 ton Gasco*n* wyne	£6

---

[1] *There is a hole in the MS. where Smythe wrote pd.*
[2] of May *is inserted above the line.*

207(L) contd.

Itm. the 4 day of Augost 30s & is for 1 h'd red wyne to be paide at all tymes	£1 10s
1547 Itm. the 27 day of Jenyver 1547 for 1 ton Gasco*n* wyne at 20 nobles, a p*ipe* of bastard at £4 6s 8d & 1 butt of seck at £4 to pay at all tymes, mo*ntith*	£15
Itm. the 22 of February for 2 h'd Gascon wyne £3 6s 8d	£3 6s 8d
1548 Itm. the 4th of May 1548 £6 13s 4d for a ton of Gascon wyne	£6 13s 4d
Itm. the 15 day of Jenyver a*nno* 1548 £5 & is for a p*ipe* of bastard sold & delyverd to hym to be paide at all tymes	£5
Itm. the 25 of February £8 for 1 ton Gascon wyne laden with Sp*ark*	£8
Itm. the 12 of June £8 for 1 to*n* Gasco*n* wyne	£8
1549 Itm. the 3 of Jenyv*er* 1549 £9 that is £5 for a butt of seck & £4 for 2 h'd Gascon wyne to be paide at all tymes	£9
Itm. the fyrst day of February £8 10s & is £5 for a butt of seck & £3 10s for 2 h'd Gasco*n* wyne to pay at all tymes	£9 ~~10s~~
Itm. the 21 of February £8 10s & is for 1 butt of seck p*rice* £5 & 2 h'd Gasco*n* wyne p*rice* £3 10s laden in Sp*arkes* bote	£8 10s

207(R)   anno 1544

W*illiam* Smothing per contra is dewe to have the 4 day of June £12 r. of hym at Bristo	£12
Itm. the 25 of July £7	£7
Itm. the 27 day of November r. of Robert Genyng*es* of Presteyne for won of the butt*es* of seck *per* contra 11 nobles	£3 13s 4d
Itm. the 1 day of December r. by J*ohn* Sp*ar*ke £9	£9
Itm. the 14 of February 1544 my wif r. of hym £5	£5
Itm. r. by Sp*ark* £5 20d	£5 1s 8d
Itm. the monthe of July 1545 he pd. for me to J*ohn* Sparck £4	£4
Itm. the 18 day of February 1545 r. of hy*m* 40s	£2
Itm. the 17 day of Ap*rell* 1546 r. of hym £8	£8
Itm. the 27 day of October r. of J*ohn* Sp*ark*	£2 6s 8d
Itm. he pd. me in November 1546 in mon*ney* & bord*es*	£2 9s 8d
Itm. the 22 day of February r. of John Sp*ark* for hym £4	£4
Itm. the 7 day of M*arche* a*nno* 1546 r. of W*illia*m Smothing in Bristowe 40s	£2
Itm. the 22 day of Ap*rell* a*nno* 1547 r. of hym at Bristowe £6 13s 4d	£6 13s 4d
Itm. the 16th day of June he paide to my wif at Bristowe £6 13s 4d	£6 13s 4d
Itm. the 17 day of June he pd. to my wif	£3 6s 8d
[1]Itm. the 23 day of July 1547, r. of hym 53s 4d	£2 13s 4d
Itm. r. of hym the seide day 20 nobles	£6 13s 4d
Itm. r. of hym the 26 day of November 20 nobles	£6 13s 4d
R. the 25 day of Jenyver of W*illia*m Smothing £6 10s	£6 10s
Itm. r. of hym for the fyrst of Gascon wyne £6 13s 4d	£6 13s 4d
Itm. the [2] day of [2] my wif r. of hym	£8 6s 8d
1548 Itm. the 24 day of July r. of hym	£6 13s 4d
Itm. the 1 day of Jenyver r. of hym 5 m*arkes*	£3 6s 8d
Itm. the 14 of February £5 which Henry Sett*er*ford r. of hym at Harvart for to pay unto Philip Symons tann*er* there	£5
Itm. the 11 of June 1549 r. of hym £8	£8
Itm. the 25 of July r. of hym £4	£4
Itm. the 30 day of December a*nno* 1549 r. of hym at Bristowe £4	£4
Itm. the 1 of ~~Jenyver~~ February r. of hym	£9
Itm. the 19 of Ap*rell* 1550 r. of hym at Bristowe £9	£9

208(L)   anno 1543

James Chester of Bristowe m*archant* o*with* the 5th day of M*arche* £3 16s 8d & is for a pipe of bastard solld & d'd to hym at the same price, mon*tith*	£3 16s 8d

---

[1] *Marginal note*, 2. 13. 4.
[2] *Blank in MS.*

208(L) contd.   anno 1544

Thomas Bick of Arlyngam clothiar owithe the 26 day of July £8 10s & is
30s for 1 h'd of iren & £7 for a pipe of oyle, to be paide at Candellmas next.
John Sparck of Newneham is shew*er*ty   £8 10s

208(R)   anno 1544

   Jamys Chester p*er* contra is dewe to have the 5 day of
   Augost £3 16s 8d & is for so myche r. in redy mon*n*ey   £3 16s 8d

        anno 1544

   Thomas Bick p*er* contra is dewe to have £8 10s which
   J*oh*n Sp*ar*k of Newneham have pd. me for hym in a
   reckenynge   £8 10s

209(L)   anno 1543

Thomas Hawle of B*ar*ckley owith the 6 daye of M*ar*che £3 10s & is for a butt
seck solld & d'd to hym to be paide at all tymes   £3 10s

        a*nn*o 1549

George Burnell owth £25 for my hows apo*n* the Wayer   £25

        anno 1543

Giles Dane of Bristowe s*er*chor owith the 14 day of Marche 11 nobles which
is for 1 butt seck to be pd. the 26 day of May next com*m*yng   £3 13s 4d

        anno 1544

Sawnders Appowell dwelling at the George in the High Streate of Bristowe
ow*ith* the 5th day of June £4 to be paide at all tymes requyrid. I have a sallt
seller p*ar*cell gyllt in pledge   £4

209(R)   anno 1544

   Thomas Hawle p*er* contra is dewe to have the 3d daye of
   Augost 40s which he paide to my wif   £2
   Itm. the 12 of Septemb*er* my wif r. of hym 20s   £1
   Itm. the 19 day of May a*n*no 1545 r. of hym 10s   10s

        a*nn*o 1549

   George Burnell of Bristowe sleymaker is due to have the
   fyrst day of February[1] £4 which I r. in p*ar*te of payment of
   £25 which he must pay me for my hows apon the Wayer at
   Mydsomer next com*m*yng or ells not to have the hows &
   allso lese his seid yernes, as in my shop booke more at large
   do apere   £4
   Itm. the 23 of M*ar*che r. of hym £5   £5
   Itm. the   [2] of June 1550 r. of hym £16 & so made
   to hym & to his heyres a state in fee symple of my hows
   apon the Wayer   £16
                                                                            ―――
                                                                            £25

        anno 1544

   Giles Dane p*er* contra is dewe to have the 9 daye of Octob*er*
   1544 40s which Robert Leight r. of hym   £2

---

[1] the fyrst day of February *is inserted above the line.*
[2] *Blank in MS.*

209(R) contd.   **anno 1544**

Sawnders Appowell per contra is dewe to have the 28 of Augost 40s which he paide to my wif	£2
Itm. the 28 day of November my wif r. 40s	£2

210(L)   **anno 1543**

Jeffrey Arndell of Bridgewater owith the 17 daye of Marche £3 16s 8d & is for a but seck sent hym in Nycolas Lanemans bote	£3 13s 4d
1544 Itm. the 26 daye of July anno 1544 £3 13s 4d & is for a butt of seck at 11 nobles to be pd. at all tymes	£3 13s 4d

anno 1549

John Buckland of West Hartry gentyllman owithe the ~~fyrst~~ last day of February £11 which I paide unto hym in yerenes & part of payment of 2 tons lead to be d'd by thend of the next weke at £6 6s 8d per ton	£11
Itm. the 12 day of February paide to his sarvant 39s 8d	£1 19s 8d

210(R)   **anno 1544**

Jeffrey Arndell per contra is dewe to have the 27 day of June £3 13s 4d which my wif r. from hym	£3 13s 4d
Itm. the 9 day of Jenyver r. by Spyring	£3 13s 4d

anno 1549

John Buckland per contra is due to have the fyrst day of Februarye £6 13s & is for 1 ton led r. at Bristowe, more 1 C. I sey £6 13s	£6 13s
Itm. the 12 day of February £6 6s 8d for 1 ton led	£6 6s 8d

211(L)   **anno 1543**

Thomas Pawllmer of Higley troweman owith the 19 daye of Marche 5 ~~markes~~ nobles & is for 1 h'd 3 li. iren of S.S. d'd to hym in yernes & part of payment of serteyne tymber which I have bowght of hym	£1 13s 4d

anno 1549

Henry Wyeth of Hawxbery by Coventry owith £7 for 1 ton of Gascon wyne which I lode in William Woodwalls trowe as in my shop booke aperithe the 28 of Jenyver	£7
1550 Itm. the 31 day of May anno 1550 £29 & is for 1 ton of oyle which I sent unto hym in Richard Pawlmers trowe of Bewdeley. More £14 & is for 2 ton Gascon wyne laden in the same trowe in 5 h'd claret wyne, 2 h'd whyte wyne & 1 h'd red wyne, montith all £43, to pay ½ at Bartyllmewtyde & ½ at Myghellmas next commyng	£43
Itm. the seyde daye laden in Hugh Skelars trowe of Bewdeley, 3 ton, more 7 li.[1] of S.S. iren conteynyng 296 endes at £12 10s per ton, montith £37 10s, to be pd. ½ at Seynt Jamystide next commyng & the other hallf at Mighellmas next after that	£37 10s 9d ob

211(R)   **anno 1544**

Thomas Pallmer per contra is dew to have the 16 day of June 5 nobles discowntyd & r. in tymber	£1 13s 4d

anno 1549

Henry Wyeth per contra is due to have 18 of Marche £7 r. of Robert Howytt, sarvant to his brother Robert Wyeth	£7

---

[1] *more 7 li. is inserted above the line.*

211(R) contd.

Henry Wyeth per contra is due to have £80 10s 9d ob for so
myche I do make his brother Robert Wyeth debytor for,
becaws the seid Henry have writen unto me by his letter
that his seide brother have r. for his owne use all the
goodes which I lode in Pawllmers & Skelars trowe the 31
day of May as per contra dothe apere & allso as it may apere
to the seid Robert Wyeth in debito folio 186   £80 10s 9d ob

212(L)   **anno 1543**

Cristyan White of Bristowe wyddo owith the last daye of Augost £50 13s 8d
which is for 4 tons S.S. iren at 20 nobles the ton & 4 tons more 6 li. Rendry
iren at £6 the ton & 4 tons more 6 li. Rendry iren at £6 the ton d'd to
Thomas Harrys in her name   £50 13s 8d
Itm. the 5th daye of Marche £74 13s 4d & is for 16 buttes of seck at 11 nobles
the butt & 4 pipes bastard at £4 the pipe which I d'd in her name to Thomas
Harrys, montith   £74 13s 4d
1544 Itm. the fyrst day of Aprell anno 1544 £40 & is for the freight of 30
tons iren at 26s 8d the ton from Spayne in my ship this viage, montith £40

                                   anno 1549

Cristover Digton of Wursettor vyntnar owithe the 5th of August £8 & is for
1 ton Gascon wyne to be paide at Allhaloutide next commyng, as it may
apere by his byll   £8

212(R)   **anno 1544**

Cristyan White per contra is dewe to have the 4th daye of
Aprell £20 & is for so myche reddy money r. by Hamond for
the hallf frett of 30 tons iren   £20
Itm. the 9 day of May my wif r. of her   £20
Itm. the 2d day of Augost r. by the handes of T. Harrys   £40
Itm. the 3 day of December r. of T. Harrys £20   £20
Itm. the 18 day of February 1544 my wif r. by the handes
of Thomas Harrys £60   £60
Itm. the 14 day of Marche 1544 r. by the handes of Thomas
Harrys £5 7s 8d   £5   7s

                                   1549

Cristover Dyton per contra is dewe to have the 5 of
December £8 r. of hym at Bristowe in ready monney   £8

213(L)   **anno 1543**

8   Tayntz for my owne acowmpt, 8 pipes r. the 1 daye of
pipes   Marche owt of a hulk calld the Swan owith 19 V. 080 M. for
          so myche it cost clere abord, for freight 28s per ton & for
          averes 3s 4d per ton, for costom of 3 tons at 3s per ton, for
          hallyng 4d per ton & for hopyng 14d per ton   £20 7s
          Itm. the 28 of Aprell 1544 £11 9s 8d where of I do make
          the cownt of gaynes creditor fo. 200   £11 9s 8d

                                                          S. £31 16s 8d

213(R)   **anno 1543**

          Tayntz per contra is dewe to have the 1 day of
     1   Marche £4 which is for a pipe of taynt solld to
          A. Bosgrove 68   £4
     1   Itm. the same day for a pipe to A. Stanbanck
          206 for   £4

213(R) contd.

1	Itm. for a pipe taken to the prize, mon*tith*	£4		
1	Itm. the 13 of M*arche* for a pipe to J*oh*n Roxby fo. 162	£4		
1	Itm. *the* same day a pipe to W*illiam* Smothing 207 for	£4		
1	Itm. the 19 of M*arche* r. of W*illiam* Preston for a pipe £4	£4		
1	*1544* Itm. the 22 of Aprell 1544 1 p*ipe* to W*illiam* Northe 141 for	£3	16s	8d
1	Itm. the 28 of the same to J*oh*n Roxby fo. 162 1 pipe for	£4		
8 pipes				
	S.	£31	16s	8d

214(L)   **anno 1544**

Thomas Wheteley of Bristowe scryvynar ow*ith* the 5 of Aprell £3 13s 4d & is for a butt of seck to be paide at Mighellmas next & J*oh*n Barns s*ar*vant his father in the law is shew*er*ty   £3 13s 4d[1]

anno 1544

Nicholas Murton of Bristowe rop*er* ow*i*the the 9 day of Aprell £3 13s 4d & is for 2 butt*es* of seck, to pay 11 nobles at Mighellmas next com*m*yng & 11 nobles at Candellmas next after that   £3 13s 4d

214(R)

1

anno 1544

Nicolas Murton p*er* contra is dewe to have the 20 day of December 40s which I r. of hym in 5 angells nobles   £2
Itm. the 22 day of December r. of hym 20s   £1
Itm. the 17 day of Jenyver r. of hym 13s 4d   13s 4d

215(L)   **anno 1544**

Elno*r* Higgyns of Bristowe wedo ow*i*th the 17 day of Maye 45s which is for 1 h'd Gascon wyne to be paide at Mydsom*er* next com*m*yng   £2 5s

anno 1544

Antony Payne of Bristowe groc*er* ow*i*th the 23 of May £19 10s & is for 1 ton[2] Gascon wyne at £8 13s 4d the ton to pay at Whitsontide next   £8 [3]
Itm. the 5th day of June 40s which is for 1 h'd Gasco*n* wyne solld & delyv*er*d to hym   £2
Itm. the 25 day of November & 5th daye of December for 5 h'd Gasco*n* wyne at £7 the to*n* to pay at all tymes requyrid   £8 15s

215(R)   **anno 1544**

Elnor Higgyns p*er* contra is dewe to have the 16 of July 45s & is for 1 h'd Gascon wyne r. p*er* co*n*tra   £2

anno 1544

Antony Payne p*er* contra is dewe to have the 9 daye of M*ar*che £10 which he paide me for Roger in allowance of

---

[1] *There is no credit entry for Wheteley.*
[2] 1 ton *apparently altered from* 2 ton 1 h'd.
[3] £19 10s *erased.*

215(R) cont.

and part of payment of £20 for Roger Abyndon	£10
Itm. the 10 day of September 1546 £7 for so myche r. of hym in reddy monney	£7
Itm. the 11 day of September in reddy monney 16s 9d & more I r. of hym the last Lent in ffische that came from London, as by the acowmpt may appere 18s 3d. So montith the hole 35s	£1 15s

216(L)   anno 1544

Griffithe weyver of Presteyne owith the 6th day of June 40s which is for 1 h'd Gascon wyne to be pd. at Seynt Jamystide next commyng   £2

anno 1550

John Lane of Pride in the parische of West Hartry husbandman owith the 29 day of Marche anno 1550 £21 6s 8d to be pd. in 4 tons led delyverd at Bristowe at Mydsomer next. (Henry Northen is his suertye) passed to my newe booke fo. 11 the 2de day of July anno 1550   £21 6s 8d

anno 1544

Syr John Seyntlo knyght owthe the 6th day of June £4 & is for 2 h'd claret wyne to be paide at all tymes	£4
Itm. he owith by 2 bylls herto annexid of olld	£1 13s 3d½
Itm. paide to John Wyllis the 23 day of December 1544 for 8 gallons & 1 pottell of seck at 12d the gallon & for 8 gallons of mawmessey at 16d the gallon & for 2 barells to fyll it in 18d, montith the hole 20s 8d	£1 8d
Itm. the 17 of Jenyver d'd to his sarvant 9 gallons & 1 pottell of mawnsey that cost to William Jones 16d the gallon	12s 8d
Itm. the 4th day of Aprell anno 1547 £6 & is for 1 ton of Gascon wyne d'd to his sarvant Thomas Evan	£6
1548 Itm. the 25 day of Jenyver anno 1548 delyvered Ewyn Master Seyntlos sarvant 2 tons Gascon wyne at 20 nobles the ton, whereof r. £10, rest £3 6s 8d	£3 6s 8d
Itm. the 7 of February to the seide Ewyn 2 h'd Gascon wyne at 20 nobles the ton, montith	£3 6s 8d
Itm. the 11 day of February 1548 d'd for hym to his sarvant 2 h'd of Gascon wyne price £4	£4
Itm. the 13 day of Marche delyverd for hym[1] to Umffrey Gamon his sarvant 2 ton Gascon wyne at £8 the ton	£16
1549 Itm. the 21 of December 1549, for 2 h'd Gascon wyne d'd to his sarvant Yewyn after £8 the ton	£4
Itm. the 24 of Jenyver £12 for 6 h'd Gascon wyne d'd for hym to his sarvant Yewyn to be pd. at all tymes requyryd	£12
Itm. the 10th of February for 2 h'd wyne d'd for hym to Yewyn	£4
Itm. the 14 of May 1550 for 2 tons at £7 10s per ton	£15

216(R)   anno 1544

Griffithe weyver per contra is dewe to have the 9 day of August 40s which I r. of John Spark   £2

1550

John Lane per contra is due to have the 28 of June £10 13s 4d, & is for 2 ton led conteynying 35 peces Mendyp weight   £10 13s 4d

---

[1] hym is inserted above the line.

216(R) contd.   **anno 1545**

Syr John Seyntlo per contra is dewe to have the 3d day of May £4 which Frances Codryngton paide me for hym in acowmpt	£4
Itm. the 21 day of Jenyver 1547 of Yowen Master Seyntlows sarvant £9 6s 7d ob	£9 6s 7d ob
Itm. the 23 day of February anno 1548 r. of John¹ Ewyn £4 in part of payment of 20 nobles	£4
Itm. the 13 day of Marche 1548 r. of Umfrey Gamon £10	£10
Itm. r. the 24 day of December 1549 from Master Seyntlo by thandes of Thomas Wekes & in presence of his sarvant Ewyn, £16 13s 4d	£16 13s 4d
passed this cowmpt to my newe booke the 2de day of July 1550 in fo. 11	

217(L)   **anno 1544**

John Genynges of Kermerdyne marchant owith the 9 of June £3 to be pd. at Seynt Jamistide next commyng ffor the rest of 3 buttes seck & 2 h'd Gascon wyne, montith	£3
1545 Itm. the 1 day of June 1545 £3 13s 4d which is for the rest of 1 pipe bastard & 2 h'd Gascon wyne to be pd. at Seynt Jamystide next	£3 13s 4d

anno 1544

Frances Woosley marchant of Bristowe owthe the 1 day of Aprell £4 which is for the freight of 3 tons iren in my ship the Trynte, to paye hallf in hand & hallf at thend of 3 monthes next commyng	£4
1548 Itm. the 3d day of May anno 1548 the seid Frances Wosley & his brother Nycolas Wosley owith £40 to pay it ageyne by theyre obligacion made by John Sare at Mydsomer next commyng & is for so myche lent in ready monney to his brother Nicholas Wosley	£40

217(R)   **anno 1544**

John Genynges here ageynst is dewe to have the 21 day of Augost £3 for so myche r. of hym in redy monney & so delyverd to hym his byll	£3
Itm. the 15 day of Augost 1545 my wif r. of hym	£3 13s 4d

anno 1544

Frances Woosley per contra is dewe to have the ² day of Augost 40s for so myche redy monney r.	£2
Itm. the last day of October his wyf pd. 20s	£1
Itm. the 24 day of December 1544 r. of his wyff 20s	£1
1548 R. the 23 day of July of Frances Wosley £40	£40

218(L)   **anno 1544**

Thomas Coper of Bristowe owith the 16 day of June £10 which is £6 for 1 ton Rendry iren at £6 the ton & 2 h'd Gascon wyne at £4 to be all paide at Mighellmas next commyng	£10
Itm. the 19 day of September £12 & is for 2 tons Rendry iren laden for hym in Gryffyth weyvars trow of Wursettor, to be paide at Cristmas next commyng	£12
Itm. the 13 day of October £6 7d & is for 1 ton 12 li. Rendry iren after £6 the ton, to be paide at Candellmas next commyng	£6 7d
Itm. the 12 day of Marche for 1 ton 6 li. iren of S.S. at 20 nobles the ton, montith	£6 13s 8d
anno 1548 Itm. the 9 daye of Jenyver anno 1548 £5 & is for a butt of seck to be pd. at Whitsontyde next commyng	£5

---

¹ John is inserted above the line.
² Blank in MS.

218(L) contd.

Itm. the fyrst day of February £5 & is for a butt of seck to be paide at the seide Whitsontyde £5

Itm. the 10th of September anno 1549 £22 & is for 2 pipes wull oyle to be paide at Owr Lady Day in Marche next commyng £22

1549 Itm. the 24 day of December 1549 £10 & is for 2 buttes of seck sold & delyverd to hym to be paide [1] £10

Itm. the 7 of Marche £5 for a butt of hullock solld & d'd to hym £5
passed to my newe[2] boke the 2de day of July anno 1550

anno 1544

William Pepwell of Bristowe grocer owithe £21 which is for 2 ton iren d'd for hym to Nicholas Kelly hoper the 18 of June & 1 ton to the seid Nycholas the 22 of July, montith 3 tons at £7 the ton & the seid Pepwell is bownd by a byll fyrmyd & sealid with his hand to pay the same £21 at Allhaloutyde next commyng, montith £21

1548

Master Davyd Broke serjant at the lawe owith the 11 day of February £4 for 2 h'd Gascon wyne d'd for hym to his sarvant Walker £4

Itm. the 1 day of July 1549 40s & is for 1 h'd white wyne which was delyverd for hym to his sarvant John Waren poyntmaker £2

218(R)   **anno 1544**

Thomas Cowper per contra is dewe to have the 19 day of September £6 which I r. from hym by Griffith weyvar of Wursettor, montith £6

Itm. the 12 day of October r. by his sarvant Morrys £4

Itm. the 9 day of Marche r. by thandes of [1] late Master Antony Paynes sarvant £12 £12

Itm. the 28 day of September r. of John Sebright in redy money £11, more the seid Coper sent me oken bordes which cost 26s 2d, so montith the hole £12 6s 2d   £12   6s   2d[1]

Itm. r. of hym 15s

Itm. the 16 day of Augost anno 1549 £5 for so myche receavyd by thandes of John Cutt marchant of Bristowe £5

Itm. the 9th of September r. of hym £5 £5

Itm. the 6 day of Marche £22 for so myche r. of hym in ready monney £22

anno 1544

William Pepwell per contra is dewe to have the 16 day of Jenyver £10 which his sarvant pd. to my wif £10

Itm. my wif r. from hym by his sarvant & of hym seallf at 2 tymes £11 £11

1549

Master Broke per contra is dewe to have the 15 of June £3 10s 10s I geve hym in the price, so montith all £4

219(L)   **anno 1544**

William Bemer of Langford owith the 4 day of July £4 which is for a butt of seck, to pay 40s at Mighellmas next commyng & 40s at Allhaloutyde next after that. Richard Pryn is shewerty £4

---

[1] Blank in MS.
[2] newe is inserted above the line.

219(L) contd. *anno* **1547**

Edmond & ⟨¹⟩ Jones of Bristowe hallyars o*with* the 20th day of
September *anno* dicto £20, to be paide ageyne at Mighellmas next com*m*yng,
which £20 I delyv*er* unto them to thentent & *a*pon agrement made byfore
M*aster* Rog*er* Cooke all*d*erman, that they & ev*er*y of them shulld at all
tymes wynter & sommer have provysyon of seme wood & tale wood lying
apon the Back of Bristow, for to sarve the com*m*ons plentyfully withou*t*
grudging or denyall by the pen*n*y worthe & hallf pen*n*y wurck, that is to sey
7 shides of seme wood for a pen*n*y & 14 shides of tale wood for a pen*n*y £20

anno **1544**

Will*ia*m Appowell of Bristowe m*a*rchant owthe the 22 day of Augost 8
m*a*rkes sterling which is for the rest of 1 ton 2 li. Rendry iren, as it may
apere in my shop boke, to be pd, in this maner followyng, that is to sey,
4 nobles at Cristmas next com*m*yng & 4 nobles at O*w*r Lady Day in Lent
M*a*rche next after that & 4 m*a*rkes at Seynt Jamistide next after that. He have
left with me in pledge for thassuran*ce* of the seid som won olld covering for
a bed of flow*er* warck & 22 ownzes of plate in a standyng cupp gillt & six
sylver spones knopyd with postells gyllt & a lytell smawle sallt of sylver
with his cover   £5 6s 8d

219(R)   *anno* **1544**

Will*ia*m Bem*er* of Langford is dewe to have the 14 day
of November £3 which he paide to my wif   £3
Itm. the 29 of July 1545 my wif r. of hym   £1
²

anno **1544**

Will*ia*m Appowell *per* contra is dewe to have the 14 day
of Jenyver 4 nobles which his wif paide to my wif & r. the
6 spones & the litell smawle sawllt mencyonyd *per* contra   £1 6s 8d
Itm. r. by my wif of hym seallf the 20 of Ap*r*ell 1545   £2
Itm. the 24 day of July anno 1545 40s which he paide to
me in reddy mon*n*ey   £2

220(L)   *anno* **1544**

Seck*es* for my owne acowmpte o*with* the 26 day of July
£31 & is for 12 butt*es* seck & 1 butt hullock of hole wyne
20   & 7 butt*es* seck of corrupt wyne that rest to sell of
acowmpt fo. 202   £31
Itm. the monthes of Jenyver & Feverell a*n*no 1544 r. ow*t*
of the Samson of Ankewes, master under God Will*ia*m
Jonson, 14 butt*es* seck, 1 pipe taynt & 6 pipes of basta*r*d
which cost clere abord   ¹

220(R)   *anno* **1544**

Seck*es per* contra be dewe to have the 28 of
2   July £7 6s 8d & is for 2 butt*es* solld to J*o*hn
     Hamon fo. 77   £7 6s 8d
2   Itm. the same day £7 6s 8d for 2 butt*es* to Alson
     Bisshop 152   £7 6s 8d
2   Itm. the 2d day of September for 2 but*es* to
     J*o*hn Roxby 162   £7 6s 8d
2   Itm. the 10th of September for 1 but hullock & 1
     but seck to Will*ia*m Northe fo. 141   £7 6s 8d

---

¹ *Blank in MS.*
² *There is no credit entry for Jones.*

220(R) contd.

1	Itm. the 16 of September for 1 but to John Wade 133	£4		
1	Itm. the 8 of November for 1 but to Robert Jacson	£3	13s	4d
1	Itm. the 17 of November r. of John Americkes wif for 1 but	£3	13s	4d

221(L)   anno 1544

30 L clothes
3 northen cottons
16 ton 5 C led

Viages to Spayne in Guyposcoa owithe the monthe of Aprell £192 10s & is for 30 London clothes, 3 northen couttons, 16 ton 5 C led in 291 peces, all whiche I lode in the John Baptist of the Rendry & the Peter of the Passage & commyttyd it to the governance & rule of my prentes Hewgh Hamon & it cost me clere abord as above seid as it may apere in viages fo. 196   £192 10s

582 fanegas whete
12 hides cow & stere
213 doz. calve skuyns

Itm. the 19 day of June £150 10s & is for 582 fanegas wheat, 12 hydes cow & stere & 213 dozens of calve skuyns, the which Tyndall left with the seid Hamon of myne to sell at Spayne, as it may apere to viages in credito fo. 196   £150 10s

Itm. £18 9s 1d which the seid Tyndall left in Spayne with the seid Hamon to be r. of serteyne debtors for my acowmpt, as it may apere by the seid Tyndalls reckenyng   £18 9s 1d

30 L clothes
6 clothes truckers
10 whit kerssis
150 Manchester cottens
80 hides ox
540 hides cow & stere
59 doz ½ calve skuyns

Itm. the 9 day of Augost laden by the grace of God 20 clothes of John Yerberys & 10 clothes of William Buchar which cost clere abord £120, more 6 truckers of John Yerberys which cost clere abord £18, more 10 whit kerssis which cost clere abord £8 10s, more 150 Manchester cottons which cost clere abord £112 10s, more 8 dicker of ox lether which cost clere abord £25 14s 8d, more 54 dicker cow & stere which cost clere abord £125 14s, more 59 dozens ½ calve skuyns which cost clere abord £17 18s, montith the hole £428 6s 8d   £428 6s 8d

This forseid clothes, kersys, Manchesters, hides & calve skuyns war laden in 2 good ships of the Rendry, the on callid the San Johannes of the Rendry, masters John de Beroby & Mighell de Arsavalo

221(R)   1545

Viages per contra is dewe to have the 12 day of May for the nete sale of 50 clothes of John Yerberys penny hewes & 10 clothes of William Buchars makyng & 6 truckers of John Yerberys makyng & for 10 whit kerssys & for 120 Manchester cottons & 3 northen dozens 545 V. 557 M. as it may apere by acownt subscribyd by my sarvantes Robert Tyndall & Hewgh Hamon r. the afore seid day, montith sterlyng £363 14s 1d   £363 14s 1d

Itm. for the neate sale of 80 ox hides, of 552 hides cowe & stere, & of 272 dozens calve skuyns 430 V. 572 M. ½, as it may apere by the aforeseid reckenyng gevyn by Tyndall & Hamon   £287   11d ob

Itm. for the neate sale of 16 tons 5 C led, 109 V. 362 M. ½, as it may apere by the foreseid reckenyng   £72 18s 2d

Itm. for the neate procedewe of 582 fanegas wheate 93 V. 876 M. as it may apere by the foreseid reckenyng   £62 11s 8d

Itm. for the neate sale of 30 Manchester cottons which Martyne Grevys solld in Andaluzia   [1]

Itm. £18 9s 1d that is for 27 V. 657 M. that Tyndall & Hamon make me creditor of, as it[2] maye apere by the foreseid acownt   £18 9s 1d

---

[1] Blank in MS.
[2] it is inserted above the line.

222(L)

anno 1544

27 ton 1 h'd

Wynes of Gascon for my owne acowmpt 27 ton 1 h'd r. in May owt of the John of the Passage & Mary of S.S., masters Jonot de Villa Viciosa & Diego de la Rua owith 182 V. 261 M. for so myche it cost clere abord with the shewrance, for freight 20s per ton, for averes [1] per ton, for costom 3s per ton, for lysence & other costes [1] per ton, for hopyng 8d per ton, for hallyng & strekyng 4d per ton

[1]

222(R)

anno 1544

8	Wynes per contra be dewe to have the 14 day of May £16 for 2 ton sold to John Roxby fo. 162	£16	
2	Itm. the 17 of May for 2 h'd to Elnor Higgyns fo. 215	£2	5s
4	Itm. the 19 of May for 1 ton to Antony Stanbanck 206	£8	
1	Itm. the 21 day of May I gave 1 h'd to Edward Stanbanck	[1]	
1	Itm. the same day for 1 h'd to T. Lawnsdon fo. 86	£2	
4	Itm. the 23 of May for 1 ton to Antony Payne fo. 215	£8	
6	Itm. the same day r. of Richart Smythe of Coventry for 6 h'd	£12	5s
2	Itm. the 26 day of May r. of Mastres Wynter for 2 h'd	£4	
2	Itm. the 27 of May r. of Jamys Grene for 2 h'd	£4	
4	Itm. the same day for 1 ton to William Northe fo. 141	£7	10s
4	Itm. the 5th of June for 1 ton to William Rowley fo. 87	£8	
2	Itm. the same day to William Smothing fo. 207 2 h'd	£8	
2	Itm. the same day for 2 h'd to Sawnders Appowell fo. 209	£4	
1	Itm. the same day for 1 h'd to Antony Payne fo. 215	£2	
4	Itm. the 6 of June for 1 ton to Jerom Grene, fo.[1]	£8	
1	Itm. r. of Spark for Gryffith weyver for 1 h'd	£2	
1	Itm. r. of Robert Genynges for 1 h'd	£2	
2	Itm. the 7 day of June for 2 h'd to my Lady Seyntlo 216	£4	
4	Itm. the 9 day of June r. of John Hoper for 1 ton	£8	
2	Itm. the same day for 2 h'd to John Genynges fo. 217	£4	
3	Itm. the 10 of June r. of Richard Hodges for 3 h'd	£6	
2	Itm. the 14 of June for 2 h'd to Antony Stanbank 206	£4	
12	Itm. the same day for 3 tons to John Wyllis fo. 73	£24	
4	Itm. the same day for 1 ton to John Roxby fo. 162	£8	
2	Itm. the 16 of June for 2 h'd to Thomas Copar fo. 218	£4	
1	Itm. the 18 of June for 1 h'd to John Awells fo.[1]	£2	
1	Itm. the same day r. of William Appowell grocer for 1 h'd	£2	
1	Itm. the 20 of June r. for 1 h'd Gascon wyne	£2	
2	Itm. the 25 of June r. of Myles Willson for 2 h'd	£4	

[1] *Blank in MS.*

222(R) contd.

1	Itm. the 26 of June r. of the wif of the 3 tons for 1 h'd	£2
4	Itm. the 28 of June for 1 ton to John Web of Syssetor fo.[1]	£8
1	Itm. the same day £2 for 1 h'd to John Wellsche fo. 74	£2
4	Itm. the 29 of June r. of my Lord Harbardes sarvant for 1 ton	£8
2	Itm. the 30 of June r. for 2 h'd of William Powell grocer	£4
1	Itm. the 8 of July r. of Master Northole for 1 h'd	£2
1	Itm. the 10 of July r. in acowmpt of John Spark for 1 h'd	£2
4	Itm. the 25 of July r. of Richard Carryck for 1 ton	£7
1	Itm. the same day for 1 h'd to William Smothing fo. 207	£2
1	Itm. the 26 of July I gave 1 h'd to Doctor Owen	[1]
1	Itm. 1 h'd which I ocupyed in my howse, £2	[1]
3	Itm. 3 h'd for ylladge	[1]
27 ton 1 h'd		

222(A)

A small loose sheet approx 5" × 4" in Smythe's hand

4 spones weying 3 ownces & hallf a quarter   3 oz.
1 flate pece wying 16 oz. ½
1 flat pece pece[2] 10 oz. ½
a standyng cupp 33 oz. ½
a nut coveryd 22 oz. rebate for the shell 1 oz. & ½. Rest 20 oz. ½.

222(B)(L)

A loose sheet not in John Smythe's hand

1541

Master Smithe owithe £6 19s 2d and ys ffor his quarter parte lissaunce of 38 weys wheat, 20 weyes beannes bowt of Master Stanbancke Whereof 30 weyes wheate, 20 weys beannes was entred in the Trenyte, and you enjoyed the hallff and your parte was but 1 quarter so that you rest owing 7 weys ½ wheat and 2 weys ½ beannes and of [1] the rest off the lissaunce was entread in Anton de Astiasso 8 weys wheat 3 weys beannes, whereof you enjoyed your quarter and the rest of the holle lissaunce was 7 weys beannes which was solld to William Tyndall by your conssent whereof you r. your quarter. So that you rest owing as abovesseyd 7 weys hallff wheat, 2 weys ½ beannes	£6 19s 2d £4 15s 10d
Itm. ffor lissaunce of 31 weys in the Harrye att 7s 2d qr. per wey	£11 3s 5d
Itm. ffor ffreight of 40 ton oylle and serteyn soppe	£40 1s 11d
Itm. ffor 2 peces of tymber delyverid your pursser 3s 4d	3s 4d
Itm. ffor a plancke[3]	1s [4]
Itm. more you owe me ffor 1 tierce of a weye wheat, or 1 tierce whiche was laden in the Trenyte	8s
Itm. for 9 ton 19 C freight in the Hary	£11 17s 6d[4]
	£75 19s 02d[4]

---

[1] *Blank in MS.*
[2] *Smythe repeats pece.*
[3] *There is a sign here which is undecipherable.*
[4] *Another hand has filled in these totals.*

222(B)(R)

Master Smithe per conntra ys dewe £5 5s 6d and ys ffor so moche r. in parte of payment of the quarter parte of lissaunce bowght of Master Stanbancke, montith	£5	5s	6d
Itm. ffor lissaunce of 4 weys beannes att 7s 6d per weye	£1	10s	
Itm. ffor lissaunce and costes of 32 weyes in the Trenyte att 8s per weye, montith	£12	16s	
Itm. 15s 2d ffor hallff Hamons costes to London, montith and 33s 4d for ½ of 5 markes to Master Stanbancke and 16d ffor 4 mates ¹ the Harrye	£2	9s	10d
Itm. ffor lissaunce of 7 dicker lether £4 13s 4d	£4	13s	4d
Itm. ffor ffreight of 40 ton iren in the Trenyte, montith	£26	13s	4d
Itm. the 12th daye of Dessember anno 1541 ffor ffreight in the Trenyte of 6 ton ffrom the Condado at 25s the ton, montith	£7	10s	
Itm. £1 10s and is for 1 h'd iren which you shall r. of Thomas Hikes	£1	10s	
Itm. for 4 ton ded freight £1 10s	£1	10s	
Itm. the 24 day of Dezember 1541 £11 12s 2d for so muche redy money r. for the rest and clozinge up of this acowmpt, montith²	£11	12s	2d
	£75	19s	02d

222(C)

A loose bifolium written on three sides
The account of John Wyllis

p. i

anno 1547

Master John Smyth marchaunt

Receved the ffyrste day of January one toon of Gaskyn wyne price	£6	13s	4d
Receved the 7th of January 2 hoggeddes	£3	6s	8d
Receved the laste day of January 3 toon price the toon £6 13s 4d amontith	£20		
Receved the 18 day of September 3 buttes of secke price	£12		
More Master Smyth ys due³ to have owte of the Chamber for his hole yeres ffee due at Myghelmas	£36		

Summa £78

Master Smyth owith unto me John Wyllie as yt aperith be my hows booke which have ben delyvered at dyverse tymes		34s	1d
Plus for 7 C of led price the hondrith which was delyveryd from Master Tyndall stor hows			⁴
Plus for 2 C qr. 14 li. lede⁵ which was delyveryd be thandes of James Chester ffor this Master Paynes copullment, more there ys 20 foders and ys due to me for I lackyd so myche of my copulment			⁴
Plus for £8 6s 8d which I payd to Master ⁴ of London for 25 yardes of cloth for ys sergent ys lyverye	£8	6s	8d
Plus for £3 8s delyveryd to Robert Cater at Trinite Terme	£3	8s	
Plus for £2 that I d'd to Master Curtys	£2		
Plus for £2 13s 4d pd. by ys eom comandment to Sir Water Jaye	£3	13s	4d⁶

p. ii

Master John Smyth marchaunt

Plus for pavyng before ys 3 tenementes in Brode Streate	15s 6d ob qr.
Plus for pavyng in Grope Lane befor Wylliam Lantros hows as it may aper	4s 1d ob

---

¹ *There is a sign here which is undecipherable.*
² *The handwriting changes for the last three items.*
³ due *is inserted above the line.*
⁴ *Blank in MS.*
⁵ lede *is inserted above the line.*
⁶ *sic.*

222(C) p. ii contd.

Plus for vestementes of the chapell of the brydge	£2	6s	8d
Plus for Thomas Cooke ye sarvant for hys burges money			[1]
Plus for serteyn tymbers delyveryd at dyverse tymes due to the chamber			[1]
Summa that I doo amont	£56	15s	1d

p. iii

John Horner, Aldred Fitzjamys, Nycholas Fitzjames, Antony Gilbert, esquyers	£78		
	£21	7s–	5d
56 – 15 – 1		4s	11d

222(D)

A loose sheet in Smythe's handwriting

anno 1549

7 ton 12 C led
30 dozens
10 calve skyns

Viages to Andaluzia owith the 11 day of March for my acowmpt in the Hart of Chepstowe[2] £67 7s 2d & is for 7 tons 12 C led conteynyng 130 peces powncyd & markyd as my shop booke may apere, every ton whereof cost clere aboorde £7 16s 8d, which amontith to £51 8s 8d. More 1 fardell of calve skyns markyd with my mark in the margent conteynyng 30 dozens & 10 skyns which cost clere aboorde 10s per dozen. So montith the hole   £67 7s 2d

Itm. the 8 daye of June 1550 I lode by Godes grace in the

2 fyne hulynges
10 sortyng clothis
35 northen streightes
1 pece of black lynard
1 dozen of calve skyns
15 tons 4 C 1 qr. 22 li. led conteynyng 263 peces

Savyor of Bristowe 1 fardell of clothe under this mark conteynyng 2 fyne hewlynges in buckeram which cost aboorde £14 & 10 sortyng clothes which cost aborde £62, I sey £62, more in woon other fardell under my seide mark 35 northen streightes which cost abord 19s the pece, montith £33 5s, more 1 black pece of lynyng which was wrapper to the fardell of clothe that cost 9s, more 1 dozen of calve skyns valent 9s, more 15 tons 4 C 1 qr. 22 li. led conteynyng 263 peces markyd thus   & powncyd thus   which cost aboord £7 5s per ton, montith £110 7s.[3] So montith all £220 10s. to all the whiche goodes so laden in the Savyor, Hugh Hamon is my factor   £220 10s

passed all this cowmptes the 2de day of July anno 1550 to my new boke fo. 21

223(L)   anno 1544

George Graye of Bristowe inholder owith the 22 day of September 46s 8d & is for the rest of a pipe of bastard apon the lyes solld to hym for 7 markes & it must be paide at Cristmas next commyng   £2 6s 8d

Itm. the 7 day of June anno 1547 30s and is for 1 h'd of Gascon wyne to be paide at Seynt Jamystide next comyng   £1 10s

anno 1545

Nicholas Baylif of Stawntondrewe owithe £3 13s 10d ob which is for the rest of 12 C 3 qr. 26 li. iren of S.S. & of the Rendry solld to hym the 13 & 22 dayes of Aprell, to be pd. at Myddsomer next, as by my shop boke may apere   £3 13s 10d½

---

[1] *Blank in MS.*
[2] in the Hart of Chepstowe *is inserted above the line.*
[3] 7s *is inserted above the line.*

223(L) contd.

Itm. the 12 day of October £6 13s 4d which is for the rest of 21 C 14 li. iren which he promes to pay at Allrode Day in May next com*m*yng, mo*ntith* £6 13s 4d

Itm. the 8 day of July 1546 £6 13s 4d which is for a ton of S.S. iren to be paide at Allhaloutyde next com*m*yng £6 13s 4d

223(R)   **anno 1544**

George Gray p*er* contra is dewe to have the 24 of December 46s 8d & is for so myche mon*n*ey r. of hy*m* £2 6s 8d

Itm. the 28 of July 1547 r. 30s £1 10s

1545

Nicholas Baylif is dewe to have £3 3s 10d ob & is for so myche he pd. to my wif .... £3 3s 10d ob

Itm. my wif r. of hym the 20 day of June 1546 £6 13s 4d £6 13s 4d

r. by my wif which Bayly pd. to her £6 13s 4d £6 13s 4d

224(L)   **anno 1544**

John Chambers of Kyngsnorton owith the 18 day of September £12 to be paide at all tymes whiche is for 2 ton Rendry iren sent unto hym in Thomas Asevarns trowe, mo*ntith* £12

Itm. the 9 day of December £6 for 1 ton Rendry iren laden in Thomas Pawlmers trowe £6

224(R)   a*n*no 1545

John Chambers p*er* contra is dewe the 19 day of August £12 which I r. of hym at Bristowe £12

Itm. the 15 day of December r. by Thomas Harrys m*ar*chant £6

225(L)   **anno 1544**

John Walker of Sissetor vyntener owithe the 11 of October £14 which is for 2 pipes wull oyle sent to hym by J*oh*n Byrco*m* of Dodyng carryer, to be paide at Candellmas next com*m*yng £14

                                        anno 1544

John Wynter Tresorer of the Kyng*es* navy owith the 21 day of Marche £6 6s 8d & is for 1 ton of iren d'd by his com*m*awndement to J*oh*n Snyg £6 6s 8d

225(R)   **anno 1544**

John Walker p*er* contra is dewe to have the last daye of February £7 which I r. by thand*es* of John Byrco*m* £7

Itm. r. of Byco*m* the carryer in M*ar*che £7

John Wynter is dewe to have £6 13s 4d & is for so myche he paide in acowmpt to my s*ar*vant Leight[1] £6 13s 4d

226(L)   **anno 1544**

John Bircom of Dodyngton carryar owithe the 11 day of October £6 13s 4d & is for a ton of S.S. iren to be paide at Holyrode Day in May next com*m*yng £6 13s 4d

Itm. the 5 day of June a*nn*o 1545 for 1 ton of S.S. iren price £6 13s 4d to pay at Crist*m*as next £6 13s 4d

---

[1] *This entry is undated.*

226(L) contd.

Itm. the 6 day of June £7 for 1 but of seck to be paide at Mighellmas next	£4
1546 Itm. the 9 day of Aprell anno 1546 £6 13s 4d & is for a ton of iren of S.S. to be pd. at Mighellmas next commyng	£6 13s 4d

226(R)   **1545**

John Byrcom per contra is dewe to have the 29 day of May £6 13s 4d which I r. of hym in redy monney	£6 13s 4d
Itm. the 24 day of July 1545 r. of T. Web of Sysseter for the but seck per contra £4	£4
Itm. the 23 day of Jenyver 1545 r. of hym at Bristowe £6	£6
Itm. the 12 day of Marche r. of hym 13s 4d	13s 4d
Itm. the 19 day of November 1546 r	£6 13s 4d

227(L)   **anno 1544**

William Preston of Bristowe hosemaker owithe the 20 day of October 26s 8d to be paide at Seynt Androwstide next commyng which is for the rest of a pipe of muscadell sold to hym for 14 nobles	£1 6s 8d

anno 1549

Bastyan de Sansust marchant of S.S. in Spayne owith the 14 of Jenyver anno dicto £50 & is for so myche ready monney whiche I lent to hym to be paide at all tymes requyred	£50

anno 1549

Edward Mathewe otherwise Capper of Tawnton owith the 15th of Jenyver £7 which is for a ton of Gascon wyne to pay at Easter next commyng passed to my newe boke the 2de day of July 1550.	£7

227(R)   **anno 1544**

William Preston per contra is dewe to have the 8 day of Jenyver 26s 8d which he pd. to my wif	£1 6s 8d

anno 1549

Bastyan de Sansust per contra is due to have the 17 day of February £50 which he paide unto me in ready monney¹	£50

228(L)   **anno 1544**

Robert Genynges of Presten owith the 1 day of December £3 which is for a pipe iren to be paide at all tymes requyrid	£3
Itm. for the rest of 2 buttes seck 40s	£2
Itm. the 28 day of Marche 1545 for 1 but seck at £4 & for 2 h'd Gascon wyne £4, montith	£8
Itm. the 28 day of Aprell £8 10s that is £4 for 1 butt of seck & £4 10s for 1 pipe bastard	£8 10s
Itm. the 15 day of Jenyver 1545 £3 which is for the rest of 2 buttes of seck d'd for hym to John Spark	£3
Itm. £3 13s 4d for 2 h'd Gascon wyne	~~£3 13s 4d~~
Itm. the 19 day of February for 1 butt seck £4 ~~and for 2 h'd gascon wyne £3 15s~~ montith	£4
Itm. the 17 day of Marche for 1 h'd 1 qr. 12 li. Rendry iren 32s 2d & for 2 h'd, 2 tierces Gascon wyne £6 5s, montith the hole £7 17s 2d to pay at all tymes	£7 17s 2d
1546 Itm. the last day of Aprell £8 for 2 butes seck	£8

---

¹ *There is no credit entry for Mathewe.*

228(L) contd.

Itm. the 3th day of May for 2 but*tes* sec*k price* £8	£8
Itm. the 28 day of July 30*s* which is for 1 h'd Rendry ire*n* to be paide at all tymes	£1 10s
Itm. the 12 day of December a*nno* 1546 £8 which is for 2 but*tes* of seck*es* to be paide at all tymes	£8
Itm. the 5 day of February £8 for 2 but*tes* seck	£8
Itm. the 24 of M*arche* £8 for 2 but*tes* seck	£8
Itm. the 6 day of Aprill 1547 for 1 to*n* Gasco*n* wyne	£6
Itm. the 5th day of Maye £14 & is for 2 but*tes* seck*es* at eiche £8 & 1 ton Gascon wyne at £6, to be pd. at all tym*es*	£14
Itm. the 4 day of Augost a*nno* 1547 laden for hym in J*ohn* Sparck*es* bote 2 but*tes* seck at eiche £4 & 3 h'd Gascon wyne at eiche 30s, mo*ntith* £12 10s to pay at all tymes requyrid	£12 10s
Itm. the 19 day of Augost laden in J*ohn* Sp*arkes* bote 2 but*tes* of seck p*r*ice £8 to pay at all tymes	£8
1547 Itm. the 10th day of February a*nno* 1547 £20 3s 4d & is for 1 ton Gascon wyne at 20 nobles & for 2 but*tes* seck £8 & for a but of mawmessey at £5 10s, to be pd. at all tymes requyrid	£20 3s 4d
1548 Itm. the 11 day of Ap*r*ell a*nno* 1548 £11 6s 8d & is for 2 but*tes* of seck at eich £4 & for 2 h'd Gascon wyne at £3 6s 8d	£11 6s 8d
Itm. the 25 day of May £17 10s & is for 3 but*tes* of seck at eich £4 & for 1 butt of mawmesey at £5 10s	£17 10s
Itm. the 26 of July £7 15s & is for a but of seck at £4 & 2 h'd Gascon wyne after £7 10s p*er* ton to be paide at all tymes requyrid	£7 15s
Itm. the 9 day of Jenyver 1548 £10 & is for 2 but*tes* of newe seck*es* at £5 the butt to be paide at all tymes, mo*ntith*	£10
	S. £182 ~~15~~ 2s 2d

228(R)   anno 1544

Robert Genyng*es* p*er* contra is dewe to have 40s which my wif r. of his boy	£2
Itm. she r. the 28 day of Ap*r*ell 1545 £3	£3
Itm. she r. the seid day of hym in p*art* of payement of 1 butt seck & 2 h'd Gascon wyne p*er* contra 40s	£2
Itm. the 26 day of July my wif r. of hym £6	£6
Itm. my wif r. of hym in December 1545 £8 10s	£8 10s
Itm. the 17 day of Marche a*nno* 1545 r. of hym in Bristowe	£3
Itm. the last day of Ap*r*ell 1546 r. of hym at Bristowe in ready mon*ney* £8	£8
Itm. £8 which my wif r. from hym by J*ohn* Sp*ark* the 16 day of June 1546	£8
The 28 day of July my wif r. of hym £4	£4
Itm. the [1] day of [1] 1546 my wif r. of J*ohn* Sp*ark* & his s*ar*vant £5 2s 2d	£5 2s 2d
Itm. the 28 day of Ap*r*ell 1547 r. of hym at Bristowe £10	£10
Itm. the 26 day of July r. of hym £20	£20
Itm. the 12 day of October 1547 my [1] r. of hym £7	£7
Itm. the 9 day of February 1547 r. of hym £20	£20
Itm. the 10th day of February 1547 r. of hym £7 10s	£7 10s
Itm. the 25 day of May 1548 r. of hym £8	£8
Itm. the 26 day of July r. of hym £20	£20
Itm. the 12 day of October 1548 for 44 dozens of calve skuyns bowght of Water Byrd at 6s 8d p*er* dozen, for carriage to Newneham 10s, for a shurt clothe 3s 4d	£15 6s 8d
Itm. r. of his s*ar*vant the [1] day of Jenyver 1548 £10 in testorns	£10

---

[1] *Blank in MS.*

228(R) contd.

Itm. the 13 daye of February a*nno* 1548, r. of Robert Gen*y*n*ges* £13 8s 4d ffor the hole & full payment of this acow*m*pt	£13	8s	4d
I sey £182 2s 2d S.	£182 ~~15~~ 2s	2d

229(L)   **anno 1544**

Wynes of Andaluzia for the acowmpt of Robert Tyndall, that is to sey 8 butt*es* seck, 1 pipe of teynt & 3 pipes bastard r. the monthes of Jenyver & February ow*t* of a hulk callid the Samson of Ankewes, m*aster* W*i*lliam Jonsson owith for costom at Chepstowe   [1]   , for bote hyer to Bristowe   [1]   , for the Kyng*es* custom   [1]   , for freight 26s 3d p*er* ton & for averes   [1]   p*er* ton.   [2]

an*no* **1549**

Will*i*am Northe of Bruto*n* owithe the 14 of Octo*ber* £7 14d & is for the rest of acowmpt as it may apere to hym in credito fo. 239	£7	1s	2d
Itm. the last day of Decem*ber* a*nno* dicto £8 10s & is for 1 but seck p*r*ice £5 & 1 h'd Gasco*n* wyne p*r*ice £3 10s	£8	10s	
Itm. the 25 of Jenyver for 2 h'd Gasco*n* wyne p*r*ice £3 10s	£3	10s	
Itm. the 28 of Jenyver £34 that is £10 for 2 butt*es* of seck & £24 10s for 3 ton p*i*pe Gascon wyne at £7 p*er* ton	£34	10s	
	£53	11s	2d

229(R)

[1]

1549

W*i*lliam North, Itm. the ~~20~~ [1] day of Jenyver £10 which he pd. for me to Will*a*m Brydg*es* of Weston clothiar	£10		
Itm. more he have pd. to Brydg*es* £20	£20		
Itm. the 16 of May r. from hym by my s*a*rvant W*i*lliam Clerk £23 10s	£23	10s	
Itm. more 14d which he seyeth I do owe hym for a rest of iren		1s	2d
S.	£53	11s	2d

230(L)   **anno 1545**

John Sparck of Newneham in the Forrest of Deane yeoman owith the 29 day of May £5 19s 9d & is for 19 C 3 qr. 23 li. Rendry iren at £6 the ton, to be paide at all tymes	£5	19s	9d
Itm. the 12 day of July £22 11s 8d & is for £4 which he r. for me of W*i*lliam Smothe & he r. of me £18 11s 8d, mon*tith*	£22	11s	8d
Itm. the last day of October £8 which Smothyng paide to hym for me for the acowmpt of Jamys Webster, mon*tith*	£8		
Itm. more he r. of the smythe of Homlass £3 & of my wif £40	£43		
Itm. for 2 ton iren at £6 the ton, d'd the 8 of October[3]	£12		
Itm. for 1 p*i*pe ire*n* d'd the 21 day of November	£3		

---

[1] *Blank in MS.*
[2] *There is no credit entry for wines.*
[3] *d'd the 8 of October is inserted above the line.*

230(L) contd.

Itm. the 5 of December 1545 for 6 h'd Gascon wyne	£11		
Itm. the 15 day of Jenyver for 2 bute*s* seck	£8		
Itm. the 3d day of February 1545 £3 4s	£3	4s	
Itm. the 18 day of February for 1 butt of seck p*rice*	£4		
Itm. the 17 day of Marche £4 for 1 h'd meate oyle	£4		
1546 Itm. the 3d & 30 dayes of May for 3 pec*es* resyng*es* of Malaga at 8s the pece, 24s	£1	4s	
Itm. the 29 day of May for 1 ton pi*pe* 3 li. Rendry ire*n* £9 2d & the 15 day of July for 1 pi*pe* 3 li. Rendry iren £3 2d, amon*tith* all £12 4d	£12		4d
Itm. for spic*es* sett at Master Powells at *Crist*mas 1546 36s	£1	16s	
S.	£139	15s	8d

230(R)   anno 1545

John Sparck of Newneham in the Forrest of Dean yeoman is dewe to have the 13 day of June £22 11s 8d, & is for 17 dozen of calve skuyns which I rest owyng to hym at 5s p*er* doze*n* & 15 dicker ox hid*es* at 46s 8d p*er* dicker & for 15 dicker cowe & stere, of the which 10 dick*er* do cost 33s 4d p*er* dicker & 5 dicker at 40s the dicker, as it may apere in a pap*er* which I have d'd to hym wrytten with my owne hand   £22 11s 8d

I sey that I owe the seid £22 11s 8d for the rest of the foressed calve skuyns & le*ther*.

Itm. £3 which he paide to my wif the 25 of July	£3		
more he pd. for the smythe of Homelass	£3		
Itm. the 20 day of October for 33 dicker 7 tand hides at 40s the dicker, of the which war 3 dicker ox, mon*tith* £67 8s	£67	8s	
Itm. for 7 dicker 3 hid*es*, of the which be 3 dicker & more of ox at 40s the dicker & 21 doze*n* calve skuyns at 5s the dozen, mon*tith* £19 17s, which le*ther* rest yet in his hows	£19	17s	
Itm. for ~~brynging lether abord~~ the 8 C of ellm bord*es* at 7 grot*es* the C & 4d for metyng, mon*tith*[1]		19s	
Itm. for 74 foote of ellme bord*es* at 2s 4d the ~~foote~~ C, & 1049 fote of oke bordes at [2] the ~~fote~~ C, mon*tith* the hole[1]		[2]	
Itm. the 10 day of November £7 ~~18s~~ 5s & is for 3 dicker ~~& 7~~ tand hid*es* at 40s the dicker & 6 dozens of calve skuyns at 5s the dozen, mon*tith*	£7 ~~£7 18s~~	5s	
Itm. 14s pd. to M*aster* Goldsmythe for oken bord*es* & 13s 4d for carage of oken bord*es* from Harvart to Newman & 16s 4d for 7 C ellm boord*es* & 4s for bote hier of boord*es* to Bristowe, 24s for 120 rent bord*es* & 9s 4d for 4 C oken bord*es*, mon*tith* all	£4		
Itm. for rest of shepe 4s 8d		4s	8d
Itm. the 24 day of M*arche* 1546, r. of hym		10s	4d
Itm. the 24 day of M*arche* £11 for the rest & closyng up of this cowmpt whereof I make the seid J*ohn* Sp*ark* debitor in fo. 264	£11		
S.	£139	15s	8d

231(L)   anno 1544

Will*iam* Appowell of Bristowe grocer owith the 9 day of February £12 13s 7d & is for 1 ton Rendry iren at £6 the ton & 1 ton 4 li. S.S. iren at £6 13s 4d the ton, to be paide at Mydsomer next com*m*yng, mon*tith*   £12 13s 4d

---
[1] *These two items are crossed through.*
[2] *Blank in MS.*

231(L) contd.

1545 Itm. the 28 day of March a*nn*o 1545 for 1 h'd of Gascon wyne 40s £2
Itm. the 5th day of November 1545 £13 6s 8d & is for 2 tons iren which his s*a*rvant r. to be pd. at Easter next £13 6s 8d
Itm. the 3de day of October 1549 £40 & is for 60 C of Yland woode at 13s 4d p*e*r C, to be paide £20 at Candellmas next com*m*yng & £20 at Easter next after that £40
passed this cownt the 2de of July 1550 to my newe boke fo. 13

231(R)   anno 1545

Willi*a*m Appowell p*e*r contra is dewe to have the 3 day of July £10 13s 4d[1] which my s*a*rvant Hamon r. of hy*m* £10 13s 4d
Itm. I entryd apo*n* his lisence 5 dicker le*t*her at 6s 8d p*e*r dicker £1 13s 4d
Itm. 12s 6d for 2 C ½ of corck 12s 6d
Itm. for spyc*es* that John Sp*a*rk had at *Crist*mas for M*a*ster Baskyrdfyld £1 16s
Itm. the 14 day of Aprell a*n*no 1546 r. of hym by my sa*r*vant Henry Setterford £10 18s 2d £10 18s 2d
Itm. the 8 day of February 1549 r. fro*m* hym by thand*es* of Nycolas Frema*n* 20 m*a*rkes in ready money £13 6s 8d
Itm. the 13 day of May a*nn*o 1550 r. fro*m* hym by thand*es* of Jo*h*n Beyt his s*a*rvant 20 m*a*rk*es* £13 6s 8d

232(L)   anno 1545

148 Manchester cottons

Viag*es* for my owne acowmpt to Biscay & dyrectid & consygnyd to my s*a*rvant Robert Tyndall owithe the 11 daye of Ap*r*ell £101 3s 4d & is for 148 Manchester cottons of dyvers collow*r*es laden in 4 pack*es* under my m*a*rk in the Trynte of the Rendry, m*a*ster under God John Ware de Amassa, mon*tith* £106 3s 4d
Itm. 6 d*u*cat*ts* which Hewgh Hamon left with Tyndall for to shewere a C d*u*cats & it was not shewryd £1 10s

31 clo*thes*
2 Manchesters
188 dozens ½ of calve skuyns
180 ox hid*es*
250 hid*es* cow & stere

Itm. the 12 day of June laden in the San J*oh*n of the Rendry, ma*s*ter John de Beroby, & in the Nycolas of Orio, m*a*ster Domyngo de Segura, 3 fardells *conteynyng* 30 clothes of John Yerberys pen*n*y hews which cost clere abord £120, more 2 Manchester cottons which cost 28s, more a clothe of Jo*h*n Ravyns makyng which cost £4 12s, more 188 dozens & ½ of calve skuyns which cost clere abord £56 11s 8d, more 18 dick*er* of ox hid*es* & 25 dicker cowe & stere which cost clere aborde £97 11s 8d, mon*tith* all £280 3s 4d

40 Ma*n*chester cottons

Itm. the 17 day of June lode by God*es* grace in the San J*oh*n of the Rendry, m*a*ster under God Miguell de Arysabalo, 1 fardell of Mancher cottons *conteynyng* 40 which cost clere abord £29, mon*tith* £29

232(R)[2]

233(L)   anno 1545

John Yerbery of Bruto*n* o*with* the 3 day of July £16 17s 6d which is paide in p*a*rt of payment of the £26 17s 6d dewe the fyve of May last past, more the 14 of July pd. to hym sellf at Bristow £10, mon*tith* the hole £26 17s 6d £26 17s 6d
Itm. the 9 day of Septemb*e*r £17 18s 4d which his son Willi*a*m r. for a payment dewe at Seynt Jamistide last past & so I r. my byll £17 18s 4d

---

[1] *13s 4d is inserted above the line.*
[2] *Fo. 232(R) is blank in the MS.*

233(L) contd.

Itm. paide to John Yerbery by thandes of William Northe in 3 parcells £31 4s 10d ~~that~~ as it may apere in the backside of my byll datyd the 3 day of July 1545, more pd. the last day of September to John Yerbery the yonger £20 as it may apere in the back side of the same byll, more paide to the same John Yerbery the yonger the 3d day of November £20 8s 6d. So montith the hole £71 13s 4d & is for the payment in hand for a byll datid the 3 day of July last past, as per contra aperithe £71 13s 4d

Itm. he r. of William Northe the 18 day of February £16 12s 10d, more of a smythe of Waynstrowe 20s, more of me the 15 day of Marche anno 1545 £9 4s 8d, montith £26 17s 6d payable at Seynt Androwstide last past & so I r. my byll of his son John Yerbery £26 17s 6d

1546 Itm. the 10 day of May William Northe pd. to hym for me £11 & the 18 day of the same I paide to hym £24 16s 8d, montith £35 16s 8d dewe for the payemet at Candellmas last past £35 16s 8d

Itm. the 18 day of May anno 1546 £7 6s 8d & is for 1 pipe wull oyle sold to hym to pay at Seynt Jamistide next £7 6s 8d

Itm. the 29 day of July 1546 £3 6s 8d which he is content to r. of William Petter smythe, as it maye apere to hym in credito 77 & £25 3s 4d which I pay at Bristowe to hym in reddy money & this quyte for all maner reckenynges untyll this day £28 10s

S. £215

233(R)   anno 1545

John Yerbery of Bruton clothiar is dewe to have the 2d day of June £71 13s 4d & is for the rest & closyng up of his acowmpt fo. 201 to be paide in this maner followyng, that is for the last payment of a byll datide the 14 day of Augost ~~£17 18s 4d~~ to pay at Seynt Jamistide anno 1545 & by a byll datid the 15 day of November anno 1544 ~~£53 15s~~ to be paide ~~£26 17s 6d~~ the end of May last past £26 17s 6d to be pd. at Seynt Androwstide in anno 1545. So montith the hole as before seid ~~£71 13s 4d~~

Itm. the 3 day of July £143 6s 8d & is for 40 penny hewes at 5 markes 5s the clothe, to pay ~~£71 13s 4d in hand~~ & ~~£35 16s 8d~~ at Candellmas next & £35 16s 8d at Seynt Jamystide in anno 1546, as it may apere by my bill, montith £143 6s 8d

S. £215

234(L)   anno 1544

Iren for my owne acownt owith the 22 day of Augost £177 18s 10d, & is ffor 29 ton 10 C 1 qr. 17 li. iren which rest to sell in my hows unsolld for the closyng up of acowmpt fo. 198 £177 18s 10d

29 ton
10 C
1 qr.
17 li.

Itm. the 20 day of November r. owt of the Sancta Maria of the Rendry, under God master Francis de Subita 300 kyntalls iren of the Rendry & Fontraby which made by my weightes 21 tons 11 C 1 qr. 10 li. conteynyng 2166 li.,[1] which cost clere abord in Spayne 131 V. 340 M., for freight of 20 tons at 20s per ton, for averes [2] per ton, for costom 2s 6d per ton, for halyng & weying 4d per ton, montith [2]

21 tons
11 C 1 qr.
10 li.

---

[1] Smythe has written li. in mistake for endes.
[2] Blank in MS.

234(L) contd.

5 ton 2 C ½ 21 li.	Itm. the 14 day of March anno 1544 I bowght of Pedro de Verrotazan, master of the Marieta 71 kyntalls ½ Rendry iren which made by my weightes 5 tons 2 C ½, 21 li. conteynyng 498 endes & it cost	£28	4s
50 ton pipe 7 li.	anno 1545 Itm. the fyrst day of May anno 1545 r. owt of the San John of the Rendry, master Johannes de Beroby, & owt of the San Nicholas of Orio, master Domyngo de Segura, 150 kyntalls iren of S.S., 150 kyntalls of Fontraby & 398 kyntalls ½, 74 li. of the Rendry, which made by my weightes 50 tons 10 C 7 li. conteynyng 4827 li.,[1] which cost in Spayne clere abord 321 V. 531 M., for shewrance of 300 ducats 18 ducats, for freight of 46 ton pipe & 1 kyntall at 20s per ton, for averes in the San John & Nycolas at 8d per ton, for costom 2s 6d per ton, for halyng & weying 4d per ton	£273	6s 2d

234(R)[2]

235(L)   1545

Wynes of Gascon for my owne acowmpt 38 tons 1 h'd 2 tierces r. in November owt of a good ship callid the Sancta Maria of Fontraby, under God master & ownar Luyes de Abadia, owith for freight at 5 ducatts 1 qr. per ton & for the averes of beyend the see 2 rialls of plate, all which montith £52 7s 9d
Itm. for the averes & prisage, gawging & lighterage £4 18s ob
Itm. for the lisence costom & other pety costes at 5s 2d per ton £9 19s 4d
Itm.   [3]   ducatts which the seid wyne cost clere abord   [3]

235(R)   1545

	Wynes per contra is dewe to have for ylladge, that is for [3] tons [3] drawen owt			[3]
4	Itm. the 17 of November for a ton to the prize £7 11s	£7	11s	
9	Itm. the 21 of November for 2 tons 1 h'd to William Jay, fo. [3]	£15	15s	
4	Itm. the same day to Thomas Chester 1 ton at £7 10s, fo. [3]	£7	10s	
8	Itm. the 22 of November & the 4 of December to Rychard Vere 2 tons at eich £7 6s 8d, montith fo. [3]	£14	13s	4d
3	Itm. the 24 of November r. of the goodman of the George in Bristowe for 3 h'd wyne after £7 10s per ton	£5	12s	6d
5	Itm. the 25 of November for 1 ton 1 h'd after £7 to Master Payn	£8	15s	
2	Itm. the 27 of November 2 h'd after £7 6s 8d to Master Roxby	£3	13s	4d
4	Itm. the fyrst day of December for 1 ton to William Eyre	£7	10s	
6	Itm. the 2d day of December for 6 h'd to John Roxby	£11		
16	Itm. the 3d of December to John Chanseler 4 tons	£28		
5	Itm. the 4th of December for 5 h'd to John Hulat	£9	3s	4d
6	Itm. the 5th of December for 6 h'd to William Smothyng	£11		
8	Itm. the 7th of December for 2 tons to William Northe	£14	13s	4d

[1] *Smythe has written* li. *in mistake for* endes.
[2] *Fo. 234(R) is blank in the MS.*
[3] *Blank in MS.*

235(R) contd.

2	Itm. the 10th of December for 2 h'd to T. Web of Sysseter	£3	16s	8d
6	Itm. the 14 of December for 6 h'd to Richard Caryck	£11		
1	Itm. the 15 of December for 1 h'd to William Yong grocer	£2		
$3\frac{1}{3}$	Itm. the 18 of December for 3 h'd 1 tierce to Sir John Seyntlo, r. it	£6	17s	6d
4	Itm. the same day for 1 ton to Nycolas Mawrewood	£7	6s	8d
1	Itm. the same day d'd to John Spark for Master Baskyrdffylld 1 h'd claret wyne			[1]

236(L)   anno 1545

John Roxby of Wells skynner owithe the 2 day of December £15 which is for the rest & closyng up of his cowmpt fo. 162   £15

Itm. the same day £11 for 6 h'd Gascon wyne at £7 6s 8d per ton   £11

Itm. the 20 day of Jenyver for 3 buttes seck & 1 pipe bastard at eich £4   £16

Itm. the 15 day of Marche £4 for 1 pipe bastard to be paide at all tymes requyrid   £4

Itm. the 6 day of Aprell anno 1546 £20 & is for 5 buttes seck at eiche £4 to be paide at all tymes   £20

Memorandum the 17 daye of Jenyver anno 1548, I John Smythe am contentyd at the request of Master Pikes, Mayer, & allso movyd with pytty & charyte, consydering the povertie of thabove namyd John Roxby, that where the seide Roxby oe me £23, nowe I am content to r. in hand 40s & £4 13s 4d at Candellmas next commyng & 4 h'd of corrupt wyne which he sent to Bristowe to be d'd unto me & so I to geve aquyttans to hym & he to me from the begynyng of the worlld untyll this day.

Itm. r. of the seide Roxby in presence of Thomas Morgan tayllor of Bristowe the 18 day of Jenyver the 40s above mensyonyd to be paide in hand [2]

236(R)   anno 1545

John Roxby per contra is dewe to have the 21 daye of Jenyver 40s which he payeth to me in Bristowe	£2	
Itm. the 20 day of Marche £8 which he paid me in monney	£8	
Itm. the 5th day of May 1546 r. from hym by William Sarche of Bristowe £8	£8	
Itm. the 21 day of May 1546 r. of hym £8	£8	
Itm. the 30 day of July r. of hym at Bristowe £5 Itm. the 1 day of September by John Pikes the yonger £3	£8	
Itm. the 12 day of October 1546 r. by Symon taylor	£9	[2]

237(L)   anno 1545

Thomas Heyward of Bristowe diar owith the 6 daye of February 43s ob which is for the rest of all maner of reckenynges betwen hym & me untyll this day   £2 3s ob

passed this cowmpt the 2de day of July 1550 to my newe booke fo. 1

anno 1549

John Dare of Shepton Mallett owithe the 17 day of Jenyver £5 & is for a butt of seck payable at Mydsomer next commyng   £5

passed this cownt the 2de of July to my newe boke fo. 14

---

[1] *Blank in MS.*
[2] *All the entries on this folio are crossed through.*

237(R)[1]

238(L)   an*no* **1545**

William Ballard of Bristowe ma*r*chant owthe the 12 day of Awgost
£6 6s 8d which is for 1 ton of iren d'd by his com*m*awndement to W*illiam*
Nasche of Chewestoke to be pd. at all tymes requyrid   £6   6s   8d

                                an*no* **1545**

Stevyn Rodwey of Waynstrowe smythe o*with* the 21 day of September 20s
for the rest of 11 C 11 li. ire*n*, to pay at all tymes   £1
1546 Itm. the 3d day of Aprill a*nno* 1546 40s whiche is for the rest of a ton
4 li. iren of S.S. to be paide at Seynt Jamistide next com*m*yng   £2

238(R)   an*no* **1545**

       Will*i*am Ballard p*er* contra is dewe to have the 8 day of
       February £6 6s 8d r. in mon*n*ey by thand*es* of his son in
       the lawe   £6   6s   8d

                                 an*no* **1545**

       Stevyne Rodwey p*er* contra is dewe to have the 15 day
       of Ma*r*che 20s for so myche J*ohn* Yerbery r. of hym for
       myne acowmpt, as it may appere to Yerbery in debito fo.
       233   £1
       Itm. the 29 day of September 1546 r. of hym £2   £2

239(L)   an*no* **1545**

Will*i*am Northe of Bruton vyntnar owe the last day of Augost ~~49~~ 39s 6d & is
for 6 C S.S. iren d'd for hy*m* to Lockyar waynma*n*   £1   19s   6d
Itm. the 7 day of Dece*m*ber for 2 to*n* Gascon wyne at £7 6s 8d p*er* ton   £14   13s   4d
Itm. the 11 day of February for 1 ton p*i*pe of Gascon wyne at £7 6s 8d
p*er* ton to pay at all tymes   £11
Itm. the 10th day of June £4 3s 4d & is for the rest of 6 h'd Gascon wyne
to be pd. at all tymes   £4   ~~3s~~   ~~4d~~
1546 Itm. the 12 day of December a*nno* 1546 ~~£7 13s 4d~~ £8 whiche is for   £8
2 butt*es* of seck to be pd. at all tymes   ~~£7 13s – 4d~~
Itm. the 17 day of February £4 for a p*i*pe bastard at   £4
Itm. the 22 of February a*nno* 1547 for a p*i*pe of bastard at £4 & for 3 butt*es*
of seck at eche £4 & for 1 h'd 3 tersses & 1 quarto*n* of Gascon wyne after
20 nobles p*er* ton, mo*n*t*ith* all £21 16s 8d whereof he paide £7, rest   £14   16s   8d
Itm. the 3 day of October 1548 £4 2s & is for the rest of 2 tons 4 C 13 li.
S.S. ire*n*, as in my shop boke may appere, to be pd. at all tymes   £4   2s
1548 Itm. the 15 of Jenyver 1548 £10 & is for 2 butt*es* of seck delyverd
~~unto hym~~ to hym to pay at all tymes   £10
Itm. the 7 of Ma*r*che £4 for 2 h'd Gascon wyne   £4
1549 Itm. the 5th of July a*nno* 1549 for 1 ton Gascon wyne £8 & for 1 ton
2 C ½, 3 li. iren of S.S. at £11 p*er* ton, mo*n*t*ith* all   £20   7s   10d
Itm. the 14 of October £4 for 2 h'd Gascon wyne   £4

                                   S.   [2]

                               an*no* **1545**

Will*i*am Eyre of Septo*n* Malet owe the 1 day of Dece*m*ber for 1 to*n*
Gascon wyne £7 10s, to pay at Candellmas next   £7   10s
Itm. the 20th day of February £7 15s & is for 1 pipe bastard at £4 &
2 h'd Gascon wyne at £3 15s   £7   15s
1546 Itm. the 24th day of July a*nno* 1546 £13 6s 8d & is for 1 tons oyle, to
be paide at Candellmas next   £13   6s   8d

---
[1] *Fo. 237(R) is blank in the MS.*
[2] *Blank in MS.*

239(L) contd.

Itm. the 2d day of March £14 10s & is for 2 pipes of wull oyle, to be paide at Whitsontide next commyng	£14	10s
1547 Itm. the 29 of February 1547 £14 & is for a ton of wull oyle to be pd. at all tymes requyrid	£14	
1549 Itm. the 11 day of September 1549 £22 & is for 1 ton of wull oyle in 2 pipes, to be paide at Cristmas next	£22	
Itm. the 17 of Jenyver £8 & is for 1 but seck £5 & 2 h'd claret wyne price £3 10s, montith £8 10s, to be pd. at all tymes	£8	10s

It was delyverd the 26 of Marche next after as in my shop booke may apere passed this cownt the 2de day of July 1550 to my newe boke fo. 14

239(R)   **anno 1545**

William Northe per contra is dewe to have the 15 day of Marche £16 12s 10d & is for so myche he paide for me to John Yerbery	£16	12s	10d
Itm. the 10 day of May 1546 £11 which he paide for me to John Yerbery as it may apere in fo. 233	£11		
the 13 of October 1546 r. of hym £4	£4		
Itm. of Master Sylk 4 marckes	£2	13s	4d
Itm. the 4th of Jenyver 1547 r. of hym in Bristowe which he paide unto my wif £9 6s 8d	£9	6s	8d
Itm. the 29 daye of August 1548 r. of William Northe at Bristowe £14 6s 8d in ready monney & more I allowed hym in the price of 3 buttes seck 10s, montith the hole £14 16s 8d	£14	16s	8d
Itm. the 15 day of Jenyver r. of William Northe at Bristowe	£4	2s	
Itm. the 18 day of May anno 1549 r. of Penny for William Northe £4 10s	£4	10s	
Itm. the 18 day the seid Penny pd. £9 10s all in testons	£9	10s	
Itm. the 5th of July r. of William Northe £14	£14		
Itm. £3 6s 8d which he pd. for me to my Lady Arundell	£3	6s	8d
Itm. the 4th of October £7 14d which I pass to hym in debito, fo. 229	£7	1s	2d

[1]

anno 1545

William Eyre per contra is dewe to have the 19 day of February £7 10s r. of hym in redy money	£7	10s	
Itm. the 24 of July 1546 r. of hym at Bristowe	£7	15s	
Itm. the [1] day of [1] my wif r. of hym	£13	16s	8d
Itm. the last of July 1547 56s for a pece of dulas	£2	16s	
Itm. the 11 day of September r. of his sarvant £11	£11		
Itm. the 18 day of September r. of hym		14s	
Itm. the 27 of July 1548 r. of hym £14	£14		
Itm. the 17 of Jenyver r. of his son	£22		

240(L)   **anno 1545**

Thomas Chester owith the 21 day of November £7 10s that is for 1 h'd Gascon wyne to pay at all tymes	£7	10s

1545

Richard Vere of Coventre owith the 4th day of December £7 6s 8d & is for 1 ton Gascon wyne to pay at Ester day next	£7	6s	8d

---

[1] *Blank in MS.*

240(R) anno 1546

Thomas Chester per contra is dewe to have the [1] daye of Aprill £6 16s 11d r. in redy money of hym by the handes of Beryn his sarvant, montith £6 16s 11d
Itm. more the same day by acownt he send me by his seid sarvaunt 10s gevyn for my part to serchors & 2s 6d for my part of his costes to London for to get a lisens & 7d for my part of a messenger to Bridgewater

Richard Vere per contra is dewe to have the 29 day of Aprill anno 1546 £6 r. of hym in redy monney £6
Itm. the [1] day of Jenyver 1546 r. of hym £1 6s 8d

241(L) anno 1545

John Chanceller of Bristowe marchant owith the 3d daye of December £18 which is for the rest of 4 tons Gascon wyne to be paide at Candellmas next commyng £18

anno 1548

Thomas Furss of Oxfford owithe the 12 day of Marche £5 6s 8d & is for a butt of seck d'd to hym by Fowlar the carryar to be paide at all tymes requyred[2] £5 6s 8d

anno 1549

Thomas Furs of Oxfford owith the 13 day of Jenyver anno dicto £12 10s & is for a butt of seck £5 & 1 ton Gascon wyne price £7 10s £12 10s
1550 Itm. the 7 of May 1550 for 1 but seck £5 6s 8d & for 2 h'd claret wyne £3 15s which I d'd to Robert Fowlar £9 1s 8d
Itm. the last day of May £9 20d for 1 but seck, 1 h'd claret & 1 h'hd white, d'd to the seid Robert Fowlar £9 1s 8d
Itm. the 19 of Aprell £9 1s 8d for 1 butt seck, 2 h'd Gascon wyne £9 1s 8d
[3]
passed this cownt to my newe boke fo. 15, the 2de day of July 1550

anno 1545

Thomas Web of Sysseter ynholldr owith the 10 day of December 56s 8d & is for the rest of 2 h'd Gascon wyne as in my shop boke may apere £2 16s 8d
Itm. the 5th day of February d'd for hym to John Byrcom carryar, 1 butt seck price £4 6s 8d, 11 h'd red & 1 h'd claret Gascon wyne at 40s the h'd £8 6s 8d
1546 Itm. the 9 day of Aprell anno 1546 for 1 but seck £4 6s 8d & for 1 ton of Gascon wyne £8 6s 8d, montith the hole £12 13s 4d, to be paide at Mydsomer next commyng £12 13s 4d
It is but £12 6s 8d

241(R) anno 1545

John Chawncellor hereageynst is dewe to have the 18 of Marche £10 for so myche r. of hym at Bristowe in redy money £10
Itm. the 29 day of Aprell 1546 r. of hym in redy monney £8 £8

Thomas Furrs per contra is due to have the 15 of May £10 which I r. from hym by Robert Fowlar £10 13s 4d
Itm. the [1] day of [1] r. of Fowlar £10 13s 4d

1545

Thomas Web per contra is dewe to have 50s which I r. of hym at Sysseter the 20 day of February £2 10s

---

[1] *Blank in MS.*
[2] *The whole of this entry is crossed through.*
[3] *Marginal note*, 3 ton 1 but.

241(R) contd.

Itm. the 12 day of March r. of Byrcom 6s 8d		6s	8d
1546 Itm. the 8 day of Aprell 1546 r. of hym	£8	6s	8d
Itm. the 11 day of July 1546 r. of hym seallf at Bristowe £8 6s 8d	£8	6s	8d
Itm. r. of hym when I went to Oxfford	£3	13s	4d

242(L)   **anno 1545**

William Wylett of Bristowe owith the 21 day of Jenyver for 1 but seck
£4 3s 4d to be pd. as by his byll may apere   £4   3s   4d

Itm. the 2d day of Marche 1546 £12 & is for 3 buttes of seck sold & d'd to
hym at £4 the butt, to pay £4 at Seynt Jamistide, £4 at Mighellmas and
£4 at Allhaloutide which wylbe in anno 1547   £12

Itm. the 17 day of May 1547 £14 13s 4d & ys for 1 ton wull oyle, to pay
4 markes in hand & 40s within a monnethe next enshewyng & £5 at
Cristmas next after & £5 at Candellmas next after that, as by his severall
bylls may apere   £14 13s 4d

1547 Itm. the fyrst day of February 1547 £4 to be pd. at all tymes
requyryd & is for a butt of seck sold & delyverd unto hym ~~I sey at Ester next commyng~~   £4

passed the rest of this cowmpt the 2de day of July to my newe boke in fo. 16

1545

Pedro Gonzalez Portugez owith the 21 day of Jenyver £8 for 2 buttes seck
which I solld to hym for his oste of Tawnton, to be pd. at all tymes
requyrid   £8
Itm. the [1] day of [1] anno 1548 £25 lent hym in ready monney   £25

242(R)   **anno 1546**

William Wyllet per contra is dewe to have the 12 day of Aprill £4 3s 4d r. of hym in redy monney	£4	3s	4d
Itm. the 17 day of May 1547 r. of hym 53s 4d	£2	13s	4d
Itm. r. the 24 of July 40s	£2		
Itm. the 8 daye of August r. of hym £4	£4		
Itm. the 26 daye of Jenyver 1547 r. of hym for 2 buttes of the seck per contra d'd the 2d day of Marche 1546 £8	£8		
Itm. the 7 day of Aprell 1548 my wif r. by thandes of his wif £5	£5		
Itm. the 24 daye of December 1548 I r. of William Wyllet £5. I sey ffyve powndes	£5		

anno 1545

Pedro Gonzalez per contra is dewe to have the 18 day of
Marche £8 r. of hym in reddy monney   £8
Itm. the [1] day of [1] 1548 r. £25   £25

243(L)   **anno 1545**

Piers Taylor dwellyng before Seynt Petters pliump[2] in Bristowe owith the
23 day of Jenyver £8 6s 8d, that is £4 for a pipe bastard & 13 nobles for a
but seck, to pay £4 at Mydsomer next & £4 6s 8d at Seynt Jamystide next
after   £8   6s   8d

1548

Sir Henry Long knight owithe the 22 day of Marche £4 for 2 h'd of Gascon
wyne which Griffith carter chose for hym & the same wyne was delyverd
to Master Longes sarvant   £4

---

[1] *Blank in MS.*
[2] *Smythe has written 'pliump' in error for 'plump', see glossary.*

243(L) contd.

1549 Itm. the 24 of Jenyver 1549 £7 10s & is for 1 ton of Gascon wyne sold & delyverd for hym to his s*a*rvant Kyrye at £7 10s, to be pd. at O*wr* Lady Day in M*a*rch next com*m*yng £7 10s
passed the rest of this cownt the 2de day of July to my newe booke fo. 16

anno 1545

Stevyn Cole of Bristowe o*with* the 23 day of Jenyver £4 3s 4d to be paide at all tymes which is for 1 butt seck d'd to hym £4 3s 4d
1548 Itm. the 15 day of Phebruary a*n*no 1548 for a but of seck £5 payable at all tymes which but his wif r. in his name £5
1549 Itm. the 24 of December 1549 £10 & is for 2 butt*es* of seck sold & delyverd to his wif to be paide at all tymes £10
Itm. the 10th of Jenyver 1549 for 2 butt*es* sold & delyverd for hym to his wif at £5 the butt £10
passed the rest of this cowmpt the 2de day of July 1550 to my newe booke fo. 16

243(R)
anno 1546

Piers Taylo*r* p*er* contra is dewe to have the 29 daye of Ap*r*ell £4 r. by thand*es* of Edward Knotsford £4
Itm. the 10 day of Augost r. by Edward Knotsford £4 6s 8d

a*n*no 1549

S*ir* Henry Long p*er* contra is dewe to have the 7 day of Decemb*er* a*nno* dicto £4 which he sent unto me by his sarvant £4

a*n*no 1546

Stevyn Cole p*er* contra is due to have the 22 day of Augost £4 3s 4d
Itm. the 22 of Decemb*er* 1549 £5 r. of his wif £5
Itm. the last of Marche a*n*no 1550 r. of hym by thand*es* of his wif in ready money 10 l*i*bra, I sey ten pownd*es* £10

244(L)
anno 1545

John Swan of Bristowe m*a*rchant owithe the 1 day of February £4 which is for a but of seck, to pay at thend of 2 monthes next enshewyng £4
1546 Itm. the 29 day of Ap*r*ell 1546 £4 6s 11d ob & is for 14 C 1 qr. 27 li. Rendry ire*n* at £6 the ton, to be paide at all tymes £4 6s 11d½
Itm. the 13 day of August 1547 £3 13s 4d which is for a pipe ire*n* after £7 13s 4d p*er* to*n*, to pay at Mighellmas next com*m*yng £3 13s 4d
Itm. the 14 of September for 4 C grene woode at 12s p*er* C, mo*ntith* 48s, to pay at Allhaloutyde next com*m*yng £2 8s
Itm. the 25 day of M*a*rche 1550 £8 8s that is for 2 yeres rent of my hows he dwell yn, due this p*r*esent day £8 8s

244(R)
anno 1546

John Swan p*er* contra is dewe to have the 24 day of Ap*r*ell £4 which he paide unto me in redy money £4
Itm. my wif. r. of hym in Nove*m*ber 1546 £4 6s 11d ob
Itm. the 7 day of June 1548 r. of hym £3 13s 4d £3 13s 4d
Itm. the 26 of M*a*rche a*n*no 1550 £6 which I r. of his wif £6
Itm. the 15 day of Ap*r*ell r. of his wyffe £4 4d £4 4d
Itm. more for rent of a sellar 3 quarters of a yere 15s 15s
Itm. more 8d which I have not r. but gave it in *the* payment 8d

245(L)   1546

Will*a*m Smythe of Marlbrowe ow*ith* the 30 day of M*a*rche 53s 4d for the rest of a ton 1 C 1 qr. 27 li. ire*n* of S.S., to be paide at Mydsomer next com*m*yng   £2 13s 4d

anno 1549

Henry Clows of Faryngton ynkep*er* owithe the 16 day of Jenyver £3 to be paide at all tymes & is for the rest of seck & Gasco*n* wyne, as it may apere in my shop booke   £3

anno 1546

~~Will*i*am~~ Phellip Hunt of Shepton Mallet smythe owithe the 19 day of July 30s which is for 1 h'd of Rendry iren, to be paide at Mighellmas next com*m*yng, & Jo*h*n Lovell of the same towne is shew*er*ty for *the* payme*n*t   £1 10s

245(R)   an*n*o 1546

Will*a*m Smythe p*er* contra is dewe to have the 14 day of Julye 53s 4d for so myche mon*n*ey he pd. to my wif   £2 13s 4d

an*n*o 1550

Henry Clows p*er* contra is due to have the 30 of M*a*rche a*n*no dicto £3 which my s*a*rvant W*illia*m Clerk r. of hym for to carry to my sons at Oxfford   £3

1546

Phillip Hunt p*er* contra is dewe to have the [1] day of Octob*er* 30s which my s*a*rvant Henry r.   £1 10s

246(L)   anno 1546

M*emo*randum that my mother Alice Smythe wedo dep*a*rtyd ow*t* of this worlde to Godward the 16 day of Ap*re*ll 1546 abow*t* 5 of the clock at afternoone & was buryed the next day betwen 10 & 11 of the clock before none in the crowde of the p*a*risch churche of Seynt Leonard*es* in Bristowe. The inventorye of the which my mothers good*es* hereafter do ffollowe:
Inp*ri*mis, in ready mon*n*ey ~~£97~~ £173   £173
Itm. in plate, won standyng cup with a cover p*a*rcell gyllt waying 31 oz. ½ & 2 sallt*es* with a cover p*a*rcell gyllt waying 30 oz. & 2 ale cupps p*a*rcell gyllt waying 16 oz., ~~a gyllt nutt with a black shell waying 11 oz. 1 qr.~~, a lytell sylver cupp made hornelike waying 5 oz., 2 flatt sylver pec*es* p*a*rcell gyllt waying 24 oz., a flat pece with Seynt Androws cross waying 7 oz. 1 qr., 12 sylv*er* spones knoppid with lyons gylltyd waying 18 oz. ½, & 3 ale pott*es* with a cover all gyllt waying 36 oz. So mo*n*tith ~~143~~ 132 oz. ½ p*a*rcell gyllt & white plate & 36 oz. gyllt plate, valeut. I sey 132 oz. 1 qr. of whit & p*a*rcell gyllt, the on at 4s 6d the oz. & the other at 5s the oz.   £38 15s 1d½
Itm. 7 Bristowe fryses valent £7 & 1 pece of red clo*the* valent £3 & a blewe clo*the* ~~blewe wull~~ valent £4, mo*n*tith   £14
Itm. debt*es* owyng to her amont won £100   £100
Itm. all her howsolld stuff valuryd in   1
Itm. wull dyed & undyed that she left valent & yern   1

246(R)   1546

M*emo*randum that I must pay for my mothers bequest*es* by her testament & last wyll, this p*a*rcells followyng
Inp*ri*mis to Hewgh Smythe my son   25 m*a*rkes
Itm. to my son Mathewe Smythe   25 m*a*rkes

---

[1] *Blank in MS.*

246(R) contd.

Itm. to my son Nycholas Smythe 25 markes
Itm. to my dowghter Ann Smythe 25 markes & more my mothers too second gyrdills, a peyre of bedes of corral, her best gowne, her best & second kyrtylls
Itm. my mother bequethe to Joan my wife her best gyrdill & best bedes
Itm. more, I must pay to her old sarvant Margret Higgyns 16s every yere duryng her naturall lif.
& as for the rest of all her legaces I have pd. & d'd, that is to sey £12 to poore pepull & 10s to the Trynyte churche, to Master Sylk her curat 5s, to the proctors of Seynt Leonardes churche 10s, to Syr Nycholas Jones her gohestly father 6s 8d, to Nycholas Kelly hoper her best gold ryng made hopelike, to Margery Wellsche a gold ryng with a turquez in hym, to Alice Caps a gold ryng with a perle in hym, to Margett Hyggyns her rownd gowne furryd with black lambe, a flock bed, 2 blanckettes, & 2 peyre of canvas sheettes, to Elzabethe Wylkes her sarvant 13s 4d for a token.

247(L) anno 1546

Master William Sharyngton tresorer of the Kynges Majestes Mynt in the Cite of Bristowe owithe the 5th daye of Maye for 52 oz. of awngell gold at 50s 6d the oz. & for 4 oz. ½ of crusado gold at 47s 8d the oz. & for hallf an oz. of crownes sold at 48s the oz. montith the hole £148 8s, to be pd. within a monethe next enshewyng

£143 1s
~~£148 – 8s~~

anno 1548

Master Morice Walsche of Chepyng Sodbery esquyer owith the 16 day of Phebruary £4 for 2 h'd Gascon wyne d'd for his use to his sarvant William Martyne, to be pd. at all tymes requyrid £4
Itm. the 8 of June for 4 h'd Gascon wyne d'd for hym to his sarvant John Huntt after the price of £8 the ton, montith £6
Itm. the 30 day of October 40s for 1 h'd red wyne £2
[1]Itm. the 7th of February 1549 £12 & is for 6 h'd of Gascon delyverd for hym to his sarvant William Francom, to be paide at all tymes £12
passed this cownt the 2de day of July 1550 to my newe booke fo. 17

anno 1546

George Knight of the Mynt owithe the 14 day of July for Edward Rowley £15 9s 9d & is for serteyn gold & sylver he r. of hym in money, as by his bills may apere £15 9s 9d

247(R) anno 1546

William Sharynton per contra is dewe to have the 11 daye of June £143 12d which Hewgh Hamon r. of hym £143 1s

anno 1549

Master Wellsche per contra is dewe to have the 4th of September £10 which he paide unto me in ready monney £10

anno 1546

George Knyght per contra is dewe to have the 20 day of September £15 9s 9d & is for so myche he paide for me to Hamon £15 9s 9d

---

[1] Marginal note 7–10.

248(L)   **anno 1546**

Edward Rowley of Kyngsnorton ow*ithe* the 14 day of July £18 2d ob which is for the rest & closyng up of his acowmpt fo. 167	£18	2d½
Itm. the 15 day of July £57 11s 4d & is for 8 tons pipe 1 qr. 4 li. Rendry iren at £6 the ton & 1 ton 1 qr. 23 li. S.S. iren at 19 nobles the ton, to be paide at all tymes requyrid	£57 11s	4d
Itm. the last day of Apr*ell* 1547 sent hym in Gryffithes trowe of W*ursett*or 2 ton Rendry iren, more d'd to hymseallf the 24 day of May 3 ton 5 li. Rendry iren & 3 ton 4 li. ire*n* of S.S. at £7 3s 4d p*er* ton & the Rendry at 20 nobles the ton, mo*ntith* all £54 17s 3d	£54 17s	3d
Itm. the 10 day of August £50 7s & is for 4 tons 12 C 3 qr. 7 li. Rendry iren at £7 the ton and for 1 ton 17 C ½, 11 li. S.S. ire*n* at £7 10s p*er* ton & for 10 C 7 li. smawle ire*n* at 8s p*er* to I sey p*er* C, which iren is payable at all tymes. The hole is 7 ton 1 qr. 25 li. iren to be paide at all tymes	£50	7s
1548 Itm. the 24 day of Apr*ell* 1548 for 1 ton 8 C ½, 13 li. smawle iren at £10 the ton & for 4 to*n* 12 C ½, 4 li. of S.S. ire*n* at £9 13s 4d the to*n* & for 3 ton of Rendry ire*n* at £9 the ton, mo*ntith* all £86 7d, to be paide betwext this & Allhaloutide next, mo*ntith*	£86	7d
Itm. the 24 of July £57 & is for 6 ton of iren at £9 10s the ton, to be paide betwex this & Candellmas next com*m*yng	£57	
Itm. the 12 day of June 1549 £55 & is for the rest of 6 to*n* 1 qr. 11 li. ire*n* to be paide by his byll, hallf at Mighellmas next & tho*ther* hallf at Cris*tm*as next after that, as in my shop boke more largely ap*erithe*	£55	
Itm. the 8 of May 1550 £60 9d ob & is for 3 tons more 9 li. iren of S.S. & 2 tons iren of the Rendry at £12 the ton won with another, to be paide at all tymes requyred	£60	9d ob

passed this cowmpt to my new[1] booke fo. 18 the 2de day of July 1550

248(R)   **anno 1546**

Edward Rowley p*er* contra is dewe to have the [2] of Dece*m*ber £18 r. by Grevys	£18	
Itm. the 21 day of Jenyver r. by Letes fa*ther*	£17 10s	
Itm. the 25 day of May a*nno* 1547 r. of hym at Bristowe £40 & I rebate to hym 18d ob, mo*ntith* all	£40 1s	6d ob
Itm. the 8 day of Augost r. of hym at Bristowe £37	£37	
Itm. the 11 day of August £9 13s which I must r. for hym to this acowmpt of M*aster* Marshall goldsmythe	£9 13s	
Itm. 7s which I allowe hym for a pece of resyng*es*	7s	
Itm. the same day r. of hym 17s 3d	17s	3d
Itm. r. the [2] day of February by Leight*es* father	£30	
Itm. r. the 22 day of Apr*ell* 1548 r. of E. Rowley hymseallf at Bristowe £27 7s	£27 7s	
Itm. the 23 day of July a*nno* 1548 r. of hym at Bristowe £72	£72	
Itm. the 28 day of December r. by his s*arvant* Jo*h*n Hossyar £54 in testons & £17 in grot*es*	£71	
Itm. the 3de day of October a*nno* 1549 r. of hym at Bristowe £27 10s	£27 10s	
Itm. the 22 of February r. from hym by the hand*es* of his neighbur Jo*h*n Lett	£27 10s	

249(L)   **anno 1546**

Humfrey Cowlchester of Brymyjam tanner ow*ith* the 18 day of May £36 & is for 6 tons Rendry iren at £6 the ton, to be paide 3 dayes after Mighellmas next com*m*yng, as by his byll may apere	£36

anno 1549

S*ir* Antony Kyngston knight ow*ithe* the 24 of Decemb*er* £17 & is for 1 butt of seck price £5 & 6 h'd Gascon wyne price £12 solld & delyv*er*d for his use

---

[1] new *is inserted above the line.*
[2] *Blank in MS.*

249(L) contd.

to his sarvant John Barckley of Wutton under hedge, to be pd. at all tymes £17
Itm. the 5th day of February £8 for 4 h'd Gascon wyne delyverd for hym
to his seide sarvant £8
passed this cownt the 2de day of July anno 1550 to my newe boke fo. 17

anno 1546

Thomas Slocom of Bristowe draper owith the 6th day of Julye £6 for a ton
of iren, to be pd. by his & Master Reynolldes byll at Allhaloutyde next
commyng £6

249(R)   **1546**

Humfrey Colchester per contra is dewe to have the 12
day of Jenyver £36 r. by his son in the lawe £36
[1]

anno 1546

Itm. the 19 day of November r. of hym £6   £6

250(L)   **anno 1546**

John Fowlls of Warmyster owith the 25 day of May £3 3s 4d & is for a pipe
iren, to be paide at Mighellmas next. M. Bayle & Robert Fowlls be his
shewertes as in my shop boke may apere   £3   3s   4d
Itm. the 5 day of Julye anno 1547 £3 10s & is for the [2] of 15 C
14 li. ½ iren, to be paide at Mighellmas next, for the which som he & Robert
Fowlls his father of Chewe Stoke husbandman standith bownden   £3 10s

anno 1546

Robert Crosby Kendallman owith the fyrst day of July £5 for 3 h'd Gascon
wyne to be paide at Mighellmas next commyng, montith £5
Itm. the 26 day of July for 3 h'd Gascon wyne £4   6s   8d

250(R)   **1546**

John Fowls per contra is dewe to have the [3] day of
[3] £3 3s 4d which my wif r. of hym   £3   3s   4d
Itm. the 11 day of October 1547 r. at Bristowe of hym
£3 10s   £3 10s

1546

Robert Crosby per contra is dewe to have the [3] day
of December £7 6s 8d for so mych my wif r. of hym   £7   6s   8d
Itm. the 5 day of February r. of Robert Crosby 40s   £2

251(L)   **anno 1546**

Master Roger Wigmoore conptrowler of the Mynt in
Bristowe owthe the 13 day of July £22 5s 11d and is for
iren d'd at dyvers tymes by his wyll & comawndement to
Mathewe Wyllsson smythe for woorck of the seid Mynte,
as by the cowmpt the same parcells may apere   £22   5s   11d

---

[1] *There is no credit entry for Kyngston.*
[2] *Smythe has omitted* rest.
[3] *Blank in MS.*

251(L) contd.   **Anno 1549**

68 butt*es*

Seck*es* for my owne acowmpt, *that* is to sey 68 butt*es* laden for me in the Hart ow*ith* the 19 day of December [1] M. clere abord, which be sterlyng mon*n*ey at 6s the ducatt [1], more for the freight at 35s p*er* to*n* of 33 tons p*i*pe & for av*er*es of the same 4s 1d p*er* ton, for hawllyng & stowyng of the same 6d p*er* to*n*, for hopyng of the same 12d p*er* ton, for custom of the same 3s p*er* ton. [1]

10 butt*es* seck

Itm. 10 but*es* of seck r. owt of the San J*o*hn of the Rendry owith for freight & av*er*es £8 12s 6d which I pd. to the purs*er* callyd Gaspar de Pontira, for hawlyng & stowyng 6d p*er* ton, for hopyng 12d p*er* ton, for custom 3s p*er* ton & more the same 10 butt*es* cost in Andaluzia putt aboord the shipp [1] M. [1]

251(R)   **anno 1546**

M*aster* Rog*er* Wigmoore p*er* contra is dewe to have the 11 day of October £22 15s 11d r. by the hand*es* of Mathewe Willson, smythe   £22 5s 11d

anno 1549

1	Seck*es* p*er* contra is dewe to have the 20 of December £5 which is for 1 but of seck paide to *J*ohn Wyllis chamberlayne for a but which I had of hym in M*ar*che last past	£5
1	Itm. the same day r. £5 for a butt to W*illiam* Cowp*er*	£5
1	Itm. the same day, for 1 but to Rog*er* Amner fo. 277 price £5 8s 8d	£5 8s 8d
1	Itm. the 21 of December £5 for a butt to J*o*hn Sp*ar*k fo. 267	£5
3	Itm. the same day r. of J*o*hn Rede of Swaynse for 3 butt*es* £14 10s	£14 10s
1	Itm. the 24 of December £5 for a butt of seck to Si*r* Antony Kyngsto*n* fo. 249	£5
2	Itm. £10 for 2 butt*es* seck to Stevyn Cole fo. 243 sold *the* same day	£10
2	Itm. the same day £10 for 2 butt*es* to Thomas Cowp*er* fo. 218	£10
1	Itm. the same day £5 for 1 butt to Giles White fo. 42	£5
1	Itm. the same day for 1 butt seck taken to *the* p*r*ize	£5
10	Itm. the 30 of December 10 butt*es* to Antony Stambanck fo. 206	£48 6s 8d
1	Itm. the last of December for 1 butt to Robert Genyng*es* fo. 262	£5
1	Itm. the same day for 1 butt to W*illiam* Northe fo. 229	£5
1	Itm. the 3d of Jenyver for 1 but to W*illiam* Smothing fo. 207	£5
1	Itm. for 1 but that the m*ar*chant*es* dranck a see	[1]
4	Itm. the 8 of Jenyver to Antony Stanbanck fo. 206 4 butt*es*	£18 13s 4d
2	Itm. the 10th of Jenyv*er* for 2 butt*es* to Stevyn Coles fo. 243	£10
1	Itm. the 13 of the same for a butt to Thom*a*s Furrs fo. 241	£5
1	Itm. the same day to Rog*er* Amner of Wells fo. 277 1 butt	£5

---

[1] *Blank in MS.*

251(R) contd.

2	Itm. the 15 of Jenyver for 2 buttes to John Hamon fo. 296	£10
2	Itm. the same day for 2 buttes to John Morice fo. 263	£10
2	Itm. the 16 day of Jenyver for 2 buttes to Henry Clows fo. 295	£10
1	Itm. the same day for 1 butt to John Dare fo. 237	£5
1	Itm. the 17 of Jenyver for 1 butt to Edmond Hancottes fo. 279	£5
3	Itm. the same day for 3 buttes to Antony Stanbanck fo. 206	£14
1	Itm. the 18 day of Jenyver to Robert Jenynges fo. 262 1 butt	£5
5	Itm. to this present day is drawen clene owt to ylladge 5 buttes	[1]
1	Itm. to William Eyre fo. 239 1 butt price £5	£5
1	Itm. the 22 of Jenyver 1 but to Robert Sternal fo. 256	£5
3	Itm. the same day to Antony Stanbanck fo. 206 3 buttes	£14 10s [1]
1	Itm. more to yladge 1 butt seck	
2	Itm. the 28 of Jenyver £10 for 3 buttes of seck to William Northe 229	£10
3	Itm. the last day of Jenyver for 3 buttes to Robert Jenynges fo. 262	£15
1	Itm. the fyrst of February for 1 butt to William Smothe fo. 207	£5
4	Itm. r. 10 Dunsters of Henry Lowghford for payment of 4 buttes at £5 the but	£20
4	Itm. the 3d day of February r. of Cristover Geffreys of Bristowe for 4 buttes seck £19 18s	£19 18s
2	Itm. the 21 of February to Robert Genynges fo. 207 2 buttes seck	£10
1	Itm. for my provysyon 1 but	£5

252 (L)   anno 1546

Elsabeth Croston otherwise Bradhewe wedo of Ludlo owthe the 28 day of July £4 16s 8d for a pipe of rackyd muscadell, to be paide at Allhaloutide next commyng   £4 16s 8d

anno 1548

Master Robert Kellwaye esquyer, Recorder of Bristowe, owithe the 19 day of Marche £9 & is for 1 butt of seck which I had of the Chamberlayne at £5 the butt & £4 for 2 h'd of Gascon wyne   £9

252(R)   1546

Elsabeth Croston per contra is dewe to have the 15 day of November £4 16s 8d r. by the handes of William Yong of Bristowe grocer   £4 16s 8d
[2]

253(L)   anno 1546

25 clothes trukers

John Yerbery of Bruton clothiar owithe the 3 day of August for 21 C Ylland wood delyverd to hym for & in part of payment of 25 of his clothes callid trukars which I have

---

[1] Blank in MS.
[2] There is no credit entry for Kellwaye.

253(L) contd.

bowght of hym after 4 C wood for every clothe, which amon*tith* to a 100 kyntalls
Itm. the 7 day of Augost £6 13s 4d[2] & is for a ton of iren d'd by his com*m*awndement to Robert Edwardes of Hynedon smythe to be paide at all tymes   £6 13s 4d
Itm. the 19 day of October for 4 C wood, the 3d day of November 4 C wood, the same day for hym to a wayneman 11 C wood, the 19 day of November 4 C wood, the 30 day of November 3 C wood, the 8 day of December 3 C, the 12th day of Jenyver 3 C & the 10th day of May 47 kyntalls, mon*tith* all the parcells in this itm. 79 kyntalls
1548 Itm. the 12 daye of Maye anno 1548 £10 18s 6d & is for 1 ton 3 C 5 li. S.S. iren at £9 10s the ton, which was d'd to his sarvant Penny for a smythe of Bruton   £10 18s 6d
Itm. the 23 day of November £10 10s which is for a ton of S.S. iren that he is shewerty for John Jacob of Cadbery, to pay at Owr Lady Day in Lent next commyng   £10 10s
1549 Itm. the fyrst day of October anno 1549 for 3 C Ylande woode at 13s 4d per C d'd for hym to his servant Penny, the 12 of October for 3 C, the 19 of October 12 C woode, the 12 of November for 2 C woode

253(R)   anno 1546

John Yerbery per contra is dewe to have the 28 day of Augost 4 C Ylland wood for 1 clothe
25 clothes trucker r. from hym, the 10 day &[3] 25 of
truckers September r. 3 clothes truckers, the 9 of October r. 1 clothe trucker, r. the 19 day of November 2 clothes truckers.
Itm. more r. from hym at sundry tymes untyll the 6th day of June anno 1548 18 clothes truckers
Itm. r. the [1] of [1] 1546 of his son in the fawe dwellyng apon the bridge for the ton of iren per contra £6 13s 4d   £6 13s 4d
Itm. £10 18s which he discowntyd unto me in the payment of 5 clothes penny hewes which I bowght of hym   £10 18s
Itm. the month of September r. in trucker clothes £10 10s   £10 10s

254(L)   anno 1546

50 tons   Viages to Andaluzia owith for my owne acowmpt the 20
10 C 1 qr.   day of September Anno dicto, £402 18s that is for 960
12 li. led   peces or smawle sowse of led powncyd with my pownce & marck, which peces wayith 50 tons 10 C 1 qr. of a C &
1 fyne hewlyng   12 li. which cost clere aborde £5 6s 8d per ton, more one
3 truckers   fyne hewlyng clothe valent £4, more too clothes truckers
150   valent £6, more one red clothe as a trucker[4] valent £3,
Manchesters   more 150 Manchester cottons valent £112 10s and 7
7 Bristowe   Bristowe ffrises valent £8 3s 4d. Of the which foreseid
fryses   goodes be laden in the Mary Conception, under God master Richard White, 390 peces led conteynyng 21 tons 3 qrs. of a C 1 li. & a 100 Manchester cottons & 1 fyne hewlyng clothe. More is laden of the foreseid goodes in the Marieta of Fontraby, under God master Johannes

---

[2] *Blank in MS.*
[2] *13s 4d inserted later.*
[3] *10 day & inserted later.*
[4] *as a trucker inserted later.*

254(L) contd.

de Veroby, 370 peces led waying 19 tons 2 C 8 li. & 50 Manchester cottons, 7 black Bristowe fryses, 2 truckers of John Yerberys makyng & one red of my mothers makyng. More is laden of the foreseid goodes in the Trynte of Wales, under God master Thomas Boysse, 200 peces of led waying 10 tons 7 C ½, 3 li. All this goodes I have commendyd to the governaunce of my sarvantes Hewg Hamon and Robert Leight & specyally to Hewgh Hamon, as by my remenbrance hit may apere. I pray God send it all home ageyne in saftye. £402 18s

Itm. more my seid sarvantes shall r. for my acowmpt at Andaluzia of Hewgh Tipton by vertewe of a byll of exchawnge of E. Prins which I sent by the purser of the seid ship within my letter dyrectyd to my seid sarvantes, a 100 ducatts £25

Itm. the 4 day of May 1547 £38 16s 4d, & is for so myche goten by this acowmpt, as it may apere to gayenes in credito fo. 200 £38 16s 4d

S. £466 14s 4d

254(R)   anno 1547

Viages per contra is dewe to have the 4th day of May £310 10s 4d & is for 465 V. 775 M. the neate procedewe of the sale of the 50 tons 10 C 1 qr. 12 li. led per contra as by Hewgh Hamons, r. of hym this day do specifie. To hym in debito fo. 271 — *50 tons 10 C 1 qr. 12 li. led* — £310 10s 4d

Itm. the same day £15 8s 10d & is for the nete sale, that is to sey 23 V. 165 M. ½ of 1 fyne hewling & 3 truckers per contra as by the seid Hamondes cownt may apere. To hym in debito 271 — *1 fyne hewling clothe, 3 truckers* — £15 8s 10d

Itm. the same day £107 7s 5d & is for 161 V. 57 M., the nete procedewe of the sale of a 150 Manchester cottons as by the seid Hamondes cownt dothe apere. To hym in debito 271 — *150 Manchester cottons* — £107 7s 5d

Itm. the same day £8 7s 9d & is for 12 V 579 M., the neate procedewe of 7 Bristowe fryzes as by the seide Hamondes cownt may apere. To hym in debito 271 — *7 Bristow fryses* — £8 7s 9d

Itm. £25 which Hamon r. for E. Prin of Tipton, as it may apere to Hamon in debito 271 £25

S. £466 14s 4d

255(L)   anno 1546

1 do. buttes secks
15 pipes bastard
3 pipes taynt
3 buttes seck

Seckes, bastardes, hullock & taynt owith the monthe of ~~December &~~ Jenyver, that is for 12 buttes seck in the Katalyne of the Passage, master Jonot de Villa Viciosa & owt of the Mysericordia de Villa de Conde 68 buttes seck, 1 butt hulloc & 1 pipe taynt & owt of the Harry of Bristowe 6 buttes of seck & owt of the Trynte of Wales 10 buttes of seck & owt of the Mary Conception of Bristowe 2 buttes seck, 15 pipes of bastard & 2 pipes of taynt & owt of the Mawdelen Cutt 1 butt of seck & the 14 of May 1547 r. owt of the Savyor of the Rendry, master Domyngo de Subieta, 3 buttes seckes, all the which aforeseid seckes, bastardes & tayntes cost clere abord 315 V. 326 M. ½, as by Hewgh Hamondes cowmpt dothe apere £210 4s 4d

255(L) contd.

2 buttes	Itm. for 2 buttes bowght[1] of Hewgh Hamondes	£8
	Itm. for custom of ² buttes ² , for averes in the Katalyne of the Passage at 8s 2d ob per ton & in the Miserycordia at 3s 11d per ton & in the Harry at 3s 4d per ton & in the Trynte of Wales at ² per ton & in the Mary Conception at 4s 10d[3] per ton & in the Mawdelen Cutt at ² per ton, & in the Savyor of the Rendry at ² per ton	²
	Itm. for freight in the Katalyne of the Passage at 28s 9d per ton & in the Mysericordia at 21s 8d per ton & in the Harry at 30s per ton & in the Trynte of Wales at 35s per ton, & in the Mary Conception at 30 per ton & in the Mawdelen Cutt at ² per ton & in the Savior of the Rendry at ² per ton, montith all	²
	Itm. for hawlyng & stowyng of all the foreseide wyne at 4d per ton, montith	²
	Itm. for hopyng	²

255(R)   anno 1546

	Seckes, bastardes, hullockes & tayntes per contra is dewe to have the monthes of			
2 b	December & Jenyver for 2 buttes seck left for the freight, that is 1 butt in the Catalynota & 1 butt in the Myseriicordia			²
2 b 1 pipe b	Itm. £12 & is for 1 butt seck in the Harry & 1 butt seck in the Trynte of Wales & 1 pipe bastard in the Mary Conception taken all to the prize	£12		
2 b	Itm. the 12 day of December to Robert Genynges fo. 228 2 buttes seck price £8	£8		
2 b	Itm. the same tyme to William Northe fo. 239 2 buttes seck	£7	13s	4d
10 b	Itm. the 18 of Jenyver to Jamys Rogers fo. 76 10 buttes	£38	6s	8d
1 b	Itm. the same day to Thomas Crossway fo. 257 1 butt seck	£4	1s	8d
1 b	Itm. the 22 day of Jenyver to Master Owen fo. 171 1 butt seck	£4		
1 b 1 pipe b 1 pipe T.	Itm. the 24 of Jenyver to William Smothyng fo. 207 1 but seck & 1 pipe bastard at eich £4 & 1 pipe taynt at £4 13s 4d, montith the hole £12 13s 4d	£12	13s	4d
2 b	Itm. the 25 of Jenyver r. of Roxbys wif for 2 buttes seck	£8		
2 b	Itm. the 26 day of Jenyver to William Mytton fo. 258 2 butes	£8		
15 b 5 pipes b 1 pipe T.	Itm. to Antony Stanbanck fo. 206 the 29 of Jenyver 6 buttes seck & the 11 day of February 9 buttes seckes, 5 pipes bastard & 1 pipe taynt, the seckes & bastardes at £4 the pece & the pipe of taynt at £4 13s 4d, montith the hole £84 13s 4d	£84	13s	4d
2 b	Itm. the 5 of February to Robert Jenynges fo. 228 2 buttes	£8		
4 b 1 pipe b	Itm. the 17 of February r. of William Northe for 4 buttes seck £15 6s 8d, more to hym fo. 239 1 pipe bastard price £4, montith all £19 6s 8d	£19	6s	8d

---

[1] bowght *inserted above the line.*
[2] *Blank in MS.*
[3] 4s 10d *inserted above the line.*

255(R) contd.

1 b	Itm. the 25 of February for 1 butt to W*illiam* Mytto*n* fo. 258	£4
10 b 1 p*ipe* T 1 p*ipe* b	Itm. the 2d day of M*a*rche for 3 butt*es* to W*illiam* Wyllet fo. 242 & the 5th of M*a*rche to Jamys Rog*er*s fo. 76 4 butt*es* & the 7 of M*a*rche to W*illiam* Smothyng fo. 207 3 butt*es*, the same r. of *John* Priest of Ross £8 13s 4d for a p*ipe* taynt & 1 p*ipe* bastard, mon*tith* all £48	£48
1 b 1 p*ipe*	Itm. the 14 of M*a*rche to Nycholas Bathe fo. 263 1 but seck & 1 p*ipe* bastard at eich £4	£8
2 butt*es*	Itm. the 24 of M*a*rche for 2 butt*es* to Robert Genyng*es* fo. 248	£8
1 b	Itm. the 19 of Apr*i*ll 1547 for 1 butt to Croswey fo. 257	£4
2 b	Itm. the 22 of Apr*i*ll for 2 butt*es* to Garberet fo. 267	£7 13s 4d
1 b	It*m*. the same day for 1 butt to W*illiam* Smothing fo. 207	£4
2 b	It*m*. the 5th of May for 2 butt*es* to Robert Genyng*es* fo. 228	£8
2 b	It*m*. the 17 of May for 2 butt*es* to Roger Amner fo. 270	£8
1 b	Itm. the 25 of May to [1] Busgrove fo. 260 1 butt	£4
1 b	Itm. the 17 of June to Nycolas Bathe fo. 263 1 butt	£4

256(L) anno 1546

Robert Sternal of Bristowe hop*er* owithe the 17 day of Augu*s*t £8 for the rest of acowmpt dewe to my mother Alice Smythe, as may apere by a boke which I made of her debt*es*[2] £8

Itm. the 30 day of October for 17 C 3 qr. 2 li. ire*n* at 6s the C, mon*tith* £5 6s 8d[2] £5 6s 8d

M*emorandum* that the foreseide Robert Sternall r. the above seide 20 m*a*rkes for & in full payment of the legac*es* of Thomas Smythe hop*er* bequethid to his son Mathewe Smythe, & the seid Robert in won with Will*ia*m Sprat m*a*rcha*nt* of Bristowe & Will*ia*m Bullock of Elmore in Glocestershire yeoman, be bownd in a obbligacio*n* datyd the 27 of October an*no* E*dwardi* sexti pr*i*mo for to pay the seide mo*ney to me[3] *John* Smythe, his eyeres or assyngnes, when the seide Mathewe co*m* to his lawffull aige

Itm. the 22 day of Jenyver a*nn*o 1549 for 1 but of seck at £5 to be paide at all tymes, which but I sold & d'd unto hym[2] £5

Itm. £5 which my wif lent to his wif in ready mon*n*ey[2] £5

passed the itm. co*n*sernyng Mathewe Smythes legac*es* to my new boke fo. 19 the 2de day of July 1550

an*no* 1549

Robert Sternall of Bristowe hop*er* owith the 8 day of M*a*rche (besyd*es* Mathew Smythes legac*es* before menceonyd) £3 8s 8d for the rest of all reckenyng*es* betwen hym & me untyll *this* day, as in my shop boke it may appere £3 8s 8d

Itm. the same day I lent to hym in ready mon*n*ey to pay at Ester next & he left with me for pledge 1 flat sylver pece & 6 syllver spones knoppyd with postells gyllt, which cup & spones wayith 16 oz. 3 qrs. £4

Itm. 16s d'd to hym in money the same day for to bestowe hit for me in drye ffische 16s

---

[1] *Blank in MS.*
[2] *These four entries are crossed through.*
[3] me *is inserted above the line.*

256(L) contd.

Itm. the 21 day of March £6 which I lent to his wif in ready monney to be paide at all tymes requyrid   £6
Itm. the 17 day of May 1550 £4 which I lent to hym   £4
passed the rest of this cownt the 2de day of July 1550 to my new boke in fo. 19

256(R)   anno 1550

Robert Sternall per contra is due to have the 4th of Aprell £4, for so myche my wif r. of hym in part of payment of £6 lent to his wif the 21 of March last past as per contra aperithe   £4
Itm. the last day of March r. 6 cople of dry lyng & myllwell at 13s   13s
Itm. more the 10 of Aprell £4 which my wif r. of hym   £4

256(A)

A small loose sheet between pp. 256(L) & 256(R)

John Smythe

In the Savyor 12 ton oyle	45s		
in the Trynyte of Rendrye, 5 ton ierne	12s	6d	
In the John of S. Sabastyan 11 ton wyne	26s	3d	
Itm. 5 ton iron	12s	6d	
In the Santa Marya Fountrabye 5 ton iron	12s	6d	
In the Santa Maria of Rendry 4 ton iron	10s		
in the Concepcon 4 ton oyle	15s		
In the Portyngall 2 ton oyle	8s		
In the Maria Fountrabye 10 clothes	11s	8d	
In the S. John 10 clothes	11s	8d	
In the Savyor 10 clothes and 25 streytes	16s	7d	
Itm. 13 fudder lead	52s		
Itm. 1 dozen calve skyns		2d	

Summa r. £11 13s 10d for
Ester quarter anno Regni. Regis Edwardi Sexti 4°
per me William Syms

257(L)   anno 1546

Thomas Horner of Mells esquyer owithe the 18 day of Jenyver 27s 6d for 1 h'd claret wyne to be pd. at all tymes   £1 7s 6d
1549 Itm. the 12 day of February 1549 £3 10s & is for 2 h'd of claret wyne d'd to his carryar to be paide at all tymes   £3 10s
Memorandum Itm. the last of Jenyver for 2 h'd Gascon wyne which 2 h'd John Horner had   £3 10s
passed this cowmpt the 2de day of July anno 1550 to my newe booke fo. 17

anno 1546

Thomas Crossway of Mells owthe the 18 day of Jenyver £2 that is for the rest of a butt of seck, to be paide the weke after Easter next commyng. Master Thomas Horner is shewerty   £2
Itm. the 19 daye of Aprell anno 1547 £3 10s & is for the rest of a butt of seck & 1 h'd Gascon wyne to be pd. at Seynt Jamystide next as in my shop booke doth apere   £3 10s
Itm. the 26 of Augost for a but seck £4 20d for a butt seck   £4 1s 8d
Itm. the 30 day of Jenyver anno 1547 £7 8s 4d & is for a butt of seck at £4 20d & for 2 h'd of Gascon wyne at £3 6s 8d sold & delyverd to hym, to pay at all tymes, montith   £7 8s 4d
Itm. the 27 day of July anno 1548 £4 3s 4d & is for 1 butt seck to be paide at Allhaloutide next   £4 3s 4d

257(R)

anno 1547

Thomas Horner per contra is dewe to have the 22 day of Augost 27s 6d r. by T. Crossway	£1	7s	6d

anno 1547

Thomas Crosway is dewe to have the 13 day of Aprill anno 1547 40s. r. of hym in redy monney	£2		
Itm. the 25 daye of July 1547 r. of hym	£3	10s	
Itm. the 10th of Jenyver r. £4 20d	£4	1s	8d
Itm. the 19 day of Aprell r. of hym 5 nobles	£1	13s	4d
Itm. the 25 of July r. at Bristowe of the seid Crossway £4 20d	£4	1s	8d
r. from Master Horner 5 nobles of which I gave 40d	£1	13s	4d
Itm. John Horner r. of hym for me £4 3s 4d as it may apere to John Horner in debito fo. 284	£4	3s	4d

258(L)

anno 1546

William Mytton of Bathe in the cowntie of Somersett owithe the 26 day of Jenyver £6 & is for the rest of 2 buttes seck, to pay 40s at Candellmas next & £4 the begynyng of Lent	£6
Itm. the 25 of February £4 for a butt of seck to be paide at Easter next commyng	£4

anno 1547

Syr Edward Gorge knight owithe the 23 day of June 28s 4d and is for a h'd claret wyne to be pd. at Mighellmas next commyng	£1	8s	4d
Itm. the ¹ day of ¹ 1548 £13 6s 8d to be paide at ¹ next, as may apere by his obligacion²	£13	6s	8d

anno 1549

Sir Edward Gorge knight owithe the last day of December 40s & is for a hogshed of clarett wyne to pay at all tymes	£2
Itm. the 10th of February for 1 h'd claret wyne delyverd to his sarvant to be paide at Owr Lady Day in Lent next commyng	£2
Itm. the 9th of May anno 1550 £4 & is for 1 h'd claret & 1 h'd red wyne d'd to his sarvant for hym, to be pd. at all tymes	£4
passed this cownt the 2de day of July 1550 to my new booke into fo. 20	

258(R)

anno 1546

William Mytton per contra owithe the 24 day of February £3 which his wif paide unto me for hym	£3
Itm. the 8 of December 1547 r. of Master Bathe 20s	£1

anno 1547

r. the 18 of Marche by his sarvant 4 nobles	£1	6s	8d

259(L)

anno 1546

Roger Phillpot otherwise Roger Myllar of Bristowe grocer owithe the 26 day of February £8 10s 10d & is for 20 loves of fyne sugar waying 2 C 5 li. at 10d the li., to be paide within this 10 dayes, montith	£8	10s	10d

---

¹ Blank in MS.
² The whole of this entry is crossed through.

259(L) contd.

anno 1549

31 tons 1 h'd	Wynes of Gascon owith the 20ti day of December ¹ ducatts which it cost clere abord & is for 16 ton 1 h'd r. owt of the Mary of the Rendry, master John Peres de Dareta, & 15 tons owt of the San John of S.S., master Martyne de Hernando, more for freight & averes of the 16 ton 1 h'd in the Mary with the wyndage £22 10s 10d ob, & for the freight, averes & wyndage of 15 tons in the San John £22 15s, for custom of 19 tons 3s per ton & lysence of 19 tons at 4s per ton, for hawlyng 6d per ton, for hoopyng 12d per ton	¹
03 tons, pipe, 1 h'd	Itm. the 7th day of February bowght of Bastyan de Sansust 8 h'd Gascon wyne at £5 10s per ton & 3 pipes 1 h'd of Rochell wyne at 11 nobles per ton, montith all £17 08s 4d	£17 8s 4d
06 tons	Itm. the 21 day of Marche £36 & is for 6 tons Gascon wyne bowght & r. of a Portyngall at £6 the ton	£36

259(R)

anno 1546

Roger Phillpot per contra is dewe to have the 18 day of Marche £8 10s 10d which he paid to my wif   £8 10s 10d

anno 1549

	Wynes of Gascon per contra ys due to have the 20 daye of December £4 & is for 2 h'd of	
2	Gascon wyne sold to Roger Amner of Wells fo. 277	£4
1	Itm. for 1 h'd to John Cutt fo. 27 for 40s	£2
2	Itm. the 21 of December for 2 h'd to Master Seyntlo fo. 216	£4
6	Itm. the 24 of December for 6 h'd to Master Kyngston fo. 249	£12
1	Itm. the last of December for 1 h'd to Sir Edward Gorge, fo. ¹	£2
2	Itm. the same day to Robert Genynges fo. 262 2 h'd	£3 10s
2	Itm. for 2 h'd to William Northe fo. 229	£3 10s
2	Itm. the 3d of Jenyver for 2 h'd to William Smothing fo. 207	£3 10s
6	Itm. for 6 h'd to Edmond Hancotes fo. 279 at £7 per ton	£10 10s
1	Itm. the 4th of Jenyver gevyn to Master Kelly 1 h'd	¹
2	Itm. taken to the prize 1 h'd owt of the Mary and 1 h'd owt of the San John	£3 10s
4	Itm. the 13 of Jenyver for for² 4 h'd to 241 Furrs fo. 241	£7
4	Itm. the 15 of Jenyver for 4 h'd to Edward Mathew fo. 227	£7
4	Itm. the 16 of Jenyver for 4 h'd to Henry Clows fo. 245	£7
2	Itm. the 17 of Jenyver r. of John Dare for 2 h'd	£3 10s
2	Itm. for 2 h'd to William Eyre fo. 239	£3 10s
2	Itm. for 2 h'hd to Edmond Hanckockes fo. 279	£3 10s
2	Itm. the 18 of Jenyver for 2 h'd to Robert Genynges fo. 262	£3 10s
2	Itm. the 22 of Jenyver £3 10s for 2 h'd to Master Clerk fo. ¹	£3 10s
4	Itm. the 24 of Jenyver for 4 h'd to Master Long fo. 243	£7 10s

---
¹ *Blank in MS.*
² *Smythe repeats* for

259(R) contd.

2	Itm. the 25 of Jenyver for 2 h'd to William Northe fo. 229	£3	10s
6	Itm. for 6 h'd to Master Seyntlo fo. 216	£12	
14	Itm. the 28 of Jenyver for 3 ton pipe to William Northe fo. 229	£24	10s
4	Itm. for 4 h'd to Henry Wyeth fo. 211	£7	
2	Itm. the last of Jenyver for 2 h'd to T. Horner fo. 257	£3	10s
5	Itm. the same day for 5 h'd to Robert Genynges fo. 262	£8	15s
2	Itm. the fyrst day of February £4 for 2 h'd to Smothing 207	£4	
4	Itm. the 5th of February £8 for 4 h'd to Sir A. Kyngston 244	£8	
6	Itm. the 7th of February for 6 h'd to Master Wellsche fo. 247	£10	10s
4	Itm. the 10th of February for 2 h'd to Master Seyntlo fo. 216	£4	
2	Itm. the 12th of February for 2 h'd to Master T. Horner, fo. 257	£3	10s
1	Itm. the 5th of Marche for 1 h'd to Master T. Payne fo. 274	£1	15s
2	Itm. the 8th of Marche for 2 h'd to John Hamon fo. 296	£3	10s
1	Itm. the same day to Edmond Hancottes for 1 h'd fo. 279	£1	15s
2	Itm. the 19th of Marche for 2 h'd to Robert Wyethe fo. 186	£3	10s
1	Itm. the 20th of the same for 1 h'd to Long Aischeton for my provicion[1]		
18	Itm. the 22 of Marche for 4 ton pipe r. of Richard Hammorsley	£30	

260(L)   anno 1546

Nicholas Mawrewood of Bristowe poynt maker owithe the 2d day of Marche for a pipe of wull oyle £7 10s, to be paide 15 dayes next after Seynt Jamistide next commyng   £7 10s

1548 Itm. the 25 day of Jenyver anno 1548 £10 & is for a pipe of wull oyle solld & delyverd to hym at £20 per ton, to be paide at Mydsomer next commyng   £10

Itm. the 14 day of June 1549 £12 which I lent hym in ready monney to be paide by his byll the 26 day of this present[2]   £12

anno 1547

1   Bosgrove of Wells wyddo owith the the[3] 25 day of Maye £5 & is for the rest of 1 butt seck at £4 & 2 h'd clarett at £3, to be paide at all tymes requyrid   £5

260(R)   anno 1547

	Nicholas Mawrewood per contra is dewe to have the 19 day of Augost £7 10s r. of hym in redy monney	£7 10s
	Itm. the 1 day of July anno 1549 r. £15[2]	£15

anno 1547

R. for   1   Bosgrove here ageynst the 8th day of February by thandes of Master Bramspton of Wells 40s   £2

---

[1] *Blank in MS.*
[2] *The whole of the account of Mawrewood is crossed through.*
[3] *Smythe repeats* the

261(L) anno 1546

Viages to Burdes for my owne acowmpt owith the 10 day of November
£95 2s 4d & is for 116 awngell nobles after 8s 8d the angell & crownes of the
son after 5s the crowne & 5s sterlyng in white monney. More 10 dicker
lether cowe & stere which cost clere aborde £25, 27 dozens of calve skuyns
at 6s the dozen clere abord & 3 clothes of Yerberys truckers after 50s the
clothe clere abord, all the which my sarvant Henry Setterford have r. to be
employed in Gascon wynes. God send all thinges saff £95 2s 4d
Itm. the 5 day of May 1547 lode in San John of the Passage, master
Johannes de Moro, 10 tons 1 C 18 li. led in 204 peces, more in the Sancta
Maria of Fontraby, master Johannes de Berobie, 15 tons 14 C 3 qrs. led in
300 peces, montith the whole 25 tons 15 C 3 qrs 18 li. led in 504 peces which
cost me clere abord after £6 the ton, montith £154 16s 5d £154 16s 5d
Itm. more in the seid Sancta Maria one fardell conteynyng 2 clothes of
Yerberys truckers which cost me clere abord £6
Itm. the 4 day of June lode in the Savyor of the Rendry, master Domyngo
de Subieta, 1 fardell conteynyng 34 northen stretes & kerssys of dyvers
cullurs which cost me clere abord 20s 6d the pece, more one other fardell
conteynyng 10 clothes penny hewes of Hasches makyng & 1 white Aburgeyne
which cost clere a borde £43 8s, more in the seid ship, I sey in the Barka
de la Conception of Portogalete, master Coles de Myranda, 10 hides & 10
dozen calve skuyns which cost clere aborde £5 15s, montith the hole £84 £84
Itm. Henry Setterford owith me for the rest of his cownt anno 1545, in
monney 33 V. 817 M., more 82 dozens calve skuyns valent [1]
more 19 tand hides valent [1]
Itm. more 800 ducatts which Hamond sent hym from Andaluzia, that is to
say, by Tyndall in monney 600 ducatts & more 200 ducatts in bylls of John
Swetynges to be pd. at Bylbo in Robert Jeffarson marchant of London £200
Itm. the 29 day of July 1547 laden in *the* Mawdelen, master Anton
d'Altamyra, 1 fardell clothe conteynyng 5 clothes truckers & 17 Manchester
cottons which cost £28
Itm. the 20 of October 1547 laden in Mary George master John Crock, 5
truckers, 1 fyne clothe, 20 weys whete less 8 busshells, 9 dicker ox, 11 dicker
8 hides cowe & stere, 99 dozens of calve skuyns, all which cost clere aborde
£149 £149

261(R)[2]

262(L) anno 1546

Thomas Haynes of Bristowe berebruar owith the 8 day of Marche
£15 5s 10d & is for the rest of acowmpt subscrybyd with his hand, as well
for all maner bere, lyme, stones & brawne which I have had of hym as allso
for all maner iren that he had of me & allso money which my mother
Alice Smythe, whose sowle God pardon, lent hym, which £15 5s 10d is
payable at all tymes requyrid £15 5s 10d

anno 1548

Robert Jenynges of Presteyne marcer is dewe to have owithe the 14 day of
February anno dicto £24 10s & is for 2 buttes of seck at ech £5 5s & 7 h'd of
Gascon wyne at 40s the h'd, to be paide at Whitssontyde next commyng, as
it maye apere by his bill, montith £24 10s
1549 Itm. the 14 of June anno 1549 £9 10s which is for a butt of seck price
£5 13s 4d & 1 h'd claret & 1 h'd white wyne at 40s the h'd, montith
£9 13s 4d, whereof r. 3s 4d, so rest as above seid £9 10s, to be pd. by his byll
at Mighellmas next £9 10s
Itm. the 21 day of September £7 13s 4d & is for 1 but of seck price
£5 13s 4d & 1 h'd Gascon wyne price 40s, to be pd. at all tymes £7 13s 4d
Itm. the last daye of December £8 10s & is for 1 but seck £5 & for 2 h'd
Gascon wyne £3 10s £8 10s
Itm. the 18 of Jenyver £8 10s & is for 1 butt of seck & 2 h'd Gascon wyne £8 10s

---

[1] *Blank in MS.*
[2] *Fo. 261(R) is blank in the MS.*

262(L) contd.

Itm. the last day of Jenyver £23 15s & is for 3 butt*es* seck at ech £5 & 5 h'd Gascon wyne at £7 the ton, mon*tith* all	£23 15s
Itm. the 21 day of February £15 5s & is for 2 butt*es* of seck at eche £5 & 3 h'd Gasco*n* wyne after £7 p*er* ton	~~£15 5s~~
Itm. the last of May £7 for 1 ton Gasco*n* wyne	£7

262(R)

¹

anno 1549

Robert Genyng*es* p*er* contra is dewe to have the 28 of September for 42 dozens of calve skyns at 8s p*er* dozen Itm. more for 32 dozens of calve skuyns r. in Nove*m*ber at 8s p*er* dozen Itm. more the 30 of December for 20 dozens calve skuyns at 8s p*er* doze*n* which he must bryng to J*ohn* Sp*ar*k*es* hows	£37 12s
Itm. the last day of Decembe*r* r. of Thom*as* Harrys his son in the lawe £4 4s 8d	£4 4s 8d
Itm. the 30 day of May r. of hym at Bristowe £16 in gold passed the rest of this cowmpt, being £31 15s, the 2de day of July a*n*no 1550 to my new booke into folio 23.	£16

263(L)   **anno 1546**

Nicholas Bathe otherwise Jobyne² of the cite of Bathe p*re*st ow*ith* the 14 day of Marche £8 for 1 but of seck & for a pipe of bastard, to pay 40s in hand & £6 at Seynt Jamistide next com*m*yng, mon*tith*   £8
Itm. the 17 day of ~~July a*n*no~~ June a*n*no 1547 £5 10s & is for 1 butt seck at £4 & 1 h'd Gascon wyne at 30s, to pay hallf at Mighellmas next com*m*yng & th*other* hallf at Allhaloutyde next after that   £5 10s
Itm. the 22 of Augost for 2 butt*es* seck £8 to pay £4 at Cris*t*mas next com*m*yng & £4 at Candellmas next after   £8
1547 Itm. the 11 day of Jenyver 1547 for 1 butt of seck £4   £4

Anno 1549

John Morys of Bristowe rughmason owithe the 15 day of Jenyver £5 for a butt of seck to paye at Mydsomer next com*m*yng. Thomas Hort the baker is shewerty   S. £5

263(R)   **anno 1546**

Nicholas Bathe of the cite of Bathe clerck is dewe to have the 14 day of Marche ~~40s~~ 20s r. of hym in redy mon*n*ey in p*ar*te of payment of a but seck price £4	£1
Itm. the same day r. of hym 20s in yernes of 1 pipe of bastard	£1
Itm. the 16th daye of June a*n*no 1547 40s receavyd of hym in Bristowe	£2
Itm. the 4th day of Augost r. of hym at Bristoll £4	£4
Itm. the 18 day of Augost r. of hym at Bristowe £3 in ready mon*n*ey	£3
Itm. the 18 day of October 1547 my wif r. of hym at Bristowe £4 10s	£4 10s

---

¹ *There is no credit entry for Haynes.*
² *otherwise Jobyne is inserted above the line.*

263(R) contd.

Itm. the 14 day of November 1547 r. of S*i*r Nycolas Bathe £4	£4
Itm. the 6 day of December r. of M*aster* Bathe at Bristowe 40s	£2
Itm. the 8 of Jenyver 1547 r. of Bathe £2	£2
Itm. the 26 day of July 1548 r. of hym at Bristowe £4	£4
Itm. the 3de daye of June 1550 £5 r. of J*oh*n Moryce wif, Thomas Hort being preasent[1]	
	S. £5

264(L)   **A*n*no 1546**

John Sp*ar*k of Newenham in the Forrest of Deane yeman owith the 24 day of M*ar*che £11 for the rest & closyng up of his cowmpt fo. 230	£11		
Itm. more the same day for 3 tand hid*es* 12s		12s	
Itm. the 4th day of June £6 16s 8d & is for a ton of the Rendry iren, to be pd. at Seynt Jamistide next	£6	16s	8d
Itm. the 20 day of July £4 10s & is for 3 hogshed*es* Gascon wyne at £6 the ton	£4	10s	
Itm. the same day £20 which my wif delyver to hym in redy mon*n*ey for to by tand hid*es* for me	£20		
Itm. the 3 day of September £7 13s 4d for 2 butt*es* seck	£7	13s	4d
Itm. for a h'd ire*n* after £7 the to*n*, mon*tith*	£1	15s	
Itm. the 17 of September 1547 d'd & paide to hym in ready mon*n*ey £20	£20		
Itm. the last day of November 1547 pd. to J*oh*n Sp*ar*k in Bristowe £20 14s in redy mon*n*ey	£20	14s	
1547 Itm. the 24 of M*ar*che a*n*no 1547 £3 18s 4d for a butt of seck	£3	18s	4d
1548 Itm. the 13 day of Ap*r*ell £4 for a butt seck & £7 10s for a pipe of wull oyle	£11	10s	
Itm. £10 which my wif d'd to hym the 25 of July	£10		
Itm. the 23 of Augost my wif delyverd unto hym £40 for to by sckyns & lether	£40		
Itm. the 10th day of September my wif paide to hym	£20		
M*e*morandum Itm. the 26 of July £4 for a butt of seck, 3.16.8[2]	£4 £3	16s	8d
Itm. the 22 day of August 45s & is for 1 h'd iren after £9 the ton	£2	5s	
~~Itm. the 7 day of September for 2 butt*es* 1 pipe & 2 h'd lery cask. p~~rice			
Itm. the 17 day of October a*n*no 1548 pd. to hym £20 13s 4d	£20	13s	4d
Itm. the 15 day of M*ar*che 1548 paide to hym in redy money £5	£5		
Itm. the 15 day of Ap*r*ell 1549 £9 6s 8d which is 16 nobles for a butt of seck & £4 for 2 h'd Gascon wyne	£9	6s	8d
Itm. £6 which I paide for his hows in Newneham	£6		
Itm. the 13 daye of July paide to hym 49s 4d	£2	9s	4d
Itm. the last day of Augost 1549 £20 for so myche he r. of my wif in ready mon*n*ey	£20		
	S. £248		

264(R)   **anno 1547**

John Sp*ar*k p*er* contra is dewe to have the 4 day of June for 10 dozen calve skuyns at eiche 5s 8d & for 1 dick*er* hid*es* whereof hallf was ox le*ther* 46s 8d & more for bryngyng of the same abord the Barka de la Co*n*ception of Portugalete, mon*t*ith £5 40d & the carage 16d	£5	4s	8d
Itm. 20s for 9 C of bord*es* & for the carage of the same which was forgoten ow*t* of the last cowmpt	£1		
Itm. for 2 C oken bord*es* 4s 4d		4s	4d
Itm. for bote hyer for le*ther* at on tyme 26s 8d	£1	6s	8d

---

[1] *This should be a separate entry for Moryce.*
[2] *3.16.8 inserted later.*

264(R) contd.

Itm. the 26 day of October for 20 dicker of hides, whereof 4 dicker of great ox that cost £12 13s 4d, more 16 dicker ½ whereof was 5 dicker ox & 11 dicker ½ cowe & stere which cost won with a nother 46s 8d the dicker & 6s 8d apon all the seid 16 dicker, & 99 dozen calve skuyns that cost won with a nother 6s 8d the dozen, of the which there be 30 dozens wurth in Yngland 10s per dozen, more 3 hides price 12s, montith all £85 02s	£85	2s	
Itm. for bote hyer of the same abord Master Gorneys ship		14s	
Itm. for 11 dozen calve skuyns clerely browght aborde the ship £7 10s & is for the pipe of oyle per contra	£7	10s	
Itm. for 80 dozens calve skuyns at 7s 6d per dozen & 80 dozens at 7s per dozens & 17 dicker lether whereof was 4 dickers ox lether which cost one with another 4 markes per dicker, all which 160 dozens calve skuyns & 17 dicker lether was laden the 5 day of October 1548 in Guyllem de Londres is ship	£103	6s	8d
Itm. for bryng the seid skuyns & lether abord Guyllem de Londres	£1	6s	8d
Itm. the 5th day of Aprell anno 1549 for 3 dicker 4 hides at 4 markes per dicker & for 4 dozens calve skuyns at 7s 4d per dozen	£10	10s	8d
Itm. paide for bryngyng of 16 dicker 6 hides to Newneham		18s	8d
Itm. for bote hyer that is to sey on tyme abord Sebastyan de Sansust ship & the other tyme aborde the Hart 40s	£2		
Itm. the 28 of September for 60 dozens calve skyns at 8s per dozen, montith	£24		
Itm. for bryng the seide skyns & other 12 dicker lether[1] to the som of 191 dozens aborde Gabarrero in October 1549			
Itm. for puttyng of 30 dicker lether aborde the Mary Conception the [2] day of November 1549 & all other botynges	£3	9s	
Itm. 14s which he lent to my sarvant Harry, 14s		14s	
Itm. the 5th day of December 1549 20s which lackyd in monney that I delyverd unto hym to pay Symons of Harvart & 3s 8d which John Spark pay unto me this day for the fynisching & closyng up of this acowmpt, montith	£1	3s	8d
	£248		

265(L)   anno 1547

138 h'd	Wynes of Gascon for my owne acowmpt owith the monthe of Marche for 10 tons r. owt of the Thomas Seymar & for 24 tons pipe owt of the Elzabeth of Harwytche. £80 6s 4d pd. for the seid wynes clere abord in 963 ffranckes 47 a. Burdalez, as by my sarvant Henry Setterffordes cowmpt may apere. More £40 15s 2d that is for freight in the Thomas Seymor at 23s 4d per ton & averes 4s per ton & for freight in the Elzabethe 18s per ton & averes 3s 8d per ton, more for custom £4 10s, more for hawlyng & stowyng 11s 6d, more for hopyng 25s, montith all £127 8s 4d	£127	8s	4d
	Itm. more for my sarvant Henrys costes this viag	£5		
	Itm. for 1 pipe of bastard £4	£4		
017 h'd	Itm. for 4 tons 1 h'd Gascon wyne which I bowght of Symon Wyllinges at £4 3s 4d per ton	£17	14s	2d

---

[1] 12 dicker lether inserted above the line.
[2] Blank in MS.

anno 1547

3	Wynes of Gascon per contra is dewe to have £4 10s & is for 1 h'd wyne to prize in the Elzabeth & 2 h'd in the Thomas Seymar at £6 per ton Itm. to yllage untyll the 7 of Aprell	£4 10s [1]
4	Itm. the 30 of Marche 1 ton to Master T. Clerck, fo. [1]	£6
4	Itm. the same day 1 ton to John Wellshe fo. 74	£6
4	Itm. the last day of Marche 1 ton to Garbret fo. 267	£6
4	Itm. the 4 of Aprell, 1 ton to Sir John Seyntlo fo. 216	£6
2	Itm. the same day 2 h'd to William Jay fo. 269	£3
4	Itm. the 6 of Aprell r. of a man of Harvart for 1 ton	£5 10s
1	Itm. the same day r. of Master Soper for 1 h'd	£1 10s
4	Itm. the same day to William Smothing fo. 207 1 ton	£6
4	Itm. the same day 1 ton to Robert Jenynges fo. 228	£6
2	Itm. the 16 of Aprell for 2 h'd to Master M. Wekes 112	£3
2	Itm. the same day r. of Master Buttlar of Badmanton for 2 h'd £3	£3
1	Itm. the 19 of Aprell for 1 h'd to Thomas Crossway fo. 257	£1 10s
20	Itm. the 20 of Aprell for 5 tons to Richard Smythe r.	£27 10s
20	Itm. the same day for 5 tons to Jamys Rogers fo. 76	£27 10s
2	Itm. the 22 of Aprell for 2 h'd to William Smothing fo. 207	£3
1	Itm. the same day for 1 h'd which I geve to Master Skydmore	£1 10s
4	Itm. the 5th of May r. of John Preste for 1 ton wyne	£5 10s
4	Itm. the same day for 1 ton to Robert Genynges fo. 228	£6
2	Itm. the same day r. of Master Clerck for 2 h'd £3	£3
4	Itm. the 10th of May for 1 ton to Hernand Evans fo. 268	£6
2	Itm. the 12 of May for 2 h'd to Sir Edward Gorge fo. 36	£2 16s 8d
4	Itm. the 17 of May for 1 ton to Roger Amnnar fo. 270	£6
4	Itm. the 20 of May for 1 ton to William Pawle fo. 268	£6
1	Itm. the 20 of May r. of Master Scropers sarvant for 1 h'd	£1 10s
2	Itm. the 25 of Maye for 2 h'd to [1] Bosgrove 260	£3
2	Itm. the 4 of June r. of John Spark for 2 h'd	£2 15s
1	Itm. the 7 of June for 1 h'd to George Graye fo. 223	£1 10s
4	Itm. the 8 of the same for 1 ton to Garbran fo. 267	£6
4	Itm. the 16 of June for 1 ton to William Smothing fo. 207	£6
1	Itm. the 17 of June for 1 h'd to Nycolas Bathe fo. 263	£1 10s
1	Itm. the 23 of June for 1 h'd to Sir Edward Gorge 258	£1 10s

[1] Blank in MS.

265(R) contd.

12	Itm. the 8 of July r. of Antony Stanbanck for 3 tons	£18		
3	Itm. the 20 of July to J*ohn* Sp*ark* fo. 264 3 h'd	£4	10s	
2	Itm. the 26 of July r. of J*ohn* Sp*ark* for 2 h'd £3	£3		
3	Itm. the 4 of August 3 h'd to Robert Genyng*es* fo. ¹	£3	10s	
	Itm. the 4 of Augost 1 h'd to W*illiam* Smothing fo. ¹	£1	10s	

265(A)

A small loose sheet between fo. 265(L) and fo. 265(R). It is not in Smythe's handwriting

a*nno* 1547

Gascon wyne beyng in my m*asters* howse full & un sold the 7 daye of Apr*i*ll a*n*no dicto

Imprimis 74 h'd c*laret* wyne	074
Itm. 9 h'd r*ed* wyne	009
Itm. 14 h'd w*hite* wyne	014
Itm. 1 h'd w*hite* which is hicollorid & lackythe 5 ynches another w*hite* yllage *conteynyng* 14 ynches wyne	002
Itm. 1 h'd c*laret* wyne yllaage *conteynyng* 5 ynches wyne	001
more ther ar drawyn ought to yllage 2 h'd c*laret*, 1 h'd w*hite*, 1 h'd r*ed*	004
Itm. takyn to the prise 1 h'd r*ed* ought of the Isbell & 2 h'd w*hite* ought of the Thomas Semar	003
Itm. ther ar sowld as bi the shop boke dothe a pere 31 h'd*s conteynyng* in colloris, 6 w*hite*, 7 r*ed* 18 c*laret*, montith	031
	138

266(L)   **a*nno* 1547**

W*illia*m Clerck of Blackford in the p*arrische* of Wedmore in the cownty of Somerzet husbandman o*with* the 2d day of June £5 which he have r. of me in earness of 20 barrells of good & lawfull butt*er* at 22s the barrell, to be d'd at Wyndgods Pill by Rookesbridge in Bryntm*arche* at Bartyllmewetide next com*myng*, mon*tith*   £5

Itm. the 29 day of June £3 paide to hym in ready money at Bristowe apon the seide bargeyne   £3

a*nno* 1549

Henry North*en* of Chuton under Mendyp o*with* the 24 day of Decemb*er* £11 6s 8d for so myche ready money paide to hym at Bristowe for 2 tons led, to be d'd at Bristowe within fortenight next com*myng* & allso at *that* tyme I bowght of hym 6 tons led at £6 the ton, to be d'd at Bristowe a thisside Easter next com*myng*   £11 6s 8d

266(R)

R. p*er* contra 5 barrells of butt*er* at 2 tymes at 22s the barell   £5 10s

a*nno* 1549

Henry Northen hereageynst is due to have the 18 day of Jenyver £11 6s 8d for 2 to*n* led r. from hym in 37 pec*es*   £11 6s 8d

---

¹ *Blank in MS.*

267(L) anno 1547

Garbran of Oxford bokebynder owith the last day of Marche £6 & is for
1 ton Gascon wyne at £6 the ton sent hym by Roger Jones of Oxford caryar £6
Itm. the 22 day of Aprell £7 13s 4d & is for 2 buttes seck at eytche
11 nobles 40d sent to hym by Robert Parker of Wapply carryar £7 13s 4d
Itm. the 8 of June £6 & is for 1 ton Gascon wyne sent hym by Fowlar of
Dodington carryar[1] £6

anno 1549

John Sparke of Newneham in the Forrest of Deane yeoman owthe the 21 day
of December £5 & is for a but of seck solld & d'd to hym, to be paide at all
tymes requyrid £5
Itm. the 30 day of May anno 1550 £3 10s to be pd. at all tymes & is for 2 h'd
of Gascon wyne sold & d'd to hym £3 10s
passed to my newe booke, folio 23, the 2de day of July 1550

267(R) anno 1547

Itm. r. the 24 of July from Garbran by Jamys Dodwell
of Oxford £7 £7
Itm. the same day r. by Master Pawle mancypulle of Newe
Colledge in Oxfford £7 £7
Itm. £3 18s which he have d'd to my sons at thre sundry
tymes & 2s which I owe for a boke of phisick which
Master Towlly sent me £4
Itm. 20s which Hewgh Smythe r. of hym in September
1547 £1
Itm. 13s 4d which I geve hym in the price[1] 13s 4d

anno 1550

John Spark per contra is due to have £5 & is for 30s
which he paide for me at the Backhawle for a kerssy &
16s for mawllt which he sent unto my wif & 54s which I
r. of John Spark at Bristowe the 30 day of May anno dicto £5

268(L) anno 1547

William Pawle of Oxford owith the 20 day of Maye £6 & is for 1 ton
Gascon wyne to be pd. at all tymes[2] £6

anno 1547

Harmande Evans of Oxford owith the 10th day of Maye £6 for 1 ton
Gascon wyne to be paide at all tymes sent to hym by John Fowlar the
carryer £6
Itm. the 27 of February £4 & is for a butt of seck sent unto hym by Fowlar
the carryar £4
Itm. the 9 of Maye £4 for a butt seck d'd to the seid Fowler[2] £4

268(R) anno 1547

William Pawll per contra is dewe to have the 27 daye of
Maye £3 r. from hym by thandes of Fowlar the carryar[2] £3

anno 1547

Harmande Evans per contra is dewe to have £6 which he
have paide in Oxfford at sundry tymes to my sons Hewgh
& Mathewe Smythes[2] £6

---

[1] *The whole account for Garbran is crossed through.*
[2] *The accounts for Pawle and Evans are crossed through.*

269(L) anno 1547

William Jaye of Bristowe marchant owithe the 4th day of Aprell £3 & is for
2 h'd Gascon wyne, to be paide at all tymes   £3

anno 1547

William Kyng of Brymygam ffullar owithe the 24 day of May £21 & is for
2 tons of Rendry iren at £7 the ton, to pay £10 10s at Mighellmas next &
£10 10s at Cristmas next after that, as it may apere by his obligacion   £21
Itm. the 22 day of June anno 1548 £19 6s 8d which is for the rest of 2 ton
1 qr. iren at £9 13s 4d per ton, to be pd. at all tymes   £19 6s 8d
Itm. the 13 day of September £42 & is for 4 tons of S.S. iren, to be pd. by an
obligacion at Mydssomer next commyng   £42

269(R) anno 1547

William Jaye per contra is dewe to have the 27 day of June
£3 for so myche readie monney whiche my wif r. of hym   £3

anno 1547

William Kyng per contra is dewe to have the 2d day of
October £10 10s r. in redy money by his messenger
callide John Marsche   £10 10s
Itm. the 22 of Jenyver r. by his neighbur William
Peynton buchar £10 10s & delyverd the obligacion that
Kyng was bownd in to me for the seide som of £21   £10 10s
Itm. the 15 day of September 1548 £19 6s 8d r. of hym at
Bristowe   £19 6s 8d
Itm. the 15 of June anno 1549 r. of hym £42   £42

270(L) anno 1547

Richard Grevys of Kyngsnorton owithe the 24 day of Maye £7 6s 8d & is for
a ton iren of S.S. to be paide at thassumption of Owr Ladye next commyng   £7 6s 8d
Itm. the 10th of August £7 & is for the rest of 1 ton Rendry iren to be paide
at Allrode Day next commyng   £7

anno 1547

Roger Amner of Wells owithe the 17 day of Maye £14 for 2 buttes seck at
eitche £4 & 1 ton of claret wyne at £7, to pay 40s in hand & £12 at
Mighellmas next commyng, montith £14   £14
Itm. the fyrst day of September £8 & is for 2 buttes seck sold & d'd to
hym, to be paide at Seynt Thomas Day befor Cristmas next commyng   £8
Itm. the 11 day of Jenyver December for 1 ton Gascon wyne £6 13s 4d, to
pay 40s in hand & the rest to be paide at Owr Lady Day in Lent next
commyng   £6 13s 4d
Itm. the 16 of Jenyver for 1 butt seck £4 & for a pipe bastard £4 6s 8d,
montith   £8 6s 8d
Itm. the 21 day of Jenyver for 6 h'd Gascon wyne after 20 nobles the ton
& 1 butt of mawmesey at £5 10s, montith £15 10s   £15 10s
Itm. the 22 of Marche £12 6s 8d & is for 2 buttes seck at eich £4 & 1 pipe of
bastard at 13 nobles   £12 6s 8d
1548 Itm. the 3d of May for the rest of 1 ton Gascon wyne   £3 13s 4d

                                                                     S. £66 10s

270(R) anno 1547

Richard Grevys per contra is dewe to have the 11 day of
July £7 6s 8d r. of hym in redy monney   £7 6s 8d
R. the 15 of June 1548 £7   £7

270(R) contd. anno 1547

Roger Amner per contra is dewe to have the 17 daye of May 40s which he paide to me in ready monney	£2
Itm. the last day of Augost r. of hym £8 & is for the hole & full payment of 2 buttes seck sold the 17 of May last past, as per contra aperithe	£8
Itm. the apon Mighellmas Day 1547 r. of hym at Bristowe £4	£4
Itm. the 11 day of ~~Jenyver~~ December r. £8	£8
R. in part of payment of the ton Gascon wyne the 11 day of ~~Jenyver~~ December 40s	£2
Itm. the 16 day of Jenyver r. for the but seck	£4
R. for the rest of the ton Gascon wyne sold the 11 day of December last past £4 13s 4d	£4 13s 4d
Itm. the 22 day of Marche r. of hym £12	£12
Itm. the 17 of Aprell 1548 r. of hym £7 16s 8d	£7 16s 8d
Itm. the 6 of June r. by thandes of Henry Setterford £8	£8
Itm. the 6th day of June anno 1548 £8 & is for so myche I makyng debyttor of in fo. 277 for the rest & closyng up of this acowmpt	£8
	S. £66 10s

271(L) anno 1547

Hewgh Hamon owith the 4th day of Maye for the neate sale of 50 tons 10 C 1 qr. 12 li. led 465 V. 775 M. & for the neate sale of a sortyng clothe & 3 truckers 23 V. 165 M. ½ & for the neate sale of 150 Manchester cottons 161 V. 057 M. & for the neate sale of 7 Bristowe fryses 12 V. 579 M., montith as by his reckenyng may apere 662 V. 576 M. ½, valent sterling £441 1s   £441 1s

Itm. more the seide day £25 & is for one 100 ducatts which he r. of Edward[1] at Andaluzia by thandes of Hewgh Tipton for my cowmpt of the Yland wood[2]   £25

Itm. the seid day 2891 M. ½ & is for 1 pipe of bastard that he chargith more in the Mary Conception then I r., montith sterlyng 38s 6d ob qr.   £1 18s 6d ob qr.

Itm. more the seide day for the rest of his reckenyng consernyng my foreseide cabbowe 12 V. 452 M. montith sterlyng   £8 5s 8d qr.

Itm. more the seide tyme for the neate of my wifes cabow 9 V. 375 M., montith sterlyng £6 5s   £6 5s

271(R) anno 1547

Hewgh Hamon per contra is dewe to have the 4th day of Maye for 104 buttes of seck laden clere aborde 259 V. 016 M. & for 50 peces of resynges of Malaga 16 V. 073 M. & for 16 pipes of bastardes 46 V. 264 M. & for 3 pipes of taynt 10 V. 046 M. & for 22 kyntalls 2 arrovas & 11 li. allom 23 V. 670 M. & for a chest of shewgar waying neate 14 arrovas 8 li., 17 V. 894 M. & for smawle tryffylls 7 V. 536 M. & for Castano das Costes for to r. monney in Sevill 2 V. 250 M. & for 12 ducatts d'd to Robert Leight to pay his costes & for Hewgh Hamondes owne costes 9 V. 750 M. & for 8[3] ducatts sent for myne acowmpt to Guyposcoa, that is to sey 600 ducatts in ready monney by Robert Tyndall & 200 ducatts in a byll of exchange of John Swetynges of Cales to be pd. at Vyllbao in Roger Jeffar marchant of London, montith thole as it may apere by the Hamondes reckenyng consernyng the premysses 696 V. 999 M. ½, montith sterlyng   £464 13s 4d

---
[1] Edward Pryn.
[2] See fo. 149.
[3] Smythe should have written 800.

272(L)   anno 1547

27 tons 11 C 10 li.

Iren for my owne acowmpt r. the 20 day of Aprel ow*t* of the Sancta Maria of Fontraby, m*aster* Alonsso de Castaneda & ow*t* of the San J*o*hn of the Passage, m*aster* Joha*nn*es de Moru 379 k*yntall*s Spanische weight, which made by my weight*es* 27 tons 11 C 10 li., ow*ith* [1]   M. which it cost putt clere abord, for freight 15s p*er* ton, for the hole aver*es* in bothe shipps [1] , for custom 2s 6d p*er* ton, for halyng 2d p*er* ton, for weying 1d p*er* to*n*.   [1]

04 ton 5 C 1 qr. 7 li.

Itm. the 16 of June r. ow*t* of the Mawdelen of the Passage, m*aster* Anton de Altamyra, 59 k*yntall*s less 28 li. ire*n*, weight of Fontraby, which made by my weight*es* 4 to*n* 5 C 1 qr. 7 li., which ow*ith* for freight at 15s p*er* ton & for aver*es* & lighterage [1] p*er* ton, for costom 2s 6d p*er* ton & for halyng & weying 3d p*er* ton.   [1]

7 to*n* 11 C ½ 6 li. iren

Itm. r. ow*t* of the Mary Conception the 17 day of May 105 k*yntall*s Rendry ire*n* which made by my weyght*es* 7 ton 11 C ½ 6 li., which ow*ith*   [1]

272(R)[2]

273(L)   anno 1547

Led bowght for my owne acowmpt, 44 greate sowys ow*ith* the 22 day of Julye & conteynyng 392 C 1 qr. 14 li., £103 19s 4d paide to Antony Payne customer of Bristowe after the rate of £5 40d the fudder, which fudd*er* is cowmptid after 19 C ½ the fudder, made in smawle sowyes 367, whiche made by my weight*es* [1] . For hawlyng to the storehows & for hallyng to the pytt & fro*m* the storehows home to my hows 3d p*er* ffudder, mo*ntith* 5s, & for castyng 8d p*er* fọdder, for a laborer 2 dayes 10d & for a laborer at my hows to pile hit 5d   [1]

anno 1547

Willi*a*m Pill of Bristowe groc*er* owithe the 13 day of Julye £7 & is for 30 pec*es* reasyns of Malaga at 4s 8d the pece, to be paide at C*ris*tmas next com*m*yng   £7

Itm. the 8th day of February £14 16s 9d ob and is for the rest of 4 C ½ 14 li. ½ shewg*ar* at 11d ob the li., to be pd. at Whitsontyde next com*m*yng   £14 16s 9d ob

273(R)[3]

1547

Wi*ll*i*a*m Pill p*er* contra is dewe to have the 24 of Jenyver £7 r. of hym in ready mon*n*ey   £7

Itm. the last day of July 1548 r. of hym in redy mon*n*ey at Bristowe £14 16s 9d ob   £14 16s 9d ob

273(A)

Small loose sheet between pp. 273(L) and 273(R)

Rygth worshyppfull M*aster* Smythe, after most hu*m*ble com*m*endatyons & harty thank*es* for yo*u*r gentylnes, ye shall p*er*ceyve that present I have receyvyd thys p*re*sent Fryday from y*o*u by Joh*n* Fowler a tun*n*e of Gaskon wyne, the pryce £7 13s 4d, which mony ye shall receve by Joh*n* Fowler. I dyd send y*o*u £10 13s 4d for 2 butt*es* of secke by Fowler at hys last beyng here. I marvell that ye made no me*n*cyon of the receyt of hyt yn yo*u*r letter. Ye shall p*er*ceyve that I have receyvyd from y*o*u yn the hoole syns Chrystmas the p*r*ices £21 6s 8d[4] 4 butt*es* of secke and 3 tun*n*e & halffe of Gaskyn wynes

---

[1] *Blank in MS.*
[2] *Fo. 272(R) is blank in the MS.*
[3] *There is no credit entry for lead.*
[4] the prices £21 6s 8d *inserted above the line.*

(273A) contd.

wyth thys at thys tyme. And your sonnys have recevyd of me at dyvers tymes the hoole summe of £15 and I have send unto you by Fowler afore thys tyme £21 6s 8d and at thys present tyme £7 13s 4d for thys tunne of Gaskon wyne and yet am I yn your dett whyche I trust to dyscharge at Saynt Jamys tyde, God wyllyng, who ever preserve you & yours, thys present Fryday beyng the 20 day of June

by yours Thomas Fursse

               90 1s 8d
               3.15s – 3.9.4

Unto Rygth worshyppfull
Master Smythe off Brystowle
thys be d'd with spede.

274(L)   anno 1547

An Abeck owith the 23 day of February owith £56 5s pd. to her sarvant Thomas Higgyns as it aperithe in the back side of my byll   £56 5s
Itm. the 27 day of July anno 1548 paide to her sarvant John Higgyns £56 5s & r. my byll of the £112 10s per contra   £56 5s

anno 1549

Master John Wynchecom of Newbery kersymaker owithe the 22 daye of October anno dicto £6 & is for 9 C of Ylande woode which I sent unto hym for a saye by John Burnell of Hannam after 13s 4d the C montith, to be pd. at all tymes requyred   £6
Itm. the 4th daye of December anno 1549 for 22 C woode delyverd for hym to Water Taylor & others at 13s 4d the C   £14 13s 4d
passed the rest of this cownt to my olde the 2de of July to my newe boke fo. 20

anno 1549

Thomas Payne gentleman owithe the 5 day of Marche 35s & is for a h'd Gascon wyne d'd for hym to Giles Reade   £1 15s

274(R)   1547

An Abeck of Manchester with the cowntie of Lancashire wydo is dewe to have the 28 day of July £112 10s & is for a 150 Manchester cottons of dyvers collowrs r. of her sarvant Thomas Higgyns at 15s the pece, to pay £56 5s at Candellmas next commyng & £56 5s at Seynt Jamystide next after that which wyllbe in anno 1548, as by my byll may apere   £112 10s

Itm. the 13 day of June anno 1550 r. from Master Wynschecom per contra by thandes of John Pernell of Bristowe marcer £10   £10

anno 1550

Thomas Payne per contra is due to have the 24 of Maye anno dicto 35s r. from hym by his sarvant Thomas Curtys   £1 15s

275(L)   1547

Roger Tayler per contra owithe the 3d daye of February £17 10d which I paide to hym at Brystowe in ready monney & putt hit in the back side of his byll   £17 10s
Itm. the 27 day of July anno 1548 £17 10s & is for so myche paide to hym at Bristowe in redy money   £17 10s

275(L) contd.

Itm. the 7 day of May a*nno* 1550 £29 10s[1] for 2 p*ipes* of wull oyle to be paide at Bartyllmewetide next, as by his byll maye appere passed this cownt the 2de day of July 1550 to my newe boke fo. 24   £29 10s

275(R)

Ro*ger* Taylor of Bolton in Lancashire clothiar is dewe to have £35 & is for the rest of 70 Manchester cottons, to pay £17 10s at Candellmas next & £17 10s at Seynt Jamystide next after that, as by my bylls may apere   £35

Itm. the 7 day of May 1550 £29 10s & is for 2 pipes of wull oyle to be pd. at Bartyllmewetide next as by his byll aperithe   £29 10s

276(L) an*no* **1547**

Wynes of Gascon for myne owne acowmpt, that is to sey 31 ton 2 t*ierces* of dyvers collow*res* r. the mo*nthes* of Decembe*r* & Jenyver ow*t* of the Mary Holla*nd* of Darckmowthe, m*aster* Jo*hn* Smithe, owithe for freight after 21s 6d p*er* ton mo*ntith* £33 11s 10d, for averes after 4s 5d p*er* ton mo*ntith* £6 19s 4d, for hallyng & stowyng at 3d p*er* ton mo*ntith* 7s 10d, for hopyng 13s 4d, for costom after 3s p*er* ton of 28 tons £4 4s, more that the same wyne cost at the fyrst pen*ny* clere aboorde after 29 ffrancke*s* 17 a. p*er* to*n*, mo*ntith* sterling £76 10s   [2]

an*no* 1548

Philip Symons of Harvarteste tan*ner* ow*ith* the 14 day of February £10 & is for so myche which my s*arvant* Henry Setterford paide unto hym in p*art* of payment of the 16 dicker & 16 hid*es* p*er* contra   £10
Itm. the 18 day of M*arche* paide to hym in Newnam £22, *that* is £15 pd. ow*t* of £20 d'd to John Sp*ar*ke & £7 of Henry Skuynnars money which I have repaide to Henry Skuynars s*arvant* the 28 of M*arche*   £22
Itm. paide to J*ohn* Sp*ar*k the 27 of Aprell for to delyv*er* unto hym £12 5s 4d   £12 5s 4d

276(R)[3] **an*no* 1548**

Phillip Symons of Harvarteste tan*ner* is dewe to have the 14 day of February £44 6s 4d & is for 16 dicker 6 hid*es* cowe & stere which my s*arvant* Henry Setterfford bowght of hym for me at 4 m*ar*kes p*er* dicker as it may apere to lether in debito fo. 285   £44 5s 4d

277(L) **an*no* 1548**

Ro*ger* Amner of Wells yeoman otherwise vyntnar owith the 6th day of June a*nno* dicto £28, to pay £10 thereof at Bartyllmewetide next com*myng* & £10 at Cawstons fayre then next after & £8 at Seynt Androwstide next after that & is for £8 ffor the rest of his cownt fo. 270 & £4 for a butt of seck & £5 10s for a butt of mawmesey & £4 13s 4d for a p*ipe* of bastard rackyd & £5 16s 8d for the rest of won ton Gascon wyne, all which p*ar*cells may appere in my shop booke   £28
Itm. the 25 day of July £5 10s & is for a butt of mawnssey to be pd. at all tymes   £5 10s
Itm. the 8 day of October for 2 butt*es* mawmesey at 17 nobles the butt, mo*ntith* £11 6s 8d   £11 6s 8d

---

[1] 10s *is inserted above the line.*
[2] *Blank in MS.*
[3] *There is no credit entry for wines.*

277(L) contd.

Itm. £4 10s pd. to Master Yong for a butt seck	£4 10s
Itm. the 2d day of Jenyver 1548 £10 & is for 2 buttes of seck of this vyntage to be pd. at all tymes. I sey to pay at Easter next commyng	£10
Itm. the 7th day of May sold & d'd to hym 1 ton Gascon wyne price £8 to be pd. at Seynt Jamystide	£8
Itm. the 19 of June anno 1549 £5 13s 4d & is for a pipe of bastard to be pd. at Allhaloutyde next	£5 13s 4d
Itm. the 20 day of December £7 & is for the rest of a butt of seck & 2 hogshedes of Gascon wyne to be paide at all tymes, as by my shop booke may apere	£7
Itm. the 13 of Jenyver 1549 £5 for a butt of seck to be paide at all tymes	£5

passed the rest of this cownt the 2de day of July 1550 to my newe booke fo. 24

277(R)   anno 1548

Roger Amner per contra is dewe to have the 25 of July anno dicto £8 r. of hym in Bristowe	£8
Itm. the 7 day of October 1548 r. of hym £12	£12
Itm. the same day & tyme r. £5 10s for the butt of mawmesey d'd the 25 of July last past as per contra aperithe	£5 10s
Itm. the 14 of December r. £12 10s	£12 10s
Itm. the 3d day of Jenyver r. £6	£6
Itm. the 6th day of February r. £5 6s 8d	£5 6s 8d
Itm. the 6 day of May 1549 Henry Setterford r. of hym £10	£10
Itm. the 28 of ~~August~~ July r. £8 by thandes of my wif	£8
1549 Itm. the fyrst day of November r. of Roger Amner at Bristowe £5 13s 4d	£5 13s 4d
Itm. the 13 of Jenyver r. £7 which restyd to pay the 20 day of December last past as per contra aperithe	£7

278(L)   anno 1547

John Wyllye of Bristowe chamberleyne owith the 28 of December anno dicto £6 13s 4d to be paide at all tymes & is for 4 h'd Gascon wyne delyverd for hym to his wif	£6 13s 4d
Itm. the 23 of Jenyver £3 6s 8d & is for 2 h'd Gascon wyne for Master Bromeley	£3 6s 8d
Itm. the 21 day of Jenyver £20 & is for 3 ton of Gascon wyne sold & delyverd to hym	£20
Itm. the 20 day of September £12 for 3 buttes of seck	£12
Itm. for my ffee of mayrallte dewe at Mighellmas anno 1548 £36[1]	£36 [2]
Itm. for 1 h'd to Mr. Kyngston is company at the tyme of the uprore	£2
Itm. £13 6s 8d lent at the same tyme in redy monney for thuse of the Chamber of Bristowe	£13 6s 8d
Itm. for Master Bowen 5 nobles the prinsypall & the costes 3s 7d	[3]
Itm. for 1 ton [3] li. led delyverd the 11 of Jenyver 1549 in 17 peces, whereof I owe for his brother 13 C	[3]
Itm. 7s for a capp	[3]

278(R)[4]

279(L)   anno 1547

Master John Bonham of Bristowe customer owith the 23 day of Jenyver anno dicto £10 to be paide at all tymes & is for 6 h'd Gascon wyne which he have bowght of me for Sir William Harbart	£10

---
[1] Smythe was Mayor for the year 1547 to 1548.
[2] All the entries before this are crossed through.
[3] Blank in MS.
[4] Fo. 278(R) is blank in the MS.

299

279(L) contd.

Itm. the 28 of June 1549 £4 & is for 2 h'd Gascon wyne solld & d'd for hym to John Love of Bradeffort £4

anno 1547

Edmonde Hancotes of Bristowe taylor owith the 27 of Jenyver anno dicto £6 13s 4d, to be paide at all tymes & is for 1 ton Gascon wyne d'd to hym at 20 nobles the ton £6 13s 4d
1549 Itm. the 3d day of Jenyver 1549 £10 10s & is for 6 h'd Gascon wyne at £7 the ton to be paide at all tymes £10 10s
Itm. the 17 day of Jenyver £8 10s & is for 2 hogsshedes of Gascon wyne at £7 the ton & 1 butt of seck price £5, to be paide at Easter next £8 10s
Itm. 35s for 1 h'd clarett wyne delyverd the 8th of Marche to be paide at all tymes £1 15s
Itm. the 18 of June anno 1550 £14 for a pipe of wull oyle to be paide at Cristmas next commyng £14
passed this to my ~~acowmpt~~ newe boke fo. 25 the 2de day of July 1550

279(R)   **1549**

Master John Bonham per contra is dewe to have the 8 day of Aprell £10 for so myche that his sarvant William Jones allowed unto me in the my costom £10
Itm. the 2de day of May anno 1550 r. of hym by the handes of William Vynsy clerck £4 £4

1548

Edmond Hanckottes per contra is dewe to have the 1 day of Augost anno dicto £6 13s 4d which his wif paide unto me in ready money £6 13s 4d
Itm. the 6 daye of Marche anno 1549 r. of his wyf £11
Itm. the 5th day of May 1550 r. of his wif £8 £8

280(L)   **anno 1548**

Margery Wellsche of Bristowe wyddo owithe the 18 day of May anno dicto £6 3s 4d which is for a pipe of rackyd bastard £4 10s & for a h'd claret wyne at 5 nobles to be paide at eny tyme requyrid £6 3s 4d
Itm. the 27 day of Augost £4 & is for a butt of hullock to be paide at all tymes requyrid £4
Itm. the 9th of Jenyver anno 1548 the seid Margery now namyd by her husband Margery Herbard, owith £10 & is for one butt of seck & one pipe of bastard at eiche £5, to be paide at all tymes requyred £10
Itm. the fyrst day of Marche £8 for 1 ton Gascon wyn £8

anno 1547

Water Davys of Bristowe joyner owith the 28 of September 19s 8d & is for the rest of serteyne iren which he bowght & r. of me as by my shop boke more playnly may appere 19s 8d
Itm. the 5th day of October 20s & is for so myche I lent hym in ready money to be repaide at all tymes requyrid £1
Itm. the 6 day of Marche 40s for so myche lent to hym in ready monney to be paide at Easter next commyng £2

£3 19s 8d

280(R)   **anno 1548**

Margery Wellsche per contra is dewe to have the 6 day of Augost anno dicto £6 3s 4d r. of her in redy monney £6 3s 4d

280(R) contd.

Itm. the 15th of December she pd. to my wif £4	£4
Itm. the 1 day of Marche r. £5 of her	£5
Itm. the 15 of May 1549 my wif r. of her maide £4	£4
Itm. the 22 of June r. of Master Herbert £6	£6
Itm. the last daye of July 1549 r. of her £3	£3

anno 1550

Water Davys per contra is due to have by his reckenyng declared unto me the 3d day of Aprell anno dicto, that is for syllyng of a 120 fote in my cownter, being 13 yerdes 7 fote acowmptyng 9 fote for a yerde at 2s the yerd, montith, I lowyng for 14 fote — £1 8s

Itm. for makyng a frame & a borde for my shop 4s, more for 2 dayes wurck abowt my shop wyndos at 10d a daye, more for a coffer for Thomas Horner 2s 4d & for the lock 12d, for a frame for my table in the parlar 5s, montith all 14s — 14s

[1]Itm. the 28 of July r. of hym in my hows 37s 8d — £1 17s 8d

S. £3 19s 8d

281(L)   anno 1548

John Capps marchant of Bristowe owith the 18 day of Aprell anno dicto £34 16s 8d paide unto hym in full payement of 20 pipes of salt samon at the saff arryvall in the port of Bristowe from Lasroye of the Trynte Gurney of Bristowe, which is after 5 nobles every pipe & 18d for every pipes custom, which bargeyne to perfform he stondith bownden in a hundreth marckes sterlyng by his bill obligatory as it maye apere — £34 16s 8d

anno 1549

John Penny of Bruton owith the fyrst day of October anno dicto £11, & is for 1 ton of S.S. iren d'd by his wyll to [2] smythe of Bruton, to be paide at Cristmas next — £11

281(R)

My foreseid cabow being employed was taken with Scottes — £34 16s 8d

anno 1549

John Penny per contra is dewe to have £11 & is for so myche Master John Yerbery paide to my sarvant William Clerck the 22 of Jenyver — £11

282(L)   anno 1548

Iren for my owne acowmpt owith the 7th day of June anno dicto £172 10s[3] that for 15 C ½, 12 li. conteynyng 70 endes which restide of old in the hows £10 6s & for 300 kyntalls r. owt of John de Berobys ship which made by my weightes 21 ton 16 C 3 qr. conteynyng 1969 endes with the prinsypall costes and charges £162 4s, montith all as is aforeseide — £172 10s

22 ton 12 C
1 qr. 12 li.

2039 endes

---

[1] Marginal note, 37s 8d.
[2] Blank in MS.
[3] 10s is inserted above the line.

282(L) contd.   **1550**

15 tons 6 C 27 li. ire*n* of S.S.

5 to*n* 8 C ire*n* of the Rendry

Ire*n* for my acownt r. in May a*n*no dicto 285 k*yn*ta*ll*s 104 li. which made by my weight*es* 20 tons 14 C 27 li. ow*ith* for 75 k*yn*ta*ll*s 25 li. of S.S. r. ow*t* of Gaberrero after 23 f*ran*ck*es* p*er* k*yn*tall, & 75 k*yn*ta*ll*s 15 li. of Rendrye r. ow*t* of the Trynte of the Ren of the Rendry,[1] m*aster* John Myguell, & 60 k*yn*ta*ll*s 20 li. of S.S. r. ow*t* of the Mary of the Rendry, m*aster* Mygell de Arysavalo, & 75 k*yn*ta*ll*s 44 li. S.S. ow*t* of the San Jo*h*n of S.S., m*aster* Myn*a*r de Hernando

282(R)[2]

283(L)   anno 1548

pd.

John Faye of Bristowe haberdassher owithe the 24 day of July £18 14s 9d & is for 6 serons of Sevyll sope weying nete 10 C 1 qr. 18 li. at 36s the C, to be pd. by a byll within too monethes next com*m*yng[3]	£18 14s	9d

anno 1548

William Wyllye of Chuton, otherwise William Taylor of Chuton under Mendipp husbandman[4] ow*ith* the 24 day of Novemb*er* a*n*no dicto £100 for so myche that I paide for hym to his brother John Wyllie of Bristowe Chamberlayne for the whole & full payment of 20ti tons of Mendipp led to be delyverd at Redclif Hill clerely dischargid of all carage, cost & charge at £5 the ton, whereof he must bryng th*ether* before Cristmas next 5 tons & all the rest by Candellmas daye next after that. The seid Jo*h*n Wyllie is shewerty unto me for the p*er*forma*u*nce of this bargeyne   £100

1549 Itm. the 22 day of June 1549 £50 for so myche delyverd to hym for the full payment of 10 ton led to be d'd at Temple Gate within 15 dayes after Seynt Jamystide next, as it may apere by a remenbrans wryte*n* by his brother Jo*h*n Wylly   £50

Itm. the 21 day of Dece*m*b*er* £6 delyv*er*d to hym in p*ar*t of payment of 3 tons led to be d'd to me in Bristowe before Candellmas after £6 the ton   £6

Itm. the 22 of February paide to hym 4s 8d   4s 8d

283(R)

[5]

anno 1548

Willi*a*m Wylly p*er* contra is dewe to have the 21 day of Jenyver 52 pec*es* led which wayed the fyrst day of February & made 3 tons more 14 li. which after £5 the ton mon*tith* £15 7d ob	£15	7d ob
Itm. r. at dyvers tymes untyll the 19 day of June a*n*no 1549 as it may apere by my shop boke by Willi*a*m Wylly & for hym of his brother Jo*h*n Wylly of Bristowe Chamberlayne 15 tons 14 C 17 li. led aft*er* £5 p*er* ton mon*tith*	£78 10s	9d

1549 Itm. r. the last day of July r. 2 tons, ½ a C, 18 li. led, more the 17 day of Septe*m*ber by thand*es* of his brother

---

[1] *Sic.*
[2] *Fo. 282(R) is blank in the MS.*
[3] *The whole account for Faye is crossed through.*
[4] husbandman *is inserted above the line.*
[5] *There is no credit entry for Faye.*

283(R) contd.

    1 ton 19 C $\frac{1}{2}$, 22 li. led, more the 30 day of September
    1 ton, $\frac{1}{2}$ a C, the fyrst of October 15 C 26 li. led, more the
    8 day of October by thandes of his brother 1 ton 3 C 19 li.
    led, more r. from Temple Gate 1 ton led the 9 of October,
    the 16 of October 18 C $\frac{1}{2}$, 4 li. led, the 16 of November
    2 tons 19 li. led, the 21 of December r. 1 ton 3 qr. 1 li.   [1]
    Itm. the 22 of February r. 1 ton 3 qr. 5 li. lead at £6 the ton,
    montith £6 4s 8d   £6 4s 8d

283(A)

A small loose sheet inserted between pp. 283(L) & 283(R).

(*Recto*).
led of Wyllys from the last of July unto the 21 of December 1549

2	0	2	18	
1	19	2	22	
1	00	2		
0	15	0	26	
1	03	0	19	
1	00	0	00	90
0	18	2	04	84
2	19	0	00	—
1	00	3	01	06
12	17	2	06	
18	14	1	03	
31	11	3	09	

(*Verso*).

1	2	3	4	5	6	7	8
2	4	6	8	10	12	14	16
3	~~9~~ 6	~~18~~ 9	~~24~~ 12	~~30~~ 15	~~36~~ 18	~~42~~ 21	~~48~~ 24
4	8	12	16	20	24	28	32
5	10	15	20	25	30	35	40

284(L)   **anno 1548**

John Horner of Stoke Myhell in the cowntie of Somerzet gentleman owithe
the 27 day of September by his byll sealid & syngnyd £40 which I lent hym
in gold for to be repayd in golld 15 dayes after Myghellmas day next
commyng   £40
Itm. the 26 day of November £40 for so myche I send unto hym by his
son Thomas Horner for & in part of payement of 20 tons of Mendipp led
to be delyverd at Redclif Hill clere of all costes & charges for £5 the ton   £40
Itm. fyrst day of December ~~£80~~ £40 for so mych sent hym unto Wells by
his seyde son ffor the full payment of the seide 20 tons led   £40
Itm. the 22 of December £20 which is yet restyng to pay of £80 lent hym
the same day   £20
Itm. the 18 day of Jenyver 1548 paide to his son George £20 in part of
payment of 6 clothes which I must have of John Strowde of Shepton   £20

---

[1] *Blank in MS.*

284(L) contd.

Itm. £4 3s 4d which he r. for me of Thomas Crossway of Mells as it may apere to hym in credito fo. 257 — £4 3s 4d
Itm. the 2de day of October 1549 40s & is for 1 h'd red wyne sent to hym — £2

S. £166 3s 4d

Anno 1549

John Horner thellder of Stoke Myghell in the cownty of Somerzet gentyllman owithe the 23 day of Jenyver anno dicto £19 3d ob & is for the rest of his cowmpt as per contra may apere which monney he have promesyd me to pay in led d'd at Redclif Hyll with in this fortnight or 3 wekes at £6 the ton — £19 3d ob

Itm. more the 4 day of the same moneth £24 which I pd. to hym at Bristowe in ready monney to be paide in led att the tyme & price next before reherssyd — £24

Itm. the 11 daye of February 8s 4d which I payde for 20 cople of Newlande fische at 5d the cople, montith — 8s 4d

Itm. for 2 h'd wyne at one tyme £3 10s — £3 10s

Itm. the 28 of June 1550 £40 which I lent unto hym in £30 of white monney & £10 in gold, to be pd. by his byll within 10 dayes ffollowyng — £40

£86 18s 8d ob

284(R)   anno 1548

John Horner per contra is dewe to have the ffirst day off November £20 for so myche r. in golld of Thomas Pickes his sarvant & son in the lawe — £20

Itm. the 22 day of Marche r. from hym at 5 sundry tymes as by my shop boke may apere 8 tons 1 C 1 qr. 21 li. led at £5 the ton, montith £40 7s 2d — £40 7s 2d

Itm. the last day of Marche anno 1549 £20 which John Strowde allowyd me for the seid John Horner in the payment of 6 clothes which the seide Strowde sold unto me — £20

Itm. r. at 4 sundry tymes untyll the 10th day & the 10th day of September 6 ton 3 qr. 8 li. led as by my shop boke may apere, montith — £30 3s 9d

Itm. the 2de day of October r. from hym 2 ton 1 C 20 li. led, the 12 of October 1 ton 1 qr. 7 li., the 22 of October 1 ton 1 qr. 14 li., the 23 of October 19 C 1 qr. 3 li., the 24 of December 1 ton 14 li. led, the 15 of Jenyver 1 ton 1 qr. 14 li. led, montith 7 tons 1 C ½, 16 li., whereof 5 tons 17 C 3 qr. 5 li. is at £5 the ton & 1 ton 3 C 3 qr. 11 li. is at £6 the ton, montith — £36 12s 1d½

Itm. £19 3d ob which is for the rest & closyng up of this cowmpt the 23 day of Jenyver 1549 (as it apere to hym in debito in a new cowmpt wryten yn per contra) — [1]

S. £166 3s 4d

anno 1549

John Horner per contra is dewe to have the 21 day of February £6 for 1 ton led r. from hym the 13 of May for 2 tons, ½ a C, 11 li. montith 3 tons at 19 nobles 40d per ton — £19 10s

---

[1] *Blank in MS.*

284(R) contd.

Itm. the 6th of June 1 ton lead 3 qr. 22 li. more the 7 day of June 19 C ½, 17 li. mon*tith* 2 ton*s* at 20 nobles p*er* ton, mon*tith*	£13	6s	8d
Itm. the 2de day of July 1550 £54 23d ob for so myche that I make hym debytor of in my newe booke, fo. 32, & for the makyng evyn & shuttyng up of this cownt	£54	1s	11d ob
	£86	18s	7d ob

285(L)   an*no* **1548**

90 hid*es* 13 doze*n* sku*yns*	Lether for myne owne acowmpt bowght the 12 daye of November of Phillip Symons of Harvarteste tanner owthe £27 1s & is for 9 dicker le*ther* cowe & stere which my sarvant Henry Setterfford bowght of hym at 50s the dicker & for 13 dozens of calve skyns at 7s the dozen, mon*tith* as aforeseid	£27	1s	
33 doze*n* sku*yns*	Itm. the 3d day of December £11 11s & is for so myche pd. to J*oh*n Sp*ar*k for 33 dozens calve skuyns at 7s p*er* dozen	£11	11s	
	Itm. the same day pd. to the seide Sp*ar*k for carrage of the foresseid 9 dicker le*ther* & 13 doze*n* skuyns fro*m* Harvart to New*n*eham		9s	
20 hid*es* 5 doze*n* sku*yns*	Itm. the 18 day of Jenyver £7 20d & is for so myche pd. to J*oh*n Sp*ar*k for 2 dicker of large le*ther* at 4 m*ar*kes the dicker & 5 doze*n* calve skuyns at 7s p*er* dozen	£7	1s	8d
166 hid*es*	Itm. the 14 day of February £44 5s 4d & is for 16 dicker & 6 hid*es* cowe & stere bowght by Henry Sett*er*ford for me of Phillip Symons of Harvarteste tanner at 4 m*ar*kes p*er* dicker as it may apere in credito fo. 276	£44	5s	4d
3 dozen skuyns	Itm. for 3 dozens calve skuyns had of J*oh*n Sp*ar*k at 7s 4d the dozen	£1	2s	
10 dicker le*ther*	Itm. pd. the 16 day of M*ar*che a*nno* 1548 to Richard Nycolls of Ross tann*er* for 10 dicker le*ther* cow & stere £25	£25		
	Itm. paide to J*oh*n Sp*ar*k the 15 of M*ar*che £5 in p*ar*t of payment of ¹ dicker le*ther* at			¹

285(R)²

286(L)   an*no* **1548**

6 fyne clothes	Brode clothes for my owne acowmpt o*with* the 17 day of Jenyver a*nno* dicto £41 paide to J*oh*n Tovey of Wyngfford for 1 fyne blewe *conteynyng* 27 yerd*es* at the water & for one hewlyng of 27 yerd*es* & for another hewlyng *conteynyng* 25 yerd*es*, more 1 azar *conteynyng* 25 yerd*es* & 1 other azar *conteynyng* 24 yerd*es* & 1 hewlyng *conteynyng* 24 yerd*es*	£41		
10 clo*thes* pen*ny* hewes	Itm. the 5th day of February a*nno* 1548 ~~33~~ £53 6s 8d & is for 10 clothes penny hewes of W*illiam* Bryd*ges* of Batcom at £5 6s 8d p*er* clothe which money I have this p*re*sent day to his s*ar*vant Thomas Togood, mon*tith*	£53	6s	8d
05 clo*thes* pen*ny* hewes	Itm. paide to Water George for 5 clothes of his makyng penny hewes at £5 6s 8d the clothe r. from the fyrst day of M*ar*che untyll the 18 day of the same	£26	13s	4d
02 clo*thes* truckers	Itm. the 5 day of M*ar*che pd. to J*oh*n Strowde for 2 truckers £6	£6		

---

¹ *Blank in MS.*
² *Fo. 285(R) is blank in the MS.*

286(L) contd.

05 penny hewes	Itm. r. from Thomas Hasche from the 6th day of March untyll the 19 day of the same 5 clothes of his penny hewes at £5 10s per clothe whereof I paide to George Horner for his father £20 & to Thomas Asche at Bristowe the 27 of March anno 1549 £7 10s	£7 10s	
01 fyne clothe	Itm. the 9 day of March pd. to Richard Degge of Wytcom for a fyne hewlyng	£6 16s 8d	

286(R)[1]

287(L)

anno 1548

29 buttes seck	Wynes of Andaluzia for my acowmpt owithe the 2d daye of Jenyver anno dicto 108 V. [2] M. for so myche that 29 buttes of seck r. owt of the Mary Conception cost clere abord in Andaluzia which montith sterlyng £86 8s, more for freight at 30s per ton & for averes 5s 8d per ton & for custom 3s per ton & for halyng 4d per ton & for hopyng 8d per ton	£115 5s 2d	
12 pipes bastard	Itm. the 3de day of Jenyver 34 V. 7 M. ½ & is for so myche that 12 pipes of bastard r. owt of the Thomas Seymor cost clere aborde which montith sterlyng £27 6s, more for freight 5 nobles per ton, for averes 6s 1d ob per ton, for custom 3s per ton, for hawlyng 4d per ton, for hoopyng 8d per ton, montith all £40 6s 9d	£40 6s 9d	
10 buttes seck	Itm. the monthe of February r. owt of the Harry of Bristowe 10 buttes seck which cost clere abord in Spaygne 36 V. 375 M. which amontith sterlyng at 6s per ducatt £29 2s, for freight 5 nobles per ton, for averes 4s 6d per ton, for costom 3s per ton, for hawlyng 4d per ton & for hoopyng 8d per ton	£39 11s 2d	
10 buttes	Itm. the seide monethe r. owt of the Savyor of Bristowe 10 buttes of seck which cost clere aborde the ship 36 V. 375 M. valuet after 6s per ducatt £29 2s, for freight 5 nobles per ton, for averes 18s 10d ob, for costom 3s per ton, for hawlyng 4d per ton, & for hoping 8d per ton, montith all	£39 7s 6d ob	

287(R)

anno 1548

	Seckes per contra is dewe to have the 2de of Jenyver anno dicto £5 that is for so myche r. of		
1	William Smothing for 1 butt seck	£5	
1	Itm. the same day r. of John Asston for 1 but seck £5	£5	
2	Itm. the same daye £10 for 2 buttes seck to Roger Amner fo. 277	£10	
4 pipes	Itm. the 5th day of Jenyver £20 for 4 pipes bastard to Antony Stanbanck fo. 206	£20	
7	Itm. the 8th of the same £35 for 7 buttes to the seide Antony fo. 206	£35	
1	Itm. the same day, r. of Thomas Kemp for a butt seck £5	£5	
1	Itm. the 9 day of Jenyver £10 for 1 but seck & 1		
1 pipe	pipe bastard to Mastres Herbart fo. 280	£10	
1	Itm. the same day to Thomas Cowper fo. 218 1 butt price £5	£5	
2	Itm. the same day to Antony Stanbanck fo. 206 2 buttes price £10	£10	
2	Itm. the same day to Robert Jenynges fo. 228 2 buttes price £10	£10	

---

[1]*Fo. 286(R) is blank in the MS.*
[2]*Blank in MS.*

287(R) contd.

1 pipe	Itm. the 15 of Jenyver to William Smothing fo. 207 1 pipe bastard price £5	£5	
1 pipe	Itm. the same day to John Asston fo. 140 1 pipe bastard price £5	£5	
2	Itm. the same daye to William Northe fo. 239 2 buttes price £10	£10	
2 3 pipes	Itm. the 17 day of Jenyver drawn for ylladge 2 buttes & 3 pipes	[1]	
1	Itm. the 25 of Jenyver r. of Thomas Blascheffyld for 1 butt price £5	£5	
1	Itm. the fyrst of February to Thomas Cowper fo. 218 1 butt price £5	£5	
11	Itm. the 7 of February for 11 buttes seck to Antony Stanbanck fo. 206	£55	
2	Itm. the 13 of Phebruary for 2 buttes to Robert Jenynges fo. 262	£10	10s
1	Itm. the same day r. of the same Jenynges for 1 butt £5 5s	£5	5s
1	Itm. the 15 of the same for a but to Stevyne Cole fo. 243	£5	
1	Itm. the 25 of Jenyver to Robert Kemp fo. 166 1 butt price £5	£5	

288(L)

anno 1548

50

Lycens for Gascon wyne bowght the 28 of Jenyver anno dicto of Water Robertz wif owith £10 1s that is for 50 tons lysence at 4s per ton & 12d over which 12d I paide to Water Robertes wif & £10 I paide by her commawndement to Mastres Shipman of Bristo wedo. These licens remaynith in the custom hows of Bristowe[2]   £10 1s

anno 1550

John Sprynt of Bristowe pottycarry owithe the 13 day of Maye anno dicto £15 & is for a pipe of meate oyle solld and delyverd unto hym, to be paide at Cristmas next commyng passed this acowmpt the 2d day of July 1550 to my new boke fo. 20   £15

288(R)

1549

Lisence per contra is dewe to have for 36 tons 1 h'd sarved in the custom howse of Bristowe untyll the 25 of June It is all sarvyd[2]   £7 6s

[3]

289(L)

anno 1548

40 h'd

Wynes of Gascon for my owne acowmpt, that is to sey 10 tons r. the monthe of ~~Jenyver~~ February ow*i* of the Jhesus of S.S., master Guyllem de Londres, owith 112 ducatts ½ for so myche they cost in Spayne clere aboorde the ship, for custom 3s per ton, for lycens 4s per ton, for freight 20s per ton, for averes for averes[4] 6s 1d per ton, for halyng 4d per ton, for hopyng 12d per ton, montith £50 16s 2d   £50 16s 2d

---

[1] Blank in MS.
[2] This account is crossed through.
[3] There is no credit entry for Sprynt.
[4] Smythe repeats for averes.

289(L) contd.

23 h'd	Itm. the same moneth r. ow*t* of a good ship callyd the Sancta Cruz, m*aster* Bartholome de Ygneldo, 5 ton 3 h'd wyne which cost clere abord 11 du*catt*s p*er* ton, for freight & averes of the hole £9 9d, for custom 3s p*er* ton, for lisens 4s p*er* ton, for hawlyng 4d p*er* ton & for hoopyng 12d p*er* ton, mo*ntith* £30 7s 5d	£30	7s	5d

289(R)   **anno 1548**

14 h'd	Wynes p*er* contra is dewe to have the fyrst day of February an*no* dicto £28 for 3 ton p*ipe* sold to Antony Stanbanck at £8 p*er* ton as it may apere to hym in debito fo. 206	£38	
3	Itm. £6 for 3 h'd taken to *the* prize in Guyllem de Londres	£6	
2	Itm. the 11 of February to S*ir* John Seyntlo fo. 216 2 h'd p*r*ice	£4	
2	Itm. the same day, to M*aster* Serjant Brooke fo. 218 2 h'd p*r*ice	£4	
2	Itm. the 12th of Phebruary r. for 2 h'd of M*aster* Gorge	£3 18s 4d	
7	Itm. the 13th of Phebruary for 7 h'd to Robert Jenyng*es* fo. 262	£14	
2	Itm. the 16 of February for 2 h'd to M*aster* Wallsche. fo. 247	£4	

289(A)

A loose sheet between pp. 289(L) & 289(R) not in Smythe's hand.

The accompt of Gascon wine r. in an*no* 1548 & made out this 9th day of M*arch*		
R. out of the Jh*es*us of S.S.	10 tons	
R. out of the Santa X	5 ton	3 h'd
R. out of the Mathew of S.S.	18 ton	3 h'd
	34 tons	2 h'd
Taken to p*r*ize	1 ton	
Sold at dyvers tymes as may apere by the shopp boke to Antony Stanba*n*ck	10 ton	
d'd to M*aster* Sentlo is s*ar*vaunt		2 h'd
d'd to M*aster* Brokes s*ar*vant		2 h'd
Sold to M*aster* Gorge		2 h'd
Sold to Robert Jenens	1 ton	3 h'd
d'd to M*aster* Welshes s*ar*vau*n*t		2 h'd
Sold to Will*ia*m Smothinge	1 ton	
To John Ashton	1 ton	
To Bartelemew Poyns	2 ton	
To Mastres Herberd	1 ton	
To Will*ia*m Northe		2 h'd
Resteth in the grett seller to selling all full saving 1 h'd c*l*aret wyne which is a nowghty caske	5 ton	2 h'd
In the seller within dorres	4 ton	2 h'd
In the pament within 3 h'd which be not good nor full		3 h'd
Drawen out to yllage 3 ton saving ther yet remayneth in 3 h'd in ech a kantell. Yt is 1 w*h*ite, 1 r*ed*, 1 c*l*aret	3 ton	1 h'd
Itm. 1 h'd r*ed* wine taken for the howse		1 h'd
I do not accow*m*pt herin the ton you bowght in the Back Hall		
	34 ton	2 h'd

290(L)   **1549**

27 pen*n*y hewes 09 fyne clothes 02 truckers	Viag*es* to Andaluzia ow*ith* the 5th of Aprell a*nno* dicto & is for 17 clothes pen*n*y hewes at £5 10s p*er* clothe for 2 truckers at 5 m*ar*kes p*er* clothe, for 19 tons, 14 C ½, 23 li.

290(L) contd.

02 northen streightes	led at £5 10s per ton, 1 northen streight 13s 4d, for 16 yerdes yelow lynyng at 11s 4d, for ½ a way wheat 26s 8d, montith all £211 5s 4d, ~~I have laden~~ all which goodes gothe laden in the Savyor of Bristowe, master John Fischepill	£211	5s 4d
32 yerdes yelowe lynyng 24 busshells wheat 200 hides 22 tons 15 C 1 li. led	Itm. laden the seide tyme in a good ship callyd the Hart 10 clothes penny hewes at £5 10s the clothe, 9 fyne clothes at £8 the clothe, one northen streight at 13s 4d, 16 yerdes lynyng at 11s 4d & 20 dycker of lether cow & stere at £3 the dicker, montith all £188 4s 8d	£188	4s 8d
	Itm. laden laden[1] in the Mary Conception 3 tons 1 qr. 5 li. led at £5 10s the ton montith £16 13s	£16	13s
21 sortyng clothes 02 sortyng clothe of Suffolk blewes 1 fyne clothe a Suffok muster 2 fyne clothes of my owne makyng 3 fyne clothes of John Toveys makyng	Itm. the 18 day of September anno 1549 laden & sent in the Hart of Bristowe with Hewgh Hamon my sarvant 3 fardells of clothe markyd with my mark thus ⌘ conteynyng 21 clothes penny hewes of William Bridges & Thomas Nasshis makyng which cost clere aborde £6 per clothe, 2 clothes blewes of Suffolk makyng at £6 per clothe, 1 fyne muster of Suffolk makyng which cost £7 & 3 fyne clothes of John Toveys makyng which cost aborde £8 per clothe & 2 fyne clothes of my owne makyng that £7 10s per clothe, montith all	£184	
251 peces led conteynyng 14 tons 2 C ½ 9 li.	Itm. more laden in the saide ship the Hart, 251 peces of led powncyd with this mark ⌘ & allso markyd with this mark ⌒ which do conteyne in weight 14 tons 2 C ½, 9 li., montith clere abord at £6 per ton	£84	15s 6d
3 sortyng clothis of Suffolk 3 truckers of Yerberys 34 peces led conteynyng 1 ton 9 C ½, 22 li. 420 hides 40 ducatts of monney	Itm. laden in the Mary Conception, master under God John Boshar, with my sarvant Robert Leight one fardell of clothe under this my mark ⌘ conteynyng 3 musters Suffock clothes which cost clere aborde £6 per clothe & 3 of John Yerberys truckers which cost aborde £4 10s per clothe, more 1 ton 19 C ½, 22 li. led conteynyng 34 peces[2] which cost clere aborde £12, more 42 dicker lether under my pownce which cost clere aborde £3 per dicker, more 40 ducatts of ready monney to be r. of Master Thomas Harrys sarvant, montith all in this shipp £179 10s	£179	10s
2 sortyng clothes 3 truckers 247 peces led conteynyng 14 ton 1 C 3 qr. 12 li. ½	Itm. laden in the Savior of Bristowe 1 packet of clothe under my mark, conteynyng 2 sortyng clothes 2 valent £12 & 3 truckers valent £12 & 14 tons 1 C 3 qr. 12 li. ½ led conteynyng 247 peces markyd as aforesseide, which cost abord £6 per ton	£84	12s
40 tons led conteynyng 687 peces	Itm. the 9th day of Marche anno 1549 laden in the Hart of Bristowe, master under God Thomas Boyse, 40 tons lead conteynyng 687 sowes or peces every pece markyd with a markyn iren thus ⌒ & powncyd thus ⌘ Every ton cost laden abord £6 16s 8d & it gothe consygnyd in the absence of Hugh Hamond or Robert Lett to Hugh Tipton & to John Shipman. God send hit saff	£273	6s 8d
2 fyne clothes 8 sortyng clothes	Itm. the 13 of Marche laden in the Mary James of Bristow 1 fardell & 1 packet of clothes under my owne markes, conteynyng 1 sad blewe & 1 hewlyng of Webs makyng of Shepton which cost aboorde £22, more 8 sortyng clothes which cost clere abord £6 3s 4d per clothe,		

---

[1] *Smythe repeats* laden.
[2] *conteynyng* 34 peces *is inserted above the line.*

290(L) contd.

10 Dunsters 18 yerdes of yelow syngle lynyng 6 yerdes of duble yelow lynyng	more 18 yerdes yelowe lynyng at 9d the yerde, more 10 Dunsters & 6 yerdes doble yelow lynyng which cost all aborde £21 14s, mon*tith* all	£93 7s 6d

290(R)[1]

291(L)   a*n*no 1549

Cristoffer Dyghton of W*ur*setter vyntner o*with* by his byll datyd the 5th day
of Augost £8 & is for a ton Gascon wyne, to be paide at Allhaloutyde next
com*m*yng   £8

a*n*no 1549

Lord M*ar*kez Dorzet owithe the 7 day of June £45 & is for 6 tons Gascon
wyne solld & d'd for his lordeship to Geffrey Kyntney his s*ar*vant to be
paide £20 in hand and £25 at Mighellmas next com*m*yng   £45
1550 Itm. the 17 day of May a*n*no 1550 £15 to be pd. at all tymes & is for
2 tons of Gascon wyne delyverd for hym to Henry Northen   £15
passed this to my newe boke fo. 25 the 2de day of July a*n*no 1550

291(R)   anno 1549

Cristover Dighto*n* p*er* contra is dewe to have the 23 day
of Nove*m*ber £8 r. of hym at Bristowe in ready money   £8

anno 1549

Lorde M*ar*kez Dorzet is dewe to have the 10 day of July
£20 & is for so myche r. of his s*ar*vant Henry Northen by
thand*es* of John Cutt m*ar*chant of Bristowe   £20
Itm. the 12 day of November r. of Henry Northe*n*   £25

292(L)   anno 1549

Willi*a*m Cock*es* of Shepton Mallet owithe the last day of July a*n*no dicto
40s & is for 3 C Yland wood at 13s 4d the C d'd to hym this day & the 30
of the same as ın my shop boke may apere   £2

1550

Jo*h*n Mychell of Bruto*n* smythe o*with* the 13 day of June a*n*no dicto £12 10s
for 1 to*n* of S.S. ire*n* delyverd to hym to be paide at Mighellmas next com*m*yng
& W*illia*m Brydg*es* of Weston clothiar is shurty for the payment   £12 10s
passed this cownt the 2de day of July a*n*no 1550 to my new boke fo. 25

a*n*no 1547

Henry Smythe of Bristowe hop*er* of Bristowe owith the 27 day of October
a*n*no Principis E*dw*ardi 6ti 20 m*ar*kes to be pd. to me John Smythe or to
W*illia*m Smythe his bro*ther* at his lawfull aige, as it may hapere by an
obligacio*n* of £20 with a condycion made by Jo*h*n Sare nottary wherein
W*illia*m Sprat of Bristowe m*ar*chant & W*illia*m Bullock of Ellmore in
Glocestershire stande bownd in won with the seide Henry Smythe for the
payment of the same   £13 6s 4d
Itm. the 7 of August 1549 £10 & ys for 1 ton Rendry ire*n* sold & delyverd
to hym to be paide at Crist*m*as next com*m*yng   £10
passed this cownt the 2de day of July a*n*no 1550 to my new booke into
folio 26

---

[1] *Fo. 290(R) is blank in the MS.*

292(R)

anno 1549

William Cockes per contra is dewe to have the 27 day of
October 40s r. from hym in ready monney   £2

[1]

anno 1549

Henry Smythe per contra is dewe to have the last daye of
Jenyver £10 r. of hym at Bristowe   £10

293(L)

anno 1549

William Bridgges of Weston in the cownty of Somerzet clothiar owithe the
16 day of August for 3 C grene woode at a marck the C. Itm. more the 10th day
of September 3 C wode. Itm. more the 23 of September 3 C woode, montith   £6
Itm. the 18 of September £22 & is for 2 pipes wull oyle   £22
Itm. the fyrst day of October for 13 C woode, more the 2de day of October
10 C woode, the last of October for 3 C wood, the 20 of November for 3 C,
the 11 day of Jenyver for 3 C woode, the 26 of Jenyver 3 C, the 18 of
February for 3 C woode, the 25 of February 3 C woode, the 10th of Marche
3 C woode, the 18 of Marche 3 C woode, I sey thre hundreths woode, the
1 day of Aprell 4 C woode, montith   £34
Itm. the 8 day of November pd. to his wif by my wif for the hole & full
payment of the 5 clothes per contra r. the 15 of Awgost & 16 of October 40
markes, montith   £26 13s 4d
Itm. r. of William Northe the   [2]   day of Jenyver £10   £10
Itm. paide to his wif the 23 day of Jenyver at Bristowe £20   £20
Itm. more he have r of William Northe £20   £20
Itm. the 26 of Marche 1550 pd. to his wif at Bristoll   £10
Itm. the 3de day of May pd. to hym at Bristowe £72 in ready monney   £72
Itm. the 5th day of Maye pd. to hym at Bristowe £32 13s 4d   £32 13s 4d
Itm. the 13 of June 1550 £40 paide to hym in ready money for the 3 clothes
per contra & in part of payment of the rest of the 20 clothes in the other
syde mencyoned   £40
Itm. the 27 of June £10 which I d'd for hym to E. Curll past[2]   £10

293(R)

anno 1549

William Bridges per contra is dewe to have for 3 clothes
penny hewes r. from hym the 15 of August at £5 6s 8d per
clothe, montith   £16
Itm. the fyrst day of October for 2 clothes at £5 6s 8d,
which 2 clothes I have not recevyd. The 16 day of October
1549   £10 13s 4d
Itm. the 20 of November 1549 r. from hym by his sarvant
Edmonde Crull 5 sortyng clothes toward the complyment
of 40 clothes bowght of hym the fyrst day of October last
past, to be delyverd unto me by Candellmas next commyng
after £5 13s 4d the clothe, as it may appere in my
memoryall more at large   £28 6s 8d
Itm. the 26 of December r. from hym 5 clothes penny
hewes at 17 nobles the clothe   £28 6s 8d
Itm. the 11 day of Jenyver r. from hym 5 penny hewes at
£5 13s 4d per clothe   £28 6s 8d
Itm. the 26 of Jenyver r. from hym 5 clothes at eich
£5 13s 4d   £28 6s 8d
Itm. the 18 of February r. 3 clothes, the 25 of February
r. 6 clothes, the 10th of Marche 2 clothes, the 18 of
Marche 5 clothes   £90 13s 4d

---

[1] *There is no credit entry for Mychell.*
[2] *Blank in MS.*

293(R) contd.

The 24 of Marche r. of E. Curll 1 sortyng clothe, the last of Marche r. of E. Curll 2 clothes, the 18 of Aprell 1 clothe at £5 13s 4d per clothe	£22 13s 4d
Itm. the 12 day of June anno 1550 £18 & is for 3 penny hues r. of hym at at £6 the clothe in part of the complyment of 20 clothes which I must have of hym of the fyrst clothes that he do make	£18
Itm. the 27 day of June r. by Curll 2 clothes, the last day of June r. of the seide Curll 3 sortyng clothes, the 30 day of June r. 3 clothes, montith 8 clothes at £6 per clothe passed the rest of this cowmpt to my newe boke fo. 27 the 2de day of July 1550	£48

294(L) *anno* **1549**

William Mathews, otherwise William Spryngold of Cawlme in the cowmpty of Willshire haburdessher owith the 4 day of September £22 & is for 2 pipes of wooll oyle, to pay £11 at Cristmas next commyng & £11 at Owr Lady Day in Marche next after that as may apere by his byll   £22
passed this the 2de of July 1550 to my newe booke fo. 25

anno **1549**

William Berryn of Bristowe sopemaker owith the 10th day of September £21 & is for a ton of wull oyle, to be paide at Cristmas next commyng   £21
Itm. the 2de daye of June anno 1550 £28 & is for 2 pipes of oyle sold & delyverd unto hym to pay at all tymes requyred   £28
passed this cowmpt the 2de of July anno 1550 to my newe booke into fo. 28

294(R) *anno* **1549**

William Mathewes per contra is due to have the 29 of Jenyver anno dicto £11 which I r. of hym at Bristowe in ready money   £11

anno **1549**

William Beryng per contra is dewe to have the 11 day of December anno dicto £21 for so myche ready money r. by thandes of his wif   £21

295(L) *anno* **1549**

Robert Sallsbury of Bristowe diar owith the 28 of Augost 53s 4d & is for 4 C grene woode at 13s 4d per C. Itm. more the 11 of September for 3 C woode, montith all 7 C	£4 13s 4d
Itm. the 28 of September £26 13s 4d & is for 40 C of Yland woode at 13s 4d per C to pay at Easter next commyng	£26 13s 4d
Itm. in money at one tyme 40s & at another tyme 12s	£2 12s
the 2de day of July anno 1550 passed this cownt to my newe booke fo. 36	

anno **1549**

John Strowde of Shepton Malett clothiar owithe the 15 day of September £10 10s for 1 pipe of wull oyle to be paide at all tymes	£10 10s
Itm. the 24 of September for 3 C Yland woode at 13s 4d per C. More the 3de day of October 12 C woode, more the 16 of October 15 C, montith £20 passed the rest of this cowmpt to my new boke fo. 28 the 2de day of July 1550	£20

295(R)   **an*no* 1550**

Robert Salusbery p*er* contra is due to have for grasyng,
woodyng, madderyng & orchellyng of s*er*teyne clothes sens
the 28 of Jenyver in a*nno* 1548 untyll this 29 day of Marche
a*nno* 1550, that is to sey for woodyng & agrasyng a
hewlyng of Toveys makyng to a sad grene 20s, for a vyolet
12s, for 3 tawnes with the woodyng at 12s the clothe, for
maderyng one red coverlett 3s, for woodyng, maderyng &
pewkyng of a kerssy of 12 yerd*es* 5s, for woodyng of £176 li.
of wooll at 1d p*er* li. & for grasyng of 7 sortyng clothes
whereunto I fownd the alle*m* at 3s p*er* clothe, of 20 sortyng
clothes whereunto the dyar fownd alle*m* & all ma*n*er stuff
at 4s p*er* clothe, mo*ntith* all £9 11s 8d £9 11s 8d
Itm. the 4th day of Aprell r. of hym in ready mo*nn*ey £14 ... £14
Itm. the 24 day of May 1550 r. of hym £8 .... £8

anno 1549

John Strowde p*er* contra is dewe to have the 9 of Augost
£6 & is for 2 clothes truckers r. of hym at £3 the clothe £6
Itm. the 25 of September r. of hym 1 trucker p*ri*ce £3 .... £3

296(L)   **anno 1549**

Will*ia*m Pikes of Bristowe groc*er* & now mayo*r* of the same Bristowe owith
the 18 of Septemb*er* £44 & is for 4 p*i*pes wull oyle to be paide at all tymes £44
Itm. the 2 daye of May a*nno* 1550 £140 & is for 5 tons of oyle at £28 p*er* ton
to be paide at Seynt Jamystide next co*mm*yng £140
passed this cowmpt the 2de day of July a*nno* 1550 to my new booke fo. 29

anno 1549

John Hamon of Bridgewater m*a*rchant owithe the 18 of Septemb*er* 40s &
is for 3 C of Yland woode d'd for hym to his son Hewgh Hamon to be paide
at all tymes requyrid £2
Itm. the 15 day of Jenyver £10 & is for 2 butt*es* of seck at eich £5 to be paide
at all tymes requyrid £10
Itm. the 08 day of M*a*rche £3 10s for 2 h'd of Gascon wyne solld & d'd for
hym to his son Thomas Hamon to pay at all tymes £3 10s
past this the 3de day of July a*nno* 1550 to my newe booke fo. 29

296(R)   **an*no* 1549**

Will*ia*m Pickes p*er* contra is dewe to have the 7 day of
Jenyver £44 r. of hym in ready mo*nn*ey by the hand*es* of
his sarvant Will*ia*m Yate £44

an*no* 1550

John Hamon p*er* contra is due to have the 20 daye of
Maye 40s for so myche r. by thand*es* of his son Hugh
Hamo*n* £2

297(L)   **anno 1549**

Edmonde Guar of Costom in Somerzetshire clothiar ow*ith* the 19th day of
September 40 m*a*rkes & is for 40 C woode of the Ylandes at 13s 4d 4d[1] the C
to pay 20 m*a*rkes at Cristmas next co*mm*yng & 20 m*a*rkes at Candellmas next
after that, of the which woode he have r. the 23 of September 14 C. Itm. the
25 of the same 2 C, more the 30 day of September 6 C, more the 2de day of
October 6 C, more the 14 of October 6 C, more the 23 daye of October 6 C
woode. So mo*ntith* all 40 C which after 13s 4d the C mo*ntith* 40 m*a*rkes
mo*nn*ey of Ynglande £26 13s 4d

---

[1]*Smythe repeats* 4d.

297(L) contd.   an*no* **1549**

Willi*am* Myllord of ~~Chewton~~ Cowmpto*n* M*a*rtyn owthe the 21 day
Decemb*er* £12 & for & in p*ar*t of payment of 30 tons led at £6 the to*n* d'd
in Bristowe, 20 ton thereof by Easter next com*m*yng & 10 ton by Mydsomer
next after that. I say of Cowmpto*n* Martyn   £12
Itm. the 24 of December £24 & is for so myche paide to Jo*h*n Myllord his
son   £24
Itm. the 11 day of Jenyver paide to hym £12   £12
Itm. the 26 of Jenyver £12 which I paide to hym at Bristowe   £12

an*no* **1549**

Richart Edmond*es* of Bristowe tucker owithe the 25 of Septemb*er* £4 & is
for 6 C Ylande woode at 13s 4d the C to be pd. at Candellmas next
com*m*yng. M*aster* Sexy drap*er* is shewerty ffor it   £4

297(R)   an*no* **1549**

Edmonde Guar p*er* contra is due to have the 13 day of
February 20 m*ar*kes r. at Bristowe in redy money pd. by
Jo*h*n Gibs his sarvant   £13   6s   8d
1550 Itm. the 24 of Aprell r. of Jo*h*n Guar for his father
20 m*ar*kes   £13   6s   8d

an*no* **1549**

Willi*am* Myllord p*er* contra is due to have the 15 of
Jenyv*er* £48 & is for 8 ton led r. from hym at 4 tymes ~~sens~~ the
24 day of Decemb*er* untyll this day as by my shop booke
may appere   £48
Itm. the 26 day of Jenyver r. from hym 2 ton led whiche
was weyed the 29 day of the same monethe   £12

an*no* **1549**

Richard Edmond*es* p*er* contra is due to have the 1 day of
M*a*rche £4 which my s*a*rvant Thomas Horner r. of M*aster*
Sexy for hym   £4

298(L)   an*no* **1549**

John Web of Shepto*n* Mallet owithe the 29 day of
Novemb*er* 40s & is for 3 C Iland woode sent unto hym by
his messeng*er* Thomas Sage carryar after 13s 4d p*er* C to
pay at all tymes requyrid   £2
Itm. the 11 day of Decemb*er* £18 which he r. of my wif in
ready mon*n*y   £18

a*n*no **1549**

Cristover Warren of Coventry   [1]   ow*ith* the 28 day
of Novemb*er* a*n*no dicto for 91 C 3 qr. 26 li. of Iland
woode at 13s 4d the C, which 91 C 3 qr. 26 li. woode I
delyverd to Jo*h*n Estwyck of Twexbury troweman toward
the co*m*plyment of 200 hundrethis, that is to sey 10 tons
of the same woode which the seide Cristover have bowght
of me at the foreseid price, to pay one hundreth m*ar*kes
sterlyng at ~~Mydsomer~~ Easter next and one hundreth
m*ar*kes at Bartyllmewetide next followyng after that. More
d'd the 21 day of Decemb*er* for & in his name to Willi*am*

---

[1] *Blank in MS.*

298(L) contd.

169½   Blaston his sarvant 77 k*yntall*s 3 qr. 1 li. ½ woode at 13s 4d
27 li.½   the C. Mon*tith* £113 3s 4d   £113   3s   4d

passed this cowmpt to my new booke fo. 30 the 2de day of July 1550

298(R)

anno 1549

John Web hereageynst is dewe to have the 11 day of December £20 & is for a fyne blewe clo*the* £11 & for a fyne hewlyng £9, which clothes *conteyn* at the water eche 17 yerd*es*   £20

anno 1550

Cristover Warren per contra is due to have the 10th of May a*nno* dicto £50 & is for somyche r. for hym of Willi*am* Tyndall m*a*rchant of Bristowe, as by my bill made to the seid Tyndall for the receypt of the same may appere   £50

299(L)[1]

229(R)

Written by Smythe on the last page of the ledger.

                 A Receypt for to make one gallon of good ypocras

Yow muste take 3 ownc*es* of synamon or 2 ownc*es* if hit be very good
Itm. of gyng*er* hallf an ownce
Itm. of galyngale hallf an ownce
Itm. of clovys a quarter of an ownce
Itm. of long pep*er* a quarter of an ownce
Itm. of graynes hallf a quarter of an ownce
Itm. of shewg*ar* 3 li. & if the wyne be dowzet 2 li. wyll s*er*ve
Itm. of good red wyne one gallon

300(A)

A sheet added inside the back cover, not in Smythe's hand.

Suche as be m*a*rchaunt*es* and hath sporonge of m*a*rchaunt*es* I thinck not to be denyed to be of the mystery

M*aster* Smythe
M*aster* Jaye
M*aster* Brampton
M*aster* Richard Pryn
M*aster* Spratte
M*aster* Ballard
M*aster* Codrington
M*aster* Gorney
Willia*m* Car
William Tyndall
Thomas Harris
Edward Pryn
William Jones
Thomas Tyzon
William Appowell
Thomas Hick*es*
John Cut

---

[1] *Fo. 299(L) is blank in the MS.*

300(A) contd.

Thomas Harris
John Capes
Gill*es* Whitt
Thom*as* Shipman
Robert Butler
Water Robert*es*
John Pill
Allen Hill
James Chester
William Harvest
George Snyg
Henry Wyett
James Baileye
W*illiam* Cook*es*
Fraunc*es* Wosley
Richard Hentley
John Pryn
William Kyeck
John Swanne
John Chauncello*r*
Lawrence Vyne
John Symond*es*
Robert Presey
Barth*olom*ew Poynard
John Whitt
Hewg Hamond
George Wynter
William Blacke
William Preston
William Baret
John Souche
Alexand*er* Casy
John Barbor
John Browne

300(B)

Back of first sheet of merchants.

Thomas Chester
Erasimus Prin
Martin Grevys
Edward Weedon
Fraunc*es* Rowley
Randell Wilburn
Martyn Asted
Sampson Amersley
John Draper
Robert Alton
Marcke Leyche
Frye
Barlow
J*oh*n Bondell
Thomas Aldwo*r*th
Nicho*l*as Warre
John Sachefeld
George Badram
John Stone
Manyng*es*
Hewgh Draper
Arthure Smyth
Richard Maunsell
Water Standfast
T. Hemyng

300(B) contd.

Ric*hard* Moest
Pope
Domynyck Chester
Robert Smythe
Edmond Smyth
Robert Taillo*r*
William Yong
William Yong
M*aster* Cary
William Pepwell
William Yonge
John Northeall
M*aster* Jarvis
M*aster* Stone
M*aster* Saxy
the Wilsones
Mighell Sondley
Parnell
J*oh*n Watkyns
Steven Bragdon
Robert Ashe
Thomas Seward
W*illiam* Coper
Smythe the boke bynder
Thomas Cutt
Ric*hard* and Ric*hard* Carie
Slocome
Paynnes sonne
George Knight
Humfrey Cole
Rober*tes* the taillo*r*
Henry Skynner
Edmond Woode
John Shryst
Howlet
Edmond Jonys
J*oh*n Jonys
Robert Newburn
W*illiam* Pottell
Nic*ho*las Kelley
Nic*ho*las Sheth
Lantrow
M*aster* Davis sonne
John Sebright
Robert Sothewell
Lewis Robyns
T. Symound*es*
Robert Jeffreis
Watte the baker
N*ic*h*o*las Crosby

APPENDIX I

The Family of Smythe of Long Ashton, Somerset

A: Genealogical Tree

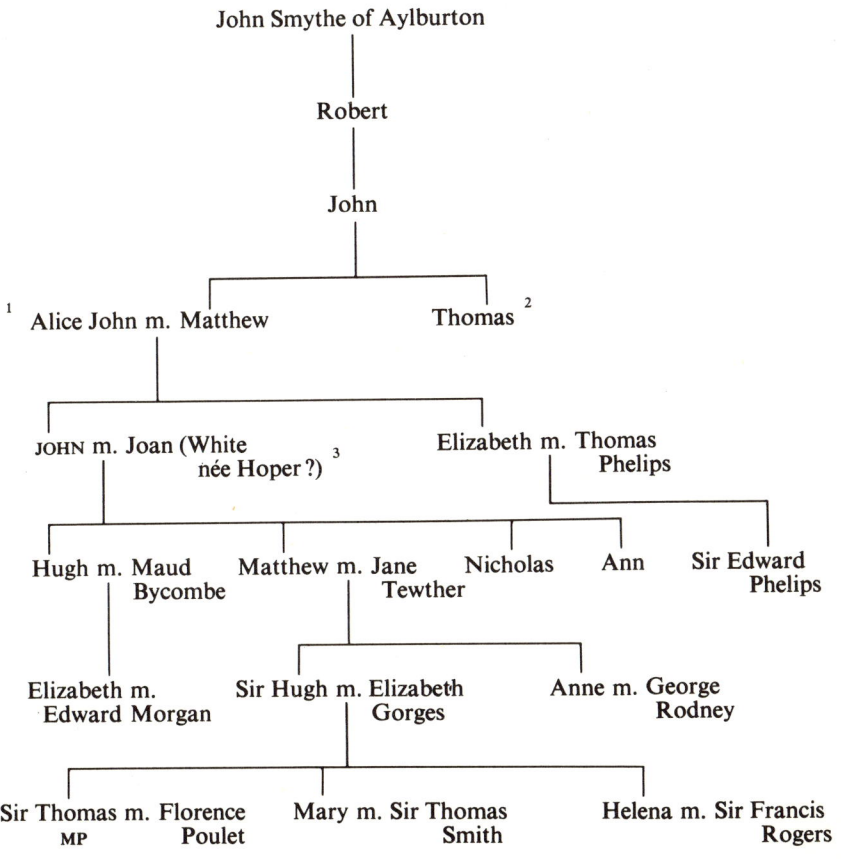

[1] J. COLLINSON, *The History and Antiquities of the County of Somerset* (Bath 1791) Vol. II p. 292 and L. U. WAY, *Family Album* B.A.O. AC/F1/4 give Alice, daughter of Charles Harvard Esq. of Herefordshire.
[2] See Ledger fos. 256 and 292 for Thomas and his family.
[3] Collinson and the *Family Album* give Joan, daughter of John Parr, Esq., but see above p. 3.

B: Grant of Arms to John Smythe, 1544 (see p. 26)

The Armes and Creste of John Smythe of Bristowe, gent*leman*, of the Lordship of Long Aisheton in the Cou*nty* of Somercet; he bereth geules two gemell*es* unde silv*er* betwene two gryffons passant golde, the wyng*es* levant langued and armed asur; betwene the saide gemell*es* a bull*es* hed golde, on eyther syde a mollet silv*er* persed of the felde; upon his helme on a torse asur and golde a gryffons hed rasyd geules beked and berded, the eres presled golde, abowt his neke a gemell unde silver manteled asur dobled silver as more plainly apereth depicted in this margent. Yeven and graunted by me, Thomas Hawley, Clarencieulx, the 9th daye of Maye in the 36ti yere of the Reigne of o*ur* sovereyne Lorde King Henry the Eight etc. . . . .

APPENDIX II

Bristol Occupations as shown in the Ledger

TRADE

merchant	144[1]
mercer	1
mercer/grocer	1
grocer	11
grocer/merchant	4
draper/merchant	3
draper/tailor	1
tailor/merchant	1
haberdasher	1
apprentice/servant	51

CLOTH INDUSTRY

weaver	1
friezemaker	1
dyer	7
tucker	3
shearman	3
cardmaker	1
sleymaker	1
hosemaker	1
pointmaker	6
coverlet maker	2
bedder	1
tailor	7

OTHER INDUSTRIES & CRAFTS

apothecary	2
soap maker	6
rope maker	4
beer brewer	4
baker	3
baker/merchant	1
smith	4
hooper	6
gun maker	1
saddler	2
haulier	3
rough mason	1
skinner	2
tanner	1
shoe maker	1
book-binder/merchant	1
carver	1
joiner	1
surgeon	1

THE LAW

lawyer	4
(including town officials)	
notary	2
scrivener	1

THE CHURCH

The Bishop of Bristol	Paul Bush
The Dean of Bristol	William Snowe
priest	1
clerk	2
curate	1
bailiff	1
(to the Abbot and to the Bishop)	

ROYAL OFFICIALS

Treasurer of the Navy	John Wynter
Treasurer of the Mint	William Sharyngton
Controller of the Mint	Roger Wigmore
Official at the Mint	1
customer	2
searcher	6

OTHER OCCUPATIONS

yeoman	4
vintner	1
inn holder	3
iron broker	1
ship owner	1
ship's master	15
purser	4
bosun	1

---

[1] I.e. merchants mentioned by name as 'merchant of Bristol'. Merchant-grocers, etc. are not included in this total.

APPENDIX III

A Comparison between the Customs Accounts and the Ledger

P.R.O. K.R. CUSTOMS E 122/21/10   LEDGER

Imports 1541–1542

Date	Customs Account	Ledger fo.	Ledger entry
14 Nov.	*Margaret of Bristol* 8 tons, pipe, h'd wine	fo. 144	10 tons, h'd
15 Nov.	*Bonaventure of Plymouth* 8 tons, pipe, h'd wine	fo. 144	10 tons, 2 h'd 1 tierce
16 Nov.	*Mary Fortune of Gloucester* 8 tons wine	fo. 144	10 tons
	Anne of London	fo. 144	9 tons, 3 h'd
22 Nov.	*Trinity of Bristol* 11 tons, pipe wine 1 ton corrupt wine 4 tons wine (with J. Pryn)	fo. 118	16 tons, pipe
28 Nov.	*Trinity of Caerleon* 8 tons, pipe wine	fo. 145	10 tons
3 Dec.	*Mary Bonaventure* 7 tons wine 6 tons, pipe wine (with Butler)	fo. 145	8 tons
6 Dec.	*Anne of London* 8 tons, pipe wine (with Shipman) 22 ½-bales woad 4 tons wine (with J. Welsh)	fo. 145 fo. 52	1 ton 24 ½-bales woad
7 Dec.	*Mary of Penmark* 5 tons, pipe wine (with J. Chauncelor)	fo. 145	4 tons
12 Dec.	*Harry of Bristol* 19 tons, pipe wine (with Thorne)	fo. 145	10 tons
18 Dec.	*Saviour of Northam* 90 pieces fruit 1 ton, h'd wine	fo. 146	90 pieces raisins
5 Apr.	*Andrew of Plymouth* 71 tons iron (with J. Shipman & others)	fo. 153	16 tons, 8 C, 18 li.
13 Apr.	*Trinity of Bristol* 125 tons iron (with others)	fo. 153	86 tons, 3 C, 1 qr. 10 li.

P.R.O. K.R. CUSTOMS E 122/21/10   LEDGER

8 May	*Primrose of Bristol* 80 tons, pipe iron (with W. Ballard & others)	fo. 153	8 tons, 15 C, 3 qr. 14 li.
14 June	*Harry of Bristol* 84 tons woad of the 30 tons islands (to Pryn, Gonsalves & others)		no record
17 July	*Mary Conception* 4 tons, pipe oil 2½ C soap (with Yong)	fo. 84	6 pipes oil
14 Aug.	*Trinity of Bristol* 122 tons iron (with T. White & others)	fo. 153	68 tons, 3 h'd, ½ C, 8 li.

Exports 1541–1542

8 Oct.	*John the Baptist* 3 cloths s.g.	fo. 173	3 cloths
28 Nov.	*Primrose of Bristol* 34 cloths s.g. (with Codrington)	fo. 173	19 cloths
13 Jan.	*Trinity of Bristol* 10 tons lead 33 cloths s.g. 18 dickers leather	fo. 173	12 tons, 4 C lead 44 cloths 40 dickers leather 152 doz. skins 3 weys. 9 bus. peson
3 Feb.	*Mary Bride* 19 cloths (with T. Shipman)	fo. 173	15 cloths
19 May	*Trinity of Bristol* 8 tons lead 45 cloths s.g. 5 dickers leather	fo. 173	10 tons, 3 C lead 52 cloths 23 dickers leather 67 doz. skins 2 hides 2 weys wheat
22 Sept.	*Trinity of Bristol* 6 tons lead 8 weys corn 18 cloths s.g.	fo. 136	7 tons, 1 C lead 23 weys wheat

APPENDIX IV

A Table of Prices to show the Effects of Inflation

DATE	GASCON WINE		ANDALUSIAN WINE		IRON	
	purchase[1]	sale[2]	purchase[1]	sale[2]	purchase[1]	sale[3]
1539	3. 10. 1	4. 10. 0	4. 18. 2	7. 0. 0	5. 19. 6	6. 4. 11
1540	3. 13. 6	4. 13. 4	4. 5. 6	6. 13. 4	5. 1. 7	6. 3. 8
1541	4. 6. 6	5. 6. 8	5. 0. 7	7. 6. 8	5. 3. 3	6. 1. 0
1542	no account		5. 11. 3	8. 0. 0	5. 4. 0	6. 1. 8
1543	no account		5. 7. 4	7. 6. 8	5. 5. 2	6. 4. 10
1544	incomplete	8. 0. 0	incomplete		5. 12. 0	6. 4. 2
1545	incomplete	7. 6. 8	no account		5. 8. 3	6. 5. 7
1546	no account		incomplete	8. 0. 0	no account	6. 3. 4
1547	4. 11. 7	incomplete	no account		no account	7. 1. 8
1548	5. 3. 1	8. 0. 0	7. 13. 10	10. 0. 0	7. 12. 7	9. 11. 1
1549	incomplete	7. 0. 0	incomplete	10. 0. 0	no account	uncertain
1550	no account[4]		no account		incomplete	12. 0. 0

[1] Total purchase price per tun/ton including all costs.
[2] The normal selling price per tun. An average would be distorted by one or two unusually high or low prices in several of the accounts.
[3] The form of the accounts makes it impossible to give anything but an average price per ton here. The prices for the years 1545–1550 are based on the accounts of Edward Rowley, fos. 167, 248.
[4] Prices of Gascon wine seem to have been affected as much by war and uncertainty as by inflation. The 1548 consignment was brought from Spain in Spanish ships and not direct from Bordeaux.
[5] The purchase price of Toulouse woad is given per ballette without any indication of the total weight of the consignment. The ballette was not of a standard weight. The prices for 1539 and 1542 are Smythe's own valuation of stock and probably above the actual cost price.
[6] The normal sale price per C. Average sale price of a ballette during this period was about £1. 10. 0.
[7] Average purchase price per C.
[8] Average sale price per C.

DATE	OIL		TOULOUSE WOAD		AZORES WOAD	
	purchase[1]	sale[2]	purchase[5]	sale[6]	purchase[7]	sale[8]
1539	12. 5. 11	15. 0. 0	1. 10. 0	17. 0	no account	
1540	10. 6. 0	12. 0. 0	1. 2. 11	17. 0	6. 11	10. 0
1541	10. 11. 6	12. 0. 0	1. 3. 9	17. 0	no account	
1542	9. 18. 11	12. 10. 0	1. 5. 0	17. 0		
1543	10. 5. 1	15. 0. 0	no account			
1544	10. 1. 11	14. 0. 0				
1545	no account					
1546	no account					
1547	no account					
1548	14. 11. 10	20. 0. 0				
1549	16. 14. 4	22. 0. 0			10. 1	13. 4
1550	21. 16. 6	28. 0. 0				13. 4

Glossary

a. abbreviation for a Bordeaux coin worth $\frac{1}{60}$ franc, probably the 'hardi' or farthing, valued at 3 deniers tournois, see CURRENCY.

ABORGEYNE, ABURGEYNE, see CLOTH.

ABYLLYMENTES, obsolete form of HABILIMENTS, the fitting, equipment or rigging of a ship. The plural form was commonly used for munitions or apparatus of war and in this sense the 'h' was often omitted.

ALBRISTEY HERRING, unidentified.

ALLEM, ALLOM, obsolete forms of ALUM, whitish, transparent mineral salt used as a mordant in dyeing, also used in medicine and in tawing skins.

ALNES, obsolete form of AUNE, an ell, see WEIGHTS AND MEASURES.

ANGEL NOBLES, AWNGELL NOBLES, an English gold coin first issued in 1465, see CURRENCY.

ANGELL GOLD, AWNGELL GOLD, gold of the fineness used in minting the angel noble. Before 1544 this was 23 ct. $3\frac{1}{2}$ gr. and from 1544 to 1552 it was reduced to 23 ct.

ANGELOTES, the ANGELET was an English gold coin worth half an angel.

ARROBA, ARROVA, a Spanish weight of a quarter of a quintal or approximately 25 lbs.

AT THE WATER, the stage in the fulling process when the cloth was thoroughly wet and was measured to comply with the statute.

AVATONSYD, possibly EVITONSYD, that is evidenced or shown.

AVENTURE, obsolete form of ADVENTURE, a term used in commerce of an undertaking or an investment involving a certain risk.

AVERES, the AVERIA, a Spanish tax first imposed in 1518; also in Mediterranean shipping a duty or tax charged on goods or any charge over and above the freight incurred in the shipment of the goods and payable by their owner.

AVYDING, using up, therefore making void.

AZAR, see CLOTH.

BALETTE, BALLETTE, a half bale, see WEIGHTS AND MEASURES.

BARBYNG, clipping or trimming, in cloth-making part of the process carried out by the shearman.

BARREL, BARRELL, a wooden cask often used as a measure of particular commodities, see WEIGHTS AND MEASURES.

BASTARD, see WINE.

BASYNE, BAZYNE, with a LAVER, a large basin used for washing the hands.

BASYS, obsolete form of BASES, small breech-loading culverin often used to repel boarders.

BEDDAR, obsolete form of BEDDER, a bed-maker or upholsterer.

BETAKLE CANDELLS, BYTAKLE, candles for the BITTACLE or BINNACLE lantern near the box which contained the compass on board ship.

BEVERAIGE, obsolete form of BEVERAGE, any common liquor for the sailors, for example, small cider. This name was also given to the liquor made by pouring water over the pressed grapes after the wine had been drawn off.

BILL, BYLL, a promissory note, a bill of debt or a bill obligatory, acknowledging a debt and promising to pay it at a specified time.

BOLLTES, obsolete form of BOLTS, the arrows of a cross-bow or any similar projectiles.

BROADCLOTH, see CLOTH.

BRODE YERD, a BROAD YARD, possibly a yard of cloth 63 inches wide.

BRYNGYNG UP, a cloth process carried out by the tucker, who also did all the rowing of the cloth. This was probably a similar process of raising the nap.

BUCKERAM, see CLOTH.

BUGE SKUYNS, imported lamb skins, originally from Bougie in North Africa, dressed with the wool outwards.

BURDEN, a measure of fish, 20–22 fishes.

BURGES MONEY, BURGESS MONEY, the fee paid on receiving the freedom of the town, for example on successful completion of apprenticeship.

BUTT, a cask for wine, in the Ledger it is used only for Spanish wines, see WEIGHTS AND MEASURES.

C. a hundredweight, in the Ledger 112 lbs; a hundred, used in sums of money and meaning 100 and not the long hundred of 120.

CABBOWE, CABOW, goods, merchandise.

CAHISSE, a Spanish weight, QAFIS or CAHIZ, containing 12 fanegas or about 18 bushels of English weight.

CANDELL BARRELL, unidentified.

CAPASSO, from Spanish CAPAZO, a large frail or basket often made of esparto grass or rushes, in the Ledger always used for packing woad.

CAPRICK, see WINE.

CAPUZ, from Spanish CAPUZ, an old-fashioned cloak with a hood or CAPUCHO, a cowl or hood.

CARDE MAKER, the maker of an instrument for raising a nap on cloth consisting of teasel heads set in a frame.

CARG, CARGG, from Spanish CARGA, a load, often used as a measure of weight, 400 lbs. in 2 bales of 200 lbs. each. In the Ledger a carg always contains 8 capassos of woad.

cha. abbreviation for a coin used in N. Spain and valued by Smythe at $\frac{1}{60}$ ducat, probably a 'chamfron' or 'shamfron', a coin of Portuguese origin, see CURRENCY.

CHAYERS, obsolete form of CHAIRS.

CHEST, a box or case in which certain commodities are packed, for example sugar, and sometimes used as a variable measure of quantity for such commodities.

CHYMES, obsolete form of CHIME, the projecting rim of a cask formed by the ends of the staves.

CLARET, CLARETT, see WINE.

CLOTH,

ABORGEYNE, ABURGEYNE, cloth made in Abergavenny, Monmouth.

AZAR, a clear, light blue cloth, dyed with woad only.

BROADCLOTH, a traditional heavy woollen cloth, 28 to 30 yards long and 63 inches wide and, when fulled and dried, weighing 90 lbs.

BUCKERAM, obsolete form of BUCKRAM, in the Middle Ages and the sixteenth century an expensive and delicate fabric, sometimes cotton, sometimes linen. Sometimes wrongly used for a coarse cotton cloth made in W. Europe.

COSTOM CLOTH, COSTON CLOTH, unidentified.

DOZENS, Northern dozens were 12 to 13 yards long and 63 inches wide and weighed 33 lbs. Devonshire dozens were lighter kerseys weighing only 14 lbs.

DULAS, obsolete form of DOULAS, a coarse linen cloth originally from Doulas in Brittany.

DUNSTERS, a woollen cloth from Dunster in Somerset.

FRISE, FRIZE, FRYSE, FRYZE, obsolete forms of FRIEZE, a coarse woollen cloth with a nap.

HEWLYNG, this seems to be any coloured cloth.

KERSSY, KERSY, KERSYE, KERSSEY, KERSEY, a woollen cloth originally from Kersey in Suffolk. It was 17 to 18 yards long, and weighed 20 lbs.

LONDON CLOTH, possibly cloth of the quality usually supplied by the Somerset and Wiltshire clothiers for the London market.

LYNARD, obsolete form of LINING.

MOTLEY, a coloured cloth sometimes also called MEDLEY, the interwoven colours having been dyed in the wool.

MUSTER CLOTH, a grey woollen cloth, originally called Musterdevillers from Montivilliers in Normandy.

NORTHERN COTTONS, MANCHESTER COTTONS, coarse woollen cloths, light-weight, cheap and brightly-coloured. It is unlikely that they contained any cotton; the name referred to a process in raising the nap, peculiar to Lancashire, Westmorland and some Welsh goods.

PENNY HEWES, HEWS, HUES, a kind of coloured woollen cloth.

PEWKE, a cloth dyed with woad, madder and other dyes to produce a colour between russet and black.

PLONKETTE, a grey or greyish-blue cloth, probably from plonquié—lead coloured.

SAD BLEWE, SAD GRENE, cloths dyed to a dull blue or dull green colour. The 'sad' effect was produced by dipping in an alkaline solution after dyeing.

SORTYNG CLOTHES, slightly heavier kerseys.

STRETES, STREIGHTS, were STRAITS or narrow cloths, 17 to 18 yards long, 1 yard wide and 24 lbs. in weight.

SUFFOCK, SUFFOLK, SUFFOK, cloths from Suffolk.

TAWNES, cloths called TAWNIES were dyed with woad, madder and other dyes to a grey or fawn colour.

TRUCKERS, TRUKARS, a kind of woollen cloth.

COCCET, COCQUET, COCQUETT, the COCKET was a receipt given for money received by the Customer. In the case of exports the document was sealed with the 'cocket' or custom house seal.

COFERAR, obsolete form of COFFERER, a maker of coffers, boxes or chests.

COMPERTENARS, obsolete form of COMPARTIONER, a co-partner.

COMPLYMENT, the COMPLEMENT, full allowance or equipment, especially of a ship; Smythe uses it to denote his share of the freight.

CONFESS A FYNE, to acknowledge to be legally valid a FINE or Final Concord, the agreement which recorded the transfer of freehold property.

CONTRATACION, contract or bargain.

COPULLMENT, possibly an error for COMPLEMENT.
CORDAVAN, CORDAVON, CORDOVAN SKUYN, Spanish leather, made originally at Cordova of goat skins tanned and dressed.
CORRANT, silver pennies of CURRENT money.
CORREDOR, Spanish term for broker or commercial agent.
CORREO, Spanish term for messenger, courier or postman.
CORTEYNE, obsolete form of CURTAIN.
COSTOM CLOTH, see CLOTH.
COTTON CLOTH, see CLOTH, NORTHERN COTTONS.
CURRENCY, see p. 336.

DREASSYD, obsolete form of DRESSED, the part of the cloth finishing process carried out by the shearman.
DUCAT, DUCATT, a Spanish gold coin first issued in 1497, valued by John Smythe at 5/- to 6/8, see CURRENCY.
DULAS, see CLOTH.
DUNSTERS, see CLOTH.

EARNESS, ERNES, YERENES, YERNES, obsolete forms of EARNEST, a pledge, a sum of money paid as an instalment, especially for the purpose of securing a bargain or contract.
EGAR, obsolete form of EAGER, sharp or sour.
ELL, a measure of length varying in different countries. An English ell was 45 inches, see WEIGHTS AND MEASURES.
ELLMYNE BORDES, obsolete form of ELM BOARDS. Elmyn was the usual adjective for elm wood or elm boards.
ENDES, from Spanish CABO—an end, iron exported from Northern Spain in bars each weighing approximately 22 to 24 lbs. called by the Spaniards 'cabos', by the French 'bouts'.
EVENING, part of the process of dyeing cloth. From the Statute 3 Henry VIII c. 6 it seems to mean drying and tentering the cloth to an even shape.
EWAR, HEWER, obsolete forms of EWER, a pitcher with a wide spout used to bring water for washing the hands.

FACTOR, the agent of a merchant abroad, authorised by letter of attorney and with a salary or allowance for his care. The same man might be a factor for several merchants. John Smythe's apprentices acted as his factors abroad and in the Ledger are called 'factor' or 'apprentice' indiscriminately.
FANEGA, a Spanish measure of grain approximately 1.8 bushels, see WEIGHTS AND MEASURES.
FARDELL, a FARDEL was a pack or bundle of indeterminate quantity.

FEE SYMPLE, a tenant in fee simple held an absolute inheritance, clear of any condition, limitation or restriction to particular heirs.
FET, obsolete form of FETCH.
28 FLORYNGES WARANTIEZ, WARANTES, the quality of woad was measured in 'florins'. The highest quality was 30 florins at the beginning of the sixteenth century and 40 florins by 1560.
FLOWER WARCK, an embroidered or tapestry design of flowers.
FODER, FODDER, FUDDER, FFUDDIR, obsolete forms of FOTHER, a measure of lead, usually 19½ cwt., see WEIGHTS AND MEASURES.
FORFFETT, obsolete form of FORFEIT, John Smythe paid as surety, conditions of sale not having been fulfilled.
FOTT, obsolete form of FETCHED.
FRANCKES, the FRANC was a French gold coin, valued by John Smythe at 1/8d, see CURRENCY.
FRISE, FRIZE, FRYSE, FRYZE, see CLOTH.

GAGE, obsolete form of GAUGE, the inspection of casks of wine to ascertain their contents. This was carried out by a Royal official and no wine could be sold unless the cask bore the gauger's mark.
GAIGE, obsolete form of GAGE, a pawn or pledge.
GALYNGALE, obsolete form of GALINGALE, an aromatic root of certain East Indian plants much used in medicine and cookery.
GASCON, see WINE.
GRAPER, obsolete form of GRAPPER, a grappling hook.
GRASSYNG, GRASYNG, GRAZYNG, GRAZING, a process in dyeing green cloth.
GRAYNES, obsolete form of GRAINS, capsules of Amomum Meleguetta or Guinea grains from West Africa, used as a spice and in medicine.
GROTE, GROTTE, obsolete forms of GROAT, an English silver fourpenny coin issued regularly from 1351, see CURRENCY.

HAND, a process in the dyeing of violet cloth.
HEWER, see EWER.
HEWLYNGES, see CLOTH.
HOGSHEAD, a cask for wine, see WEIGHTS AND MEASURES.
HOPES, obsolete form of HOOPS, circular bands of wood or flattened metal for binding together the staves of casks.
HULK, a large ship of burden, a transport or store ship.
HULLOC, HULLOCK, HULOK, HULLOK, see WINE.

ILAND WOOD, woad from the Islands of the Azores.

JEANER WOOD, woad from Genoa, usually written JEANES WOAD.
JOBBER, unidentified.
JORNAL, obsolete form of JOURNAL, a merchant's day-book into which all items from the shop-book are copied in separate accounts.

K. a Bordeaux coin valued by Smythe at about 1¼d sterling. This could be a fifteenth century 'Gros au K', a 'Karolus' dizain or, more probably a Bordeaux demi-gros minted after 1540 when the mint there was allotted the 'K' mark, see CURRENCY.
KANTELL, obsolete form of CANTLE, a canful.
KERCHO, KERCHOW CLOTHE, obsolete form of KERCHIEF, a cloth used to cover the head, formerly a woman's head-dress.
KERSEY, see CLOTH.
KINTAL, KYNTALL, an early form of QUINTAL, a weight of 100 lbs., see WEIGHTS AND MEASURES.
KNEES, KNES, a naturally crooked timber cut from the crotch of a tree, much used in ship-building.
KNOPS, KNOPPID, knobs, protuberances, buttons. SPONES KNOPPID WITH LYONS GILT, spoons with gilt lions' heads on the handles.
KYNTERKYN, obsolete form of KILDERKYN, a cask for wine or beer, see WEIGHTS AND MEASURES.

LATHES, LAYTTES, obsolete forms of LATHS, thin, narrow strips of wood, not sawn but rent or riven, used to form ground work on which to fasten slates or tiles or a plaster roof or ceiling.
LAVER, a wash hand basin or water jug usually of metal.
LERY, obsolete form of LEERY, empty or containing empty spaces or hollows.
LESS, LESSES, in book-keeping, debit entries.
LIGHTER, LIGHTERAGE, a large, open, flat-bottomed boat used to carry goods to or from ships; a charge for the hire of the lighter.
LONDON CLOTH, see CLOTH.
LOWSE WOOD, woad from Toulouse.
LYES, obsolete form of LEES, dregs, sediment deposited in the containing vessel from wine and some other liquids.
LYNARD, see CLOTH.
LYNG, obsolete form of LING, a deep-water fish, largely used for food, either split and dried as stock-fish or salted.

MADDER, a herbaceous climbing plant, the roots of which were much used for a red dye.
MANCHESTERS, see CLOTH, NORTHERN COTTONS.
MARAVEDI, Spanish money of account based on an earlier coin of Moorish origin, see CURRENCY.
MARK, MARCK, English money of account, 13/4d, originally representing a mark weight of silver.
MARLYNE, obsolete form of MARLINE, a small line of two strands, very little twisted.
MATTES, mats of a coarse weave were largely used in the stowage of corn, biscuit and other articles on board ship.
MAWMESEY, MAWMESSEY, MAWNSEY, MAWNSSEY, see WINE.
MEATE OYLE, METE OYLE, a fish oil, by the sixteenth century usually cod-liver oil, often known as 'train-oil'.
MEMORYALL, the MEMORIAL was the merchant's shop-book in which all transactions were immediately recorded in detail.
MENDYP WEIGHT, possibly special weights used at the four courts to which all lead mined in the Mendip area had to be taken before despatch, see WEIGHTS AND MEASURES.
METHEGLYN, METHEGLIN was a spiced or medicated variety of mead originally peculiar to Wales.
METYNG, METING, measuring, portioning out.
MILRES, in Portuguese money of account, 1,000 res, see CURRENCY.
MONYCIONS, obsolete form of MUNITIONS, military stores, especially powder and shot.
MORYS PIKES, obsolete form of MORRIS PIKES OR MOORISH PIKES, a form of pike supposed to be of Moorish origin.
MOTLEY, see CLOTH.
MUSCADELL, see WINE.
MUSTER CLOTH, see CLOTH.
MYLLWELL, obsolete form of MULVEL, cod.

NEST, a set of objects one inside the other.
NETE, net, clear of all deductions or charges.
NETE OYLE, unidentified, possibly an error for METE OIL.
NEWLANDE FISH, obsolete form of NEW-FOUNDLAND FISH.
NOBLE, English gold coin first issued in 1344 and valued at 6/8. In 1464 its value was raised to 8/4 and in 1526 a new 'George' noble was issued again valued at 6/8, see CURRENCY.
NUT, NUTTES, a cup formed of the shell of a coco-nut mounted in metal, also one made of metal to resemble this.

OB, OBOLUS, a half-penny, see CURRENCY.
OCAM, obsolete form of OAKUM, the coarse part of the flax separated, old ropes untwisted and picked to pieces, principally used in caulking the seams, for stopping leaks and for making into twice-laid ropes.

OLLROWNS, obsolete form of OLERONS, sailcloths made of a kind of coarse canvas originally from the Isle of Oléron in France.

ORCHILL, ORCHIL, a red or violet dye prepared from certain lichens.

OSSEY, see WINE.

OYLE BERYS, obsolete form of OIL BERRIES, olives.

PAMENT, obsolete form of PAVEMENT, paved surface or courtyard.

PARCEL-GILT, partly gilded.

PARTIDO, from Spanish PARTIDA, an entry or item in book-keeping.

PECE, obsolete form of PIECE, a variable measure. As a cask it was usually a butt or two hogsheads; of dried fruit 40 pieces made a tun, see WEIGHTS AND MEASURES.

PENNY, AT THE FIRST PENNY, the prime cost, cost price, especially without counting interest on delayed payments. This may have originated in 'God's Penny', the first money to change hands in earnest of a bargain or to seal a contract.

PENNY HEWES, see CLOTH.

PENS OF TWO PENS, these may have been English coins minted before the debasement and worth double the value of 1547–1548 coins.

PEPPER, LONG PEPPER, a pungent, aromatic condiment, native of Malabar and Bengal, the fruit is hottest in its immature state and is gathered while still green and dried in the sun.

PERCEDEWE, PERCIDO, PROCEDEWE, from obsolete Spanish word PROCEDIDO, proceeds, profits; net result.

PESON, PESSON, PEZON, peas; original plural of pease.

PEWKYNG, dyeing cloth with woad, madder and other dyes to produce pewke, a colour between russet and black.

PIPE, a large cask used for wine, beer, cider, beef, fish, etc., see WEIGHTS AND MEASURES.

PIX, obsolete form of PYX, a box or coffer; the vessel in which the host or consecrated bread of the sacrament is reserved.

PLONKETTES, see CLOTH.

PLUMP, obsolete form of PUMP.

PORT PECES, an ancient piece of ordnance, a small version of the cannon perier, mounted on wooden wheels, breech loading and weighing about 10 cwt. They were useful only at short range and were more often used to repel boarders.

PORTUGESIS, a PORTUGUEZ was a gold coin of John II of Portugal of the value of 10 crusados and struck to commemorate the voyages of exploration, see CURRENCY.

POSTELLS, POSTILLS, obsolete form of APOSTLES.

POTTELL, obsolete form of POTTLE, measure of capacity, 2 quarts; a little pot; a 2 quart measure.

POWLEDAVY, obsolete form of POLDAVIS, a coarse canvas or sacking, linen or sailcloth, originally woven in Brittany and named apparently from Poldavide on the south side of Douarnenez Bay on the coast of Brittany.

POWLES, obsolete form of POLES, possibly for masts.

POWNCE, POWNCYD, to emboss plate or other metal as a decoration or distinguishing mark; embossed.

PREMYSSES, obsolete form of PREMISES, the aforesaid, a previous statement.

PRENTIS, PRENTES, obsolete form of APPRENTICE, John Smythe uses the words 'prentis' and 'servant' indiscriminately and also continues to call the young men 'prentis' even when their actual term of apprenticeship is over.

PRINCIPAL, Smythe uses this for the amount lent on one occasion but he also seems to use it for the cost price of a consignment of goods.

PRISE, PRIZE, obsolete form of PRISAGE, the right of the Crown to take 2 tuns of wine out of every English vessel bringing 20 or more tuns of wine to England.

PROCEDEWE, see PERCEDEWE.

PRUYENES, obsolete form of PRUNES, dried plums.

PURSER, the ship's officer who kept the accounts and in general supervised the financial records of the voyage. It seems from the Ledger that the task was frequently given to an apprentice.

QUARTERON, obsolete form of QUARTERN, a quarter of anything, especially a quarter of a cwt., see WEIGHTS AND MEASURES.

QUARTON, obsolete form of QUART (also ¼ pipe, 31½ galls.), see WEIGHTS AND MEASURES.

RACKYD, RECKYD, RECKYNG, the transfer of wine from one cask to another in such a way that the lees or sediment in the bottom of the first cask are kept out of the second.

RATLYNE, obsolete form of RATLINE, a thin rope used for 'ratlines', small lines fastened horizontally on the shrouds and serving as steps by which to climb the rigging.

REBATYNG, unidentified.

RECK WYNTAIGE, obsolete form of RACK VINTAGE, in January or February the wines which remained at Bordeaux were 'racked' or strained off their lees and shipped to England after the March Fair. These wines 'of the reck' were of a better quality and clearer than those sent immediately after the Autumn vintage.

RENT BORDES, obsolete form of RENT BOARDS, split or riven boards, made by splitting with wedges instead of sawing. They were used in building, like clap-boards, and for barrel-staves.

RES, a Portuguese coin, see CURRENCY.

RESPECT, in consideration of, because of.

RIALL, RYALL, REAL, a Spanish silver coin worth 34 maravedis. A Portuguese real was worth 40 res, see CURRENCY.

ROCKELL, obsolete form of ROCHELLE, see WINE.

ROSYNE, ROZYN, obsolete form of ROSIN, resin.

ROWYNG, REWYD, obsolete forms of ROWING, ROWED, drawing out the loose fibres from the cloth with teasels so as to raise a nap on the surface.

RYALL, obsolete form of ROYAL, an English gold coin first issued in 1465 and then valued at 10/-. In 1544 its value was raised to 12/-, see CURRENCY.

S. a Bordeaux coin, its value not clearly defined by the context, see CURRENCY.

S., see also SOMMA.

SAD BLEWE, SAD GRENE, see CLOTH.

SALTES, salt-cellars.

SARCHER, SERCHER, SERCHOR, obsolete form of SEARCHER, the third officer of the customs house after the customer and controller, his duties included checking the cargo with the cockets or receipts to see that the two agreed and so prevent smuggling.

SARPLARS, wrappers of sack cloth or other coarse material for packing merchandise.

SCUCHYN, obsolete form of ESCUTCHEON, shield, coat of arms.

SEAME, SEME, obsolete forms of SEAM, a pack-horse load of timber by weight, the actual quantity varied according to locality, see WEIGHTS AND MEASURES.

SECK, SECKES, see WINE.

SERON, a bale made of animal hide used for the transport of exotic products, a basket or pannier for a pack-horse, see WEIGHTS AND MEASURES.

SETTING, the preparation of the woad vat in dyeing cloth, once properly 'set' it can be used for many months.

SHEREHOKES, obsolete form of SHEAR-HOOKS, a hook used to destroy the enemy's rigging, a barbed hook sometimes fitted to the yard-arm of a fireship to destroy the rigging of any ship it collided with.

SHEREMAN, SHERMAN, obsolete forms of SHEARMAN, the workman whose task it was to cut off the surplus nap of woollen cloth to give a smooth appearance to the surface.

SHEVERS, BRAZYN SHEVERS, obsolete form of BRASS SHEAVES, the wheels on which the rope works in a pulley or block, often made wholly or partly of brass.

SHEWRANCE, obsolete form of INSURANCE.

SHIDE, a measure of wood, see WEIGHTS AND MEASURES.

SHOMAMAKER, probably an error for SHOE-MAKER, but SHOME referred to the metal parts of harness so this could be a harness maker.

SLEY-MAKER, the sley was a movable wooden frame designed on the principle of a comb with a large number of dents through which several strands of the warp were drawn to keep them in position.

SLYNGES, obsolete form of SLINGS, a small culverin, smaller than the port piece and also used to repel boarders.

SOMMA, S., SOLMID, SOLMD, forms of SUMMA, the total.

SORTYNG CLOTHES, see CLOTH.

SOWSE, SOWYES, obsolete forms of SOWS, a large, oblong mass of solidified metal as obtained from the blast or smelting furnace, in the Ledger always used for lead.

SPEKES, obsolete form of SPIKES, metal bars driven into the touch hole of a cannon to render it useless.

SPLETYNG, unidentified.

STANDYNG CUPPS, cups usually of metal having a foot, a base or a stem on which to stand.

STREKYNG, STRYKYNG, obsolete forms of STRIKING, lowering casks or other goods or cargo into the hold of a ship or into a cellar.

STRETES, STREIGHTS, see CLOTH.

SUFFOCK, SUFFOK, see CLOTH.

SWAYGID, obsolete form of SWAGED, having an ornamental groove or moulding, shaped with a swage or die.

TABLES, table allowance, expenses.

TALE WOOD, a pack-horse load of timber by number rather than by weight.

TARE, the weight of the wrapping, receptacle or conveyance containing goods; an allowance from the gross weight of goods in consideration of the weight of the receptacle.

TASSELL JENTYLL, obsolete form of TERCEL GENTLE, male of any kind of hawk, in Falconry especially of the peregrine falcon and the goshawk.

TASTAR, TASTER, a shallow, silver cup for tasting wine.

TAWNES, see CLOTH.

TAYNT, TEYNT, see WINE.

TERCIAN, TERTIAN, a cask for wine, 84 galls., see WEIGHTS AND MEASURES.

TESTON, TESTORN, the TESTON was an English silver coin first issued in 1504 and worth 12 pennies except during the debasement 1544–1560.

TIERCE, TERSSIS, TERSSES, a TIERCE was one-third of a pipe of wine or of a wey of wheat, see WEIGHTS AND MEASURES.
TON, TUN, a cask for wine, 252 galls.; in the Ledger 'ton' is used both for wine and for iron, see WEIGHTS AND MEASURES.
TRANSSCRIPT, obsolete form of TRANSCRIPT, the copy of any original writing or deed, a copy of a legal record.
TRATE, obsolete form of TREAT, to deal, bargain or negotiate.
TROW, TROWE, a clinker-built, flat floored sailing barge used on the Severn.
TRUCK, trading by exchange of goods, barter.
TRUCKERS, TRUKARS, see CLOTH.
TRUSS, TRUSSIS, a bundle of hay or straw, the weight varying at different times and places, see WEIGHTS AND MEASURES.
TULLUS WOOD, woad from Toulouse.

ULLADGE, ULLEDGE, ULLAIGE, YLLAGE, YLLADGE, YLLAIGE, YLLAIDGE, obsolete forms of ULLAGE, the amount of wine or other liquor by which a cask or bottle falls short of being quite full. To fill the cask, often blending in another kind of wine.

VARE, a Spanish linear measure, John Smythe reckoned the vare at 30½ ins., the customs Book of Rates at 32 ins., see WEIGHTS AND MEASURES.
VATES, the VAT was a cask or vessel; when used as a measure in the coal trade it was 9 bushels.
VERSSOS, PORTYNGAL VERSSOS, a Portuguese version of the English 'bases', breech-loading boarder repellers of different sizes.
VINTAAGE, VYNTAGE, VYNTAIGE, WYNTAG, WYNTAIGE, obsolete forms of VINTAGE, the gathering of the grapes.
VYTAYLLS, obsolete form of VICTUALS, foodstuffs.

WATER, AT THE WATER, see AT.
WATER MEASURE, the Bristol measure of salt, see WEIGHTS AND MEASURES.
WEIGHTS AND MEASURES, see p. 334.
WEY, a measure of corn, see WEIGHTS AND MEASURES.
WHITE MONEY, possibly silver money as opposed to gold coins.
WINDAGE, WYNDAGE, VYNDAG, payment for loading or unloading a ship, from vindass (Norse), guindas (Old French) a windlass, used for hauling or hoisting.
WINE,
　BASTARD, BASTARDES, a sweet, Portuguese wine, so called from the Portuguese grape Bastardo, it may be either white or tawny.

CAPRICK, unidentified.
CLARET, CLARETT, the name by which the red wines of Bordeaux have been known in England since the twelfth century.
GASCON, the wines from Bordeaux, either claret, white or red as described by Smythe in the Ledger.
HULLOC, HULLOCK, HULLOK, HULOK, a Spanish wine, very dark in colour, and often used to colour other wines.
MAWMESSEY, MAWMESEY, MAWNSEY, MAWNSSEY, obsolete forms of MALMSEY, a sweet, rich wine, originally from Crete, later from Madeira, the Canaries and Mediterranean vineyards.
MUSCATELL, MUSCADELL, a sweet dessert wine, MUSCATEL, made from Muscat grapes, popular in England from early times.
OSSEY, OSSY, OSSES, OSSY SECK, a Portuguese wine, possibly from Azoia (in French Osoye or Oseye), a coastal region south of Lisbon.
ROCKELL WINE, the wine of LA ROCHELLE, a favourite white wine in the Middle Ages.
SECK, SECKES, a dry amber wine, originally spelt SECK, later SACK, imported mostly from Cadiz or Jerez in Spain, it became known as 'Sherry sack'.
SWETE WYNE, the sweet wines differ from the fortified wines in that they are made from such sweet grapes that some of the original grape sugar in the must is unable to ferment without spirit being added.
TAYNT, TEYNT, TENT, this wine was called TENT or TEINT and was the darkest of all Spanish red wines, sometimes nearly black. It was imported from southern Spain, especially Alicante, and was mainly used for colouring other wines.
WOOD, Smythe's usual spelling of WOAD.
WULL OYLE, Smythe's usual spelling of WOOL OIL, olive oil.

YELLIS, eels.
YERNES, YERENES, see EARNESS.
YLAND WOOD, woad from the islands of the Azores.
YLLAGE, YLLADGE, YLLAIGE, YLLAIDGE, see ULLADGE.
YPOCRAS, obsolete form of HIPPOCRAS, a drink made from white or red wine in which different aromatic ingredients were infused. It was filtered through a bag known as 'Hippocrates' Sleeve' from which it took its name.

Saints' Days and Festivals used in dating

ALLHALOUTYDE, All Hallows, All Saints' Day, 1st November.
ALLRODE DAY IN MAY, Inventio Sancte Crucis, 3rd May.
ST. ANDROWSTIDE, ANDROWTISTIDE, ANDROSTIDE, ANDROWSTYDE, St. Andrew's Day, 30th November.
ANNUNCIATION OF OWR BLESSYD LADY, Lady Day, 25th March.
BARTYLMEWTIDE, BARTYLMEWETYDE, St. Bartholomew's Day, 24th August.
CANDLEMAS, 2nd February.
CORPUS CRISTITIDE, Corpus Christi Day, the Thursday after Trinity Sunday.
HOLYRODE DAY, Holy Rood Day, Exaltatio Sancte Crucis, 14th September.
ST. JAMISTYDE, ST. JAMYSTYDE, St. James' Day, 25th July.
ST. KATERYNSTYDE, St. Katherine's Day, 25th November.
LAMMAS DAY, 1st August.
MIGHELLMAS, Michaelmas, 29th September.
OWR LADY DAY, 25th March.
SHRAFTYDE, Shrove Tuesday, the Tuesday before Quinquagesima Sunday, the Tuesday before Lent.
ST. THOMAS DAY (before Christmas), 21st December.
TRINITE TERM, began the Monday after Trinity Sunday for formal business, the full term began the following Friday.
TWELLSTIDE, Twelfth Day, 6th January.

FAIRS

THE FAYRE AT BRISTOWE, Bristol Fair began on 20th June, but the entry is dated 4th February so this may refer to the Candlemas Fair.
CAWSTONS FFAYER, FAYRE, FEYER, possibly at Corston in Somerset.
LENT FAYER, unidentified.
PHELIPS NORTON FAYER, 2 fairs were held each year at Norton St. Philip, Somerset, one beginning on 1st May, the other on 29th August.
STURBRIDGE FAYER, held at Stourbridge, near Cambridge, on 24th September.

Weights and Measures

CLOTH

PIECES

Broad cloth, 28–30 yards long, 63 inches wide and 90 lb weight when fully dried and dressed.
Coloured cloths, 28–30 yards long, 63 inches wide and 80 lb weight.
Whites and reds of Wilts., Glos. and Som. 26–28 yards long, 63 inches wide and 64 lb (white) and 60 lb (coloured).
Coloured broad cloth in Wilts., Glos. and Som. 25–27 yards long, 63 inches wide and 68 lb weight.
Ordinary Kerseys, 17–18 yards long and 20 lb weight.
Sorting Kerseys, 17–18 yards long and 23 lb weight.
Broad cloth from Taunton, Bridgwater, 12–13 yards long, 63 inches wide and 34 lb weight.
Straits, 17–18 yards long, 1 yard wide and 24 lb weight.
Welsh frieze, 36 yards long, $\frac{3}{4}$ yard wide and 48 lb weight.
Dozens, 12–13 yards long, 63 inches wide and 33 lb weight.
Manchester, Lancashire and Cheshire cottons, 22 yards long, $\frac{3}{4}$ yard wide and 33 lb weight.

ELL, a linear measure, the English ell was 45 inches.
VARE, from the Spanish VARA, in England the Vare was reckoned at 30–33 inches.
NAIL, $\frac{1}{16}$ yard or $2\frac{1}{4}$ inches.
FARDELL, a bundle of unknown quantity.
ALNE, possibly from the French AUNE, an ell, the English ell plus a nail, $47\frac{1}{4}$ inches.

LEATHER

LAST, 20 dickers.
DICKER, 10 hides.

LEAD

FOTHER, originally a cart-load of lead, lime, etc., containing 150–200 stones. By the sixteenth century it was defined for lead, as in the Ledger, as $19\frac{1}{2}$ cwt.

MENDIP WEIGHT, 35 pieces Mendip weight—2 tons.
SOWS, These seem to have been small amounts of lead; sows of iron were over 10 cwt.

STONE

VAT, a cask or vessel of indeterminate quantity. When later used in the coal trade it was 9 bushels.

WHEAT

WEY, 48 bushells.
TIERCE, $\frac{1}{3}$ wey.
BUSHELL, 4 pecks.
PECK, 2 gallons.
FANEGA, a Spanish measure of grain, 1.5 to 1.8 bushells.

HAY

TRUSS, old hay   56 lb
       new hay   60 lb
       straw   36 lb
LOAD, 36 trusses.

TIMBER

SEAM, a pack-horse load sold by weight.
TALE, a pack-horse load sold by number.
SHIDE, $\frac{1}{2}$ cu. foot of timber or firewood.

BUTTER

BARREL, 256 lb including the cask.

FISH

LAST of herrings, 12 barrels, 12,000 fish.
BURDEN ling, 20–22 fishes, cod and ling had 134 fish to the C.
PIPE, PIECE, of salmon, an 84 gallon cask.

SALT (Water Measure of Bristol)

TON, 40 bushells.
BUSHELL, 5 pecks.
PECK, 2 gallons.
CAHISSE, a measure of grain or oil in Spain, used by Smythe as a measure of salt. It contained 12 fanegas or about 18 English bushells.

GUNPOWDER

LAST, 24 barrels.
BARREL, 100 lb.

WINE

TON, TUN, 252 galls.
PIPE, 126 galls.
BUTT, 126 galls. (used for the wines of Spain and Portugal).
TERTIAN, 84 galls.
HOGSHEAD, 63 galls.
TIERCE, 42 galls.
QUARTON, $31\frac{1}{2}$ galls.
KILDERKIN, $\frac{1}{2}$ barrel, usually 16 galls.
CANTLE, a small amount, a canful.
POTTLE, 2 quarts.

WOAD

TON, 8 bales.
BALE, 2 balettes, $\frac{1}{2}$-bales.
CARG, CARGG, Spanish measure of weight, a load, sometimes 400 lb, often 2 bales each of 200 lb.

CAPASSO, a large frail or basket used for packing woad.
KINTAL, QUINTAL, 100 lb, often treated as if synonymous with the C.

IRON

TON, 20 cwt or 2 pipes.
PIPE, 4 hogsheads.
C., cwt, 4 qr.
QUARTER, 28 lb.
ENDES, bars of iron of about 22–24 lb.

SOAP

BARREL, 280 lb.
SERON, a bale of animal hide used for packing the soap. In the Ledger there are usually $1\frac{1}{2}$ to 2 C. to the seron.

ALUM AND SUGAR

ARROBA, ARROVA, a weight used in Spain of about 25 lb, a quarter of a quintal.
CHEST, a case or box sometimes used as a variable measure for sugar.

FRUIT

SORT, 3 pieces.
PIECE, 4 quarterons.
TUN, 40 pieces of figs.
CARGG, held 2 pieces of Malaga raisins.

Currency

I: ENGLISH

		VALUES IN THE LEDGER		
MARK	13s 4d			
RYALL OF GOLD	10 0			
after 1544	12 0			
ANGEL, ANGEL NOBLE	7 6	1542	7s	6d
		1544	8	0
		1546	8	8
NOBLE	6 8			
CROWN OF THE DOUBLE ROSE	5 0			
CROWN OF THE ROSE	4 6			
ANGELET	3 9			
TESTON	1 0			
GROAT	4			
OBOLUS	½			

II: SPANISH

DUCAT	11 reals	1 M.	1540	5 0
		375 M.	1548	6 0
			1550	6 8
REAL		34 M.		
(real of plate)				
MARAVEDI			for convenience Smythe reckoned:	
(Smythe used a sign like a V. for 1,000 maravedis			1500 M.	£1 0s 0d
and another sign for 1 maravedi which I have			75 M.	1 0
transcribed as M.)				
CHAMFRON		6¼ M.		
(a Portuguese coin used in northern Spain)		$\frac{1}{60}$ ducat		

III: PORTUGUESE

		VALUES IN THE LEDGER	
PORTUGUESE	10 crusados		
MILRES	1,000 res		
CRUSADO	400 res	1540	5 0
		1549	6 0
REAL	40 res		
RES			

IV: BORDEAUX

CROWN OF THE SUN (1540)	36 sous 3 deniers tournois	4	8
(1550)	40 sous	5	0
FRANC	20 sous	1	8
GROS	2 sous 6 deniers tournois		
DEMI GROS	1 sou 3 deniers tournois		
GRAND BLANC (DOUZAIN)	1 sou (12 deniers tournois)		
DIZAIN	10 deniers tournois		
(dizain of Charles VII called a 'Karolus')			

PETIT BLANC (SIZAIN)	6 deniers tournois
DEMI DIZAIN	5 deniers tournois
HARDI (FARTHING)	3 deniers tournois
DOUBLE TOURNOIS	2 deniers tournois
DENIER TOURNOIS	1 denier tournois
MAILLE	½ denier tournois

A good many other coins, particularly those of the English occupation, remained in circulation at Bordeaux throughout the sixteenth century.

Index

The recommendations of R. F. HUNNISETT in *Indexing for editors*, 1972 (British Records Association: Archives and the User, No. 2) are generally followed.
Entries under occupations give one entry only for each individual person: the number of that page on which the name and occupation are first linked.

Abadia, Luyes de 266
Abbis, Richard 15
Abeck, Ann (An), widow, of Manchester 297
   John, servant to Thomas Abeck 206
   Thomas, of Manchester 6, 206, 207, 217, 240, 241
Abergavenny (Aborgeyne, Aburgeyne) 30, 31, 43, 47, 57, 83, 84, 105, 106, 164, 287
abergavenny cloth 84, 105, 106, 287
Aberley, Thomas 160
Abingdon (Abyndon, Abyngton), Richard 43
   Roger 24, 233, 250
Aborgeyne *see* Abergavenny
Abowen, Ris 178
   Ris Moris, gentleman, of Carmarthen 36
   Thomas, gentleman, of Cardiff 178
Aburgeyne *see* Abergavenny
Abyam, William, of Bath 112
Abyndon, Abyngton *see* Abingdon
Abynon, Thomas 213
accountancy v, 1, 16–22
Adeane, John 76
Adventure to the Azores 191
Aerysavalo *see* Arisavalo
Aflete (Afelt, Aflette, Flete), Thomas, trowman, of Worcester 33, 34, 41, 42, 65, 76, 124, 150, 199, 205, 230
Alberton *see* Elberton
albristey herring 70
Aldworth, Thomas 316
Alicante 9
All Hallows (All Saints') Church, Bristol 222
Allen, Edmond 160
   Richard 160
Allsega *see* Alsegar
Allveley *see* Alveley
almonds 10
Almondsbury (Amesbury) 174
Alsegar (Allsega), Martyne de 106
Altamyra, Anton de 234, 287, 296
Alton, Robert 316
alum 5, 10, 80, 96, 210, 223, 295, 313
Alveley (Allveley) 109
Amassa, John Huar de (John Ware de) 107, 264
Americk, David, yeoman, of Cardiff 64, 65
   John 159, 254
Amersley, Sampson 316
Amesbury *see* Almondsbury
Ammanford (Amford) 201

Amner (Amnar), Roger, vintner/yeoman, of Wells 277, 282, 285, 291, 294, 295, 298, 299, 306
Amsterdam (Hansardam, Hanserdame) 233, 235, 238
anchors 9n, 14, 15, 97, 101, 152
Andalusia 3, 20, 47, 61, 72, 90, 91, 95, 97, 100, 111, 112, 120, 125, 126, 131, 133, 144, 145, 168, 169, 176, 177, 186, 188, 204, 210, 219, 221, 229, 232, 233, 235, 254, 258, 262, 277, 279, 280, 287, 295, 306, 308, 309, 310
Andros *see* Androws
Androwe, John 193
Androws (Andros), Richard, smith, of Banwell 117, 118, 119
Ankewes (Ankewis) *see* Enkhuisen
Antonio (Don Antonio) of Portugal 17n
Antwerp 3, 7
ap Gornay *see* Gorney
apothecaries 10, 37, 307
Apowell (Appowall, Appowell), John, purser, of the *Trinity* of Caerleon 112, 145, 167
   Moris, smith, of Bristol 17, 100–1
   Sawnders 246, 247, 255
   William, merchant/grocer, of Bristol 23, 74, 142, 253, 255, 256, 263, 264, 315
Aprise (Apris), Richard, of Hereford 185, 187, 189, 197
Arana, John Peres de 85
Arden (Ardeyn), Robert, of Mangotsfield 228, 242
Arisavalo (Aerysavalo, Arsavalo, Arysabalo), Miguell (Mighell) de 212, 236, 254, 264, 302
Arlingham (Arlyngam) 246
Arllnolld of Wells 142
Arlyngam *see* Arlingham
arms *see* weapons
Arndell (Arnedell) *see* Arundell
Arnold *see* Arllnolld
arrowhead makers 119
arrows 81, 97
Arsavalo *see* Arisavalo
Arundell (Arndell, Arnedell), Master, the Queen's Chancellor 182, 209
   Lady 269
   Geoffrey (Geffrey, Jeffrey), of Bridgwater 33, 239, 240, 247

339

Arundell—*continued*
  wife of Geoffrey   33
  Sir Thomas   25, 185
Arysabalo   *see* Arisavalo
Asche (Assh)   *see* Hasche
Aschemore, John   123
Asevern (Asevarn, Sevarn), John   119
  Thomas, trowman, of Shrawley   41, 42, 60, 119, 150, 205, 214, 259
  son of Thomas   60
Ashe, Robert   317
Ashmore   *see* Aschemore
Ashton, Long (Long Aischeton, Aschton, Ashton)   7, 25, 26, 27, 28, 29, 130n, 286
Ashton Court   1, 2n, 7, 27   *see also* Ashton, Long
Ashton, John   *see* Aston, John
Ashton Merriettes   25, 27
assurance   *see* insurance
Asteacu (Astiasso), Anton de   85, 89, 90, 96, 97, 256
Asted, Martin (Martyn)   316
Astiasso   *see* Asteacu
Astodillo, Alvaro de   6, 108
Aston (Ashton, Asston, Astone), John, of Hereford   181, 306, 307, 308
  Simon (Symond), of Bewdley   33, 70, 71, 124
  Thomas, of Shrawley   71
attorneys   144, 145
Atwood, William, servant to Sir Edward Gorge   68, 69
Auger, John   186, 188
averia   10, 74, 86, 88, 94, 103, 107, 117, 120, 123, 130, 135, 141, 142, 152, 158, 169, 185, 186, 189, 193, 204, 214, 215, 216, 217, 220, 221, 224, 229, 233, 235, 236, 238, 240, 248, 255, 262, 265, 266, 277, 281, 285, 290, 296, 298, 306, 307, 308
Avon, river   5, 7
Awells, John, sheriff of Bristol   42n, 255
Awood, John, tucker, of Bridgwater   87, 165, 190
Aylburton   1
Ayre   *see* Eyre
azar   90, 156
Azores   9, 61, 85, 91, 133, 136, 141, 142, 146, 184, 191, 207, 208, 226, 227, 264, 278, 279, 295, 297, 310, 312, 313, 314
  company to import woad   191

Babor, John   86
  William, of Congresbury   86
the Back, Bristol   253
Back Hall, Bristol   293, 308
Bade, Morgan, smith, of Caldicot   78, 79
Badminton (Badmanton)   291
Badram, George   316
Baileye, James   316
bailiffs   36, 37
Baker, Richard, of Bristol   61
bakers   4, 43–4, 199, 288
Ball   *see* Bawle

Ballard (Ballart), William, merchant, of Bristol   9, 34–5, 67–9, 168, 191, 197, 268, 315
Bane, Richard   204
Banwell   117, 118
Barbarigo, Andrea   17, 18
barbing   93, 198–9
Barbor, John   316
Barckeley (Barckley) (Glos)   *see* Berkeley
Barckley, John, of Woton-under-Edge, servant to Sir Antony Kingston   276
Barcley (Glos)   *see* Berkeley
Baret   *see* Barret
Barkyn Hundred   *see* Barton
Barlow   316
  Roger   17
Barn (Barne, Barns), John   249
  Richard   114
  Richard, of Bromyard   31, 32
  William, of Stow on the Wold   76
Barnsgrove   *see* Bromsgrove
Barnstaple (Bastaple)   122, 169, 176, 186
Barret (Baret), William   231, 316
Barrett, William   29
Barton (Barten, Bartyne, Barkyn Hundred)   228, 229, 242
Base   *see* Bays
Baskerfyld (Baskyrdffylld), Master   264, 267
Bassett, Master   139
Bastable   *see* Barnstaple
bastard (bastardes)   9, 21, 39, 44, 48, 55, 60, 61, 66, 68, 69, 70, 75, 79, 94, 95, 98, 104, 106, 107, 109, 110, 111, 112, 114, 115, 117, 120, 129, 130, 133, 139, 143, 147, 150, 154, 156, 157, 158, 159, 167, 170, 181, 182, 186, 188, 189, 190, 192, 194, 196, 197, 198, 200, 206, 215, 217, 218, 219, 220, 223, 224, 228, 235, 237, 240–2, 243, 244, 245, 248, 251, 253, 258, 260, 262, 267, 268, 271, 280–2, 288, 290, 294, 295, 298, 299, 300, 306, 307
Batcock, Thomas   17
Batcombe (Batcom)   5, 30, 70, 142, 207, 208, 305
Bath   4, 25, 112, 284, 288
Bathe *alias* Jobyne, Master Nicholas (Nycolas), priest, of Bath   282, 284, 288, 289, 291
Bawle (Ball), John, yeoman, of Bristol   138, 139
  William, pointmaker, of Bristol   138, 139
Bayle, M   276
Baylif (Bayle, Baylys), James, merchant, of Bristol   60, 61
  Nicholas, of Stanton Drew   258, 259
  William, weaver, of Whitnest   216, 232
Baynes, John   60
Bays (Base, Bayse, Bayss), Clement, pointmaker, of Bristol   22, 73–4, 78, 79, 87, 189, 190, 231
  Richard, servant to Clement Bays   79
beans   6, 15, 80, 81, 84, 89, 90, 96, 97, 105, 106, 127, 128, 162, 256, 257
Beare, Humphrey (Humfrey), merchant, of Chepstow   36
  wife of Humphrey   36

Beck *see* Abeck
Beckington 4
bedders 70
Bedminster (Bedmister, Bedmyster) 11, 26, 30, 180
beef 15
beer 15, 36, 41, 47, 70, 84, 112, 116, 117, 287
Bell, Master, of Gloucester 75
   John, Bishop of Worcester 185, 191
   Thomas, the younger, of Gloucester 97–8, 121, 136, 149, 155, 239, 241
Bellshire, William, vintner, of Wickwar 62
Belton 12
Bemer, William, of Langford 252, 253
Benett (Benet), John 72
   William, hooper 168
Berkeley (Barckeley, Barckley, Barcley) 6, 62, 76, 107, 116, 169, 194, 197, 246
Bermy, Diego de 148
Beroby (Berobie, Veroby), Johannes de 236, 254, 264, 266, 280, 287, 301
Beryn (Beryne, Beryng, Berryn), William, soapmaker, of Bristol 10, 123, 124, 125, 222, 224, 270, 312
beverage 72
Bewdley (Bewdeley) 11, 40, 50, 51, 70, 171, 225, 247
Bewley, Thomas, servant 67, 76
Beyt, John 264
Bick (Byck), Thomas, clothier, of Arlingham 216, 246
Bideford (Bydeffort) 154
Bilbao (Bilbo, Bylbo, Vyllbao) 4n, 14, 20, 89, 212, 287, 295,
Bircom *see* Byrcom
Birmingham (Brymygam, Brymyjam) 9, 58, 76, 275, 294
Biscay 3, 6, 7, 8, 14, 19, 105, 106, 117, 133, 161, 210, 211, 212, 233, 234, 235, 254, 264
biscuit 15, 41, 44, 203
Bishop (Bisshop, Bysshop), Alis (Alson, Allsson) 44, 45, 155, 159, 186, 187, 188, 192, 218, 239, 241, 253
   Robert, of Bridgwater 44, 45, 118, 192
Biss (Bissis) *see* Bysse
Bisshop *see* Bishop
Black Friars, Bristol 22
Black (Blacke), William 316
Blackford 292
Blake, Thomas 181
Blanckeley, Frances 9, 191
Bland (Blande), John senior, merchant tailor, of London 12
   John junior 12
Blascheffyld, Thomas 307
Blaston, William 315
boards *see under* timber
boats
   of William Brethern 80
   of Bullock 195
   of Robert Chew 80, 81
   of Thomas Davy 115
   of John Davys 44, 70, 80

boats—*continued*
   of John Dee 80
   of Free 115
   of Thomas Fylde 80, 174
   of Granger 44, 45, 63, 69
   of Hawle 170, 194
   of Luyes Haynes 167, 192
   of Thomas Jesse 80
   of Nicholas Lanesman 115, 167, 192, 247
   of — Lewis 167, 192
   of David Lewis 44, 115
   of David Smythe 57
   of John Spark 97, 109, 181, 192, 196, 261
   of Luyes Upricharde 115, 192
   of David Watkyn 64, 133, 209
   of — White 44
   of White the cofferer 167, 192
Bollona, Diego de, merchant, of Gibraltar 177
Bolton 6, 298
Bondell, John 316
Boner, John, kendal cloth maker 119
Bonham, John, customer, of Bristol 299, 300
book of physic 293
bookbinders 293, 317
Bordeaux (Burdes) 3, 7, 8, 9, 10, 13, 14n, 15, 20, 21, 35, 36, 47, 61, 79, 86, 90, 95, 96, 105, 106, 119, 120, 125, 126, 127, 130, 132, 133, 145, 146, 148, 149, 152, 184, 287
Borromeo ledger 1
Borwyck, Henry 42
Bosgrove (Bosgro, Busgrove) — 282, 286, 291
   Alexander, of Wells 103–5, 118, 121, 122, 149, 155, 185, 187, 188, 218, 239, 240, 248
Boshar, John 309
Boulogne 16
Bourgneuf, Bay of 8n
Bowen, Master 19, 299
Bowyer, Thomas, of Berkeley 194
Boyse (Boysse), Thomas 141, 280, 309
Bradford (Bradeffort, Brodeford, Brodefort) 72, 240, 241, 300
Bradhewe *see* Croston
Bradston, Robert 25
Bragdon, Stephen (Steven, Stevyne), grocer, of Bristol 198, 199, 317
Braghyng (Braughyng, Brawghyng), John, vintner, of Worcester 124, 149, 150–1, 155, 159, 160, 185, 186, 187, 188
Brampston, Master, of Wells 164, 286
Brampton, Master 315
Bramyerd *see* Bromyard
Braughyng (Brawghyng) *see* Braghyng
brawn 92, 287
Brecon (Brecknock) 75
Brent Marsh (Bryntmarche) 292
Brethern, William 80
brewers 4, 69, 84, 113, 116, 236
Bridges (Brydges), Master 55
   William of Batcombe 305
   William of Hereford 153, 154
   William, carrier, of Wanhope 192

Bridges—*continued*
    William, clothier, of Weston   5, 142, 222, 262, 309, 310, 311
Bridgwater (Bridgewater)   2, 3, 4, 9, 11, 12, 16, 25, 32, 38, 44, 45, 63, 69, 76, 115, 118, 128, 142, 165, 167, 168, 190, 192, 218, 247, 270, 313
    Saracens Head (Saserns Hed)   69
Bristol, All Hallows (All Saints') Church   222
    the Back   253
    Back Hall   293, 308
    Bishop of,   *see under* Bush
    Black Friars   22
    Bristol Bridge   70, 279
    Broad Street   257
    Candlemas Fair   23
    Chamber   23, 257, 258, 299
    Chapel on the Bridge   24, 258
    Christmas Street   61
    Corn Street (Cornestret)   2, 3, 12, 25, 26, 27, 61
    Court of Staple   18, 23
    Customs House   307
    customs accounts   11, 12, 283, 322, 323
    George Inn   101, 246, 266
    Groper Lane   257
    High Street   246
    Hungroad   6, 7n, 56, 126, 161, 162, 170
    Kaye (Key)   *see* Quay
    Kingroad   126
    Lawfords Gate (Laffordes Yate)   76
    Merchant Venturers' Company   4
    Mint   205, 274, 276
    New Inn (Newe Yn)   83, 84
    Newgate Prison   113
    officials   2, 4, 18, 22, 23, 24, 28, 42, 66, 110, 164, 168, 205–6, 222, 228, 231, 233, 255, 257, 258, 267, 274, 276, 277, 278, 299, 313
    Quay (Kaye, Key)   56, 111, 141
    Redcliff (Redcliff Hill)   5, 7, 302, 303, 304
    riot   23, 299
    St. Augustine's, Abbot of   37
    St. Augustine's (St. Awsten's) Green   208
    St. Leonard's Church   2, 273, 274
    St. Nicholas' Church   22
    St. Peter's Pump   271
    St. Thomas' Church   22
    St. Werburgh's Church   27, 28, 29, 75
    Small Street   25, 26, 27, 79
    Staple Court   18
    Temple district   5
    Temple Fee   23
    Temple Gate   302
    Three Tuns   256
    Tolzey Court   18, 24, 28
    Trinity Church   274
    Weir (Wayer)   246
    Welsh Back   6, 10n, 11, 148
    White Friars   229
bristol cloth   3–6, 148, 177, 178, 211, 212, 273, 279, 280
bristol frieze   *see* frieze

Broad Street, Bristol   257
broadcloth   100, 305
Brodeford (Brodefort)   *see* Bradford
Broke (Brooke), Master David, Serjeant at law   252, 308
brokers   162, 177
Bromeley, Master   299
Brommyche   *see* Bromwich
Bromsgrove (Barnsgrove)   33, 54, 203, 205, 229
Bromwich, West (Brommyche, West Bromwich)   124
Bromyard (Bramyerd)   31, 32
Brooke   *see* Broke
Brown (Browne, Brune), Henry, servant to Robert Pole   94, 152, 153, 177
    John of Bristol   13, 17, 316
    John of Ilchester   75
    John of Pershore   240
    Richard, grocer, of Bristol   151, 187
Bruton   4, 5, 54, 55, 56, 76, 81, 100, 115, 142, 146, 147, 166, 181, 182, 201, 208, 222, 223, 237, 238, 262, 264, 265, 268, 278, 279, 301, 310
Brydges   *see* Bridges
Brymygam (Brymyjam)   *see* Birmingham
Bryntmarche   *see* Brent Marsh
Bryntniche   76
Buchar   *see* Butcher
Buckland, John, innkeeper, of Reading   51, 52
    John, gentleman, of West Harptree   247
buckram   258
Bulkeley, Master   186
Bullock, William, yeoman, of Elmore   6, 66, 87, 126, 127, 160, 173, 174, 195, 216, 282, 310
Burbo, Martyne (Mynar) de   85
Burdes   *see* Bordeaux
Burge, Thomas, carrier, of Batcombe   208
Burges, Thomas   143
Burgos   148
Burnell, George, sley-maker, of Bristol   246
    John, of Hanham   297
Burton on Trent   67
Busgrove   *see* Bosgrove
Bush, Paul, Bishop of Bristol   28, 168
Butcher (Buchar), John, son of William, of West Harptree   31, 142, 190, 226, 227, 228n
    John, nephew of William   31
    Thomas, of Sherrold   143
    William, clothier, of Cowley   5, 31, 32, 87, 93, 142, 144, 183, 190, 199, 210, 226, 227, 232, 254
butchers   294
Butler (Buttlar, Buttler), Master, of Badminton   291
    Edward, merchant, of Bristol   72
    Robert, merchant, of Bristol   4, 9, 190, 316
butter   292
Buttlar (Buttler)   *see* Butler
Byccombe, Hugh, of Crowcombe   27
    Maud (Mawde)   27

342

Byck *see* Bick
Byddell, — 165
Bydeffort *see* Bideford
Bylbo *see* Bilbao
Byrcom (Bircom), John, carrier, of Dodington 11, 259, 260, 270, 271
Byrd, Walter (Water) 261
Byscay *see* Biscay
Bysse (Biss, Bissis), James, clothier, of Stoke Lane, Bristol 5, 93, 144, 156
Bysshop *see* Bishop
Byttbay 187
Byttun, William, smith, of Calne 197, 198

Cadbury (Cadbery) 279
Cadiz (Cales) 4n, 20, 295
Caerleon (Carlion, Carlon, Carlyon) 68, 111, 112, 150, 186
Caerphilly (Carffile, Carffyll) 162, 231
Calais (Calleise) 16
Caldicot (Calicot, Callycot) 78, 79
Cales *see* Cadiz
Calicot *see* Caldicot
Calleise *see* Calais
Callycot *see* Caldicot
Calne (Cawllme, Cawlne) 197, 312
Camon, Johannes de 211
Candlemas Fair, Bristol 23
Canynges, William 3
Capes *see* Caps
Capper *alias* Mathew, Edward 260
caprick 52
Caps (Capes, Capps, Cappys), Alice 274
  John, merchant, of Bristol 52-3, 89, 122, 301, 316
capuz *see* cowl
Car, William, merchant, of Bristol 9, 35, 96, 97, 191, 196, 315
Cardiff (Kerdif) 56, 64, 75, 133, 162, 209, 232
Cardiff (Cardif), Phillip, of Mitford 59
cardmakers 59
Carew, Master 27
Carffile (Carffyll) *see* Caerphilly
Carick *see* Carrick
Carie *see* Cary
Carlon (Carlion, Carlyon) *see* Caerleon
Carmarthen (Kermerdyne) 36, 43, 50, 75, 95, 135, 147, 212, 251
Carn, Hugh, merchant, of Bristol 52
Carpenter (Carpynter) *alias* Copar, Joan (Johan), widow, of Bristol 154, 156, 157
  Thomas, merchant, of Bristol 138, 156, 157
carpenters 76
carriage 34
Carrick (Carick, Carryck, Caryck), Richard, of Tewkesbury 65–6, 126, 149, 155, 185, 187, 188, 218, 239, 240, 241, 256, 267
carriers 11, 30, 103, 104, 153, 181, 192, 208, 270, 271, 283, 293, 314
  see also waggoners
Carryck *see* Carrick

Carter, Bryan, kendalman 154
carters *see* carriers
carvers 4, 146
Cary (Carie), Master 317
  Richard 317
  William, draper, of Bristol 46
Caryck *see* Carrick
Castaneda, Alonsso de 296
Castellnethe *see* Neath
Castille 4
Castilenethe (Castillneathe, Castilneth) *see* Neath
Casy, Alexander 316
Cater (Cator) *alias* Taylor, Robert 208, 225, 257
Catherine Parr, Queen of England 209
Catyssby, Mistress 69
Cawllme *see* Calne
Cawstons Fair 56, 298
cellarage 123
Chack 201
chairs 73
Chamber (Chambers), John, of Kingsnorton 259
  Richard, yeoman, of Kingsnorton 41–2
  Thomas, son of Richard 41, 42, 43
Chancellor (Chanseler, Chauncellor, Chawncellor), John 95, 266, 270
chanters 102
Chapel on the Bridge, Bristol 24, 258
Chapel (Chapell), Richard, of Northam 176, 186, 191
chapmen 102
Charles V, Emperor 15
charterparties 95, 96, 112, 125, 127, 139, 156, 171, 184, 228
Chartrons, Bordeaux 8
Chauncellor (Chawncellor) *see* Chancellor
cheese 228
Chepstow (Chepsto, Chepston, Chepstowe) 36, 76, 107, 146, 152, 167, 170, 192, 213, 262
Chepyng Sodbery *see* Sodbury
Chester, Master 123, 184
  Dominic (Domynyck) 317
  James (Jamys), merchant, of Bristol 241, 245, 246, 257, 316
  Thomas 28, 266, 269, 270, 316
  William, pointmaker, of Bristol 39, 66, 67
Chew (Chewe), Robert, of Langley 80, 81, 126
Chewestoke 268, 276
Chewton Mendip (Chuton under Mendyp) 292, 302
Cheyne, William, of London 240
Chick, Stephen (Stevyn), of Bruton 20, 81, 82, 123, 124, 237
Chipping Sodbury *see* Sodbury
Christmas Street, Bristol 61
Christophle, Jehan Ympyn 1
Chuton under Mendyp *see* Chewton Mendip
cider 15, 85, 234
Cirencester (Sisseter, Sissetor, Sysseter) 11, 256, 259, 260, 267, 270

343

Clara, Estevan (Stevan) de Sancta   see Sancta Clara
claret (clarett)   8, 35, 39, 44, 47, 50, 62, 63, 65, 67, 68, 69, 70, 72, 103, 110, 112, 134, 147, 181, 192, 196, 199, 215, 223, 225, 228, 229, 247, 250, 267, 269, 270, 283, 284, 286, 287, 292, 294, 300, 308
   see also under gascon wine
Clark, Thomas   224
Clement, John, smith, of Wolston   84
clergy   2, 15, 28, 36, 37, 38, 45, 71, 74, 163, 172, 185, 197, 288
Clerk (Clerck), William, husbandman, of Blackford   292
   William, servant of John Smyth   12n, 208, 262, 273, 301
Cley, William   165
Closetorshire   see Gloucestershire
cloth   2, 3–6, 8, 11, 20, 21, 32, 49, 71, 75, 80, 81, 83, 85, 89, 94, 100, 131, 132, 136, 144, 145, 148, 176, 177, 178, 183; 198, 199, 202, 208, 210, 211, 212, 220, 227, 232, 233, 234, 237, 254, 257, 258, 261, 279, 283, 303, 305, 309
   see also dyeing; abergavenny cloth, azar, bristol cloth, broadcloth, buckram, costom cloth, dunsters, frieze, kersey, london cloth, lining cloths, muster cloth, northern cottons, northern dozens, penny hewes, plonkette, sortyng cloth, suffolk cloth, truckers; wool, wrappers
clothiers   5, 31, 32, 52, 62, 70, 100, 142, 246, 298, 312, 313
Clows, Henry, innkeeper, of Farrington Gurney   273, 278, 285
Cockes (Cookes, Cox) —, carrier   181
   —, servant of William Taylor   57
   Richard   66
   William, merchant, of Bristol   139, 140, 316
   William of Shepton   142, 310, 311
cocket   7, 44, 74, 108, 167, 173
cod liver oil   see train oil
Codrington (Codryngton, Codrynton), Francis, merchant, of Bristol   9, 13, 20, 35, 89, 96, 97, 108, 141, 160, 161, 191, 196, 251, 315
Cogan (Gogan), Gilbert, merchant, of Bristol   87, 124, 180, 181, 189, 190
   Stephen (Stevan)   134
Coke   see Cook
Colchester (Cowlchester), Humphrey. (Humfrey), tanner, of Colchester   275, 276
Cole (Coles), Henry   46
   Humphrey (Humfrey)   317
   John, merchant, of Tenby   46–7
   John, smith, of Tenby   164, 165
   Stephen (Stevan, Stevyn, Stevyne), lawyer, of Bristol   162, 163, 272, 277, 307
Collwell, John   62
Collymore, Richard, clothier, of Sodbury   62
Combe, John, of Brecon   75
commodity accounts   21, 86–9, 106–7, 121–2,

commodity accounts—continued
   123–4, 141–3, 148–50, 154–6, 158–61, 168–9, 184–90, 192–4, 210, 213–14, 215–19, 221–2, 223–5, 233, 235–6, 238–42, 248–9, 253–4, 255–6, 265–7, 277–8, 280–2, 285–6, 290–2, 296, 298, 301–2, 305–8
Company to import woad   9, 191
Compton Martin (Cowmpton Martyn)   314
Condado   158, 257
Congresbury (Cumsbery)   86
Cook (Coke, Cooke), Master, Mayor of Bristol   110
   John   178
   Roger, Alderman   24, 253
   Thomas   204, 258
Cookes   see Cockes
Cooper (Copar, Coper, Cowper), Richard, of Ammanford   201
   Thomas, of Bristol   157, 222, 251, 252, 255, 277, 306, 307
   William   277, 317
cooperage   41
Copar (Coper)   see Cooper
cordage   141
cordovan (cordavan) skin   see leather
cork   264
corn   96, 97, 98, 152, 177
Corn Street (Cornestret), Bristol   2, 3, 12, 25, 26, 27, 61
Cornwall (Cornewall, Cornwale)   147, 173
corredors   see brokers
correos   177
Corston (Costom)   142, 313
Coster, Garet   233, 235, 238
Costes, Castano das   295
Costom   see Corston
costom cloth   89, 90, 105, 106
Cotes, Thomas, of Eyssam   47–8, 85, 118, 121, 136, 149, 155, 187
Cotton, Benett, servant to Sir Edward Gorge   68, 69
Court of Augmentations   7, 16, 24
Court of Star Chamber   22
Coventry (Coventre)   114, 142, 186, 215, 247, 255, 269, 314
coverlet makers   174, 175
Coves, John   149
   Robert, yeoman, of Malmesbury   151
Cowbridge (Cowebridge)   139
Cowlchester   see Colchester
Cowley (Cowlley)   5, 31, 32, 190, 227
cowls   72
Cowmpton Martyn   see Compton Martin
Cowper   see Cooper
Cox   see Cockes
Coyder, Watkyn   38
cranage   41, 44, 167
Crane, Sir Thomas, priest, of Bridgwater   2, 38
Crickelet, John   75
Crock, John   287
Cromwell, Thomas   15, 22, 23, 25
Cropthorne   204

344

Crosby (Krosby), Edward   62
　Nicholas   317
　Robert, chapman, of Kendal   87, 102, 276
Cross, Robert   168
crossbows   *see* weapons
Crossway (Croswey), Thomas, of Mells   281, 282, 283, 284, 291, 304
Croston *alias* Bradhewe, Elsabeth, widow, of Ludlow   278
Croswey   *see* Crossway
Crowcombe   27
Crull   *see* Curll
Cumsbery   *see* Congresbury
Curll (Crull), Edmond (Edmonde)   311, 312
curtains   131
Curtys, Master   257
　Thomas   297
Customs House, Bristol   307
customs   2, 7, 8, 9–10, 11–12, 53, 74, 86, 94, 98, 101, 102, 105, 107, 108, 117, 122, 123, 130, 135, 141, 154, 158, 169, 185, 186, 189, 193, 210, 213, 214, 215, 216, 217, 221, 224, 233, 235, 236, 238, 240, 248, 255, 262, 265, 266, 277, 281, 285, 290, 296, 298, 301, 306, 308
customs officials   108, 113, 142, 179, 184, 189, 198, 209, 239, 246, 270, 296, 299
Cutler (Cuttlar), Watkyn, of Cardiff   75
Cutt (Cut), John, merchant, of Bristol   2, 26, 58, 104, 105, 129, 200, 217, 242, 252, 285, 310, 315
　Thomas   317
Cuttlar   *see* Cutler

daggers   *see* weapons
Daiper   *see* Ledaiper
Dale, William   22
Dane, Giles, searcher, of Bristol   239, 246
Darby   *see* Derby
Darck, William   96
Darckmowthe   *see* Dartmouth
Dare, John, of Shepton Mallet   267, 278, 285
Dareta, John Peres de   285
Dartmouth (Darckmowthe)   149, 298
Datini, Francesco di Marco   1, 19n
David (Dave, Davis, Davith, Davy, Davyd, Davys) — (Davy)   80
— (Davis)   317
　Henry, tailor, of Bristol   138, 139
　John (Davy)   81
　John (Davys)   44, 70, 80, 152, 197
　John, of Carmarthen   43, 44
　Martin (Martyne)   147
　Morgan, of Carmarthen   95, 135
　Morgan, smith, of Bristol   45, 46
　Robert, merchant, of Haverford West   59
　Thomas (David)   68, 69, 162, 231
　Thomas (Davys)   238
　Thomas, of Lisvane   68, 69, 156
　Thomas, smith, of Lisvane   115, 231
　Walter (Water), joiner, of Bristol   300, 301
Dawkin, Philip, dyer   113
de   *for names with this prefix see the main element*

Deacon (Decon, Dekyn), Thomas, yeoman, of Bristol   85, 113
Dean, Forest of   1, 2, 6, 9, 11, 14, 32, 76, 107, 195, 196, 225, 262, 263, 289, 293
Dean (Deane), Alison (Allson), widow, of Shirehampton   49, 50
debts   3, 13, 20, 21–2, 28, 30, 33, 54, 72, 75–6, 91, 102, 113, 267
Decon   *see* Deacon
Dee, John   80
Degge, Richard, of Whitcombe   306
Dekyn   *see* Deacon
Delisardy, Johannes   212
　Pedro   211
Depontyra, Johannes, of Renteria   76
Derby (Darby), John, Master of the *Trinity*   49, 101, 105, 145, 148, 152, 161, 168, 210, 234, 235
Deventer (Develing)   214
Devizes (The Vise)   77
Devon (Deveshire)   191
Deyrancu, Johannes   169
daipers   43, 57, 164
Diar   *see* Dyer
Diez, Antonio   40
Dighton (Digton, Dyghton, Dyton), Christopher (Cristoffer, Cristover), vintner, of Worcester   114, 248, 310
Dison, James (Jamys)   111
Dissom, —, of Winchcombe   239
Docquett, Robert, tailor   105
doctors   25, 26, 29, 36, 149, 153, 209
Dodington (Doding, Dodyngton)   11, 153, 259, 293
Dodwell, James (Jamys), of Oxford   293
Dodyngton   *see* Dodington
Don Antonio of Portugal   *see* Antonio of Portugal
Dorset (Dorzet), Marquis of   *see* Grey
Douding   *see* Dowding
doulas   269
Doule, James (Jamy)   243
Dover   16
Dowding (Douding), Elizabeth née Hoper   3
　John   3, 76
　Thomas, of Bridgwater   128
Draper, Hugh (Hewgh)   316
　John   316
drapers   46, 51, 67, 163, 204, 214, 276
　see also tailors
Dudgyne, Master, chanter, of Wells   102
Dunster   75, 310
dunsters   310
Durban, Robert, merchant, of Bristol   94–5, 96, 118
Durleigh   25
Dutson, Henry, of Hereford   163, 164
Duttsson, Antony, dyer, of Gloucester   49, 50, 87
dyeing   5, 20, 49–50, 80, 92–3, 144, 313
Dyer (Diar), William, of Carmarthen   75
dyers   35, 48–50, 72, 79, 113, 142, 174
Dyghton   *see* Dighton
Dymock, William   65, 98, 134, 194

345

Dyngley, Thomas, of Eyssam 76, 118, 121, 134, 135
Dyton *see* Dighton

Easton (Eston in Barkyn Hundred) 228
Edmondes, Richard, tucker, of Bristol 142, 314
Edward VI, King of England 4, 16, 25, 282, 283, 310
Edwardes, Robert, smith, of Hinton 279
  William, of Dunster 75
eels 53
Egerton, William, gunmaker 127
Elberton (Alberton) 40
Elmore (Ellmore, Ellmoore) 6, 126, 173, 174, 282, 310
Ely, Master 233
Enderby, William, of Coventry 142
Enkhuisen (Ankewes, Ankewis) 106, 253, 262
Enyon, John, purser of the *Mary Grace* 15, 36
esquires 59, 153, 164, 178, 274, 283
Eston *see* Easton
Estwyck, Griffith 60, 119
  John, trowman, of Tewkesbury 314
Etloe (Ettloe) 76
Evans (Evan), Herman (Harmande, Hernand), of Oxford 291, 293
  Thomas 250
Everson, Henry 238
Ewyn (Yewyn, Yowen), John 250, 251
Eyre (Ayre), William, of Shepton Mallet 222, 266, 268, 269, 278, 285
Eyssam 47, 48, 76, 85, 134
Eyssham, Robert, tailor 55

fardelling 105
Farnalls, William, purser of the *Hart* 102
Farrington Gurney (Faryngton) 273
Fasshyn, Thomas 136
Faye, John, haberdasher, of Bristol 302
Fayrebarn, Robert 75
Fels, Thomas, of Bryntniche 76
Fernandez, Alvers 238
  Antony 106
figs 10, 21, 233, 235, 237, 242, 243
Filld *see* Fylde
Fischepill, John 309
fish 2, 10, 15, 36, 47, 85, 198, 250, 282, 283, 301, 304
  see also hake, herring, salmon
fishers 45, 70, 83, 84
Fitzjames (Fitzjamys), Master, Esquire, Town Clerk 164
  Master, Doctor, of Wells 149, 153
  Aldred 258
  Nicholas, Esquire 153, 258
Flete *see* Aflete
Florence 19n
Floyde, William, ship's master 30
Fontraby *see* Fuenterrabia
foreign currency 11, 13, 14, 19, 20, 47, 72, 83, 84–5, 86, 89, 90, 91, 94, 106, 112, 117, 122, 127, 129, 132, 141, 142, 144,

foreign currency—*continued*
  145, 146, 148, 149, 152, 158, 167, 168, 169, 176, 177, 184, 186, 187, 188, 191, 193, 197, 204, 209, 210, 211, 212, 213, 214, 215, 216, 217, 220, 221, 223, 224, 233, 235, 236, 240, 248, 254, 264, 265, 266, 274, 277, 280, 285, 287, 290, 295, 298, 306, 308, 309
Forest of Dean *see* Dean, Forest of
Fountrabye *see* Fuenterrabia
Fowler (Fowlar), Francis, factor to John Smythe 9, 91, 141, 191
  John, carrier, of Dodington 293, 296, 297
  Robert, carrier 270
Fowls (Fowlls), John, of Warminster 276
  Robert, husbandman, of Chewstoke 276
Framilode (Fromyland) 175, 211, 213
France 1, 3, 8n, 15, 16, 21
Francis I, King of France 15
Francom, William 274
Free, — 115
freight 10, 11n, 19, 21, 35, 40, 47, 60, 61, 68, 72, 86, 93, 94, 95, 102, 106, 117, 119, 120, 125, 126, 127, 128, 129, 130, 131, 135, 136, 139, 140, 141, 143, 149, 152, 154, 156, 157, 167, 169, 170, 171, 186, 188, 191, 193, 195, 196, 208, 210, 213, 214, 215, 216, 219, 220, 221, 224, 229, 235, 236, 238, 248, 255, 262, 277, 281, 285, 296, 298, 306, 307, 308
Freman, Nycolas 264
frieze 6, 37, 59, 89, 90, 105, 106, 148, 177, 178, 211, 212, 273, 279, 280, 295
friezemakers 102
Frome (Som) 4
Fromyland *see* Framilode
fruit 8, 18
  see also figs, raisins
Frye, — 316
Fuenterrabia (Fontraby, Fountrabye) 169, 192, 265, 266, 283, 287, 296
fullers 294
Furs (Furrs, Furss, Fursse), Thomas, of Oxford 270, 277, 285, 297
Fylde (Filld), — 61
  Thomas 80, 174

gains accounts 132–3, 237
Gamon, Humphrey (Umffrey) 250, 251
Gane, John, the younger of Bristol, merchant 30
Garbran (Garberet, Garbret), bookbinder, of Oxford 282, 291, 293
Garlick, Evan 215
gascon wine 7–8, 16, 21, 35, 38, 39, 47, 48, 49, 51, 52, 53, 54, 55, 58, 61, 65, 66, 67, 68, 69, 70, 72, 73, 95, 97, 103, 104, 109, 110, 111, 112, 114, 116, 119, 120, 125, 126, 127, 128, 129, 130, 133, 134, 139, 143, 147, 148, 149, 150, 151, 152, 153, 156, 157, 163, 170, 171, 181, 182, 184, 191, 197, 200, 219, 225, 242, 243, 244, 245, 247, 248, 249, 250, 251, 252, 255–6,

gascon wine—*continued*
    257, 258, 260, 261, 262, 263, 264, 266–7, 268, 269, 270, 272, 273, 274, 275, 276, 278, 283, 285–6, 287, 288, 289, 290–2, 293, 294, 295, 296, 297, 298, 299, 300, 307–8, 310, 313
    see also under claret, red wine, white wine
Gascony 3–5
Gatcombe (Gatcom) 194
gauging 266
Gawlle, John 145
Gay, Nicholas, merchant, of Bristol 47, 135
Geffreys (Jeffreis), Christopher (Cristover), of Bristol 278
    Robert 317
Genoa (Jeaner) 9, 17, 82
gentlemen 36, 62, 111, 162, 174, 178, 180, 225, 247, 297, 303
Genynges (Jenens, Jenynges), John, merchant, of Carmarthen 107, 240, 251, 255
    Robert, mercer, of Presteigne 245, 255, 260, 261, 262, 277, 278, 281, 282, 285, 286, 287, 288, 291, 292, 306, 307, 308
George Inn, Bristol 101, 246, 266
George, Walter (Water) 305
Gervis, John, grocer, of Bristol 44
    John, waggoner, of Winterbourne 62
Gest, Giles 152
    William 205
Gibbs, Richard 168
Gibraltar (Gibralltar, Gybrawlltar) 177, 186
gibraltar wine 186
Gibs (Gibbs, Gybs), John 314
    John, of Bridgwater 69–70, 118, 121, 122, 136, 150, 155, 159, 160
    Richard 80
    Susan, widow of John Gibs, of Bridgwater 70, 167, 168, 187, 189, 218, 239, 241
Gilbert, Master 149
    Antony 258
girdle 30
Glazynbe, Thomas, dyer, of Bristol 79, 80, 86
Gloucester (Glocester) 7, 36, 49, 75, 93, 94, 97, 98, 108, 151, 152, 153, 160, 170, 174, 175, 177, 184, 185, 197, 210, 232
Gloucestershire (Glocestershire, Closetorshire) 4n, 6, 25, 40, 126, 153, 161, 173, 174, 178, 232, 282, 310
Gogan *see* Cogan
gold 4, 20, 205–6, 242, 274
goldsmiths 153, 275
Gonsalves (Gonsalez), Pedro 9, 10n, 191, 271
Goodman, Master John, Dean of Wells 163, 164
goodmen *see* innkeepers
Goodwyne (Goodyng), Richard, smith, of Pershore 194, 195, 204
Gorge (Gorges), Master 150, 185, 308
    Sir Edward 68, 69, 284, 285, 291
    Lady 69
Gorney (ap Gornay), Master 290, 315
    John, merchant, of Bristol 127, 128, 181, 182, 186, 217
Goseling, John 81

Gosselet (Goselett, Goselet), John, of Marshfield 239, 240, 241, 242
Gowgh (Gowghe), David (Davy, Davyd), diaper, of Abergavenny 57, 164
    James (Jamys), merchant, of Waterford 174
    Patrick, hooper, of Bristol 119, 123
    Robert, hooper, of Bristol 168, 187
Gozelyng, Thomas, of Langley 80
Granger (Grawnger), — 44, 45, 63, 69, 115
    Robert, yeoman, of Bristol 75
    William, smith, of Wolverton 66–7
grassyng (grasyng) *see* dyeing
Gray (Graye), George, innkeeper, of Bristol 258, 259, 291
grazing (grazyng) *see* dyeing
Green (Grene), James 255
    Jerome (Jerom) 255
    Philip (Phillip) 157
Greve, Myles, tailor, of Bristol 62
Grevys, — 43, 275
    Master 275
    Martin (Martyne) 219, 235, 254, 316
    Richard, of Kingsnorton 294
Grey, Agnes 231
    Henry, 3rd Marquis of Dorset, later Duke of Suffolk 310
    William 227
Grice, Gilbert 16
Griffith (Griffithe, Griffythe, Gryffith, Gryffyth), —, carter 271
    —, weaver, of Presteigne 250, 251, 252, 255, 275
    David, servant to John David 43
    John, roper, of Bristol 188, 202
    Philip (Phillip), bailiff successively to (1) the Abbot of St. Augustine in Bristol and (2) the Bishop of Bristol 37, 113, 168
    Walter (Water) 132
grocers 34, 44, 59, 63, 74, 103, 125, 151, 162, 198, 214, 235, 284, 296
Groper Lane, Bristol 257
Grossgrene, John, carpenter, of Chepstow 76
Gryffith (Gryffyth) *see* Griffith
Guar, Edmond, clothier, of Corston 142, 313, 314
    John 314
Guinea 14
gunmakers 127
Gunnyng (Gunwyn), John, of Easton 228, 242
    Robert, of Barton 228
gunpowder 15, 41, 220, 228
Gunwyn *see* Gunnyng
guns *see* weapons
Guyposcoa 254, 295
Guytten (Guytton, Guyttons), Hugh (Hewgh) 212
    Robert, merchant, of Bristol 113, 123, 124, 138, 139, 170, 171
Gybrawlltar *see* Gibraltar
Gybs *see* Gibs

haberdashers 302, 312

347

hake 47, 84, 198
halliers *see* hauliers
hallyng *see* hauling
Hamlyn (Hamlyng), Master 159, 188
Hammorsley, Richard 286
Hamond (Hamon, Hamonde), Hugh (Hew, Hewg, Hewgh, Hughe) 11, 13, 20, 28, 36, 45, 50, 52, 58, 61, 70, 80, 89, 90, 94, 95, 96, 97, 101, 102, 108, 116, 120, 126, 127, 128, 130, 138, 140, 141, 142, 143, 157, 158, 176, 177, 182, 186, 190, 204, 220, 224, 234, 248, 254, 257, 258, 264, 274, 280, 281, 287, 295, 309, 316
   John senior, merchant, of Bridgwater 12, 115–16, 117, 118, 123, 124, 142, 187, 218, 219, 239, 240, 253, 278, 286, 313
   John junior 116
   Robert, of Bridgwater 45
   Thomas 313
Hampton *see* Southampton
Hancot (Hanccott, Hanckockes, Hanckot, Hanckotes, Hanckott, Hanckottes, Hancotes, Hancottes), —, fisher 33, 45
   Edmond, tailor, of Bristol 224, 278, 285, 286, 300
   Lawrence, of Bromsgrove 33, 34, 54, 160, 161, 203, 205, 211, 229, 230, 240
   Nicholas, fisher, of Wellington 83, 84
   Simon (Symon, Symond), tailor, of Bristol 33, 34, 118, 119, 164
Handley (Handeley, Hanley Castle) 45, 109, 150
Hanham (Hannam) 162, 297
Hansardam (Hanserdame) *see* Amsterdam
Harbarde *see* Herbert
Harptree, West (West Harptree, West Hartry) 7, 142, 175, 227, 247, 250
Harris (Hares, Harrys, Herris, Herrys), David, apothecary, of Bristol 37, 39
   Richard 137
   Robert, of Wells 143
   Thomas, merchant, of Bristol, subsequently sheriff of Bristol 42, 43, 115, 177, 219, 220, 228, 229, 240, 248, 259, 309, 315, 316
   Thomas, son-in-law of Robert Genynges 288
   Thomas, of Wells 142
Hart (Hert), David (Davy), shearman, of Bristol 5, 92, 93, 155, 187, 198, 199, 218, 239, 241
   Thomas, merchant, of Bristol 95
Harvart (Harvardeast, Harvarteast, Harvarteaste, Harvarteste) *see* Hereford
Harvart West *see* Haverfordwest
Harvest, William 119, 122, 232, 316
Harwich (Harwytche) 290
Hasbery (Hassbery), Thomas, of Bromsgrove 188, 203, 230
Hasche (Asche, Assh, Hassh, Hasshe), Thomas, clothier of Batcombe 5, 70, 71, 91, 93, 142, 183, 198, 199, 207, 210, 211, 287, 306, 309
   see also Nasche

hauliers 17, 24, 253
hauling 21, 41, 44, 74, 78–9, 86, 88, 107, 117, 120, 122, 123, 130, 135, 141, 149, 154, 158, 167, 169, 185, 186, 188, 193, 210, 213, 214, 215, 216, 217, 221, 224, 233, 235, 236, 238, 240, 248, 255, 265, 266, 277, 281, 285, 290, 296, 298, 306, 307, 308
Haverfordwest (Harvart West) 57, 59, 135
Hawes, Richard (Richart) 73
hawks 53
Hawkesbury near Coventry (Hawxbery) 142, 247
Hawkyns, Richard (Rychart), smith 62
Hawle, — 170, 194
   John 184
   Thomas of Berkeley 62, 160, 239, 246
Hawxbery *see* Hawkesbury
hay 60, 70, 74
Haynes (Hayenes, Heynes), — 78, 79
   Lewis (Luyes), of Chepstow 167, 192
   Thomas, brewer, of Bristol 116, 117, 123, 156, 287, 288n
Hazard, William, dyer, of Gloucester 87, 174
   William, his kinsman 174
Hemmyng, — 96
   T 316
Henry VIII, King of England 7, 14, 15, 16, 23, 25, 40, 60, 107, 110, 113, 130, 131, 174, 204, 209, 231, 259, 262, 274
Henry, Prince of Wales 2
Hentley, Richard 316
Herbert (Harbarde, Herbart, Herberd), Lord 256
   Master 301
   Mistress 306, 308
   Sir William 299
Hereford (Harvardeast, Harvart, Harvarteast, Harvarteaste, Harvarteste, Herfort, Hervorteste) 10, 31, 109, 153, 154, 163, 181, 192, 197, 243, 244, 245, 263, 290, 291, 298, 305
Hernando, Martyne (Mynar) de 285, 302
herring 31, 70, 223
Herris (Herrys) *see* Harris
Hert *see* Hart
Hervorteste *see* Hereford
Heward (Hewart, Heyward), Thomas, dyer, of Bristol 48–50, 87, 155, 187, 190, 240, 267
Heynes *see* Haynes
Heyward *see* Heward
Hickes (Hicks, Hikes), Thomas, merchant, of Bristol 4, 18, 96, 140, 141, 196, 257, 315
Hickman, Henry, saddler, of Bristol 58
   Richard, arrowhead maker, of Wolverhampton 119
Hicks *see* Hickes
hides *see* leather
Higgins (Higgyn, Higgyns, Hyggyns), Eleanor (Elnor) 249, 255
   George 26
   John 206, 297

Higgins—*continued*
  Margaret (Margret)   274
  Thomas   206, 207, 297
Higgley (Higley)   *see* Highlea
High Street, Bristol   246
Highlea (Higgley, Higley)   60, 65, 205, 247
Hikes   *see* Hickes
Hill (Hyll), Allen, merchant, of Bristol   123, 157, 158, 217, 316
  William, searcher   189
Hinton (Hynedon, Hynton, Hyntyne)   197, 279
hippocras, recipe for   315
Hobbs (Hobs), David (Davy), grocer, of Bristol   63
Hodges, Richard   255
Holder (Hollder), John   178
Holmelacy (Homelass, Homlass)   132, 262, 263
hoods   72
hoopers   2, 39, 119, 168, 219, 282, 310
hooping   41, 217, 221, 238, 240, 248, 255, 277, 281, 285, 290, 298, 306, 307, 308
Hoper, Clement (Clementes)   103
  John   255
  Thomas, merchant, of Bridgwater   2, 3, 12, 38
  Tristram   3n
Hopkyns (Hopkynges), Lewis (Luyes, Luys), of Carmarthen   135, 164
Horner, George   303, 306
  John   258
  John of Stokelane   12, 283, 284
  John senior, gentleman, of Stoke St. Michael   303, 304
  Thomas   12, 13, 301, 303, 314
  Thomas, esquire, of Mells   283, 284, 286
horse hire   52, 108
horsemeat   40, 66
horses   8, 13, 52, 80, 81, 86, 89, 90, 103, 145, 146
Hort, Thomas, baker   288, 289
hosemakers   260
Hosyer (Hossyar), John   205, 275
Howell (Howel) Thomas, brewer, of Bristol   69, 70, 84, 87, 140, 141
  Thomas of London   17
Howlat, John, draper, of Wolverhampton   51-2, 66
Howlet, —   317
Howytt, Robert   247
Hubbardine, William   22
Huchyn, Nicholas   149
Hulat, John   266
hulloc (hullock, hullok, hulok)   110, 117, 181, 182, 188, 217, 252, 253, 280-2, 300
Hungroad, Bristol   6, 7n, 56, 126, 161, 162, 170
Hunt (Huntt), John   274
  Philip (Phillip, Phellip), smith, of Shepton Mallet   273
Huntley (Hunteley, Huntly, Untley), Master   119
  John, Esquire, of Gloucestershire   123, 124, 178, 232

Huntspill   25
Huntt   *see* Hunt
husbandmen   7, 32, 52, 161, 276, 292, 302
Husse, John, merchant, of London   76
Hutchyn, John, of Martock   75
Hutton, John   24
Hwet, John   147
Hyggyns   *see* Higgins
Hyll   *see* Hill
Hynedon (Hynton, Hyntyne)   *see* Hinton

Iceland   10n
Iland   *see* Azores
Ilchester (Yllchester)   75
Inner Temple, London   26
innkeepers   51, 258, 266, 270, 273
insurance   10, 20, 21, 85, 86, 255, 264, 266
Ireland   2, 3, 10n, 21, 72
iron   8, 9, 11, 18, 21, 30, 32, 33, 34, 35, 36, 40, 41-2, 43, 45, 46, 47, 49, 50, 51, 53, 54, 55, 56, 57, 58, 59, 61, 64, 65, 66, 67, 68, 69, 70, 72, 73, 74, 75, 76, 77, 78, 79, 80, 81, 82, 83, 84, 85, 87-9, 92, 93-4, 95, 96, 100, 101, 102, 103, 107, 111, 113, 114, 115, 116, 117, 119, 120, 121, 124, 125, 126, 127, 128, 129, 130, 131, 132, 133, 134, 135, 137, 138, 139, 143, 146, 147, 151, 152, 156, 157, 162, 163, 164, 165, 168, 169, 170, 171, 172, 173, 176, 178, 179, 180, 181, 191, 192-3, 194, 197, 198, 199, 202, 203, 204, 205, 208, 209, 211, 212, 213, 214, 215, 219, 221, 222, 223, 225, 227, 229-30, 231, 232, 235-6, 237, 242, 246, 247, 248, 251, 252, 253, 257, 258, 259, 260, 261, 262, 263, 264, 265-6, 268, 272, 273, 275, 276, 279, 283, 287, 289, 294, 296, 300, 301-2, 310
Irun (Vryn)   192, 193
Islands   *see* Azores
Isles of Scilly   *see* Scilly

Jacob, John, of Cadbury   279
Jackson (Jacksson, Jacson), Robert, haulier, of Bristol   17, 178-9, 240, 254
James (Jamys), Thomas   222
Jarvis, Master   317
Jay (Jaye), Master   315
  Benet, merchant, of Bristol and Malmesbury   176
  Sir Walter (Water)   257
  William, merchant, of Bristol   241, 266, 291, 294
Jaymes, Antonye   148
Jeaner   *see* Genoa
Jeffar, Roger   295
Jeffarson, Robert   20, 287
Jeffreis   *see* Geffreys
Jenynges (Jenens)   *see* Genynges
Jerez (Sherys)   154
Jesse, Thomas   80
jewellery,   84, 242, 274
Joachym (Joahim), Christopher (Christover), tanner   60
  Thomas, Sheriff of Bristol   42n, 66n

Jobyne *see* Bathe
John, Lewis, merchant, of Bristol 2
   Roger William, of Abergavenny 57
Johnson, — 79
joiners 300
Jones (Jonys), — 253
   Master 91
   Edmond 317
   Edmond, haulier, of Bristol 253
   Edward, of Abergavenny 31, 47, 57, 58, 225
   John 317
   John, of Chepstow 146
   Lewis (Luys), of Abergavenny 83
   Maud (Mawde) widow, of Bristol 74
   Sir Nicholas (Nycolas) 274
   Roger, carrier, of Oxford 293
   Walter (Water) son-in-law of David Americk 65
   William, gentleman, of Caerleon 111, 112
   William, merchant, of Bristol 157, 218, 250, 315
   William, motleymaker, of Cardiff 56
   William, servant to John Bonham 300
Jonson (Jonsson), William, master of the *Sampson* of Enkhuisen 106, 253, 262
Jonys *see* Jones
Justice, R 217

Kaye, Bristol *see* Quay
Kekar (Keker), John, of Haverfordwest 57, 135
Kelly (Kelley, Kellwaye, Kelway), John, of Petherton 192
   Nicholas 317
   Nicholas (Nicolas, Nycolas, Nycholas), hooper, of Bristol 109, 219, 222, 223, 274
   Richard, smith, of Cardiff 75
   Robert, Recorder of Bristol 24, 278, 285
Kemer, William 240
Kemp, Robert, draper, of Winchcombe 204, 307
   Thomas 306
Kemys, John, of Oldbury 52
   Thomas, gentleman, of Bedminster 180
Kendal (Kendale, Kendall) 6, 62, 102, 119, 150, 154, 198, 276
kendal cloth makers 6, 119, 154
Kent, Mary 164
   Matthew (Mathewe), merchant, of Bristol 130, 131
kerchiefs 46, 244
Kerdif *see* Cardiff
Kermerdyne *see* Carmarthen
kersey 37, 106, 137, 138, 148, 210, 211, 212, 254, 287, 293, 313
kerseymakers 297
Key, Bristol *see* Quay
Keynes, John 235
Keynsham 25
Keynsham (Keynssam), Thomas, shearman, of Bristol 76, 86, 136

King (Kyng), William, fuller, of Birmingham 294
king's subsidy 204, 231
Kingroad (Kingrode, Kyngrode) 7, 126, 161, 162, 170
Kingsnorton *see* Norton, King's
Kingston (Kyngston), Master 23, 285, 286, 299
   Sir Anthony 28, 275, 276n, 277
Kirby (Kyrby), Richard, of Wedmore 75
Knight (Knyght), George, of the Mint 205, 274, 317
   John, pointmaker, of Bristol 184
Knutsford (Knotsford), Edward 13, 272
Knyght *see* Knight
Krosby *see* Crosby
Kyeck, William 316
Kyng *see* King
Kyngesnorton *see* Norton, King's
Kyngrode *see* Kingroad
Kyngston *see* Kingston
Kyntney, Geffrey 310
Kyrby *see* Kirby
Kyrye, — 272
Kyttells Wood 226

Lacon, Richard 61
Laffan, Thomas, of Gatcombe 194
Laffordes Yate *see* Lawfords Gate
Lamb, Thomas 66
lambskins 119
Lancashire 298
Lane, John, husbandman, of Priddy 7, 250
   Richard, brewer, of Bristol 113
Lanesman (Laneman), Nicholas (Nycolas) 115, 167, 192, 247
Langford (Langffort) 76, 252, 253
Langley (Langney) 80, 81, 161, 162
Langston, Richard, servant to the Sheriff 42, 130
Lanssdon, —, waiting man to William Grawnger 69, 168
Lantro (Lantrow), William 257, 317
Lasroye 301
Lasye, John 137, 138
Latche, Thomas 193
Latimer, Hugh 22, 28
Laughton (Lawghton), John, trowman, of Handley 45, 65, 150, 160, 203, 204
Lawfords Gate (Laffordes Yate), Bristol 76
Lawghton *see* Laughton
Lawnsdon (Lawnston), Thomas, grocer, of Bristol 125, 255
Lawrence, John, dyer 5, 35
   Robert 130, 131, 187, 235
   William, of Stapleton 228
Lawton, Master 26
lawyers 8, 32, 138, 162
Le, Thomas 178
lead 7, 8, 13, 16, 21, 81, 175, 176, 210, 211, 234, 247, 250, 254, 257, 258, 279, 280, 283, 287, 292, 295, 296, 302, 303, 304, 305, 308–9, 314

leather   6, 7, 11, 13, 21, 33, 34, 51, 52, 58, 62, 63, 70, 74, 84, 85, 89, 90, 94, 103, 105, 106, 108, 109, 116, 131, 133, 160, 161, 170, 180, 194, 195, 204, 210, 211, 212, 216, 225–6, 228, 230, 233, 234, 254, 257, 258, 261, 263, 264, 283, 287, 288, 289, 290, 298, 305, 309
Lecknor, Tristan, searcher, of Bristol   108, 113, 179, 180
Ledaiper, William, of Kingsnorton   42
Leicester (Lysetter)   225
Leight (Let, Lett, Leyght, Leyt, Leyte, Leytt), John   205, 275
  Robert   12, 38, 42, 43, 48, 54, 58, 60, 61, 63, 66, 67, 69, 81, 94, 95, 96, 98, 102, 103, 105, 111, 112, 120, 126, 128, 130, 137, 139, 140, 147, 151, 152, 153, 154, 157, 171, 172, 173, 174, 196, 198, 205, 208, 219, 224, 228, 230, 231, 243, 246, 275, 280, 296, 309
Leighton, Robert, merchant, of Bristol   79–80
Leke, Henry, tailor, of Bristol   135, 164, 165, 240
Leland, John   9
lemons   204
Lesso, Domyngo de   89, 211, 213
  Guyllem de   214, 233
Let (Lett)   see Leight
Lewis (Luyes, Luys), —, tanner   160
  David (Davyd), boatman, of Bristol   44, 167, 192
  David (Davy, Davyd), servant to John David   44, 115, 209
  John, smith, of Tewkesbury   65, 66, 118, 121
  William Davyd, of Haverfordwest   59–60
Leyche, Marcke   316
Leyght (Leyt, Leyte, Leytt)   see Leight
licences   6–7, 16, 20, 21, 74–5, 86, 96, 97, 98, 101, 105, 108, 152, 160, 174, 175, 255, 256–7, 266, 270, 285, 307, 308
lighterage   266, 296
lining cloths   6, 84, 138, 233, 234, 258, 309, 310
ling   180
Lions (Lyons), Sir Stephen (Stevan), priest, of Sturminster   74
Lisbon (Luxborn, Luxbron)   8, 90, 91, 144, 145, 152, 176, 177, 178, 199, 232
Lisle   see Plantagenet
Lisvane (Liswayne, Llyswen, Lyswayn, Lyswayne)   68, 69, 162, 231
Litell (Lytell), Richard, smith, of Bristol   85
Littleton (Litellton)   153
Litton (Lytton)   142
Llyswen   see Lisvane
loans of ready money   19, 25, 30, 31, 35, 37, 38, 40, 43, 48, 52, 54, 63, 72, 92, 101, 110, 127, 174, 179, 180, 223, 242, 271, 282, 283, 287, 299
Lockiar, —   55
Lockyar, —, wainman   55, 268
  Thomas   184
Logan, William, ship's master   15, 41

London   3, 5, 6, 11, 12, 17, 20, 24, 26, 27, 28, 54, 55, 74, 76, 108, 111, 127, 130, 131, 148, 158, 174, 177, 184, 187, 209, 210, 211, 235, 238, 240, 250, 257, 270, 287, 295
London, Inner Temple   26
London, Middle Temple   26, 27
london cloth   71, 84, 89, 90, 91, 105, 106, 210, 212, 233, 234, 238, 254
London, Thomas a, *alias* Scales   101, 102
Londres, Guyllem de   290, 307, 308
Long, Master   283
  Sir Henry   271, 272
Long Ashton (Aschton, Aischeton)   *see* Ashton, Long
Lord, William, merchant, of Bristol   63
Loughborough (Lughburn)   225
Love, John, of Bradford   300
Lovell, Joan, widow, of Bridgwater   32, 63
  John, of Shepton Mallet   273
Lowe, Charles, merchant, of Bristol   146, 147
Lowghford, Henry   278
Lowse   see Toulouse
Ludlow (Ludlo)   278
Lughburn   see Loughborough
Luxborn (Luxbron)   see Lisbon
Luyes (Luys)   see Lewis
Lydney   1
Lyncoll, Thomas, of London   184
Lyndon (Lynedon), John, draper, of Kingsnorton   42, 43, 205, 214
Lyons   see Lions
Lysetter   see Leicester
Lyswayn (Lyswayne)   see Lisvane
Lytell   see Litell
Lytton   see Litton

Machet (Machyn, Machyne), Thomas, tanner, of Berkeley   6, 62, 63, 107, 123, 124, 160, 161, 169, 170, 194, 197, 216, 239, 241
madder   5, 10, 48, 62, 169, 170, 194, 313
maddering   see dyeing
Maggott, John, cardmaker, of Bristol   59
Maginsfield   see Mangotsfield
Malaga (Mallaga)   58, 103, 125, 188, 189, 191, 198, 233, 243, 263, 295, 296
Malmesbury (Mawnsbery, Mawnsbury)   151, 176
malmsey (mawmesey, mawmessey, mawnsey, mawnssey)   47, 111, 127, 250, 261, 294, 298, 299
malt   293
Manchester (Mawnchester)   6, 215, 220, 235, 297
manchester cottons (manchesters)   see northern cottons
manciples   293
Mangotsfield (Maginsfield, Mangunfflld)   228, 242
Manuela, Antonio de   6, 108
Manynges, —   316
Marchant   see Merchant

351

Marke, John   194
marks of ownership   1n, 20, 167, 258, 309
Marlborough (Marlbrowe)   273
marmalade   10, 48
Marsche, John   294
Marshall, Master, goldsmith   275
Marshfield (Marschefilld)   242
Martin (Martyne), Thomas   170
  William, servant to Dr. Owen   25
  William, servant to Morice Welsh   274
Martock (Martoc)   32, 38, 75
Martyne   *see* Martin
Mary, Queen of England   16, 28
Master, Richard, smith, of Westbury on Severn   32, 33
mats   96, 98, 108, 173
Matthew (Mathew, Mathewe), Edward   260, 285
Matthews (Mathewes, Mathews) *alias* Spryngold, William, haberdasher, of Calne   222, 312
Maunsell, Richard   316
mawmesey (mawmessey)   *see* malmsey
Mawnchester   *see* Manchester
mawnchesters   *see* northern cottons
Mawnsbery (Mawnsbury)   *see* Malmesbury
mawnsey (mawnssey)   *see* malmsey
Mawrewood, Nicholas (Nycolas), pointmaker, of Bristol   147, 190, 222, 267, 286
Mayo, Dorothy, widow of John Mayo   72
  John, dyer, of Bradford   72
  Thomas, son of John Mayo   72
mead   *see* metheglyn
medicine   37
Medina Sidonia, Duke of   8
Melcombe Regis   2
Melksham (Mylksam, Mylkssam)   76, 178, 180
Mellis, John   17
Mells   4, 76, 224, 283, 304
metheglin   56
Mendip (Mendipp, Mendyp)   7, 250, 302
mercers   137, 287, 297
Merchant (Marchant), Robert   148
Merchant Venturers' Company, Bristol   4
Mertyllcom   168
Methwey, John   108
Middle Temple, London   26, 27
Middleton (Myddellton), James (Jamys)   114, 115
Milford (Myllford, Myllfort)   59
milk pans   204
Millior (Myllyor), Sebastian (Bastian)   144, 186
Minehead (Mynnet)   11, 135
Mint, Bristol   205, 274, 276
Moest, Richard   317
Mollynez, Diego, corredor, of Gibraltar   177
money lending   *see* loans of ready money
Montacute (Montagew)   2, 38
More (Moore), Thomas, brewer, of Bristol   236, 237
Morgan, Thomas, tailor, of Bristol   267
Morice (Moryce, Morys), John, roughmason, of Bristol   278, 288, 289

Moro (Moru), Johannes de   287, 296
Morrys, —   252
  Thomas   127
Mors (Mos), Lewis   2
  Richard, baker, of Bristol   124, 199
  Richard, William Ballard's servant   68, 197
Moru   *see* Moro
Moryce (Morys)   *see* Morice
motleymakers   56
Mowllton, John   54
Mumbles (Mummells, Mummylls)   107, 191, 192
Murton, Nicholas, roper, of Bristol   240, 249
muscatel (muscadell, muscatell)   38, 39, 44, 73, 75, 110, 114, 120, 126, 154, 181, 185, 192, 200, 206, 243, 244, 260, 278
muster cloth   309
Mychell, John, smith, of Bruton   310, 311n
Myddellton   *see* Middleton
Myguell, John   302
Mylkssam   *see* Melksham
Myllar   *see* Phillpot
Myllars, Nicholas (Nycolas)   72
Myllford (Myllfort)   *see* Milford
Myllord, John   314
  William, of Compton Martin   314
Myllward, —, carrier   72
Myllyor   *see* Millior
Mylton   *see* Mytton
Mynnet   *see* Minehead
Myranda, Coles de   287
  Sebastyan de   85
Mytton (Mylton), William, of Bath   281, 282, 284

Nappar, John, husbandman, of Martock   32, 33, 38
Narcote, Richard, of Shepton Mallet   11, 117
Nasche, John, of North Petherton   184
  Richard, son-in-law of Thomas Turbot   54
  Robert, searcher, of Bristol   142, 184
  Thomas (possibly Thomas Hasche), clothier, of Batcombe   86, 87, 92, 93, 142, 144, 176
  William, notary, of Bristol   138, 218, 219, 224, 225, 235, 241
  William, of Chew Stoke   268
Naviejas, Thomas de   211
Nawle, William, of Bromwich   124, 125
Neath (Castellnethe, Castilenethe, Castillneathe, Castilneth)   175, 218, 227, 239
Nervol, John, of Bruton   208
Netherlands   5, 15
New College, Oxford   293
New Inn (Newe Yn), Bristol   83, 84
Newborn (Newburn), Robert   113, 317
Newbury (Newbery)   297
Newenham   *see* Newnham
Newfoundland (Newland)   10n, 15, 36, 47, 304
Newgate Prison, Bristol   113
Newman (Glos)   *see* Newnham
Newman, Thomas, servant to Gregory Showlyng   77

Newnham (Newenham, Newham, Newman, Newnam, Newneham) 6, 11, 14, 25, 33, 34, 103, 154, 187, 194, 196, 225, 230, 246, 261, 262, 263, 289, 290, 293, 298, 305
Newport 122
Nice, Truce of 15
Nivelle, J 1
Norfolk 16
North Petherton *see* Petherton, North
North (Northe), Edward, 1st Baron North, Chancellor of the Court of Augmentations 16
 William, vintner, of Bruton 20, 54–5, 56, 58, 81, 82, 107, 116, 118, 121, 122, 136, 149, 155, 159, 166, 181, 182, 185, 186, 187, 188, 201, 218, 233, 237, 238, 239, 241, 249, 253, 255, 262, 265, 266, 268, 269, 277, 278, 281, 285, 286, 307, 308, 311
Northall (Northol), Margery, dyer, of Bristol 48, 49, 155
Northam (Northeham) 186, 188, 191
Northeall, John 317
Northen, Henry, of Chewton Mendip 250, 292
 Henry, servant of the Marquis of Dorset 310
northern cottons (manchester cottons, manchesters, mawnchesters) 5, 6, 89, 90, 91, 105, 106, 176, 177, 178, 206–7, 211, 212, 220, 232, 233, 234, 235, 254, 258, 264, 279, 280, 287, 295, 297, 298
northern dozens 6, 11, 87, 145, 176, 177
northernmen 6, 42, 204
Northol *see* Northall
Northole, Master 256
Norton, King's (Kingsnorton, Kyngesnorton) 9, 12, 33, 41, 42, 204, 214, 259, 275, 294
Norton St. Philip (Phelips Norton, Phillips Norton) 43, 164
notaries *see under* lawyers
Nunny, Lawrence 177
Nycolls, James (Jamys), trowman, of Alveley 109, 110
 Richard 305

oakum 58
obits 58
oil 2, 8, 10, 10n, 11n, 18, 58, 80, 81, 97, 112, 115, 120, 122–4, 125, 131, 132, 133, 137, 141, 144, 171, 177, 194, 204, 215, 216, 219, 220, 221, 222, 223, 224–5, 235, 237, 238, 246, 247, 256, 268, 283, 290, 313
Oldbury (Oldebury) 52
olive oil *see* wool oil
olives 10, 150
Oporto (the Porte of Portyngal) 106, 223
orchelling *see* dyeing
orchil 10, 58, 61, 313
ore 61
Orio 266
ossey (osses, ossy, ossy seck) 9, 21, 38, 48, 55, 73, 97, 110, 114, 132, 135, 136, 150

Ostriche, William, merchant, of London 6n, 17, 76, 91, 131, 132
Owen, George, the King's Physician 23, 25, 27, 209, 256, 281
 see also Abowen
oxen 38, 127
Oxford (Oxfford) 11, 26, 28, 112, 253, 270, 271, 293
 New College 293

Packer (Packar), Richard, tanner, of Berkeley 62, 116
Pacy, Master, Mayor of Bristol 24, 110, 239
 Thomas 113, 233
Paget, William, 1st Baron Paget of Beaudesert, the King's Secretary 6, 174
Palmer (Pallmer, Pawllmer, Pawlmer), — 65, 230
 Richard 225, 247, 248
 Thomas, trowman, of Higley 42, 60, 65, 205, 230, 247, 259
Panmarck *see* Penmarch
pans 204
paper 1
Parcar, John 192
Parker, James 16
 Robert, carrier, of Wapply 293
Parnell, — 317
Parr, Catherine, Queen of England 209
 Joan 3n
 John 3n
Parssons, Edward 123
 Roger, carrier, of Littleton 153
Pasajes (the Passage, the Passaige) 61, 85, 88, 89, 97, 105, 148, 211, 212, 226, 234, 254, 255, 281, 296
Pavy, John, weaver, of Bristol 55, 56
Pawle (Pawll), Master, manciple, of New College, Oxford 293
 William 291, 293
Pawllmer (Pawlmer) *see* Palmer
Payne (Paynne), — 317
 Master 257, 266
 Anthony, customer, of Bristol 296
 Anthony, grocer, of Bristol 16, 59, 124, 197, 198, 249, 252, 255
 Thomas, gentleman 286, 297
peas 210, 211, 212
Peasley, John, saddler, of Bristol 58
Pekes, Master 63
Pembroke (Penbrooke) 165
Penmarch (Panmarck) 186
Penny, John, of Bruton 201, 208, 222, 269, 279, 301
penny hewes 5, 6, 71, 81, 83, 91, 93, 166, 167, 177, 183, 202, 210, 238, 254, 264, 265, 279, 287, 305, 306, 308, 309, 311, 312
Pensford 4
Pensson, — 205
Pepwell, Robert, of Tewkesbury 53, 65, 195
 William, grocer, of Bristol 162, 163, 252, 317

353

Perciar (Percyar) *see* Pershore
Peres de Arana, John *see* Arana, John Peres de
Pernell, John, mercer, of Bristol   297
Pershore (Perciar, Percyar)   53, 54, 194, 204, 240
personal accounts   19, 21, 86–9, 98–100, 117, 120, 122–3, 132–3, 135–6, 144–5, 148–50, 154–6, 158–61, 168–9, 176–8, 184–90, 192–4, 210, 211, 213–4, 221–2, 223–5, 232–5, 235–6, 238–42, 248–9, 253–4, 255–6, 265–7, 277–8, 287, 290–2, 296, 298, 301–2, 305–8
Peryman, Richard, smith, of Westerleigh   120, 122
    Robert   122
Peryngton, Thomas   147
Peter (Petter), William, smith, of Bruton   81, 115, 116, 166, 265
Petherton, North (Pethirton, North Petherton)   75, 184, 192
Peynton, William, butcher   294
Phillips (Phelips), Sir Edward   2
    Elizabeth   2
    Richard, esquire, M.P. for Melcombe Regis   2, 59
    T, son of Richard Phillips, esquire   59
    Thomas of Montague, brother-in-law to John Smythe   2, 38, 59
    Walter (Water)   198
Phillips Norton
    see Norton St. Philip
Phillpot, *alias* Myllar, Roger, grocer, of Bristol   284, 285
Pick, —, son of Master Pick, of Bristol   52
Pickes (Pikes), —   39, 52
    Master   39, 267
    John, grocer, of Bristol   124, 214, 215
    John junior   267
    Thomas   304
    William, mercer, of Bristol   123, 124, 137, 222, 224, 313
Picket (Pickett, Piggott, Pyket), Antony, Master of the *Harry*   97, 105, 122, 127, 141, 144, 154, 186, 216
Pignall, John, smith, of Cardiff   118, 133, 134
Pikes   *see* Pickes
Pill, John   316
    William, grocer, of Bristol   296
pilotage   106
pitch   46
Plantagenet, Arthur, Viscount Lisle   6, 23, 24, 110
plate   16, 19, 23, 24, 37, 40, 83, 98–100, 127, 128, 148, 174, 209, 246, 253, 256, 273, 282
pledges   37, 40, 174, 209, 242, 246, 253, 282
plonkette   100
Plumley, John, clothier, of Bruton   142, 146, 147
Plymouth (Plymowthe)   184, 185, 193
pointmakers   4, 24, 39, 67, 73, 138, 147, 184, 252

Pole (Poole), Reginald, Cardinal   15
    Robert, merchant, of Gloucester   6, 36, 93–4, 108, 149, 151, 152, 153, 170, 175, 177, 197, 198, 210
poles   40, 51, 171
Pollowghan (Polloghan, Polloughan), Watkyn, smith, of Abergavenny   57, 58, 164
    William, smith, of Abergavenny   43, 44, 164
Pollton, John   116
Pontira, Gaspar de   277
Poole   *see* Pole
Pope, —   317
Popley, John, priest, Chancellor of St. Davids   36, 37
Porte of Portyngal   *see* Oporto
Portsmouth   15, 16
Portugal (Portyngal)   9, 11n, 14, 17, 37, 40, 53, 67, 97, 99, 141, 142, 271, 285, 287, 289
Pottell, William, ropemaker, of Bristol   113, 317
Powell   *see* Apowell
powncing   1n, 7, 258, 279, 309
Poynard, Bartholomew   316
Poyntz (Poyns), Master   121
    Bartholomew (Bartelemew)   308
    Jon   25, 185
    Sir Nicholas   25
Poyrou, Nicolas   13n
Prell, William of Litton   142
Preste, John   291
Presteigne (Presten, Presteyne)   250, 260, 287
Preston, William, hosemaker, of Bristol   242, 249, 260, 316
Presy (Presey, Pressy), Robert, merchant, of Bristol   75, 219, 316
Price   *see* Aprise
Priddy (Pride)   7, 250
Priest, John, of Ross   282
priests   *see under* clergy
Prin   *see* Pryn
Prince (Prynce), Richard, clerk of All Hallows Church, Bristol   218, 222, 223
prisage   102, 107, 155, 159, 185, 218, 248, 266, 277, 281, 285, 291, 308
profit and loss accounts   132–3, 237
prunes   229
Pryn (Prin), Edward, merchant, of Bristol   4, 9, 10n, 17, 20, 28, 58, 61, 108, 128–9, 130, 132, 137, 140, 191, 280, 295, 315
    Erasmus (Erasimus)   316
    John, merchant, of Bristol   129, 139, 140, 316
    Richard, merchant, of Bristol   124, 195, 196, 216, 252, 315
Prynce   *see* Prince
Pullton, —   48, 65
Pyket   *see* Picket
pyling   88, 107, 193, 235, 236
Pyncket, William, of Tetbury   222

Quay (Kaye, Key), Bristol   56, 111, 141

rack vintage 8, 112
raisins 10, 21, 55, 58, 103, 112, 125, 133, 182, 188, 189, 191, 198, 233, 235, 237, 242, 243, 263, 275, 295, 296
Raleigh, Sir Walter 27
Ranscombe (Rancom, Rancum) 222, 223
Raven (Ravyn), John, searcher, of Bristol 198, 209, 210, 264
Reade, Giles 297
Reading (Reding) 11, 51, 52
Record, Richard, merchant, of Tenby 165
red wine 8, 39, 149, 152, 160, 181, 245, 247, 274, 284, 292, 304, 308
  see also under gascon wine
Redcliff (Redcliff Hill), Bristol 5, 7, 302, 303, 304
Rede, John, of Swansea 189, 277
  Nicholas 183
Redhed, Bartholomew (Bartillmewe, Bartyllmewe) 209
Reding *see* Reading
Reece *see* Aprise
Renteria (the Rendry) 76, 136
  see also under iron
resin 33, 50, 59, 72, 95, 96, 104
Reynold (Reynolldes), Master 276
  William, of Kingsnorton 42, 43
  William, yeoman, of Newnham 185, 196, 240
Rhys *see* Aprise
Richardes, John, purser 220, 228
Richmond (Richemond), Ralph (Raf) 36
Riddall, Marry, widow, of Birmingham 76
Robbyns (Robyns), John, smith, of Cropthorne 204
  John, of Mumbles 192
  Lewis (Luyes), skinner, of Bristol 129, 131, 132, 317
Roberts (Robarts, Robertes, Robertz), — 317
  Thomas 96, 140
  Walter (Water), merchant, of Bristol 56, 76, 147–8, 151, 159, 185, 307, 316
rochell wine 285
Rochelle (Rochel, Rockell) 8, 10, 89, 285
Rode 4
Rodryguez, Alexander, correo, of Gibraltar 177
Rodwey, Stephen (Stevan, Steveyne), smith, of Wanstrow 237, 238, 265, 268
Rogent 73
Rogers, Henry (Harry) 114, 115
  James (Jamys), merchant, of Coventry 107, 114, 115, 118, 121, 136, 142, 159, 185, 281, 291
Rokesby (Roxby), John, skinner, of Wells 38–9, 40, 107, 117, 118, 121, 136, 142, 149, 150, 155, 159, 160, 185, 186, 187, 188, 199, 200, 218, 239, 240, 241, 249, 253, 255, 266, 281
Romessey, Thomas, tailor 43
Romney *see* Rumney
Rooksbridge (Rookesbridge) 292
ropemakers 113, 140, 202, 249

Ross 282, 305
roughmasons 288
rowing 5, 92, 93, 183
Rowley (Rowly), Edward, of Kingsnorton 9, 33, 204, 205, 230, 274, 275
  Frances (Fraunces) 316
  William, merchant, of Bristol 126–7, 159, 255
Roxby *see* Rokesby
royal arms 14, 60
rozyne *see* resin
Rua, Diego de la 255
Ruiz, Simon 17
Rumney (Romney), Walter (Water) of Tetbury 187, 196, 218, 240, 241
Russell, — 160
  , —, kinsman 80, 81
  John, husbandman, of Langley 161–2
  John, mariner, of Mumbles 107, 191
Ruyfrere, —, merchant, of Lisbon 90–1
Ryve, John, of Petherton 75

Sachefylld *see* Satchefilld
sack *see* sherry
saddlers 58
Sage, Thomas, carrier 314
St. Augustine's, Bristol, Abbot of 37
St. Augustine's (St. Awstens) Green, Bristol 208
St. Davids 36
St. Fagans 209
St. Leonard's Church, Bristol 2, 273, 274
St. Lo (St. Loe, Seyntlo), Lady 255
  Sir John 28, 72–3, 149, 150, 159, 185, 187, 250, 251, 267, 285, 286, 291, 308
St. Nicholas' Church, Bristol 22
St. Peter's Pump, Bristol 271
St. Thomas' Church, Bristol 22
St. Werburgh's Church, Bristol 27, 28, 29, 75
Sala, John de la, shipmaster 61, 86, 88, 105, 148
Salisbury (Sallsbury, Salusbery), Robert, dyer, of Bristol 142, 312, 313
salmon 21, 52, 53, 132, 143, 170, 301
salt 8, 8n, 10, 13, 21, 41, 52, 55, 76, 89, 132, 152, 172
Salusbery *see* Salisbury
Samwest, Robert, of Bruton 76
San Lucar de Barrameda 8, 17, 91, 131, 167
San Sebastian (Sabastyan) v, 9, 13, 14, 89, 260
  and see under iron
Sancist *see* Sansust
Sancta Clara, Estevan (Stevan) de 211, 213
Sansust (Sancist), Sebastyan (Bastyan), merchant, of San Sebastian 162, 260, 285, 290
Sandyfford, Henry 113
Saracen's Head (Saserns Hed), Bridgwater 69
Sarche *see* Serche
Sare, John, notary, of Bristol 32, 53, 54, 67, 113, 171, 251, 310
Satchefilld (Sachefeld, Sachefylld), John, merchant, of Bristol 169, 217, 316

355

Sawll, Thomas 108
Sawnders, Richard, merchant, of Bristol 220
    William, vintner, of Burton-on-Trent 67
Saxy *see* Sexy
Scales, Thomas *alias* Thomas a London 101–2
Scilly (Sylly), islands 184
Scottish pirates 21, 301
scriveners 249
Scroper, Master 291
Scudamore, John 7
searchers 108, 142, 179, 189, 198, 239, 246, 270
Sebright, John 23, 252, 317
seck *see* sherry
Segura, Domyngo de 264, 266
Sekeford *see* Setterford
Septon Malet *see* Shepton Mallet
Serche (Sarche), William 113, 267
Serjeant (Sergant, Serjant, Serjent), Sir Thomas, vicar, of Sodbury 172
serjeants at law 252
Sessyll, John 113
Setterford (Sekeford, Setterfort), Henry 12, 14, 20, 127, 138, 148, 152, 181, 232, 233, 235, 245, 264, 287, 290, 295, 298, 299, 305
Sevarn *see* Asevern
Severn, river 6, 7, 9, 10, 11
Seville 4, 6n, 8, 10, 17, 37, 137, 177, 188, 189, 295, 302
Seward, Thomas 317
Sexy (Saxy), Robert, draper, of Bristol 67, 128, 136, 137, 138, 142, 314, 317
Seymour, Edward, 1st Earl of Hertford, Duke of Somerset 24
Sharington (Sharyngton), William, treasurer of Bristol Mint 274
Sharstons Poole 81, 162
shearing 93, 198–9
shearmen 57, 76, 92
Shee, Nicholas, soapmaker, of Bristol 10, 113, 203, 224
Shepherd (Shepard, Sheppard, Shepward), — 190
    John, servant to Clement Bays 73, 74
    Maurice (Morys, Mawrice), gentleman, of Almondsbury 174
Shepton Mallet (Septon Malet, Shepton Mallard) 4, 117, 142, 267, 268, 273, 303, 309, 310, 312, 314
Shepward *see* Shepherd
Sherehampton *see* Shirehampton
Sherrold 143
sherry (sack, seck) 8, 9, 11n, 21, 35, 38, 39, 44, 47, 48, 49, 50, 51, 53, 54, 55, 56, 62, 65, 66, 69, 70, 73, 75, 92, 94, 97, 98, 103, 104, 106, 107, 109, 110, 111, 112, 113, 114, 115, 117–8, 120, 125, 127, 130, 131, 132, 133, 134, 135, 150, 151, 153, 154–5, 156, 159, 167, 169, 174, 175, 181, 182, 183, 186, 187, 191, 192, 194, 196, 197, 198, 200, 203, 204, 206, 209, 215, 217, 218, 220, 222, 224, 225, 227, 229, 230,

sherry (sack, seek)—*continued*
    235, 237, 238, 239–40, 242, 243, 244, 245, 246, 247, 248, 249, 250, 251, 252, 253–4, 257, 260, 261, 262, 263, 267, 268, 269, 270, 271, 272, 273, 275, 277–8, 280–2, 283, 284, 286, 287, 288, 289, 293, 294, 295, 296, 298, 299, 300, 306–7, 313
Sherwood, William 243
Sherys *see* Jerez
Sheth, Nicholas 317
Sheward, William, carrier, of Bedminster 11, 30, 31, 38, 39, 59, 103, 104, 153, 200
Shewring (Showlyng, Showryng, Shrewryng), Gregory, smith, of Melksham 76, 77, 178, 179, 180
Shipman, Mistress 307
    John senior, merchant, of Bristol 52, 125, 309
    Thomas, servant to John Smythe 12, 13, 14, 44, 69, 75, 83, 84, 85, 98, 106, 140, 145, 146, 148, 149, 168, 174, 181, 183, 184, 316
    William, merchant, of Bristol 5, 12, 13, 35–6, 96, 140
ships,
    Anton de Asteacu's ship of Pasajes 89, 90, 256
    John de Beroby's ship 301
    ship of Car, Hickes and Codrington 196
    Gabarrero's ship 290, 302
    Master Gorney's ship 290
    Domyngo de Lesso's ship 89
    ship of Thomas Lincoln of London *see* Ann of London
    ship of London 75
    Guyllen de Londres' ship 290
    Robert Poole's ship 170
    Portuguese ships 9, 81, 126, 129, 162, 217, 218, 235, 283
    Bastyan de Sansust's ship 162, 290
    Androwe of Plymouth 193
    Ann of London 86, 145, 184, 185
    Antony of the Porte of Portyngal 106
    Barka de la Conception of Portugalete 287, 289
    Brytten (*Brytton*) 154, 186
    Christopher of Dartmouth 149
    Clement of Framilode 175, 211, 213
    Conception 283
    Elizabeth of Harwich 290, 291, 292
    Harry (*Hary, Harrye, Henry, Herry*) of Bristol 10n, 96, 97, 108, 122, 127, 141, 144, 145, 154, 155, 161, 186, 187, 215, 256, 257, 280, 281, 306
    Hart of Bristol 102, 141, 221, 277, 290, 309
    Hart of Chepstow 258
    Isbell 292
    Jelyan 235, 238
    Jesus of Barnstaple 122
    Jesus of Bideford 154
    Jesus of Bristol 61, 75, 90, 132, 141, 144, 154, 158, 186, 187
    Jesus of San Sebastian 307, 308

ships—*continued*
  Jesus of Tor   148, 149
  John of Pasajes   211, 255
  John of San Sebastian   283
  John Baptist   97, 117, 210
  John Baptist of Renteria   169, 234, 254
  Katalyne of Pasajes   280, 281
  Kateryn of Barnstaple   117, 118, 169
  Margaret of Bristol   72, 130, 144, 145, 154, 155, 184, 185, 232
  Margaret of Minehead   135
  Margaret Bonaventure of Plymouth   184, 185
  Marieta of Fuenterrabia   266, 279
  Mary of Penmarch   186
  Mary of Renteria   285, 302
  Mary of San Sebastian   255
  Mary Bonaventure of Bristol   95, 96, 186
  Mary Bride   90, 95, 117, 210, 217
  Mary Bulleyne   216, 235, 238
  Mary Christopher   90, 91, 117, 122, 125, 154
  Mary Conception of Bristol   84, 90, 105, 108, 120, 123, 177, 204, 216, 217, 218, 220, 223, 224, 228, 229, 232, 235, 279, 280, 281, 290, 295, 296, 306, 309
  Mary Fortune of Gloucester   152, 170, 177, 184, 185, 210
  Mary George of Bristol   127, 128, 287
  Mary Grace   15, 36
  Mary Holland of Dartmouth   298
  Mary James of Bristol   80, 177, 216, 232, 235, 309
  Mathew of San Sebastian   308
  Mawdelen   287
  Mawdelen of Pasajes   61, 86, 87, 88, 105, 148, 296
  Mawdelen of Renteria   106
  Mawdelen Cutt   280, 281
  Murderer   15n
  Mysericordia of Villa de Conde   280, 281
  Nicholas of Bristol   14, 15, 60
  Peter of Pasajes   234, 254
  Primrose of Bristol   20, 105–6, 120, 128, 129, 130, 148, 149, 193, 210, 211, 212
  Sampson of Enkhuisen   106, 253, 262
  San John   283
  San John of Pasajes   211, 212, 226, 287, 296
  San John of Renteria   204, 211, 212, 213, 236, 254, 264, 266, 277
  San John of San Sebastian   285, 302
  San Nicholas of Orio   264, 266
  Sancta Cruz   308
  Sancta Maria of Fuenterrabia   266, 283, 287, 296
  Sancta Maria of Renteria   211, 213, 226, 265, 283
  Sancta Maria of San Sebastian   235
  Sancta Maria de Misericordia of Villa de Conde   238
  Sant Espiritus of the Porte of Portyngal   223, 224
  Saviour of Barnstaple   176
  Saviour of Bristol   15, 117, 120, 122, 221, 223, 258, 283, 306, 309

ships—*continued*
  Saviour of Northam   186, 188
  Saviour of Renteria   280, 281, 287
  Swan of Amsterdam   233, 235, 238, 240, 248
  Thomas Seymour   290, 291, 292, 306
  Trinity of Caerleon   20, 68, 91, 111, 112, 144, 167, 186, 280, 281
  Trinity of Deventer   214
  Trinity of Newport   122
  Trinity of Renteria   107, 214, 233, 264, 283, 302
  Trinity Gurney of Bristol   301
  Trinity Smythe of Bristol, account of   97
  Trinity Smythe, iron work for the ship   101
  Trinity Smythe, provisions for the ship   41, 85, 116, 117, 141, 172, 203
  Trinity Smythe, timber for the ship   72, 120, 138, 226
  Trinity Smythe, in the King's service   15, 16, 40
  Trinity Smythe, sold to the King   7, 16, 130n and *passim*
Shirehampton (Sherehampton)   49
shoemakers   4, 74, 76
Shoots (Shuttes) [an obstruction or race in the River Severn]   33
Shorcom, Geffrey   116, 168
Showlyng (Showryng)   *see* Shewring
Shrawley (Shrawle, Shravell)   71, 119
Shrewsbury   6n, 10
Shryst, John   317
Shuche   *see* Sowche
Shuttes   *see* Shoots
Shyne   77
Silk   *see* Sylk
silver   205–6, 274
Sisseter (Sissetor)   *see* Cirencester
Skelar, Hugh   225, 247, 248
Skellton, Alexander   38
skinners   38–9, 113, 131
skins   *see* leather
Skydmore, Master   291
Skynner (Skuynnar, Skynnar), Henry   298, 317
  John   118, 155
  Lewis (Lueys)   216
Slake, —   204
Slattery, Edmund, of Waterford   174
sleymakers   246
Slocom (Slocome), Thomas, draper, of Bristol   276, 317
Small Street, Bristol   25, 26, 27, 79
Smith   *see* Smythe
smiths   4, 17, 30, 32, 45, 57, 58, 62, 65, 66, 75, 76, 78, 81, 83, 84, 85, 117, 120, 133, 162, 163, 164, 194, 197, 204, 209, 229, 231, 237, 262, 263, 273, 276, 279, 301, 310
Smothing (Smothe, Smotheng, Smothyng), William, of Hereford   109, 118, 121, 149, 150, 155, 159, 163, 185, 187, 188, 215, 218, 219, 225, 239, 240, 241, 244, 245, 249, 255, 256, 262, 266, 277, 278, 281, 282, 285, 286, 291, 292, 306, 307

smuggling 7, 12
Smythe, — book-binder 317
—, servant 73
—, of St. Fagans 209
Alice, mother of John Smythe 2, 16, 26, 99, 170, 190, 200, 221, 273, 274, 280, 282, 287
Alison (Allson), widow, of Shirehampton 49, 50n, 218
Ann, daughter of John Smythe 26, 274
Arthur (Arture, Arthure), merchant, of Bristol 51, 91, 123, 156–7, 316
David (Davyd) 57
Edmond 317
Edward 172
Henry, hooper, of Bristol, cousin of John Smythe 310, 311
Hugh (Hewgh), son of John Smythe 26, 27, 28, 112, 232, 273, 293, 297
Joan, wife of John Smythe 3, 23, 26, 27, 28, 178, 181, 274
and passim
trading on her own account 178, 181
John, merchant, of Bristol,
family and early life 1–3
land and property 23, 25, 26, 40, 52, 61, 64, 79, 121, 130n, 181, 208, 229, 246, 257, 272, 286, 289, 301
house used as store 88–9, 143, 230, 235, 301
stores skins in house of John Spark of Newnham 225–6, 288
Sheriff 3, 22
Mayor 23, 24, 110, 111, 257, 258
inventory of plate 98, 99, 100
grant of arms 26, 320
sons at Oxford 112
John (son of John Smythe) 26
John, of Hinton 197
John, of Shyne 77
John, smith, of Winterbourne, tenant of John Smythe 64–5, 229
John, of Devizes 77
John, of Wollston 40
John, ship-master 298
Matthew, merchant and hooper, of Bristol, father of John Smythe 1, 2, 12n
Matthew, son of John Smythe 25, 26, 27, 28, 112, 273, 293, 297
Matthew, cousin of John Smythe 282
Maurice (Morys) 72, 140, 208
Nicholas, son of John Smythe 26, 274
Richard, of Bromyard 31, 32
Richard, merchant, of Coventry 186, 215, 216, 218, 255, 291
Robert, smith, of Abergavenny 164
Robert, of Bristol 317
Thomas, merchant, of Bristol 74, 108, 143
Thomas, hooper, of Bristol, uncle of John Smythe 2, 39, 132, 143, 151, 189, 191, 196, 230, 282
Thomas, of Sodbury 172, 173
William, cousin of John Smythe 310
William, of Lawfords Gate 76

Smythe—*continued*
William, of Marlborough 273
William, Dean of Bristol 197, 198
Snygg (Snyg), George 98, 172, 316
John, merchant, of Bristol 40, 124, 125, 172, 259
soap 4, 8, 10, 13, 17, 21, 37, 76, 137, 188, 189, 220, 256, 302
Sodbury (Chepyng Sodbery, Chipping Sodbury, Sodbery, Sodebury, Soodbery) 62, 172, 173, 274
Sodebery, William 37
Sodebury *see* Sodbury
Somerset 9, 11, 12, 25, 27, 32, 156, 175
Somerset, Duke of *see* Seymour
Sondley, Mighell 317
Soodbery *see* Sodbury
Soper, Master 291
sortyng cloth 227, 258, 295, 309, 311, 312, 313
Sothewell, Robert 317
Southampton (Hampton) 136
Sowche (Shuche, Souche), John, merchant, of Bristol 231, 316
Spain (Spagne, Spayne) 3, 4, 5, 6, 7, 8, 9, 11n, 13, 14, 17, 37, 58, 61, 68, 76, 84, 88, 89, 94, 96, 99, 105, 116, 125, 127, 128, 129, 131, 133, 136, 137, 140, 148, 152, 168, 169, 171, 184, 193, 208, 211, 212, 220, 234, 235, 248, 254, 260, 265, 266, 306, 307
Spark (Sparck, Sparke), John, yeoman, of Newnham 6, 11, 14, 25, 32, 34, 97, 103, 109, 132, 151, 154, 162, 181, 187, 188, 192, 194, 195, 196, 215, 218, 225, 226, 230, 233, 245, 246, 250, 255, 256, 260, 261, 262, 263, 264, 267, 277, 288, 289, 290, 291, 292, 293, 298, 305
spices 8, 235, 263
Spillman (Spyllman), William 208
spletyng 44
Sprat (Spratt, Spratte), John, mariner, of Mumbles 107, 108
Nicholas, son of William 61
William, merchant, of Bristol 9, 14, 60–2, 125, 191, 219, 282, 310, 315
Spryngold *see* Mathewes
Sprynt, John, apothecary, of Bristol 224, 307
Spyllman *see* Spillman
Spyring, William, fisher 63, 70, 168, 247
Staffordshire 9
Stanbank (Stambanck, Stanbanck, Stanbancke, Stanebanck), Antony 75, 107, 108, 241, 242, 243, 248, 255, 256, 257, 277, 278, 281, 292, 306, 307, 308
Edward 255
Standfaste, Walter 26, 316
Stanley, Nicholas (Nycholas) 48
Stanshawes 25
Stanton Drew (Stawnton Drewe) 258
Stapleton (Stapillton) 228
Sternall (Sternal), Robert, hooper, of Bristol 138, 278, 282, 283
Stile, William, of Mells 76

Stoke 52
Stokelane 5, 12, 156
Stoke St. Michael (Stoke Myhell, Stoke Myghell) 303, 304
Stone, Master 316
　John, dyer 191
　John, merchant 316
Stoneaston 25
Stonebagg, Edward 96, 108
Store, Robert, weaver, of Bridgwater 76
Stour, West (Stowrewestover, West Stour) 52
Stourbridge (Sturbridge) 147
Stovey, Roger 77
Stow (Stowe) on the Wold (Stowe the Old) 76
stowing 10, 21, 107, 117, 120, 122, 130, 135, 149, 158, 185, 186, 215, 216, 238, 240, 277, 281, 290, 298
Stowremynster see Sturminster
Stowrewestover see Stour
straking 154, 158, 217, 255
Strovit, John 142
Strowd (Strowde), John, clothier, of Shepton Mallet 222, 303, 304, 305, 312, 313
Sturdon 25, 28, 121
Sturminster (Stowremynster) 74
Subieta (Subueta, Subita), Domyngo de 280, 287
　Francis (Francisco) de 136, 265
Suche, Lord 242
　Richard 242, 243n
Suffell, Thomas, smith, of Hereford 163
suffolk cloth 16, 309
sugar 110, 111, 235, 284, 295, 296
Sumpter, John, merchant, of Bristol 72
Surryes (Surys) see Azores
Sutton, John, of Bristol 57
　John, merchant, of Haverfordwest 57
　John, kinsman of John Sutton of Haverfordwest 57
　William, of Berkeley 76
　William, shearman, of Bristol 57
Swan (Swanne), John, merchant, of Bristol 272, 316
Swansea (Swaynse) 277
sweet wine 109
Swetynge (Swetyng), John 20, 287, 295
Swift, Humphrey (Humfrey), servant to John Smythe 12n, 36
Sylk (Silk), Master, of Bristol 39, 269, 274
　Thomas, friezemaker, of Bristol 86, 87, 102, 103
Sylly see Scilly
Symons (Symondes, Symoundes), James (Jamys), tucker, of Bristol 190, 227, 228
　John 316
　Philip, tanner, of Hereford 181, 245, 290, 298, 305
　T 317
Syms, Richard 216
　William, soapmaker, of Bristol 220, 283
Sysseter see Cirencester

Tailor (Taillor, Tallor, Tayler, Tayller, Tayllor, Taylor), Henry, draper, of Hereford 163, 164
　John, servant to Thomas Phillips 38, 59
　Piers, of Bristol 271, 272
　Robert 317
　Robert, alias Cator, yeoman, of Bristol 208, 225, 257
　Roger, clothier, of Bolton 224, 297, 298
　Simon (Symon, Symond) 105, 192, 200, 267
　Walter (Water) 297
　Watkyn, of Tenby 30
　William 65
　William, of Tewkesbury 48, 56–7, 65
　William, of Worcester 67
　William alias Wyllys see Wyllys, William
tailors 26, 33, 34, 43, 62, 105, 135, 138, 267, 300
　see also drapers
taint see tent
tallow 137, 138, 171
tanners 4, 6, 60, 62, 103, 116, 181, 223, 275
tare 37, 137
Taunton (Tawnton) 4, 260, 271
Tawler,— 65
taynt see tent
Tedbery see Tetbury
teint see tent
Tenby (Tymby, Tymbye, Tynby) 30, 46, 89, 90, 105, 106, 164, 165
tent (taint, taynt, teint, teynt) 9, 21, 38, 39, 50, 52, 70, 97, 104, 106, 107, 110, 114, 133, 149, 150, 158, 160, 182, 200, 217, 218, 235, 237, 243, 244, 248–9, 253, 262, 280–2, 295
Tetbury (Tedbery, Tedbury) 196, 222
Tewkesbury (Twexbury) 11, 48, 56, 65, 66, 126, 152, 194, 195, 204, 314
teynt see tent
Thames, river 16
Thomas, John 30, 31
　John, of Abergavenny 164
　Philip (Phillip, Phelip, Phellip) 141, 144, 154, 158, 186, 187
　Robert 45, 91, 192
　William, goldsmith, of Hereford 149, 153–4, 155, 187, 189, 218, 239, 241, 263
Thorne (Thorn), Nicholas (Nycholas, Nycolas), merchant, of Bristol 9, 17, 24, 27, 28, 119, 120, 191, 208, 214
　Robert 317
Thornton, George 186
Thurston (Thurstone, Thuston), Thomas, soapmaker, of Bristol 10, 124, 202, 203, 216, 224
tiles 181
timber 11, 14, 15, 24, 72, 86, 120, 138, 148, 172, 226, 245, 247, 252, 253, 256, 258, 263, 289
Tippar, Richard (Richert), tucker, of Bristol 5, 86, 87, 92–3, 183, 188, 189, 198, 218, 239

Tipton, Hugh (Hewgh)   14, 17, 20, 221, 280, 295, 309
Tizon (Tyzon), —   176
  James, son of John   40, 196, 217
  Joan, widow, of Bristol   73
  John, yeoman, of Elberton   40
  Nicholas (Nycolas), merchant, of Bristol   124, 145, 167, 168, 195, 196, 217
  Thomas, merchant, of Bristol   67, 95, 96, 181, 315
Togood, Thomas   305
Tonell, Richard   24
Tor   148, 149
Toulouse (Lowse, Tullus)   31, 47, 49, 50, 52, 56, 61, 70, 71, 72, 73, 79, 81, 85, 86, 87, 92, 100, 102, 136, 147, 148, 165, 173, 174, 180, 189, 190, 206, 221, 227, 231, 237
Tovey (Tovy), —   313
  John   142
  John, of Rogent   73, 74, 86
  John, of Winford   305, 309
  Richard, clothier, of Stoke   52, 53
Towlly, Master   293
Towsan (Towssan), John, mariner, of Plymouth   184
Traharan (Traharine, Traheryn),   *see* Treheren
train oil   150, 224, 263, 307
Trawnter, William, yeoman, of Langley   80–1
Trayguss, Thomas   224
Treheren (Traharan, Traharine, Traheryn, Treharen, Treharine, Treheryn), John Thomas, son of Thomas   51, 213
  Thomas, merchant, of Carmarthen   50, 51, 86, 212, 213
trowmen   45, 119, 199, 247, 314
trows,
  of Thomas Aflete   33, 34, 41, 42, 65, 150, 205, 230
  of Thomas Asevern   41, 42, 150, 205, 214, 259
  of Simon Aston   33, 124
  of Richard Barns   114
  of William Dymock   65, 98, 134
  of Griffith   251, 275
  of John Laughton   65, 150, 160
  of James Nycolls   109
  of Richard Palmer   225, 247, 248
  of Thomas Palmer   42, 65, 205, 230, 259
  of Pensson   205
  of Robert Pepwell   53, 65
  of Pullton   48, 65
  of Hugh Skelar   225, 247, 248
  of William Tailor   48, 65
  of Tawler   65
  of William Woodwall   247
trows [*owners not indicated*]   9, 10–11, 33, 34
Troyes   1
truckers   5, 81, 82, 83, 87, 90, 91, 92, 93, 100, 131, 132, 144, 145, 146, 166, 167, 183, 190, 199, 210, 237, 254, 278, 279, 280, 287, 295, 305, 308, 309, 313

Tucker, John, of Bruton   142, 222, 223
tuckers   5, 142, 165, 227
Tullus   *see* Toulouse
Turbot, Thomas, merchant, of Pershore   28, 53–4, 118, 121, 156, 185, 186, 218
Turlo, John, of Ranscombe   222, 223
turpentine   37
Twexbury   *see* Tewkesbury
Tynby (Tymby, Tymbye)   *see* Tenby
Tyndall (Tyndal), Master   256
  Robert   12, 13, 14, 15, 20, 28, 36, 84, 85, 89–90, 99, 105, 106, 107n, 110, 111, 116, 137, 148, 161, 168, 182, 184, 192, 194, 210, 211, 212, 233, 234, 235, 236, 254, 262, 264, 287, 295
  William, chamberlain, of Bristol   13, 107, 110, 111, 161, 194, 231, 256, 315
Tyzon   *see* Tizon

ullage   107, 120, 124, 130, 136, 150, 155, 159, 185, 186, 187, 217, 218, 222, 225, 240, 241, 256, 266, 278, 291, 292, 307, 308
Ullarhampton   *see* Wolverhampton
Ullaston   *see* Wolston
Ullerhampton   *see* Wolverhampton
Untely   *see* Huntley
Updavith (Updavithe), Thomas, of Cowbridge   139
Upgenckyn (Upgenckyng, Upgenkyne), Alice *alias* Watkyn   30, 31
  Thomas, smith, of Abergavenny   30, 31
Uphall, Richard (Rickart), servant to Sir John St. Loe   72, 73
Upricharde (Uprichard), Lewis (Luyes)   115, 192
  Thomas, smith, of St. Fagans   209, 232
Upyevan, Jenkyn, servant of Thomas Trehern   50
  Ris, mariner, of Mumbles   107
Usk (Uske)   156

Vaghan, Ris David, shoemaker, of Bristol   76
Vale, Richard   30
Vele, John, carver, of Bristol   146
Venice   17, 18, 21
Vere, Richard (Rychard), of Coventry   107, 114, 266, 269, 270
Veroby   *see* Beroby
Verrotazan, Pedro de   266
vestments   258
Vicarye, David, of Pembroke   165
Valla de Conde   238, 280
Villa Viciosa, Jonot de   255, 280
vintners   62, 67, 110, 150, 182, 248, 259, 298
Vise   *see* Devizes
Vowell, Master   185
voyage accounts   18, 20, 90–2, 105–6, 144–6, 176–8, 191, 210–12, 232–5, 254, 258, 264, 279–80, 287, 308–10
Vryn   *see* Irun
Vyllbao   *see* Bilbao

Vyne, Lawrence, merchant, of Bristol   130, 131, 220, 316
Vynsy, William   300

Wade, John, coverlet maker, of Bristol   155, 174, 175, 188, 254
waggoners (wainmen)   62, 268, 279
   see also carriers
Wale, Thomas, of Hereford   243
Wales   9, 11, 78, 91, 107, 112, 139, 144, 156, 162, 167, 209, 231, 280, 281
Walker, —   252
   John, vintner, of Cirencester   217, 259
   Roger, soapmaker   76
Walsche   *see* Welsh
Wanhope   192
Wanstrowe (Waynstrowe)   237, 265, 268
Wapply [possibly Codrington Wapley]   293
Waren, John, pointmaker   252
Warminster (Warmyster)   242, 276
Warre, Nicholas   316
Warren, Christopher (Cristofor, Cristover), of Coventry   142, 143, 314, 315
Warwick (Warwyck)   50
Waterford (Waterfford)   174
Watkyn, Alice   30, 31
Watkyns (Watte, Wattes, Watkynges), —   317
   David (Davy, Davyd), of Cardiff   64, 133, 134, 209
   John   125, 317
   Thomas   77, 179
Waynstrowe   *see* Wanstrow
weapons   14, 23, 52, 53, 62, 67, 76, 81, 97, 141
weavers   2, 55, 59, 76, 232, 250
Web (Webb), John, of Cirencester   256
   John, of Shepton Mallet   142, 309, 314, 315
   Thomas, master of the *Trinity*   6, 98, 105–6, 135, 148, 175, 176, 177, 192, 193, 210, 215, 217
   Thomas, innkeeper, of Cirencester   260, 267, 270
   Thomas, yeoman, of West Harptree   175
Webster, James (Jamys), of Manchester   109, 215, 240, 241, 262
Webster, Nicholas (Nycholas), smith, of Birmingham   58
Weddington, John   20
Wedmore   75, 292
Weedon, Edward   316
weighing   74, 169, 213, 214, 236, 265, 266, 296
Weke (Wekes), Master   121
   Nicholas, esquire, of Dodington   149, 153, 291
   Thomas   251
Wekewar   *see* Wickwar
Wellington (Wellyngton)   83
Wells   4, 11, 24, 25, 38, 39, 102, 103, 104, 105, 142, 143, 149, 153, 199, 200, 267, 277, 285, 286, 294, 303
Wells, Dean of   *see* Goodman
Wells, John, of Bristol
   John, weaver, of Worcester   59, 60

Wells—*continued*
   John a, soapmaker, Sheriff of Bristol   42n, 66n, 89, 123, 124, 171, 172, 216, 221
   John   *see also* Awells, John
Wellyngton   *see* Wellington
Welsh (Wallsche, Welch, Wellsche, Wellsh, Wellsshe, Welshe), Master   208, 286, 308
   Henry, gentleman, of Worcester   62
   John, merchant, of Bristol   28, 53, 107, 111, 112, 121, 123, 144, 145, 149, 169, 188, 256, 291
   Margery, widow, of Bristol subsequently Margery Herbert   112, 239, 241, 274, 300
   Maurice (Morice, Morys), esquire, of Chipping Sodbury   274
West Bromwich   *see* Bromwich
West Harptree (West Hartry)   *see* Harptree
West Stour   *see* Stour, West
Westbury on Severn (Wesbery)   32
Westen, John, of Langford   76
Westerleigh (Westerley)   120
Westmorland   102
Weston   5, 142, 262, 310, 311
Weylland, William   242
Weysford, Nicholas   211
Whaley (Whaly), Thomas, surgeon, of Bristol   36
   Thomas, tanner, of Bristol   223, 224
wheat   6–7, 8, 11, 15, 21, 43, 45, 56, 84, 85, 89, 90–1, 96, 97, 98, 105, 106, 108, 111, 126, 127, 144, 145, 152, 160, 161, 162, 173, 174, 175, 176, 177, 178, 194, 195, 197, 203, 210, 211, 212, 233, 234, 254, 256, 287, 309
Wheeler (Whelar), Edward, servant, to Robert Leighton   80
   William, merchant, of Bridgwater   32, 33
Wheteley, Thomas, scrivener, of Bristol   107, 240, 249
White (Whit, Whitt), —, cofferer   44, 167, 192
   Christian (Cristyan)   220, 239, 241, 248
   Giles, servant to John Smythe   11, 12, 13, 14, 45, 47, 53, 58, 70, 74, 75, 76, 90, 91, 97, 108, 112, 122, 131, 144, 145, 154, 158, 168, 169, 176, 177, 178, 186, 192, 199, 277, 316
   John, of Bristol   12
   John junior   316
   John, merchant, of Cardiff   162, 163
   John, smith, of Wolston   84
   Margaret, of St. Stephen's parish, Bristol   36
   Richard   154, 177, 186, 279
   Simon   312
   Sir Thomas, priest   45, 70
   Sir Thomas, alderman of London   111
   Thomas, merchant, of Bristol   24, 131, 132
white wine   8, 70, 72, 149, 199, 243, 247, 270, 287, 292, 308
   see also under gascon wine
Whitnest   222

Whitsson, Robert 238
Wickwar (Wekewar) 62
Wigmoore, Roger, Controller of the Mint 276, 277
Wilburn, Randell 316
William, Robert, husbandman, of West Stour 52
Williams (Wyllams, Wylliams, Wyllyams),
    David (Davy), baker, of Bristol 43–4, 187, 188, 203
  Eleanor (Ellnor) 199
  John, coverlet maker 175
  John, shipmaster 130, 144, 154
  John, skinner, of Bristol 113
  John, of New Inn, Bristol 83, 84
  John, of Neath 175, 218, 227, 228, 239
  Martin (Martyne), smith, of Caerphilly 68, 162, 163, 231
  Richard, ropemaker, of Bristol 140, 141
  Thomas, grocer, of Bristol 198, 199
  Thomas, tailor, of Bristol 26
Willis see Wyllys
Willshire see Wiltshire
Willsson (Wyllson, Wyllsson), George 213
  Matthew (Mathewe), smith 276, 277
  Miles (Myles), chapman, of Kendal 102, 150, 151, 198, 215, 255
  Miles (Myles), merchant, of Chepstow 213
Wilschere see Wiltshire
Wilsone 317
Wiltshire (Willshire, Wilschere, Wyllshire), Richard, broker 3, 4, 5, 9, 162, 172, 176, 218, 312
Winchcombe (Wynschecom, Wyncheton) 204, 239
Winchcombe (Wynchecom, Wynschecom), John, kerseymaker, of Newbury 142, 297
wine 2, 7–8, 11, 18, 20, 26, 52, 53, 56, 58, 70, 72, 78, 79, 90, 95, 97, 102, 104, 109, 120, 121–2, 126, 127, 130, 134, 140, 141, 148, 149, 150, 151, 157, 182, 184, 185, 186, 219, 220, 229, 255, 256, 262, 285, 286, 290, 291, 292, 298, 304, 306, 307, 308
  see also bastard, caprick, claret, gascon wine, gibraltar wine, hulloc, malmsey, metheglin, muscatel, ossey, red wine, rochell wine, sherry, sweet wine, tent, white wine
Winford (Wyngfford) 305
Winter (Wynter), Master 32
  Mistress 41, 255
  Arthur (Arture), son of John 40
  George, merchant, of Bristol 40, 102, 103
  John, merchant, of Bristol 15, 32, 40–1, 123, 259
Winterbourne (Wynterborn) 25, 28, 62, 64, 229
Wishart, George 24
Wissetorshire see Worcestershire
Witcombe (Wytcom) 306
woad 5, 8, 9, 9n, 10, 10n, 11, 13, 18, 21, 31, 36, 47–8, 49, 50, 52, 60, 61, 69, 70, 71, 72, 73, 74, 79, 81, 82, 83, 85–7, 92, 96,

woad—*continued*
  100, 114, 129, 130, 133, 136, 141, 142, 143, 146, 147, 148, 165, 166, 173, 174, 180, 181, 184, 189–90, 191, 206, 207, 208, 211, 222, 225, 226, 227, 231, 237, 264, 272, 278, 279, 295, 297, 310, 311, 312, 313, 314, 315
woading see dyeing
Wollston (Wolston, Ullaston) 40, 84
Wolverhampton (Ullarhampton, Ullerhampton) 12, 51, 66, 119
Wood see under Atwood, Awood
wood see timber
Woode, Edmond 317
Woodhows, Master 130
Woodwall (Woodoll, Woodwal), Richard, of Warwick 50, 51, 155
  William 51, 247
Wookey 25
wool 5, 6, 10, 35, 184, 273, 313
  see also under cloth and specific materials
wool oil (olive oil) 5, 11, 21, 21n, 40, 58, 62, 63, 67, 91, 111, 112, 114, 115, 116, 119, 122, 123, 124, 137, 147, 156, 157, 170, 171, 172, 173, 178, 180, 194, 195, 197, 202, 203, 206, 207, 214, 215, 221, 223, 225, 232, 237, 252, 259, 265, 269, 271, 286, 289, 298, 300, 311, 312, 313
Woosley see Wosley
Worcester (Wursetter, Wursettor) 33, 59, 62, 66, 67, 76, 123, 150, 151, 160, 199, 248, 251, 252, 275, 310
Worcester, Bishop of see Bell
Worcestershire (Wissetorshire) 11, 204
Wosley (Woosley), Francis (Fraunces), merchant, of Bristol 251, 316
  Nicholas (Nycolas) 120, 251
Wottley, Thomas, of Batcombe, yeoman 30
Wotton under Edge (Wutton under Hedge) 276
wrappers 6, 144, 204, 211
Wutton under Hedge see Wotton under Edge
Wye, river 10
Wyeth (Wyethe, Wyett, Wyot), Henry, of Bristol 316
  Henry, of Coventry 142, 224, 226, 239, 241, 247, 248, 286
  Robert, gentleman, of Loughborough 225, 226, 247, 248, 286
Wyllams (Wylliams) see Williams
Wyllet (Wyllett), William, merchant, of Bristol 76, 136, 180, 271, 282
Wyllinges, Simon (Symon) 290
Wyllkes, Elizabeth (Elzabethe) 274
Wyllshire see Wiltshire
Wyllsson see Willsson
Wyllyams see Williams
Wyllys (Willis, Wylles, Wyllie, Wyllis, Wylly, Wyllye), John, vintner, of Bristol 18, 107, 110, 111, 121, 136, 138, 149, 160, 189, 239, 241, 250, 255, 257, 277, 299, 302, 303

362

Wyllys—*continued*
   William *alias* Taylor, husbandman, of Chewton Mendip   302, 303
Wynchecom   *see* Winchcombe
wyndage   107, 285
Wyndgods Pill   292
Wyngfford (Wyngford)   *see* Winford
Wynschecom (Wynscheton)   *see* Winchcombe
Wynter   *see* Winter
Wynterborn   *see* Winterbourne
Wyot   *see* Wyeth
Wyrreat, Roger, servant, to Master Sheward   59
Wytcom   *see* Witcombe

Yate, William   313
Yellis of Surrys   *see* Azores
yeom   30, 40, 41, 75, 80–1, 85, 126, 138, 151, 173, 175, 196, 208, 225, 298
Yerbery (Yerberi), John, clothier, of Bruton   5, 9, 19n, 20, 49, 55, 56, 74, 81, 82, 87, 90, 91, 92, 93, 100, 105, 106, 115, 116, 131, 142, 144, 147, 166, 167, 176, 177, 182, 183, 190, 198, 199, 201, 208, 210, 211, 216, 217, 223, 232, 234, 237, 238,

Yerbery (Yerberi), John, clothier, of Bruton—*continued*
   254, 265, 268, 269, 278, 279, 280, 287, 301, 309
   John, the younger   81, 82, 166, 201, 265
   Stephen (Stevy)   237
   Thomas   223
   William   201, 237, 264
Yerwith, William, grocer, of Bristol   34, 35
Yevan   *see* Upyevan
Yevers, William   176
Yewyn   *see* Ewyn
Ygneldo, Bartholome de   308
Yland (Yllandes, Yles, Ylls)   *see* Azores
Yllchester   *see* Ilchester
Ympyn, Jehan   1
Yong, Master   299
   John, gentleman, of Hanham   162, 163
   John, servant of Thomas Asevern   119
   Thomas, grocer, of Bristol   235
   William, grocer, of Bristol   103, 189n, 233, 239, 241, 242, 243, 267, 278, 317
   William junior   103, 317
Yowen   *see* Ewyn
Yrancu, Johannes de   210, 234

m5